Advances in
Input-Output
Analysis

Advances in Input-Output Analysis

Edited by
Karen R. Polenske
Jiri V. Skolka

Proceedings of the Sixth International
Conference on Input-Output Techniques, Vienna, April 22–26, 1974

Ballinger Publishing Company • **Cambridge, Mass.**
A Subsidiary of J.B. Lippincott Company

This book is printed on recycled paper.

International Standard Book Number: 0–88410–277–7

Library of Congress Catalog Card Number: 75–19295

Printed in the United States of America

Library of Congress Cataloging in Publication Data

International Conference on Input-Output Techniques, 6th, Vienna, 1974.
  Advances in input-output analysis.

  1. Interindustry economics—Mathematical models—Congresses. 2. Linear programming—Congresses. I. Polenske, Karen R. II. Skolka, Jiri. III. Title.
HB142.I58 1974   339.2'3   75–19295
ISBN 0–88410–277–7

Table of Contents

List of Figures

List of Tables

Editors' Note

The papers in this book were selected from those presented at the Sixth International Conference on Input-Output Techniques held April 22–26, 1974, in Vienna. More than 300 economists and statisticians participated in the meetings which were sponsored jointly by the Secretariat of the United Nations and the Battelle Institute.

The editors wish to express their deep gratitude to Irene Raught and M.N. Lewis for their valuable and painstaking assistance in editing the papers and to Susan Hart and Page Shepard for standardizing the lists of references and for handling the many tedious details in preparing the papers for publication.

Karen R. Polenske
Jiri V. Skolka

Program of the Sixth International Conference on Input-Output Techniques Vienna, April 22-26, 1974

April 22, 1974

Session 1 Problems of the Environment

*John H. Cumberland and Bruce N. Stram (United States)
Empirical Results from Application of Input-Output Models to Environmental Problems
*Rainer Thoss (Federal Republic of Germany)
A Generalized Input-Output Model for Residuals Management
R.U. Ayres, S.B. Noble, and M.O. Stern (United States)
Input-Output in Environmental Protection Agency's Strategic Environmental Assessment System (SEAS)
Martino Lo Cascio (Italy)
Anti-Pollution Policy: The Effects on Costs and Prices in Italy

Session 2 Problems of Energy and Pollution

Alan S. Manne (United States)
Waiting for the Breeder
*Karen R. Polenske (United States)
Regional Interactions Between Energy and Transportation
F. van Scheepen (EEC)
An Input-Output Approach to the European Energy Sector
*H. den Hartog and A. Houweling (Netherlands)
Empirical Results of Input-Output Computations for the Netherlands
W.A. Reardon (United States)
Input-Output Analysis of U.S. Energy Consumption

*These papers were selected for inclusion in this volume.

Session 3 Studies of National Applications

H. Krinjse Locker and M. Le Grontec (EEC)
  Some Comparisons of Economic Structures Between EEC Countries
J. Lamel, J. Richter, W. Teufelsbauer, and K. Zelle (Austria)
  Comparative Analysis of Mathematical Methods for Updating Input-Output
  Tables
E.F. Baranov (USSR)
  Analysis of the National Economy Sequence of Branches in the USSR Economy
G.J.A. Mensink (Netherlands)
  Methods of Estimating the Input Structure for Separate Product Groups of
  Heterogeneous Industries
Bohuslav Sekerka (Czechoslovakia)
  Problem of Relations Among Balances in Various Classifications
Kattamuri S. Sarma (United States)
  Comparison of Alternative Methods of Improving Input-Output Forecasts: A
  Simulation Study
Jacqueline Fau (France)
  Income and Financial Assets Description by Input-Output Tables

Session 4 Technology, Production, Investment

J. Sojka, E. Holub, and M. Sysák (Czechoslovakia)
  A Simulation Approach to the Construction of Investment Coefficients
*Iwao Ozaki (Japan)
  The Effects of the Technological Changes on the Economic Growth of Japan,
  1955–1970
*A. Duval, N. Jeantet, and G. McNeill (Switzerland and France)
  Recent Research into the Wigley Production Function for Use in a Static
  Equilibrium Multisector Model Applied to France
William Peterson (United Kingdom)
  Factor Demand Equations and Input-Output Analysis
Paul M.C. de Boer (Netherlands)
  A Generalization of Input-Output Analysis Based on C.E.S.-Type of Production Functions
*Thomas Reimbold (United States)
  Testing a Dynamic Input-Output Model by Simulation
Kari Levitt (Canada)
  The Leontief Input-Output Multiplier as a Measure of General Interdependence

Session 5   Business Applications

C.B. Tilanus (Netherlands)
Where Short-Term Budget Meets Long-Term Plan—Solving Conflicts by the
Multiproportional RAS Method
*Thomas Vietorisz (United States)
The Use of Input-Output Information at the Process Level for Chemical Indus-
try Programming on a Time-Shared Computer System
John H. Morawetz (United States)
An Application of Input-Output: Estimating and Forecasting of Building Ma-
terials Demand
*Margaret Buckler (United States)
Industrial Applications of the University of Maryland Input-Output Model
Carl W. Nelson and Axel von Pochhammer (United States and Federal Republic
of Germany)
Difficulties in Implementing Input-Output Techniques in Multinational Pro-
ducing Enterprises: A Summary Report
Jay M. Gould (United States)
The Use of the EIS Data Base in Economic Research
*A. George Gols (United States)
The Use of Input-Output in Industrial Planning

Session 6   Models of Interregional Relations

*R.B. Hoffman and J.N. Kent (Canada)
Design for a Commodity-by-Industry Interregional Input-Output Model
*M. Jarvin Emerson (United States)
Interregional Trade Effects in Static and Dynamic Input-Output Models
*R. Courbis and D. Vallet (France)
Building and Use of an Interindustry, Interregional Table for a Regional-
National Model of the French Economy
A.G. Granberg (USSR)
The Development and Application of Interregional and Interindustry Models
in the USSR
*D. Vanwynsberghe (Belgium)
The Spatial Element in Sectoral Analysis

Session 7   Optimization Models

*D.A. Livesey (United Kingdom)
Optimization Techniques in the Cambridge Growth Model
K.K. Val'tukh (USSR)
Multisectoral Dynamic Models Maximizing Consumption

J. Tsukui, T. Watanabe, and Y. Kobayashi (Japan)
An Optimal Programme for Structural Changes
*Iu. N. Ivanov (USSR)
A Dynamic Optimal Plan of Economic Growth

Session 8 Income Distribution

*Richard Weisskoff (United States)
A Multi-sector Simulation Model of Employment, Growth, and Income Distribution in Puerto Rico: A Re-evaluation of "Successful" Development Strategy
*R.M. Goodwin (United Kingdom)
The Use of Normalized General Coordinates in Linear Value and Distribution Theory
Irma Adelman and L. D'Andrea Tyson (United States)
A Model of Income Distribution Determination in Yugoslavia
Luz Maria Bassoco and Roger D. Norton (Mexico and United States)
A Quantitative Agricultural Planning Methodology
Kjeld Bjerke (Denmark)
The Distribution of Personal Incomes in Denmark
*Felix Paukert, Jiri V. Skolka, and Jef Maton (Switzerland, Austria, Belgium)
Redistribution of Income Patterns of Consumption and Employment: A Case Study of the Philippines
Brian P. O'Connor (United States)
An Income Side to an Input-Output Model of the United States
Masa Aoki (Japan)
Dual Stability and the Normal Rate of Profit

Session 9 Applications in Developing Regions and Countries

Gustav Schachter and Franco Pilloton (United States and Italy)
I-O Tables for a Dynamic Interregional Analysis of Development Policies for the Italian South
*A. Kuyvenhoven (Netherlands)
Sector Appraisal Where Trade Opportunities Are Limited
*Siegfried Schultz (Federal Republic of Germany)
Intersectoral Comparison of an Approach to the Identification of Key Sectors
Shinichi Ichimura and Yukio Kaneko (Japan)
Practical Use of Input-Output for Development Planning
Max Börlin and Halder Fisher (Switzerland and United States)
The Generation of an Input-Output Linear Programming Model of the Economy of Iran
D. McMenamin and Joseph A. Haring (United States)
An Appraisal of Nonsurvey Techniques for Estimating Regional Input-Output Models

Session 10   Forecasting Models

*Shuntaro Shishido and Akira Oshizaka (Japan)
  Inventory Adjustment in a Quarterly Input-Output Model for Japan
Lawrence M. Horwitz (United States)
  A Quarterly Input-Output Model of the United States
*Ronald G. Bodkin (Canada)
  The Use of Input-Output Techniques in a Large-Scale Econometric Model of
  the Canadian Economy (CANDIDE)
*T.S. Barker (United Kingdom)
  Projecting Alternative Structures of the British Economy
Peter Glattfelder (Hungary)
  Forecast of the 1975 Hungarian Input-Output Table with a Special Variety of
  the RAS Method

Session 11   Modeling Social Systems

Richard Stone (United Kingdom)
  Random Walks Through the Social Sciences: Input-Output and Markov Mod-
  els in Social Research
H. Aujac (France)
  Towards a New Social Input-Output Table: The Dynamics of Social Groups
  and Institutions.
Emilio Fontela (Spain)
  Uses of Input-Output Techniques for the Analysis of Intuitive Information

Session 12   Prices

*V.A. Volkonskii (USSR)
  On a Possibility of Discount Rate Determination by Intersectoral Models
*B.D. Haig and M.P. Wood (Australia)
  A Computable Model for Analyzing Price Changes in an Input-Output System
Masahiro Kuroda (Japan)
  An Application of a General Equilibrium Model to the Japanese Economy,
  1955–1965
*Per Sevaldson (Norway)
  Studies in the Stability of Input-Output Relationships: Price Changes as
  Causes of Variations in Input-Output Coefficients
P.D. Lowe (United Kingdom)
  The Conflict Between Profitability and Threshold Wage Policy in Containing
  the Inflation of an Input-Output Economy
*David Gilmartin (United States)
  Price Forecasting in an Input-Output Model

Session 13 International Trade

*K. Tokoyama, Y. Kobayashi, Y. Murakami, and J. Tsukui (Japan)
  Structures of Trade and Production and Development
*Peter Petri (United States)
  A Multiregional Model of Japanese-American Trade
*V.R. Panchamukhi (India)
  A Multisectoral and Multicountry Model for Planning of Production and
  Trade Among the Countries of the ECAFE Region
J.W. McGilvray and D. Simpson (United Kingdom)
  Intermediate Goods and the Theory of International Trade and Investment
H.D. Evans, N. Klijn, and G.A. Meagher (Australia)
  A General Equilibrium Analysis of Protection of Australia (Revised): Work in
  Progress and Some Preliminary Findings

List of Authors

(Listed affiliation is as of the time of the Sixth International Conference on Input-Output Techniques, April 1974.)

T.S. Barker
Department of Applied Economics
University of Cambridge
England

Ronald G. Bodkin
CANDIDE Project
Economic Council of Canada
Ottawa, Canada; and
Department of Economics
University of Western Ontario
London, Ontario, Canada

Margaret B. Buckler
Interindustry Forecasting Project
University of Maryland
College Park, Maryland, United
States

Raymond Courbis
Groupe d'Analyse Macroéconomique Appliquée (GAMA)
Université de Paris-X
Nanterre, France

John H. Cumberland
Bureau of Business and Economic
Research
University of Maryland
College Park, Maryland, United
States

A. Duval
Department of Physics and Electronics
Battelle Centre de Recherche de
Genève
Geneva, Switzerland

M. Jarvin Emerson
Department of Economics
Kansas State University
Manhattan, Kansas, United States

David Gilmartin
Department of Budget and Fiscal
Planning
Treasury Building
Annapolis, Maryland, United States

A. George Gols
  Arthur D. Little, Inc.
  Cambridge, Massachusetts, United
    States

R.M. Goodwin
  University of Cambridge
  Cambridge, England

B.D. Haig
  Research School of Social Sciences
  Australian National University
  Canberra, Australia

H. den Hartog
  Central Planning Bureau
  The Hague, The Netherlands

R.B. Hoffman
  Structural Analysis Division
  Statistics Canada
  Ottawa, Canada

A. Houweling
  Central Planning Bureau
  The Hague, The Netherlands

Iu. N. Ivanov
  Institute of Control Sciences
  U.S.S.R. Academy of Sciences
  Moscow, USSR

N. Jeantet
  Institut National des Statistiques et
    des Etudes Economiques (INSEE)
  Paris, France

J.N. Kent
  Structural Analysis Division
  Statistics Canada
  Ottawa, Canada

Y. Kobayashi
  Economic Planning Agency
  Tokyo, Japan

A. Kuyvenhoven
  Centre for Development Planning,
    Netherlands School of
    Economics
  Erasmus University, Rotterdam
  Rotterdam, The Netherlands

D.A. Livesey
  Department of Applied Economics
  University of Cambridge
  Cambridge, England

Jef Maton
  Centre for Development Planning
  University of Ghent
  Ghent, Belgium

G. McNeill
  Union Carbide
    Europe, S.A.
  Geneva, Switzerland

Y. Murakami
  University of Tokyo
  Tokyo, Japan

Akira Oshizaka
  Data Control and Analysis Division
  Economic Planning Agency
  Tokyo, Japan

Iwao Ozaki
  Department of Economics
  Keio University
  Tokyo, Japan

V.R. Panchamukhi
Department of Economics
University of Bombay
Bombay, India

Felix Paukert
Employment and Development
Department
International Labour Office
Geneva, Switzerland

Peter A. Petri
Department of Economics
Brandeis University
Waltham, Massachusetts, United
States

Karen R. Polenske
Department of Urban Studies and
Planning
Massachusetts Institute of Tech-
nology
Cambridge, Massachusetts, United
States

Thomas C. Reimbold
Interindustry Forecasting Project
University of Maryland
College Park, Maryland, United
States

Siegfried Schultz
Department of Western Industrial-
ized and Developing Countries
Deutsches Institut für Wirtschafts-
forschung
Berlin, Federal Republic of
Germany

Per Sevaldson
Central Bureau of Statistics of
Norway
Oslo, Norway

Shuntaro Shishido
School of Social Engineering
University of Tsukuba
Ibaraki-ken, Japan

Jiri V. Skolka
Austrian Institute for Economic
Research
Vienna, Austria

Bruce N. Stram
Bureau of Business and Economic
Research
University of Maryland
College Park, Maryland, United
States

Rainer Thoss
Institut für Siedlungs und
Wohnungswesen
Universitat Münster
Münster, Federal Republic of
Germany

K. Tokoyama
Hitotsubashi University
Kunitachi, Tokyo, Japan

J. Tsukui
Institute of Social and Economic
Research
Osaka University
Osaka, Japan

Dominique Vallet
Groupe d'Analyse Macroéconom-
ique Appliquée (GAMA)
Université de Paris-X
Nanterre, France

D. Vanwynsberghe
  Regional Economic Council of
    Brabant
  Brussels, Belgium

Thomas Vietorisz
  Research Center for Economic
    Planning
  New School for Social Research
  New York, New York, United
    States

V. Volkonskii
  Central Economic-Mathematical
    Institute
  U.S.S.R. Academy of Sciences
  Moscow, USSR

Richard Weisskoff
  Department of Economics
  Iowa State University
  Ames, Iowa, United States

M.P. Wood
  Research School of Social Sciences
  Australian National University
  Canberra, Australia

Introduction

Karen R. Polenske and Jiri V. Skolka

A few months before the Sixth International Conference on Input-Output Techniques convened in Vienna, in April 1974, the Royal Swedish Academy of Science had awarded the 1973 Nobel Memorial Prize in Economic Science to Wassily Leontief as the "sole and unchallenged creator of the input-output technique." News of the award was welcomed wholeheartedly by all who in the past three decades had worked with Leontief's model of economic interdependence and whose experience confirmed it to be one of the most fruitful contributions to empirical economic research. This publication of selected papers from the 1974 input-output conference offers an excellent opportunity to briefly review the growth of input-output analysis from its childhood to its maturity and thus to trace the important phases and trends in its development.

Leontief and His Model

Professor Leontief was born in St. Petersburg in 1906. He studied in his native city and graduated from the University of Leningrad in 1925 with the title of "Learned Economist." He then continued his studies abroad and in 1928 earned a doctorate in economics at the University of Berlin. That same year—1928—he joined the staff of the National Bureau of Economic Research in New York City as a Research Associate. He went to Harvard University as an instructor in 1932 and remained on the Harvard faculty through June 1975. During those forty-odd years, he was incredibly busy with research, teaching, and writing, as well as giving lectures around the world on the input-output technique that he had developed—and this is not to mention his many other activities, such as his work as an economic adviser to the government. In 1948 he established the Harvard Economic Research Project (officially called the Research Project on the Structure of the American Economy). Here, numerous students worked in a dynamic environment on input-output and related research. Scholars from many countries visited the Project for periods of a few hours to several years. The Project was closed in 1972 and Leontief left Harvard in June 1975. His input-output and related research is being continued under his direction at New York University. He is working now on a world model for the United Nations concerned with the Impact of Prospective Environmental Issues and Policies on the International Development Strategy.

Leontief had not grown up in an intellectual vacuum. His father was an economist, and Leontief was well informed of the ongoing statistical accounting research in the USSR in the early 1920s. In fact, before leaving the USSR, he wrote an article, "The Balance of the Economy of the USSR," published in 1925, in which he explained the attempt made by a small group of Russian statisticians, headed by Popov, to construct a simple national accounting system that provided also some information on the interdependence of the economic sectors. Leontief knew, of course, of previous efforts to understand and depict the interdependence of economic activities. Such efforts go back as far as 1758, when the Tableau Economique by François Quesnay was published, and include Karl Marx's nineteenth century analysis of the interdependence of economic activities in a two-sector model of reproduction and Leon Walras' construction of a mathematical multisector general equilibrium model of production, which was extended and improved by Gustav Cassel.

All new ideas have ancient roots, but they take fresh forms as they are developed and applied in new ways. This is true for input-output analysis. Leontief used elements from previous studies on economic interdependence and made a unique contribution by simplifying the Walrasian system of equations. Thus he created a new, simple, and elegant system for which statistical information could be compiled with relative ease and which brought many new insights into the interdependence of prices, outputs, and incomes in different sectors of the economy.

Leontief concluded the preliminary research on the construction of his empirical input-output system in 1931 while he was a Research Associate at the National Bureau of Economic Research. After he had been appointed an instructor at Harvard University in 1932, he began the statistical assembly of data for the 1919 table. The research was funded from 1932–1939 by the Committee on Research in the Social Sciences. In 1936, he published the first empirical article on interdependence in the U.S. economy in *The Review of Economics and Statistics.* This article was followed five years later (1941) by his first book, *The Structure of American Economy, 1919–1929,* which was revised in 1951 in an enlarged edition that expanded the analysis to 1939.

When Leontief's 1936 article on input-output theory and analysis was published, the world was just recovering from the Great Depression and was searching for ways to prevent such economic disaster in the future. The publication in the same year of Keynes' general theory was not at all accidental. It was "awaited"; it also made it clear that depressions cannot be avoided without government intervention. Leontief's model soon proved to be one of the best techniques for analyzing economic policies, including those related to depression policies.

It should be added, perhaps, that Leontief also had some luck on his side: Electronic computers, which made fast numerical solutions of large systems of equations possible, were to be invented soon. (The relay computer developed by Howard Aiken provided the basis for the development of the ENIAC electronic computer by von Neumann et al. Both were developed by the mid-1940s.)

In 1941, the U.S. Bureau of Labor Statistics (BLS) started an investigation of employment readjustments that would occur at the end of World War II. This led to the construction between 1942 and 1944 of a 1939 U.S. input-output table for 96 industries, under the direction of Leontief at Harvard University. The first official U.S. government application of input-output data—that of the 1939 table—was made by the BLS in 1944 for the Planning Division of the War Production Board to determine the anticipated distribution of employment in December 1945 under an assumption that the war would end June 30, 1945.

In 1949, four years after the war ended, a group ranging from 50 to 75 people began work at the BLS on the construction of the 1947 input-output table—the first really large table (500 industries). By August 1952, that compilation was basically complete, and the data were aggregated for use in the U.S. 190-industry Emergency Model.

It is quite understandable that input-output analysis soon began to spread to other countries. Leontief's publications were widely read in many of them, and their scholars came to the Harvard Economic Research Project to learn how to compile and use input-output tables. During the 1950s, input-output tables were first assembled in countries of Western Europe and Japan as well, and later, after varying delays, by countries with centrally planned economies and by the developing world. The number of countries without at least one input-output table is now very small indeed. In 1968, input-output tables became an integral part of the System of National Accounts recommended by the United Nations. Attempts to construct sets of internationally comparable input-output tables for several countries were made by two organizations, the Statistical Office of the European Communities and the Economic Commission for Europe.

International Input-Output Conferences

With the rapid spread of input-output analysis, there emerged theoretical and practical problems that indicated a pressing need for practitioners in this field to exchange experiences and search together for solutions to the problems they were encountering. And so the first international input-output conference was convened in 1950 in Driebergen, in the Netherlands. Between that first modest gathering, attended by 15 participants (in addition to the Dutch hosts), and this sixth and largest conference—with 320 participants—lies a time span of nearly a quarter of a century. To a large extent, the success story of input-output analysis in the third quarter of the twentieth century can be followed in the proceedings of the international conferences held during this period.[1] The second conference was held in 1954 in Varenna, Italy; the third was held in 1961, the fourth in 1968, and the fifth in 1971—these were held in Geneva. Various sponsors have contributed money, facilities, and services to make these conferences possible. They include the Netherlands Economic Institute, the Rockefeller Foundation, the University of Pisa, the Varenna Foundation, the Secretariat of the United Nations and of the United Nations Organization for Industrial Development, the Harvard Economic Research Project, the Ford Foundation, the Battelle Memorial Institute, Brandeis University, and the Austrian government.

The picture of the development of the input-output technique emerging from the proceedings of the international conference is complemented by two books by Leontief, published in the 1950s, and by publications of the proceedings of various national and regional conferences, such as the 1952 U.S. conference organized by the National Bureau of Economic Research, the 1961 conference held in Hungary, the 1965 Indian conference in Poona, and the United Kingdom conferences held in 1968, 1971, and 1975. The excellent input-output bibliographies prepared during the 1960s by the Harvard Economic Research Project and published by the United Nations provide still more evidence of the growth in importance of the input-output approach.

During the past twenty-five years, important progress has been made in many areas of input-output analysis, little or none in other areas. Certain problems considered in the past as difficult are no longer discussed at all: for example, the methodology and organization of the statistical compilation of national input-output tables, computer calculations, and consistency between input-output and national accounting data. Statistical services in many (although not all) countries have been instituted and improved, even though the international comparability of input-output data is still largely unresolved. It was at the 1961 conference in Geneva that the problem was discussed for the first time at an international conference, but only the Statistical Office of the European Economic Community and, to a lesser extent, the United Nations Economic Commission for Europe, gave it serious consideration. Until it is resolved, differences between national input-output tables, both in the industry classifications and in the definitions used, will continue to hinder comparisons of consumption and production structures between countries. The dimension of this problem can be clearly seen in this book by comparing the differences in industrial classifications used in the empirical studies. But standardization of input-output tables is a problem that must be investigated and solved by statistical officers who work with international organizations—participants at input-output conferences can do little more than discuss it.

The effects of rapid advances in computer technology are implied in the

_____

1. See Reference entries 2 through 7 for a listing of the published proceedings of the first five conferences.

papers delivered at the present conference—none of which dealt explicitly with computational problems. They are best illustrated by comparing computation times for inverting input-output matrices in 1950 with those in 1969. In 1950, at the First International Input-Output Conference, Leontief reported that

> A generalized solution of a complete set of 38 simultaneous linear equations took *only* [italics added] 56 hours of operation on Dr. Aiken's Harvard Mark II calculator.

By 1969, however, the time had been reduced drastically; it took about 36 seconds to invert a 100-sector table on the IBM 7094, 26 seconds on the IBM 360/65, and only 10 seconds on the CDC 6600. At present (1975), computational problems are centered more on the organization of large data bases and on portraying the results of calculations involving large quantities of data than on the speed of the calculations themselves.

The Sixth Conference Papers

Three basic versions of the input-output model emerged from the work of the late 1940s and early 1950s: the open static model, the closed static model, and the dynamic model. The open static model proved to be the one best able to cope with a great variety of economic problems. The closed static model, proposed by Leontief in his very early studies, has been virtually abandoned. However, as the paper by Paukert, Skolka, and Maton proves, a partial closing of the model can still be useful in certain cases, such as for the study of the interdependence between personal income and private consumption. The elegant dynamic model proposed originally by Leontief was too rigid to cope with all the multiple aspects of economic growth. Subsequent efforts to further develop the dynamic model have, basically, gone in two different directions, one theoretical, the other more pedestrian.

The theoretical approach was used to design more and more sophisticated tools, such as the calculation of the turnpike, linear programming, or dynamic programming. The most advanced, from the standpoint of usefulness for economic policy, is the turnpike model, which can soon become operational, as is illustrated in the Japanese study by Tokoyama, Kobayashi, Murakami, and Tsukui. Other studies, such as Volkonskii's, remain at a very abstract level. Earlier development of this theoretical approach can be followed through Tsukui's contributions to the 1968 and 1971 input-output conferences, from Bródy's paper at the 1968 conference, and from other publications of these two and other authors.

There is no paper in this volume on the combination of linear programming with quasi-dynamic input-output models. These optimal planning models were rather popular in the 1960s, especially in countries with centrally planned economies. Their drawbacks were mainly the subjective determination of the objective function, the restriction to selecting only one target (while economic policymakers must work with multiple economic goals), and an unclear economic interpretation of their dual solution. It is difficult to imagine that projects can be selected on the basis of one set of criteria (shadow prices) and successfully implemented with the help of another set of criteria (current prices, interest rates, and wage rates).

The attempt to combine input-output techniques with dynamic programming, although interesting, is still far from operational, as illustrated by the theoretical study reported here by Ivanov. In this vein, the paper by Goodwin should be mentioned, which uses input-output as a useful framework for the discussion of certain purely theoretical questions.

The other line of development was less abstract and more pedestrian. It tried to meet the demand of economic policymakers for models of economic development in which industries were treated as many separate sectors of the economy rather than as an aggregate. One of the pioneering contributions here was the Cambridge growth model, the description of which was published by Stone and Brown in 1962. The contemporary state of economics in this area in Cambridge, England, is demonstrated in this volume by the contributions of Barker and Livesey. The Cambridge model incorporates the Wigley function, which was also developed in Cambridge and which is discussed in the paper by Duval, McNeill, and Jeantet. But Cambridge is not the only place where such models are constructed. Two dynamic input-output models are described in this book, one for Canada, in the paper by Bodkin, the other for the United States, in the paper by Buckler, Gilmartin, and Reimbold at the University of Maryland. An earlier version of the Maryland model was described by Almon at the 1971 input-output conference, as was a Norwegian long-term input-output model constructed by Schreiner. Similar studies have also been carried out, for example, in France, Finland, Hungary, Japan, and the USSR. The ex post analysis of the structural changes in the Japanese economy, provided in this volume by the Ozaki paper, belongs to this class of studies, as does the contribution by Weisskoff, in which he analyzes the employment effect of industrialization in Puerto Rico.

All the presently operational dynamic input-output models are surprisingly similar in their general framework. Therefore, an almost standard input-output dynamic model may finally emerge. This model will contain either consecutive input-output tables for all years being reviewed, or, alternatively, only the base input-output table and a table projected for the final year. Investment matrices will link tables for different years. Attention will be paid to the prediction of final demand, in particular foreign trade, and to changes in input-output coefficients. Forecasts of absolute or relative prices will most likely be among the results provided by the calculations. One tendency to be observed in recent dynamic interindustry models is, however, alarming. They are becoming too large. Both the compilation of data and the handling of the results of the calculations are becoming more and more difficult.

One of the essential problems of dynamic input-output analysis is the prediction of changes in the input coefficients. Leontief was aware of the importance of the stability of the coefficients even before he started to write about the dynamic model. In the pioneering years of input-output analysis, the time lag (usually 5 to 15 years) between the reference year and the year in which the table became available did not really justify the assumption of constant coefficients even in the use of the static model. Since then, the efficiency of the statistical services has improved, and a few countries (the Netherlands and Norway, for example) have been able to prepare series of comparable input-output tables on a yearly basis and so have collected considerable data on changes in the coefficients over time. Other countries, like the Federal Republic of Germany and Denmark, have started to follow this example. In the United States, updated input-output tables will be published on an annual basis.

Discussions of input-output coefficient stability now appear regularly on the programs of the international input-output conferences. For example, Sevaldson's paper in the present volume deals with the impact of price changes on the stability of input-output relationships. There are several monographs on this subject, among them those by Arrow and Hoffenberg, and Carter. But in spite of all the research, the most successful approach is very pedestrian—information about expected changes in technology is collected from trade journals, interviews with engineers, research reports, and other sources and then translated into coefficient adjustments.

Time is one dimension in economics, space is the other. Economists working with input-output techniques started very early to develop the open static model in this direction, first as regional input-output analyses, later on as analyses of the interdependence of countries linked by trade flows. At the 1954 conference in Varenna, Chenery reported on a two-region input-output study for Italy. Unfortunately, most of the regional studies are still for single regions, as evidenced by the Emerson paper in the present volume, and are primarily concerned with problems of data assembly or estimation rather than with the results of applying the models to particular issues. Only a few countries have operational multiregional models that embrace all regions, separated according to administrative districts or other areas suitable for economic planning purposes. Four multiregional studies are presented in this book—one for France, in the paper by Courbis and Vallet; one for Belgium, in the paper by Vanwynsberghe; one for Canada, in the paper by Hoffman and Kent; and one for the United States, in the paper by Polenske. In the first two papers, the methods of assembling or estimating the multiregional data are presented. The Canadian contribution provides the first information on the use of rectangular matrices (used also for the national Canadian table) for interregional studies. In the U.S. contribution, the multiregional model, which had already been described at the 1971 conference, is used to analyze the interrelations between transportation and energy in the United States. Although no papers were presented at this conference on the

Japanese multiregional work, Japan has the most complete set of regional statistics, with two sets of 9-region, 25-industry data assembled (1960 and 1965) and a third set (1970) that will be available soon. Nor is the regional work in the USSR represented in this volume. It is hoped that important studies will emerge from the USSR as their analysts have available to them the improved regional input-output statistics resulting from the preparation of the 1972 USSR input-output table.

The linkage of national input-output tables by trade-flow matrices is methodologically similar to multiregional input-output analysis. The first attempts in this direction can be traced back to 1961, when Wonnacott published his study on the Canadian-American interdependence between Canada and the United States. Later on, the network of intercountry trade flows was dealt with in a book by Linnemann. The topic also appeared on the programs of the 1968 and 1971 input-output conferences. In this book, Petri analyzes the trade interdependence between the United States and Japan, and Panchamukhi discusses the linkage of the economies of the countries of the ECAFE region.

Three papers in this volume concern the application of input-output analysis to the problems of developing countries, which, unfortunately, is a topic not frequently studied. The Panchamukhi paper deals with trade relationships; the papers by Schultz and Kuyvenhoven deal with similar topics—the use of the input-output technique for determining sectors whose promotion would most accelerate economic development.

The family of input-output studies on other than the national level includes, besides studies on regional and multicountry levels, sectoral or enterprise studies. A distinction must be made, however, between three different uses of input-output techniques at the enterprise level. The first is the application of results of macroeconomic input-output projections for enterprise planning. An example of this application can be found in the present volume. It was used in the Maryland input-output model, described by Buckler, Gilmartin, and Reimbold. The second is the construction of input-output models depicting the activities of a particular enterprise or of a whole industry. At the 1961 conference, the only one at which this topic has been discussed, two papers were given on the use of input-output analysis for agriculture. (Input-output models do, however, seem to be used often in some of the centrally planned economies for analyzing the activities of individual firms.) The third is the organization of large data banks for commercial market research, the organization of which reflects the logical structure of the input-output model. This last application is a very recent invention—an American one. It is described here in the contributions of Vietorisz and Gols.

Another area in which input-output analysis has been applied only recently is environmental protection. It was dealt with for the first time at an international input-output conference in a paper presented by Leontief and Ford in 1971. Three such investigations appear in the present volume: one for the United

States, by Cumberland and Stram; one for the Netherlands, by den Hartog and Houweling; and one for the Federal Republic of Germany, by Den Hartog and studies stress one point: the estimated costs of environmental protection and pollution abatement in the industrialized countries are not prohibitive.

Another new development is the use of input-output models for short-term forecasting and business-cycle analysis, which is very difficult, mainly because of the influence of the short-term fluctuations in the use of labor and capital or of the changes in inventories. So it happens that this volume is the first among the proceedings of the international input-output conferences to include papers describing quarterly input-output models. The Japanese study, reported by Shishido and Oshizaka, constitutes an important breakthrough in this direction. The Australian paper by Haig and Wood puts more emphasis on the quarterly simulation price movements and on the role of feedback from (and time lag between) the changes in the cost-of-living index and in the wage level.

Before concluding this introduction, an additional point—quite different, but equally important—should be mentioned. It concerns the geographical distribution, as well as the content, of the contributions to the conference proceedings. This presents a difficult problem for those who prepare the program, and possibly an even more difficult problem for those who must make a balanced selection from a very large number of papers for publication in a volume of manageable size, while judging each paper for its applicability to input-output analysis and the relevance of the substantive issues discussed. The editors have endeavored to include a selection of papers that covered the latest theoretical developments and their applications and that were representative of input-output studies being conducted throughout the world. They believe they have achieved the first of these goals. They have been less successful in achieving the second—that of geographical balance. The United States, Western Europe, and Japan were well represented at the conference. Most of the U.S. contributions were of high quality. This is also true of the contributions from Japan. Although there were numerous contributions from Western Europe, they were limited to certain countries. Considering the high standard of the statistics in most of these countries, and the importance of their governmental policy measures, many more contributions might have been expected from them. The participation of East European countries in the international input-output conferences has never corresponded to the level of research that is carried out there, particularly in countries like Hungary and Poland. Participants from the developing world appeared at the input-output conferences for the first time in 1961; the proceedings of the 1961 conference (the third) contain contributions from Egypt, Israel, and Latin America. But since then, in spite of the efforts of the organizers, the number of contributors from the developing countries has not increased. On the contrary, most studies of the use of input-output analysis in development planning were presented at this conference by participants from industrialized countries. This book necessarily reflects this geographical imbalance.

Conclusion

The editors of the previous conference volumes have already praised the remarkable flexibility of input-output analysis, which was able to provide a suitable framework for the analysis of many aspects of the economy, ranging from international to national to regional issues, from output to price variations, from the global problems of country development to the micro problems of industrial-firm expansion. The present editors join in this praise. In introducing this volume, however, we should like to emphasize that input-output analysis reflects very well Leontief's philosophy concerning the role of economic science in modern society. This philosophy—perhaps shaped by the experience he gained over many years—is fully consistent with his development of the input-output method and is excellently articulated in his Presidential address delivered at the eighty-third meeting of the American Economic Association in 1970. He drew attention to the inadequacy of the scientific means by which economists try to solve practical problems: "The weak and slowly growing empirical foundation clearly cannot support the proliferating superstructure of pure . . . speculative economic theory." And he repeated the old truth, unfortunately often forgotten in academic circles: "True advance can be achieved only through an iterative process in which improved theoretical formulation raises new empirical questions and the answers to these questions, in their turn, lead to new theoretical insights."

This volume is called *Advances in Input-Output Analysis.* We hope that it contains also some modest, but useful, advances in our knowledge of the functioning of the contemporary economic systems.

REFERENCES

1. Arrow, K.S., and M. Hoffenberg. *A Time Series Analysis of Interindustry Demands.* Amsterdam: North-Holland Publishing Company, 1959.

2. Barna, Tibor, ed. *Structural Interdependence and Economic Development.* London: MacMillan & Co., Ltd., 1963.

3. Barna, Tibor, ed. *Structural Interdependence of the Economy.* New York: John Wiley & Sons, Inc., 1956.

4. Bródy, A., and A.P. Carter, eds. *Input-Output Techniques.* Amsterdam: North-Holland Publishing Company, 1972.

5. Carter, Anne P. *Structural Change in the American Economy.* Cambridge, Mass.: Harvard University Press, 1970.

6. Carter, A.P., and A. Bródy, eds. *Input-Output Techniques.* Vol. 1, *Contributions to Input-Output Analysis.* Amsterdam: North-Holland Publishing Company, 1970.

7. Carter, A.P., and A. Bródy, eds. *Input-Output Techniques.* Vol. 2, *Applications of Input-Output Analysis.* Amsterdam: North-Holland Publishing Company, 1970.

8. European Community. *Methodologie der Gemeinschaften der Input-Output Tabellen, 1965* [Methodology of the Input-Output Tables of the European Community, 1965]. Brussels: European Community, 1970.

9. European Economic Community. *Input-Output Tabellen für Länder der Europäischen Wirtschaftsgemeinschaft* [Input-Output Tables for the Countries of the European Economic Community]. Brussels: European Economic Community, 1965.

10. Gossling, W.F., ed. *Input-Output and Throughput: Proceedings of the 1971 Norwich Conference.* London: Input-Output Publishing Company, 1975.

11. Gossling, W.F., ed. *Input-Output in the United Kingdom.* London: Cass, 1970.

12. Keynes, John Maynard. *The General Theory of Employment, Interest, and Money.* London: MacMillan & Co., Ltd., 1936.

13. Leontief, W. "The Balance of the Economy of the USSR." In *Foundations of the Soviet Strategy for Economic Growth: Selected Soviet Essays, 1924–1930.* Edited by Nicholas Spulber. Bloomington, Indiana: Indiana University Press, 1964. Pp. 88–94.

14. Leontief, W. "Quantitative Input-Output Relations in the Economic System of the United States." *The Review of Economics and Statistics* 18, no. 3 (August 1936): 105–125.

15. Leontief, W. *The Structure of American Economy, 1919–1929.* New York: Oxford University Press, 1941.

16. Leontief, W. "Theoretical Assumptions and Nonobserved Facts." *American Economic Review* 61, no. 1 (March 1971): 1–7.

17. Leontief, W., et al. *Studies in the Structure of the American Economy.* New York: Oxford University Press, 1953.

18. Linnemann, H. *An Econometric Study of International Trade Flows.* Amsterdam: North-Holland Publishing Company, 1966.

19. Lukács, O.; C. Cukor; P. Havas; and Z. Román, eds. *Input-Output Tables— Their Compilation and Use: Scientific Conference on Statistical Problems.* Budapest: Publishing House of the Hungarian Academy of Sciences, 1962.

20. National Bureau of Economic Research. *Input-Output Analysis: An Appraisal.* Princeton: Princeton University Press, 1955.

21. The Netherlands Economic Institute, eds. *Input-Output Relations: Proceedings of a Conference on Inter-Industrial Relations.* Leiden, Holland: H.E. Stenfert Kroese, 1953.

22. Stone, R., and J.A.C. Brown. *A Computable Model of Economic Growth.* Ser. No. 1. *A Programme for Growth.* London: Chapman & Hall, 1962.

23. United Nations. *Input-Output Bibliography, 1955–1960.* New York: United Nations, 1961.

24. United Nations. *Input-Output Bibliography, 1960–1963.* Statistical Papers, series M, no. 39. New York: United Nations, 1964.

25. United Nations. *Input-Output Bibliography, 1963–1966.* Statistical Papers, series M, no. 46. New York: United Nations, 1967.

26. United Nations. *Input-Output Bibliography, 1966–1970.* 3 vols. Statistical Papers, series M, no. 55. New York: United Nations, 1972.

27. United Nations. *Standardized Tables of ECE Countries for Years Around 1959.* Geneva: United Nations, 1972.

28. United Nations. *A System of National Accounts.* New York: United Nations, 1968.

29. Wonnacott, R.J. *Canadian-American Dependence: An Interindustry Analysis of Production and Prices.* Amsterdam: North-Holland Publishing Company, 1961.

Part One

National Economic Development Studies

Chapter One

Projecting Alternative Structures of the British Economy

T. S. Barker

One of the original aims of the Cambridge Growth Project was the examination of possibilities of stimulating the rate of growth of the British economy and the problems to which this would give rise [13]. The development of the research as regards economic policy has, however, been more general than this: it might now be summarised as the presentation and examination of feasible alternatives regarding the future of the economy. One of these alternatives is faster growth; but others, such as higher levels of public services or a more egalitarian distribution of income, are not precluded from our work.

We have chosen from the outset to tackle these problems by means of an input-output model of the economy. The first projections were made by Brown [7] and relied on a model with three main sets of relationships: current industrial inputs were determined by the input-output matrix; capital inputs by a set of incremental capital–output ratios; and imports by row and column vectors of coefficients. Since then, the foreign trade sector has been elaborated with the introduction of price-sensitive trade functions in parallel with the development of price generation in the model, as explained in a paper by Barker and Lecomber [4]. And, later still, in a paper by Barker and Woodward [5], production functions and consumption functions have been introduced to allow more explicitly the simulation of fiscal instruments. However, it should be noted that from the beginning the projections were never intended to be "forecasts of what is most likely or statements of what is most desired" [13, p. 3], but rather attempts to follow through in detail the consequences of particular sets of assumptions. The assumptions, however, should be realistic (or feasible if they concern economic policy) if the projections are to be of value in guiding decisions.

The author wishes to thank his colleagues in the Cambridge Growth Project for their advice while this paper was being written and for help when he was generating the projections reported in it.

The model has developed in this way in acknowledgement of the fact that to get the most out of the projections of the economy, the policies adopted in response to them must be incorporated as part of the model. For example, the project began by setting out the consequences of alternative rates of growth of consumers' expenditures during the period 1960–1970 [7] and asking the questions: What would output growth be if these rates of growth were achieved? And what investment would be needed to sustain the output growth? But when these questions were answered there remained the problem of the policies needed to increase consumers' expenditures (different policies having different effects on employment and the balance of foreign trade), the problem of balancing foreign payments if exports are not sufficient to pay for the import requirements, and the problem of ensuring that any level of investment required for growth is forthcoming.

The model is a combination of technical relationships explaining current and capital transactions and behavioural relationships explaining consumption, foreign trade, and prices. As such, it bears some resemblance to the models developed for the Norwegian economy by Johansen and Schreiner [9; 10] and for the American economy by Almon and others [1; 2]. The Norwegian model emphasises the problems of long-term development of the economy; the American model emphasises the dynamic adjustment between investment and output; the British model, as it has developed over the past three years, emphasises the problems of economic policy in controlling the medium-term future.

This paper is about two alternative 1980 projections of the British economy: one allows for faster growth by increasing investment; and the other has more social services, incurring higher levels of public current and capital expenditures. The increase in investment is brought about directly by more spending in public industries and indirectly by increases in incentives for private investment. The paper investigates the structures of supplies of and demands for commodities and labour that are implied by these alternatives.

These calculations, however, must be set in the context of the British economy and the model we have estimated to represent that economy. This paper continues with a description of the model. Then a view of the economy in 1980 is adopted as a standard that can be used to compare the two alternatives. The effects of changes in policy instruments in the model are crucial to the realism of the alternative projections and these are measured and examined to ensure that they conform to a priori expectations. Particular values of the instruments are chosen in such a way as to display the alternatives on a consistent basis, that is, with internal and external balance corresponding to that in the standard view of the economy. The alternatives are described and compared in the final section of the paper.

A Computable Model of the Economy

Our model is intended to represent the underlying structure of the economy for the purpose of projecting four to six years in the future. Accordingly, we almost completely ignore the short-term dynamics of the economy and concentrate on the long-term outlook with a given structure and a given set of exogenous variables but with alternative assumptions about economic policy. The solutions of the model represent the economy as almost fully adjusted to the assumptions about exchange rates, taxes, public expenditures, and other instruments of policy. Thus, they do not represent the actual state of the economy at any one point in time, but the hypothetical economy where outputs, incomes, and expenditures are adjusted to, *inter alia,* a particular growth in wages and particular levels of exchange rates and taxes.

The Main Relationships
The following six sets of relationships describe the main features of the model.

COMMODITY SUPPLIES AND DEMANDS

$$A_1 M + Q \equiv U + A_2 V + \Delta^* S + A_3 G + A_4 C + X \equiv D \tag{1-1}$$

INPUT-OUTPUT RELATIONS

$$U = A_5 Y \tag{1-2}$$

$$Y = A_6 Q \tag{1-3}$$

IMPORT AND EXPORT FUNCTIONS

$$\log M = B_0 + \hat{B}_1 \log D + \hat{B}_2 \log [\hat{P}_a^{-1} P_m^*] \tag{1-4}$$

$$\log X = B_3 + \hat{B}_4 \log D_f + \hat{B}_5 \log [\theta(\hat{P}_f)^{-1} P_x] + \hat{B}_6 \log [\hat{P}_q^{-1} P_x] \tag{1-5}$$

INVESTMENT AND EMPLOYMENT FUNCTIONS

$$V \qquad = (A_7 + A_8 \Delta^* Y)i \tag{1-6}$$

$$\hat{Y}^{-1} \Delta^* Y = \hat{B}_7 \hat{L}^{-1} \Delta^* L + (I - \hat{B}_7 \hat{B}_8^{-1}) \hat{B}_9^{-1} \hat{Y}^{-1} V \tag{1-7}$$

CONSUMPTION FUNCTION AND
LINEAR EXPENDITURES SYSTEM

$$i' E_1 = \epsilon = \alpha_1 \omega_1 + \beta_1 \mu_1 + \beta_2 \mu_2 \tag{1-8}$$

$$E_1 \quad = B_{10} + \hat{P}_{e_1}^{-1} B_{11} (\epsilon \pi_\epsilon - P'_{e_1} B_{10}) \tag{1-9}$$

PRICE FORMATION

$$P_y \quad = A'_5 P_h + W + P_r + T_y + M_y \tag{1-10}$$

$$P_h = \hat{K}_1 P_q + \hat{K}_2 P_m^* + \hat{K}_3 P_x \tag{1-11}$$

$$W = B_{12} \hat{Y}^{-1} L\rho \tag{1-12}$$

$$P_r = \hat{B}_{13} W \tag{1-13}$$

$$P_c = A_4' P_h + F_c + T_c + M_c \tag{1-14}$$

$$\log P_x = B_{14} + \hat{B}_{15} \log [P_f \theta^{-1}] + \hat{B}_{16} \log P_q \tag{1-15}$$

In these equations, capital letters represent matrices and vectors, and Greek letters represent scalars. A vector that is transformed into a diagonal matrix is denoted by ^, and a forward first difference operator is denoted by Δ^*. The parameters and variables in order of appearance are as follows.

A_1 to A_8 = matrices of parameters, with A_5 being the input-output matrix

B_0 to B_{16} = vectors of parameters

$\alpha_1, \beta_1, \beta_2$ = scalar parameters

M = a vector of imports

Q = a vector of commodity outputs

U = a vector of industrial demands for commodities

V = a vector of fixed investments, classified by the investing industry

$\Delta^* S$ = a vector of stockbuilding

G = a vector of government current expenditures

C = a vector of consumers' expenditures divided into expenditures on nondurables and on durables

X = a vector of exports

D = a vector of total demands

Y = a vector of industrial outputs

P_q = a vector of prices of domestic outputs

P_m^* = a vector of prices of imports adjusted for customs duties

D_f = a vector of foreign demands for commodities

θ = the "effective" exchange rate

P_f = a vector of competitor countries' prices

P_x = a vector of UK export prices

$\Delta^* Y$ = a vector of changes in industrial outputs

L = a vector of employment by industry

E_1 = a vector of consumers' expenditures per capita on nondurables [If E_2 is consumers' expenditures on durables, then $(E_1 + E_2) \cdot$ population $= C$]

ϵ = total consumers' expenditures per capita on nondurables

ω_1 = the permanent component of wealth per capita

μ_1, μ_2 = permanent and transitory components of disposable income per capita

P_{e_1} = a vector of prices of consumers' expenditures on nondurables

π_ϵ = the overall price index appropriate to ϵ

P_y = a vector of prices of industrial outputs

P_h = a vector of prices of domestic absorptions

W = a vector of labour earnings per unit of output

P_r = a vector of profits per unit of output

T_y, M_y = vectors of taxes and imports per unit of output

K_1, K_2, K_3 = vectors of weights, where $K_1 + K_2 + K_3 = i$, the unit vector

ρ = the average industrial wage

F_c, T_c, M_c = vectors of labour inputs, taxes, and imports per unit of consumers' expenditures

This set of equations is not a comprehensive account of the model, but it does show the principal interactions between variables.[1] The basic sets of identities in the model are those embodied in the economic accounts: commodity demands equal supplies in constant and current prices; the value of industrial outputs equals that of inputs; and all incomes of the various institutional sectors of the economy (government and the corporate and personal sectors) are equal to expenditures plus savings. Only the first of these identities is shown above— in equation (1-1)—but the others are implicit in the price relationships, [equation (1-10)], or included, if only to estimate savings by institutional sectors, as residuals. In the commodity identities, the matrices of parameters are classifica-

---

1. The computer program of the model is in fact more complicated, as it includes details of the tax and subsidy system and special treatment for some of the imports and industrial outputs.

tion converters, which convert vectors from a function classification to a commodity classification.

The input-output coefficient matrix, A_5, is rectangular, showing inputs of commodities per unit of output of industries. For a vector of industrial outputs given at any stage in the solution of the model, the matrix is used to calculate industrial demands for commodities [see equation (1-2)]. This procedure requires that the industrial production mix of each commodity output is also calculated [equation (1-3)].

The foreign trade relationships, equations (1-4) and (1-5), are log linear so as to incorporate constant-elasticity price effects. The parameters in the model are based on time-series regression estimates in which the estimated equations included lagged price terms, capacity terms, and time trends.[2] The overall price elasticities depend on the mix of imports and exports, but the average price elasticity for imports works out at about -0.45 and that for exports at -1.35.

The investment coefficients, equation (1-6), in matrices A_7 and A_8 represent replacement investments and incremental capital–output ratios for each industry by type of asset. The replacements are estimated from asset lives; the incremental capital–output ratios are estimated from a study of investment and changes in output in the period 1949-1965.

The production function, equation (1-7), has been developed by Wigley [22]. We have adopted the vintage approach to technical change, assuming that once equipment is installed, the capital-output and labour-output ratios are fixed, at least for normal utilisation of capacity. Hence increases in productivity are assumed to be entirely dependent on gross investment or the scrapping of old equipment. The parameters of the functions are estimated on each industry's investment and its long-term growth rate in output and employment during the period 1954-1968.

The consumption function in the model is described by Stone [12]. Total consumers' expenditures on nondurables are determined by wealth and by permanent and transient components of income, equation (1-8). This total is divided into expenditures in functional categories using the linear expenditures system, equation (1-9), as described by Stone [11]. The parameters of the system have been estimated by maximum likelihood for 1954-1970 data with linear time trends in the vector of parameters $\hat{B}_{11}$. (This is described by Deaton [8].)

Industries set their prices in the model by passing on all costs, equation (1-10), and maintaining profits as a constant share of value added in each industry, equation (1-13). Costs per unit of output consist of the cost of material and service inputs, the cost of labour inputs—which are related to employment and the average industrial wage, equation (1-12)—taxes, and direct imports. A set of prices is needed to value material and service inputs. This is formed by weighting the domestic output prices, import prices, and export prices so that the identity of commodity supplies and demands in current prices is satisfied, equation

---

2. The import functions have been published in Barker [3]; the export study is not yet completed. Both sets of functions are being reestimated to include the period 1967-1972.

(1-11). Consumer prices and other prices of domestic demands are also formed from these prices of domestic absorptions, adding in unit values of factor inputs, taxes, and imports, equation (1-14). Export prices are related to both home prices and competitors' prices, allowing for exchange-rate variations, equation (1-15).

The Solution of the Model

The model in its present operational form contains 693 technical and behavioural relationships, not including the detail of interindustry flows or the elements of the classification converters. The model is nonlinear and an algebraic solution does not exist. The numerical solution is a simple Gauss-Seidel one, holding stored values to a minimum: the method is to solve for a set of prices, given the quantities, then use the prices to recalculate the quantities, and so on. The whole process takes 12-14 seconds on an IBM 370/165 computer, and there have been no problems of convergence as long as reasonable starting values have been adopted.

Two economic aggregates are especially interesting in each solution of the model. The first is the balance of trade in goods and services, which is calculated by subtracting the value of imports from that of exports, where import volumes, export volumes, and export prices are all solved in the model. However, there is no built-in constraint preventing this balance from becoming large and negative. If this does happen, it may well indicate that the solution is very unrealistic as a projection of the economy, but then the model is not intended to do the work of the economist—only to guide his judgement. The second economic aggregate of interest is the level of employment, which is found by adding employment in industry to that in government and in the personal sector. Again, there is no constraint on this total so that a projection can indicate requirements for employment greater than the working population.

These solutions all have the characteristic that economic policy is assumed to be exogenous to the model. However, the program solving the model has been developed so that particular targets of government policy, for example, full employment, are reached in the solutions by appropriate adjustment to instruments of economic policy, for example, the standard rate of personal income tax. These "target" solutions, with economic policy now endogenous to the model, are the relevant ones in comparing alternative economic structures.

The British Economy to 1980

For the comparison of alternative projections of the economy, we require a "standard view" which represents the outcome of a set of assumptions chosen as the most realistic of the assumptions we regard as feasible.[3] The standard view

---

3. The data, assumptions, and projections presented and described in this and the following sections were as of March 1974. In the light of subsequent developments and changes in our assumptions (particularly those relating to hours worked in manufacturing and productivity in services) they must be regarded as highly optimistic.

should also reflect the achievement of two targets for policy, viz., internal and external equilibrium as measured by full employment and a balance of foreign payments and receipts. These two targets are treated differently from others, such as faster growth, for two reasons: first, both meet with general agreement and, second, both should perhaps be considered more as constraints on policy rather than as targets. To achieve both targets we require two instruments, and we have chosen the standard rate of income tax and the exchange rate on the basis that these have been used in the past.

The Assumptions

The assumptions underlying the standard view are in general rather conservative: unless there is strong evidence to the contrary, we have assumed that long-term trends in past behaviour will continue and that the present fiscal system will remain substantially unchanged. The principal assumptions insofar as they can be quantified are listed in Table 1-1. They are divided into assumptions about the British economy and those about the rest of the world.

The population of the United Kingdom (UK) is expected to rise more quickly in the period 1975-1980 than in the period 1970-1975. The age structure also changes so that the working population, which declined between 1965 and 1971, is expected to rise again, giving an extra one million workers by 1980. This is an important factor, which, together with the assumption that actual hours worked will remain constant, raises the underlying rate of growth of productive potential over the next few years. The assumption about UK cost inflation is embodied in the figure for the average wage (UK average earnings per man-year). This is shown as growing at 10.6 percent per annum from 1973 through 1980, which is compared with 12.1 percent per annum from 1970 through 1973 and 6.7 percent per annum from 1960 through 1970.

The other assumptions concern the fiscal system and the exchange rate. The standard rate of tax must fall to 25 percent to maintain full employment in 1980. (This is after the single and married allowances have been increased pro rata with the consumers' expenditures price index.) Other tax rates, allowances, and exemptions have been held at the levels of the 1973 budget, incorporating the changes in that budget. This means that by 1980, as a result of inflation, the real values of specific duties on alcohol, tobacco, and mineral oil are nearly half what they were in 1973. Public expenditures on goods and services follow the projections of the White Paper of December 1973 [18]; and the current transfers by government, the main one of which is pensions, are assumed to rise in line with the average wage. The special cuts in public expenditures announced in December 1973 and subsequent revisions have not been included in these projections.

The level of the exchange rate is determined by events in the rest of the world as well as in the United Kingdom. In the standard view of 1980, it is 6 percent lower than its 1974 level in relation to other currencies. The volume of world

Table 1-1. Principal Assumptions: Projections of the British Economy to 1980

Year	UK Population (millions)	UK Average Earnings per Man-year (£)	UK Policy Instruments — Income Tax Standard Rate[a] (percent)	UK Policy Instruments — Value added Tax Standard Rate (percent)	Sterling Exchange Rate (Dec. 1971 = 100)	Volume of World Production	Import Prices[b] (1963 = 100) — Total	Import Prices — Food	Import Prices — Raw Materials	Import Prices — Fuel	Manufactures	United Kingdom's Competitors' Prices
1955	50.95	—[c]	33.5	—	109	65	105	98	113	116	100	92
1960	52.35	570	30.1	—	115	83	99	94	104	107	102	98
1965	54.18	759	30.1	—	114	116	104	102	110	93	105	103
1970	55.41	1096	32.1		98	159	128	119	149	101	138	117
1973	(55.98)[d]	(1546)	30.0	10	(85)	(183)	(179)	(182)	(217)	(166)	(177)	(158)
Projections												
1975	56.33	1910	28.3	10	82.5	190	231	213	216	381	218	195
1980	57.42	3250	25.1	10	75	225	309	282	291	594	294	287

[a]Adjusted to the 1973 definition of "basic rate."
[b]Nonferrous metals have been included in raw materials.
[c]Not available or not calculated.
[d]Numbers in parentheses are estimates.

Sources: United Kingdom Central Statistical Office, *Annual Abstract of Statistics* (London: H.M.S.O.); United Nations, *Monthly Bulletin of Statistics*; *Yearbook of National Accounts*; *Yearbook of Statistics* (New York: United Nations).

production, which is an important assumption for UK export volumes, is expected to continue to increase following the 1974–1975 setback. The increase in UK import prices in 1973 was sustained in 1974 partly as a result of the oil price; but from 1975, the growth in import prices is much slower, so that the net effect is a considerable improvement in the UK terms of trade. The oil price for 1980 is about 3.5 times its average level in 1973. UK exports are also affected by inflation in competitor countries, and this is assumed to accelerate after 1972, so that the competitive advantage of sterling is maintained.

The Use of Resources

The use of resources for the UK in 1970 and the projections for 1975 and 1980 are shown in Table 1-2, together with selected growth rates in each component for 1955–1980. The rapid growth in consumers' expenditures in 1971–1973 is not expected to continue, but any slowdown in 1974–1975 will have to be followed by further increases to maintain full employment unless public expenditures or investment is increased above the levels we have projected, given current assumptions about the growth of the economy. The slower growth in public expenditures in the late 1970s reflects the decisions taken in 1973. Investment is expected to continue to grow relatively fast to 1975, but the long-term growth is expected to be slower than that from 1955–1965. Both imports and exports increased by 9 percent in 1973 over 1972. This was due to the exceptional growth in the UK economy and in world production as a whole; this expansion is already at an end. However, we are still anticipating an increase in foreign trade well above past performance.

The 1975–1980 growth rate in gross domestic product reflects the higher utilisation of capacity in 1980 as compared with 1975 because previously unemployed resources are reemployed and result in higher actual as well as potential growth. The longer-term growth rate of 4.0 percent per annum during the period 1970–1980 represents an improvement over the rate of 3.1 percent per annum during the period 1960–1970. However, this higher growth is concentrated in the second half of the decade and can be traced to four factors: first, there is the substantial increase we have assumed in the working population between 1975 and 1980; second, the assumed recovery of hours worked to the 1969 level means that the labour supply is further augmented; third, the projected investment growth between 1975 and 1980 has a direct effect on increasing the productivity of labour; and fourth, the exploitation of North Sea mineral resources changes the mix of output towards the highly productive oil and gas sectors. Since we are projecting a fully employed economy in 1980, these additional resources are reemployed and result in higher actual as well as potential growth.

The faster growth in full-employment gross domestic product is also dependent on a rise in productivity in the service industries which was in evidence in the 1960s but has been much more uncertain since then. It is worth noting that if the growth rate in service productivity slows down appreciably, then the growth

Table 1-2. Gross Domestic Product and the Use of Resources, United Kingdom, 1955-1980

Year	Con- sumers' Expen- ditures	Public Authori- ties' Current Expen- ditures	Gross Fixed Capital Forma- tion	Stock- build- ing	Exports of Goods and Services	Less Imports of Goods and Services	Gross Domestic Product at Market Prices
			(£ million 1963 prices)				
1970	23,447	5,889	7,152	266	8,627	8,356	37,025
Projections							
1975 (full employment)	26,770	6,698	8,358	338	11,409	10,622	42,952
1980 (standard view)	33,973	7,902	11,982	408	15,607	15,031	54,842
			(growth rates percent per annum)				
1955-1960	2.8	-0.1	5.6	15.8	2.7	4.4	2.5
1960-1965	2.9	2.6	6.2	-9.8	3.6	3.0	3.3
1965-1970	1.9	1.6	2.9	-6.8	6.2	4.9	2.9
1970-1971	2.6	3.7	0.5	n.c.[a]	7.1	4.8	2.4
1971-1972[b]	(5.9)	(3.8)	(1.7)	n.c.	(3.1)	(10.2)	(2.3)
1972-1973[b]	(4.6)	(3.2)	(6.0)	n.c.	(8.6)	(9.0)	(5.3)
Projections							
1970-1975	2.7	2.5	3.3	4.9	5.7	4.9	3.0
1975-1980	4.9	3.4	7.5	3.8	6.5	7.3	5.0
1970-1980	3.8	3.0	5.3	4.4	6.1	6.0	4.0

[a]n.c. = not calculated.

[b]Numbers in parentheses are provisional estimates that are based on the data in *Monthly Digest of Statistics,* February 1974 [15] and *National Income and Expenditure, 1973* [16]. The data were converted from 1970 prices to 1963 prices.

Source: United Kingdom, *National Income and Expenditure* (London: H.M.S.O., 1972).

in output will be reduced in the projection period 1975-1980 by as much as 1 percent per annum.

Employment and the Balance of Trade

Tables 1-3 and 1-4 show the targets for employment and the balance of trade in 1980 and their implications for employment in different sectors of the economy and for the volumes and unit values of exports and imports. The employment target represents our definition of full employment for a working population of 26,300,000, that is, an unemployment rate of 2 percent. The distribution of this employment shows a continuation of past trends towards the service industries and government.

Table 1-3.   Employment, United Kingdom, 1958–1980 (thousands)

Year	*Industry*		*Govern-ment*	*Personal Sector*	*Total*	*Unem-ployment*	*Working Population*
	Goods	*Services*					
1958	12,035	8,539	2,944	760	24,278	406	24,684
1968	11,876	9,155	3,517	735	25,283	542	25,825
Projections							
1975 (full employment)	n.c.[a]	n.c.	3,861	735	25,107	512	25,619
1980 (standard view)	11,303	9,504	4,230	735	25,774	526	26,300

[a]n.c. = not calculated.

Source: United Kingdom, *Annual Abstract of Statistics* (London: H.M.S.O., 1972).

The balance-of-trade target of £600 million in 1980 is intended to be large enough to cover interest payments on the earlier borrowing required to cover the oil deficit. Larger surpluses will have to be generated in the 1980s to repay these loans. The surplus is partly a result of the improvement in the terms of trade, which are assumed to recover from 94.0 in 1973 to 97.5 in 1980. Because the price of oil has risen so much relative to other import prices, the terms of trade are more sensitive than before to the quantity of oil imported, and (because we have assumed a fixed production of North Sea oil) to the growth in UK demand. At the prices assumed for oil in these projections, North Sea oil makes a gross contribution to the balance of trade in 1980 of nearly £5000 million. This is reduced by net profits and transfers paid abroad by the oil companies; nevertheless, it is the main factor leading to the transformation of the UK balance of payments by 1980. North Sea oil production is estimated at 125 million tons in 1980, representing 70 percent of total UK supplies. This is priced at the same level as imports, resulting in exceptional profits for the oil companies. If these were taxed away, our implicit assumption is that the tax revenues would not be spent by the government.

To achieve the targets, it was necessary to reduce the standard rate of tax from 30 percent to 25 percent and to reduce the effective sterling exchange rate from 80 to 75 (December 1971 = 100). With the December 1973 tax rates and exchange rates and retaining all the other assumptions for 1980, the model produces unemployment of over one million people and a surplus on the balance of trade of £2500 million.

Alternative Projections

The preceding sections provide the background for the calculation of alternative projections. But before these are presented, it is worth considering how the model reacts to the changes in economic policy that may be required.

Table 1-4.   The Balance of Trade in Goods and Services, United Kingdom, 1955-1980

Year	Exports of Goods and Services			Imports of Goods and Services			Terms of Trade (1963 = 100)	Balance of Trade (£ million)
	(£ million)	(£ million 1963 prices)	(unit value 1963 = 100)	(£ million)	(£ million 1963 prices)	(unit value 1963 = 100)		
1955	4,177	4,664	89.6	4,481	4,571	98.0	91.4	-304
1960	5,147	5,327	96.6	5,554	5,669	98.0	98.6	-407
1965	6,561	6,343	103.4	6,861	6,577	104.3	99.2	-300
1970	11,344	8,627	131.5	10,844	8,356	129.8	101.4	500
1971	12,601	9,065	139.2	11,804	8,738	135.1	103.1	797
1972	13,229	9,248	143.0	13,430	9,543	140.7	101.6	-201
1973[a]	(16,683)	(10,043)	(166.1)	(18,383)	(10,402)	(176.7)	(94.0)	(-1,700)
Projections								
1975 (full employment)	23,412	11,409	205.2	24,523	10,622	230.9	88.9	-1,112
1980 (standard view)	47,091	15,607	301.8	46,491	15,031	309.4	97.5	600

[a]Numbers in parentheses are provisional estimates.

Sources: United Kingdom, National Income and Expenditure (London: H.M.S.O., 1972) and Preliminary Estimates of the Balance of Payments 1967 to 1972, Cmnd. 5261 (London: H.M.S.O., March 1973).

The Effects of Fiscal Instruments

The model contains a large number of instruments for controlling the economy. In this section, five of the more important instruments are each varied in turn and their effects on the main aggregates are measured. This provides a check on the plausibility of the model and also shows up its main characteristics. The five policy instruments are as follows:

1. The exchange rate: The effective sterling exchange rate had already depreciated by 18 percent in the two years following the Smithsonian agreement of December 1971. Further depreciation of 8 percent is needed to achieve the required surplus in the 1980 balance of trade.
2. The standard rate of income tax: This was at 30 percent in 1973, but in the projections it is reduced to 25 percent, although the rate would be higher if all the personal allowances in the tax system were adjusted for inflation.
3. The basic rate of value-added tax: This was at 10 percent in 1973 with food and fuels having a zero rate and various services exempted; this system is fully represented in the model.
4. Investment incentives: Allowances are given to industrial investors, enabling them to write off investment costs against profits in calculating tax payable. In 1973, initial allowances for plant, machinery, and vehicles were 100 percent and for buildings 40 percent. Further allowances were given to development areas and to special industries. We have assumed that the value of these incentives is changed so as to reduce the effective price of capital goods by 10 percent. This works out for plant and machinery as an increase in initial allowances of approximately 11 percent, whilst for buildings and works, the initial allowance must be raised to 60 percent to produce the same result. The effects of incentives are introduced into the model by changing industrial investment according to parameters estimated in investment functions.[4]
5. Public expenditures on health, education, and other social services plus all investment in dwellings: Defence and spending on new roads have both been excluded. Table 1-5 shows the projections compared with past figures.

Table 1-6 shows the effects on the level of employment and the balance of trade of increasing the level of each instrument by 10 percent. The exchange rate and investment allowances are both instruments that affect employment and the balance of trade in the same direction, that is, deflation accompanies a deterioration rather than an improvement in the balance of trade. The contrast between the exchange rate, traditionally used to control the balance of foreign trade, and the income tax rate, traditionally used to control employment, is

4. The treatment of investment in the model was changed after the projections reported in this paper were finished, with the existing functions, equation (1-6) being replaced by investment demand functions incorporating price effects. The effects of changes in investment incentives were calculated from these functions and added to the investment levels in the standard view.

Table 1-5. Public Expenditures, United Kingdom, 1960–1980 (£ million 1963 prices)

				Projections		
Public Expenditures	*1960*	*1965*	*1970*	*1975 (full employ- ment)*	*1980 (stan- dard view)*	*(higher public services)*
Current expenditures on goods and services:						
Military defence	1,724	1,846	1,511	1,551	1,735	1,735
National health services	923	1,045	1,232	1,382	1,637	1,801
Education	780	958	1,181	1,514	1,867	2,054
Other	1,333	1,547	1,959	2,251	2,663	2,929
Total	4,760	5,396	5,883	6,698	7,902	8,519
Capital expenditures on goods and services:						
Education	138	230	(240)[a]	258	373	410
National health services	40	83	(95)	122	145	160
Roads, etc.	94	185	(377)	295	430	430
Other public services	124	211	(337)	379	575	632
Dwellings: public sector	301	526	585	1,140	1,500	1,650
private sector	524	652	530			
Total	1,221	1,887	2,164	2,194	3,023	3,282

[a]Numbers in parentheses are estimated.

Source: United Kingdom, *National Income and Expenditure* (London: H.M.S.O., 1972).

surprising: the exchange rate has more powerful effects on employment, through the increase in exports; and the income tax rate has more powerful effects on the balance of trade, through the decrease in imports. Changes in the value-added tax rate appear to be very similar to those in income tax rates, and allowances with a 10 percent increase in the value-added rate seem to reduce employment about half as much as a 10 percent increase in the income tax rate. Investment allowances reduce employment because of the substitution of capital for labour; but the balance of trade is worsened because investment and domestic output increase and draw in more imports. However, the increase in output is not enough to reemploy all the labour made redundant by the extra investment.

Table 1-7 shows the effects of changing the levels of the instruments on the use of resources. It is a feature of the model that all the components of gross domestic product tend to move together in the same direction, with employment varying with output unless there is a sharp structural change (as in the case of more investment incentives). The revaluation of sterling has the largest effect on gross domestic product, with the reduction in exports causing a chain reaction on consumers' expenditures, investment, and imports. The other instruments

**Table 1-6. Changes in Fiscal Instruments and the Targets, United
Kingdom, 1980**

1980 Projections	*Employment (thousands)*	*Balance of Trade (£ million)*
Target	25,773	600
The effect of a 10 percent increase in		
Exchange rate	−694	−288
Income tax, standard rate	−147	+902
Value-added tax rate	−72	+407
Investment incentives	−119	−172
Public expenditures	+677	−1,584

Note: The exact definition of the instruments in the table is provided in the text.

also affect exports, but only indirectly through their effects on UK prices. Income tax and value-added tax both concentrate their effects on consumers'
expenditures, which is their primary target. Investment incentives also increase
consumers' expenditures and exports, but this is mainly an indirect effect of
higher growth on the price level in the model. The changes in public expenditures
have primary effects of increases of £617 million in current expenditures and of
£260 million in investment (both figures in 1963 prices). The secondary effects
on consumers' expenditures are particularly high because of the increase in
government employment and wages.

The small changes in exports shown in most of these tests are a result of
slightly higher or lower domestic price levels. Prices move inversely with the
level of gross domestic product projected by the model because of the assumption of fixed average earnings, irrespective of the level of unemployment. Hence,
a higher level of employment with fixed earnings per person means that unit
costs for labour are reduced, and since we assume that prices are formed from
unit costs, these are also reduced. This effect is most marked when investment
incentives are increased so that the level of gross domestic product increases and
domestic unit costs fall by as much as 1 percent.

Alternative Structures for the Economy

Social choice regarding the future of the economy involves a political process
and political and social judgements about the alternatives as well as economic
ones. And a real choice requires the equal and simultaneous presentation of these
alternatives. We are now in a position to do this for three alternatives.

1. The standard view: This alternative, which has been described earlier, involves
   a substantial increase in private consumers' expenditures to absorb the available economic resources.
2. Higher growth: This alternative can be achieved by increasing investment
   incentives, always assuming that the response of investment incorporated in

Table 1-7. Changes in Fiscal Instruments and the Use of Resources, 1980

1980 Projections	Con- umers' Expen- ditures	Public Authori- ties' Current Expen- ditures	Gross Fixed Capital Forma- tion	Stock- building	Exports of Goods and Services	Less Imports of Goods and Services	Gross Domestic Product at Market Prices
	(£ million 1963 prices)						
Standard view	33,973	7,902	11,982	408	15,607	15,031	54,842
The effects of 10 percent increase in							
Exchange rate	−975	0	−746	−81	−946	−191	−2,559
Income tax, standard rate	−860	0	−243	−9	−39	−286	−865
Value added tax rate	−383	0	−118	−5	−24	−127	−403
Investment incentives	+301	0	+154	+13	+135	+91	+511
Public ex- penditures	+877	+617	+647	+14	+39	+497	+1,695
	(as percentages of the standard view)						
The effects of 10 percent increase in							
Exchange rate	−2.9	0	−6.2	−19.9	−6.1	−1.4	−4.7
Income tax, standard rate	−2.5	0	−2.0	−2.2	−0.2	−1.9	−1.6
Value added tax rate	−1.1	0	−1.0	−1.2	−0.2	−0.8	−0.7
Investment incentives	0.9	0	1.3	3.2	0.9	0.6	0.9
Public ex- penditures	2.6	7.8	5.4	3.4	0.2	3.3	3.1
	(as percentages of the change in gross domestic product)						
The effects of 10 percent increase in							
Exchange rate	38.1	0	29.2	3.2	37.0	7.5	100
Income tax, standard rate	99.3	0	28.1	1.0	4.5	33.0	100
Value added tax rate	95.0	0	29.3	1.2	6.0	31.5	100
Investment incentives	58.9	0	30.1	2.5	26.4	17.8	100
Public ex- penditures	51.7	36.4	38.2	0.8	2.3	29.3	100

our model is correct. The extra investment must use up some of the resources that would otherwise have gone to consumption, whether public or private, but it also increases the productive capacity of the economy.

3. Higher public services: This alternative can be achieved by increasing public expenditures at the expense of private consumption.

These alternatives are compared by building them into a model of the economy and ensuring that internal, as well as external, equilibrium is maintained for the projection year. Table 1-8 shows how the exchange rate and the standard rate of income tax (the two instruments chosen to maintain equilibrium) must vary if this condition is fulfilled by the projections. For higher growth, the exchange rate must be depreciated even more than is necessary in the standard view, because investment is more import-intensive than consumption. The income tax rate, however, is only slightly above the rate in the standard view, because the extra investment increases productive capacity sufficiently to allow extra consumption as well. For higher public services in 1980, both the exchange rate and the income tax rate remain at their December 1973 levels. The use of extra resources by the government rather than by private consumers reduces the volume of imports and any need for further sterling depreciation.

The changes in the composition of gross domestic product for the alternatives are shown in Table 1-9. Higher growth increases the underlying growth in gross domestic product from 3.9 to 4.1 percent per annum for the period 1969-1980 and results in an absolute increase in consumption greater than that in investment in order to maintain employment. Higher public services require lower private consumption and also reduce the growth rate as labour must be diverted from industries into government service. However, the reduction in the growth rate (from the standard view of 3.9 to 3.7 percent per annum for the period 1969-1980) must not be taken as a reduction in the growth of welfare for two reasons. First, national accounting conventions measure the output of government by expenditures, so that if productivity improved it would not show in the figures and the difference in the (corrected) growth rates may not exist. And second, public goods may contribute more to welfare than private goods, so that the change in the composition of final output more than compensates for the reduction in its total.

The reasons for these differences become clearer when the structures of output and employment are examined for the alternatives. These are shown in Table 1-10. Higher public services require over 400,000 workers to move into govern-

Table 1-8. Changes in the Exchange Rate and the Income Tax Rate to Meet the Targets, 1980

Year	Exchange Rate *(Dec. 1971 = 100)*	Income Tax *Standard Rate (percent)*
1973	85.0	30.0
1980 Projections		
Standard view	75.2	25.1
Higher growth	73.8	25.4
Higher public services	79.5	29.9

Table 1-9. Alternative Structures of the Gross Domestic Product, 1980

1980 Projections	Consumers' Expenditures	Public Authorities' Current Expenditures	Gross Fixed Capital Formation	Stock-building	Exports of Goods and Services	Less Imports of Goods and Services	Gross Domestic Product at Market Prices
	(£ million 1963 prices)						
Standard view	33,973	7,902	11,982	408	15,607	15,031	54,842
	(absolute changes from standard view)						
Higher growth	+393	0	+286	+30	+335	+100	+943
Higher public services	-1,331	+617	-258	-51	-586	-175	-1,436
	(percentage changes from standard view)						
Higher growth	1.2	0.0	2.4	7.4	2.1	0.7	1.7
Higher public services	-3.9	7.8	-2.2	-12.5	-3.8	-1.2	-2.6

ment rather than industry—almost half of the growth in the working population from 1975 to 1980. This reduces industrial output and investment below what they might have been. One of the industries least affected is construction, since much of the extra public expenditures directly affects this industry.

Higher growth has the effect of reallocating labour within the industrial sector towards the engineering and allied industries and away from services. One of the main reasons for the very favourable response of the growth rate to extra investment is the assumption we make about the productive process. All extra output is assumed to arise from new equipment; and changes in labour productivity are assumed to take place through gross investment and the scrapping of old equipment. Thus, extra investment directly increases productivity; and, since full employment is maintained, this directly increases the growth rate of the economy. This does not mean that extra investment is costless, because it must be undertaken in advance of the extra output being produced, and at that stage (not represented in the 1980 projections) consumption must be less than it would otherwise be.

Conclusion: Models and Reality

Many of the results given in this paper convey a false impression of precision. We are very uncertain about events in the rest of the world (in particular whether 1974 and 1975 will see the emergence of a world depression), about wage inflation in the British economy, and about the responses to income and price changes we have incorporated in the model. Alternative assumptions, rather than

Table 1–10. Alternative Structures of Output and Employment, 1980

Industry[a]	Primary Increase in Investment for Higher Growth (£ million 1963 prices)	Gross Output			Employment		
		Standard View	Change from Standard		Standard View	Change from Standard	
			Higher Growth	Higher Public Services		Higher Growth	Higher Public Services
		(£ million 1963 prices)			(thousands)		
1 Agriculture, etc.	4	2,156	+17	-32	270	+1	-11
2 Coal mining b	2	662	+13	-20	308	+4	-8
3 Mining, n.e.s.	11	1,259	+11	-9	95	-3	0
4 Cereal processing	0	1,206	+4	+1	266	0	1
5 Food processing, n.e.s.	1	1,577	+13	-24	328	+1	-4
6 Drink	2	1,522	+27	-71	125	-2	-2
7 Tobacco manufacture	0	135	-1	+7	11	0	1
8 Coke ovens	0	261	+7	-12	18	0	0
9 Mineral oil refining	2	1,718	+51	-81	19	0	-1
10 Chemicals, etc.	9	4,455	+133	-205	343	+2	-15
11 Iron & steel	5	2,911	+86	-152	410	+16	-33
12 Nonferrous metals	2	1,241	+30	-52	183	+2	-6
13 Engineering	8	8,061	+248	-446	2,146	+27	-88
14 Shipbuilding, etc.	0	514	+15	-30	181	+4	-9
15 Motor vehicles, etc.	3	3,724	+104	-200	592	+3	-18
16 Aircraft	1	1,011	+33	-62	327	+6	-14
17 Vehicles, n.e.s.	0	306	+6	-12	118	+2	-6
18 Metal goods	1	1,615	+53	-90	541	+11	-22
19 Textile fibres	2	674	+29	-46	35	-2	-1
20 Textiles, n.e.s.	4	1,962	+68	-135	560	+18	-41
21 Leather, clothing, etc.	1	1,243	+43	-96	466	-3	-1
22 Building materials	4	1,436	+32	-25	116	-4	1
23 Pottery & glass	0	352	+9	-15	101	-1	0
24 Timber & furniture	1	1,000	+16	-19	257	-1	-2
25 Paper & board	1	616	+18	-27	86	0	-2
26 Printing & publishing	2	2,206	+36	-57	656	+4	-12

27	Rubber	1	596	+12	−23	93	−1	−1
28	Manufactures, n.e.s.	1	872	+27	−48	238	0	−4
29	Construction	8	8,380	+168	−58	2,010	−4	−9
30	Gas	2	1,953	+19	−31	186	+1	−6
31	Electricity	17	3,234	+57	−105	151	+2	−19
32	Water	3	223	+3	−6	66	+1	−2
33	Transport & communic.	36	7,128	+136	−241	1,615	−5	−32
34	Distribution	16	6,380	+88	−192	2,858	−28	−18
35	Misc. services	47	12,449	+238	−511	5,031	−48	−33
	Total industries	197	85,038	+1,850	−3,125	20,807	+3	−417
	Other sectors	n.c.^c	n.c.	n.c.	n.c.	4,965	0	+420
	Total	n.c.	n.c.	n.c.	n.c.	25,772	+3	+3

aThe industries are defined in a monograph by Barker and Lecomber [4].
bn.e.s. = not elsewhere specified.
cn.c. = not calculated.

policies, would give a range to the projections which would in turn give a range in the combinations of exchange rate and tax rate to achieve equilibrium. Even so, given a different standard view, the alternatives of higher growth or higher public services and the trade-off between them and the standard view should still be in the same direction and have a similar relative magnitude. The aim of this paper is to make discussion of the choice between these alternatives more informed.

References

1. Almon, C. *The American Economy to 1975.* New York: Harper & Row, 1966.

2. Almon, C.; L. Atkinson; and T.C. Reimbold. "Dynamic Interindustry Forecasting for Business Planning." In *Input-Output Techniques.* Edited by A. Bródy and A.P. Carter. Amsterdam: North-Holland Publishing Company, 1972. Pp. 518–530.

3. Barker, T.S. *The Determinants of Britain's Visible Imports, 1949–1966.* In *A Programme for Growth.* Vol. 10. Edited by Richard Stone. London: Chapman and Hall, December 1970.

4. Barker, T.S., and J.R.C. Lecomber. *Exploring 1972 with Special Reference to the Balance of Payments.* In *A Programme for Growth.* Vol. 9. Edited by Richard Stone. London: Chapman and Hall, July 1970.

5. Barker, T.S., and V.H. Woodward. "Inflation, Growth, and Economic Policy in the Medium-Term." *National Institute Economic Review* no. 60 (May 1972): 37–55.

6. Bródy, A., and A.P. Carter, eds. *Input-Output Techniques.* Amsterdam: North-Holland Publishing Company, 1972.

7. Brown, A. *Exploring 1970: Some Numerical Results.* In *A Programme for Growth.* Vol. 6. Edited by Richard Stone. London: Chapman and Hall, July 1965.

8. Deaton, A.S. *Models and Projections of Demand in Post–War Britain.* London: Chapman and Hall, 1975.

9. Johansen, L. *A Multisectoral Study of Economic Growth.* Amsterdam: North-Holland Publishing Company, 1964.

10. Schreiner, P. "The Role of Input-Output in the Perspective Analysis of the Norwegian Economy." In *Input-Output Techniques.* Edited by A. Bródy and A.P. Carter. Amsterdam: North-Holland Publishing Company, 1972. Pp. 449–475.

11. Stone, J.R.N. "Linear Expenditure Systems and Demand Analysis: An Application to the Pattern of British Demand." *Economic Journal* 64, no. 255 (September 1954): 511–527.

12. Stone, R. "Personal Spending and Saving in Postwar Britain." In *Economic Structure and Development.* Edited by H.C. Bos et al. Amsterdam: North-Holland Publishing Company, 1973. Pp. 75–98.

13. Stone, R., and A. Brown. *A Computable Model of Economic Growth.* In *A Programme for Growth.* Vol. 1. Edited by Richard Stone. London: Chapman and Hall, July 1962.

14. United Kingdom Central Statistical Office. *Annual Abstract of Statistics.* London: H.M.S.O.

15. United Kingdom Central Statistical Office. *Monthly Digest of Statistics.* London: H.M.S.O.

16. United Kingdom Central Statistical Office. *National Income and Expenditure.* London: H.M.S.O., annual.

17. United Kingdom Central Statistical Office. *Preliminary Estimates of the Balance of Payments, 1967 to 1972* (Cmnd. 5261). London: H.M.S.O., March 1973.

18. United Kingdom Chancellor of the Exchequer. *Public Expenditure to 1977–78* (Cmnd. 5519). London: H.M.S.O., December 1973.

19. United Nations. *Monthly Bulletin of Statistics.* New York: United Nations.

20. United Nations. *Yearbook of National Accounts.* New York: United Nations.

21. United Nations. *Yearbook of Statistics.* New York: United Nations.

22. Wigley, K.J. "Production Models and Time Trends of Input-Output Coefficients." In *Input-Output in the United Kingdom.* Edited by W.F. Gossling. London: Frank Cass and Company, 1970. Pp. 89–118.

Chapter Two

A Large-Scale Input-Output Econometric Model of the Canadian Economy (CANDIDE)

Ronald G. Bodkin

The CANDIDE model is a large-scale model of the Canadian national economy, fitted to annual data, with an outlook that is medium-term in nature.[1] Two characteristics of the model should be mentioned immediately. First, it is intended to be a general-purpose model, onto which satellite models can be grafted as a particular need arises. It is not a panacea for all policy problems, however. And, in particular, a general-purpose model should not be confused with that nonexistent entity, an all-purpose model. Second, such a large system is obviously computer oriented. With the simultaneous core of CANDIDE Model 1.0 exceeding some 1000 nonlinear equations, and the entire model containing more than 1500 equations, a model like CANDIDE would have been impossible to manage before the age of the high-speed computer. CANDIDE Model 1.0 is block-recursive, with a small number of equations that can be solved before and another small number after calculations have been made for the bulk of the model.

The characteristic of the CANDIDE model that concerns us most in this paper is the fact that it is (by the standards of the literature on macroeconometric models, though not necessarily by the standards of practising industrial

The author wishes to thank Michael C. McCracken, who first suggested that this paper be written; H. Bert Waslander, for helpful criticisms on preliminary drafts; Lou Auer and Dominique Vallet, whose hard work underlies the research described here; and the editors of this volume, for their helpful comments at the final stages of this piece. Of course, all of the foregoing are absolved of any errors of omission or commission.

1. The acronym is (appropriately enough) bilingual in the two official languages of Canada and represents, in English, *CAN*adian *D*isaggregated *I*nter-*D*epartmental *E*conometric [model or project]. (The acronym in French is: [modele ou projet] *CAN*adien *D*ésagrégé *I*nter-*D*épartemental *E*conométrique.) At present, there are two generations of the CANDIDE model, Model 1.0 and Model 1.1, respectively. Only the older model (Model 1.0) has been documented publicly, and consequently the discussion of this paper will focus primarily on Model 1.0. A statement in some depth of the salient features of CANDIDE Model 1.0 may be found in M.C. McCracken [10]. Further details may be found in CANDIDE Project Papers Nos. 2 through 17 [6], not all of which have been published at this writing. This paper draws heavily from the Project Papers by Auer and Vallet [2; 3].

economists) a highly disaggregated one. The disaggregation is basically twofold; namely, it is carried out on the side of real magnitudes (quantities) and also on the side of prices. However, a moment's reflection will persuade the reader that there are, at least potentially, some difficulties to be surmounted. On the issue of real magnitudes, demand is generally modelled by ultimate use (for example, consumer demand for a particular category of expenditures, demand for machinery and equipment by a particular investing industry, or government or export demand for particular categories of expenditures), while supply is generally filled from producing industries. Except in rare cases, the two classifications (commodities and industries) will not coincide, and so we must face squarely the issue of how to bridge this gap. Similar problems arise on the side of prices, and these problems are in a sense the dual of the problem with real magnitudes. In general, we think of price formation as occurring in the industries that produce the real output; thus an appropriate price concept for structural explanation would appear to be some variant of an industry selling price. However, final users do not pay (directly) industry selling prices; they pay for the classes of commodities (categories of expenditures) that they purchase directly, and accordingly (with even a modest degree of aggregation) the concept of price that becomes relevant from the demand side is the implicit deflator of a particular expenditures category. Thus, once again, the model builder must face an analogous problem: how to bridge the gap between producer prices and the prices paid by final users.

In the CANDIDE model, the approach to each of these two problems is based on the use of a moderately large input-output submodel that is rectangular in nature.[2] This input-output submodel is incorporated directly into the basic model itself, and indeed the key equations of the input-output submodel (on both the side of real outputs and the side of implicit deflators) are part of the large simultaneous core of some 1000 nonlinear equations, mentioned earlier. While other solutions to the problems raised in the preceding paragraph can (at least in principle) be envisaged, we have found the option selected to be reasonably satisfactory, from both a theoretical and a practical viewpoint. In particular, the use of an input-output submodel guarantees that we can take the duality of pricing and real output decisions into account in our modelling procedures, where we wish to do so.

First, a brief and selective review of the literature is given. Then, the uses of input-output techniques in the determination of real output by industry and in the determination of the final demand deflators are discussed. Next, some important interrelationships between the input-output portions and the more conventional sectors of CANDIDE Model 1.0 are discussed. The concluding

---

2. This submodel is essentially the result of the labours of the Input-Output Research Division of Statistics Canada. The submodel is, in effect, a condensation of the large rectangular input-output system for Canada described in *The Input-Output Structure of the Canadian Economy, 1961* [5].

section is a cursory summary of some of our experiences in utilizing the input-output portions of the model.

Antecedents in the Literature

The problem outlined in the introductory section does not arise until econometric models attain a certain scale. In particular, if we can consider the various components of final demand as the output of a sole industry, then the distinctions suggested above become unimportant. Thus, in the early stages of econometric model building, there was no need to take interindustrial relationships into account. As far as could be determined, input-output techniques were first combined with conventional macroeconometric modelling in the Brookings econometric model of the U.S. economy [7; 8]. In this section, the use of input-output techniques in the Brookings Model is discussed, along with two other antecedents in the literature.

In the relevant chapter of the Brookings Model volume [7], input-output techniques are utilized for "output conversion" (as it is termed) along the following lines. The components of final demand by category of use (consumption of nondurables excluding foods, nonfarm residential construction expenditures, net exports, etc.—there were 19 in total) served selectively as explanatory variables for constructed series of final demands (the input-output concept) for each of the seven major producing sectors. In turn, final demands by producing sector were related to gross industry outputs by the usual input-output relationships. Finally, the assumption of constant shares of value added in gross industry outputs yielded estimates of real gross national product originating in the seven producing sectors of the economy. In a later version of the Brookings model described in a book by Fromm and Taubman [8, pp. 15-16, 139-140], a second, improved estimate of gross national product originating in a particular producing sector was obtained by regressing the measured level of product originating in each of the sectors of the model on the respective first-round estimate and on the lagged value of the discrepancy between the measured value and the first-round estimate. On the side of prices, the duality of the price-conversion process with the output-conversion process was clearly recognized. With the coefficients obtained in the above regressions, the Brookings authors were able (after some aggregation) to generate first estimates of the implicit deflators of nine categories of final demand expenditures as linear and homogeneous functions of the industry prices for the seven major producing industries. Refined estimates of the implicit deflators were obtained by regressing these final demand deflators on their respective first estimates and the lagged discrepancies between the actual deflators and their respective first estimates.

Another early use of input-output analysis, in combination with conventional macroeconometric modelling, may be found in a 1965 monograph prepared by a committee of ten Japanese econometricians [4]. The committee sets forth a sequence of five econometric models, in which the time horizon gradually shortens and the degree of detail (including, of course, industrial detail) progressively increases. The final two models in this finite sequence (the interindustry model and the integrated model for macroeconomic and interindustry projection) make extensive use of analysis for what the Brookings authors would term "real side conversion" (output conversion). Indeed, the problem of translating final demand by category of final use, through the medium of final demand by product (industry) into output by some 60 industries, is the principal focus of the interindustry model. After gross value added (or gross domestic product) in real terms is calculated for the 60 industries or producing sectors, these outputs are aggregated to some 25 "ownership" sectors, for which labour and capital requirements are calculated. (The labour requirements are calculated by a log-linear relationship between the real wage and the average product of labour; the capital requirements are obtained by inverting a Cobb-Douglas production function which allows for neutral technological change.) These developments are carried further in the case of the integrated model.

The integrated model extends the analysis of the interindustry model (which is conducted exclusively in real magnitudes and relative prices) by adding a prices block, a number of equations for determining functional shares of income, and some final demand equations, which are specified in nominal terms. In this integrated model, a number of repercussions of industrial output levels on the determination of final demand can be taken into account. A striking example of this is the comparison of the investment requirements implied by the inverted production functions of some 25 ownership sectors (which make use of output levels for the 60 industries of the input-output table) with the results of an aggregative investment function emphasizing financial variables. On the prices side, there appears to have been virtually no use made of input-output analysis, despite the fact that the prices block seeks to explain the implicit deflators of some 16 consumption categories and of some 6 export demand categories, in addition to some 5 other more aggregative price level variables. Indeed, the price side seems less well thought out and articulated than the real output side, and the approach would appear to be largely an empirical one. Two other systems that integrate input-output analyses and conventional macroeconometric modelling may be mentioned explicitly. The path-breaking work of Professor Richard Stone and his associates in Cambridge, England, appears in [12]. It may be observed that not only does the Cambridge model use input-output analysis to convert demands by category of final use into output originating by industry, but the techniques are also applied on the side of prices, in order to take interindustrial repercussions into account. Secondly, Clopper Almon [1] combined input-output analysis with behavioural relationships estimated by regression techniques, in order to study problems in the allocation of labour among industries.

The use made of input-output analysis techniques by Ross S. Preston in *The Wharton Annual and Industry Forecasting Model* [11, pp. 26-28, 77-91] is quite similar to their uses in CANDIDE Model 1.0, which is not surprising in view of the fact that the CANDIDE model builders took a good part of their inspiration from Preston's seminal work. Indeed, the principal differences between Preston's approach and that used in CANDIDE are the fact that Preston uses a square input-output system, while a rectangular system is utilized for CANDIDE, and the fact that Preston's model is a model of the U.S. economy.

On the side of output conversion, Preston takes 19 categories of final demand by ultimate use and converts them first into final demand by industry, then, using the standard Leontief inverse, into gross output originating (gross of intermediate inputs) by industry, and finally into gross national product originating by some 50 industries. Although they are conceptually distinct, Preston collapses these three matrices by the simple technique of matrix multiplication. As Preston has observations on the coefficients of these three matrices for one single year, 1958, it becomes possible to generate predictions of gross national product originating in the 50 industries, under the assumption of constant coefficients of these matrices and a given structure of final demand. These series can be compared with the national income estimates (prepared by the U.S. Department of Commerce) of the actual amount of gross national product originating in these 50 industries. Preston solves what he calls the "changing coefficient problem" by a set of adjustment equations that model the discrepancies between the measured and the calculated levels of gross national product originating, for each of the 50 industries.

On the side of price determination, Preston makes use, in principle, of the duality principle inherent in the use of an input-output model for the determination of real output by industry. Starting with seven major sector price levels, which represent the sector deflators of the 50 industries of his model and which are either exogenous or determined elsewhere in the model, Preston forms linear combinations to obtain first estimates of the expenditures deflators. These linear combinations are obtained, in principle, from the transpose of the *C* matrix (the product of the three matrices mentioned above) used in the determination of real output by industry in Preston's model.[3] Finally, these first estimates are subjected to an autoregressive correction equation.[4] In a typical equation, the actual level of the expenditures deflator under consideration is "explained" by the first estimate of the expenditures deflator on the basis of the input-output

3. In comparing the theoretical section vis-à-vis the empirical section [11, pp. 26–28, 77–91], it is not at all evident that this is what Preston has done. However, from conversations with Preston, the author has ascertained that Preston aggregated the three appropriate matrices to dimensions suitable to seven major industries, reinverted the new (smaller) Leontief matrix $(I - A)$, and multiplied the three required matrices together, thus obtaining a new *C* matrix (in Preston's terminology) with the required dimensions. Accordingly, the theory developed in Preston's analytical section still applies, but with the dimension of 7 industries, not 50.

4. Special treatment is accorded to the deflator of imports and of the physical change in inventories. Accordingly, the input-output prices side submodel is applied to only 17 of the 19 categories of final demand by ultimate use.

model, the lagged value of the discrepancy between the actual deflator and its first estimate, and a time trend. Thus, Preston's treatment of price conversion is, as he notes, a development of procedures employed at an earlier date by the Brookings model builders.

Determination of Industry Outputs in CANDIDE
Model 1.0

In CANDIDE Model 1.0, final demand by category of ultimate use is determined for 41 consumption expenditures categories, 6 categories of government expenditures on current account, 39 machinery and equipment investment categories, 40 categories of investment in structures, 12 categories of imports, 25 export categories, and 3 categories of inventory investment—166 categories of final demand altogether. Government spending on capital account appears in one of several investment expenditures categories, while there is one more category of investment in structures than of machinery and equipment investment expenditures because residential construction expenditures are obviously a category of structures investment for which there is no apparent counterpart with regard to machinery and equipment investment. Finally, one of the three categories of inventory investment, Used motor vehicles & scrap, is a source of supply, not of demand, and so is treated in a suitable manner.

In the following discussion, Figure 2-1 may serve as an aid to understanding. It presents a flow chart of the process of output determination for the 43 industries for which real gross domestic product originating in the industry in question is determined in the model. The first stage in the determination of industrial outputs is to convert demand by the 166 categories of final use into demand classified by some 84 commodities. As an aid to the exposition, we may define the following two vectors: let f_j ($j = 1, 2, \ldots, 166$) be the level of final demand expenditures in constant dollars by category of ultimate use j, and let y_i ($i = 1, 2, \ldots, 84$) represent real final demand (according to the commodity classification) for commodity i ($i = 1, 2, \ldots, 84$). Finally, let t_{ij} represent the amount of final demand category j that takes the form of commodity i. We have data for these fine classifications only for one year (1961); for every other year for which the model is run, these magnitudes are unobserved constructs. Now, because total final demand for commodity i is obviously the sum of the demands for this commodity over all possible ultimate uses (that is, over all final demand expenditures categories),[5] we have

5. Actually, this point is not really obvious at all. Since we interpret y_i as the total of final demand requirements for commodity i from domestic production, we must actually *subtract* from total final demand requirements those requirements that are filled from sources other than domestic production. In our framework, there are two such alternative sources: competing imports and the category of Used motor vehicles & scrap. We ensure that equation (2–1) remains correct by defining the final demand expenditures categories that are alternative sources of supply (and their associated t_{ij}'s) to have negative signs; thus, properly interpreted, the identity, equation (2–1), continues to hold. Finally, we note that, in practice, many of the t_{ij}'s are actually zeros.

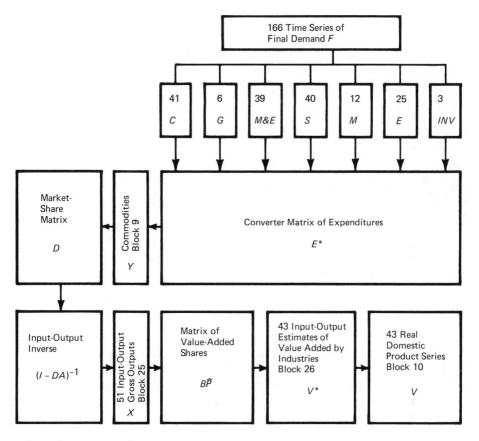

C   = Consumer expenditures
G   = Government expenditures (on current account)
M&E = Machinery and equipment investment
S   = Investment in structures
M   = Imports
E   = Exports
INV = Inventory changes
A   = Industry technology matrix (matrix of technical coefficients)
$\hat{P}$ = Diagonal matrix of shares of gross domestic product in industry gross outputs
B   = Aggregation matrix
V*   = Input-output estimates of value added by industry
V   = Measured gross domestic product by industry
Y   = Final demand by commodity
X   = Gross output by industry

Figure 2-1. Relationship Between Demand and Industry Output, Blocks 9, 10, 25, and 26 of CANDIDE Model 1.0.

$$y_i = \sum_{j=1}^{166} t_{ij} \quad (i = 1, 2, \ldots, 84) \tag{2-1}$$

If we define a new expenditures matrix E^* by allowing its coefficients to be defined by

$$e_{ij}^* = t_{ij}/f_j \quad (i = 1, 2, \ldots, 84; j = 1, 2, \ldots, 166)$$

we may rewrite equation (2-1) as

$$y_i = \sum_{j=1}^{166} e_{ij}^* f_j \quad (i = 1, 2, \ldots, 84) \tag{2-2}$$

Such a definition is permissible because all f_j's are strictly positive, and hence we do not violate the conventions of mathematics by dividing by zero. Finally, in matrix terms (interpreting all vectors as column vectors), we may write equation (2-2) as

$$Y = E^* \cdot F \tag{2-3}$$

Equation (2-3) is the essence of Block 9 of CANDIDE Model 1.0; it is essentially a mechanism for converting final demand categories classified by ultimate uses into final demand requirements by commodities, both vectors being in constant dollars. In practice, there are several important details that are worthy of attention. In particular, the actual equations of the model have two vectors of constant terms, to take account of problems associated with the conversion of inventory investment. (See Auer and Vallet [2], especially their section in · Chapter 2 on inventory change.) It is worth noting that equation (2-3) has a two-fold interpretation. For the actual data of 1961, it is simply a tautology, an identity that must hold because of the way the variables are defined. However, for the other years for which the model is run (or even for the year 1961, in a simulation of the full model), equation (2-3) can best be regarded as a definition of the vector Y. Accordingly, these relationships of the model remain as identities, but the interpretation changes. Moreover, with this change in interpretation, we have slipped in some very strong assumptions about the constancy of certain ratios, assumptions that may well be debatable. Even though we attempt to correct for the rigidity of these assumptions at the end of the process (compare the discussion below), the reader should be aware of the strong assumptions that we have made.

Next, we may proceed to the determination of gross outputs by the 51 industries of the input-output classification used in CANDIDE Model 1.0. Let the total amount of commodity i that is produced domestically be given by q_i ($i = 1, 2, \ldots, 84$), and let the total (gross) output of domestic industry j be given by x_j ($j = 1, 2, \ldots, 51$). (As we shall see in a minute, we can differentiate the output of domestic industries either by commodities or by industries.) Finally, let u_{ij} represent the amount of commodity i that is used as an intermediate input in industry j. Equating total commodity requirements to the sum of intermediate uses plus final requirements, we have

$$q_i = \sum_{j=1}^{51} u_{ij} + y_i \quad (i = 1, 2, \ldots, 84) \qquad (2\text{-}4)$$

We may introduce the well-known "industry technology" assumption and postulate that the ratios of intermediate commodity inputs to total industry outputs are (provisionally) constant.

$$u_{ij}/x_j = a_{ij} \quad (i = 1, 2, \ldots, 84; j = 1, 2, \ldots, 51) \qquad (2\text{-}5)$$

where the a_{ij}'s are regarded as constants, to a first approximation.[6] (The associated matrix, of dimension 84×51, is denoted by A.) Substitution of equation (2-5) into equation (2-4) yields

$$q_i = \sum_{j=1}^{51} a_{ij}x_j + y_i \quad (i = 1, 2, \ldots, 84) \qquad (2\text{-}6)$$

which in turn can be expressed in matrix notation as

$$Q = AX + Y \qquad (2\text{-}7)$$

To complete the algorithm for the determination of gross outputs by industry, we must obtain a second relationship between the vectors Q and X. Let z_{ij} be the amount of the output of industry i that takes the form of commodity j. Then, since the total output of a particular industry is distributed over all possible commodities (many of these possibilities will, in the event, be zeros), we must have

$$x_i = \sum_{j=1}^{84} z_{ij} \quad (i = 1, 2, \ldots, 51) \qquad (2\text{-}8)$$

6. As the x_j's are always strictly positive and hence nonzero, the division in the definitional condition is always permissible.

We may now introduce the moderately strong assumption that industries maintain (to a first approximation) their shares in the total outputs of the various
domestically produced commodities. Let us define provisional constants, d_{ij}
($i = 1, 2, \ldots, 51; j = 1, 2, \ldots, 84$), as the ratios z_{ij}/q_j; these parameters are the
elements of the "market shares" matrix D, of dimensions 51×84. Utilizing this
definition, equation (2-8) can be rewritten

$$x_i = \sum_{j=1}^{84} d_{ij}q_j \quad (i = 1, 2, \ldots, 51) \tag{2-9}$$

In matrix notation, this becomes

$$X = DQ \tag{2-10}$$

The algorithm for Block 25 may now be presented quickly. The substitution
of equation (2-7) into equation (2-10) yields

$$X = D(AX + Y) = DAX + DY \tag{2-11}$$

In turn, equation (2-11) may be written as

$$(I - DA)X = DY \tag{2-12}$$

where I is the identity matrix of order 51. In fact, it is not difficult to show
(under certain reasonably "realistic" conditions) that the generalized Leontief
matrix is in fact nonsingular and so possesses an inverse matrix which, moreover,
has a standard matrix series approximation. (On these points, see Appendix C of
Auer and Vallet [2].) Given the existence of the inverse of the generalized
Leontief matrix $(I-DA)$, we may obtain the (unique) solution of equation (2-12)
as:

$$X = (I - DA)^{-1}DY \tag{2-13}$$

Equation (2-13) is the algorithm (51 scalar equations) that comprises Block 25.
It is worthwhile to pause momentarily to interpret equation (2-13). For the
actual data pertaining to the year 1961, equation (2-13) is simply an interpretation of the accounting identities among the measured flows of industrial outputs
and inputs for that year. It is therefore simply a special identity in this context.
For other years of the sample (or in simulations of the model), equation (2-13)
can be regarded as defining the (unobserved) x_j variables; it thus remains an
identity, although the interpretation changes. In particular, underlying these

definitional relationships are the assumptions of constant values of the elements in the A and D matrices. Thus, despite the adjustment procedures carried out further on, we assume provisionally the validity of the "industry technology" and the "market shares" postulates.

Next, we calculate the first approximations, according to the input-output model, of real gross domestic product (real value added) originating in some 41 industries of the economy.[7] This is done by assuming the constancy of the shares of gross domestic product in gross industry outputs. Let p_j be the share of gross domestic product in the gross output industry j ($j = 1, 2, \ldots, 51$); again, we have estimates of the p_j's for the year 1961. The p_j's are obtained by subtracting from unity the column sums of the appropriate a_{ij}'s, after allowing for the non-factor primary inputs as well. We may denote the first estimates of real domestic product originating in the 43 national accounts industries of the economy by v_i^* ($i = 1, 2, \ldots, 43$). Then the first 41 equations of Block 26 are given by (2-14).[8]

$$v_i^* = p_i x_i \quad (i = 1, 2, \ldots, 19)$$

$$v_i^* = p_{i+2} x_{i+2} \quad (i = 20, 21, \ldots, 33)$$

$$v_{34}^* = \sum_{j=36}^{43} p_j x_j$$

$$v_i^* = p_{i+9} x_{i+9} \quad (i = 35, 36, \ldots, 41) \tag{2-14}$$

The final two estimates of real gross domestic product originating in a national accounts industry refer to two industries—public administration and the non-commercial portion of community, business, and personal services—outside the input-output framework, and so these two estimates are calculated directly from the relevant categories of final demand expenditures (the relevant elements of the F vector).

Finally, the difficulty that Ross Preston refers to as the problem of "changing coefficients" is tentatively resolved by an approach very similar to his. Over time, the coefficients of the industry technology matrix (the A matrix) can change for a number of reasons, such as technological change, compositional

7. In going from the stage of gross output to real gross domestic product originating, we aggregate the eight construction subindustries into one industry. Also, we lose three other industries for technical reasons, the details of which need not concern us here. Accordingly, the 51 input-output industries are collapsed into 41, at the stage of real gross domestic product originating. As mentioned below, we add first estimates of real gross domestic product originating in two industries outside the input-output framework, so that we have 43 national accounts industries in total.

8. This statement has to be qualified by the fact that these equations also carry multiplicative factors, which adjust for conceptual differences between the national accounts and the input-output concepts of gross domestic product originating in the particular industries.

shifts (within our fairly broad classifications), or possibly relative price changes. The elements of the market shares and the expenditures matrices (the D and E^* matrices, respectively) can also change for these reasons, and they might shift as well because of changes in tastes. In Model 1.0, we have over 10,000 nonzero coefficients in our three input-output matrices. It is easier to model the results of the process of output determination than it is to model explicitly changes in a large number of input-output coefficients. In particular, in Block 10, we have used autoregressive adjustment equations for the determination of real gross domestic product originating in the 43 industries, which schematically take the form

$$v_{it} - v_{it}^* = \alpha_i + \beta_i t + \gamma_i (v_i - v_i^*)_{t-1} + \delta_i (v_i - v_i^*)_{t-2} + u_{it}$$
$$(i = 1, 2, \ldots, 43, \text{ all } t) \tag{2-15}$$

where

v_i = the national accounts estimate of real gross domestic product originating in industry i

t = (as a variable) a time trend variable

t = (as a subscript) the date of an observation

u_{it} = a random disturbance referring to industry i at time t

v_i^* = the input-output estimate of real gross domestic product originating in industry i

and $\alpha_i, \beta_i, \gamma_i$, and δ_i are parameters peculiar to industry i (which are presumed to be independent of time).

These autoregressive adjustment equations are thus intended to correct, in one pass, for the deficiencies inherent in assuming constancy in the elements of the input-output matrices in all possible uses of the model. How well does it work? The results are reasonably satisfactory in those cases for which the basic model is well specified, so that the discrepancies of the actual data from the first estimates on the basis of the input-output approximations can reasonably be described in terms of the traditional trend and cyclical movements. However, this is not to say that some problem areas are not present and that in certain instances ad hoc solutions to definite difficulties have not had to be adopted.

Determination of Implicit Deflators of Certain
Final Demand Categories

In this section, we can only briefly sketch the process of determining some of the final demand implicit deflators in CANDIDE Model 1.0. Wage formation takes place in 12 major industries of the Canadian economy, using a wage adjustment function or a modified Phillips curve as a general approach. In a typical function, the variables explaining the rate of change of industry wages would be the unemployment rate, the rate of change of consumer prices, and perhaps the rate of change of the corresponding U.S. wage rate. Industry price formation is strongly cost oriented, with industry price levels, which are the implicit deflators of industry gross domestic product, being explained by unit labour costs or unit total costs, at times supplemented by demand-type or U.S. price variables. These 12 industry prices are then expanded into estimates of the deflators of value added for the 51 input-output industries, which then serve as one of the major inputs into the input-output submodel on the prices side. A second major input into this submodel is a set of import prices. Import prices are essentially exogenous in CANDIDE Model 1.0, but the model contains mechanisms for expanding the major foreign prices, which are generally exogenous, into the price levels of competing import commodities. These, along with the price level of noncompeting imports, are the second major input into the input-output prices-side submodel. Supplementary inputs include the price level of government goods and services (the deflator of value added in public administration) and a tax deflator, which measures the average impact, year by year, on commodity prices of indirect taxes (and subsidies) levied (paid) before the retail stage.

With values of these inputs at hand, we are ready to enter the input-output submodel on the prices side. This submodel is highly cost oriented, and essentially asserts that costs at various stages of production will be fully passed on. The submodel can also be interpreted as making essential use of the duality in the determination of industry outputs and in price formation.[9] With the complete set of inputs, the algorithms of the submodel enable us to compute estimates of the price levels of 84 domestically produced commodities. We also simultaneously determine the vector of price levels of gross outputs for the 51 input-output industries. (This variable is not used elsewhere in the model.) We can then work through the expenditures matrix to obtain first estimates of the deflators for the categories of consumption expenditures, government expenditures, residential construction, and business fixed investment. Three rates of retail sales taxation also appear as determinants of the input-output estimates of the consumption final demand deflators at this stage of the analysis. Finally, the first estimates of all of these implicit deflators are subjected to autoregressive correction equations, which are designed to correct for the shortcomings of the input-output submodel over time, analogously to what was done on the side of real output by industry.

9. In the input-output analysis of price formation, we introduce an additional strong assumption, namely, the postulate that the share of imports in the total disposition of the various commodities is independent of the industry or the final demand use to which the various commodities may be put. This assumption is not needed in the real-side input-output submodel.

Interrelationships Among the Input-Output Submodels
and the More Conventional Portions of CANDIDE
Model 1.0

As suggested by the earlier discussion, the inputs into the industry output submodel (roughly consisting of the input-output real-side submodel, together with autoregressive industry output equations) come exclusively from the final demand portions (9 computer blocks out of a total of 38 blocks) of the model. Thus, for example, 38 (out of 39) machinery and equipment investment demand functions and 38 (out of 40) investment demand functions for structures are based on a variant of Professor Jorgenson's "neoclassical" theory of investment [9], which is implemented in Blocks 4 and 32 of the model.[10] Thus the process of industry output determination makes use of the final demand functions that have been the traditional foci of econometric model builders. We may now ask about the role of the industry output determination mechanism as inputs into other portions of the model. In other words, where do the variables representing the levels of real gross domestic product (at factor cost) by industry (or aggregations of these levels of industry output) go, elsewhere in the model?

We can distinguish four major ways in which the industry outputs are used in the remaining portions of CANDIDE Model 1.0. First, the Jorgenson-type theory of business fixed investment, as applied by investing industry, requires a measure of industry output; accordingly, there is an important feedback from the real-side input-output submodel. (To a lesser extent, the process of industry output determination has repercussions on the final demand mechanism through the functions for inventory investment and some of the functions of import demands by categories.) Second, industry output determination plays a role, through the use of inverted production functions, in the determination of labour requirements, both by number of employees and by total manhours. Third, once we have both output and employment (or manhours) by industry, we can compute labour–productivity ratios for individual industries (or for suitable aggregations thereof). These labour–productivity ratios are an important component of our unit labour cost variables, which are used in the determination of an industry price level for each of the 12 major industries.[11] Finally, the estimates of real

---

10. This theory (see [9]) is applied only to business demand (by investing industry) for plant and for machinery and equipment separately; thus, a different theory is employed to explain governments' capital investment demands and the demands of households (and, in small part, of governments) for residential construction. Also, it should be noted that a separate approach is used for the determination of inventory investment. The use of the Jorgenson model of business fixed investment in CANDIDE Model 1.0 is described by White [13].

11. As noted earlier, these 12 industry prices are then expanded to obtain industry prices for the 51 input-output industries, in order to be able to put the prices submodel in motion. Thus there is this (indirect) link between the two input-output submodels utilized in the full model. The details of the processes of industry price determination are discussed by Wolfgang M. Illing and C. Dewaleyne [6].

output by industry and the corresponding implicit deflators enable us to construct one measure of gross national product from the side of production (incomes). Elsewhere in the model, another estimate of gross national product (that coming from the expenditures side) is constructed and compared with the estimate from production, and then a balance is struck to obtain the final estimate, in the model, of Canada's gross national product (in both current and constant dollars).

Turning to the prices side, we may again ask, how are the implicit deflators of the various categories of final demand expenditures used elsewhere in the model? Their immediate use is to convert the constant-dollar levels of various expenditures categories into current-dollar values. From this conversion (and of course also from certain aggregations), the model obtains estimates of the implicit deflators of broad categories of expenditures, such as all consumption expenditures or all investment expenditures; the broadest implicit deflator obtained is that for gross national expenditures itself. (In general, the implicit deflators of such broad expenditures categories can be regarded as weighted averages, with current-period weights, of the component deflators.) Moreover, the process of "pricing up" the constant-dollar expenditures levels generates a first estimate of gross national product from the side of expenditures, which is used in conjunction with the first estimate from the side of production to obtain the final estimate of this magnitude. In addition, the implicit deflators of the various final demand categories are also used directly, in the two income blocks of CANDIDE Model 1.0 (Blocks 18 and 19), to "price up" certain constant-dollar magnitudes, and thus serve in the process of explaining certain items of governmental revenues and private (nonwage) incomes. Finally, the effects of the final demand deflators are also felt (to some extent) in the final demand equations (in constant dollars) for the various categories of expenditures, since whatever relative price effects we present in the model are found in these functions. Thus, we find the implicit deflators of consumption expenditures categories utilized heavily in the functions of consumption expenditures by detailed categories, while the implicit deflators of plant investment expenditures (and also the implicit deflators of machinery and equipment investment outlays) have an important role in implementing the Jorgenson-type model of business fixed investment. The implicit deflators determined in the prices submodel are also used in the mechanism explaining residential construction outlays in the final demand expenditures portion of CANDIDE Model 1.0.

From this discussion, it can be seen that the input-output submodels are central to the functioning of CANDIDE Model 1.0. In particular, it is impossible to compute solution values of aggregative measures of interest (unemployment rate, real gross national product, the consumer price index, etc.) without also computing the basic 43 industrial outputs and the 127 implicit deflators generated by the use of input-output submodels on the real side and on the prices side, respectively. (Of course, it is not necessary to *present* all of the results in detail, but this is definitely a secondary issue.)

Conclusion

In this final section, we shall attempt to provide some further measure of evaluation of the input-output submodels employed in CANDIDE Model 1.0. The reader is advised to discount for the biases of the author, who served as manager of the CANDIDE Project between mid-1972 and mid-1974.

In general, the process of real output determination in the 43 individual industries appears to function reasonably well, at least in terms of reproducing the experience of the sample period. As indicated in the relevant CANDIDE Project Paper, this seems to be true for both the typical individual industry [2, ch. 4] and for aggregations across industries, such as the level of real gross national product for the entire Canadian economy [2, ch. 5]. Of course, reproduction of sample-period experience is only one test—and in general not the most rigorous test—to which a model can be put, as we are always forcing the fit (to a certain extent) when we attempt to "track" historical experience with a model whose parameters are estimated from the same time period. We can also consider other more difficult (but in general more subjective) tests, such as the behaviour of the model in counterfactual historical simulations (such as the calculation of certain dynamic multipliers) or in conditional or unconditional extrapolation of the determinants of the model beyond the sample period.[12] How does the industry output determination mechanism fare, with regard to these admittedly subjective tests? Very briefly, calculation of dynamic multipliers in general yields reasonable results, at least to a first approximation. As for the results in projection exercises (conditional simulations), the mechanism functions reasonably well, with the resulting distributions of real gross domestic product originating in the individual industries of the economy being believable ones, at least for the disaggregation down to 13 major industries. Some of the projections for output originating in several of the detailed industries are somewhat less believable, and such evidence of weakness must be candidly admitted. A model with the dimensions of CANDIDE 1.0 is not, in the view of this author, a suitable vehicle for unconditional forecasting, if only because obtaining defensible values for more than 300 exogenous variables is a horrendous task. (In any case, at the Economic Council of Canada, we have never used the model for this purpose.)

As for the mechanism for determining final demand deflators, the reproduction of sample-period experience is almost (but not quite) as good as that with

12. In principle, unconditional extrapolation of its (jointly) dependent variables can yield an objective test of a model, since (if we extrapolate to a period beyond the sample but in the past) we can use measured values of the exogenous variables and compare predicted values of the dependent variables with the actual observations. In practice, things are rarely this simple. Generally, we use every available bit of information; accordingly, forward extrapolation will generally be for some future period, for which the true values of the exogenous variables are unknown. Projection backward to a period before the sample period proper is also possible in principle, but in practice this test often breaks against the hard rock of structural change.

regard to industry output determination. Finally, we may observe that holistic criteria, based on the functioning of the input-output submodels within the full model, are possible. Indeed, in one point of view, these are the most relevant criteria. The weakest test is the issue of whether these two distinct strands of modelling an economy have been successfully combined, in the sense of producing an operational model. (Given the fact that the combination of these two approaches is still in an experimental stage, one can argue that this is not a trivial question.) For CANDIDE Model 1.0 (and also for its successor, CANDIDE Model 1.1), this admittedly weak test is passed: the model is operational, in the sense that the equations have been estimated and that definite solutions can be obtained from the model, given the appropriate inputs. On a deeper level, the evaluation of the input-output submodels becomes essentially a problem (with perhaps varying degrees of emphasis) of the evaluation of CANDIDE Model 1.0. This topic is obviously beyond the scope of this paper.

References

1. Almon, Clopper. *The American Economy to 1975.* New York: Harper & Row, 1966.

2. Auer, L., and D. Vallet. *CANDIDE Model 1.0: Industry Output Determination.* Edited by Ronald G. Bodkin and Barbara A.M. Young. CANDIDE Project Paper No. 8. Ottawa: Economic Council of Canada for the Interdepartmental Committee, Information Canada, 1974.

3. Auer, L., and D. Vallet. *CANDIDE Model 1.0: Final Demand Deflators.* Edited by Ronald G. Bodkin, Stephen M. Tanny, and Barbara A.M. Young. CANDIDE Project Paper No. 12. Ottawa: Economic Council of Canada for the Interdepartmental Committee, Information Canada, 1975.

4. Committee on Econometric Methods. *Econometric Models for Medium-Term Economic Plan, 1964–1968.* Japan: Economic Planning Agency, Government of Japan, August 1965.

5. Dominion Bureau of Statistics [Statistics Canada], Input-Output Research and Development Staff. *The Input-Output Structure of the Canadian Economy, 1961.* Vol. 1. Ottawa: The Queen's Printer, 1969.

6. Economic Council of Canada (for the Interdepartmental Committee). CANDIDE Project Papers 2–17. Ottawa: Information Canada, 1973 through 1975.

7. Fisher, Franklin M., Lawrence R. Klein, and Yoichi Shinkai. "Price and Output Aggregation in the Brookings Econometric Model." In *The Brookings Quarterly Econometric Model of the United States.* Edited by James S. Duesenberry, Gary Fromm, Lawrence R. Klein, and Edwin Kuh. Chicago: Rand McNally; Amsterdam: North-Holland Publishing Company, 1965. Pp. 652–679.

8. Fromm, Gary, and Paul Taubman. *Policy Simulations with an Econometric Model.* Washington, D.C.: The Brookings Institution, 1968.

9. Jorgenson, Dale W. "Anticipations and Investment Behavior." In *The Brookings Quarterly Econometric Model of the United States.* Edited by James

S. Duesenberry, Gary Fromm, Lawrence R. Klein, and Edwin Kuh. Chicago: Rand McNally; Amsterdam: North-Holland Publishing Company, 1965. Pp. 35–92.

10. McCracken, M.C. *An Overview of CANDIDE Model 1.0.* CANDIDE Project Paper No. 1. Ottawa: Economic Council of Canada for the Interdepartmental Committee, Information Canada, 1973.

11. Preston, Ross S. *The Wharton Annual and Industry Forecasting Model.* Philadelphia: Economics Research Unit of the University of Pennsylvania, 1972.

12. Stone, Richard, ed. *A Programme for Growth.* Vols. 1–6. London: Chapman and Hall, 1962 through 1965.

13. White, Derek A. *CANDIDE Model 1.0: Business Fixed Investment.* CANDIDE Project Paper No. 5. Ottawa: Economic Council of Canada for the Interdepartmental Committee, Information Canada, 1974.

Chapter Three

Inventory Adjustment in a Quarterly Input-Output Model for Japan

Shuntaro Shishido
Akira Oshizaka

In view of the growing need for consistent sectoral projections connected
with aggregative demand management, a quarterly input-output model has been
constructed that can be linked to key macroeconomic policy variables. The purpose of the present paper is to focus attention on the problems of inventory
adjustment and the dynamic responses of sectoral demand and supply, each of
which is of vital importance for short-term sectoral forecasts and policy formulation. Shortage of specific products, for example, gives rise to a decline in inventories, an increase in imports, and changes in output of various related products
with different lag responses. Certainly, if inflationary pressures on the economy
are to be prevented, a fiscal stimulus of the Keynesian type must be reexamined
from a sectoral viewpoint for its likely impacts on (and the corresponding lagged
responses of) critical sectors, such as energy or construction.

In this context, conventional inventory studies have been concerned with
either highly aggregative aspects of inventory analyses or those aspects that can
be disaggregated but are limited to finished inventories of specific sectors. Short-
term macroeconomic studies have primarily concentrated on the "institutional"
type of inventories—raw materials, work-in-process, finished inventories held by
producers and traders, etc. [2; 10]. While recently developed industry models
(such as those for steel or automobiles, which contributed greatly to empirical
studies of business behavior) deal with finished inventories, those inventories
held by traders and consuming sectors are neglected [3].

Dynamic Leontief models usually include an inventory matrix for longer-
term projections, but they do not provide satisfactory results for short-term

This research was done under the sponsorship of the Japan Economic Research Center
(JERC). The authors are grateful to M. Ide and Y. Ikeda for research and programming and
to A. Kinoshita, H. Matsumoto, A. Nomura, N. Takahara, and Y. Yoshizoe for data estimation. They are also grateful for the encouragement they received from Professor T. Uchida
and Mr. Y. Fujimura. The views expressed in this paper are those of the authors and do not
necessarily reflect the views of the Japanese government.

sectoral analyses because of the unavailability of data and rigidity of the acceleration principle assumption.

The model presented in this paper aims first at an analysis of short-term responses of sectoral inventories and production, using the consistent framework of the Leontief input-output system with exogenous changes in final demand. Another aim of the model is an analysis of the dynamic responses of macroeconomic policy variables by integration of the model with a quarterly macromodel. Although the model is eventually intended to include endogenously such variables as sectoral prices, wage rates, and capital costs (as well as business investment, private consumption, and money), the present paper is confined to the real sectors with special reference to quarterly adjustments of inventories and supplies. Introduction of the sectoral price changes into the present system is to be undertaken in the next stage of our model building.[1]

Scope of Inventory Analysis

Empirical study of inventory adjustment in the Leontief model has been treated rather casually, as users of the model have been mainly concerned with longer-term annual movements of real sectors. A difficulty is created by the fact that the input-output model requires not only the finished products, but also products held by traders and various consuming sectors. For example, steel products in the inventory adjustment vector in the final demand of the static Leontief model consist strictly of products held by (i) steel producers (and include work-in-process); (ii) wholesalers; and (iii) various consuming industries, such as the engineering and construction industries. While such inventory data—which are available only for key products—include all product stages, most of the analysis is related to the "finished" inventories, which usually account for less than one-third of the total inventories. The data provided by wholesalers and retailers are most unsatisfactory for consistent input-output analyses.

Conventional inventory matrices, on the other hand, are estimated with a simple assumption of constant sectoral inventory-output coefficients. Not only is this assumption too rigid, it is also not operational for quarterly econometric analysis, since we are more concerned with the total inventory change for each sector, regardless of its institutional stages or consuming sectors. A decline in a retailer's inventory of a specific product due to a sudden rise in final demand might be offset by a quick response in accumulation of the producer's inventory, with little change in total inventories of this product. In the case of agricultural products, where there is a slow response in supply, even a quick rise in retailers' inventories in anticipation of increased final demand is likely to be cancelled by a quick reduction in wholesalers' and producers' inventories.

These considerations require the construction of a new model whereby the changes in sectoral inventories are dealt with in the framework of dynamic

1. For this improvement in the annual model, see two earlier papers [11; 15].

response of sectoral supply to demand, whatever its institutional stages—such as producer or traders—or its consuming sectors.

Unlike the conventional approaches, our new approach assumes that the sectoral changes in the inventory vector are derived as the difference between supply (domestic output plus imports) and demand (intermediate plus final demand, excluding inventory changes). Thus, the dynamic response of sectoral supply to these final and intermediate demands plays a key role in our quarterly Leontief model.[2]

Statistical Data Estimation

Since the inventory data in the Japanese national accounts are estimated quarterly on an institutional statistical basis, such as corporation surveys and farmers' household surveys, they are only available as an aggregate benchmark and are not useful for sectoral input-output analyses. The method used in our study is one that is indirect, but operational, so as to avoid the difficulties in estimating quarterly sectoral inventory changes in all institutional stages, that is, producers, traders, and consumers.

First, the estimation of quarterly data was undertaken at a 60-sector level for output, imports, and exports in 1960 constant prices. These quarterly series were then adjusted for seasonal variation and calculated at an annual rate in order to link to macroeconomic variables. The output data, originally based on the estimates used for the annual Leontief model by the Economic Planning Agency (EPA) [15], were derived by quarterly disaggregation of the annual series by means of newly estimated quarterly indices in 1960 prices. These quarterly index series, together with those for exports and imports, have been made available after two years of laborious research by the Japan Economic Research Center (JERC) in collaboration with many sectoral experts [12].

In regard to sectoral final demand, our model is specified for 60 industrial sectors ($i = 1, \ldots, 60$), 16 consumption expenditures categories ($j = 1, \ldots, 16$), and 15 government expenditures categories ($k = 1, \ldots, 15$).

$$Y_i = C_i + C_{si} + I_{hi} + I_{pi} + G_i + \bar{E}_i \tag{3-1}$$

$$C_i = \kappa_{oi} + \sum_j \kappa_{1,ij} C_j \tag{3-2}$$

$$C_j = f(\bar{p}_j, \bar{C}) \tag{3-3}$$

$$C_{si} = \beta_i \bar{C}_s \tag{3-4}$$

2. Lovell constructed a theoretical model, a multisector buffer-stock model, to evaluate the stability of the economy [4]. Though simplified for formal analysis, it is the first attempt to make the Leontief model dynamic with respect to inventory and sales anticipation.

$$I_{hi} = \gamma_i \bar{I}_h \tag{3-5}$$

$$I_{pi} = \delta_i \bar{I}_p \tag{3-6}$$

$$G_i = \sum_k \phi_{ik} \bar{G}_k \tag{3-7}$$

where

Y = final demand, excluding change in inventories

C = private consumption, by type of expenditures j

$\dot{p}$ = relative price of consumption

C_s = business consumption expenses

I_h = private housing construction

I_p = private business investment

G = government purchases, by type of expenditures k

E = exports (exogenous)

Variables with overbars are exogenous in the present input-output model but endogenous in the macromodel.

The parameters (β, γ, δ, and ϕ) are not fixed, but are made gradually changeable over time in view of their structural changes in the long run, and κ is a consumption expenditures coefficient.

The changes in inventories, our main interest in the present paper, are estimated indirectly from the following formulae:

$$J_i = Z_i - \sum_j a_{ij} X_j - Y_i - \epsilon_i \tag{3-8}$$

$$Z_i = X_i + M_i \tag{3-9}$$

where

J = change in inventories

Z = supply

a_{ij} = technical coefficients (changing over time)

X = output

M = imports

ϵ = adjustment dummy variables ($\sum_i \epsilon_i = 0$)

The dummy variables were used for those sectors in which changes in a_{ij} do not fully represent actual changes.

In these formulae, technical coefficients have been estimated by explicitly taking account of changes in technologies, which are mostly based on more detailed input-output tables available every five years and time series information on current production statistics. In aggregative terms, the following macro-economic identity in equation (3-11) is obtained, as total real value added in equation (3-10) can be derived from equations (3-8) and (3-9):

$$V_j = \sum_i (1 - a_{ij}) X_j \tag{3-10}$$

$$\sum_i J_i = \sum_i V_i + \sum_i M_i - \sum_i Y_i \tag{3-11}$$

Although minor statistical errors are likely to exist due to errors in estimation of final demand and technical changes, our test on the global balance in equation (3-11) and side analyses, such as incremental inventory–sale ratios for major sectors, have indicated that our inventory estimates are fairly accurate for most of the sectors, especially those in which changes are subject to wide business fluctuations.[3]

The Quarterly Dynamic Model

With special reference to short-term adjustment of inventories, it is essential first to distinguish between the sectoral responses of supply induced (i) by final demand, excluding inventories, and (ii) by changes in inventories. Our system thus can be stated as

$$Z = Z_Y + Z_J \tag{3-12}$$

$$X = X_Y + X_J \tag{3-13}$$

$$M = M_Y + M_J \tag{3-14}$$

where

Z = total supply

X = output

M = imports

3. For a few sectors, whose incremental inventory–supply ratios are unusually high or low, parameters in supply–adjustment functions (discussed later) are likely to be somewhat biased. These sectors, however, are insignificant for analytical purposes.

These are divided into two groups of column vectors: (i) Z_Y, X_Y, and M_Y, derived from final demand, excluding changes in inventories; and (ii) Z_J, X_J, and M_J, induced by changes in inventories. Since supply and demand are in balance in our version of the Leontief system, we obtain

$$Z = AX + Y + J \qquad\qquad (3\text{-}15)$$

where A is the technical input coefficient matrix and Z, X, Y, and J are column vectors of supply, output, final demand, and change in inventories, respectively. In the above final demand, Y is exogenously given, while others are all endogenous.

From equations (3-12) through (3-15), we can derive

$$Z_Y = AX_Y + Y \qquad\qquad (3\text{-}16)$$

$$Z_J = AX_J + J \qquad\qquad (3\text{-}17)$$

Since equation (3-16) is a static system without inventory adjustment and time lags, the system can be easily solved by adding import functions and identities, which have no time lag:

$$M_Y = f(Z_Y) \qquad\qquad (3\text{-}18)$$

$$Z_Y = X_Y + M_Y \qquad\qquad (3\text{-}19)$$

From this static Leontief system, we can now build a dynamic adjustment system in which these static variables form the basis for demand anticipation.[4] As equation (3-17) still remains unsolved, we need to introduce a reduced form of the supply-adjustment function with the aid of demand variables, $Z_{Y(t)}$

$$Z = f(Z_{Y(0)}, Z_{Y(-1)}, \ldots, Z_{Y(-i)}, \ldots, Z_{Y(-n)}) \qquad\qquad (3\text{-}20)$$

where it is assumed that total supply, including output and imports, tends to adjust itself in response to the changes in demand, final or intermediate, with a certain pattern of lagged responses. With the difference between $Z_{(t)}$ and $Z_{Y(t)}$ being $Z_{J(t)}$, this equation provides a basis for obtaining J in equation (3-17). In order to analyze its theoretical basis, this reduced form needs to be further transformed into its original formula, in which the dynamic adjustment is explicitly defined with expectation variables. First, we must simplify our model by assuming a constant relationship between AX_J and J in equation (3-17),

4. For related discussions on inventory and sales expectations and adjustment lags, see Lovell [5], Modigliani and Sauerlander [6], Moriguchi [7], Pashigian [8], Shinkai [9], and Watanabe and Kinoshita [14].

although it is subject to change in primary sectors, whose products depend largely on consuming industries. After this simplification, the original formula of equation (3-20) can be revised as

$$Z = Z^e + \eta(Z_Y - Z_Y^e) \tag{3-21a}$$

$$Z^e = (1 + a)J^e + Z_Y^e \tag{3-21b}$$

where Z^e, J^e, and Z_Y^e are expected values, η is an adjustment parameter of supply for correcting for errors in demand expectation, and a is a ratio of AX_J to J.

Since equation (3-21a) represents a realization function of supply expectation Z^e, it can be further elaborated by introducing prices and monetary variables, as discussed later. Equation (3-21b) is derived from equation (3-17). From these two basic equations, we obtain

$$Z = [(1 + a)J^e + \theta(Z_Y - Z_Y^e)] + [Z_Y^e + \gamma(Z_Y - Z_Y^e)] \tag{3-21c}$$

where θ and γ are also adjustment parameters for expectation errors and $\theta + \gamma = \eta$. In this formula, the first term is related to the expected and unexpected changes in inventories and the second term to the total demand or sales to final and intermediate users, which also consist of expectation, Z_Y^e, and its adjustment $(Z_Y - Z_Y^e)$. While the parameter γ is positive around unity, θ can be either positive or negative, depending on the speed of response of supply Z and error adjustment of $(Z_Y - Z_Y^e)$. Generally, the θ tends to be significantly negative, and thus unexpected changes in inventories take place in cases where the adjustment response of supply, η, is low and yet the value of γ is nearly unity, as in primary sectors. At the other extreme, the supply adjustment becomes highly sensitive to final demand changes if there is a positive adjustment of errors in inventory expectation, as in steel and capital goods industries. To be more specific, equation (3-21) can be changed further for statistical estimation:

$$Z = \alpha + (1 + a)k\Delta Z_Y^e + \theta(Z_Y - Z_Y^e) + \beta Z_Y^e + \gamma(Z_Y - Z_Y^e) \tag{3-22a}$$

$$Z_Y^e = \lambda_1 Z_{Y(-1)} + \lambda_2 Z_{Y(-2)}, \ldots, + \lambda_i Z_{Y(-i)}, \ldots, \lambda_n Z_{Y(-n)} \left(\sum_i^n \lambda_i = 1 \right) \tag{3-22b}$$

where k is the desired incremental inventory-sales ratio; λ_i is a distributed lag of the demand expectation, Z_Y^e; and α is a constant.

Use of the accelerator for inventory changes is required because of the relative unreliability of the stock data. Besides, owing to the lack of anticipation data, we attempted to estimate the values of λ_i on the basis of supply-adjustment parameters in equation (3-20), as discussed in the next section. No a priori assumption was made with regard to the type of lag distribution, such as rational or adaptive expectation. Instead, we attempted to derive the pattern empirically by using the method of polynomial lag distribution because of its flexibility [1]. The values k and γ were derived independently, while β, which is $\Sigma\beta_i$, was assumed to be a sum of distributed lag coefficients of equation (3–20), which is around unity.

An alternative approach for supply adjustment is to introduce the idea of stock adjustment by using incremental inventory–sales ratios instead of absolute level of stock of inventories. This approach was adopted for some sectors with relatively more reliable inventory data. In this case, equation (3–22) becomes

$$Z = (1 + a)\left[\alpha + k\,\delta Z_Y^e - \epsilon\left(\frac{K_j^*}{Z_Y}\right)_{-1} + \theta\,\delta k(Z_Y - Z_Y^e)\right]$$
$$+ [Z_Y^e + \gamma(Z_Y - Z_Y^e)] \tag{3-22'}$$

where δ is the speed of inventory adjustment and K_j^* is the accumulated increase in inventories. Since ϵ is $\delta \cdot \bar{Z}_Y$ and $\bar{Z}_Y$ is the average of Z_Y, the adjustment speed, δ, can be obtained if ϵ is properly estimated.

Once sectoral supply Z is obtained from the above formulae and Z_J thereby becomes available in equation (3–12), we can close our system by introducing import functions, which also contain a dynamic adjustment, as below:

$$M = f(Z, Z_{(-1)}, \ldots, Z_{(-i)}, \ldots, Z_{(-n)}) \tag{3-23}$$

Since X and X_J can be obtained from equations (3–9) and (3–13), a column vector for inventory changes, J, is finally obtained from equation (3–17).

As readily noted, the dynamic core of our short-term model is in equation (3–20), and is based on equations (3–21) and (3–22'), whose parameters determine all the time patterns of sectoral output and imports, as well as inventory adjustment, in a consistent framework of the Leontief system. As mentioned above, these functions can be further elaborated by introducing additional explanatory variables, such as interest rate, prices, and inventory-supply ratios. Although domestic price data are not yet available, our final version of equation (3–20) has become

$$Z_{(t)} = f\left[Z_{Y(t-i)}, \ldots, r_{(t-i)}, \ldots, P_{m(t-i)}, \ldots, \left(\frac{K_j^*}{Z_Y}\right)_{(t-i)}\right] \tag{3-24}$$

where r is interest rate on bank loans and P_m are the import prices. The last variable, K_j^*/Z_Y, is used only for certain sectors related to equation (3–22'), where inventory data are relatively reliable.

Main Structural Parameters

Since our model requires the estimation of various types of structural parameters that cannot be discussed in detail in the present paper, we briefly mention only key parameters in the context of the dynamic adjustment of our system.

Supply Adjustment

Although there is room for further elaboration of the parameters in final demand, such as private consumption and business investment by type, our main interest here lies in the sectoral supply adjustment function in equation (3-24). The results of our estimation distinguish three types of response pattern.[5] Generally, manufacturing sectors have faster responses than primary sectors. Among the former, basic metals, machinery and equipment (excluding shipbuilding), and consumption goods sectors (such as dairy products, tobacco, printing and publishing, rubber, and sundry goods) tend to adjust much faster than other manufacturing sectors. These faster responses are partly attributable to rapid economic growth. Slower responses are observed for most of the primary sectors, except for fishing and coal, because of the longer production period or long-term supply contracts from abroad. The slowest responses are noted for agricultural crops, crude oil, and mineral ores. In these sectors, inventories tend to be unintentionally reduced during the early quarters, in sharp contrast to most of the manufacturing sectors.

Import prices are introduced as indicators of foreign market conditions for forestry and iron ores, where positive signs are interpreted as speculative variables for accelerating those imports. Financial variables are also significant for several basic products, such as wool, lumber, iron and nonferrous ores, textiles, and steel, where inventory adjustments by traders are usually active. Positive signs for the interest rate in nonferrous metallic ores and natural textiles imply that they are highly sensitive to the financial market for speculative purposes despite their slower supply responses to final demand.

Finally, it should be noted that some sectors, such as iron and steel, furniture, and rubber products, tend to respond not only quickly but also too sensitively, thus resulting in somewhat unstable oscillation, as discussed later.

Expectation and Error Adjustment

Next we analyze the basic adjustment mechanism that underlies the above parameters of our supply adjustment function. As discussed earlier, changes in final demand affect sales expectation and inventory planning, and both of them are likely to be readjusted in realization. The supply response pattern can thus be differentiated into demand expectation, as shown in Table 3-1, and its error adjustments of demand and inventories, as shown in Table 3-2.

The lag distribution of demand expectation in Table 3-1 is estimated on the basis of our supply response pattern and the theoretical assumptions implied by equations (3-22) and (3-22′). Because of the questionable reliability of inventory

5. For details of the results, see Watanabe and Kinoshita [14].

Table 3-1.   Parameters of Demand Expectation

Sector Number	λ_1	λ_2	λ_3	λ_4	λ_5	λ_6	λ_7	λ_8	λ_9	λ_{10}	λ_{11}	λ_{12}
2			0.29	0.38	0.33							
3	0.27	0.29	0.26	0.18								
4	0.06	0.12	0.17	0.18	0.17	0.14	0.16					
6	0.50	0.50										
8	0.29	0.38	0.33									
9	0.03	0.07	0.11	0.14	0.15	0.16	0.14	0.20				
10	0.16	0.21	0.21	0.18	0.13	0.11						
11	0.01	0.03	0.05	0.07	0.09	0.11	0.12	0.13	0.12	0.11	0.16	
15	0.03	0.07	0.12	0.17	0.20	0.19	0.22					
20	0.16	0.20	0.21	0.20	0.15	0.08						
21	0.13	0.19	0.21	0.18	0.14	0.09	0.06					
24	0.24	0.76										
27	1.21	-0.21										
28	0.29	0.71										
29	0.52	0.48										
31	0.08	0.12	0.14	0.14	0.14	0.12	0.10	0.08	0.05	0.03	0.01	0.02
32	0.57	0.35	0.08									
34	0.51	0.34	0.13	0.02								
35	0.44	0.56										
36	0.60	0.40										
37	0.91	0.09										
38	1.24	-0.24										
39	1.14	-0.14										
40	0.31	0.69										
41	0.18	0.40	0.42									

Note: See equations (3–22) and (3–22′). For sector numbers and titles, see Appendix 3A.

data, we select here only sectors with a relatively longer demand expectation. However, in view of their importance in short-term analysis, the parameters of error adjustment for the excluded sectors are given in Table 3–2. If the distributed lag coefficients, λ_i, given in Table 3–1 were plotted, the demand expectations would be quite different in shape. There are only a few cases where the conventional hypotheses, such as exponential weighted averages, can be supported. For instance, slower responses and longer patterns of lag distribution are observed for most of the primary and light manufacturing sectors, such as food and textiles. Most of the engineering and rubber industries, on the other hand, show a highly sensitive expectation, implying that they are strongly subject to the fluctuations of business conditions and external markets. Unlike the other primary sectors, the fishing industry indicates a fairly sensitive demand expectation, while basic chemicals and paper industries show relatively slower patterns of expectation.

The next problem is to analyze how expectations are likely to be adjusted in the course of this realization. Usually, anticipations tend to be affected by (i)

Table 3-2. Parameters of Error Adjustment

Sector Number	β_O	Parameters θ	γ	Sector Number	β_O	Parameters θ	γ
1	0	-0.72	0.72	22	0.39	n.s.	n.s.
2	0	-1.53	0.92	23	1.75	0.77	0.98
3	0.59	-0.11	0.68	24	0.51	-0.38	0.89
4	0	-0.94	0.94	25	0.95	0.07	0.88
5	0.42	-0.19	0.61	26	0.66	0.33	0.33
6	1.04	n.s.[a]	n.s.	27	1.42	0.71	0.71
7	1.11	0.69	0.42	28	0.35	-0.61	0.96
8	0.18	-0.74	0.92	29	0	-0.99	0.99
9	0	-1.04	1.04	30	0.75	-0.20	0.95
10	0.13	-0.89	1.02	31	0.09	-0.89	0.98
11	0	-0.99	0.99	32	0.45	-1.19	0.95
12	1.05	0.30	1.02	33	1.42	0.43	0.80
13	0.56	0.03	0.53	34	0.77	-0.37	0.92
14	0.62	0.19	0.43	35	0.12	-0.88	0.91
15	0	-0.99	0.99	36	0.38	-1.74	0.99
16	0	n.s.	n.s.	37	0.92	0.00	0.92
17	1.44	0.53	0.91	38	0.96	0.05	0.91
18	0.08	-0.59	0.67	39	0.87	0.13	0.74
19	0.57	-0.22	0.79	40	0.34	-0.35	0.69
20	0.11	-0.69	0.96	41	0	-1.57	0.94
21	0.14	-0.86	1.00	42	0.62	-0.30	0.92

[a]n.s. denotes that the coefficients are not satisfactory.
Note: For sector numbers and titles, see Appendix 3A.

monetary conditions and the external market and (ii) their self-correction for errors in forecasting demand and inventories. In Table 3-2, this second factor of error adjustment is shown for the first quarter to analyze the immediate impact of these errors on revising the original forecast. As noted earlier, the parameter γ is independently estimated, while θ is obtained as the difference between β_O ($=\eta$) and γ, where β_O denotes the first quarter coefficient of Z_Y in the supply-adjustment function. First, it should be noted from this table that γ is fairly stable, around 0.5 to 1.0, whereas θ is either negative or positive, depending on the value of β_O. This implies that a slower and milder pattern of demand expectation in most of the primary sectors tends to be positively adjusted in the course of its realization, but the negative adjustment in inventory changes, as shown by the negative value of θ, again tends to delay their supply adjustment, thus giving a lower value of β_O. This clearly accounts for the delayed supply response, as noted in the previous section. Similarly, the quick and sensitive supply response in some of the metal and engineering industries can be attributed to a highly positive error adjustment in both inventory and demand expectations, especially in terms of the positive value of θ. A similar pattern of an active inventory adjustment is also observed for the tobacco, rubber products, and furniture industries.

The basic tendency noted above can be tentatively summarized thus: (1) Fast-growing manufacturing sectors tend to have a more sensitive expectation in response to demand impact and also to be flexible in revising their expectation of both demand and inventories. (2) Primary sectors and stagnant manufacturing sectors tend to have a more stable expectation, which is nevertheless adjustable to demand but is somewhat rigid in inventory adjustment, thus causing unintended inventory changes and wide price fluctuations.[6]

The Results of Ex Post Simulation

In order to test its performance, we first simulated our model for our sample period of 32 quarters for 1963 to 1970. As shown in Figures 3-1 and 3-2, two types of test were conducted: (i) short-term simulations for 8 quarters and (ii) long-term simulations for the entire period. Although in both cases lagged endogenous variables are generated within the model, the first test naturally gives fewer errors because of its shorter simulation period.

In aggregative terms at the 7-sector level, Figure 3-1 indicates fairly satisfactory performance for sectoral estimates of total supply, that is, output plus imports. At the 60-sector level, relative errors in the percentages are also small, with only 5 sectors exceeding 5 percent and 42 sectors being below 3 percent. Although the errors tend to be a little higher in the long-term simulation, they are still below 3 percent for 36 sectors and exceed 5 percent for only 10 sectors.

With regard to inventory changes, Figure 3-2 indicates fairly good estimates using the short-term simulations, with a relatively lower performance using the long-term simulations. The larger errors in the latter case are for the most part due to those in heavy manufacturing and are chiefly accounted for by basic steel products. The errors in the mining sectors are also partly attributable to those errors. The average relative error is about 22 percent for the short-term and about 38 percent for the long-term simulations.

Although there is some room for further elaboration in estimating the lag structures, the results of our test roughly indicate the workability of our model for short-term forecasts of sectoral supply and inventory adjustment. This is especially the case for supply forecasts at the 60-sector level in view of the small relative errors in our short-term simulation. While the errors in basic steel are significant in the long-term simulation, most of the other sectors tend to have much smaller errors.

Multisector Multiplier Analysis

As part of the ex post simulation, we simulated the model to derive dynamic multipliers so as to evaluate its dynamic property. Here we introduce two types

6. A similar association of forecast error adjustment with growth rate among different commodity groups was noted in the Japanese steel industry by Watanabe and Kinoshita [14].

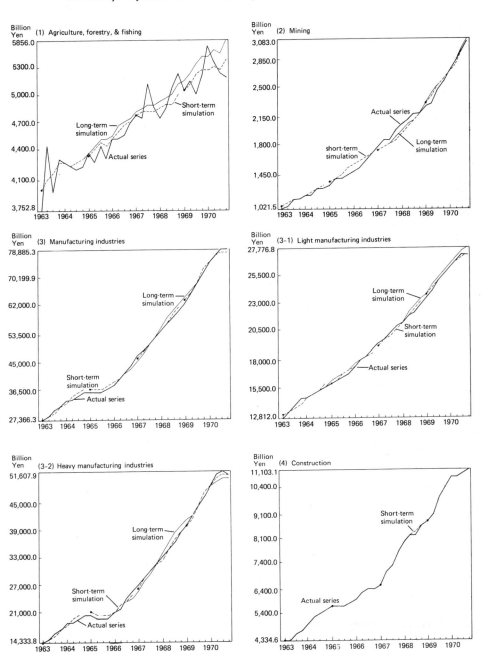

Figure 3-1. Short-Term and Long-Term Simulations Compared with Actual Total Supply (7-Sector Level).

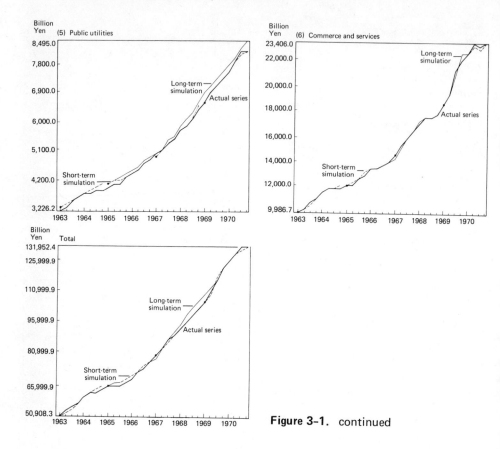

Figure 3-1. continued

of multipliers: (1) multipliers of specific sectors in final demand and (2) composite multipliers of macroeconomic policy variables—such as public investment and its derived private investment and consumption. Multipliers of the first type are useful for the Leontief system of input-output analysis, where the inventory vector is treated as endogenous but other elements in final demand are assumed to remain unchanged. Multipliers of the second type are more comprehensive and realistic for dynamic analysis of policy effects, since various final demand aggregates are treated as mutually dependent in the integrated framework of input-output and macroeconometric systems.

Multipliers of Selected Sectors in Final Demand

Due to limited space, we introduce only two multipliers—those for the automobile industry and those for the apparel industry. These multipliers are obtained as a difference between standard and revised simulations during our sample period. They can be interpreted as dynamic impacts of an increase in

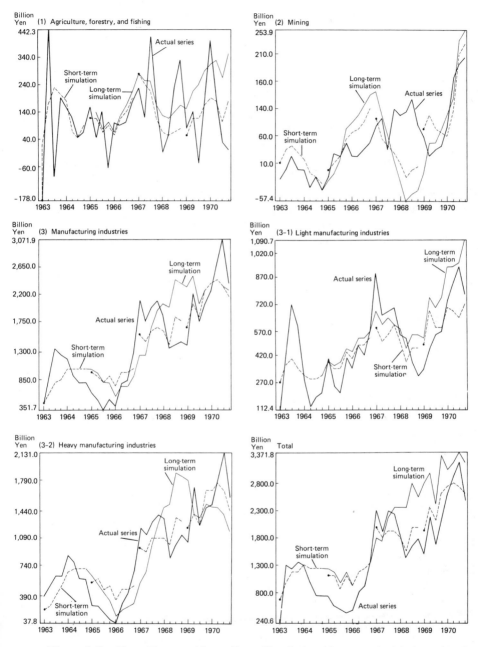

Figure 3–2. Short-Term and Long-Term Simulations Compared with Actual Inventory Changes (7-Sector Level).

exports of automobiles or apparel in cases where the induced final demand for consumption or investment is disregarded.

As shown in Table 3–3, total induced supply by the automobile industry is 2.4 in the first quarter; then it rises to 3.7 in the second quarter, gradually declines to 2.3 in the twelfth quarter, and again rises—to 3.8—in the twentieth quarter. This oscillatory move is chiefly accounted for by the sensitive behavior of the steel industry. Except for the second quarter, a rather stable supply is observed for the machinery industries, while slow but gradual adjustments are noted for steel products, nonferrous metals, and iron ores. A slow but slight oscillation is indicated in ceramics, while a gradual declining trend is observed for rubber products, such as tires. As for inventories, gradual moves in total supply tend to produce rather sensitive changes in total inventories. There are two peaks, in the second and sixth quarters, which fall sharply and hit the bottom in the twelfth quarter and then rise till the twentieth quarter. These sharp oscillatory moves are again accounted for by volatile moves in the heavy industries, especially in steel.

These interesting differences in response pattern and adjustment can also be observed in the apparel industry. Table 3–4 indicates a slower response of the total supply and milder adjustment of the inventories. (This is what we can easily expect from the coefficients in Tables 3–1 and 3–2.) In total supply, the first peak is shown in the seventh quarter and after a slight decline it again rises—to 3.6—in the last quarter. This slow adjustment is due mostly to the apparel sector itself, but partly to natural and other textiles. A quicker response is noted for basic chemicals and leather products for the earlier period, but they continue to rise slowly until the last quarter.

As for inventories, the slow adjustments give rise to a sharp decline, unintended, for the first four quarters, and there is a milder inventory build-up afterwards, accompanied by a mild oscillation.

Composite Multipliers

Finally, we will discuss briefly the results of our composite multipliers, which are obtained by linking the present Leontief-type model to a Keynesian-type macroeconometric model of the Japan Economic Research Center [13]. Since the data are also seasonally adjusted at an annual rate in the latter model, we can simulate both quarterly models in a consistent way so as to derive composite multisector multipliers.

Due to limited space, we introduce here only one of our simulations—multipliers of public investment. In evaluating the results, it should be noted first that the dynamic property of the entire system is subject to that of the macromodel, which tends to vary slightly according to the difference in specification. The macromodel simulation in Figure 3–3 indicates adjustment patterns of related final demand in 1965 prices, which are affected by an increase in public investment in current prices. The declining tendency of public investment in real terms

Table 3-3. Multipliers for a 100 Billion Yen Increase in Automobile Final Demand—60-Sector Level (billion yen)

Year and Quarter		61 Total Supply	39 Automobile	38 Electrical Machinery	37 Machinery	34 Steel Products	32 Ceramics	27 Rubber Products	8 Iron Ores	Inventory Changes
1965	I	242.5	115.2	7.9	22.4	14.2	1.0	15.3	0.2	-17.3
	II	367.3	170.5	11.2	32.4	27.8	2.1	19.4	0.5	28.9
	III	324.2	138.4	8.3	24.9	34.0	2.6	10.4	0.9	16.4
	IV	324.6	138.7	8.2	24.4	31.6	2.7	10.1	1.3	17.5
1966	I	336.6	139.3	8.2	24.3	29.9	3.0	9.9	1.5	21.1
	II	348.8	139.9	8.2	24.1	38.5	4.6	9.7	1.5	25.7
	III	336.2	140.3	8.1	24.0	34.2	4.0	9.5	1.5	22.2
	IV	313.9	140.7	8.1	23.9	21.9	3.5	9.3	1.6	14.8
1967	I	286.0	141.2	7.9	23.8	9.7	3.1	9.1	1.6	5.9
	II	265.3	141.6	7.9	23.7	-1.8	2.5	8.9	1.6	-0.9
	III	243.7	142.0	7.8	23.6	-14.2	1.3	8.7	1.6	-7.5
	IV	230.4	142.5	7.7	23.5	-23.0	0.8	8.4	1.6	-11.3
1968	I	231.6	143.0	7.7	23.4	-24.1	0.5	8.2	1.5	-11.1
	II	245.8	143.5	7.7	23.2	-17.1	0.3	8.0	1.5	-7.3
	III	269.3	144.1	7.7	23.1	-3.0	0.5	7.8	1.4	-1.1
	IV	300.3	144.8	7.7	23.0	16.9	1.1	7.6	1.4	6.6
1969	I	330.8	145.4	7.7	22.9	38.5	1.7	7.4	1.4	13.9
	II	356.8	146.1	7.7	22.8	57.6	2.2	7.2	1.5	19.7
	III	374.3	146.7	7.7	22.7	71.8	2.7	6.9	1.5	23.2
	IV	380.3	147.3	7.7	22.6	77.8	3.0	6.7	1.6	24.0
1970	I	375.3	147.9	7.7	22.5	74.9	3.1	6.5	1.7	22.3
	II	359.6	148.4	7.6	22.3	63.7	3.0	6.2	1.7	18.4
	III	335.3	148.8	7.6	22.1	44.8	2.7	6.0	1.7	12.9
	IV	307.4	149.3	7.5	22.0	22.4	2.5	5.8	1.7	6.9

Supply

Table 3-4. Multipliers for a 100 Billion Yen Increase in Wearing Apparel Final Demand—60-Sector Level (billion yen)

Year and Quarter		61 Total Supply	21 Wearing Apparel	28 Basic Chemicals	26 Leather Products	20 Other Textiles	19 Chemical Textiles	18 Natural Textiles	3 Live-stock for Textiles	2 Industrial Crops	Inventory Changes
						Supply					
1965	I	75.3	14.0	7.3	4.2	6.0	3.8	1.6	2.3	1.0	-72.7
	II	146.2	35.1	15.4	6.6	14.3	6.7	3.1	4.6	0.8	-46.7
	III	203.9	58.0	22.5	6.0	24.7	6.6	5.6	7.0	0.7	-24.7
	IV	256.9	78.5	22.2	6.1	41.9	6.6	8.5	9.8	3.7	-3.5
1966	I	299.6	94.1	21.8	6.1	54.2	6.7	11.8	10.1	6.8	12.8
	II	333.5	103.8	21.7	6.1	63.4	6.7	15.3	10.5	9.4	26.5
	III	345.3	107.9	21.7	6.2	67.8	6.7	18.6	9.0	10.3	30.8
	IV	341.9	108.3	21.7	6.2	67.4	6.8	21.8	6.9	9.4	28.4
1967	I	333.6	108.4	21.6	6.2	65.9	6.8	24.6	4.0	8.1	23.8
	II	327.6	108.6	21.6	6.3	64.8	6.9	27.0	1.9	6.8	20.5
	III	321.0	108.7	21.7	6.3	63.6	6.9	28.8	0.1	5.7	17.4
	IV	316.4	108.8	21.8	6.4	62.5	7.0	29.9	-1.3	4.7	15.4
1968	I	315.4	109.0	22.2	6.5	61.4	7.1	30.2	-2.1	3.9	15.0
	II	317.5	109.2	22.7	6.6	60.4	7.2	29.6	-2.5	3.4	16.0
	III	322.4	109.4	23.3	6.7	59.7	7.3	29.0	-2.1	3.0	18.5
	IV	330.0	109.6	23.9	6.8	59.0	7.4	28.5	-1.7	2.7	21.8
1969	I	338.1	109.8	24.5	7.0	58.7	7.5	28.0	-1.1	2.4	25.6
	II	345.5	110.1	25.1	7.2	58.6	7.7	27.5	-0.4	2.3	29.3
	III	351.7	110.4	25.8	7.4	58.6	7.9	27.1	0.3	2.1	32.8
	IV	356.1	110.7	26.5	7.6	59.0	8.0	26.6	0.8	2.0	35.9
1970	I	359.2	111.1	27.3	7.9	59.5	8.3	26.2	1.3	1.9	38.7
	II	360.8	111.5	28.1	8.2	60.4	8.5	25.9	1.5	1.8	41.3
	III	361.7	112.0	29.2	8.6	61.7	8.8	25.6	1.6	1.6	43.8
	IV	363.4	112.5	30.3	9.0	63.3	9.2	25.3	1.6	1.5	46.8

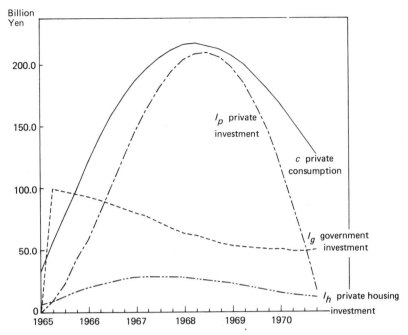

Figure 3-3. Multipliers of Public Investment (an increase of 100 billion yen in current prices).

implies that there is a rising trend in the price deflator for public investment. In terms of response, housing investment appears to respond more rapidly than do other items, while private investment tends to respond most slowly.

After price levels are adjusted from 1965 to 1960 prices, all the final demand aggregates are fed into our Leontief model for use in dynamic sectoral analysis. As indicated in Figure 3-4, the construction sector has the fastest response, as would be expected, while heavy manufacturing has the slowest adjustment because of the time lag in business investment. Among basic sectors, agricultural sectors tend to respond quickly, while mining sectors, which are strongly affected by business investment, respond slowly. Public utilities and service sectors appear to respond nearly as quickly as the total supply.

Looking into the details at the 60-sector level in Figure 3-5, it is evident that there are several groups that clearly depend on different types of final demand. The public construction sector (group A) depends heavily on government investment, thus responding most quickly, while residential construction, wood products, and furniture (group B) are dependent on private housing and so respond rather less quickly.

The consumption group (group C), such as grain products, tobacco, leather

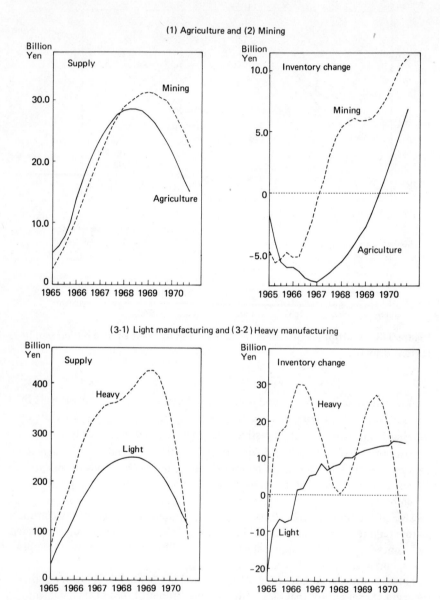

Figure 3-4.   Composite Multiplier (Supply and Inventory Changes) of Public Investment (7-Sector Level).

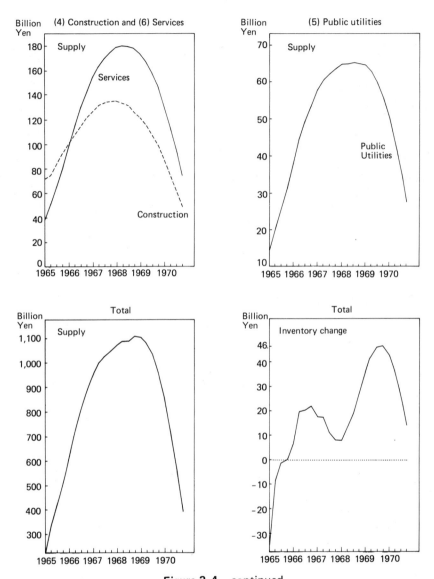

Figure 3-4. continued

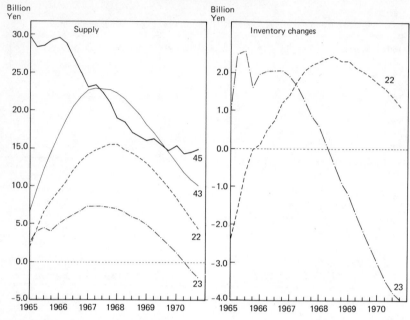

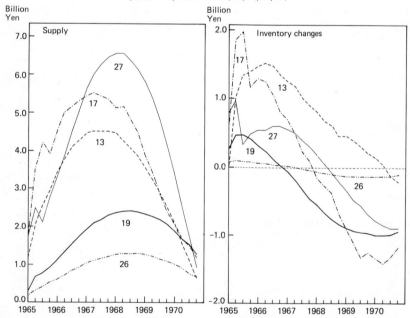

Figure 3-5. Responses by Groups.

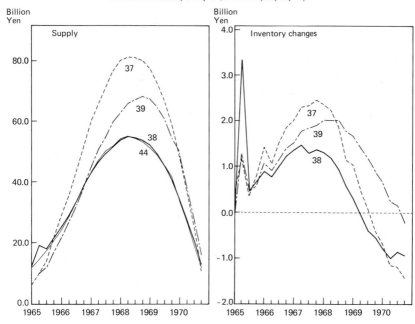

Business Investment, Group D (Sectors 37, 38, 39, 44)

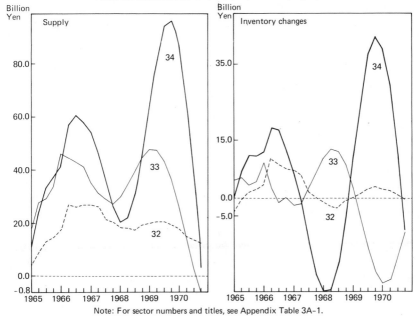

Public and Business Investment, Group E (Sectors 32, 33, 34)

Note: For sector numbers and titles, see Appendix Table 3A-1.

Figure 3-5.   continued

and rubber products, and chemical textiles, being mainly dependent on private consumption, adjust rather quickly in both supply and inventories. Capital goods, such as automobile, machinery, and business construction (group D), tend to respond more slowly because of their dependence on business investment. There are unique sectors (group E) with two peaks, as they are equally dependent on both public and private investment. Those sectors are basic iron, basic steel, and ceramics, whose changes in inventories are strongly affected by these two types of impact.

As for the total change in inventories, a similar two-peak pattern emerges because of the significance and sensitivity of heavy manufacturing, including steel and ceramics.

Concluding Remarks

The above analysis of dynamic sectoral responses in the Leontief model appears to indicate the general validity of our approach for short-term sectoral projection, although it reveals a need for further refinement in terms of data reliability and lag structures.

In summary, our findings indicate that there are various types of response pattern:

1. Capital goods with the highest growth rate and the most sensitive moves in their basic materials, such as steel and cement, respond very quickly.
2. Primary products, whether imported or produced domestically, tend to respond slowly, with an immediate unintended decline in their inventories for the early period.
3. Some of the consumption goods closely related to primary products also tend to adjust slowly, but are sensitive to financial conditions.
4. Imported raw materials usually respond rather slowly but are highly sensitive to world price conditions and the world monetary market.
5. Other types of consumption goods respond rather quickly, with moderate adjustment in inventories.

Our experiment with the link to the Keynesian-type macromodel also indicates various patterns of sectoral responses in the case of public investment. Other policy variables, such as the official discount rate, transfer payments, and exchange rate, are scheduled to be linked to our model for testing various sectoral responses.

We are planning to fully introduce the price mechanism, which is only partly incorporated at present, as in import prices. Through this extension, the model is expected to respond explicitly to external impacts on the supply side, such as cuts in imports or strikes in specific sectors. Backward interindustry demand linkage in the present model can thus be integrated with forward interindustry supply linkage through this improvement in price variables.

References

1. Almon, S. "The Distributed Lag Between Capital Appropriations and Expenditures." *Econometrica* 33, no. 1 (January 1965): 178–196.
2. Darling, P.G., and M.C. Lovell. "Factors Influencing Investment in Inventories." *The Brookings Quarterly Econometric Model of the United States.* Edited by J.S. Duesenberry, G. Fromm, L.R. Klein, and E. Kuh. Chicago: Rand McNally; Amsterdam: North-Holland Publishing Company, 1965. Pp. 131–161.
3. Klein, L.R., ed. *Essays in Industrial Econometrics.* Vol. III. Philadelphia: Economics Research Unit, University of Pennsylvania, 1969.
4. Lovell, M.C. "Buffer Stocks, Sales Expectations, and Stability: A Multi-Sector Analysis of Inventory Cycle." *Econometrica* 30, no. 2 (April 1962): 267–296.
5. Lovell, M.C. "Determinants of Inventory Investment." In *Models of Income Determination.* By the National Bureau of Economic Research. Princeton: Princeton University Press, 1964. Pp. 177–224.
6. Modigliani, F., and C.H. Sauerlander. "Economic Expectations and Plans in Relation to Short-Term Economic Forecasting." *Short-Term Economic Forecasting.* By the National Bureau of Economic Research. Princeton: Princeton University Press, 1955. Pp. 229–308.
7. Moriguchi, C. "Inventory Changes and Structure of Anticipation." *Economic Review* 16 (1965): 68–72. (In Japanese.)
8. Pashigian, B.P. "The Relevance of Sale Anticipatory Data in Explaining Inventory Investment." *International Economic Review* 6 (January 1965): 65–91.
9. Shinkai, Y. "Manufacturer's Inventory Investment in Japan." *Economic Studies Quarterly* 23, no. 2 (August 1972): 70–75. (In Japanese.)
10. Shishido, S., et al. "Policy Simulations for Supply and Demand Management with the EPA Quarterly Econometric Model." 1970. (Mimeographed.)
11. Shishido, S., and A. Oshizaka. "Simulation Analysis for Anti-Pollution Control." 1974. (Mimeographed.)
12. Shishido, S., and A. Oshizaka, eds. "Data Estimation for Quarterly Input-Output Model." Japan Economic Research Center, 1974. (In Japanese, mimeographed.)
13. Uchida, T. "Short-Term Forecasting Model of J.E.R.C." 1973. (In Japanese, mimeographed.)
14. Watanabe, T., and S. Kinoshita. "An Econometric Study of the Japanese Steel Industry." In *Essays in Industrial Economics.* Vol. III. Edited by L.R. Klein. Philadelphia: Economics Research Unit, University of Pennsylvania, 1969. Pp. 97–162.
15. Watanabe, T., and S. Shishido. "Planning Applications of the Leontief Model in Japan." In *Input-Output Techniques.* Vol. 2, *Applications of Input-Output Analysis.* Edited by A.P. Carter and A. Bródy. Amsterdam: North-Holland Publishing Company, 1970. Pp. 9–23.

Appendix 3A

Table 3A-1. Industrial Classification

60-Sector		7-Sector	
1	General crop		
2	Industrial crop		
3	Livestock for textiles	1	Agriculture, forestry, & fishing
4	Livestock		
5	Forestry		
6	Fisheries		
7	Coal mining		
8	Iron ores		
9	Nonferrous metallic ores	2	Mining
10	Crude petroleum & natural gas		
11	Other mining		
12	Meat & dairy products		
13	Grain products		
14	Manufactured sea foods		
15	Other food		
16	Beverages		
17	Tobacco		
18	Natural textiles		
19	Chemical textiles	3-1	Light manufacturing industries
20	Other textiles		
21	Wearing apparel		
22	Wood products		
23	Furniture		
24	Pulp & paper		
25	Printing & publishing		
26	Leather products		
27	Rubber products		
28	Basic chemicals	3-2	Heavy manufacturing industries
29	Other chemicals		

(continued)

Table 3A-1 continued

60-Sector	7-Sector
30 Petroleum products	
31 Coal products	3-1 Light manufacturing industries
32 Ceramics	
33 Primary iron	
34 Steel products	
35 Primary nonferrous metals	
36 Fabricated metals	3-2 Heavy manufacturing industries
37 Machinery	
38 Electrical machinery	
39 Automobile	
40 Other transport equipment	
41 Instruments & related products	3-1 Light manufacturing industries
42 Miscellaneous manufacturing	
43 Residence	
44 Nonresidence	4 Construction
45 Public engineering work	
46 Other engineering work	
47 Electricity	
48 Gas	5 Public utilities
49 Water & sanitary services	
50 Wholesale & retail trade	6 Commerce & services
51 Real estate	
52 Railway transport	
53 Road transport	5 Public utilities
54 Other transport	
55 Communication	
56 Bank & other financial institution	
57 Government service	6 Commerce & services
58 Public service	
59 Other personal services	
60 Unallocated	7 Unallocated
61 Total	8 Total

Chapter Four

A Dynamic Model for Analysing Price Changes

B. D. Haig
M. P. Wood

This paper describes a model for the dynamic analysis of quarterly price changes in an economy. The model is composed of two sets of relations—an open input-output system and equations that close the model. The two sets of relations are tested by comparing the actual changes in prices and costs in Australia from the third quarter of 1969 (1969-III) through the second quarter of 1973 (1973-II) with those predicted by each set of relations.

The model is basically a closed input-output system that describes the transmission of price changes between different industry sectors and, in addition, relates changes in costs of production (inputs into the input-output system) to changes in final prices (as determined by the input-output system). Prices are determined by a markup on historical costs of production; and prices of outputs of industries and of sales to final buyers are, therefore, based on costs of production in a previous period. This results in a dynamic input-output system in which increases in costs are passed on, after a delay, as increases in selling prices of industries. The model is closed by adding equations that express changes in some costs of production (wages and profits) to previous changes in prices of sales to final buyers.

The structure of the model follows closely the standard two-equation system that has been extensively employed in recent years in quantitative studies of the generation of inflation. A prototype of this sytem, as formulated by Lipsey and Parkin [4], is as follows:

$$P = f(W_r, M_s, Q_t) \tag{4-1}$$

$$W = f(U_u, P_v, S_w) \tag{4-2}$$

where

P = the proportionate rate of change of an index of prices

W = the proportionate rate of change of wages or earnings

M = the proportionate rate of change of import prices

Q = the proportionate rate of change of output per head

U = some function of the percentage of the labour force unemployed

S = some measure of the aggressiveness of the trade unions

and $r, s, t, u, v,$ and w are lags in quarters.

In the present model, equation (4-2) is divided into two equations, which describe cost and demand factors separately. The major innovation in this paper, however, is the use of input-output data to estimate the form of the relationship in equation (4-1), instead of relying on econometric methods of regression. Finally, the properties of the model, and conclusions about the determinants of inflation, are studied by computer simulation of the system instead of the usual econometric or analytical methods.

The plan of the paper is as follows. The next two sections develop the relationships expressed by equations (4-1) and (4-2). The fourth section gives the results of simulating the two parts of the model over a past period. The conclusions of the paper are summarised in the fifth section.

The Input-Output Relations

The input-output system is used to determine the relationship between changes in costs of industries and the subsequent changes in prices of sales to final buyers [see equation (4-1)]. This relationship is usually estimated by econometric methods of regression employing time series data. Estimates of coefficient values obtained by this method are, however, generally unsatisfactory, and the values are sensitive to the sample period.[1] The data used in the regressions usually show a general upward trend over the period, which produces considerable multicollinearity in the estimates of the coefficients for the independent variables. As a result, the estimates of the coefficients and the standard errors obtained in these studies are unreliable. In particular, the upward trend makes it difficult (or impossible) to estimate the lag structure of the variables.

The use of input-output data to estimate the relationship between changes in costs and changes in prices avoids these problems of estimation. The coefficients of the variables and the appropriate lag structures are obtained implicitly by the simulation of a model, constructed from input-output data, of actual flows of prices and costs between industries and final buyers. Moreover, the input-output procedure is based on an assumption about the theory of business behaviour, whereas the econometric approach simply uses the apparent identity between

---

1. See, for example, results presented by Pitchford [5] and Haig and Wood [3].

the income and expenditures sides of the national income accounts. The theory of business behaviour adopted in this study, however, is fairly rudimentary and relies on simple assumptions about the pricing policies of business and the rate of transmission of costs between industries. These assumptions are described below. It may be noted that the predictions of the model can be compared with actual price changes, and these provide a test of the model, including the reasonableness of the assumptions.

The input-output coefficients are assumed constant. Since the model is simulated only over a period of four or five years, this assumption is probably reasonably accurate. However, the input-output data are for 1962-1963, the latest year for which official input-output data are available. All the price series calculated by the model are based, therefore, on constant 1962-1963 weights, and it would obviously have been preferable to have adopted a more recent period as the base year.

The Determination of Prices

The main features of the model are illustrated by the flow diagram shown in Figure 4-1. In this diagram, different blocks are used to represent groups of industries and transactions, and these blocks are linked by lines to show how changes in the prices of wages, imports, and import duties affect the prices of transactions between industries and consequently the retail price index. Thus, an increase in the price of imports of a particular commodity used in manufacturing affects the retail price index by the following process. First, the price increase raises production costs and thereby the selling prices of those industries using the import. The higher selling prices are then passed on, either through higher production costs for other industries or as increased prices paid by wholesalers for final output. Then wholesalers and retailers mark up the cost of goods as they pass through the trade block. Finally, the changes in retail prices of products of different industries are translated into prices of the components of the retail price index by the consumption convertor.

Blocks 1 and 8 represent the inputs and outputs of the model. Block 1 shows the payments for primary inputs of wages, imports, and import duty, and Block 8 the value of sales to final buyers (personal consumers). Profit margins are assumed constant, and changes in profits of industries are related to changes in prime costs covering wages, imports, import duties, and purchases from other industries. Profit is therefore determined endogenously by the model. Sales to final buyers in the present model include only personal consumption expenditures. The changes in the prices of other items of final expenditures are not analysed, since they do not lead to further changes in industry costs or prices.

Blocks 2 to 6 represent groups of industries—the primary, manufacturing, services, and trade industries. The method of calculating the selling prices from costs for each of these groups of industries is described here.

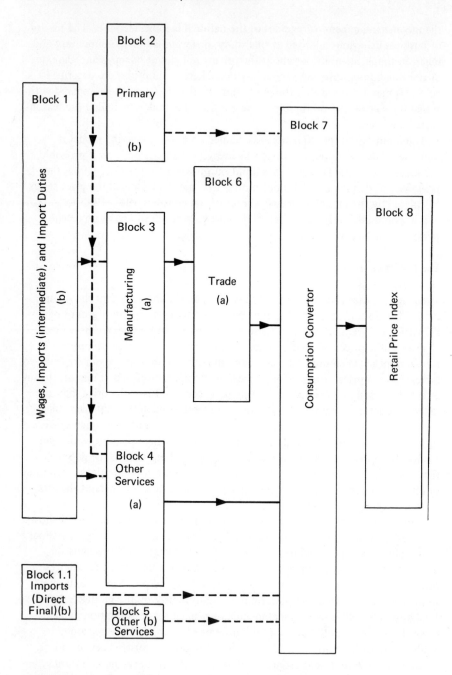

Figure 4–1. The Input-Output Relations. (a) = prices determined by the model and (b) = prices exogenous.

Primary Industries

These industries cover agriculture, pastoral, and mining. The prices of output sold to other industries and to final buyers are assumed to be exogenous, and determined by world prices or seasonal conditions.

Manufacturing Industries

Prices are assumed to be determined by applying a constant percentage mark-up to the historical cost of goods sold, which comprise the purchases from other industries, imports, import duties, and the costs of wages per unit of output. Purchases from the service industries and profit are assumed to be included in overhead costs. Thus, selling prices do not vary directly in response to changes in the prices of items of services, depreciation, interest, etc.

Costs of materials are assumed to be passed on by the period of stock turn-over and costs of wages by the period of turnover of work-in-progress. Therefore, material costs are assumed to enter only at the initial stage of production, while wage costs are assumed to be spread evenly over the stage of production of work-in-progress.

The period of turnover is calculated by relating the value of inputs or outputs of industries to the value of stock held. For those industries whose intraindustry transactions were comparatively unimportant, use was made of data on stocks by stage of processing, and ratios were calculated separately for raw materials, work-in-progress, and finished goods. The periods of turnover for each component were obtained by relating the value of stocks to the value of inputs, to the average value of outputs (less profits) and inputs, and to the value of output (less profits), respectively. This procedure allows for progressive increases in the value of stocks as they pass through the stages of production. The average length of lag in passing on increases in costs of materials was then obtained by summing the length of turnover for each of these classes of stocks. It was assumed that labour cost is spread evenly over the period of work-in-progress, and the length of lag in passing on wages costs was derived as the sum of the period of turnover of finished goods plus half the period of turnover of work-in-progress stock.[2]

For those industries whose intraindustry transactions are important, the data on stocks by stage of processing will not represent the stocks of the industry held in each category. In this case, a part of the stocks of raw materials and finished goods is properly considered work-in-progress of the industry. Hence, for those industries whose intraindustry transactions are significant (rather arbitrarily selected as industries in which 25 percent or more of sales were to firms within the industry: chemicals, textiles, paper, and wood), one overall period of stock turnover was estimated by relating the value of stocks to the total sales (excluding intraindustry sales and profit). An attempt was made, however, to estimate the length of the turnover of work-in-progress, in order to correctly allocate

2. This is basically the method used by Godley and Nordhaus [1] to estimate the length of the delay in passing on costs in British manufacturing industries.

the cost of wages to production. This was done by first estimating the period of turnover of stock, where stock represented all the raw materials and finished goods of the industry. For the estimation, an assumption was made that the ratio of raw materials and finished goods purchased by all industries to the value of their total inputs (excluding profits and intraindustry transactions) held for each individual industry. The length of turnover of work-in-progress was then calculated by subtracting the estimated period of turnover of stocks of goods, which represented raw materials and finished goods to the industry, from the estimated total period of turnover of stocks. The length of lag in passing on labour costs was assumed to equal the average of this period plus the period of turnover of finished goods.

The estimated periods of transmitting materials and wages costs by industries are shown in Table 4-1. Changes in wages costs are converted to changes in costs per unit of output by dividing the computed increase in wages by the average rate of increase in labour productivity, again calculated separately for each industry.

Trade

Selling prices are obtained by applying a constant percent markup to the prices of goods bought for resale. The turnover period for sales to final buyers is obtained as the sum of the average stock turnover period for wholesalers and retailers, and this is assumed to represent the lag in passing on increases in costs to consumers. The period of turnover is calculated separately for the products of each industry; and these are shown in Table 4-1. No information is available on the delay in interindustry transactions, and it is assumed to be nil.

Other Services

Changes in prices of other services do not affect manufacturers' costs of production (and hence selling prices of these industries) but do enter into the changes in the retail price index. The selling price of the output of service industries is calculated in the same way as selling prices of manufacturers. It is assumed that costs are passed on after one month. Comparison of changes in retail prices of services and of goods suggests that prices of services are passed on much more quickly than those of goods. The actual period assumed—one month—is not based on direct evidence.

These assumptions are sufficient to construct a model for the transmission of costs between industries and from industries to final buyers. The model also includes a "consumption convertor" (Block 7), which reclassifies changes in prices of sales to personal consumers by industry category to the components in the official retail price index. The changes in prices of these components are then added by using the weights of the components in the official retail price index. Changes in prices of sales to final buyers are therefore converted to changes in the official price index.

Table 4-1. Number of Months' Delay in Passing on Increases in Costs

		Manufacturing Industry		
Num-ber	*Industry* *Title*	*Materials*	*Wages*	*Trade*
1	Chemicals	5	1	4
2	Petroleum products	3	1	3
3	Glass, clay, & other nonmetallic products	5	1	8
4	Fabricated metal products	7	2	4
7	Leather & leather goods	7	1	7
8	Textiles	3	1	6
9	Clothing & footwear	2	1	6
10	Food manufacturing	2	1	2
11	Beverages & tobacco products	8	1	2
12	Paper & paper products, printing, & publishing	6	1	5
13	Wood, wood products, & furniture	3	1	6
14	Other manufacturing	3	1	6

The flows of exogenous costs and prices, indicated by broken lines, are:

1. Average earnings and the price of imports and duty (Block 1).
2. Prices of output of the agricultural industry (wool and food products) and forestry and mining industries (including basic metals) (Block 2). These prices are costs of inputs used by industries, but they include also the price of unprocessed food and natural gas in the official retail price index.
3. Prices of some outputs of services—rent, and radio and TV licenses (Block 5).

Equations for the Input-Output Relationships

The equations in the model are given below, with the subscript i referring to the industries whose selling prices are determined by the model. The indexes of costs and prices for each industry are based on quantity weights in 1962-1963. These and the trade margins and profit markups are calculated from entries in the input-output table for that year. The indexes of the selling prices of the output of each industry are obtained as the sum of the lagged indexes of the per unit cost of materials and labour used by the industry and the profit markup. A list of industries and a list of consumption categories are given in Appendix 4A. In equation (4-3), the cost of materials is generated as the sum of selling prices of supplying industries (determined by the model) and the exogenous prices.

EQUATIONS EXPLAINING COSTS OF INTERMEDIATE
INPUTS PER BASE-YEAR UNIT OF OUTPUT

$$IN_i = \left(\sum_{j=1}^{18} a_{ij} SA_j \right) + AG_i + FO_i + MI_i + IM_i + ID_i \tag{4-3}$$

where

IN = costs of inputs per unit of output

a = matrix of technical input coefficients

SA = selling price of supplying industries

AG = unit costs of purchases from agriculture

FO = unit costs of purchases from forestry

MI = unit costs of purchases from mining

IM = unit costs of imported inputs

ID = unit costs of duty on imported inputs

The cost of sales of each industry is determined in equation (4-4) and the selling price of sales in equation (4-5).

COST-OF-PRODUCTION EQUATIONS

$$CP_i = (IN_i \cdot MT_i)_{t-k}(W_i)_{t-\ell} \tag{4-4}$$

where

CP = cost price per unit of output

W = earnings per unit of output (determined by the changes in average earnings and labour productivity)

MT = trade margins on goods purchased from other industries and imports

k,ℓ = number of months' delay in passing on increases in costs, which differ between industries

EQUATIONS EXPLAINING SELLING PRICES

$$SA_i = CP_i \cdot MC_i \tag{4-5}$$

where

MC = profit markup on costs per unit of output

SA = selling price per unit of output

The unit price of imports (including duty), the indirect tax rate, and the wholesale and retail trade markup determine the retail price of the goods sold to consumers, as shown in equation (4-6).[3]

THE RETAIL PRICE OF GOODS SOLD TO CONSUMERS

$$C_i = (SA_i \cdot RD_i + IMC_i \cdot RM_i)_{t-m}(T_i + MS_i) \tag{4-6}$$

where

C = retail price of goods sold to consumers

IMC = price of imports allocated directly to consumers, including duty

T = rate of commodity tax

RD = relative shares of domestic goods

RM = relative shares of imported goods

MS = wholesale and retail markup

m = number of months' delay in passing on increases in costs, which differ between industries

In the final step, the retail price index is calculated from retail prices determined both exogenously and endogenously.

The Closed Model

The model is completed by the addition of two equations that form the link between the change in prices, determined by the input-output system, and the change in costs, which enters as an input into the system.

One equation completes the wage-price spiral, by making nominal wages a function of prices. The second equation explains the wage drift, or the excess of actual over nominal wages, in terms of excess demand for consumers' goods. This equation introduces demand elements into the explanation of inflation.

The first equation simply reflects the fact that nominal or negotiated wages are in fact fixed by reference to the cost of living, as measured by the official retail price index. The main difficulty is to determine the length of the delay between increases in the cost of living and the level of negotiated wages. In estimating this equation, different lengths of lag were assumed, for nil, or one, two, or three quarters. In addition, a dummy variable is included to pick up the effect of a substantial increase in award wages awarded by the Commonwealth Arbitration Court early in 1971. The best fit was obtained by the following equation, allowing for a two-quarter lag between changes in retail prices and nominal wages.

3. All import duties and indirect taxes are assumed to be ad valorem. Some are, of course, specific. It is assumed that taxes are not marked up.

$$NW = -27.676 + .733CP_{-2} + 2.726D \qquad\qquad (4\text{--}7)$$
$$(9.14) \quad (26.11) \quad\;\; (7.00)$$
$$D.W. = 1.69 \qquad R^2 = .996$$

where

NW = nominal wages (mean value, 58.0)

CP = index of retail prices (mean value, 114.7)

D = dummy variable, taking the value 0 before 1971-I and 1 in 1971-I and later periods

 Estimation of this equation obviously runs into the same problems, due to the trend in the data, that affect estimation of equation (4–1). The fit is only marginally better using a lag of two periods—F values, for example, were 1780, compared with values of 1415 for a lag of one period and 1126 for a lag of three periods. However, there are reasons for accepting a two-period lag. There is a delay before price indexes are published and there is a further delay before the wage rates are adjusted for changes in prices.

 The wage drift is explained in the model by excess demand as a result of (unintended) savings of wage earners. Excess demand (and unintended savings) is measured by the difference between wage income (less desired savings) and the money value of consumers' goods available to wage earners. This explanation for the wage drift is based on three main assumptions: (1) that there are significant changes from one quarter to the next in the ratio of wages to the money value of consumers' goods available to wage earners; (2) that this leads to a bidding-up of wages above the nominal levels; and (3) that other sources of excess demand are relatively unimportant. The explanation for differences in the timing of changes in money wages and the money value of sales of consumers' goods is provided by the open input-output model, described in the preceding section of this paper, and by the relationship expressed by equation (4–1). Exogenous increases in wages lead to a rise in prices in a subsequent period, after which, the increase in costs is transmitted through the system of input-output relationships and wholesalers and retailers to final buyers. Similarly, an exogenous increase in prices of final output (as a result, perhaps, of changes in external prices) is reflected in the average earnings after a period of time. In fact, the notion of the wage-price spiral implies that changes in wages and prices in any one period are not closely related, except, perhaps, in particular circumstances, or where the period is so long that the effect of differences in timing on the series is smoothed out.

 Nominal or negotiated wages are expressed, by equation (4–7), as a function of previous levels of retail prices.

 In equation (4–8), explaining the wage drift, the dependent variable is expressed as the ratio of average earnings to nominal wages and the independent variables as (1) the ratio of average earnings to retail prices (both in index form), and (2) the male unemployment rate.

$$AE/NW = 1.469 + .000424(AEI/CP)_{-2} - .0160UM_{-2} \qquad (4\text{-}8)$$
$$(78.55) \quad (3.50) \qquad\qquad (1.54)$$

$$\text{D.W.} = 1.49 \qquad R^2 = .469$$

where

AE = average earnings (seasonally adjusted)

NW = nominal wages

AEI = index of average earnings (seasonally adjusted)

CP = index of retail prices

UM = male unemployment rate (seasonally adjusted)

Equation (4-8) implies that the nominal or negotiated wages are bid up by the excess demand. Strictly, the effect of excess demand would be met first by a decline in inventories, increasing order books, etc. Subsequently, wages would be bid up as employers attempt to increase employment to meet the increased demand; and finally, the effect of excess demand would lead to reduced levels of unemployment.

The transmission of excess demand could occur in two ways. First, increased demands for labor by industries that produce consumption goods lead, in that sector, to higher wages, which then spread to other sectors. Second, increased demands for labor in other industries—that supply intermediate products to the consumer goods industries—induce these industries to raise wages in order to attract additional workers. In both instances, the effect of increased demand for consumers' goods would be felt after a delay. Accordingly, the mechanism would allow for some lag before excess demand is reflected in a bidding-up of the nominal wages; and experiments were made in estimating the equation to determine whether or not there was a significant lag.

Since the effect of excess demand on wages is likely to depend upon the level of unemployment, the current level of unemployment was tried as an additional explanatory variable and was found to be marginally significant.

The mechanism suggested also implies that excess demand does not lead to an appreciable increase in profit margins; consequently, there would be no point in measuring excess demand in terms of the excess of wages and salaries over the money value of the sales of consumers' goods in a particular period. This assumption underlies the open input-output system described in the preceding section. The mechanism also implies a good deal of homogeneity in the demand for labour; that is, that an increase in the demand for final goods leads to a general rise in wages.

The effects of excess demand for consumer goods by profit earners, and of excess demands for other goods, on the wage drift are ignored. It seems reasonable to assume that consumption expenditures of profit earners are relatively stable, or at least less responsive to changes in income than the expenditures by wage earners. The traditional (Keynesian) explanation of excess demand, of course, traces the demands to increases in real spending by public authorities and on investment goods (as well as on consumption goods) and allows for leakage through imports. In the mechanism suggested in this paper, changes in these other components of final expenditures are ignored; it is simply assumed that they are less important in a period of inflation than the effect of excess spending power available for personal consumption.

A Test of the Model

A comparison of the actual changes in retail prices, as measured by the official index of retail prices, with changes predicted by the model is given in Table 4-2.[4] The table also compares the actual with the predicted earnings, derived from the two wage relations described in the preceding section. In order to eliminate the effect of initial values, as shown by the input-output data, the prices and earnings for three years are simulated, using the model, before comparing the predicted values with the actual values. This comparison is made for 16 quarters—from 1969-III through 1973-II.

The predicted prices are obtained by simulating the model, using actual monthly values of exogenous variables—average earnings, prices of imports and import duties, the price of purchases by industries from the primary industries, and actual prices for some components of the retail price index. The results are converted to quarterly averages for comparison with the official index of retail prices. The simulation is dynamic; that is, no correction is made for differences between actual and predicted prices in any period, when predicting prices for the next period.

One source of difference between the actual and predicted prices for components of the price index is the use of overall average price indexes to measure the changes in prices of exogenous inputs to industries, instead of the actual changes in prices. Price indexes of costs by individual industries in Australia are not readily available. It might be assumed, however, that the use of average indexes leads to errors in prices of output of individual industries (and hence in the components of the retail price index), but the error will tend to be offsetting in the total index.

4. Comparison of actual and predicted retail prices for components of the official index of retail prices is given in Haig and Wood [2].

Table 4-2. Actual and Predicted Prices and Average Earnings

Year and Quarter		Retail Price Index (1966/67 = 100)			Average Earnings ($ per week)		
		Actual	Predicted	Residual	Actual	Predicted	Residual
1969–70	I	107.8	107.8	0.0	73.7	73.7	0.0
	II	108.7	108.5	0.2	75.1	74.1	1.0
	III	109.8	109.7	0.1	76.9	74.7	2.2
	IV	111.2	111.1	0.1	78.8	76.2	2.6
1970–71	I	111.9	112.4	−0.5	80.1	77.8	2.3
	II	114.0	113.6	0.4	82.0	79.0	3.0
	III	115.2	115.4	−0.2	86.9	83.2	3.7
	IV	117.2	117.2	0.0	88.3	86.5	1.8
1971–72	I	119.2	119.0	0.2	90.2	88.5	1.7
	II	122.0	121.0	1.0	91.7	90.1	1.6
	III	123.3	122.1	1.2	93.3	92.1	1.2
	IV	124.4	123.6	0.8	95.2	93.1	2.1
1972–73	I	126.1	125.7	0.4	98.1	94.6	3.5
	II	127.7	128.1	−0.4	100.0	96.5	3.5
	III	130.4	131.4	−1.0	102.2	99.3	2.9
	IV	134.7	135.0	−0.3	106.0	103.4	2.6

Other sources of difference between the actual and predicted prices are: (1) mistakes in the specification of the model, including the assumptions that there is a constant markup on cost and that prices are based on historical cost, and (2) errors in the estimates of the model parameters, including the rate of productivity change, the period of stock turnover, and the calculation of markups and tax rates. Ideally, it would be desirable to reduce the possibility of the second type of error as much as possible so that a check could be made on the pricing assumptions in the model. However, the reliability of the parameter estimates is considerably affected by limitations in the data available. For example, official indexes of industrial production are not available in Australia, and there are differences between the industrial classification of output and stocks of goods.

The model predicted the increase in total retail prices quite closely. The predicted prices, however, include the prices of items predicted by the model plus the actual prices of rent, unprocessed food, natural gas, and radio and TV licences. The actual prices contribute about 20 percent of the weight of the total index, and their inclusion therefore leads to a somewhat spurious accuracy in the prediction of the total price change. Moreover, the accuracy of the predictions of retail prices conceals substantial differences in the predictions of prices of components of the retail price index, which to some extent are offsetting.[5]

5. A detailed discussion of the predictions of the components of the retail price index and analysis of the reasons for the divergence between the actual and predicted prices for these components is given in Haig and Wood [2].

A large part of the discrepancy between the actual and predicted prices from one quarter to the next is due to discontinuous price changes for some items, particularly newspapers, fares of public transport, and postal charges. For example, there was a substantial increase in fares in the first half of 1971-1972, which largely accounted for the faster increases in actual than predicted prices in this period. Over the full period, of course, the effects of these discontinuous changes in prices tend to be smoothed out.

The actual and predicted levels of average wages tend to move together except that, in the first two quarters, the model underpredicts the increase in average wages. The estimated equation underpredicted the level of actual wages for the first period of the comparison, that is, 1969-III. This resulted in an apparent initial fall in the level of wages, which had the effect of damping the rates of increase in wages until 1970-I.

Conclusions

The aim of this paper was to formulate a closed input-output system for the purpose of analysing the determinants of changes in prices. The model is composed of two separate sets of relations; one describes an open dynamic input-output system, and the other describes regression equations that link changes in the price of sales to final buyers (retail prices) to the cost of primary inputs (average earnings). Results were given of the simulation of these two parts of the model.

The system described in this paper has two advantages over the traditional methods of analysing changes in prices using the static input-output model. First, it provides a method for analysing the time path of the effects of changes in primary inputs on the price of intermediate transactions and on the price of final output. Second, the model is closed and hence provides a self-generating mechanism for analysing changes in prices and costs over a particular period for given initial values and actual values of exogenous variables.

The complete system has not been simulated. The results of the simulations of the separate parts of the model suggest, however, that it will provide a useful system for the analysis of price changes over time, and of the effects on prices of intermediate transactions and the price of final output of changes in costs of primary inputs and economic policy changes affecting directly wages or costs, including changes in tax rates and statutory increases in nominal wages.

References

1. Godley, W.A.H., and W.D. Nordhaus. "Pricing in the Trade Cycle." *Economic Journal* 82, no. 327 (September 1972): 853–882.
2. Haig, B.D., and M.P. Wood. "A Dynamic Input-Output System for Analysing Price Changes." Working Papers in Economics and Econometrics No. 23. The Australian National University, Canberra, Australia, August 1974.

3. Haig, B.D., and M.P. Wood. "An Econometric Analysis of Price Changes." The Australian National University, Canberra, Australia, 1973. (Mimeographed.)

4. Lipsey, R., and M. Parkin. "Incomes Policy: A Reappraisal." In *Incomes Policy and Inflation.* Edited by M. Parkin and M.T. Sumner. Manchester: Manchester University Press, 1972. Pp. 85–111.

5. Pitchford, J.D. "An Analysis of Price Movements in Australia, 1947–1967." *Australian Economic Papers* 7, no. 11 (December 1968): 111–135.

Appendix 4A

Table 4A–1.   List of Industries

Industry

Selling Prices
Determined by
the Model

1   Chemicals
2   Petroleum products
3   Glass, clay, & other nonmetallic
    products
4   Fabricated metal products
5   Transport equipment
6   Other machinery & equipment
7   Leather & leather goods
8   Textiles
9   Clothing & footwear
10 Food manufacturing
11 Beverages & tobacco products
12 Paper & paper products, printing,
    & publishing
13 Wood, wood products, &
    furniture
14 Other manufacturing
15 Gas, electricity, & water
16 Health, education & welfare,
    & entertainment
17 Motor vehicle repairs & service
18 Transport, storage, & communi-
    cation

Selling Prices
Assumed Exogenous

1   Agriculture
2   Forestry
3   Mining (including base metals)
4   Rent

Selling Prices
Determined as a
Markup on Purchases

1   Wholesale and retail trade

Table 4A–2. List of Consumption Expenditures Categories

Industry

Prices Determined
by the Model

1 Processed food
2 Clothing
3 Household appliances
4 Furniture & floor coverings
5 Other utensils (household)

6 Personal requisites & proprietary
   medicines
7 Motoring (goods)
8 Motoring (services)
9 Tobacco, cigarettes, beer
10 Newspapers, magazines

11 Fuel, light (excluding natural
   gas)
12 Fares & postal
13 Other services

Prices Assumed
Exogenous

1 Unprocessed food
2 Rent

3 Radio & TV licenses
4 Natural gas

Chapter Five

The Effects of Technological Changes on the Economic Growth of Japan, 1955-1970

Iwao Ozaki

In the years following World War II, the Japanese economy achieved a high rate of growth and over the past twenty years has maintained its growth rate at approximately 10 percent per year in real terms. As a consequence, the economy has experienced a large amount of structural change. During this period, the size of the agricultural labor force has rapidly decreased, while the size of the labor force in the manufacturing and service sectors has increased. Also, "heavy industrialization" has been achieved within a short period in the course of this unbalanced economic growth. The Japanese experience represents an interesting pattern of industrialization.

The main purpose of the present study has been to show statistically some basic factors that have sustained the high growth rate of the Japanese economy, with emphasis on the effects of technological changes. For this purpose, four input-output tables of Japan—1955, 1960, 1965, and 1970—were used, all of which are represented in 1965 constant prices and rearranged so as to be mutually compatible [9; 10; 11; 12].

In applying input-output analysis to the economic dynamics that involve structural changes, it is mandatory to determine empirically the technology parameters of the sectoral production function and to find systematic changes in the technology along with concomitant changes in labor and capital requirements. The author presented a paper [18] at the Fourth International Conference on Input-Output Techniques in January 1968. Confining his discussion to the manufacturing sectors of the Japanese economy, he pointed out the following concerning the statistical determination of the production function in the Leontief system: (1) the usefulness and effectiveness of the factor-limitational

This paper is a result of the efforts of many people at the Keio Economic Observatory, Keio University. The author particularly wishes to thank M. Shimizu, Keio University; N. Nomura, Center for Economic Data Development and Research; and H. Tsuneki, Keio Economic Observatory. He is deeply grateful, also, to Professor Wassily Leontief for valuable suggestions concerning the research reported here.

93

type of production function for the analysis of economic dynamics, including structural change; (2) the tendency toward economies of scale in the use of labor inputs for all sectors;[1] (3) the different tendencies toward economies and diseconomies of scale in the use of capital inputs for various sectors; and (4) the existence of constant returns to scale for material inputs. In the present paper, the author attempts to analyze empirically the performance of structural change in the Japanese economy as a whole using the same type of approach.

Design of Experiments

In this study, the whole technology structure, T_c, is defined as follows:

$$T_c = \left[\begin{array}{ccccc} a_{11} & \cdots & a_{1j} & \cdots & a_{1n} \\ & & & & \\ \cdot & & & & \cdot \\ \cdot & & a_{ij} & & \cdot \\ \cdot & & & & \cdot \\ & & & & \\ a_{n1} & \cdots & a_{nj} & \cdots & a_{nn} \end{array}\right] = A$$
$$\left[\begin{array}{ccccc} l_1 & \cdots & l_j & \cdots & l_n \\ k_1 & \cdots & k_j & \cdots & k_n \end{array}\right] = C$$

(5-1)

where A represents the $n \times n$ matrix of intermediate input-output coefficients, a_{ij}, and C represents the $2 \times n$ matrix of labor and capital input coefficients, l_j, k_j. The analysis of technological changes may be divided into two parts. One concerns the changes in the intermediate input patterns, ΔA, and the other concerns the concomitant changes in the labor and capital inputs, ΔC, where the technological changes as a whole, ΔT_c, are described by the next equation.

$$\Delta T_c = \left[\begin{array}{c} \Delta A \\ \Delta C \end{array}\right]$$

(5-2)

With respect to the separability of ΔA and ΔC, some evidence has already been given in the author's earlier paper [18].

For this analysis, the following experiments have been designed: Experiment 1—analysis of technological changes in the labor and capital inputs (ΔC); Experi-

---

1. Concerning the importance of economies of scale, see Komiya and Uchida [13], Salter [21], Walters [24].

ment 2—investigation of changes over time in intermediate input patterns (ΔA); and Experiment 3—empirical determination of changes over time in the allocation of resources among various sectors by combining the results obtained in Experiments 1 and 2.

The methodology of Experiment 1 was as follows: First, the technology parameters of the production function for each sector corresponding to the 54×54 input-output tables were statistically estimated using time-series data of labor and capital inputs and output. Second, in accordance with the estimated value of these parameters, all sectors were classified into five groups with different types of technology. Third, in order to determine any systematic movement of economic variables representing the allocation of resources, the changes over time in these variables were observed in connection with the above technology types. The results obtained in Experiment 1 showed that technological changes in labor-capital inputs could be adequately explained by the effects of economies of scale and that this technological characteristic may be one of the most important factors in explaining changes in the pattern of the allocation of resources.

For Experiment 2, the changes in intermediate input patterns, ΔA, an attempt was made to verify statistically the substitution effects of new products for old products in the use of materials inputs for all sectors. Before we could proceed with the experiment, the new sectors producing new products first had to be designated in the 54×54 input-output tables of Japan. The following three—Sector 3, Petroleum refining products; Sector 4, Basic organic chemicals; and Sector 5, Artificial fiber materials—were selected as the new products for the Japanese economy in this period. The reason for this selection was that in 1957 the Japanese government had approved, for the first time, the introduction of technology associated with the production of petroleum refining products into the Japanese industries. Since then, the scale of production for these sectors has expanded by almost a geometrical progression. The introduction of petroleum refining products in 1957, therefore, can be regarded as representing a typical new technology for the analysis of the Japanese economic development since 1957.

Thus, Experiment 2 was conducted in the following way: First, using the mutually compatible input-output tables for the years 1955, 1960, 1965, and 1970 (1965 constant prices), the inverse matrices were computed:

$$B_t = (I - A_t)^{-1} \tag{5-3}$$

where t = 1955, 1960, 1965, and 1970. Second, in order to determine the substitution effects of the new products for the old products in the use of materials inputs for all sectors, the following index was computed from the elements of the matrices B_t:

$$H_j^k = \frac{\left(\sum_{i\in k} b_{ij}\right)_{1970}}{\left(\sum_{i\in k} b_{ij}\right)_{1955}} \cdot 100 \qquad j = 1, 2, \ldots, n \tag{5-4}$$

where k represents block k (for instance, the new-technology block or the traditional-technology block), and i represents the number of sectors belonging to block k. That is, if block k represents the new-products block, the summation refers to the direct and indirect inputs of the new products required for sector j. The index $H_j^k > 100$ means that the required inputs of the products of sector j belonging to block k increased, and $H_j^k < 100$ means that the required inputs of these products decreased between 1955 and 1970. The experimental results showed that the substitution effect was a dominant factor in explaining the changes over time in intermediate patterns, ΔA, in the course of the Japanese economic development between 1955 and 1970.[2]

Finally, by combining the technology group determined in Experiment 1 with the block classification used in Experiment 2, a pattern of structural change in the Japanese economy was empirically determined in Experiment 3. These results clearly showed that two dominant factors, the effect of economies of scale in the use of labor-capital inputs and the substitution effects of new for old products in the use of materials inputs, have played an important role in the structural change in the rapidly growing Japanese economy.

Data for 1955, 1960, 1965, and 1970

Two sets of basic data were used to estimate the technology parameters and also to test the substitution effects of new products for old products. One was the set of time-series data for gross output, X; labor input, L; real capital stock, K; exports, E; imports, M; and each of their deflators, P_X, W, P_E, P_M, except P_K, over the period 1951–1968. The other was the mutually compatible Japanese input-output tables for the years 1955, 1960, 1965, and 1970 published by the Japanese government [9; 10; 11; 12]. The tables were aggregated to 54 sectors for the analysis of the coordinated data sets of labor and capital inputs and exports and imports. The reconstruction and development of these two sets of data were performed through the joint research efforts of members of the Center for Economic Data Development and Research.[3]

2. For an analysis of technical change in the American economy, see Carter [2; 4].
3. The Center for Economic Data Development and Research was established in April 1970 as an independent organization in response to the practical needs arising in this era of highly advanced economic theory and the information revolution. It helps contribute to the

Experiment 1: Statistical Determination
of Types of Technology

Let us start with the statistical estimation of the technology parameters of the production function. As mentioned earlier, the usefulness and effectiveness of the factor-limitational production function have been tested for the manufacturing sectors but not for the other industries. We estimated the parameters of the production function for all sectors corresponding to the 54×54 input-output table by using the new time-series data mentioned in the preceding section. Experimental equations are as follows.

FACTOR-LIMITATIONAL TYPE

$$L = \alpha_L X^{\beta_L} \qquad K = \alpha_K X^{\beta_K} \tag{5-5}$$

LINEAR HOMOGENEOUS COBB-DOUGLAS TYPE

$$X = \alpha_o L^{1-\beta_o} K^{\beta_o} \tag{5-6}$$

GENERALIZED COBB-DOUGLAS TYPE

$$X = \alpha L^{\gamma_L} K^{\gamma_K} \tag{5-7}$$

where

X = gross output

L = labor

K = capital stock

α, β, γ = parameters

On the basis of the results obtained in this estimation, the following five types of technology were identified: K(I), K(II), (L-K), L(I), and L(II).

Type K(I) Technology
Type K(I) technology is the case of $\beta_L < 1$ and $\beta_K < 1$ in equation (5-5). The sectors included in this type are shown in the upper part of Table 5-1. If β_L and β_K are less than unity, economies of scale prevail in both labor and capital inputs in the sector, regardless of any changes in the factor–price ratio.

---

advancement of economic theory and the spread of its practical utilization through developing an efficient high-quality data system that provides a solid data base for economic analysis and forecasting. During 1970–1972, its activity was concentrated on the reconstruction and development of the set of input-output time-series data.

Table 5-1.   Changes over Time in Economic Variables for Type   K(I) and K(II) Technologies

Num-ber	Title	Type of Technology	(1a) β_L	(1b) β_K	(2)[a] $(\bar{K}/\bar{L})_j$	(3) $\dfrac{\Delta(V_j/V)}{}\ \dfrac{1965}{1955}$	(4) $\dfrac{\Delta(L_j/L)}{}\ \dfrac{1965}{1955}$	(5) $\dfrac{\Delta(K_j/K)}{}\ \dfrac{1965}{1955}$	(6) $\dfrac{\Delta(X_j/X)}{}\ \dfrac{1965}{1955}$	(7) $\dfrac{\Delta(Y_j/Y)}{}\ \dfrac{1970}{1955}$
1	Electric power supply	K(I)	0.12	0.80	17.43	1.17	0.94	1.01	1.14	1.00
2	Gas & water supply	K(I)	0.68	0.73	2.59	1.59	2.07	0.90	1.10	2.06
3	Petroleum refining products	K(I)	0.27	0.65	14.76	2.43	1.52	1.48	2.21	3.12
4	Basic organic chemicals	K(I)	0.33	0.72	5.70	2.25	2.05	2.48	3.44	—b
5	Artificial fiber materials	K(I)	0.10	0.84	3.89	1.18	1.10	1.82	1.79	—b
6	Iron & steel	K(I)	0.30	0.80	3.86	1.14	1.44	1.40	1.44	—b
7	Nonferrous metal products	K(I)	0.38	0.73	3.84	0.85	1.45	1.03	1.22	—b
8	Ships & ship repairing	K(I)	0.07	0.80	1.19	1.26	1.04	1.27	1.57	1.97
9	Motor vehicles	K(I)	0.46	0.70	2.12	2.35	2.66	2.38	3.95	7.28
10	Machinery	K(I)	0.52	0.88	0.62	2.26	1.95	1.57	1.48	2.50
11	Electrical machinery	K(I)	0.55	0.91	1.00	2.25	2.86	2.62	2.74	6.27
12	Precision instruments	K(I)	0.53	0.97	0.59	1.34	1.96	1.94	1.61	2.07
13	Fiber spinning	K(I)	0.26	0.59	2.07	0.53	1.19	0.61	0.72	0.73
14	Beverages & alcoholic drinks	K(I)	0.33	0.79	2.26	0.75	1.18	0.91	0.88	0.60
15	Paper	K(II)	0.13	1.03	3.07	0.88	1.03	1.42	1.08	0.60
16	Pulp	K(II)	-0.29	1.23	3.94	0.61	0.61	1.24	0.88	1.09
17	Cement	K(II)	0.08	1.03	9.07	0.50	0.94	1.35	1.06	—b
18	Basic inorganic chemicals	K(II)	0.04c	1.01	2.71	0.75	0.95	1.53	1.01	0.31
19	Chemical manure	K(II)	-0.71	1.71	4.97	0.46	0.35	1.50	0.66	0.61
20	Miscellaneous coal products	K(II)	-0.09	1.67	1.50	1.57	0.72	2.43	0.98	1.18
21	Tobacco	K(II)	0.18	2.30	1.83	0.59	0.91	1.39	0.56	0.68

[a]The figures of $\bar{K}$ and $\bar{L}$ represent the annual average for the years 1955 through 1970.

[b]The values of final demand in relation to total final demand are negligibly small (less than 1 percent) for the two periods 1955 and 1970.

[c]All the figures in columns (1a) and (1b) except this figure were statistically significant at a 1 percent level.

Note: β_L, β_K = the estimated value of the technology parameters.

Source: The sector classification is from the Center for Economic Data Development and Research, Tokyo, Japan.

Accordingly, for these sectors there would always exist the incentives of expanding the production scale for the purpose of reducing unit cost. Only the saturation of the demand market would prevent the expansion of the production scale.

In order to observe the changes in allocation of resources in connection with type K(I) technology, the following indices representing the changes in composition ratios of value added, V, labor force, L, capital stock, K, gross output, X, and final demand, Y, were computed, where each composition ratio was defined as the ratio of the amount of each variable for industry j to the total amount for all industries—(V_j/V), (L_j/L), (K_j/K), (X_j/X), and (Y_j/Y), respectively. Columns (3) through (7) in Table 5-1 represent the indices of changes over time in these composition ratios between 1955 and 1965 for $\Delta(V_j/V)$, $\Delta(L_j/L)$, $\Delta(K_j/K)$, and $\Delta(X_j/X)$, and between 1955 and 1970 for $\Delta(Y_j/Y)$. The results can be summarized as follows:

1. In the period between 1955 and 1965, all composition ratios for these sectors (especially the capital composition ratio) have increased very rapidly with the exception of the indices for Sector 13, Fiber spinning, and Sector 14, Beverages & alcoholic drinks, which have both decreased.
2. The relative reduction of composition ratios for these two sectors was clearly due to the saturation of the demand market, as shown in columns (6) and (7) of the table, representing the changes in composition ratios of gross output and final demand.

Furthermore, all sectors with type K(I) technology, except Sector 10, Machinery; Sector 11, Electrical machinery; and Sector 12, Precision instruments, have the most capital-intensive methods—the high ratio of capital to labor (K/L), as shown in column (3) of Table 5-1. Therefore, $\beta_K < 1$ would mean the existence of the technical indivisibility of capital; and as a consequence, the degree of what is called "capital-embodied technical progress" may be measured by the value of $\beta_K < 1$ in terms of economies of scale.

Type K(II) Technology

Type K(II) technology is the case of $\beta_L < 1$ and $\beta_K > 1$ in equation (5-5). The sectors included in this type are listed in the lower part of Table 5-1. In this case, diseconomies of scale occur in the use of capital inputs, while economies of scale prevail for labor inputs. Consequently, in these sectors the tendency toward substitution of capital for labor through the expansion of the scale of production prevails as the factor–price ratio (w/r) increases and demand expands. The substitution occurs because of the incentive for introducing labor-saving techniques in order to lower the unit cost of these products at a time when wage rates are rapidly increasing. In columns (4) and (5) of the table, it can be observed that for sectors with type K(I) technology (Sector 13, Fiber spinning; and Sector 14, Beverages & alcoholic drinks), the saturation of the demand market has brought about relative reductions of capital inputs and increases in labor inputs, while for sectors with type K(II) technology, the increase in the factor–price ratio (w/r) and the expansion of demand have resulted in the labor-saving and capital-using tendency.[4]

Type (L-K) Technology

Type (L-K) technology is the case of $\beta_o < 1$ in equation (5–6), $X/L = \alpha_o (K/L)^{\beta_o}$. (It is theoretically irrelevant for $\beta_o > 1$ or $\beta_o < 0$.) This is the linear-homogeneous classical Cobb-Douglas production function, which is often observed in the premodern sectors, where the term "pre-modern sectors" is here defined as those small-scale industries that have divisible technology and factor substitution implied by $\beta_o < 1$ and a low capital–labor ratio, as shown in columns (1) and (2) of Table 5–2. At the beginning of the 1950s, a large part of the labor force was absorbed in these sectors, particularly in the agricultural sector. Since then, a high percentage of the labor force has shifted into the manufacturing and service sectors. This shift has been accompanied by rapid urbanization, which has accompanied a high rate of economic growth. Generally speaking, these sectors are characterized by a relative reduction in demand, and consequently, the composition ratios of value added, (V_j/V), and gross output, (X_j/X), as well as labor force, (L_j/L), have decreased.

Type L(I) Technology

Type L(I) technology is the case of $0 < \gamma_L < 1, 0 < \gamma_K < 1$, and $\gamma_L + \gamma_K > 1$, in equation (5–7), $X = \alpha L^{\gamma_L} K^{\gamma_K}$. This is the ordinary type of generalized Cobb-Douglas production function with increasing returns to scale and factor substitutability. The sectors included in this type of technology are shown in the upper part of Table 5–3.

Type L(II) Technology

Type L(II) technology is the case of $\gamma_L > 1$ in type L(I) technology. In this case, an increase of the marginal productivity of labor seems to take place. However, from the theoretical point of view, it would be an ineffective approach to introduce such an ambiguous analytical concept into the model. In this study, an alternative explanation was given for these estimated parameters of the L(I) and L(II) types of technology by using the more definite concept of "product mix." Let us now assume a factor-limitational type of production function as the basic input-output relationship for a single commodity, which formally excludes the technical substitutability of factors for a given output level. At a high level of aggregation, an apparent isoquant curve with factor substitution can sometimes be determined using time-series data as product-mix changes. This is shown in Figure 5–1.

4. Concerning the K(I) and K(II) types of production functions, see Chenery [5] and Ozaki [18].

Table 5-2. Changes over Time in Economic Variables for Type (L-K) Technology

Sector Num-ber	Title	Type of Technology	(1)[a] β_o	(2)[b] $(K/\bar{L})_j$	(3) $\dfrac{\Delta(V_j/V)\ 1965}{1955}$	(4) $\dfrac{\Delta(L_j/L)\ 1965}{1955}$	(5) $\dfrac{\Delta(K_j/K)\ 1965}{1955}$	(6) $\dfrac{\Delta(X_j/X)\ 1965}{1955}$	(7) $\dfrac{\Delta(Y_j/Y)\ 1970}{1955}$
22	Agriculture, forestry, & fisheries	L-K	0.67	0.46	0.50	0.59	0.65	0.41	0.24
23	Coal & lignite	L-K	0.56	0.90	0.31	0.44	0.78	0.41	0.65
24	Mining	L-K	0.64	0.56	0.82	0.91	1.95	0.96	–
25	Silk reeling & spinning	L-K	0.70	0.59	0.59	0.42	0.70	0.40	0.01
26	Vegetable & animal oil & fat	L-K	0.69	1.91	0.68	0.80	2.37	0.94	0.08
27	Wood milling	L-K	0.78	0.68	0.81	1.09	0.89	0.71	0.13

[a] All the figures in column (1) were statistically significant at a 1 percent level.
[b] The figures of K and L represent the annual average for the years 1955 through 1970.

Table 5-3.   Changes over Time in Economic Variables for Type L(I) and L(II) Technologies

Number	Title	Type of Technology	(1a) γ_L	(1b) γ_K	(2)ᵃ $(\bar{K}/\bar{L})_j$	(3) $\dfrac{\Delta(V_j/V)\ 1965}{1955}$	(4) $\dfrac{\Delta(L_j/L)\ 1965}{1955}$	(5) $\dfrac{\Delta(K_j/K)\ 1965}{1955}$	(6) $\dfrac{\Delta(X_j/X)\ 1965}{1955}$	(7) $\dfrac{\Delta(Y_j/Y)\ 1970}{1955}$
28	Building & construction	L(I)	0.75	0.45	0.25	1.54	1.64	2.26	1.32	1.54
29	Meat	L(I)	0.44	0.61	1.52	2.42	2.95	1.10	1.11	1.27
30	Seafood, preserved	L(I)	0.90	0.48	0.59	1.37	1.07	0.76	0.63	0.60
31	Transport services	L(I)	0.70	0.67	1.04	1.22	1.45	1.07	0.95	1.51
32	Paints	L(I)	0.58	0.73	1.51	1.35	1.35	1.86	1.21	1.54
33	Rubber products	L(I)	0.99	0.63	0.99	1.14	1.75	1.41	1.46	1.26
34	Grass products	L(I)	0.44ᵇ	0.88	1.46	1.18	1.37	1.57	1.35	—
35	Miscellaneous industrial products	L(I)	0.83	0.93	0.78	2.30	2.27	1.30	2.38	2.79
36	Other transport equipment	L(I)	1.31	0.54	1.01	1.22	1.18	1.17	0.87	0.81
37	Metal products	L(II)	1.35	0.30ᵇ	0.49	2.37	2.05	2.26	1.74	3.38
38	Leather products	L(II)	2.21	-0.07ᵇ	0.40	1.01	1.52	0.90	1.07	1.18
39	Furniture & fixtures	L(II)	1.82	0.44	0.40	1.34	1.43	0.88	1.24	1.83
40	Other wood products	L(II)	2.33	0.68	0.26	0.85	1.11	0.69	0.98	0.57
41	Paper articles	L(II)	1.29	0.56	0.72	1.81	2.04	1.89	2.32	1.84
42	Pottery, china, & earthenware	L(II)	1.39	0.55	0.51	1.76	1.24	1.05	1.02	1.29
43	Structural clay products	L(II)	1.59	0.96	0.57	1.35	0.79	1.17	0.86	—
44	Other nonmetallic mineral products	L(II)	1.87ᵇ	0.19ᵇ	1.15	2.28	1.96	1.38	2.25	1.70
45	Medicine	L(II)	1.20ᵇ	0.80	1.25	1.70	1.41	2.13	2.07	2.38
46	Weaving & other fiber products	L(II)	1.75	0.63	0.79	0.98	1.04	0.76	0.75	0.50
47	Footwear & wearing apparel	L(II)	1.93	0.28ᵇ	0.31	0.97	1.47	0.89	1.28	0.82
48	Printing & publishing	L(II)	1.43	0.27ᵇ	0.57	0.91	1.42	1.64	1.08	0.46
49	Other food, prepared	L(II)	1.26	0.35	0.65	0.61	1.10	1.14	0.67	0.54
50	Trading	L(II)	1.95	0.84	0.65	0.99	1.31	0.69	1.36	1.19
51	Finance & insurance	L(II)	1.60	0.22ᵇ	0.70	1.44	1.66	1.92	1.40	1.98
52	Communication services	L(II)	3.38	0.08ᵇ	0.17	1.08	1.12	2.37	1.03	1.46

ᵃThe figures of $\bar{K}$ and $\bar{L}$ represent the annual average for the years 1955 through 1970.

ᵇAll the figures in columns (1a) and (1b) except these figures were statistically significant at a 1 percent level.

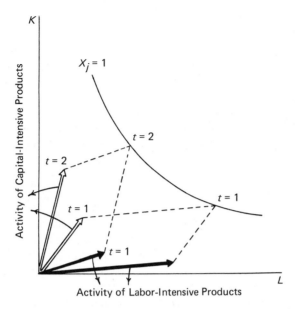

Figure 5-1. Apparent Isoquant Curve Determined Using Time-Series Data. Change over time in product-mix results in the apparent factor substitution of labor and capital inputs at a high level of aggregation: X_j is gross output for sector j at the high level of aggregation; K is capital stock; and L is labor.

When the factor substitution observed in the apparent isoquant curve is of this nature, it is immaterial whether the estimated parameters, γ_L, exceed unity or not. Along this line of thinking, the production functions with types L(I) and L(II) technology, shown in Table 5-3, were inevitably regarded more or less as apparent factor-substitutable production functions caused by the changes over time in a product mix at this high level of aggregation. But this problem could be resolved only by using the more disaggregated data set.

The results presented in Table 5-3 can be summarized as follows:

1. Those sectors with the L(I) and L(II) types of technology have the most labor-intensive production methods, as shown in the lower level of capital-labor ratio $(\bar{K}/\bar{L})$ in column (2).
2. In most cases, the products in those sectors have nevertheless increased over the average expansion for all industries, as shown in column (6), (X_j/X).
3. As a result, the composition ratios of labor and capital inputs, shown in columns (4) and (5), have increased.

In other words, a considerable degree of expansion in those sectors with the L(I) and L(II) types of technology was observed during the years 1955–1965, in spite of their having the most labor-intensive production methods. Consequently, a large part of the labor force has been absorbed in those sectors.

Thus, it can be concluded that in connection with the different technology types, (a) the larger part of capital has been concentrated in the sectors with the type K(I) technology, while the larger part of the labor force has flowed into the sectors with the type L(I) and L(II) technologies and the labor force in the sectors with the type (L-K) technology has rapidly decreased during the years 1955–1965; and (b) the technology differences among various sectors are among the most important factors causing changes over time in the allocation of resources.

Experiment 2: Changes in Intermediate Input Patterns

Let us first divide the whole economy into separate blocks in order to determine a systematic change over time in the intermediate input patterns, ΔA, of the Japanese economy for the period 1955–1970. The most important block would be composed of leading sectors, which have propelled the high rate of Japanese economic growth. Among these leading sectors, we focused on the effects of new technology. Thus, Petroleum refining products, Basic organic chemicals, and Artificial fiber materials were selected as the three new products for the Japanese economy during this period. In the present analysis, we define the sectors producing these three products as the new-technology block. Accordingly, the residual sectors could be classified together into the traditional-technology block. However, the importance of giving a definite block order in more detail for the whole economy has been pointed out by many economists.[5] Thus, in this experiment, the following block order was tentatively determined, based upon the Simpson-Tsukui results [22].

1. New-technology block	N		4. Public utility block	U
2. Employment block	R		5. Metal block	M
3. Services block	S		6. Traditional-technology block	T

In this classification, the employment block is composed of the sectors in which a large part of the labor force had been absorbed in the beginning of the 1950s and the metal block includes the sectors having metallic mineral as the origin of their raw materials.[6] Separation of the public utility block and the services block is based upon traditional classification. Finally, the traditional-technology block includes all of the residual sectors, most of them consumers' goods sectors. The

---

5. Concerning the determination of a block order for the whole economy, see Simpson and Tsukui [22].

6. At this high level of aggregation (54 sectors), it would be very difficult to determine a more precise block order. Ishida and the author attempted successfully to construct a more precise triangularization and block order, based upon the origin of raw materials and its production series, for the 1965 Japanese input-output table, using a higher level of disaggregation (about 450 sectors). See Ishida and Ozaki [19].

correspondence of block order, sector number and title, and type of technology is given in the left-hand portion of Table 5–4. In order to observe the changes over time in intermediate input patterns in connection with the above block ordering, the following indices were computed for each block, using the adjusted 54×54 input-output tables:

$$
H_j^k = \frac{\left(\displaystyle\sum_{i\in k} b_{ij} \right)_{1970}}{\left(\displaystyle\sum_{i\in k} b_{ij} \right)_{1955}} \cdot 100
$$

$$(5\text{-}4)$$

where k represents the kth block, $j = 1, 2, \ldots, 54$. In the case of $k = N$, $H_j^N > 100$ means, in sector j, the increase of the required inputs of the new products produced in block N, while $H_j^N < 100$ means the decrease of the required inputs of new products between 1955 and 1970. The computed values of H_j^k for $k = N$, R, T_r are listed in Table 5–4. In the case of a high rate of economic growth, a rapid substitution of new materials for old materials may occur in the intermediate inputs process. Thus, it would be expected that H_j^N would increase, while H_j^R would decrease in each sector. The results shown in Table 5–4 can be summarized as follows:

1. During the years 1955–1970, the total inputs of new materials produced in the new-technology block, N, had a rapid rate of growth in all sectors, as shown in column (1). Particularly, a large absorption of new products in the traditional sectors was observed, as is shown by the elements in column (1) and the rows for sectors 28 through 49, those sectors included in the traditional-technology block, T. This implies that the expansion of the traditional sectors has created a large domestic market for new products.
2. On the other hand, old materials, which have been produced in the employment block, have decreased in all sectors, as shown in column (2) of the table. These results indicate that the substitution of new materials for old materials was occurring as technology changed.
3. In column (3), it can be observed that traditional products have been increasingly used as materials inputs into almost all sectors. In other words, there would have been a considerable degree of economic maturity in the traditional sectors.

These results would imply that the introduction of new products alone was not always sufficient to sustain a high rate of economic growth and that the maintenance of economic maturity in the traditional sectors was necessary for the successful development of new technology products. In other words, the

Table 5-4. Changes over Time in the Intermediate Input Pattern, 1955-1970

Block Order	Number	Title	Type of Technology	(1) H_j^N	(2) H_j^R (1955 = 100)	(3) H_j^T
N	3	Petroleum refining products	K(I)	106.7	152.8	189.7
N	4	Basic organic chemicals	K(I)	131.2	14.1	37.3
N	5	Artificial fiber materials	K(I)	136.2	16.2	45.6
R	13	Fiber spinning	K(I)	325.1	63.4	141.5
R	14	Beverages & alcoholic drinks	K(I)	49.1	76.2	107.8
R	15	Paper	K(II)	292.8	80.7	80.5
R	16	Pulp	K(II)	297.8	71.3	109.6
R	17	Cement	K(II)	457.0	79.1	71.6
R	18	Basic inorganic chemicals	K(II)	264.1	78.5	60.9
R	19	Chemical manure	K(II)	214.3	81.2	73.0
R	20	Miscellaneous coal products	K(II)	1214.6	90.1	154.7
R	21	Tobacco	K(II)	433.2	98.1	208.9
R	22	Agriculture, forestry, & fisheries	L-K	554.3	94.2	459.5
R	23	Coal & lignite	L-K	219.6	78.9	142.7
R	24	Mining	L-K	1425.8	97.6	154.8
R	25	Silk reeling & spinning	L-K	400.5	84.7	352.6
R	26	Vegetable & animal oil & fat	L-K	270.9	62.4	222.1
R	27	Wood milling	L-K	671.4	86.7	341.1
T	28	Building & construction	L(I)	409.3	54.1	113.7
T	29	Meat	L(I)	326.8	102.9	232.9
T	30	Seafood, preserved	L(I)	474.1	74.4	111.3
T	32	Paints	L(I)	280.9	39.4	103.4
T	33	Rubber products	L(I)	687.9	32.3	103.2
T	34	Grass products	L(I)	140.9	48.3	109.2
T	35	Miscellaneous industrial products	L(I)	452.0	41.1	102.7
T	36	Other transport equipment	L(II)	341.6	52.7	120.9
T	37	Metal products	L(II)	275.3	75.5	108.2
T	38	Leather products	L(II)	385.2	61.5	123.6
T	39	Furniture & fixtures	L(II)	596.3	67.3	117.9
T	40	Other wood products	L(II)	276.1	70.9	116.7
T	41	Paper articles	L(II)	410.3	68.4	86.7
T	42	Pottery, china, & earthenware	L(II)	183.0	41.7	111.0
T	43	Structural clay products	L(II)	257.4	54.4	106.7
T	44	Other nonmetallic mineral products	L(II)	463.9	139.8	100.3
T	45	Medicine	L(II)	152.3	28.7	92.8
T	46	Weaving & other fiber products	L(II)	378.3	63.8	107.2
T	47	Footwear & wearing apparel	L(II)	381.8	48.0	104.9
T	48	Printing & publishing	L(II)	350.8	86.7	115.3
T	49	Other food, prepared	L(II)	451.8	88.2	120.2
S	31	Transport services	L(I)	101.5	32.6	78.0
S	50	Trading	L(II)	448.0	42.1	80.7
S	51	Finance & insurance	L(II)	288.5	69.1	128.8
S	52	Communication services	L(II)	283.2	89.4	151.5
S	53	Real estate & rents	–	1258.5	136.1	270.1

Table 5-4. continued

Block Order	Num- ber	Title	Type of Technology	(1) H_j^N	(2) H_j^R	(3) H_j^T
		Sector			*(1955 = 100)*	
S	54	Miscellaneous manufacturing & other business & personal services	–	547.4	147.1	320.2
U	1	Electric power supply	K(I)	608.6	73.7	95.6
U	2	Gas & water supply	K(I)	326.2	32.2	187.2
M	6	Iron & steel	K(I)	185.8	79.3	113.6
M	7	Nonferrous metal products	K(I)	495.6	61.7	205.8
M	8	Ships & ship repairing	K(I)	142.0	25.4	104.1
M	9	Motor vehicles	K(I)	341.8	47.3	92.0
M	10	Machinery	K(I)	267.7	54.2	137.6
M	11	Electrical machinery	K(I)	199.8	28.2	97.6
M	12	Precision instruments	K(I)	207.0	43.0	97.8

combined expansion in both the new-technology block and the traditional block have made it possible to accelerate economic growth.

Experiment 3: Structural Change

Combining the results obtained so far, a typical pattern of structural change can be introduced in the analysis of Japanese economic development. In Table 5-5, the changes in the composition ratios for value added, labor force, capital

Table 5-5. Percentage Changes over Time in the Composition Ratios for Value Added, Labor Force, Capital Stock, and Exports, 1955-1965 (percent)

Technology Group	V_j/V 1955	V_j/V 1965	L_j/L 1955	L_j/L 1965	K_j/K 1955	K_j/K 1965	E_j/E 1955	E_j/E 1970
K(I)	17.0	23.1	7.1	12.3	27.9	35.2	28.5	63.4
K(II)	4.8	3.0	1.0	0.8	3.1	4.5	3.9	3.4
L-K	26.5	13.0	52.2	31.1	30.9	21.2	11.8	2.4
L(I) + L(II)	51.7	60.9	39.7	55.8	38.1	39.1	55.8	30.8
Total	100.0	100.0	100.0	100.0	100.0	100.0	100.0	100.0

Note: The total (100 percent) for each column shows the total amount of all sectors, except for the following two sectors: Sector 53, Real estate & rents, and Sector 54, Miscellaneous manufacturing & other business & personal services. For these two sectors, it was impossible to statistically determine the type of technology, due to the lack of capital stock data.

stock, and exports are listed for each technology group. The results obtained in the table can be summarized as follows:

1. Between the years 1955 and 1965, a large part of capital investment was concentrated in the sectors with type K(I) technology by taking advantage of economies of scale in both labor and capital inputs (27.9 to 35.2 percent).
2. On the other hand, the greater part of the labor force (39.7 to 55.8 percent) was absorbed into the sectors with the L(I) and L(II) types of technology.
3. In the sectors with type (L-K) technology, rapid reductions in the composition ratios for both the labor force (52.2 to 31.1 percent) and capital stock (30.9 to 21.2 percent) were observed.
4. As a consequence, the export of products with type K(I) technology rapidly increased (28.5 to 63.4 percent). In addition, as previously noted, a considerable degree of economic growth in the traditional sectors supported the expansion of demand for new products produced in the new-technology block.

These four points would give the most advantageous conditions for the maximization of the growth rate as well as the maintenance of full employment. These structural changes are shown in Figure 5-2, a sketch diagram of the interdependency and mutual relations among the various blocks. In this figure, channel 1 shows that capital investment was concentrated in blocks N and M with technology type K(I) and at the same time, propelled the growth of block M. Channel 2 shows the decrease of the labor force in block R against the increase of the labor force in block T. Channel 3 shows that the material substitution effects of required inputs in block T supported the demand expansion for new products in block N. During this period, block T has absorbed a large part of the labor force (channel 2), supplied final products to the consumption sector (channel 4), and presented a market for the new products (channel 3). Channel 5 shows that a large amount of imports of natural resources has flowed into the sectors with type K(I) technology.

Conclusion

The results obtained in this study can be summarized as follows:

1. The sustained high rate of economic growth could not be achieved without rapid structural change. The term "structural change," here, is defined as a change in resource allocation patterns caused by changes both in production technology and in demand.
2. The effects of technological change may be most effectively analyzed in terms of two factors. One is the substitution effects of new and traditional commodities in the materials input process for each sector, and the other is the effects of economies of scale in the labor and capital input processes.

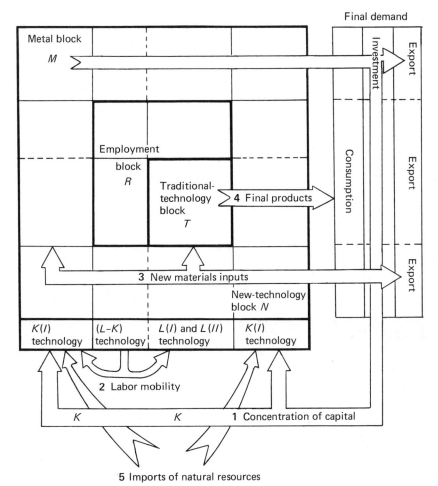

Figure 5-2. Sketch Diagram of Structural Change.

3. In this study, it was empirically verified that a considerable degree of economic maturity in the traditional sectors with traditional technology should provide the conditions essential for the successful development of the new-technology block, *N*—that is to say, the substitution of new materials for old materials in the production of all sectors necessarily have affected the demand for new products. The steady economic expansion in the traditional sectors was instrumental in introducing new technology and thereby developing new products and new markets during this period.

4. The steady growth in the traditional block, *T,* is one of the most important factors for economic growth in three ways: (i) having a large absorption of

the labor force, which satisfies the full-employment condition; (ii) having a large-scale supply of consumption goods for the final demand sector; and (iii) having a large market for new products supplied by the new-technology block.

In this study, our focus was concentrated on the statistical validity of the effects of technological changes on economic growth. Needless to say, changes in the allocation of resources would depend upon both demand and supply conditions,[7] and we have not neglected the demand side in this study. In Tables 5-1, 5-2, and 5-3, the downward tendency of the composition ratio for output, as seen in Sector 13, Fiber spinning; Sector 19, Chemical manure; Sector 22, Agriculture, forestry & fisheries; Sector 23, Coal & lignite; and Sector 24, Mining, can be interpreted as being caused by the saturation of demand. Nevertheless, on the whole it can be observed that the technology factor was a dominant force behind the leading sectors of the Japanese economy in determining the allocation of resources. Particularly in the heavy industries with type K(I) technology, the economies of scale in both labor and capital inputs may automatically give rise to increases in labor and capital productivity associated with an expanding output level. Therefore, it can be concluded that the maintenance of the high rate of growth in the Japanese economy since World War II was essentially based upon the effects of technological changes characterized by two features: the effects of economies of scale and the substitution effects of new materials for old materials in the intermediate input process of all sectors.

References

1. Cameron, B. "The Production Function in Leontief Models." *Review of Economic Studies* 20, no. 5 (1952/1953): 62–69.

2. Carter, A.P. "Changes in the Structure of the American Economy, 1947 to 1958 and 1962." *The Review of Economics and Statistics* 49, no. 2 (May 1967): 209–224.

3. Carter, A.P. "A Linear Programming System Analyzing Embodied Technological Change." In *Input-Output Techniques.* Vol. 1, *Contributions to Input-Output Analysis.* Edited by A.P. Carter and A. Bródy. Amsterdam: North-Holland Publishing Company, 1970. Pp. 77–98.

4. Carter, A.P. *Structural Change in the American Economy.* Cambridge, Mass.: Harvard University Press, 1970.

5. Chenery, H.B. "Overcapacity and the Acceleration Principle." *Econometrica* 20, no. 1 (January 1952): 1–28.

6. Chenery, H.B. "Patterns of Industrial Growth." *American Economic Review* 50, no. 4 (September 1960): 624–654.

7. Chenery, H.B., and K.S. Kretshmer. "Resource Allocation for Economic Development." *Econometrica* 24, no. 4 (October 1956): 365–399.

8. Grosse (Carter), A.P. "The Technological Structure of the Cotton Textile

7. See Chenery [6] and Chenery and Kretshmer [7].

Industry." In W. Leontief et al. *Studies in the Structure of the American Economy.* New York: Oxford University Press, 1953. Pp. 360–420.

9. Japanese Government, Administrative Management Agency and six other ministries; "The 1955 Input-Output Table of Japan." Tokyo, 1961.

10. Japanese Government, Administrative Management Agency et al. "The 1960 Input-Output Table of Japan." Tokyo, 1964.

11. Japanese Government, Administrative Management Agency et al. "The 1965 Input-Output Table of Japan." Tokyo, 1969.

12. Japanese Government, Administrative Management Agency et al. "The 1970 Input-Output Table of Japan." Tokyo, 1974.

13. Komiya, R., and T. Uchida. "The Labour Coefficient and the Size of Establishment in Two Japanese Industries." In *Structural Interdependence and Economic Development.* Edited by T. Barna. New York: St. Martin's Press, 1963. Pp. 265–276.

14. Leontief, W. "Structural Change." In W. Leontief et al. *Studies in the Structure of the American Economy.* New York: Oxford University Press, 1953. Pp. 17–52.

15. Leontief, W. *The Structure of American Economy, 1919–1939.* 2nd ed. New York: Oxford University Press, 1951.

16. Mathur, P.N. "An Efficient Path for the Technological Transformation of an Economy." In *Structural Interdependence and Economic Development.* Edited by T. Barna. New York: St. Martin's Press, 1963. Pp. 39–56.

17. Middelhoek, A.J. "Tests of the Marginal Stability of Input-Output Coefficients." In *Input-Output Techniques.* Vol. 2, *Applications of Input-Output Analysis.* Edited by A.P. Carter and A. Bródy. Amsterdam: North-Holland Publishing Company, 1970. Pp. 261–279.

18. Ozaki, I. "Economies of Scale and Input-Output Coefficients." In *Input-Output Techniques.* Vol. 2, *Applications of Input-Output Analysis.* Edited by A.P. Carter and A. Bródy. Amsterdam: North-Holland Publishing Company, 1970. Pp. 280–302.

19. Ozaki, I., and K. Ishida. "The Determination of Economic Fundamental Structure." *Mita Gakkai Zasshi* [*Mita Journal of Economics*] 63, no. 6 (June 1970): 15–35. (In Japanese.)

20. Pratten, C., and R.M. Dean, in collaboration with A. Silverston. *The Economics of Large-Scale Production in British Industry.* Cambridge, England: Cambridge University Press, 1965.

21. Salter, W.E.G. *Productivity and Technical Change.* Cambridge, England: Cambridge University Press, 1960.

22. Simpson, D., and J. Tsukui. "The Fundamental Structure of Input-Output Tables, An International Comparison." *The Review of Economics and Statistics* 47, no. 4 (November 1965): 434–446.

23. Vaccara, B.N. "Changes over Time in Input-Output Coefficients for the United States." In *Input-Output Techniques.* Vol. 2, *Applications of Input-Output Analysis.* Edited by A.P. Carter and A. Bródy. Amsterdam: North-Holland Publishing Company, 1970. Pp. 238–260.

24. Walters, A.A. "Economies of Scale; Some Statistical Evidence: Comment." *Quarterly Journal of Economics* 74, no. 1 (February 1960): 154–157.

Chapter Six

Price Changes as Causes of Variations in Input-Output Coefficients

Per Sevaldson

Analyses of input-output relations in Norwegian production sectors over the period 1949–1960 have revealed rather extensive variations in input-output coefficients, that is, the ratios between volumes of inputs and volumes of outputs [3]. Analyses of the same data have also made it clear that some part of the variations in coefficients are of a type that can be described as trends in the coefficients over the observation period [3; 4]. Those analyses have also shown that variations in the volume of output contribute little to explaining variations in input-output ratios. In other words, the model of proportionate changes in inputs and outputs has not been rejected. The 1949–1960 data also made it possible to investigate whether there were groups of inputs in particular sectors that tended to form "substitution rings," that is, to have coefficient movements that were highly correlated [6]. This was not found to be the case to any significant extent, so this simple form of substitution was rejected as a major source of coefficient variation in the data at hand. If we now survey the remaining possible sources of coefficient variation, we have the following list:

1. Substitutions of a somewhat more complicated form than those referred to above, mainly to be described as a reversible change in input proportions in order to produce a product of given specifications in the cheapest possible way
2. Reversible and irreversible changes in product mix in order to obtain an optimal combination of inputs and outputs in response to given market conditions
3. Irreversible, but sporadic changes in production techniques
4. Random changes in the distribution of market shares of establishments in a sector having producing establishments with different production techniques,

This is a slightly modified version of an article to be published together with other contributions by the same author under the common title, "Studies in the Stability of Input-Output Relationships," by the Central Bureau of Statistics of Norway.

for example, due to differences in fixed-capital structure, size, market position, location, and so on.

Hypotheses of Technology Adjustment

In the present study, we shall search for evidence about the first of these sources of coefficient change. In order to do this, it is necessary to specify the possible hypotheses that may be investigated under this heading and the precise implications of those hypotheses.

Hypothesis 1a

A production sector (or the establishments that make it up) has available to it a number of alternative vectors of input-output proportions, that is, proportions between quantities of each type of input and quantity of total output. Among these vectors, the sector will in any one year choose the one that, at the average prices of that year, gives the lowest total cost for intermediate inputs, ignoring the costs of primary inputs and possible other costs. The reasons for ignoring the costs of the primary inputs and other costs may be, for instance, that these are determined by the fixed capital structure of the sector and by the level of demand for the product, and are independent of the vector of intermediate inputs chosen.

Hypothesis 1b

A production sector (or the establishments that make it up) has available to it a number of alternative vectors of input-output proportions. Among these vectors, the sector will in any one year choose the one that, at the average prices of that year, gives the lowest total cost for intermediate inputs and wages and salaries, ignoring the costs of primary inputs other than hired labour and other possible costs. The reasons for this form of the hypothesis may be that the use of hired labour is generally conditioned by the choice of intermediate input proportions or vice versa, whereas the costs for other primary inputs, fixed capital, and self-employed labour, as well as other costs, are not dependent on the choice of the vector of labour and intermediate inputs.

Other Hypotheses 1c

There are, of course, other possibilities of substitution: The vector of input proportions for which the cost is minimized may include more of the primary inputs—for example, depreciation charges, costs of employing family labour (without direct pay), computed cost of owner participation, etc. Besides, there may be special costs associated with the use of particular input proportion vectors. There is also the possibility, suggested under point 2 above, that changes in input proportions are linked to changes in output specifications, which may imply alternative output prices. We shall not test such hypotheses here.

Hypothesis 2a
Among the vectors of input-output coefficients available to a sector in a given year are all the technologies that were actually used by the sector in a given number of previous years.

Hypothesis 2b
Among the vectors of input-output coefficients available for a sector in a given year are all the technologies that were actually used by the sector in a given number of preceding years and succeeding years.

Norwegian Data

We have two sets of data that permit some testing of the above hypotheses.

Data in 1955 Prices
Norwegian national accounts for the period 1949–1960 give, for each year, production and use of intermediate inputs in each of 79 production sectors in constant 1955 purchasers' values. This means that for each sector we can compute the total value of intermediate inputs as percentages of output in 1955 purchasers' prices for each of the years 1949–1960. If for each sector, we subtract from the recorded values of production the inputs from the trade sector, we obtain production value at constant producers' prices, and can thus compute the total value of inputs (excluding the trade and transportation margins on deliveries out of the sector) as percentages of production, valued at constant producers' prices in each sector. Assuming that the producers in a sector are adjusting to the relationship between what they receive in payment for their products and what they pay for the inputs they use, the latter percentages should be the relevant ones in comparing the costs of alternative input vectors.

The national accounts also give the number of employed wage and salary earners in each sector in each year and wages and salaries in each sector in 1955. If we assume no change in quality, we can consequently compute wage and salary costs in 1955 prices for each year in each sector and relate these costs to production in 1955 producers' prices.

These data make it possible to test the chosen hypotheses for the year 1955 with up to six preceding and up to five succeeding years. In order to test the hypotheses for other years, we would have had to convert the data to the prices of those years—a procedure for which we did not have the resources.

Data in 1964 Prices
The Central Bureau of Statistics of Norway has published input-output data in 1964 producers' prices for the years 1954, 1959, and 1964 [2]. These data contain the same kind of information for 113 production sectors for the years covered as the data in 1955 prices described above contain for 1949–1960. Con-

sequently, they make possible a comparison of the cost of parts of the input vector used in 1964 with the cost of corresponding vectors used in 1959 and 1954, all evaluated in 1964 prices. Results based on these data are not reported here.[1]

Results for the 1955 Input Vector Compared with Vectors from the Period 1949-1960

The four major hypotheses set forth earlier in the paper were tested, comparing input vectors from the period 1949-1960 with the 1955 input vector. The results of these comparisons are summarized below.

Coefficient Sums for Intermediate Inputs—
Hypotheses (1a, 2a) and (1a, 2b)

Sums of intermediate inputs (including imports) in 1955 purchasers' prices as a percent of production in 1955 producers' prices for each sector in each year during the period 1949-1960 are given in the full report of the present research [5]. Using those data, we can perform our tests by comparing the percentages for the other years with the percentage for 1955 for each sector. One test is to rank the percentages for the years under consideration from the lowest to the highest and compare the average rankings for the years. If there are no systematic changes, we would expect all years to score roughly the same average. If there is a systematic tendency to introduce new input-saving techniques, we would expect the average rankings to decrease from year to year. If there is a systematic tendency to choose the cheapest available technique, the average ranking for 1955 would be expected to be lower than the ranking for other years with techniques that are assumed to have been available in 1955. However, when the years are ordered according to their average ranking, we get the rankings shown in Table 6-1. The mean of these averages is 6.502, and their standard deviation is 0.48.[2] The average for 1955 is the highest of all and 1.8 times the standard deviation above the average. A deviation of at least this size might be expected in about 7 percent of random drawings from a normal distribution. Thus, the higher average ranking for 1955 than for all other years may be accidental, but there is certainly no indication of a lower ranking for 1955 than for the other years.

We must now try to find out if this general impression is confirmed by a further study of the figures. Let us first look at the entire period 1949-1960. The number of coefficient sums that are lower than the coefficient sum for 1955 is given for each year in Table 6-2. The number of sectors with lower coefficients

---

1. A full text for this paper, which gives an analysis of figures for the years 1954, 1959, and 1964 and two appendix tables of data, is contained in a working paper by the author [5].
2. There is a very weak positive trend in the figures, but the regression coefficient with time is only 0.05 and not statistically significant under the usual hypotheses.

Table 6-1. Average Ranking of 79 Coefficient Sums for Each Year—
Intermediate Inputs

Year	Coefficient Sum
1951	5.65
1952	5.85
1953	6.04
1957	6.14
1959	6.56
1954	6.60
1956	6.62
1950	6.65
1958	6.68
1949	6.79
1960	7.08
1955	7.37

Note: The year in which a given sector has its lowest percentage is given the ranking 1 for that sector. The year with the highest percentage is given the ranking 12. Equal figures are given the average ranking; for example, if the two lowest figures are equal, the ranking is 1.5.

than in 1955 is slightly more than half of the total in five of the six years before 1955 and in three of the five years after 1955. Assuming equal probability for sums over and under the 1955 figure in each sector for each year, three of the years before 1955 and one of the years after 1955 have figures slightly more than two times the standard deviation above the expected value of 39.5.[3]

For the years 1949-1954, the number of "sector-years" with lower coefficient sums than those of 1955 is 280, which is roughly 4 times the standard deviation above an expected value of 237, and for the years after 1955 the actual figure is 1.6 times the standard deviation above the expected value. For the entire period of 11 years the actual figure is again 4 times the standard deviation above the expected value. There is evidently no tendency for the input combination actually used in 1955 to be cheaper than the input combinations employed in other years of the period 1949-1960.

Table 6-3 gives the distribution of the 79 sectors according to the number of years with input combinations cheaper than the input combinations actually used in 1955 for periods of varying lengths. For all the periods covered in the table, the tendency is for the 1955 figure to be the highest or above average, rather than the lowest or below average.

The first three columns of Table 6-4 give the sectors distributed according to the number of years between 1955 and the nearest year with a lower coefficient sum for intermediate inputs. This "distance" is registered when all the years are taken into consideration, and also when only preceding and when only succeed-

3. With 79 sectors, the expected value in each year is 39.5, and the standard deviation is $\sqrt{(0.5 \cdot 0.5 \cdot 79)} = 4.441$.

Table 6-2. Number of Sectors with Coefficient Sums Lower than in 1955

Year	Number of Sectors[a]	Percent of Total
1949	39	49.4
1950	45	57.0
1951	47	59.5
1952	51	64.6
1953	49	62.0
1954	49	62.0
Total, prior to 1955	280	59.1
1956	50	63.3
1957	46	58.3
1958	39	49.4
1959	41	51.9
1960	37	46.8
Total, after 1955	213	53.9
Total, 1949–1960	493	56.7

[a]Of 79 sectors, the number of sectors in each year 1949–1960 for which the coefficient sum for intermediate inputs is lower than the corresponding sum for 1955.

Table 6-3. Number of Years with Coefficient Sums for Intermediate Inputs Lower than in 1955

Number of Years with Coefficient Sum Lower than in 1955	Total Period (1949–1954, 1956–1960)	Six Years Before (1949–1954)	Five Years After (1956–1960)	Four Years Before (1951–1954)	Two Years Before (1953–1954)	Two Nearest Years (1954–1956)	Four Nearest Years (1953–1957)	Six Nearest Years (1952–1958)
			Period Investigated					
11	6							
10	4							
9	6							
8	10							
7	13							
6	11	19						13
5	8	11	21					13
4	10	12	10	25			18	18
3	4	13	13	18			25	14
2	2	8	7	16	38	34	17	11
1	1	8	15	11	22	31	13	5
0	4	8	13	9	19	14	6	5
Total	79	79	79	79	79	79	79	79

Note: The 79 production sectors are distributed according to the number of years in which coefficient sums for intermediate inputs in 1955 prices were lower than in 1955.

Table 6–4. Number of Years Between 1955 and Nearest Year with Lower Coefficient Sums

Number of Sectors with Given Number of Years from 1955 to Nearest Year with

Number of Years	Lower Coefficient Sum			1 Percent Lower Coefficient Sum			2 Percent Lower Coefficient Sum		
	All Years	*Prior to 1955*	*After 1955*	*All Years*	*Prior to 1955*	*After 1955*	*All Years*	*Prior to 1955*	*After 1955*
1	65	49	50	49	35	32	27	17	18
2	8	11	12	7	11	11	16	11	15
3	1	5	0	6	6	4	6	9	2
4	1	5	4	4	6	5	7	9	6
5	0	1	0	2	2	1	1	3	0
6	0	0	–	0	1	–	2	2	–
No such year[a]	4	8	13	11	18	26	20	28	38
Total	79	79	79	79	79	79	79	79	79

[a]The year 1955 has the lowest coefficient sum.

Note: The 79 sectors are distributed according to the number of years between 1955 and the nearest year with a coefficient sum for intermediate inputs that is lower, 1 percentage point lower, and 2 percentage points lower, respectively, than in 1955.

ing years are considered. For 49 sectors, the coefficient sum in 1954 was lower than in 1955 when both are computed in 1955 prices. For 60 sectors, or three-fourths of the total number, the coefficient sum was lower than in 1955 in at least one of the two immediately preceding years, 1953 and 1954. If we consider years both before and after 1955, there were 73 of the 79 sectors that had lower coefficient sums not more than two years away from 1955.

If we disregard small differences, as given in the last six columns of Table 6-4, the distances in years to the nearest lower coefficient sum increase, and the number of sectors with no coefficient sum in other years smaller than in 1955 by more than the stipulated minimum difference increases. But the number of sectors with smaller coefficient sums in years near to 1955 remains quite high, irrespective of what period we consider (for sectors with coefficient sums both 1 and 2 percentage points lower than in 1955).

When we consider the 55 sectors that had coefficient sums of at least as much as 25 percent in 1955, as given in Table 6-5, we also find that as many as 30 of these had coefficient sums more than 5 percentage points lower than in 1955 in at least one year of the entire period; 23 had sums that much lower in at least one of the years before 1955; and 16 in at least one of the years after 1955.

In Table 6-6, we have distributed the sectors according to the size of the average coefficient sum for the entire period 1949-1960 and according to the distance in years from 1955 to the nearest year with at least a 1 percent lower coefficient sum. Since the larger coefficient sums are more important for total production costs, a finer adjustment would be expected for sectors with large coefficient sums. However, irrespective of the period considered, large coeffi-

Table 6-5. Number of Years Between 1955 and Nearest Year with 5 Percent Lower Coefficient Sum

	Number of Sectors with Given Distance to Nearest of		
Number of Years	*All Years*	*Prior to 1955*	*After 1955*
1	9	5	6
2	5	3	2
3	6	6	3
4	6	6	3
5	3	2	2
6	1	1	0
No such year[a]	25	32	39
Total	55	55	55

[a]The year 1955 has the lowest coefficient sum.

Note: The 55 sectors with coefficient sum for intermediate inputs not less than 25 percent in 1955, are distributed according to the number of years between 1955 and nearest year with 5 percent lower coefficient sum.

Table 6-6.   Number of Years Between 1955 and Years with Lower Coefficent Sum, by Size of Coefficient Sum

	Sectors by Size of Average Coefficient Sum				
Number of Years	*Less than 25.0 Percent*	*25.0- 49.9 Percent*	*50.0- 66.6 Percent*	*Over 66.6 Percent*	*Total*
	All Years				
1	9	17	13	10	49
2	2	2	2	1	7
3	3	1	1	1	6
4	1	1	1	1	4
5	2	0	0	0	2
No such year[a]	6	2	2	1	11
Total	23	23	19	14	79
	Years Before 1955				
1	9	13	7	6	35
2	0	3	5	3	11
3	1	2	2	1	6
4	1	1	2	2	6
5	1	0	1	0	2
6	1	0	0	0	1
No such year[a]	10	4	2	2	18
Total	23	23	19	14	79
	Years After 1955				
1	5	9	11	7	32
2	4	4	3	0	11
3	2	1	0	1	4
4	1	2	1	1	5
5	1	0	0	0	1
No such year[a]	10	7	4	5	26
Total	23	23	19	14	79

[a]The year 1955 has the lowest coefficient sum.

Note: The 79 sectors are distributed according to the size of the average coefficient sum (1949–1960) and the number of years between 1955 and the nearest year with 1 percent lower coefficient sum for intermediate inputs.

cient sums show rather less tendency to be smaller in 1955 compared with other years than do smaller coefficient sums.

Finally, in Table 6–7, we have compared the 1955 coefficient sums with the averages of coefficient sums over the whole period 1949–1960 and over the period 1949–1955. More than 60 percent of the coefficient sums in 1955 are above the averages for both periods. For the total period only five, and for the period 1949–1955 eight coefficient sums are less than the average by more than two times the standard deviation for the period concerned. This is 6 and 10

Table 6-7.   1955 Coefficient Sum for Intermediate Inputs Compared with the Average Coefficient Sum

	Number of Sectors, for Comparison over the Period	
	1949-1960	*1949-1955*
1955 coefficient sum equals or exceeds the average for the period	49	51
1955 coefficient sum less than the average, but exceeding the average minus standard deviation for the period	25	20
1955 coefficient sum less than the average minus 1 times standard deviation, but exceeding the average minus 2 times standard deviation for the period	4	8
1955 coefficient sum less than the average minus 3 times standard deviation, but exceeding the average minus 4 times standard deviation for the period	1	0
Total	79	79

percent, respectively, of all sector sums. Thus, there appears to be a tendency for the coefficient sum in 1955 to be higher than in other years. This might be explained if there was a tendency to increasing trends in the coefficient sums. We have not computed trends in the coefficient sums. But if we compare the averages over the period 1949-1955 with the averages for the whole period 1949-1960, the tendency to positive trends would cause the averages for the whole period to exceed the averages for the earlier seven years. However, this was the case for only 40 sectors, and we must conclude that there is no predominant tendency to increasing trends.

The conclusion concerning hypothesis 1a must be that in combination both with 2a and with 2b, it is not confirmed. Either the coefficient vectors of recent years, preceding or succeeding, are not available to a sector in a given year, or there are other considerations than minimization of unit input costs for intermediate inputs for the sector as a whole that determine the choice of input structure. However, we must also take into account the possibility of systematic errors in our figures. The tendency for the input costs to be systematically higher for the 1955 input vectors than for the vectors of other years computed in 1955 prices may indicate a tendency to underestimate price increases from the period before 1955 and to overestimate price increases after 1955. Since many of the basic price observations used in the deflation procedure are unit values, and since we must also count on a general improvement in quality over the observation period, there is considerable support for a hypothesis of general overestimation of price increases, but it is not easy to see why price increases prior to 1955 should be underestimated.

Another possibility is that hypothesis 1b is a better approximation to reality than 1a, and that an increase in the relative cost of labour has been the cause of labour-saving changes in the input structure of the production sectors, and these changes need not necessarily imply reductions in the costs of intermediate inputs.

Coefficient Sums, Including Labour Costs—
Hypotheses (1b, 2a) and (1b, 2b)

Intermediate inputs (including imports) plus wage and salary payments all in 1955 purchasers' prices as a percent of production in 1955 producers' prices, for each sector in each year 1949-1960, are given in the full report by this author [5]. In the same way as when we looked at intermediate input sums only, we used these data to perform our tests by comparing the percentages for other years with the ones for 1955 for each sector. If we now compare the average ranking for the twelve years, we find that there is a strong negative trend, as shown in Table 6-8. The falling trend reflects a falling coefficient of labour input over the period, that is, increasing labour productivity in the production sectors. This again may be explained by improved production techniques, improved quality of labour, and substitution of capital for labour, but apparently not by substitution of intermediate inputs for labour.

The observations are grouped relatively closely around the trend, and the deviation for 1955 is not more than 1.5 times the standard deviation from the

Table 6-8. Average Ranking of 79 Coefficient Sums of Intermediate and Wage and Salary Inputs for Each Year

Year	Observation	Trend Value[a]	Deviation
1949	8.31	8.07	.24
1950	7.97	7.79	.18
1951	7.11	7.50	−.39
1952	7.15	7.21	−.06
1953	6.75	6.93	−.18
1954	6.48	6.64	−.16
1955	6.82	6.36	.46
1956	5.73	6.07	−.34
1957	5.82	5.79	.03
1958	5.99	5.50	.49
1959	5.05	5.21	−.16
1960	4.83	4.93	−.10

[a]A linear trend was fitted by ordinary least squares.

Note: The year in which a given sector has the lowest percentage is given the ranking 1 for that sector. The year with the highest percentage is given the ranking 12. Equal figures are given the average rank of nearest higher and lower ranks.

trend. Still, the average ranking of the coefficient sums for 1955 is higher than the averages for the two preceding years; and whereas the average for 1955 is relatively far above the trend, the figure for 1956 is relatively far below. Thus, the figures give no indication that the production techniques of prior years or of later years are available as alternatives in a given year and are applied when they give lower sums of intermediate and labour input costs than other alternatives.

When there is a strong technological trend in the sector, there is a continuous change in the input vector, and we must assume that the coefficient sum for each year is determined by the technological development. It might therefore be of interest to study the average ranking for sectors that do not show a strong trend in the coefficient sum. As a rough criterion for the existence of a trend, we used the following: A sector is considered to have a negative trend in the coefficient sum if (1) one of the three first years (1949-1951) has the highest or second highest ranking; (2) one of the three last years (1958-1960) has the lowest or second lowest ranking; (3) none of the three first years has a lower ranking than 7 (6.5); and (4) none of the three last years has a higher ranking than 6 (6.5).

The criteria for a positive trend were defined correspondingly. By these criteria, 24 sectors were classified as having a negative trend and 7 as having a positive trend. Thus, there were 48 sectors left that were not classified as having a trend.

The classification procedure is of course rather rough and inaccurate, but very simple to apply. Probably, more refined methods would give a higher number of sectors with a trend. For the 48 sectors classified as having no trend, the average rankings are shown in Table 6-9. While the first two years still receive rankings considerably above and the last two considerably below the average, the rankings for the eight remaining years are scattered about the expected

Table 6-9. Average Rankings of 48 Coefficient Sums of Intermediate and Wage and Salary Inputs to Sectors Without a Trend

Year	Coefficient Sum
1949	7.56
1950	7.28
1951	6.46
1952	6.88
1953	6.25
1954	6.22
1955	6.96
1956	5.86
1957	6.29
1958	6.77
1959	5.69
1960	5.76

Note: The lowest percentage is given the ranking 1, highest percentage is given the ranking 12. Equal figures are given the average rank of nearest higher and lower ranks.

average of 6.5 in an apparently unsystematic way, and the average for 1955 is higher than the other seven. Thus, these figures also indicate that there is no tendency for the 1955 coefficient sum (in 1955 prices) to be lower than the corresponding sum for other years (in 1955 prices), even when the cost of hired labour is included with intermediate inputs in the coefficient sum. We must, however, again determine whether a closer study of the figures will modify the general impression.

We see from Table 6-10 that in spite of the general tendency toward a decreasing coefficient sum when the cost of labour is included, a considerable number of sectors in each of the years prior to 1955 have lower coefficient sums for that particular year than they had in 1955. In fact, as many as 42 percent of the sector years in the period 1949-1954 have lower sums than the corresponding sums in 1955. Conversely, a considerable number of sectors still had higher coefficient sums computed in 1955 prices after 1955 than in 1955. The percentage of sector years with lower coefficient sums was not higher than 65.

In Table 6-11, we have counted the number of years with coefficient sums lower than in 1955 for each sector over periods of varying length. Due to the existence of trends in a relatively large number of sectors, this table gives a more varied picture than the corresponding Table 6-3, where labour costs were not included in the coefficient sums. For periods prior to 1955, there is a tendency for the 1955 figure to be lower than the average, in particular where the longer

Table 6–10. Number of Sectors for Which the Coefficient Sum for Intermediate and Wage and Salary Inputs Is Lower than the Corresponding Sum in 1955

Year	Number of Sectors	Percent of Total
1949	25	31.7
1950	29	36.8
1951	37	46.9
1952	30	38.0
1953	35	44.3
1954	43	54.5
Total, prior to 1955	199	42.0
1956	53	67.1
1957	49	62.0
1958	46	58.2
1959	53	67.1
1960	55	69.6
Total, after 1955	256	65.0
Total, 1949–1960	455	52.4

Table 6-11. Number of Years with Intermediate and Labour Input
Coefficient Sums Lower than in 1955

Number of Years with Coefficient Sum Lower than in 1955	Total Period (1949–1954, 1956–1960)	Six Years Before (1949–1954)	Five Years After (1956–1960)	Four Years Before (1951–1954)	Two Years Before (1953–1954)	Two Nearest Years (1954–1956)	Four Nearest Years (1953–1957)	Six Nearest Years (1952–1958)
				Period Investigated				
11	1							
10	7							
9	8							
8	7							
7	9							
6	12	8						9
5	9	7	31					14
4	8	12	13	15			17	10
3	8	11	9	12			17	19
2	2	10	6	16	29	28	23	14
1	6	15	10	17	20	40	14	7
0	2	16	10	19	30	11	8	6
Total	79	79	79	79	79	79	79	79

Note: The 79 production sectors are distributed according to the number of years in which coefficient sums for intermediate inputs plus wages and salaries in 1955 prices were lower than in 1955.

periods of six and five years are considered. When we include years after 1955, we see a tendency for the 1955 figure to be the highest.

In Table 6-12, we have only included the 48 sectors that are classified as having no trend in the coefficient sum. For these sectors, there is apparently no tendency for the coefficient sum to be lower in 1955 than in preceding years.

The first three columns of Table 6-13 give the sectors distributed according to the number of years from 1955 to the nearest preceding and succeeding years with lower coefficient sums for intermediate and wage and salary inputs in 1955 prices. For 43 sectors, the coefficient sum in 1954 was lower than in 1955, and for 49 sectors the coefficient sum was lower than in 1955 in at least one of the two immediately preceding years, 1953 and 1954. This is slightly less than the corresponding number obtained when only the coefficient sum for intermediate inputs is considered (60 sectors, according to Table 6-4), but it is still 62 percent of the 79 sectors. If we consider years both before and after 1955, 71 of the sectors had lower coefficient sums not more than two years away from 1955. If we again restrict the analysis to the 48 sectors classified as having no trends in the coefficient sum, we find a distribution that is quite similar to the one we obtained when wage and salary costs were not included in the coefficient sum (see Table 6-14).

Table 6-12. Number of Years with Intermediate and Labour Input Coefficient Sums Lower than in 1955 for Sectors Without a Trend

		Period Investigated						
Number of Years with Coefficient Sum Lower than in 1955	Total Period (1949– 1954, 1956– 1960)	Six Years Before (1949– 1954)	Five Years After (1956– 1960)	Four Years Before (1951– 1954)	Two Years Before (1953– 1954)	Two Nearest Years (1954– 1956)	Four Nearest Years (1953– 1957)	Six Nearest Years (1952– 1958)
11	1							
10	7							
9	5							
8	5							
7	5							
6	6	5						7
5	1	5	14					11
4	4	9	9	10			14	2
3	7	9	7	10			7	9
2	0	8	4	11	21	17	12	10
1	6	9	6	11	12	25	10	5
0	1	3	8	6	15	6	5	4
Total	48	48	48	48	48	48	48	48

Note: The 48 production sectors without a trend are distributed according to the number of years in which coefficient sums for intermediate inputs plus wages and salaries in 1955 prices were lower than in 1955.

If small differences are disregarded, as given in the last six columns of Table 6-13, we obtain effects comparable to those that occurred when we studied coefficient sums for intermediate inputs only (compare Table 6-4).

There were 76 sectors that had coefficient sums of intermediate and wage and salary inputs of at least 25 percent in 1955 (Table 6-15), and 44 or 58 percent of these had coefficient sums 5 percentage points lower than in 1955 in at least one year in the entire period; 18 had sums that much lower in at least one of the years before 1955 and 37 in at least one year after 1955. When only 18 of the 76 sectors had coefficient sums at least 5 percent lower than in 1955 in at least one of the preceding years, this has to do with the occurrence of trends in the sums in many of the sectors. Among the 47 sectors without trends and with coefficient sums of at least 25 in 1955, 15 had a sum at least 5 percent lower than in 1955 in at least one of the preceding years, whereas the figure was only 3 out of a total of 29 sectors with trends.

In Table 6-16, we have distributed the sectors according to the size of the average coefficient sum for intermediate and wage and salary inputs over the period 1949-1960 and according to the distance in years from 1955 to the nearest year with at least 1 percent lower coefficient sums. As when we considered intermediate inputs alone, there is no indication of a tendency to find the

Table 6–13.   Number of Years Between 1955 and Nearest Year with Lower Coefficient Sums for Intermediate and Labour Inputs

Number of Sectors with Given Number of Years from 1955 to Nearest Year with

Number of Years	Lower Coefficient Sum			1 Percent Lower Coefficient Sum			2 Percent Lower Coefficient Sum		
	All Years	Prior to 1955	After 1955	All Years	Prior to 1955	After 1955	All Years	Prior to 1955	After 1955
1	68	43	53	55	28	42	38	15	30
2	3	6	6	8	11	9	11	8	12
3	1	4	2	1	2	3	4	1	4
4	3	7	5	7	11	7	6	10	7
5	1	1	3	1	2	2	4	2	4
6	1	2	–	0	1	–	0	0	–
No such year[a]	2	16	10	7	24	16	16	43	22
Total	79	79	79	79	79	79	79	79	79

[a]The year 1955 has the lowest coefficient sum.

Note: The 79 sectors are distributed according to the number of years between 1955 and the nearest year with a coefficient sum for intermediate and wage and salary inputs, that is lower, 1 percentage point lower, and 2 percentage points lower, respectively, than in 1955.

Table 6–14. Number of Years from 1955 to Years with Lower Coefficient Sums (percentage distribution)

Number of Years	Percentage of Sectors with Given Distance to Nearest Year with Lower Sum								
	Intermediate and Wage and Salary Inputs						*Intermediate Inputs Only*		
	All 79 Sectors			*48 Sectors Without a Trend*			*All 79 Sectors*		
	All Years	*Prior to 1955*	*After 1955*	*All Years*	*Prior to 1955*	*After 1955*	*All Years*	*Prior to 1955*	*After 1955*
1	86.0	54.5	67.1	87.4	60.4	64.6	82.2	62.0	63.3
2	3.8	7.6	7.6	2.1	8.3	6.2	10.1	13.9	15.2
3	1.3	5.1	2.5	2.1	6.2	4.2	1.3	6.3	.0
4	3.8	8.8	6.3	2.1	12.5	6.2	1.3	6.3	5.1
5	1.3	1.3	3.8	2.1	2.1	4.2	.0	1.3	.0
6	1.3	2.5	.0	2.1	4.2	.0	.0	.0	.0
No such year[a]	2.5	20.2	12.7	2.1	6.3	14.6	5.1	10.2	16.4
Total	100.0	100.0	100.0	100.0	100.0	100.0	100.0	100.0	100.0

[a]The year 1955 has the lowest coefficient sum.

Table 6-15.   Number of Years Between 1955 and Nearest Year with 5 Percent Lower Coefficient Sum for Intermediate and Labour Inputs

	Number of Sectors with Given Distance to Nearest of		
Number of Years	*All Years*	*Prior to 1955*	*After 1955*
1	16	6	12
2	5	2	4
3	7	4	7
4	9	5	7
5	7	0	7
6	0	1	–
No such year[a]	32	58	39
Total	76	76	76

[a]The year 1955 has the lowest coefficient sum.

Note: The 76 sectors with coefficient sums for intermediate and wage and salary inputs not less than 25 percent in 1955 are distributed according to the number of years between 1955 and nearest year with 5 percent lower coefficient sum.

smallest coefficient sums in 1955 for the sectors with high input sums more often than for those with low.

In Table 6-17, the 1955 coefficient sums are compared with the average coefficients for each sector over the whole period 1949-1960 and over the period 1949-1955. Nearly 50 percent of the coefficient sums for 1955 are equal to or exceed the corresponding average for the period 1949-1960 and nearly 40 percent are equal to or exceed the corresponding average for the period 1949-1955. No coefficient sum in 1955 is more than two times the standard deviation below the average for the whole period, and only two sectors show a deviation of that magnitude below the average for the period 1949-1955. Thus, even this test cannot be said to corroborate a hypothesis that the coefficient sum for 1955 tends to be lower than the corresponding sums for other years, when these are computed in 1955 prices.

Taken together, our data do not tend to support hypothesis 1b in combination with either 2a or 2b, that is, that the sectors in each year choose vectors of intermediate and labour inputs that are cheaper per unit of output than the vectors of preceding or of preceding and succeeding years (when these latter are computed in the prices of the year in question).

Summary and Conclusions

We have in this study investigated to what extent available data support hypotheses to the effect that changes in input-output coefficients can be explained as the effects of certain types of cost adjustments in the production sectors specified in the technology coefficient table. The cost adjustments considered are

Table 6-16. Number of Years Between 1955 and Years with Lower Coefficient Sum for Intermediate and Labour Inputs, by Size of Coefficient Sums

Number of Years	Sectors by Size of Average Coefficient Sum				
	Less than 50.0 Percent	50.0–74.9 Percent	75.0–89.9 Percent	Over 90.0 Percent	Total
			All Years		
1	9	11	23	12	55
2	1	2	3	2	8
3	0	0	1	0	1
4	1	2	3	1	7
5	0	1	0	0	1
6	0	0	0	0	0
No such year[a]	3	2	2	0	7
Total	14	18	32	15	79
			Years Before 1955		
1	6	7	8	7	28
2	1	2	5	3	11
3	0	0	1	1	2
4	1	1	8	1	11
5	0	1	0	1	2
6	0	1	0	0	1
No such year[a]	6	6	10	2	24
Total	14	18	32	15	79
			Years After 1955		
1	8	7	19	8	42
2	2	2	4	1	9
3	0	0	2	1	3
4	0	4	1	2	7
5	0	1	0	1	2
No such year[a]	4	4	6	2	16
Total	14	18	32	15	79

[a]The year 1955 has the lowest coefficient sum.

Note: The 79 sectors are distributed according to the size of the average coefficient sum (1949–1960) for intermediate and wage and salary inputs, and the number of years between 1955 and nearest year with 1 percent lower coefficient sum for intermediate and wage and salary inputs.

such as would result if the sectors for a given year always chose the vector of input-output coefficients which, in that year's prices, gave the lowest coefficient sum. Two alternative concepts of coefficient sums are considered: (1) the sum of input coefficients for intermediate inputs alone and (2) the same sum augmented by the coefficient for wages and salaries, that is, hired-labour input. Alternative assumptions are made about the extent to which input-output vectors

Table 6-17. 1955 Coefficient Sum for Intermediate and Labour Inputs Compared with the Average Coefficient Sum

	Number of Sectors, for Comparison over the Period	
	1949–1960	*1949–1955*
1955 coefficient sum equals or exceeds the average for the period	39	31
1955 coefficient sum less than the average, but exceeding the average minus standard deviation for the period	33	27
1955 coefficient sum less than the average minus 1 times standard deviation, but exceeding the average minus 2 times standard deviation for the period	7	19
1955 coefficient sum less than average minus 2 times standard deviation, but exceeding average minus 3 times standard deviation for the period	0	2
Total	79	79

(technologies) realized in preceding and succeeding years are available to the sectors in a given year.

The testing of the hypotheses consists in registering, from among the observed input-output coefficient vectors assumed to be available in a given year, co-efficient sums (computed in that year's prices) that are lower than those actually realized in that year. Two sets of data were available: The first set provided input-output coefficients in 1955 prices for 79 sectors for each of the 12 years 1949-1960. Here, assumptions of availability in 1955 of vectors from periods of varying length up to six years before 1955 and up to five years after 1955 could be tested. The second set provided input-output coefficients in 1964 prices for 113 sectors for the three years 1954, 1959, and 1964. With this set, we could only test our hypotheses under the assumptions that the 1954 and/or 1959 vectors of input-output coefficients were available in 1964.

Neither of these data sets appears to confirm a hypothesis that the realized coefficient vector is the one that gives the lowest coefficient sum of intermediate inputs alone in the given year's prices. This conclusion is independent of the assumption made about which alternative realized vectors are available.

When the input coefficient for hired labour is included in the coefficient sum, both data sets indicate a tendency for the coefficient sum of the given year to be lower than the coefficient sums for earlier years, when all coefficients are computed in the prices of the given year. This result appears to be the effect of a tendency toward declining trends in the input coefficient for hired labour. The data give no basis for deciding whether these trends are the effects of reversible adjustments to ever-rising relative prices of labour or the effects of (in the short run) irreversible technological changes associated with increasing capital intensity and technological progress. The author must admit that he subscribes to the latter—more complex—explanation. It is his belief that the observed changes (which are quite considerable) in input-output coefficients are the effects of much more complex causes than the simple types of substitution tested in this investigation. Among such causes may be mentioned technological change, changes in product mix, changes in product specifications, and changes in product distribution over producing establishments. A host of possible errors in statistical reporting, measurement, and deflation should also be mentioned as a factor. The present investigation has not weakened the author's belief in the more complex explanation. However, the value of the investigation is limited, just as is its scope. More evidence will be required, and the author is prejudiced in favour of a conclusion to the effect that the changes in coefficients may be treated as random, since such a conclusion appears to be less troublesome for the applicability of input-output models than a hypothesis of simple cost-minimizing coefficient adjustments.

References

1. Carter, A.P., and A. Bródy. *Input-Output Techniques.* Vol. 2, *Applications of Input-Output Analysis.* Amsterdam: North-Holland Publishing Company, 1970.

2. Central Bureau of Statistics of Norway. "Kryssløpstall 1954, 1959 og 1964" [Input-Output Data 1954, 1959, and 1964], NOS A 234, Oslo, 1968.

3. Sevaldson, P. "The Stability of Input-Output Coefficients." In *Input-Output Techniques.* Vol. 2, *Applications of Input-Output Analysis.* Edited by A.P. Carter and A. Bródy. Amsterdam: North-Holland Publishing Company, 1970. Pp. 207–237. And as "Artikler fra Statistisk Sentralbyrå" [Articles from the Central Bureau of Statistics], no. 32. Oslo, 1969.

4. Sevaldson, P. "Studies in the Stability of Input-Output Relationships. The Form of Input-Output Relationships." Working Paper from the Central Bureau of Statistics of Norway, IO 73/26, Oslo, 1973. (Mimeographed.)

5. Sevaldson, P. "Studies in the Stability of Input-Output Relationships. Price Changes as Causes of Variations in Input-Output Coefficients." Working Paper from the Central Bureau of Statistics of Norway, IO 74/14, Oslo, 1974. (Mimeographed.)

6. Sevaldson, P. "Substitution and Complementarity Effects on Input-Output Ratios." Working Paper from the Central Bureau of Statistics of Norway, IO 69/14, Oslo, 1969. (Mimeographed.)

Part Two

Applications in Developing Countries

Chapter Seven

Intersectoral Comparison as an Approach to the Identification of Key Sectors

Siegfried Schultz

It is the purpose of this paper to specify the methodology and present some results of a trial application of input-output techniques to identify key sectors for developing countries.[1] Aiming at an empirical determination of the relative importance of individual sectors, the mutual dependence of sectors is measured first by the extent of their intermediate demand and supply. Besides these direct spread effects in terms of backward and forward linkages, use will be made of the inverse matrix to determine the indirect effects as well. Moreover, the sectoral effects on the import dependency, gross domestic product, and balance of foreign trade are considered. Finally, by use of statistical information from outside the input-output system, the analysis is supplemented by including sectoral employment effects as well.

The results of the computation, that is, the size of the several linkage ratios, the primary input requirements, and the employment impact on a per unit level, are translated into an ordinal sequence. This ranking is carried out on the basis of a standardized 20×20 sectoral scheme for 22 input-output tables, most of which are from developing Asian countries.

With reference to their valuation, the input-output tables used in the analysis generally are valued in producers' prices. The level of aggregation is identical for all tables throughout the study.[2] Following the International Standard Industrial Classification (ISIC) definitions, a scheme of 21 standard sectors has been applied, out of which two sectors (1 and 2) stand for primary and three sectors (18-20) for tertiary production. Industrial activity is subdivided into 13 manufacturing branches (3-15) as well as Energy (16) and Construction (17). In

---

1. For an earlier attempt, see Schultz [28].
2. As to the formal aggregation procedure, see Benz [1, pp. 55-60]. Both tables for Israel were slightly changed: nonpositive intrasectoral deliveries in the aggregated version (1966, Sectors 9 and 15; 1969, Sectors 2 and 7) were deleted, and the gross outputs were adjusted accordingly. These changes did not go beyond 2.6 percent. In the case of Japan, two variations of this nature hardly affected the gross output figures (0.01 percent).

Table 7-1. Standardized Sectors (UN Classification)

Sector		ISIC	
Number	Title	1958[a]	1968[b]
1	Agriculture, forestry, & fishing	01–04	11–13
2	Mining & quarrying	11–14, 19	21–23, 29
3	Processed foods	20–22	31
4	Apparel, incl. textiles & footwear	23, 24	32, except 323
5	Leather & leather products	29	323
6	Wood & paper products & printing	25–28	33, 34
7	Rubber products	30	355
8	Chemicals	31	351, 352, 356
9	Petroleum products	32	353, 354
10	Nonmetallic mineral products	33	36
11	Basic metals, metal products	34, 35	37, 381
12	Nonelectrical machinery	36	382
13	Electrical machinery	37	383
14	Transport equipment	38	384
15	Industry not elsewhere classified	39	385, 39
16	Electricity, gas, water	51, 52	41, 42
17	Construction	40	50
18	Trade	61	61, 62
19	Transportation, storage, & communications	71–73	71, 72
20	Services	62–64, 81–85	63, 81–83, 91–94, 952, 953, 959
21	Undistributed	90	00

[a]United Nations, Statistical Office. *International Standard Industrial Classification of All Economic Activities.* Statistical Papers, Series M, no. 4, rev. 1. New York: United Nations, 1958.

[b]United Nations, Statistical Office. *International Standard Industrial Classification of All Economic Activities.* Statistical Papers, Series M, no. 4, rev. 2. New York: United Nations, 1968.

another sector (21), all those transactions have been collected that could not be allocated elsewhere; this residual has been ignored in the subsequent ranking of sectors. This classification is shown in Table 7-1.

Of the 22 tables analysed, the majority—17—are from developing Asian countries. For comparison, three additional tables have been included from developing countries outside this region and two from economically more advanced countries, as shown in Table 7-2.

Methodology: Linkage Indicators

Typically, countries with high per capita incomes have a high degree of division of labour, expressed by a dense network of intermediate supplies or deliveries. Those sectors of the economy that, owing to their close technology-related ties, are in a position to promote or generate growth in other sectors through that of

Table 7-2. Analysed Input-Output Tables

Country	Year	Abbre-viation		Number of Sectors in Original Table	Imports	
					Row	Column
India [19]	1963	IND	63	33		x
India [26]	1964–65	IND	65	77		x
Indonesia [10]	1969	IDO	69	43		x
Iran [30]	1965	IRN	65	29	x	
Korea (South) [15]	1963	KOR	63	43	x	
Korea (South) [16]	1966	KOR	66	43	x	
Malaysia (West) [18]	1965	MLY	65	31	x	
Pakistan [25]	1960–61	PAK	61	30	x	
Pakistan [36]	1963–64	PAK	64	54	x	
Philippines [21]	1961	PHI	61	29	x	
Philippines [22]	1965	PHI	65	97	x	
Sri Lanka [20]	1963	SLA	63	38	x	
Sri Lanka [2]	1965	SLA	65	41		x
Taiwan [7]	1964	TAI	64	55	x	
Taiwan [33]	1966	TAI	66	76	x	
Taiwan [34]	1969	TAI	69	76	x	
Turkey [4; 29]	1963	TUR	63	37		x
Israel [12]	1965–66	ISR	66	80	x	
Israel [5]	1968–69	ISR	69	30	x	
Yugoslavia [40]	1966	YUG	66	29	x	
Germany (West) [31]	1966	GER	66	56	x	
Japan [13]	1965	JAP	65	56		x

their own can be called strategic for achieving higher income levels. Therefore, the extent of interdependence can serve as a suitable criterion for a ranking of sectors.

Standard Notion of Backward and Forward Linkages

In the simplest approach, a sector's degree of interdependence with its economic environment can be expressed by the relation of intermediate to total transactions. Depending on whether the inputs or the deliveries are used in the numerator, the obtained ratios express the well-known sectoral linkages described by Hirschman [9, pp. 100, 105]. *Backward* linkages, u, indicate to what extent the economic branches have been specializing. Thus, coefficients are high if the sectors observed are drawing heavily on the system of industries or, vice versa, if the value added by use of primary input is relatively small. *Forward* linkages, w, which are generally weaker since the output produced is not necessarily met by adequate demand, give an indication of the direction of supply; high coefficients will typically be found with those sectors producing relatively little directly for final demand but rather for intermediate demand of other sectors. The words "high" and "low" are used interchangeably for the phrases "values above the average" and "values below (or equal to) the average," respectively.

Modifications

The above notion of linkages (u_a, w_a) can easily be computed and has been used before.[3] Besides the technological relationships expressed in these ratios, it may be desirable also to consider the size of a sector's transactions. For this reason, the analysis was supplemented by attaching *weights* to the linkage ratios: (1) the sum of intermediate input or output per sector (u_b, w_b) and (2) the share of the sectoral gross output in the output of the entire economy (u_c, w_c).

In a further variation, intrasectoral transactions were deducted before computing the linkages. The coefficients thus obtained (u_d, w_d) refer only to deliveries among different sectors. In analogy to the basic linkage version, the weighting procedure was repeated here (u_e, w_e, u_f, w_f).[4]

Allowance was made for the differing treatment of *imports* in the first quadrant of the input-output tables affecting the size of the calculated linkages: If alternative versions were on hand or the matrix cells had several entries, preference was given to the one containing domestic transactions only. In those— fortunately few—cases where competing imports were not compiled in a separate row (that is, the matrix elements comprise both domestic and imported inputs), the u's are relatively too high while the w's are properly computed after the gross output has been adjusted by the inclusion of imports (w^z).

Power of Dispersion

The simplicity of calculating the u's and w's gives the power-of-dispersion approach some attractiveness; ratios that can be computed in a "pedestrian" way allow the immediate ranking of sectors. However, this procedure addresses itself only to direct production effects as they are expressed in the technical coefficients—a drawback that can be avoided by using the inverted Leontief matrix, the use of which guarantees inclusion of total (direct and indirect) effects of a variation in the final demand vector on sectoral production levels.

In particular, use has been made here of the inverse matrix in the following way:[5] The sum of all elements in each column of the inverse, referred to as a vertical sum, indicates the extent of the increase in output in the entire economy caused by the rise of final demand in the sector under consideration. If this variation in final demand takes place one at a time for each of the *n* sectors, the inverse's vertical sums show each sector's vertical impact on overall production.

3. See, for example, Chenery and Watanabe [6]; Rasul [24]; and Chakraverti [3]. For more recent applications, see Yotopoulos and Nugent [39] and Thoburn [35].
4. Definitions are given in Appendix 7A.
5. This approach was originated by Rasmussen [23]. For an application to Indian data see Hazari [8]. Compare also Yotopoulos and Nugent [39, pp. 161 ff.].

If the sum over all column totals is divided by the number of sectors, $(1/n)C_{.j}$ denotes the average rise in output—in a sector chosen at random—which is necessary as a consequence of the increase in the observed sector j.

By standardizing the column totals for the purpose of intersectoral comparison in terms of the average of all elements of the inverse, the indicator p thus obtained is expressing the power of dispersion of the observed sector in the entire economy. So p is a measure of the effects of increased output in one sector *relative* to those of all sectors.[6] If $p < 1$, the sector in question produces only weak output stimuli for the economy; a value of $p > 1$, however, would signal that this sector is transmitting above-average impulses to other sectors through its intermediate input requirements.

Hypothetical Extraction

Again taking advantage of the features of the inverse matrix, a hypothetical extraction approach is used to determine each sector's significance. This is done by removing sectors from the interdependent system one at a time.[7] This means not only a hypothetical production shutdown in the observed sector, but also that intermediate supplies from and deliveries to other sectors would be affected. Depending upon whether the effect on production of other sectors or the effect on the sector itself is greater, the isolated sector can be described as stimulating or dependent.

The indicators can be derived as follows: A sector's exclusion begins by deleting its row and column from the input-output table. The sought sector-specific impact can be measured by comparing numerically the output levels of the economy before and after the hypothetical extraction, adjusted by the gross production of the isolated sector. Extraction is accomplished by subtracting the reduced matrix from the unity matrix, inverting the new Leontief matrix, and multiplying it by the reduced final demand vector.

The ratio of these net effects on other sectors and the intermediate deliveries of the isolated sector to others is called indicator s. If $s < 1$, the sector is dependent on impulses of other sectors; if $s > 1$, the sector can be called stimulating. Under this approach, key sectors obviously are those for which the indicator is largest.

Effects on some Economic Aggregates

The linkage coefficients help to identify sectors that, due to their important position in the interindustrial network, are significant for initiating or distribut-

---

6. Another indicator, v, a measure of "variability" (compare Rasmussen [23]) has been considered here as an auxiliary criterion only, since the prime concern was the power of dispersion irrespective of its distribution. See Appendix 7A for definitions.

7. This method was first used by Strassert [32]. Compare also Lehbert [17, pp. 63 ff.].

ing growth impulses. However, they do not indicate what variations of major economic aggregates, such as national income, trade balance, or employment, are affected through the inverse matrix by an autonomous rise in production in a particular sector and the subsequent reactions in the system of industries. For this reason, the total requirements of primary inputs (domestic and foreign) also have been calculated by means of the inverse matrix. Its multiplication by the row vectors of the direct coefficients gives us—through inclusion of the primary input content of intermediate supplies—the total of primary inputs necessary per unit of sectoral gross output.

Gross Domestic Product and Foreign Trade

The sum of each sector's net contribution to the gross domestic product (GDP) indicates the total (direct and indirect) variation of national income that occurs as a result of the initial increase of gross production in sector j minus imports. Therefore, if all initial increases are of the same size, the sectoral ranking under the GDP and the import effect must be identical. (In case intermediate inputs were mixed irrespective of their domestic or foreign origin, both effects could not be calculated.) Due to a modest disaggregation in the third quadrant of the input-output tables from developing Asian countries in the sample—only about every other country had an entry for wages and salaries—none of the GDP components were compared by sector and country.

As to foreign trade, by balancing exports and imports by sector, the value of sectoral net exports (imports) has been used to determine whether the sector under consideration is drawing on or contributing to foreign exchange reserves. The grading is based on the difference between the (direct) export ratio in sector j and the total (direct and indirect) import effects caused by the extension of production in sector j.

Employment

Finally, as a further criterion for identifying key sectors, the employment effect has been introduced for those countries that have the necessary data. The rough approximation using the sum of wages and salaries is unfit for intersectoral comparison due to substantial differences in wages. Also, the real employment impact may be underestimated, especially for the countries with lower levels of development where relatively more own-account workers (farmers, artisans) are to be found.

As to the origin and processing of the statistical information on employment, basically the data have been taken from international sources, namely the International Labour Office (ILO) [11] and the United Nations Economic Commission for Asia and the Far East (UN-ECAFE) [37], in which the results of national sample surveys are being reproduced.[8] These figures generally refer to

8. For South Korea, Germany, and Japan, use was made directly of some national employment statistics that were already adjusted to the sectoral classification of the respective input-output tables.

the total civilian labour force employed, with two main exceptions: those including military personnel and those for employees only. Since the sectoral breakdown of these employment data does not go beyond the one-digit ISIC level, while the manufacturing industry in this study is subdivided into several branches, the structure of the more detailed data in the UN industrial statistics [38] has been transformed to coincide with the ILO figures for manufacturing after being fitted to the scheme of standard sectors applied here.[9]

Indicator p can also be used here. Analogously interpreted for the "employment inverse," $(1/n)_L r._j$ stands for the average employment increase touched off in an arbitrarily chosen sector by the rise in final demand in sector j. For intersectoral comparison, $_L p$ indicates the relative importance of each sector with reference to its employment effect; for example, $_L p > 1$ means that this sector is transmitting impulses that are above normal.

Backward and Forward Linkages

The sectors can be grouped according to the size of their backward and forward linkages (u's and w's, respectively) in such a manner that all combinations of high and low values are easy to survey. It ought to be mentioned, however, that the calculated ratios for u and w are a function of the sectoral interdependence in each table, that is, the classification is country specific. A sector with the same values for u and w may, in another country, belong to another group.[10] Nevertheless, a few common features can be recognized in all countries under consideration: typically, u's are high in manufacturing industries, while they are rather low for primary production and services. Sectors that are heavily supplying others are characterized by high w's; these are generally low when production is directly for consumption and investment, that is, in industries delivering to final demand.

Therefore, still quite conventionally, sectors can be arranged according to their linkage ratios as follows:

Group	Sector Classification	Dominant Direction
I	manufacturing	final demand
II	manufacturing	intermediate demand
III	primary, tertiary	final demand
IV	primary, tertiary	intermediate demand

Analysis of the statistical correlation between the ratios for the backward and forward linkages in their basic type a and the weighted variants b and c revealed

9. ILO and UN figures may not coincide due to differing coverage in relation to employed persons above a certain age and the size of the establishment in terms of number of persons engaged.

10. The nonhomogeneous residuals in Sector 21 are disregarded here and in the following sections. The same applies to sectors with no entries.

only a loose connection: For the developing Asian countries under consideration, the average correlation between u_a and u_b (w_a and w_b) was $r = 0.63$ (0.64); between u_a and u_c (w_a and w_c) was $r = 0.62$ (0.51). Despite their different weights, however, the ratios of variants b and c correlated highly; their mean values for r were 0.95 and 0.94, respectively.

Because in some of the input-output tables transactions were concentrated in the cells on the main diagonal, these items were deducted before computing the linkages (version d). Yet the ranking of sectors varied only slightly: for the analysed sample of developing Asian countries, the correlation between linkages in version u_a and u_d (w_a and w_d) was $r = 0.97$ (0.98). Since intrasectoral transactions frequently are substantial, their share obviously is similar from sector to sector.[11]

Finally, attention must be called to an interesting possibility, raised by version c, regarding the interpretation of backward and forward linkages in the entire economy. Whereas version c represents a weighted quantification of the degree of mutual dependence of various economic sectors, the national average of all sectors (u^*, w^*) can be taken as an indicator of the division of labour and thus the level of development within a given country.[12] From a ranking according to economic integration, countries can be grouped, as shown in Table 7-3, in a way that by and large conforms to ranking according to conventional indicators of the stage of development (per capita GNP or GDP). There were, however, certain striking departures. Israel's position in this classification is relatively low, while Indonesia would appear to be ranked too high.[13] The surprisingly high ranking of Yugoslavia and the position of Japan relative to that of Germany may be explained by an intensive, growth-oriented sectoral integration, which has yet to be reflected to a corresponding degree in per capita income.

Power of Dispersion

Findings based on the empirical results of the power of dispersion, p, of the various economic sectors, as shown in Table 7-4, are as follows: Relatively strong intersectoral impulses are emitted by the various industrial sectors of developing Asian economies. In the primary and tertiary sectors, on the other hand, values of $p > 1$ are infrequent (specifically, only in India 1963, the Philippines, and Turkey). In principle, the same is true of the more highly developed countries: the most stimuli are forthcoming from the secondary sectors, although in the case of Israel, the intensity with which agriculture is conducted apparently creates a considerable stimulus for other sectors.

Of the secondary sectors, Processed foods are predominant, followed closely by Apparel and Construction. In frequency of appearance, Leather & leather

11. For more detailed results of backward and forward linkages that, due to space limitations, could not be reproduced here, see Schultz [27, pp. 14, 15].

12. Definitions for u^* and w^* are provided in Appendix 7A.

13. This first table for Indonesia is to be regarded with some reservation. The original version could not be inverted due to singularity; for this analysis, a marginal alteration was made in the intrasectoral flow of Sector 21.

Table 7-3. Country Ranking According to Combined Backward and Forward Linkages

		Combined Backward and Forward Linkages[a]		
Less than 0.30	*0.30 to 0.34*	*0.35 to 0.39*	*0.40 to 0.44*	*Greater than 0.44*
India 1963	India 1965	Indonesia 1969	Germany 1966	Japan 1965
Philippines 1961	Iran 1965	Pakistan 1961	Yugoslavia 1966	
Sri Lanka 1963	Israel 1966	Pakistan 1964		
Sri Lanka 1965	Israel 1969	Philippines 1965		
	South Korea 1963	Taiwan 1964		
	South Korea 1966	Taiwan 1966		
	Malaysia 1965	Taiwan 1969		
		Turkey 1963		

[a]Calculated as $(u^* + w^*)/2$.

Table 7-4. Sectors with Values of Indicator p Above Average

Num-ber	Title	IND 63	IND 65	IDO 69	IRN 65	KOR 63	KOR 66	MLY 65	PAK 61	PAK 64	PHI 61	PHI 65	SLA 63	SLA 65	TAI 64	TAI 66	TAI 69	TUR 63	ISR 66	ISR 69	YUG 66	GER 66	JAP 65
1	Agriculture, forestry, & fishing	★□									★								★□	★□			
2	Mining & quarrying	★□	★		★□	★□	★□	★□	★□	★□	★□	★	★□	★□	★□	★□		★	★□	★□	★□	★□	★□
3	Processed foods	★□	★□		★	★□	★	★□	★□	★□	★□	★□	★□	★	★□	★□	★□	★□	★□	★□	★□	★□	★
4	Apparel, incl. textiles & footwear	★□	★□		★□	★	★		★□	★□	★	★	★	★	★	★	★	★	★	★	★	★	★
5	Leather & leather products	★□	★□		★□	★□	★□	★□	★□	★□	★□	★□	★□	★□	★□	★	★	★□	★	★	★□	★	★□
6	Wood & paper products & printing	★			★□			★□	★□	★	★□	★□	★□	★	★□	★□	★□	★□	★□	★□	★□	★□	★□
7	Rubber products	★□	★□		★□	★□	★□	★□	★□	★□	★□	★□	★	★□	★□	★□	★□	★□			★□	★	★□
8	Chemicals	★□	★□			★	★	★□	★□	★□	★□	★□		★	★	★	★	★□			★		★
9	Petroleum products				★□																		
10	Nonmetallic mineral products	★□			★□			★□	★□	★□	★□	★□	★□	★□	★□	★□	★□	★□	★□		★□	★□	★□
11	Basic metals & metal products	★	★			★□	★	★□	★	★□	★	★	★	★	★□	★□	★	★	★	★	★	★	★
12	Nonelectrical machinery	★□	★			★	★	★□	★	★□	★□	★□			★□	★□	★□	★□			★	★	★□
13	Electrical machinery	★□	★□		★	★□	★□	★□	★	★□	★□		★□	★□	★□	★□	★□	★□	★□	★□	★□	★□	★□
14	Transport equipment	★□	★□		★□	★□	★□	★□	★□	★□	★□	★	★□	★□	★□	★□	★□	★□		★□	★□	★□	★□
15	Industry not elsewhere classified					★□	★□	★□	★□	★□	★□	★□	★□	★□	★□	★□							★□
16	Electricity, gas, water					★□	★□	★□	★□			★□	★□		★□	★□			★□	★□		★□	★□
17	Construction	★				★□	★	★□		★□		★	★			★	★□		★	★□		★	
18	Trade	★□	★□		★□	★□	★□	★□	★□	★□	★□	★□	★□	★□	★□	★□	★□	★□	★□	★□	★□		★□
19	Transportation, storage, & communication	★□																★□			★□		
20	Services																					★	

Note: ★ = p > 1; □ = even dispersion.

products; Wood & paper products & printing; and Chemicals are on nearly equal footing.[14] When the subsidiary criterion of the greatest possible evenness of dispersion of impulses (indicator v) is applied, only minor changes result with regard to the ranking of sectors according to their frequency of appearance. Of the leaders, only Apparel receives a lower rating—this apparently because only a few other sectors are drawn upon to cover intermediate input requirements (for example, in Korea and Taiwan). Sectors in which there is a high degree of vertical integration will not register high p and v values. This is clearly demonstrated in the example of Basic metals & metal products. Stimuli forthcoming from Transport equipment, Nonelectrical machinery, and Industry not elsewhere classified, by comparison, are powerful and relatively evenly distributed, not only in the industrialized countries but in some of the developing countries as well.

Hypothetical Extraction

A calculation of the impact of a hypothetical production shutdown in each sector to determine that sector's economic importance in intersectoral flows, indicator s, produces results similar to those for p as shown in Table 7–5. (Without further refinements, this method tends to result in extremely high values for those sectors that produce heavily for final demand; therefore, additional information on the share of a sector's production going directly to final demand has been provided in Table 7–5.) The secondary sectors are predominant here as well, while primary production is only modestly represented. There is a distinct departure, however, in the tertiary sectors, which show up more strongly.

Of the secondary sectors, Processed foods has an above-average indicator value in all countries in the study. Also high on this list is Leather & leather products. Transport equipment is found comparatively often among the stimulator sectors, as is Construction.[15]

Correlation of Sector Rankings with the Various Linkage Criteria

A comparison of results for the indicators p and s leads to the general observation that in the average of all countries, that is, including industrialized countries, a number of sectors are ascribed a lesser importance by s than by p. This applies in particular to Basic metals & metal products, Nonmetallic mineral products,

14. The Leather & leather products indicator is considerably higher in the developing Asian countries than in the more developed countries. This finding is confirmed by Yotopoulos and Nugent in their study of six industrialized and five developing countries [39, p. 163]. However, their finding that values for the standard sectors 1, 2, 16, and 20 in the developing countries range considerably below those of the industrialized countries is not corroborated by the results of the present study.

15. For India and Turkey, the difference in frequency between Construction and Food processing is due only to a peculiarity in the present computer programme if the final demand share increases to the extreme of 100 percent.

Table 7-5.   Sectors with Values of Indicators *s* Above Average

Num-ber	Title	IND 63	IND 65	IDO 69	IRN 65	KOR 63	KOR 66	MLY 65	PAK 61	PAK 64	PHI 61	PHI 65	SLA 63	SLA 65	TAI 64	TAI 66	TAI 69	TUR 63	ISR 66	ISR 69	YUG 66	GER 66	JAP 65
1	Agriculture, forestry, & fishing			★○					★⊕	★○	★⊕								★○	★○			
2	Mining & quarrying		★⊕	★○					★○	★○	★○	★○								★○			
3	Processed foods	★★	★⊕	★⊕	★⊕	★○	★⊕	★★	★⊕	★★	★⊕	★⊕	★★	★★	★⊕	★⊕	★★	★★		★★	★★	★○	★★
4	Apparel, incl. textiles & footwear	★★	★○		★○			★★	★○	★★	★⊕	★○	★⊕	★⊕	★⊕	★⊕	★★	★○				★○	★★
5	Leather & leather products	★○	★○	★		★○			★○	★⊕	★○					★	★⊕	★○			★○	★○	★
6	Wood & paper products & printing	★○		★					★○	★○	★○					★	★○				★		
7	Rubber products			★⊕	★○	★○	★○	★○	★⊕	★○	★⊕			★		★	★○			★	★		
8	Chemicals	★○		★	★	★⊕	★	★⊕	★⊕	★○	★○						★○			★⊕	★★		
9	Petroleum products								★⊕	★★													
10	Nonmetallic mineral products			★					★○														
11	Basic metals & metal products							★⊕	★○	★○	★⊕				★								
12	Nonelectrical machinery	★★	★⊕	★			★○		★⊕	★★	★⊕		★○		★	★○	★○		★⊕	★○	★○	★○	★★
13	Electrical machinery	★★	★⊕	★	★	★○	★○		★★	★★	★⊕	★○			★○	★★	★⊕		★★	★⊕	★○	★○	★★
14	Transport equipment	★★	★○	★	★	★○	★○		★⊕	★★			★⊕	★⊕	★○	★⊕	★⊕	★	★⊕		★⊕	★⊕	★⊕
15	Industry not elsewhere classified	★⊕		★	★⊕	★○	★○	★○	★★	★★	★○		★★	★★	★★	★★	★★	★★	★⊕	★○	★★	★○	★★
16	Electricity, gas, water			★	★⊕	★⊕	★○	★⊕	★⊕	★⊕	★○	★○			★○	★○	★○	★○	★⊕	★○	★⊕	★⊕	★○
17	Construction			★⊕	★⊕	★⊕	★⊕	★⊕	★★	★★		★○	★	★⊕	★⊕	★★	★★	★⊕	★★	★⊕	★⊕	★⊕	★★
18	Trade			★○	★⊕			★⊕											★⊕				
19	Transportation, storage, & communication	★		★○	★○	★○	★○		★○		★⊕		★⊕	★⊕		★⊕	★⊕	★⊕	★★		★○	★○	★⊕
20	Services			★○	★⊕	★⊕	★⊕						★⊕	★⊕		★⊕	★⊕		★★		★○	★○	

Note: ★ = *s* > 1;   ○ = share of final demand > 50 percent;   ⊕ = share of final demand > 75 percent.

and Chemicals and to a lesser extent to Apparel, a sector which is one of the stimulator sectors, even in the two industrialized countries—presumably due to the high share of synthetic-fibre processing.

The p and s sector rankings were tested for correlation using the Spearman coefficient.[16] The coefficient of correlation between the p and s ordinal values of each sector averaged $r = 0.49$ for the developing Asian countries. The national coefficients ranged from -0.21 (India) to 0.79 (Pakistan). All sectors of the Indonesian economy showed above-average s values and below-average p values. Presumably, this is to be explained by the lack of linear independence in the rows and columns of the original table. (Marginal corrections in the aggregated version made it possible to obtain an inverse matrix but not plausible results.)

A much stronger correlation was found to exist between the u_a and p sectoral rankings, the coefficients averaging $r = 0.95$. Among the developing Asian countries, individual figures ranged from 0.57 (Indonesia) to 0.99 (Malaysia, the Philippines). Coefficients for the other two groups were similarly high: 0.99 (Israel, Yugoslavia) and 0.96 (Germany, Japan). Thus, a good approximation of p sector rankings can be obtained by way of the more simply calculated backward linkages in the basic version.

As expected, a corresponding test of the correlation of u_a and s rankings did not turn out as well: the correlation between u_a and p is generally so close—apart from Indonesia—that indicators can be interchanged without significantly altering the result. The average coefficient of correlation is 0.49 for the developing Asian countries and even lower for the other two country groups.

The similarity of w_a and p rankings is also quite limited (-0.18). Between the w_a and s rankings, the correlation is also negative, but higher. In view of the mean correlation of -0.69, however, an approximation of s results with reciprocal w_a values (more simply derived) is not advisable.

Gross Domestic Product and Foreign Trade

For the income effect, the analysis of the average sectoral position in the international comparison is necessarily restricted to gross domestic product. The original tables vary in the extent to which they break down the national income components—in some cases, there exists only one primary input entry. A country-to-country cross-section comparison is thus pointless.

As explained earlier, the sectors are ranked on the basis of their combined coefficients of direct and indirect effects. These coefficients are standardized on the basis of gross sectoral output. Unless imported intermediate inputs are shown in the third quadrant, all GDP coefficients will equal one—and thus offer no means for comparison. For this reason, analysis of this effect is concentrated on those tables which include an import row (see Table 7-2).

16. The subsidiary criterion v was not allowed for in the test (see footnote 6).

For the average of the developing Asian countries, the highest rankings are in the tertiary and primary sectors.[17] In manufacturing, Processed foods is found most often among the leaders. By and large, a similar constellation is seen in the more advanced countries. In these countries, however, Construction also occupies a comparatively high position.

As a general observation on this criterion, it is to be noted that here the weight of the direct effects of a sector, as expressed in its input coefficients, is the dominant factor of the overall impact and the ranking.

The sectoral effects on the balance of trade are also examined. (The countries examined are the same as those examined for the income effect, with the exception of Pakistan 1961, where exports are not shown as a subgroup of final demand.) At first glance, the cross-section comparison of balance of trade effects gives about the same picture: rankings of the primary sectors in the developing Asian countries average highest. More than anything else, this is attributable to exports of mining products such as ores and crude oil and agricultural products. Of the manufacturing sectors, only Processed foods has a high ranking; the others are found farther down on the scale of net foreign exchange earners.

Employment

Evaluation of the results of the employment impact reveals the following characteristics: As expected, a marginal change in final demand, indirect effects included, produces a comparatively strong employment effect in Agriculture and Trade in all developing Asian countries.[18] As regards the dispersion of effects, impulses from Wood & paper products & printing and from Construction are generally powerful and relatively evenly distributed to other sectors, as shown in Table 7-6. Strong effects on output and employment as well are apparently felt by sectors for which, because of production-related ties or their specific employment requirement, indicator values for p and $_L p > 1$ (specially noted in Table 7-6). In the developing Asian countries, Processed foods is most frequently one of these sectors.

Due to the central importance of the employment impact, the detailed sectoral rankings, based on total effects rather than just rough groupings of above- and below-average positions, are also shown in Table 7-7. Owing to the strong direct effects, the greatest total employment effect is that of Agriculture; in second place is Processed foods. Averaged for the developing Asian countries, the employment effect of Apparel nearly equals that of Trade—a reflection of the large extent of indirect employment by the apparel industry.

17. In place of the official Turkish table, a different one—based on official figures—in which imports are presented as a row was used here in order that Turkey could be included in this section of the study.

18. Due to a difference in statistical concepts (that is, labour force as opposed to employed persons), the employment effect is presumably overestimated in the case of Turkey.

Table 7-6.   Sectors with Values of $_L p$ Above Average

Num-ber	Title	KOR 63	KOR 66	PHI 61	PHI 65	TAI 66	TAI 69	TUR 63	ISR 66	ISR 69	YUG 66	GER 66	JAP 65
1	Agriculture, forestry, & fishing	★	★	★☆	★☆	★	★	★☆	★☆	★☆		★	★
2	Mining & quarrying		★				★	★			★	★	
3	Processed foods	★☆		★☆	★☆	★☆□	★☆□	★		★☆□		★☆	★☆
4	Apparel, incl. textiles & footwear			★☆	★☆□	★☆	★☆□	★☆□	★☆	★☆	★☆	★☆	★☆□
5	Leather & leather products			★☆□	★☆□			★☆				★☆□	★☆□
6	Wood & paper products, & printing			★☆□	★☆□	★☆□	★☆□	★☆			★☆	★☆	★☆
7	Rubber products			★☆□			★					★☆□	★☆□
8	Chemicals												
9	Petroleum products												
10	Nonmetallic mineral products											★☆	
11	Basic metals & metal products											★★	
12	Nonelectrical machinery		★☆									★★	
13	Electrical machinery			★☆						★☆□		★☆	
14	Transport equipment						★□		★	★☆	★☆	★☆	★□
15	Industry not elsewhere classified			★☆	★☆	★☆			★	★☆			
16	Electricity, gas, water			★☆□	★☆□	★☆□	★☆□		★☆	★☆□		★☆□	
17	Construction	★☆□			★	★					★	★□	
18	Trade	★	★	★	★				★	★		★	
19	Transportation, storage, & communication									★	★☆	★	★
20	Services	★	★		★			★	★	★	★☆		

Note: ★ = $_L p > 1$;   □ = even dispersion;   ☆ = also $p > 1$.

Table 7-7.   Sectoral Employment Effects Compared Internationally

Sector Num-ber	Title	Total Employment Effect Sector Rank Country Groups A	B	C	Ratio of Indirect/Direct Employment Effect A	B	C
1	Agriculture, forestry, & fishing	1	6, 7	1	0.28	0.62	0.25
2	Mining & quarrying	11	11	9	1.12	0.59	0.51
3	Processed foods	2	10	6	5.75	1.92	5.64
4	Apparel, incl. textiles & footwear	4	2	2	1.39	0.90	1.64
5	Leather & leather products	14	19	10, 11	4.34	1.90	2.00
6	Wood & paper products & printing	6	12	4	1.80	0.68	1.78
7	Rubber products	9	16	7	1.10	1.18	1.51
8	Chemicals	15, 16	17	17	1.81	0.99	2.86
9	Petroleum products	19	20	19, 20	3.35	0.58	11.03
10	Nonmetallic mineral products	10	18	12	0.76	0.74	0.91
11	Basic metals & metal products	17	15	15, 16	1.10	1.06	2.09
12	Nonelectrical machinery	15, 16	8	10, 11	1.24	0.42	1.30
13	Electrical machinery	12	13	5	1.03	0.35	1.27
14	Transport equipment	13	6, 7	13, 14	1.00	0.35	2.01
15	Industry not elsewhere classified	7	4	15, 16	0.99	0.10	4.86
16	Electricity, gas, water	20	5	19, 20	1.13	0.56	2.40
17	Construction	5	9	8	0.91	0.81	1.18
18	Trade	3	3	3	0.12	0.21	0.26
19	Transportation, storage, & communication	18	14	13, 14	0.46	0.45	0.49
20	Services	8	1	18	0.22	0.12	0.57

Note: A = South Korea 1963 and 1966; Philippines 1961 and 1965; Taiwan 1966 and
           1969; Turkey 1963
       B = Israel 1966 and 1969; Yugoslavia 1966
       C = Germany 1966; Japan 1965

Whereas the ratio of indirect to direct employment varies widely from sector to sector, these ratios were shown in addition to the total employment-effect rankings. These quotients give an indication of the extent to which a sector's employment effect is underestimated whenever only direct effects are considered. While the direct effects may be regarded as sufficiently characteristic of the tertiary sectors—as well as the primary sectors in the more advanced countries—, a true grasp of the potential employment effect of most manufacturing sectors is gained only when adequate allowance is made for the induced effects.

For lack of employment data, the wages and salaries ranking might be assumed to approximate that of employment. In order to obtain some statistical evidence as to whether this would be a justified supposition, the ranking of sectors was checked for similarity in countries having data for wages and salaries as well as for the number of persons employed. The test for rank correlation showed widely dispersed values with a maximum of around $r = 0.60$. Supposedly, this is because the statistical coverage of the two approaches is so different. But even if only wage earners and salaried employees were compiled in the employment category (as with Yugoslavia), the observed correlation is very moderate ($r = 0.23$). Thus, it is not advisable to substitute the one ranking for the other.

Conclusion

The foregoing analysis is an extension of an earlier attempt to assist the determination of priorities for sectoral allocation of resources. On the basis of input-output tables from developing countries the sectors were distinguished according to the degree of their interdependencies. Working with a scheme of 20 standard sectors for all 22 tables analysed, the intensity of interindustrial linkages was taken as an indicator of a sector's basic ability to spread growth impulses to its economic environment. For this purpose, backward and forward linkages of the original Hirschman-Chenery-Watanabe type, as well as some modified versions thereof, were calculated. In addition, spread effects were computed using the inverse matrix in two approaches.

Subsequently, the sectors were classified according to their total (direct and indirect) primary input requirements per unit of final demand. Among the effects analysed are the import dependency, the gross domestic product, and the foreign trade balance. Finally, the analysis has been supplemented by determination of the sectoral employment impact in real terms, that is, by applying absolute figures for the persons engaged sectorwise.

Particularly under the linkage criterion, the obtained rankings were checked for similarity. Although some rankings were highly correlated—and thus would justify resorting to the simpler algorithms—none of the criteria under consideration proved to be superior to all others.

References

1. Benz, C.W. *PASSION* (Program for Algebraic Sequences Specifically of Input-Output Nature). San Francisco: W.H. Freeman & Company, 1971.

2. Ceylon, Ministry of Planning and Economic Affairs, Perspective Planning Division. "Input-Output Table for Ceylon—1965." UNDP Special Fund Planning Project, Colombo, 1969.

3. Chakraverti, A.K. "Input-Output Techniques in National Planning (with Special Reference to India)." *Opsearch* 2, no. 1-2 (1965): 203–230.

4. Chakraverti, A.K.; C. Çinar; and G. Canalp. *Structural Interdependence of the Turkish Economy: 1963.* Istanbul: Prime Ministry, State Planning Organization, 1970.

5. Chen, D. *Input-Output Tables 1968/69*. Special Series, No. 380. Jerusalem: Central Bureau of Statistics, 1972.

6. Chenery, H.B., and T. Watanabe. "International Comparisons of the Structure of Production." *Econometrica* 26, no. 4 (October 1958): 487–521.

7. Chiu, J.S. (Council for International Economic Cooperation and Development). "The Taiwan Economy: An Input-Output Study." *Industry of Free China* 30, no. 5 (November 1968).

8. Hazari, B.R. "Empirical Identification of Key Sectors in the Indian Economy." *The Review of Economics and Statistics* 52, no. 3 (August 1970): 301–305.

9. Hirschman, A.O. *The Strategy of Economic Development*. New Haven: Yale University Press, 1961.

10. Indonesia, LEKNAS/KYODAI. "Input-Output Table of Indonesia, 1969." Djakarta, 1972.

11. International Labour Office. *Yearbook of Labour Statistics*. 31st ed. (32nd). Geneva: International Labour Office, 1971 (1972).

12. Israel, Bank of Israel. "Input-Output Tables for 1965/66." (Computer print-outs, no date.)

13. Japanese Government, Administrative Management Agency and six other ministries. "The 1965 Input-Output Table of Japan." Tokyo: Government of Japan, 1969.

14. Katano, H. In *Economic Bulletin for Asia and the Far East* 28, no. 2 (September 1967): 23–26, Supplement to Table 1.

15. Korea, Bank of Korea (South), Research Department. *Input-Output, Interindustry Relations Tables for 1963*. Seoul: Bank of Korea, 1965.

16. Korea, Bank of Korea (South), Research Department. *Input-Output, Interindustry Relations Tables for 1966*. Seoul: Bank of Korea, 1968.

17. Lehbert, B. "Bedeutung und Auswertung regionaler Input-Output Tabellen" [Significance and Evaluation of Regional Input-Output Tables]. *Kieler Studien*, no. 105 (1970).

18. Malaysia (West), Department of Statistics. "Malaysia Barat Kira2 Perusahaan Perantaraan 1965" [West Malaysia Inter-Industry Accounts, 1965]. Kuala Lumpur (no date).

19. Mathur, P.N., et al. "Input-Output Flow Table (32X32), 1963 (at Purchaser's Prices)." *Artha Vijnana* 11, no. 2 (June 1969): 181–199.

20. Perera, D. "A Preliminary Input-Output Table for Ceylon 1963." *Central Bank of Ceylon Bulletin*, July 1967, pp. 17–34 plus Appendix.

21. Philippines, Department of Commerce and Industry, Bureau of the Census and Statistics. "Input-Output Analysis of the Philippine Economy, 1961." *Journal of Philippine Statistics* 19, no. 1 (January-March 1968): VII–XLI.

22. Philippines, Department of Commerce and Industry, Bureau of the Census and Statistics. *The 1965 Inter-Industry Relations Study of the Philippine Economy*. National Economic Council Workshop Series, Paper No. 71-2. University of the Philippines, School of Economics, Manila, 1971.

23. Rasmussen, P.N. *Studies in Inter-Sectoral Relations*. Amsterdam: North-Holland Publishing Company, 1956.

24. Rasul, G. *Input-Output Relationships in Pakistan, 1954*. Rotterdam: Rotterdam University Press, 1964.

25. Rasul, G. "A Summary of Input-Output Studies of the Economy of Pakistan." *Pakistan Development Review* 5, no. 3 (Autumn 1965): 408–460.

26. Saluja, M.R. "Structure of Indian Economy: Inter-Industry Flows and Pattern of Final Demands 1964–65." *Sankhyā* 30, ser. B, Pts. 1 & 2 (June 1968): 97–122.

27. Schultz, S. "Intersektoraler Strukturvergleich zur Ermittlung von Schlüsselsektoren" [Intersectoral Structural Comparison for Determining Key Sectors]. *DIW-Beiträge zur Strukturforschung,* no. 30 (1974).

28. Schultz, S. "Quantitative Criteria for the Determination of Sectoral Priorities." *Asian Economies,* no. 5 (1973): 27–54.

29. Şenel, Ş. *Aufstellung einer Input-Output-Tabelle und Input-Output Analyse für die Türkei* [Compilation of an Input-Output Table and Input-Output Analysis for Turkey]. Dissertation, University of Bonn, 1971.

30. Shaheen, A.S. "1965 Input-Output Table for Iranian Economy." (No place, no date.)

31. Stäglin, R., and H. Wessels. "Input-Output Tabelle für die Bundesrepublik Deutschland 1966" [Input-Output Table for the Federal Republic of Germany, 1966]. *Vierteljahrshefte zur Wirtschaftsforschung des DIW* no. 3 (1971): 215–220.

32. Strassert, G. "Zur Bestimmung strategischer Sektoren mit Hilfe von Input-Output-Modellen" [The Determination of Strategic Sectors Using Input-Output Models]. *Jahrbücher für Nationalökonomie und Statistik* 182, no. 3 (1968): 211–215.

33. Taiwan, Council for International Economic Cooperation and Development. "Taiwan's Interindustry Transactions Table for 1966." Taipei, 1969.

34. Taiwan, Council for International Economic Cooperation and Development. "Taiwan's Interindustry Transactions Table for 1969." Taipei, 1972.

35. Thoburn, J.T. "Exports and the Malaysian Engineering Industry: A Case Study of Backward Linkage." *Oxford Bulletin of Economics and Statistics* 35, no. 2 (1973): 91–117.

36. Tims, W. *Analytical Techniques for Development Planning.* Karachi: Pakistan Institute of Development Economics, 1968.

37. United Nations, Economic Commission for Asia and the Far East. *Statistical Yearbook for Asia and the Far East,* 1970 (1971). Bangkok: United Nations, 1971 (1972).

38. United Nations, Statistical Office. *The Growth of World Industry.* Vol. I, *General Industrial Statistics,* 1968 (1969, 1970). New York: United Nations, 1970 (1971, 1972).

39. Yotopoulos, P.A., and J.B. Nugent. "A Balanced-Growth Version of the Linkage Hypothesis: A Test." *Quarterly Journal of Economics* 87, no. 2 (May 1973): 157–171.

40. Yugoslavia, Savezni Zavod za Statistiku [Federal Institute of Statistics]. *Medusobni Odnosi Privrednih Delatnosti Jugoslavije u 1966* [The Interrelations Among Economic Activities in Yugoslavia in 1966]. Beograd: Government of Yugoslavia, 1969.

Appendix 7A

Definitions

Within the open static Leontief model,

$x_{\cdot j}$ = intermediate input of sector j

x_j = total input of sector j

$x_{i\cdot}$ = intermediate demand for products of sector i

x_i = total demand for products of sector i

$$x_{\cdot\cdot} = \sum_{i=1}^{n} \sum_{j=1}^{n} x_{ij}$$

$$\sum_{i=1}^{n} x_i = \sum_{j=1}^{n} x_j = x$$

$$\sum_{i=1}^{n} m_i = m \quad (m_i = \text{import of products of sector } i)$$

$$m + x = z$$

INDICATORS u AND w, DIFFERENT VERSIONS

$$u_a = \frac{x_{\cdot j}}{x_j} \qquad w_a = \frac{x_{i\cdot}}{x_i} \qquad w_a^z = \frac{x_{i\cdot}}{x_i + |m_i|}$$

$$u_b = u_a x_{\cdot j} \qquad w_b = w_a x_{i\cdot} \qquad w_b^z = w_a^z x_{i\cdot}$$

$$u_c = u_a \frac{x_j}{x} \qquad w_c = w_a \frac{x_i}{x} \qquad w_c^z = w_a^z \frac{x_i}{x}$$

$$u_d = \frac{x_{\cdot j} - x_{jj}}{x_j} \qquad w_d = \frac{x_{i \cdot} - x_{ii}}{x_i} \qquad w_d^z = \frac{x_{i \cdot} - x_{ii}}{x_i + |m_i|}$$

$$u_e = u_d x_{\cdot j} \qquad w_e = w_d x_{i \cdot} \qquad w_e^z = w_d^z x_{i \cdot}$$

$$u_f = u_d \frac{x_j}{x} \qquad w_f = w_d \frac{x_i}{x} \qquad w_f^z = w_d^z \frac{x_i}{x}$$

$$u^* = w^* = \frac{x_{\cdot \cdot}}{x}$$

respectively

$$w^{z*} = \frac{x_{\cdot \cdot}}{x + |m|}$$

INDICATORS *p* AND *v*

$$\sum_{i=1}^{n} r_{ij} = r_{\cdot j} \qquad \text{column total of the inverse matrix}$$

$$p_{\cdot j} = \frac{(1/n) \sum_{i=1}^{n} r_{ij}}{(1/n^2) \sum_{i=1}^{n} \sum_{j=1}^{n} r_{ij}} = \frac{n r_{\cdot j}}{r_{\cdot \cdot}} \qquad (j = 1, 2, \ldots, n)$$

$$v_{\cdot j} = \frac{\sqrt{[1/(n-1)] \sum_{i=1}^{n} \left[r_{ij} - (1/n) r_{\cdot j} \right]^2}}{(1/n) r_{\cdot j}} \qquad (j = 1, 2, \ldots, n)$$

INDICATOR s

$$s_e = \frac{\displaystyle\sum_{i=1}^{m} x_i - \sum_{i=1}^{e-1} x^*_{(e)i} - \sum_{i=e+1}^{m} x^*_{(e)i} - x_e}{x_e - y_e} = \frac{\displaystyle\sum_{\substack{i=1 \\ i \neq e}}^{m} (x_i - x^*_{(e)i})}{x_e - y_e}$$

$$(e = 1, 2, \ldots, m)$$

where

$x^*_{(e)i}$ is an element of a vector defined as

$$X^*_{(e)} = R^*_{(e)} Y^*_{(e)}$$

and

x_i = gross production of sector i

$R^*_{(e)}$ = inverse of the reduced matrix after elimination of column and row of the extracted sector

$Y^*_{(e)}$ = final demand vector as shortened by omission of the extracted sector

x_e = gross production of the extracted sector

y_e = final demand of the extracted sector

Chapter Eight

Redistribution of Income, Patterns of Consumption, and Employment: A Case Study for the Philippines

Felix Paukert
Jiri Skolka
Jef Maton

This paper contains the first results of an empirical investigation of the links between changes in income distribution and changes in employment. The investigation was carried out with the help of a simple input-output simulation model, using statistical data for the Philippines.

In our model, the changes in employment caused by changes in income distribution are channeled mainly through the private-consumption pattern.[1] The first stage of this link, the relation between income distribution and the level of consumption, has of course been known for a long time. It received particular attention in the late 1940s and 1950s, beginning with Lubell's study of effects of income redistribution on consumers' expenditures [12] and continuing with studies by Johnson [11]; Conrad [4]; and Bronfenbrenner, Yamane, and Lee [1]; among others. Studies of the relation between income distribution and consumption can be traced back not only to Keynesian predecessors such as Malthus, Lauderdale, and Hobson, but much further. Bronfenbrenner, Yamane, and Lee go back to 1728, when Mandeville's Fable of the Bees was published, and Johnson reaches back another hundred years to the French Physiocrat Boisguillebert, who argued that trade would be more active if taxation fell on the rich than if it fell on the poor.

The study on which this paper is based is being undertaken within the framework of the Research Programme on Income Distribution and Employment of the World Employment Programme. The views expressed in the paper are not necessarily those of the International Labour Office. The authors wish to acknowledge, with thanks, Michel Garzuel's assistance with computations.

1. The earliest version of the model was described by Paukert and Skolka [15]. We are obliged for critical comments on that version to a number of people, and in particular to Erik Thorbecke and Graham Pyatt, neither of whom, however, bears any responsibility for the subsequent changes in the model or for its application to the Philippines.

At the time of our formulation of the model, we were aware only of the earlier version described by Cline [3]. Since then, however, a number of studies of growth and employment effects of income redistribution have appeared, although none of them has as yet been published. For best, although incomplete, surveys of this "underground" literature, see Morawetz [14] and Cline [2].

The post-Keynesian examinations of the distribution–consumption relationship had a number of features in common. All were concerned with industrialised countries (where the Keynesian theory can be applied) and all examined the effects of progressive income redistribution on aggregate consumption. Progressive income redistribution transfers income from those with a high propensity to save to those with a high propensity to consume and thus increases aggregate consumption and—given the Keynesian framework—total output.

In studies of developing countries, the same argument was used against progressive redistribution of income, in view of the importance of savings and capital formation for growth in economies facing the savings gap. But in recent years, a new aspect of the relation has been discovered in the *pattern* of private consumption, through which changes in income distribution are reflected in employment. Perhaps the clearest formulation of this mechanism was contained in the International Labour Office (ILO) mission report on Colombia:

> The main way in which income distribution affects the level of employment in Colombia is through its effect on the pattern of consumption. This works in two ways: the first is through the different import content of the expenditures of the rich and the poor; the second is through the different direct labour content of those expenditures.
>
> The relation between the first element and the level of employment can be explained as follows. If we assume that the tendency to consume imported products is higher among the rich than among the poor, [Note: Strictly, we are talking about the *marginal* propensity to consume imported goods.] then the greater the degree of inequality in income distribution, the higher the demand for foreign goods and less foreign exchange is left for the capital goods and intermediate products needed to expand employment. [9, p. 145]

This description of the mechanism by which income redistribution influences employment is accepted by many writers on the subject. There are a few, however, who argue that higher income groups with demand for personal services and for elaborate handicrafts products have a more labour-intensive production pattern than do lower income groups (see Strassmann [17]).

The purpose of the model used in our study was to provide a framework for empirical testing of the impact of three effects (which might be called the "savings," "factor intensity," and "import substitution" effects) that translate the change in income distribution into a change of both volume and pattern of private consumption and thereafter into a change of employment. There is no general agreement about the most appropriate form of the savings function in developing countries, but the empirical evidence shows that the propensity to save is greater in the higher income brackets than in the lower ones, where negative savings are often reported in household budget studies. We also assume, mainly because of lack of empirical evidence, that there is no divergence between private savings and private investment.

Redistribution of income can be defined in a number of different ways. In the first version of the model described in this paper, we simply assume that an amount is taken from the richer classes and given to the poorer classes by a certain mechanism (for example, income taxes and transfer payments). This shift affects the pattern and level of private consumption.

Changes in other final uses (that is, final uses except private consumption) are not considered in the model. Also, fixed prices and wage rates are assumed, but changes in the total volume of production and the corresponding volume of total income are allowed. The total impact on employment is calculated not only as a sum of the savings, import substitution, and factor intensity effects, but also as the feedback effect of resulting changes in total output. The structure of the simplest version of the model, which has already been applied and which provided results that are described later on, can be briefly described here as follows: First, a certain *stipulated* income distribution by size (that is, by deciles of the total number of families), different from the actual distribution, is defined. In the next step we calculate the effect of the stipulated income redistribution on the volume and pattern of private consumption, on the direct imports for private consumption, and on savings. Finally, we calculate, for the new private consumption, the corresponding pattern and volume of gross output, of gross value added, personal income, intermediate imports, employment, savings, and capital stock (estimated from incremental capital–output ratios), with the help of an extended semiclosed input-output model. We use a system of exclusively linear homogeneous equations and obtain a solution by a simple matrix inversion operation.

The exercise is a *static comparative simulation* of alternative hypothetical equilibrium states of the economy, corresponding to different assumptions about income distribution by size of income recipient unit (hereafter referred to simply as income distribution by size). The model shows what the equilibrium state of the economy would look like under alternative income distribution patterns, concentrating primarily on the impact of the income redistribution on the level of employment.

The whole exercise is obviously carried out under certain assumptions, which should be kept in mind when interpreting the results. The most important assumptions (some of which will be more precisely described later on in the paper) are the following: Leontief's linear homogeneous production functions, free labour force resources and no capacity limitations, no economies of scale and constant returns to scale, constant volumes of final uses other than private consumption, and no balance-of-payments limitations. To this static and Keynesian analysis based on the Leontief model, we add a simple dynamic analysis of the consequences of the changes in the level of savings.

The structure of the model is summarized by Figure 8–1.

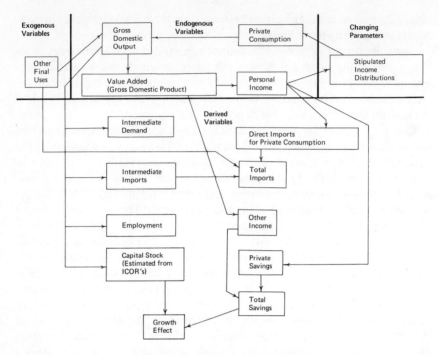

Figure 8-1. Structure of the Model.

Description of the Model

The main purpose of the model is to study the impact of changes in income distribution on the level of employment. These changes are assumed to provoke changes in the level and pattern of domestic output, imports (both final and intermediate), private consumption, private savings, personal income, and other income (corporate savings and government revenues). In this network of inter-related changes, the shift in the income distribution by size is the only exogenous element; all other changes are endogenous.

Income Distribution by Size

In analysing the effects of income redistribution, we assume that the total number of income recipients (households), h, can be divided into u income groups of size h_k ($k = 1, 2, \ldots, u$). The share of each income group in the total number of income recipients is defined as

$$g_k = \frac{h_k}{h} \quad (k = 1, 2, \ldots, u) \tag{8-1}$$

In the model, we divide the households into ten decile groups, so that $g_k = 0.1$ for all k's.[2]

The total personal income y can then be divided into income by income groups, y_k. The share of each income group in total income is then defined as

$$\lambda_k = \frac{y_k}{y} \qquad (k = 1, 2, \ldots, u) \tag{8-2}$$

The average income per one recipient unit (household) is equal to

$$\bar{y} = \frac{y}{h} \tag{8-3a}$$

and the average income per household in the income group k is equal to

$$\bar{y}_k = \frac{y_k}{h_k} \qquad (k = 1, 2, \ldots, u) \tag{8-3b}$$

The values of λ_k can be written as elements of a u-dimensional vector Λ.

In the model, we define the stipulated (desired) income distribution as a new vector Λ^*, different from Λ. The income in each income group is then equal to

$$y_k^* = y\Lambda_k^* \qquad (k = 1, 2, \ldots, u) \tag{8-4}$$

This definition of income redistribution is simple and flexible. It does not explain the mechanism of income redistribution. It allows us, however, to assume many alternative ways of redistributing income.

We use two aggregate measures of the equality of income distribution, which allow us to compare various stipulated income distributions and to rank them according to the degree of income equality. One measure is the traditional Gini coefficient, the other one is Shannon's entropy measure.

When all the h_k are equal, the Gini coefficient is defined as

$$G_1 = 1 - \tfrac{1}{2}h_k \sum_{k=1}^{u} f_k \tag{8-5a}$$

2. In another version of the model, we intend to assume income groups with unequal size of income recipient units, defined by income brackets.

where

$$f_k = \sum_{\kappa=1}^{k} \lambda_\kappa \qquad (k = 1, 2, \ldots, u; \kappa = 1, 2, \ldots, u) \qquad \text{(8-5b)}$$

The entropy measure is equal to

$$G_2 = -\lambda_k \sum_{k=1}^{u} \log \lambda_k \qquad \text{(8-6)}$$

Consumption and Savings Functions

The choice of the consumption and savings functions was not an easy one. In the model, we wanted to obtain the solution by a single matrix inversion. In order to avoid adjustment problems, we also wanted the consumption functions to fulfil the additivity condition. And the shift in the income distribution had to lead to a change in the pattern of the total private consumption and the level of total private savings (since we assumed a Keynesian savings function). Unfortunately, there is no type of consumption function that would fulfil all these three conditions simultaneously. We have therefore accepted the following solution.

We assume that the share of expenditures on private consumption of a certain commodity $(i = 1, 2, \ldots, n)$ in the total income of a certain income group, y_k, remains constant and define this share as

$$c_{ik} = \frac{e_{ik}}{y_k} \qquad (k = 1, 2, \ldots, u; i = 1, 2, \ldots, n) \qquad \text{(8-7a)}$$

where e_{ik} is the expenditures on private consumption of commodity i by income group k. In equation (8-7a), we consider the private consumption of domestically produced commodity i only. We could define analogous consumption functions for the private consumption of each directly imported commodity i, but, mainly because of lack of data, we use only one aggregate consumption function for imports:

$$c_{mk} = \frac{e_{mk}}{y_k} \qquad (k = 1, 2, \ldots, u) \qquad \text{(8-7b)}$$

where e_{mk} are direct imports for private consumption by income group k.

The definition of the savings function is then

$$c_{sk} = \frac{s_k}{y_k} \qquad (k = 1, 2, \ldots, u) \tag{8-8}$$

where s_k are private savings of income group k.

Since we assume that total expenditures on private consumption plus private savings in each income group is equal to total income of the same group, that is, that

$$\sum_{i=1}^{n} e_{ik} + e_{mk} + s_k = y_k \qquad (k = 1, 2, \ldots, u) \tag{8-9a}$$

It follows that

$$\sum_{i=1}^{n} c_{ik} + c_{mk} + c_{sk} = 1 \qquad (k = 1, 2, \ldots, u) \tag{8-9b}$$

It is then assumed that the values of the coefficients c_{ik}, c_{mk}, and c_{sk} remain constant. They can be written as elements of a matrix giving the private domestic consumption pattern:

$$C = [c_{ik}] \tag{8-10a}$$

of a row vector of the private consumption pattern of imported goods:

$$C'_m = [c_{mk}] \tag{8-10b}$$

and of a row vector of the private savings pattern:

$$C'_s = [c_{sk}] \tag{8-10c}$$

Input-Output Core of the Model

We use the type of input-output table that contains in the first (intermediate deliveries) and second (final uses) quadrants flows of domestically produced goods only. At the bottom of both quadrants there is a row of imported inter-mediate inputs by industries and by components of final uses.

In our model, however, the standard input-output framework has been slightly modified. Final uses have been aggregated into private consumption and other final uses (the former includes government expenditures, fixed capital formation, changes in stocks, and exports). The vector of other final uses is then constant and exogenous. Private consumption, on the contrary, is disaggregated by ten income groups and is endogenous. Changes have also been made in the breakdown of value added. Instead of the usual breakdown into wages and salaries and other final uses, the sum of both items was disaggregated into personal income, corporate savings, and direct corporate taxes.

In order to be able to study the effect of the income redistribution on employment as well as its likely consequences for economic growth, the standard input-output framework was extended by data on employment and information on the incremental capital–output ratios (ICORs).

From the extended input-output table, the following coefficients can be calculated:

INPUT COEFFICIENTS FOR DOMESTICALLY
PRODUCED INTERMEDIATE INPUTS

$$a_{ij} = \frac{x_{ij}}{x_j} \qquad (i, j = 1, 2, \ldots, n) \tag{8-11}$$

where

x_{ij} = intermediate deliveries of domestic output of industry i to industry j

x_j = gross output of industry j

n = number of industries in the input-output table

These coefficients are elements of a square matrix, A, of order $n \times n$.

INPUT COEFFICIENTS FOR INTERMEDIATE IMPORTS

$$a_{mj} = \frac{m_j}{x_j} \qquad (j = 1, 2, \ldots, n) \tag{8-12}$$

where m_j is intermediate imports by industry j. These coefficients are elements of an n-dimensional row vector, A_m.

GROSS VALUE ADDED COEFFICIENTS

$$a_{vj} = \frac{w_{vj}}{x_j} \qquad (j = 1, 2, \ldots, n; \quad v = 1, 2, \ldots, t) \tag{8-13}$$

where

w_{vj} = component v of value added in industry j

t = number of value added components

These coefficients can be written as elements of a rectangular matrix of order $t \times n$ of value added coefficients, A_v.

EMPLOYMENT COEFFICIENTS

$$a_{L,j} = \frac{L_j}{x_j} \qquad (j = 1, 2, \ldots, n) \tag{8-14}$$

where L_j is employment in industry j. These coefficients are elements of an n-dimensional row vector of employment coefficients, A.

In addition to these coefficients, we use a row vector of exogenously determined ICORs, R, where r_j is the ICOR in industry j.

Formulation of the Model

From the elements already defined, we can assemble the simulation model, which can be written as

$$B \cdot Z = D \tag{8-15}$$

where

B = a square matrix of model parameters or structural coefficients

Z = a column vector of the endogenous variables

D = a column vector of the exogenous variables

The solution is obvious:

$$Z = B^{-1}D \tag{8-16}$$

The meaning of particular components of the model is as follows:

Matrix of Model Parameters B: The matrix of model parameters contains the already defined matrices and vectors of various coefficients arranged in the following way:

$$
B = \begin{bmatrix}
I - A & 0 & -C & 0 \\
-A'_m & & -C'_m & \\
0 & I & -C'_s & 0 \\
-A_v & & 0 & \\
0 & 0 \quad -\Lambda^* & I & 0 \\
-A'_L & & & \\
-R' & 0 & 0 & I
\end{bmatrix}
\qquad (8\text{-}17)
$$

The size of this partitioned square matrix is as follows:

n rows corresponding to the number of industries in the input-output table

1 row of intermediate import coefficients

t rows[3] corresponding to the value added components[4]

1 row of private savings coefficients

k rows corresponding to the number of income groups (that is, 10)

1 row of employment

1 row of ICORs

The total number of rows (and columns as well) is then $n + t + k + 4$. Matrix B also contains identity or zero matrices and vectors. All elements on the main diagonal are positive and in most cases equal to one; all nonzero elements are negative and (with the exception of the employment coefficients and the ICORs) smaller than one. One can therefore expect that matrix B must have an inverse.

3. In the operational model, we added one row with data on the share of gross value added in gross output value (value added coefficients) in order to obtain in the solution the total value added corresponding to each stipulated income distribution pattern. The size of the B matrix is therefore increased by one column and one row.

4. It is important to know that the last row must always contain data on personal income, which are then linked with the column vector Λ^* (stipulated income distribution) through the unit scalar on the main diagonal.

All coefficients of matrix B are kept constant with the sole exception of the elements of the vector Λ^*, that is, the income distribution pattern by size. In each step of the simulation, the stipulated values of the elements of the vector Λ^* are set into matrix B; matrix B is inverted; and the results are multiplied by the constant vector D in order to obtain the vector of the solution Z.

Column Vector of Solution Z: The elements of column vector Z correspond to the row pattern of matrix B and include the following data:

n values of gross (domestic) output by industries

1 value of total intermediate imports and direct imports for private consumption

t values of value added components

1 value of private savings

k values of personal income by income groups (that is, 10)

1 value of total employment

1 value of capital stock estimated from ICORs

The total number of rows (and columns as well) is then $n + t + k + 4$.

Column Vector of Exogenous Variables D: The elements of this vector are the actual values of the other final uses (that is, of government expenditures, gross capital formation, changes in stocks, and exports). The values of D are kept constant.

Application of the Model for the Philippines

One of the very few developing countries for which all data required by our model are available is the Philippines. Moreover, with only one exception (household expenditures by income groups), all required data sets are available for the same year, 1965. Unfortunately, they are not mutually consistent. In the two available input-output tables (which are both for 1965), differences occur in what should presumably be identical estimates of national income and product statistics. The overall consistency, however, is one of the main features of the input-output models, and we could not avoid adjustments of these data sets by inflating or deflating them while keeping their structures intact.

Data Sources
We used the following main data sources:
Input-output tables: For 1965, two different input-output tables for the

Philippines were compiled and published, one by the National Economic Council (NEC) [6],[5] the other by the Bureau of Census and Statistics (BCS) [13]. These two independent estimates of interindustry flows differ substantially. Since the values of the principal economic aggregates in the NEC table are closer to the national accounts data, we decided to use the NEC table as the principal data framework. The table was aggregated into 64 industries, and unallocated flows were removed. The NEC table, however, does not contain the import matrix. This matrix was taken from the BCS table and adjusted to the NEC data.

The combination of the two input-output tables provided data on the pattern of intermediate flows (both domestic and imported), values of the (exogenous) other final demand, and values of total private consumption by industries. The breakdown of value added and the breakdown of private consumption by income groups were taken from other sources.

National accounts: The data of value added in the input-output tables were incompatible with the personal income and employment data. The national accounts, therefore, were used to obtain the total depreciation, indirect taxes, corporate savings, corporate income taxes, and private savings [8]. The personal income was then determined as the difference between the gross value added and the sum of the above-mentioned value added components.

Family income and expenditure statistics: Data on private consumption patterns by income groups were available only for 1971 [7]. They were first aggregated from the original 455 items into the 64-industry breakdown. Their values were then adjusted to sum to the total private consumption value given in the 1965 NEC input-output table and to the 1965 personal income distribution pattern [5]. The consumption items were also adjusted from purchasers' prices to producers' prices and separated into private consumption of domestically produced goods (by 64 industries) and direct imports for private consumption. This procedure could obviously yield only approximate estimates of the consumption pattern by income groups.

A combination of the private consumption data and data from the national accounts provided us with estimates of private savings by income deciles.

Employment statistics: The benchmark for the estimation of employment was the 1965 labour force survey. Various statistical sources were used to break down the labour force data to the industrial level. Industrial labour force data were then adjusted for unused manhours on the basis of the average number of hours worked per year as revealed by the 1971 census. A full workload was defined as 2400 hours per year (50 weeks at 48 hours per week), and unemploy-

5. This publication contains only an aggregated version with 51 industries. We had access, however, to the original table with the breakdown into 194 industries.

ment or unused manpower was determined as the difference between this norm and the actual number of hours worked. The employment vector thus refers to man-years worked.

Capital-output ratios: The capital-output ratios used are ICORs for industries. They are based on project analyses carried out by the Philippine Board of Investments.

Simulation of Income Redistribution

The purpose of the calculations was to determine the effect of changes in the income distribution on employment level and on other indicators of the level and pattern of economic activities. Various stipulated income distributions by size were considered, some corresponding to actual income distributions in certain countries, some purely hypothetical.

Table 8-1 contains the information on 23 stipulated income distributions for which the calculations have been carried out. These are ranked by the values of the Gini coefficients, proceeding from the most uneven income distribution to the most egalitarian one.

Some of the stipulated alternatives have specific meanings. Alternative 1 reflects the existing income distribution in 1965 and thus provides the "basic solution" of the model. Alternative 2, however, reflects income distribution of even greater inequality than the actual 1965 and 1971 distributions in the Philippines. Alternative 3 reflects the 1971 income distribution. Alternative 4 applies to the 1965 income distribution, but a floor of 1000 pesos is introduced, which results in increasing the share of the lowest two deciles at the expense of the share of the highest decile.

Two alternatives reflect the income distribution situation in two Pacific countries on a higher level of economic development: Alternative 5 simulates the distribution in Japan in 1962 [10] and alternative 17 the distribution in Australia in 1966-67 [16]. There are four alternatives (5, 9, 13, and 23) based on a proposal by Lubell [12], which consists of a reduction by a given percentage of the range between the arithmetic average of each decile and the arithmetic average of total population. Our alternative 5 reduces the range by 10 percent, alternative 9 by 20 percent, alternative 13 by 30 percent, and alternative 23 by 50 percent.

The remaining alternatives (6-8; 10-12; 14-22) are arbitrary and are designed to provide information about different degrees of inequality between the basic 1965 position in alternative 1 and the most radical redistribution (Lubell's 50 percent) in alternative 23.

Results of Calculations

The results of the income redistribution will now be summarized in terms of gross national product, employment, and personal income; foreign trade; savings; and economic growth.

Table 8-1.   Stipulated Alternatives of Income Distribution (in percentages)

Alternative	Shares of Deciles on Total Personal Income										Gini Coefficient	Entropy Measure
	1	2	3	4	5	6	7	8	9	10		
1	1.15	2.05	3.60	4.20	6.80	7.20	8.90	11.30	14.20	40.60	0.493	0.808
2	2.00	2.40	2.90	3.50	4.20	5.05	6.06	7.30	8.80	57.79	0.577	0.679
3	1.28	2.45	3.47	5.00	5.60	7.30	9.70	12.00	17.20	36.00	0.474	0.832
4	2.63	2.63	3.60	4.20	6.80	7.20	8.90	11.30	14.20	38.54	0.457	0.835
5	2.03	2.85	4.24	4.78	7.12	7.48	9.01	11.17	13.78	37.54	0.444	0.845
6	2.00	2.50	4.00	5.00	7.00	9.00	11.00	13.00	17.00	29.50	0.414	0.878
7	1.50	2.50	4.00	5.00	8.00	9.00	11.00	14.00	16.00	29.00	0.411	0.878
8	1.40	3.30	4.70	5.90	7.20	8.60	10.30	12.60	16.20	29.80	0.400	0.883
9	2.92	3.64	4.88	5.36	7.44	7.76	9.12	11.04	13.36	34.48	0.394	0.876
10	1.50	2.50	4.00	5.00	8.00	10.00	12.00	15.00	18.00	24.00	0.389	0.893
11	2.00	3.00	4.50	5.50	8.50	9.50	11.00	13.00	15.00	28.00	0.378	0.897
12	3.00	3.50	4.50	5.50	7.50	9.00	11.00	13.00	16.00	27.00	0.364	0.907
13	3.81	4.43	5.52	5.94	7.76	8.04	9.23	10.91	12.94	31.42	0.345	0.904
14	3.00	3.50	4.50	5.50	7.50	10.00	12.00	14.00	18.00	22.00	0.342	0.920
15	3.00	4.00	5.00	6.00	8.00	10.00	11.00	13.00	14.00	26.00	0.334	0.920
16	3.00	4.00	5.00	6.00	7.50	10.00	12.00	14.00	17.50	21.00	0.322	0.929
17	2.13	4.44	6.16	7.28	8.32	9.48	10.86	12.52	15.05	23.76	0.313	0.930
18	3.00	4.00	5.00	6.00	8.00	11.00	13.00	15.00	17.00	18.00	0.300	0.937
19	1.82	3.64	5.46	7.28	9.10	10.92	12.74	14.56	16.38	18.10	0.299	0.934
20	2.50	3.80	5.10	6.40	7.70	12.30	13.60	14.90	16.20	17.50	0.297	0.936
21	3.00	4.00	5.00	7.00	9.00	11.00	12.00	14.00	15.00	20.00	0.292	0.940
22	3.00	4.00	5.00	7.50	9.50	11.50	12.50	14.00	16.00	17.00	0.272	0.947
23	5.57	6.03	6.80	7.10	8.40	8.60	9.45	10.65	12.10	25.30	0.247	0.949

Table 8-2. Consequences of Stipulated Alternatives of Income Distribution, Ratios (1965 = 1.0)

Income Distribution Alternative	Employment	GDP	Personal Income	Private Savings	Imports
1	1.0000	1.0000	1.0000	1.0000	1.0000
2	0.9353	0.9563	0.9558	1.1602	0.9670
3	1.0145	1.0096	1.0098	0.9647	1.0073
4	1.0141	1.0088	1.0091	0.9715	1.0059
5	1.0217	1.0140	1.0143	0.9535	1.0096
6	1.0515	1.0342	1.0347	0.8790	1.0249
7	1.0552	1.0368	1.0373	0.8696	1.0267
8	1.0552	1.0365	1.0371	0.8721	1.0264
9	1.0441	1.0284	1.0290	0.9057	1.0195
10	1.0754	1.0504	1.0511	0.8197	1.0370
11	1.0691	1.0458	1.0465	0.8400	1.0329
12	1.0734	1.0481	1.0490	0.8334	1.0344
13	1.0671	1.0432	1.0442	0.8564	1.0297
14	1.0940	1.0621	1.0631	0.7825	1.0449
15	1.0882	1.0579	1.0589	0.8013	1.0409
16	1.1035	1.0682	1.0693	0.7625	1.0490
17	1.1009	1.0663	1.0675	0.7711	1.0472
18	1.1213	1.0801	1.0815	0.7203	1.0575
19	1.1237	1.0821	1.0833	0.7120	1.0592
20	1.1265	1.0839	1.0852	0.7066	1.0603
21	1.1203	1.0793	1.0807	0.7244	1.0568
22	1.1361	1.0900	1.0915	0.6857	1.0648
23	1.1152	1.0742	1.0759	0.7535	1.0511

Gross Domestic Product, Employment, and Personal Income: The most important results are presented in Tables 8-2 and 8-3. Income redistribution leads to simultaneous increases in employment, in the gross domestic product, and in personal income. The degrees of change of these three indicators are not identical, however.

The largest increase can be observed in the employment level (see Figure 8-2); the smallest in the level of personal income. The shift in the consumption patterns caused by income redistribution leads to increased demand for production of industries that are more labour intensive. As a consequence, both the gross domestic product (GDP) per employed person and the personal income per employed person decrease with more equal distributions.

Foreign Trade: The exports, which are part of other final uses, are kept constant in the model, and because of the increase in the level of the GDP, their share in the GDP is decreasing. The assumption of a constant level of exports is not so unrealistic as it seems at first glance. The model contains the assumption of no capacity constraints. In reality, the increase in the domestic private consumption caused by income redistribution may lead, in some cases, to a decrease in exports because of capacity constraints, and in other cases, to construction of

Table 8-3.   Consequences of Stipulated Alternatives of Income Distribution, Values and Shares (absolute values in pesos)

Income Distribution Alternative	GDP per Employed Person	Personal Income per Employed Person	Share of Personal Income in GDP	Share of Private Savings in Personal Income	Share of Imports in Value Added	Share of Exports in Value Added
1	2691	2234	0.8300	0.1047	0.2156	0.1893
2	2751	2283	0.8296	0.1271	0.2181	0.2070
3	2678	2223	0.8301	0.1001	0.2152	0.1857
4	2677	2223	0.8302	0.1008	0.2150	0.1860
5	2671	2218	0.8302	0.0985	0.2147	0.1841
6	2647	2198	0.8304	0.0890	0.2137	0.1769
7	2644	2196	0.8304	0.0878	0.2136	0.1761
8	2643	2195	0.8305	0.0881	0.2135	0.1762
9	2651	2202	0.8305	0.0922	0.2138	0.1790
10	2629	2183	0.8306	0.0817	0.2129	0.1716
11	2632	2187	0.8306	0.0841	0.2130	0.1731
12	2628	2183	0.8307	0.0832	0.2128	0.1723
13	2631	2186	0.8308	0.0859	0.2129	0.1740
14	2613	2171	0.8308	0.0771	0.2122	0.1678
15	2616	2174	0.8309	0.0793	0.2122	0.1691
16	2605	2165	0.8309	0.0747	0.2118	0.1659
17	2607	2166	0.8310	0.0757	0.2118	0.1665
18	2592	2154	0.8311	0.0698	0.2111	0.1622
19	2592	2154	0.8310	0.0688	0.2111	0.1616
20	2689	2152	0.8311	0.0682	0.2110	0.1612
21	2593	2155	0.8311	0.0702	0.2111	0.1625
22	2582	2148	0.8312	0.0658	0.2107	0.1594
23	2592	2156	0.8313	0.0734	0.2110	0.1640

new factories, which may export part of their production (to benefit from the economies of scale).

The results obtained for imports are rather interesting. The volume of imports increases as a consequence of income redistribution, but this increase is less pronounced than the increase in the level of the GDP, so that the ratio of imports in the GDP decreases. The deterioration of the balance of trade is therefore rather small. For this reason, we can assume that income redistribution would cause no serious balance-of-payments problems.

Savings: The data on savings are presented in Table 8-4. In 1965 (alternative 1), private savings amounted to 1943 million pesos. We can assume that in addition to private savings, the depreciation of 1658 million pesos and corporate savings of 415 million pesos were used for investment financing. The total investment resources (or total savings) thus amounted to 4016 million pesos. According to the 1965 NEC input-output table, the value of gross fixed capital formation was 4045 million pesos. Total savings and gross fixed capital formation were thus roughly in balance.

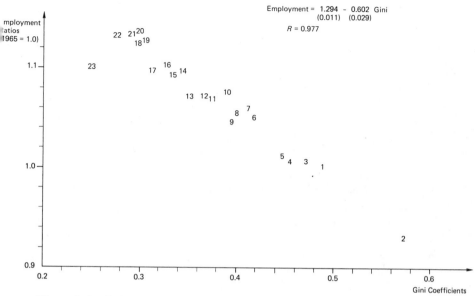

Figure 8-2. Relation Between Changes in Income Distribution and Employment.

Table 8-4. Resources for Investment Financing (million pesos)

Income Distribution Alternative	Private Savings	Depreciation	Corporate Savings	Increase or Decrease in Indirect Taxes	Increase or Decrease in Corporate Direct Taxes	Total Resources
1	1943	1658	415	−	−	4016
2	2249	1592	397	−71	−9	4158
3	1870	1666	418	+16	+2	3972
4	1883	1664	417	+13	+2	3979
5	1848	1671	419	+21	+3	3962
6	1704	1700	427	+54	+7	3892
7	1686	1703	428	+58	+8	3883
8	1690	1702	427	+57	+7	3883
9	1756	1690	424	+43	+6	3919
10	1589	1722	433	+80	+10	3834
11	1628	1715	431	+72	+9	3855
12	1615	1718	431	+75	+10	3849
13	1660	1710	429	+65	+8	3872
14	1517	1737	437	+97	+13	3801
15	1553	1731	435	+89	+12	3820
16	1478	1745	439	+106	+14	3782
17	1495	1742	438	+103	+13	3791
18	1396	1761	443	+125	+16	3741
19	1380	1764	444	+129	+17	3734
20	1370	1767	445	+132	+17	3731

(continued)

Table 8-4 continued

Income Distribution Alternative	Private Savings	Depreciation	Corporate Savings	Increase or Decrease in Indirect Taxes	Increase or Decrease in Corporate Direct Taxes	Total Resources
21	1404	1760	443	+124	+16	3747
22	1329	1775	447	+141	+18	3710
23	1461	1750	440	+112	+15	3778

As a consequence of income redistribution, the volume of depreciation and corporate taxes increases because of the increase in the level of the GDP. There is also an increase in the volume of indirect taxes and corporate direct taxes. Since the volume of government spending is assumed to remain constant, we may assume that the increase in indirect taxes and corporate direct taxes could also be used for investment financing.

The volume of private savings, on the contrary, decreases and causes a decrease in the level of total financial resources for investment financing.

Economic Growth: The input-output data were supplemented with data on incremental capital-output ratios for 64 industries. Products of these ratios and gross output values then provide capital stock estimated from ICORs by industries, and their total is the estimate of gross capital stock estimated from ICORs.

The values of total capital stock estimated from ICORs were compared with the calculated values of the GDP. The resulting values of average ICORs for the economy can be found in Table 8-5. The table shows that income redistribution causes a small decrease in the values of the capital stock estimated from ICORs. This result is complementary to the previous finding that the income redistribution leads to a shift in favour of more labour-intensive production.

The foregoing analysis of the results of the simulation of the impact of income redistribution on the Philippines economy was a pure static comparative analysis based on an input-output model. In interpreting these results, the assumptions on which this linear model is based should be kept in mind.

As mentioned earlier, one assumption was that there were no capacity constraints. This means that the instant increase in production caused by income redistribution does not require additional investment. A brief look at Table 8-5 indicates that this assumption is valid: free capacity should amount roughly to 5 percent—at the maximum, to 10 percent—of existing total capacities.

By comparing the total financial resources with the capital stock estimated from ICORs, we can derive the implied rate of growth as in the following example: The total financial resources available for gross investment in 1965 (alternative 1) are equal to 4016 million pesos (see Table 8-4). Provided that the

Table 8-5. Income Redistribution and Rate of Growth of GDP

				Implied Growth of GDP	
Income Distribu- tion Alternative	*GDP (million pesos)*	*Capital– Output Ratio*	*Capital Stock Estimated from ICORs (million pesos)*	*Absolute Increase in the First Year (million pesos)*	*Annual Rate (percent)*
1	22,350	2.388	53,374	1,682	7.53
2	21,320	2.409	51,363	1,726	8.10
3	22,511	2.376	53,492	1,671	7.43
4	22,493	2.375	53,430	1,675	7.45
5	22,607	2.372	53,630	1,671	7.39
6	23,058	2.361	54,441	1,648	7.15
7	23,116	2.360	54,545	1,645	7.12
8	23,110	2.359	54,522	1,647	7.13
9	22,928	2.362	54,167	1,659	7.23
10	23,419	2.352	55,089	1,630	6.96
11	23,316	2.354	54,876	1,638	7.02
12	23,369	2.352	54,955	1,636	7.00
13	23,259	2.353	54,720	1,646	7.08
14	23,679	2.344	55,511	1,621	6.85
15	23,586	2.345	55,318	1,629	6.91
16	23,815	2.340	55,738	1,616	6.79
17	23,775	2.341	55,650	1,619	6.81
18	24,082	2.334	56,205	1,603	6.66
19	24,125	2.333	56,289	1,601	6.63
20	24,166	2.332	56,357	1,599	6.62
21	24,064	2.334	56,160	1,605	6.67
22	24,302	2.328	56,580	1,593	6.65
23	23,949	2.333	55,875	1,619	6.76

capital stock estimated from ICORs was equal to 53,374 million pesos, this volume of financial resources secures an implied increase in the GDP of 7.53 percent. Similar calculations have been carried out for each alternative income distribution, and the implied rates of growth are shown in the last column of Table 8-5. The decrease in the implied rate of growth caused by the decrease in the volume of savings is quite small. The loss is highest for alternative 20, amounting to 0.91 percent per annum, compared with the once-for-all increase of employment of 12.65 percent (see Table 8-2). Due to the linearity of the model, that is, the constancy of the coefficients, the implied rates of growth of the GDP equal the implied rates of growth of employment.

Preliminary Conclusions

This simple semi-closed input-output model is based on 1965 input-output income distribution and employment data and on 1971 consumption data for the Philippines. It simulates the effects of alternative income redistributions on employment and output. Altogether, 22 stipulated income redistribution alternatives have been considered and compared with the solution of the model for the income distribution in 1965.

The results may be summarised as follows. The calculated employment increase caused by income redistribution amounts to about 6–7 percent for the less drastic income redistribution alternatives and to 10–13 percent for the very drastic alternatives. The employment effect shown by our results is probably somewhat greater than the employment effect of income redistribution estimated in other studies. One reason for this may be that our study is based on a disaggregated model of 64 industries.

The employment effect is mainly due to a decrease in the personal income-savings ratio and to a shift of private consumption towards more labour-intensive products. A movement towards more nearly equal distribution leads through a shift in the pattern of private consumption to less capital-intensive and more labour-intensive patterns of production and to increased employment of less skilled, less productive, and less costly labour.

The impact of income redistribution on the trade balance is negative but not very strong. The model contains the assumption that the volume of exports remains constant. On the other hand, the increase in the volume of imports is less than the corresponding increase in the GDP so the share of imports in the GDP is somewhat less. The net result is a slight deterioration in the foreign trade balance, which is not likely to be serious.

The last problem is that of savings, capital formation, and growth. As expected, the income redistribution causes a decrease in private savings, which is partly outweighed by an increase in other sources of savings (depreciation, corporate savings, and taxes). The result of both tendencies is a decrease in total savings (total financial resources available for investment). This leads, in spite of the lower capital-output ratios, to lower future rates of growth of employment and GDP. However, the decrease is rather mild.

On the basis of these results, the following trade-off can be predicted, provided that there is extra capacity and, of course, a mobile labourforce; A realistic shift in the income distribution (from a Gini ratio of about 0.5 to a Gini ratio of about 0.4) would increase employment by about 6–7 percent and the GDP by about 4.5–5.0 percent. It would cause a slight deterioration in the balance of payments and lower the rate of growth of employment and the GDP by about half a percent. All these estimates are rough, but they indicate that a redistribution of income could be a sound economic measure, leaving aside other, equally positive, social and political aspects.

References

1. Bronfenbrenner, M.; T. Yamane; and C.H. Lee. "A Study in Redistribution and Consumption." *The Review of Economics and Statistics* 37, no. 2 (May 1955): 149–159.

2. Cline, W.R. "Income Distribution and Economic Development: A Survey, and Tests for Selected Latin American Cities." Paper prepared for ECIEL International Conference on Consumption, Income, and Prices, Hamburg, October 1-3, 1973 (revised November 1973).

3. Cline, W.R. *Potential Effects of Income Redistribution on Economic Growth: Latin American Cases.* New York: Praeger Publishers, 1972.

4. Conrad, A.H. "The Multiplier Effects of Redistributive Public Budgets." *The Review of Economics and Statistics* 37, no. 2 (May 1955): 160-173.

5. Government of the Philippines. "Family Income Distribution and Expenditure Patterns in the Philippines, 1965." *Journal of Philippine Statistics* 19, no. 2 (April-June 1968): ix-xxx.

6. Government of the Philippines. "1965 Interindustry (Input-Output) Accounts for the Philippines." *Statistical Reporter* 15, no. 3 (July-September 1971): 1-14, and Table 2.

7. Government of the Philippines, Bureau of Census and Statistics, National Economic Development Authority. *Family Income and Expenditure Survey, 1971.* Manila, 1973.

8. Government of the Philippines, Office of Statistical Coordination and Standards, National Economic Council. "The National Income of the Philippines CY 1965-1967." *Statistical Reporter* 12, no. 2 (April-June 1968): 1-31.

9. International Labour Organisation. "Towards Full Employment: A Programme for Colombia." Prepared by an interagency team organised by the International Labour Office, Geneva, 1970.

10. Ishizaki, T. "The Income Distribution in Japan." *Developing Economies* 5, no. 2 (June 1967): 351-370.

11. Johnson, H.G. "The Macroeconomics of Income Redistribution." In *Income Redistribution and Social Policy,* edited by A.T. Peacock. London: CAPE, 1954. Pp. 19-40.

12. Lubell, H. "Effects of Redistribution of Income on Consumers' Expenditure." *American Economic Review* 37, no. 1 (March 1947): 157-170.

13. Mijares, T.A. "The 1965 Interindustry Relations Study of the Philippines Economy." National Economic Council Workshop Series Paper No. 71-2. University of the Philippines, School of Economics, November 24, 1971.

14. Morawetz, D. "Employment Implications of Industrialisation in Developing Countries: A Survey." *Economic Journal* 84, no. 335 (September 1974): 491-542.

15. Paukert, F., and J. Skolka. "Redistribution of Income, Patterns of Consumption and Employment: A Framework of Analysis." Geneva, August 18, 1972. (Mimeographed.)

16. Podder, N. "Distribution of Household Income in Australia." *Economic Record* 48, no. 122 (June 1972): 181-200.

17. Strassmann, W.P. "Economic Growth and Income Distribution." *Quarterly Journal of Economics* 70, no. 3 (August 1956): 425-440.

Chapter Nine

Sector Appraisal Where Trade Opportunities Are Limited

A. Kuyvenhoven

In development planning, one of the main problems to be solved at the sectoral level is to determine which sectors should be developed (in case no domestic production yet exists) or expanded, and by how much. In solving these problems, a variety of multisectoral programming models have been developed and applied, for example, Sandee [12], Manne [9], Manne and Rudra [10], Bruno [2], and Clark [4], to mention a few of a still-growing list. All these models are characterised by an input-output system as the hard core. The outcome of empirical studies of this kind for a specific country could supply planners with important data, such as the sectoral distribution of production and investment, the country's trade pattern, and a set of shadow prices for commodity groups and primary factors of production.

Planning at the Sectoral Level

The importance of the results at the sectoral level of planning is twofold. First, the results serve as a check on the outcome of planning exercises of a less disaggregative nature. Second, the results could be helpful at the micro level, where the evaluation of projects takes place. With regard to the latter, costs and benefits of a project can now be valued using the shadow prices obtained at the sectoral level, and the number of projects selected should roughly be in accordance with the planned sectoral expansions. In case significant differences arise, certain revisions at the sectoral level may be necessary, using the more detailed information acquired at the project level.

The planning procedure mentioned above, reflecting a kind of planning in stages, described in Tinbergen [13], has several advantages, but it is not without

Part of the work on this paper was done while the author was Visiting Senior Lecturer at the University of Lagos, Department of Economics, under an arrangement financed by the Netherlands Universities Foundation for International Co-operation. The cheerful computational assistance of J.H.M. Opdam is gratefully acknowledged.

problems when applied empirically, especially with regard to the relation between the sector stage and the project stage. One of the main problems in linking the two stages lies in the different degrees of disaggregation at the sectoral and project levels, and the question arises as to how useful the results of such models at the sectoral level of planning can be.

With regard to the sectoral level, the answer to this question depends to a large extent on (1) the homogeneity of the sectors distinguished, and (2) the period to which the structural coefficients refer. Theoretically, the basis for aggregating commodities is either similarity of input structure or output proportionality, as explained in Chenery and Clark [3, pp. 34–39]. It is an empirical matter whether these requirements are reasonably met, but several studies suggest that there is some room for skepticism.[1] In other words, situations where the variance in economic characteristics among commodities within the same sector is larger than among sectors themselves cannot be ruled out. As to the second point, coefficients are usually estimated on the basis of data from some recent period. This need not worry us, if developments during the planning period would only differ gradually from past developments. In developing countries, however, this may not always be the case, because additions to existing activities or the development of entirely new activities may lead to substantial changes in the commodity composition of a sector. A priori corrections of coefficients could be attempted, of course, though it should be realised that changes in the commodity composition are usually not known in advance, especially where the production of previously imported commodities is concerned.

Although most multisector models have not primarily been developed with a possible use of their results at the project level in mind, these results could nevertheless be useful to planners at the micro level, for whom this information would otherwise be hard to obtain.

Confining ourselves to cases where objectives and resources are comparable at both levels, we first consider the usefulness of sectoral information for project identification. In several countries, planners experience considerable difficulties in finding a sufficient number of well-prepared projects for inclusion in a development plan. In such a situation, the information from the sectoral level could be helpful: the attractiveness of the different sectors and their rates of expansion are, in principle, known. Unfortunately, it is the aggregation problem that could again lead to serious difficulties in interpreting the sectoral results.

Similar problems arise in the project appraisal stage when interpreting the shadow prices for commodities or commodity groups. The most reliable information is certainly that on shadow prices for factors of production. Though the degree of aggregation influences the value of the shadow prices for primary resources, some empirical results, such as those by Clark [4, ch. 9], have shown

---

1. See Verdoorn [18], Verdoorn and Meyer zu Schlochteren [19], and Balassa [1] on intrasectoral specialisation. It is interesting to note that Leontief's analysis of factor proportions in the United States' foreign trade was based on a 192-industry breakdown.

that this variation is within acceptable limits. Of course, the estimation of factor shadow prices is not necessarily linked to an advanced multisector model. Simpler methods can sometimes serve the same purpose.

Considering the various qualifications made with respect to the information that is usually available at the sectoral level, it seems worthwhile to attempt certain modifications in the planning approach. A promising attempt has been made by Clark in his study on Nigeria [4]. In a 25-sector model, he incorporates 61 new sectors based on project data. Depending on the objective function and the resource constraints, the model indicates which of the 61 new sectors should start production (first to replace imports) and whether production in the existing 25 sectors should be increased, held constant, or discontinued. Though this approach is a major improvement, it appears that the existing sectors are still too aggregated to enable a meaningful interpretation of their behaviour. A more detailed breakdown of the existing industries seems mandatory if the results are to be used for planning purposes.[2]

As the data requirements and the computational work involved increase rapidly with the size of the models mentioned above, it has been decided to construct a relatively simple model, aimed primarily at *appraising the attractiveness* of different sectors, whether existing or new, according to their contribution to the gross domestic product. This model is based on Tinbergen's semi-input-output method, the main contents of which will be briefly explained in the next section.[3]

The Semi-Input-Output Method

In a completely open economy, where all goods and services can enter foreign trade, the planning problem at the sectoral level is almost reduced to a mere application of the theory of comparative advantage. With perfectly competitive foreign trade, inputs can always be purchased and outputs always be sold abroad at fixed world market prices. Under these circumstances, sectors are appraised in complete isolation, and the resulting production and investment pattern is one of specialisation, based on the country's comparative advantage in international trade. The structure of domestic demand is irrelevant and only serves to determine the sectoral trade balances.

In reality, a substantial part of aggregate output—for most countries, up to 55 percent—is never traded internationally for technical, cultural, or institutional reasons. International trade in construction is absent because transportation costs are prohibitive. All kinds of services, domestic trade and transport, education, etc., never cross national or even state or district borders. In brief, there are

2. See, for example, Weisskopf [20], who distinguishes 147 sectors within the industrial part of the economy.
3. The method, first mentioned in Tinbergen and Bos [17, pp. 82–83], has since been described in Tinbergen [15; 16] and in many other publications. Hansen [7] has given a good analysis of the method and its relation to planning in stages.

a number of industries whose products cannot be imported or exported, because the cost of transportation, in the widest sense, would be extremely high. These industries will be called *national* industries. All other sectors are *international* industries, whose products can, in principle, be traded internationally. Most agricultural, mining, and manufacturing activities can be considered international. National activities normally include construction, utilities, trade, transport, personal and government services, and education.[4] A further elaboration of the distinction between national and international industries is given, among others, in Tinbergen [14] and Mennes et al. [11].

At the analytical level, the distinction between national and international activities has far-reaching consequences. By definition, demand for products of the national industries must be met by domestic production. If (1) there is no excess capacity in the national sectors, and (2) production in the international sectors requires inputs—on current or capital account—from some of the national sectors, capacity expansion in the international sectors necessarily leads to complementary capacity expansion in the national sectors. Hence, there is no point in considering isolated investment in an international sector; the complementary investments required in the national sectors must also be included. The investment in an international sector, together with the complementary investments in the national sectors, will be referred to as the *bunch* of investment. To estimate the exact composition of the different investment bunches, which is the core of the semi-input-output method, only a part of the complete input-output matrix—the submatrix of national sectors—is used, hence the description of the method as semi-input-output.

With regard to the appraisal of a capacity expansion in an international sector, the foregoing implies that the criterion of attractiveness used should be applied to the corresponding bunch of investment. The actual choice of the criterion is immaterial to the semi-input-output method, as argued by Tinbergen [13, p. 96]. The production pattern that results when applying the criterion of attractiveness to the international sectors is again that of specialisation through international trade, but now based on characteristics of the corresponding investment bunches. If foreign trade is perfectly competitive, complete specialisation will occur in one international sector, with the national sectors producing to satisfy home demand.

In some countries, the availability of abundant natural resources has, at least for some period of time, led to a considerable amount of such specialisation. However, the full exploitation, or the gradual exhaustion, of some of the natural resources has usually caused the development of new exporting industries. This kind of diversity presents no problem to the semi-input-output method. Essentially, it implies a restriction on the production of some of the international sectors. If, in the process of appraising sectors, investments are allocated to an international sector in which production can no longer be expanded, the re-

4. The distinction between international and national products is similar to I.M.D. Little's distinction between traded and nontraded goods. See Little and Mirrlees [8].

maining investment funds can simply be allocated to the next international sector in terms of attractiveness.

Many developing countries, however, have been forced into a different kind of diversification. Some of their export products, which are mainly primary, face competition from cheaper substitutes; for others, world demand is hardly growing or not growing at all. Moreover, exports of certain products may constitute an important part of total world supply, so that prices received are not independent of the quantities offered. In all these cases, the possibilities of increasing export volumes at given prices are restricted.[5] If such a situation occurs, part of the available investment will have to be allocated to one or more other international sectors. Are these the sectors that come next in attractiveness according to the criterion used? Not necessarily. A restriction on the export of an international sector implies that its production can still increase in response to increases in *domestic* demand, that is, its behaviour has become identical with that of a national sector. The composition of the bunches corresponding to the remaining international sectors could, therefore, change, and this may affect the ranking of the remaining international sectors according to their attractiveness. The attractiveness of international sectors having strong linkages with such "domestically producing" international sectors can be expected to change, because production expansion in these sectors will create domestic demand for products of the export-restricted international sectors.[6] The same reasoning applies, of course, when import substitution is restricted.

Thus, one of the main virtues of the semi-input-output method—its ability to handle a large number of sectors because of its computational simplicity—could in principle be lost when trade possibilities are restricted, for whatever reason. It is therefore of prime importance to know whether and to what extent the effects of trade limitations are likely to occur in reality. With the help of a relatively simple semi-input-output model, to be described in the next section, these effects will be investigated empirically in the case of Nigeria.

The Model

To formulate the semi-input-output model, the following assumptions will be made:

1. Sectors produce either national or international products.
2. Sectors are connected by input–output and capital–output relations.
3. No sector has excess capacity initially.
4. Imports can be differentiated into competitive and noncompetitive imports.

5. Actually, a nonlinear relationship is implied, but for the sake of simplicity, such a relation will be approximated by a bound.
6. See Mennes et al. [11, p. 20]. For a more rigorous treatment, see Cornelisse and Versluis [5].

5. Investment increases at a constant annual rate of growth during a planning period of 10 years.

Variables without bars refer to the terminal year, barred variables to the initial year of the planning period. A Δ indicates a change during the planning period. To simplify the exposition, assumption 1 will not be introduced immediately.

The sectoral balance equations can be written as

$$X = AX + C + F + N + E \tag{9-1}$$

where

X = vector of production levels in the terminal year

C = vector of final consumption

F = vector of fixed capital formation

N = vector of inventory changes in the terminal year

E = vector of exports minus competitive imports

A = matrix of input-output technical coefficients excluding noncompetitive imports

Competitive imports are imports that can be replaced by domestic production during the current planning period. Noncompetitive imports comprise all other imports.

Fixed capital formation in the terminal year is related to capacity or production expansions during the planning period:

$$F = \Theta K(X - \bar{X}) \tag{9-2}$$

and

$$U'M_f = \Theta K'_m (X - \bar{X}) \tag{9-3}$$

where

M_f = vector of noncompetitive imports of capital goods

K = matrix of partial capital-output ratios excluding noncompetitive imports; element k_{ij} of matrix K denotes investment of good i per unit output of sector j

K_m = vector of partial capital–output ratios for noncompetitive imports of capital goods

U = sum vector

Θ = capital stock-flow conversion factor

Capital-output ratios are average or incremental, depending on whether or not capacity exists at the beginning of the planning period. If K_s is the vector of sectoral capital-output ratios, the definition of the capital-output ratios implies that $U'K + K_m' = K_s'$.

The total investment activity during the planning period can be related to the investment flow in the terminal year—which appears in the balance equations (9-1)—through stock-flow conversion factors. Using assumption 5 and assuming no time lag between investment and production, the following relation can be derived, as shown by Manne [9] and Manne and Rudra [10]:

$$\Theta_j = \frac{r_j}{1 - (1 + r_j)^{-10}}$$

where r_j is the annual rate of investment increase in sector j. For simplicity, a constant Θ will be assumed for all sectors, applying to both fixed capital formation and inventory changes.[7]

In a similar way, inventory changes in the terminal year are related to changes in output during the planning period:

$$N = \Theta S (X - \bar{X}) \tag{9-4}$$

and

$$U'M_n = \Theta S_m' (X - \bar{X}) \tag{9-5}$$

where

M_n = vector of terminal-year inventory changes of noncompetitive imports of raw materials (and semifinished products)

S = matrix of average partial stock-output ratios; element s_{ij} of matrix S denotes stockholding of good i per unit output of sector j

S_m = vector of partial stock-output ratios for noncompetitive imports of raw materials

Inventories are differentiated into (i) raw materials and semifinished products (material inputs) and (ii) finished products. The stock of material inputs has been

---

7. The case of a linear increase in investment is dealt with by Sandee [12]. Slightly different methods for estimating Θ_j are given by Clark [4] and Weisskopf [20].

related to the corresponding annual flow of material inputs into current production through a set of multiplication factors. Within each sector, this factor is assumed to be uniform with respect to all material inputs and therefore indicates the average period over which materials are kept in stock. For example, if a sector keeps an average three-months' stock of materials, its multiplication factor will be 0.25. Stocks of finished products have been related directly to annual production. If S_s is a vector of sectoral stock–output ratios, the definition of the stock–output ratios implies that $U'S + S'_m = S'_s$.

Aggregate value added at factor cost is defined as

$$V'U = A'_o X$$

where

$$A'_o = U'(I - A - \hat{A}_m - \hat{T}) \tag{9-6}$$

V = vector of value added

A_o = vector of value added coefficients

$\hat{A}_m$ = diagonal matrix of input coefficients for noncompetitive imports of raw materials into current production

$\hat{T}$ = diagonal matrix of excise tax coefficients

Aggregate investment can easily be derived from equations (9–2) through (9–5):

$$U'J = \Theta(K'_s + S'_s)(X - \bar{X}) \qquad (J = F + N) \tag{9-7}$$

Substituting equations (9–2) and (9–4) in equation (9–1) and writing the variables as changes during the planning period gives

$$\Delta X = D\Delta X + \Delta E + \Delta C - \bar{J} \qquad [D = A + \Theta(K + S)] \tag{9-8}$$

Now we introduce assumption 1 and distinguish between national and international sectors. If the number of international sectors is F and the number of national sectors N, equation (9–8) can be reformulated as

$$\Delta X_F = D_{FF} \Delta X_F + D_{FN} \Delta X_N + \Delta E_F + \Delta C_F - \bar{J}_F \tag{9-8a}$$

and

$$\Delta X_N = D_{NF} \Delta X_F + D_{NN} \Delta X_N + \Delta C_N - \bar{J}_N \tag{9-8b}$$

Indices F and N indicate the order of vectors and matrices. Characteristically, no trade variables appear in the balance equations for the national sectors.

In order to calculate the indirect effects of a capacity expansion Δx_f of international sector f correctly, the production levels of all other international sectors should be kept constant. This means that equations (9-8a) and (9-8b) are considerably simplified:

$$(\Delta X_F)_f = D_{F,f}\, \Delta x_f + D_{FN}\, \Delta X_N + \Delta E_F + \Delta C_F - \bar{J}_F \qquad (f = 1, \ldots, F) \qquad (9\text{-}8c)$$

and

$$\Delta X_N = D_{N,f}\, \Delta x_f + D_{NN}\, \Delta X_N + \Delta C_N - \bar{J}_N \qquad (f = 1, \ldots, F) \qquad (9\text{-}8d)$$

where

Δx_f $\quad$ = capacity expansion of international sector f

$(\Delta X_F)_f$ = vector with zero elements except for the fth element Δx_f

$D_{F,f}$ $\quad$ = fth column of matrix D_{FF}

$D_{N,f}$ $\quad$ = fth column of matrix D_{NF}

With consumption exogenous, the complementary capacity expansion in the national sectors corresponding to a capacity expansion in international sector f can be found by solving equation (9-8d):[8]

$$\Delta X_N = (I_{NN} - D_{NN})^{-1}\, [D_{N,f}\, \Delta x_f + (\Delta C_N - \bar{J}_N)] \qquad (9\text{-}9)$$

The bunch of investment necessary to realize the capacity expansion in international sector f and the national sectors can be calculated from equation (9-7):

$$U'J = \Theta(k_f + s_f)\, \Delta x_f + \Theta(K'_{sN} + S'_{sN})(I_{NN} - D_{NN})^{-1}\, [D_{N,f}\, \Delta x_f + (\Delta C_N - \bar{J}_N)]$$
$$(9\text{-}10)$$

and the resulting increase in value added from equation (9-6):

$$\Delta V'U = a_{of}\, \Delta x_f + A'_{oN}(I_{NN} - D_{NN})^{-1}\, [D_{N,f}\, \Delta x_f + (\Delta C_N - \bar{J}_N)] \qquad (9\text{-}11)$$

where k_f, s_f, and a_{of} are the fth elements of vectors K_{sF}, S_{sF}, and A_{oF}, respectively. Notice that only the national part of matrix $(I - D)$ needs to be inverted

---

8. Endogenous consumption does not affect the results, provided the sectoral consumption pattern is independent of the sectoral distribution of production.

and that equations (9-3), (9-5), and (9-8c), defining the trade variables, play no role in the solution.

To appraise the capacity expansions in the international sectors, an evaluation criterion is necessary. Confining ourselves to the simple case of one scarce resource and one objective, an obvious choice would be the increase in value added at factor cost per unit bunch investment, resulting from a capacity expansion Δx_f in international sector f. In other words, sectors will be appraised according to their contribution to the growth of gross domestic product. This criterion can easily be derived from equations (9-10) and (9-11):

$$r_f = \frac{1}{\Theta} \frac{a_{of} + A'_{oN}(I_{NN} - D_{NN})^{-1} D_{N,f}}{(k_f + s_f) + (K'_{sN} + S'_{sN})(I_{NN} - D_{NN})^{-1} D_{N,f}} \qquad (9\text{-}12)$$

In the absence of national sectors, all sectors would have been appraised in isolation, and their ranking would be based on the incremental sectoral ratio of value added to capital $a_{of}/(k_f + s_f)$. With the bunch approach, the effect on capacity expansion in the national sectors, $(I_{NN} - D_{NN})^{-1} D_{N,f}$, must also be taken into account. Because each international sector has different linkages with the national sectors, $D_{N,f}$, the required complementary capacity expansion will generally be different for different international industries. This will result in nonuniform changes in the sectors' attractiveness, and could, therefore, affect their ranking.

If the best international sector according to the criterion given by equation (9-12) is subject to an export restriction, a new ranking of the remaining $F - 1$ international sectors will have to be established. The best international sector (now a "domestically producing" international sector) is considered as an additional national sector, necessitating a recalculation of criterion r_f, now with vectors and matrices of order $N + 1$. If necessary, this procedure can be repeated many times.

Application of the Model to Nigeria

This model has been applied to Nigeria to investigate the effect of restricting export and import substitution possibilities on the ranking of the international sectors. In total, 106 sectors have been distinguished—102 international and 4 national sectors (103, Utilities; 104, Construction; 105, Trade & services; and 106, Transportation). Among the 102 international sectors are 4 nonmanufacturing industries: 1, Agriculture, livestock, & forestry; 2, Fishing; 3, Mining, excluding oil; and 4, Oil mining. The 98 manufacturing sectors consist of 50 existing industries and 48 new activities (projects, including extensions of existing capacity), mainly on a commodity basis.[9]

9. A list of all sectors is given in Appendix 9A.

The year 1970 has been chosen as the initial year of the planning period. At present, this is the most recent year for which detailed information is available. In addition, 1970 is probably a fairly "normal" year in the sense that most industries were operating at near-normal rates of capacity utilization. The various coefficients have been estimated on the basis of the annual *Industrial Surveys of Nigeria* for 1963-1971 [6] for the 50 existing manufacturing sectors and Clark's data [4] for the 48 new activities and the 8 nonmanufacturing sectors.[10] Throughout, no stockholding of products of the national sectors has been assumed. The value of the capital stock-flow conversion factor Θ has been put at 0.15, implying an annual rate of growth for investment of almost 8.5 percent during the planning period 1970-1980.

Results

In the application of the semi-input-output model to Nigerian data, the following steps can be distinguished.

First step: For all 102 international sectors, the attractiveness according to the contribution to the growth of gross domestic product at factor cost per unit bunch investment is calculated [criterion r_f of equation (9-12)]. The results of these computations are included in Table 9-1, columns (1) and (2), where the 102 international sectors have been ranked according to their attractiveness (first run).

Second step: A trade limitation is imposed on the best international sector (2, Fishing). This sector now becomes a "domestically producing" international sector and is added to the four national sectors. The criterion for the remaining 101 international sectors is computed again with five sectors included in the bunch—four national sectors plus the best international sector (second run). The ranking of the unrestricted international sectors after the first and second runs can now be compared, to find out whether the ranking of one or more sectors has improved as a result of restricting trade opportunities for the best international sector in the first run.

Third step: A trade limitation is imposed on the best international sector in the second run. The number of sectors in the bunch now increases from 5 to 6. For the remaining 100 international sectors, a new value for the criterion is computed, and the ranking after the second and third run is compared. In total, 36 runs have been computed. During the last run, 39 sectors were included in the bunch (of which 35 sectors are "domestically producing" international sectors), enabling the computation of the attractiveness of the 67 remaining

10. These coefficients are available from the author upon request.

Table 9-1.   Ranking of 102 International Sectors According to Attractiveness

Sector		No Trade Limitations		35 International Sectors Subject to Trade Limitations	
Number	Title	Order of Rank (1)	Value of Criterion (2)	Order of Rank (3)	Value of Criterion[a] (4)
2	Fishing	1	21.328	1	21.328
100	Watches & clocks	2	9.216	2	9.216
1	Agriculture, livestock, & forestry	3	7.000	3	7.000
56	Soap & glycerine[b]	4	5.997	4	6.004
97	Motor body & ship-building	5	5.675	6	5.690
88	Special machinery	6	5.394	8	5.476
54	Pharmaceuticals[b]	7	5.164	9	5.241
4	Oil mining	8	5.050	11	5.054
47	Basic industrial chemicals	9	5.010	10	5.091
6	Dairy products	10	4.994	7	5.630
36	Hats[b]	11	4.869	13	4.896
95	Accumulators & batteries[b]	12	4.813	14	4.828
102	Misc. manufacturing	13	4.644	18	4.661
94	Dry cell batteries[b]	14	4.585	19	4.632
90	Sewing machine assembly[b]	15	4.513	20	4.524
15	Misc. food & animal feed	16	4.339	5	5.704
83	Metal doors, windows, etc.[b]	17	4.339	23	4.350
30	Towels & blankets[b]	18	4.190	24	4.215
5	Meat products	19	4.141	12	5.012
23	Craft weaving & dyeing	20	3.972	25	4.177
57	Perfume[b]	21	3.899	31	3.925
59	Matches[b]	22	3.838	26	4.123
86	Lamps, lanterns, etc.[b]	23	3.808	33	3.851
32	Knit goods[b]	24	3.776	34	3.839
42	Wooden furniture & fixtures	25	3.656	27	4.032
41	Saw milling	26	3.570	22	4.516
11	Bakery products	27	3.562	37	3.647
77	Hand tools[b]	28	3.545	40	3.577
101	Stationery	29	3.498	35	3.774
19	Spirit distillery & beer	30	3.494	43	3.522
67	Ceramics[b]	31	3.380	41	3.542
60	Waxes[b]	32	3.365	45	3.412
69	Bricks & tiles	33	3.275	50	3.307
79	Cast iron & steel castings[b]	34	3.269	51	3.297
40	Footwear	35	3.263	30	3.948

Table 9-1 continued

Sector		No Trade Limitations		35 International Sectors Subject to Trade Limitations	
Num-ber	Title	Order of Rank (1)	Value of Criterion (2)	Order of Rank (3)	Value of Criterion[a] (4)
93	Household appliances	36	3.262	54	3.284
46	Printing	37	3.223	55	3.260
29	Cotton bags[b]	38	3.187	36	3.691
82	Structural metal products	39	3.185	46	3.396
16	Tea[b]	40	3.112	16	4.694
20	Soft drinks	41	3.089	52	3.287
71	Concrete products	42	3.082	60	3.108
58	Other chemical products	43	3.071	47	3.368
61	Petroleum products	44	3.018	42	3.536
85	Metal drums & hoops[b]	45	3.013	64	3.043
44	Containers & paper boxes	46	2.889	61	3.085
7	Fruit canning	47	2.881	44	3.497
65	Pottery & glass	48	2.878	63	3.049
87	Wire products, nails, etc.[b]	49	2.834	70	2.896
3	Mining, excl. oil	50	2.819	72	2.850
49	Organic chemicals[b]	51	2.816	66	3.016
52	Paints	52	2.776	62	3.079
9	Vegetable oil milling	53	2.772	17	4.693
64	Plastic products	54	2.770	74	2.813
81	Metal furniture & fixtures	55	2.693	59	3.138
34	Wearing apparel	56	2.690	49	3.322
68	Sinks, tubs, & toilets[b]	57	2.668	75	2.761
37	Tanning	58	2.661	15	4.720
35	Apparel[b]	59	2.639	48	3.327
78	Metal pipes[b]	60	2.597	77	2.633
10	Grain mill products	61	2.580	71	2.887
84	Fabricated metal products	62	2.573	68	2.916
21	Tobacco manufactures	63	2.522	65	3.020
63	Other rubber products	64	2.497	53	3.286
55	Soaps, perfumes & cosmetics	65	2.493	58	3.157
76	Enamel utensils[b]	66	2.481	79	2.548
99	Railway wagon assembly[b]	67	2.477	80	2.502
62	Tyres & tubes	68	2.477	56	3.235
22	Textiles	69	2.412	29	3.959
14	Candy & confectionery[b]	70	2.400	28	4.000
92	Radio, television, etc.	71	2.325	82	2.351
96	Air conditioning assembly[b]	72	2.251	84	2.271

(continued)

Table 9-1 continued

Sector		No Trade Limitations		35 International Sectors Subject to Trade Limitations	
Num-ber	Title	Order of Rank (1)	Value of Criterion (2)	Order of Rank (3)	Value of Criterion[a] (4)
89	Machinery not else-where classified	73	2.250	76	2.677
33	Rope, cord, & nets[b]	74	2.186	38	3.601
66	Glass manufactures[b]	75	2.145	83	2.326
39	Handbags[b]	76	2.076	57	3.191
91	Machine tools[b]	77	2.039	86	2.082
25	Cotton yarn[b]	78	2.018	32	3.910
13	Sugar refining[b]	79	2.013	85	2.164
45	Paper products	80	1.922	88	2.048
72	Asbestos products[b]	81	1.897	87	2.065
28	Made-up textile goods	82	1.831	67	2.985
12	Sugar & confectionery	83	1.797	69	2.908
26	Synthetic yarns[b]	84	1.795	91	1.861
50	Fertilizer[b]	85	1.685	94	1.752
98	Motor vehicle assembly	86	1.677	90	1.895
18	Salt[b]	87	1.668	92	1.844
27	Synthetic textiles[b]	88	1.613	73	2.823
74	Steel bars & angles[b]	89	1.605	96	1.654
17	Starch[b]	90	1.584	21	4.517
24	Jute bags[b]	91	1.423	39	3.588
70	Cement	92	1.422	98	1.473
80	Basic metal products	93	1.339	95	1.722
48	Inorganic chemicals[b]	94	1.320	99	1.438
73	Steel mill & rolled sheets[b]	95	1.309	100	1.375
75	Aluminium products[b]	96	1.085	102	1.131
8	Stock fish[b]	97	1.047	89	2.045
43	Paper[b]	98	1.001	93	1.830
31	Knitted goods	99	0.938	78	2.563
53	Drugs & medicines	100	0.873	97	1.652
51	Insecticide[b]	101	0.732	101	1.233
38	Travel goods	102	0.351	81	2.378

[a]For each of the 35 international sectors subject to trade limitations—sectors with the order of rank 1–35—the value during the last run before becoming a "domestically producing" international sector has been recorded.

[b]New activities (projects, including extensions of existing capacity).

Note: Attractiveness refers to the contribution of an industry to the gross domestic product.

international sectors. The results of this run are given in columns (3) and (4) of Table 9-1.

Sector Ranking Changes

Before analysing the main results it may be useful to state, in general terms, the conditions under which changes in the ranking of the international sectors may occur. To this effect the production process of an economy is simplified into a few stages. The primary stage is assumed to consist of activities such as agriculture, livestock, forestry, fishing, mining, and quarrying; and is, as far as specific products are concerned, closely related to the natural resource endowment of a country. Next, these products are being processed in several stages by manufacturing sectors. In the final stages of manufacturing, finished products are being produced.

If the bunch ratio of value added to capital would steadily decrease when going from the final stages of manufacturing to the first stage of primary activities, the ranking of the sectors according to their attractiveness would generally be independent of trade limitations. When, for example, international sectors whose outputs consist of finished products become "domestically producing" sectors because of a trade limitation, the attractiveness of processing industries will hardly be affected, because these industries typically require negligible inputs from sectors producing finished products. Hence, as soon as the bunch ratio of value added to capital no longer decreases continuously but increases at (at least) one processing stage when moving from the final stages to the early stages in production, changes in the ranking of sectors due to trade limitations can be expected.

The Final Analysis

Turning to the computations, the main results can be summarized as follows.

1. Before establishing the attractiveness of sectors according to the criterion of equation (9-12), sectors were also appraised in isolation. A comparison of the two rankings showed substantial differences. Because national sectors 104, Construction, and 105, Trade & services, are relatively attractive, and 103, Utilities, and 106, Transportation are very unattractive, international sectors having important inputs from the last two national sectors decrease in attractiveness when the bunch approach is applied (for example, 65, Pottery & glass, changes from place 30 to 48). On the other hand, international sectors with relatively important inputs, both on current and capital account, from the first two national sectors increase their attractiveness (for example, Sector 79, Cast iron & steel castings, changes from place 50 to 34).

2. Analysing the results of run 1 indeed reveals that, broadly speaking, the attractiveness of sectors decreases when moving from the final stages of processing, where industries mainly produce finished products, to the earlier stages of processing, with one important exception. Three of the four primary sectors, 1, Agriculture, livestock, & forestry; 2, Fishing; and 4, Oil mining, are highly attractive. Of these sectors, agriculture is a major supplier (of a variety of inputs) to some 25 industries. Important manufacturing industries in the earlier stages of processing are: 22, Textiles; 25, Cotton yarn; 26, Synthetic yarns; 43, Paper; 70, Cement; and 73, Steel mill & rolled sheets. Less important processing industries include, among others: 9, Vegetable oil milling; 37, Tanning; 41, Saw

milling; and 47, Basic industrial chemicals. Of all these manufacturing processing industries, only 41, Saw milling, is relatively attractive (place 26).

3. The results of the first run also indicate that for many industry groups a less disaggregative approach would not have been justified, in view of the widely varying bunch attractiveness of sectors within the same industry group. The same applies to the distinction between existing sectors and new activities. Of course, there are some exceptions; Sectors 62, Tyres & tubes, and 63, Other rubber products, could have been aggregated, but Sectors 13, Sugar refining, and 14, Candy & confectionery, though very near in attractiveness after the first run, will behave quite differently when trade restrictions are introduced.

4. Not unexpectedly, run 4, in which the Agriculture, livestock, & forestry sector becomes a "domestically producing" international sector and is added to the bunch, shows substantial, in some cases even dramatic, changes in the attractiveness of the remaining international sectors. Among these sectors are some well-known processing industries using local raw materials as their major input, such as Sectors 9, Vegetable oil milling; 22, Textiles; 24, Jute bags; 25, Cotton yarn; 37, Tanning; 41, Saw milling; 62, Tyres & tubes; and 63, Other rubber products. In addition, almost all food, beverages, and tobacco industries, having substantial inputs from the agricultural sector show marked increases in their attractiveness. Insofar as the favourable attractiveness of Sector 1, Agriculture, livestock, & forestry, reflects the local availability of relatively cheap raw materials, for which export possibilities are limited (cocoa being the only weak exception in the case of Nigeria), the inclusion of the agricultural sector in the bunch improves the explanatory value of the semi-input-output method considerably. Of course, for planning purposes, a careful investigation should be made as to whether, during the whole planning period, local raw materials will continue to be available on the same favourable conditions. As soon as this ceases to be the case, the attractiveness of the agricultural sector will no longer be that favourable. Hence, its becoming a "domestically producing" international sector will be less likely.

5. Another important implication of run 4 is that some of the processing industries have improved their attractiveness sufficiently, in comparison with industries mainly producing finished products, that, for this reason, more changes in ranking can be expected in the next runs. This happens, indeed. In run 16, Sector 37, Tanning, enters the bunch, improving the attractiveness of Sector 40, Footwear. In run 18, the same happens to Sector 9, Vegetable oil milling, and, among others, Sector 55, Soaps, perfumes, & cosmetics, improves considerably. In run 23, Sector 41, Saw milling, is added to the bunch; and among the sectors favourably affected are Sectors 42, Wooden furniture & fixtures, and 58, Other chemical products. In runs 30 and 33, Sectors 22, Textiles, and 25, Cotton yarn, respectively, become "domestically producing" international sectors; and a fair number of textile and clothing industries in the later stages of processing improve their attractiveness.

6. During the other runs, in which mainly sectors in the final stages of processing enter the bunch, changes in ranking occur only occasionally.

7. Data on Sector 4, Oil mining, are based on price levels prevailing in the early 1970s. Taking the 1974 price level as a new base—roughly a quadrupling compared to the level in the early 1970s—an alternative computation of the attractiveness was carried out, with the capital–output ratio of Sector 4, Oil mining, at one-quarter of its original value and the other coefficients unchanged. As a result, the value of its criterion increases to 13.056, placing the Oil mining sector clearly before all other activities except Sector 2, Fishing.

Conclusions

Several main conclusions can be drawn from our empirical investigation with respect to the appraisal of sectors in the case of limited trade possibilities using the semi-input-output method.

1. If the ranking of sectors according to their attractiveness, calculated without any trade limitations, is such that the bunch ratio of value added to capital decreases steadily when going from manufacturing activities in the final stages of processing to industries in the early stages of processing and finally to primary activities, imposing trade limitations will only slightly affect the ranking of sectors.

2. If the attractiveness of sectors, in the absence of trade limitations, is such that some industries in the early stages of processing are more attractive than industries producing finished products, imposing trade limitations will generally affect the ranking of a number of sectors. If some primary activities are very attractive, substantial changes in the ranking of a considerable number of sectors can be expected.

3. If some primary activities are very attractive, imposing trade limitations could substantially increase the attractiveness of some processing industries, thereby creating new possibilities for changes in the ranking of the remaining sectors when additional trade limitations are imposed.

4. Working at a lower level of disaggregation cannot be expected to give equally reliable results.

If a situation occurs, as in the case of Nigeria, where some primary activities are fairly attractive and trade limitations are likely to occur, the following short-cut in the computations can be suggested on the basis of our empirical investigation.

(1) Compute the bunch criterion of all international sectors in the absence of trade limitations.
(2) If the ranking of the international sectors shows very attractive primary activities or industries in the early stages of processing, add these sectors to the national sectors and recalculate the criteria.
(3) If no important industries in the early stages of processing are among the more attractive international sectors, the ranking according to the attractiveness calculated under (2) can be considered the final one. If some

processing industries are among the more attractive sectors, the procedure described under (2) should be repeated. Because of the importance of Sector 1, Agriculture, livestock, & forestry, for the attractiveness of many industries in the early stages of processing, this procedure has been applied in two stages: (a) Sector 1 was added to the bunch and the criteria recalculated, and (b) eight other very attractive primary activities and industries in the early stages of processing were added to the bunch (2, Fishing; 4, Oil mining; 9, Vegetable oil milling; 22, Textiles; 25, Cotton yarn; 37, Tanning; 41, Saw milling; and 47, Basic industrial chemicals) and the criteria recalculated. The ranking of the remaining international sectors was then almost identical to the ranking after 36 subsequent runs.

As the application of this short-cut requires only a few additional computations, the effect of imposing trade limitations when using the semi-input-output method in appraising sectors does not complicate the method unreasonably.

References

1. Balassa, B. "Trade Creation and Trade Diversion in the European Common Market." *Economic Journal* 77, no. 305 (March 1967): 1–21.

2. Bruno, M. "A Programming Model for Israel." In *The Theory and Design of Economic Development.* Edited by I. Adelman and E. Thorbecke. Baltimore, Maryland: Johns Hopkins Press, 1966. Pp. 327–354.

3. Chenery, H.B., and P.G. Clark. *Interindustry Economics.* New York: John Wiley and Sons, 1959.

4. Clark, P.B. *Planning Import Substitution.* Amsterdam: North-Holland Publishing Company, 1970.

5. Cornelisse, P.A., and J. Versluis. "The Semi-Input-Output Method Under Upper Bounds." In *Towards Balanced International Growth.* Edited by H.C. Bos. Amsterdam: North-Holland Publishing Company, 1969. Pp. 175–199.

6. Federal Office of Statistics. *Industrial Survey of Nigeria, 1963–1971.* Lagos, Nigeria: Federal Office of Statistics, 1966–1974.

7. Hansen, B. *Long- and Short-Term Planning in Underdeveloped Countries.* Amsterdam: North-Holland Publishing Company, 1967.

8. Little, I.M.D., and J.A. Mirrlees. *Manual of Industrial Project Analysis in Developing Countries.* Vol. II, *Social Cost Benefit Analysis.* Development Centre Studies. Paris: OECD, 1968.

9. Manne, A.S. "Key Sectors of the Mexican Economy, 1960–1970." In *Studies in Process Analysis: Economy-Wide Production Capabilities.* Edited by A.S. Manne and H.M. Markowitz. New York: John Wiley and Sons, 1963. Pp. 379–400.

10. Manne, A.S., and A. Rudra. "A Consistency Model of India's Fourth Plan." *Sankhyā* 27, ser. B (September 1965): 57–144.

11. Mennes, L.B.M.; J. Tinbergen; and J.G. Waardenburg. *The Element of Space in Development Planning.* Amsterdam: North-Holland Publishing Company, 1969.

12. Sandee, J. *A Demonstration Planning Model for India.* New York: Asia Publishing House, 1960.

13. Tinbergen, J. *Development Planning.* London: World University Library, 1967.

14. Tinbergen, J. "International, National, Regional, and Local Industries." In *Trade, Growth, and the Balance of Payments.* Edited by R.E. Caves, H.G. Johnson, and P.B. Kenen. Chicago: Rand McNally; Amsterdam: North-Holland Publishing Company, 1965. Pp. 116–125.

15. Tinbergen, J. "Projections of Economic Data in Development Planning." In *Planning for Economic Development in the Caribbean.* Edited by Caribbean Organization. Puerto Rico: Hato Rey, 1963. Pp. 26–51.

16. Tinbergen, J. "Some Refinements of the Semi-Input-Output Method." *Pakistan Development Review* 6, no. 2 (Summer 1966): 243–247.

17. Tinbergen, J., and H.C. Bos. *Mathematical Models of Economic Growth.* New York: McGraw-Hill, 1962.

18. Verdoorn, P.J. "The Intra-Block Trade of Benelux." In *Economic Consequences of the Size of Nations.* Edited by E.A.G. Robinson. London: MacMillan and Co., Ltd., 1960. Pp. 292–329.

19. Verdoorn, P.J., and F.J.M. Meyer zu Schlochteren. "Trade Creation and Trade Diversion in the Common Market." In *Intégration Européenne et Réalité Economique* [European Integration and Economic Reality]. Edited by H. Aujac et al. Bruges: De Tempel, Tempelhof, 1964. Pp. 95–137.

20. Weisskopf, T.E. "Alternative Patterns of Import Substitution in India." In *Studies in Development Planning.* Edited by H.B. Chenery et al. Cambridge, Mass.: Harvard University Press, 1971. Pp. 95–121.

Appendix 9A

Table 9A-1. List of Sectors

	Sector			Sector	
Number	Title		Number	Title	
1	Agriculture, livestock, & forestry		32	Knit goods*	
2	Fishing		33	Rope, cord, & nets*	
3	Mining, excl. oil		34	Wearing apparel	
4	Oil mining		35	Apparel*	
5	Meat products		36	Hats*	
6	Dairy products		37	Tanning	
7	Fruit canning		38	Travel goods	
8	Stock fish*		39	Handbags*	
9	Vegetable oil milling		40	Footwear	
10	Grain mill products		41	Saw milling	
11	Bakery products		42	Wooden furniture & fixtures	
12	Sugar & confectionery		43	Paper*	
13	Sugar refining*		44	Containers & paper boxes	
14	Candy & confectionery*		45	Paper products	
15	Misc. food & animal feed		46	Printing	
16	Tea*		47	Basic industrial chemicals	
17	Starch*		48	Inorganic chemicals*	
18	Salt*		49	Organic chemicals*	
19	Spirit distillery & beer		50	Fertilizer*	
20	Soft drinks		51	Insecticide*	
21	Tobacco manufactures		52	Paints	
22	Textiles		53	Drugs & medicines	
23	Craft weaving & dyeing		54	Pharmaceuticals*	
24	Jute bags*		55	Soaps, perfumes, & cosmetics	
25	Cotton yarn*		56	Soap & glycerine*	
26	Synthetic yarns*		57	Perfume*	
27	Synthetic textiles*		58	Other chemical products	
28	Made-up textile goods		59	Matches*	
29	Cotton bags*		60	Waxes*	
30	Towels & blankets*		61	Petroleum products	
31	Knitted goods		62	Tyres & tubes	

(continued)

Table 9A-1 continued

Sector		Sector	
Number	Title	Number	Title
63	Other rubber products	85	Metal drums & hoops*
64	Plastic products	86	Lamps, lanterns, etc.*
65	Pottery & glass	87	Wire products, nails, etc.*
66	Glass manufactures*	88	Special machinery
67	Ceramics*	89	Machinery not elsewhere classified
68	Sinks, tubs, & toilets*	90	Sewing machine assembly*
69	Bricks & tiles	91	Machine tools*
70	Cement	92	Radio, television, etc.
71	Concrete products	93	Household appliances
72	Asbestos products*	94	Dry cell batteries*
73	Steel mill & rolled sheets*	95	Accumulators & batteries*
74	Steel bars & angles*	96	Air conditioning assembly*
75	Aluminium products*	97	Motor body & shipbuilding
76	Enamel utensils*	98	Motor vehicle assembly
77	Hand tools*	99	Railway wagon assembly*
78	Metal pipes*	100	Watches & clocks
79	Cast iron & steel castings*	101	Stationery
80	Basic metal products	102	Misc. manufacturing
81	Metal furniture & fixtures	103	Utilities
82	Structural metal products	104	Construction
83	Metal doors, windows, etc.*	105	Trade & services
84	Fabricated metal products	106	Transportation

*New activities (projects, including extensions of existing capacity).

Chapter Ten

Income Distribution and Export Promotion in Puerto Rico

Richard Weisskoff

Two broad sets of questions have propelled this study. The first is historical and is directed toward investigating the sources of the rapid changes in employment and income distribution in Puerto Rico during a decade of extraordinary growth from 1953 to 1963. A second set of questions is more forward-looking and seeks to evaluate the impact on the island economy both of continuing its so-called successful growth strategy and of departing from this historical path.[1]

The underlying view that guides this research begins with the proposition that a small, open, export-oriented society responds to the demands placed on it by industry and that a specific growth path is the consequence of policy choice. The generous incentives for industrial development provided by the Commonwealth of Puerto Rico have led consciously to the promotion of certain industries that are oriented toward mainland export and integrated with mainland, not Puerto Rican, production. The projections made in this study are therefore intended to show the likely range of incomes, employment, and occupational skills needed in different possible paths in the future. The projections also provide criteria against which future population growth and employment goals can be evaluated.

To anticipate the conclusions, the results of the model, which are subject to severe limitations inherent in the technique used, suggest the limited objectives which can be achieved by continuing the present path of industrialization in Puerto Rico. The anticipated labor absorption in newly created jobs may be substantially offset by labor displaced from the agricultural and service sectors. To

The author wishes to thank the editors for their helpful criticism. He is grateful for the cooperation of the Puerto Rico Planning Board and the support of the Manpower Administration of the United States Department of Labor and the National Science Foundation. None of these agencies are responsible for the opinions presented here. The conclusions summarized in this paper were originally presented by the author in the Research Report [24] to the Manpower Administration in July 1971.

1. The terms "island," "domestic," and "local," as used in this chapter, all refer to Puerto Rico, while the terms "mainland," "foreign," and "abroad" refer primarily to the United States or other economies.

pursue further export-oriented industrialization accompanied by accelerated productivity may fail even to provide a net increase in jobs and lead to continuing large-scale out-migration during the next decade.

Historical Background, Hypotheses, and Speculation

Puerto Rico's development program, known popularly as Operation Bootstrap, represents the quintessential prototype of export-oriented industrialization carried out by a small country in the shadow of a major economy. After an initial failure in the mid-1940s at direct government ownership of a few factories, the Puerto Rican developmental strategists initiated a scheme of attracting branch plants of mainland industrial companies to locate on the island in hopes of creating new employment needed to overcome the island's poverty.[2] Rising incomes stimulated during the wartime period were to be sustained in a two-stage program in which Puerto Rico was to provide the social capital and infrastructure needed for industry to locate in the industrial sites. The promotional incentives offered to new foreign industry (which have since become standard operating procedures for other industrializing countries as well), included exemptions from U.S. profits taxes, subsidized land and utility rates, and the administration of training grants, not to mention substantially lower wage rates in Puerto Rico compared with the mainland.[3]

By one set of standards, the efforts to industrialize have been remarkably successful. Capital has flowed into Puerto Rico. Over 1700 factories have been built under the promotion schemes, and a stable, productive working force has been created.[4] All forms of public services have been expanded; port and transportation facilities have been improved to handle the increasing cargo and the retail network has been modernized.[5] After some vacillation, the government plunged into tourist promotion, and its success has been marked by its impulse to the domestic construction industry and the establishment of a permanent service workforce.

Despite these efforts, the total number of jobs created has been disappointing. Neglect of the agricultural sector, especially the production of sugar cane, tobacco, coffee, and tropical food crops, has led to the out-migration of large numbers of Puerto Rican workers who could not be absorbed into the expanding

2. On the earliest industrialization efforts, compare Tugwell's discouraged accounts [21] with the later analyses of Baer [1], Ingram [10], Hanson [9], Ross [18], and Stead [19].

3. Puerto Rico lies within the trade zone of the United States and faces common duties on non-U.S. imports only. Carriage to and from the mainland is restricted to U.S. carriers. The inclusion of Puerto Rico within the U.S. Federal Reserve system obviates the possibility of foreign exchange imbalances and inconvertibility. A stable political and economic arrangement achieved, Puerto Rico has encountered little difficulty in selling government bonds on Wall Street or in attracting direct foreign investment.

4. See Reynolds and Gregory [17].

5. That is, relative to the inefficient marketing system described by Galbraith and Holton [6] of the early 1950s.

industrial sector. At the same time that the industrial promoters were imaginatively devising methods for attracting new industrial capital which boosted industrial employment by 90,000 between 1950 and 1970, the agricultural sector—which accounted for nearly half the labor force in 1950—was releasing over 140,000 workers.[6]

Conventional wisdom on the recomposition of the Puerto Rican labor force during this period maintains that female workers in the home needlework trades, once the most important cottage industry, merely stopped seeking work as male job expectations rose, and rural workers simply withdrew their labor at low agricultural rates in favor of seasonal migration to the United States.[7]

This kind of explanation, however, discounts the fragility of the mosaic of multiple income sources. In the pre-war economy, earnings from needlework were a critical supplement to low agricultural income for the rural household. With the departure of the needlework industry from Puerto Rico and the slow decline of agriculture, the delicate balance of family income was only partially maintained by the more highly paid factory employment promoted in the urban parts of the island. Workers of advanced age and those with nontransferable skills suffered most from the displacement of work opportunities and encouraged the migration of mobile and employable members of their families. Thus the illusory prosperity which resulted from the successful industrial promotion is based on the mirage of rising real incomes for the employed as the declining rural sector vented its work force. The entire process has become known popularly as "surplus labor" by conventional economists.[8] The improved living standards of those employed in the industrial sector of Puerto Rico stand in contrast to the relative impoverishment of those for whom employment was withdrawn.

The question here is one of history. The sugar and tobacco plantations had been developed on the basis of low absolute wages which rendered the crop profitable when the land was intensively farmed and manual labor extensively used. When, within a decade, these activities no longer proved profitable, one is compelled to investigate the specific policies that brought about the change and ways in which they could have been altered to preserve this source of domestic employment.

The answer to this line of inquiry lies in the prevailing strategy of development. Industry was brought in on an open-door basis with minimal interference from the state once the tax exemptions were granted. The decision had apparently been made to forego an intensive and perhaps risky program for improving tropical agriculture, that very activity which had supported the dense population of the island in the past and had been responsible for the generation of both poverty and wealth.

6. See United States Department of Commerce [22].
7. See Reynolds and Gregory [17].
8. See Reynolds and Gregory [17], ch. 10. See also Friedlander [4]; and, by contrast, Thomas [20] and Lewis [11].

A major political decision was actually being implemented in the early years of Operation Bootstrap. Rather than force reform of the sugar sector by changing tenure arrangements or by substituting vegetables or citrus fruits for sugar cane, new industry was sought that would not disturb the traditional arrangements. A political impasse was sustained: the U.S.-owned sugar companies were not to be antagonized, and the industry faced a so-called natural decline in the absence of more active intervention.

The promotion of industrialization as an alternative development strategy to agricultural reform amounts to a backing away from a revolution, not the "administration of a revolution" as depicted by a recent author [7]. This developmental strategy also required a shift from a rural to an urban proletariat while retaining a constant export orientation toward mainland markets.[9] The change from the open-air factory-like plantations to conventional mechanical factories also reduced the scale and multiplied the number of productive units, diffusing the labor force and reducing its collective bargaining power.

In the saga of the Puerto Rican industrialization, the objective of income maintenance appears to have conflicted with and triumphed over the objective of job maintenance. However, in a society in which work itself is taken as the most important factor in determining each individual's position, it is not enough to say that per capita income has risen substantially while absolute employment has barely advanced for a growing population. The ability of the unemployed and of those outside the formal labor force to survive by virtue of extensive family ties to working members and remittances of migrant's earnings from the United States may be indicative of the divergence between the so-called success of the industrialization and the actual historical process of employment displacement. Since the failure of the economy to provide employment opportunities also affects intergenerational mobility and access to public services such as education and health care, it is crucial for us to investigate the sources and causes of job destruction during the process of income creation. It is this task to which we now turn.

Historical View of the Limits of Job Creation, 1953-1963

The changes in the Puerto Rican economy from 1953 to 1963 summarize in one decade the course traversed by other developing countries in half a century. The shrinkage of the primary agriculture sector has been more extreme, the rise in per capita income more spectacular, and the outflow of population more extensive in Puerto Rico than elsewhere in the developing world.

During the decade, real per capita income rose by 90 percent although total employment increased by only 10 percent. Improved medical care lowered the death rate, birth rates remained high, and the straitjacket that had restrained the net growth of population was ripped away. The island's resident population,

9. See the introduction by Sidney Mintz in Guerra y Sánchez[8] for the formation of sugar proletariats elsewhere in the Caribbean.

free to move back and forth to the mainland, grew by a mere 10 percent in ten years, although the natural rate of increase exceeded 2.5 percent per year for the same decade.

The illusory stability in the size of the labor force masks dramatic changes which underlie its reconstitution during industrialization.[10] The compositional shifts from 1953 to 1963 are most striking in the decline in the share of male managers and laborers, both of which reflect the decline of farming, and of female operatives and service workers (Table 10-1, columns 1 and 5). The shares of craftsmen, male operatives, and clerical women rose significantly, but the increase in the ratio of male/female workers suggests that the new factory jobs for women operatives replaced but a fraction of the former female force employed in the needlework trades. The rise in both the Gini and Kuznets coefficients and the shifts in the Lorenz curves indicate deteriorating equality in the size distribution of income to persons during the decade of growth.[11]

How different might employment generation have been under alternative hypothetical conditions, however unlikely?

Two complete economies were constructed for 1953 and 1963 in constant prices. For each year, the employment and income structure, interindustry flows, and the composition of final demands were brought together in a static accounting framework. Each of these components was then successively substituted into the model for the earlier, preindustrial economy in order to observe any change in employment and income associated with the hypothesized substitution.[12]

---

10. The term illusory is applied advisedly here. Although Puerto Ricans are full United States citizens and may travel unrestrained to and from the continental United States, the stability of a labor force that is achieved by a migration encouraged if not forced by economic circumstances must certainly be an illusion.

11. Since family income and its size distribution are known to be sensitive to cyclical factors, it would be preferable to average the annual size distributions for several consecutive years during the decade. However, such information on an annual basis is scarce even in wealthier countries.

The Gini coefficient is calculated:

$$1 - \sum_i (P_i - P_{i-1}) (W_i + W_{i-1})$$

where W_i is the cumulated share of income of the ith percentile and P_i is the cumulated share of persons of the corresponding percentile.

The Kuznets coefficient is estimated:

$$\sum_i |p_i - w_i|$$

where w_i is the noncumulated share of income and p_i the corresponding share of noncumulated persons.

See Weisskoff and Figueroa [23] for comparisons of income distributions of other Latin American countries and cities.

12. See Appendix 10A for specifications and data sources. This kind of exercise has been popularized in the economic history literature, as in the examination of the decline of British exports at the turn of the nineteenth century by Conrad and Meyer [3]. A similar technique is also used in a study of U.S. technological change by Carter [2] in evaluating hypothetical materials input requirements under changing levels of final demand.

Table 10-1.   Puerto Rican Employment and Income Distribution, 1953–1963

	(1) 1953 Actual	(2) 1953A,D,J 1963 Y	(3) 1953 D, J 1963 A, Y	(4) 1953 A, Y 1963 D, J	(5) 1963 Actual
Total (thousands)	548.5	1006.4	856.3	412.0	606.2
Men (percent)*	(76.0)	(73.2)	(70.7)	(80.5)	(76.8)
1. Professionals	2.8	3.1	3.4	3.6	4.1
2. Managerial, farm, nonfarm	12.3	9.9	10.9	11.3	10.7
3. Clerical	3.4	3.5	3.4	4.7	4.7
4. Sales	6.3	4.2	6.3	6.7	7.1
5. Crafts	8.6	12.4	9.9.	8.6	10.1
6. Operatives	8.8	9.7	9.5	9.5	10.4
7. Service	4.1	4.7	5.2	4.6	5.1
8. Laborers	29.1	25.1	21.5	30.8	24.0
9. Not reported	0.6	0.6	0.6	0.7	0.7
Women (percent)*	(24.0)	(26.8)	(29.3)	(19.4)	(23.2)
10. Professionals	1.9	2.2	3.1	1.9	2.8
11. Managerial	0.9	0.7	0.9	1.0	1.1
12. Clerical	2.9	3.0	3.0	4.9	5.1
13. Sales	0.9	0.6	0.9	1.4	1.5
14. Crafts	0.1	0.2	0.1	0.3	0.4
15. Operatives	10.7	12.5	10.9	6.3	6.9
16. Service	5.6	6.8	9.6	2.5	4.3
17. Laborers	0.6	0.5	0.5	0.5	0.4
18. Not reported	0.3	0.4	0.4	0.6	0.7
Men/women ratio	3.16	2.73	2.41	4.12	3.32
Measures of income distribution:					
Kuznets coefficient	.658	.658	.495	.722	.714
Gini ratio	.428(b)	.428	.363(c)	.480	.471(a)

	Percent		Percent		Percent		Percent	
	Persons	Income	Persons	Income	Persons	Income	Persons	Income
Lorenz	6.0	1.1	7.5	1.9	13.4	2.7	10.8	2.0
curves:	20.0	5.7	28.5	11.5	40.5	12.8	37.3	11.5
	34.7	12.3	49.4	24.6	58.1	23.4	55.6	22.0
	74.2	41.3	87.9	64.4	68.5	32.4	66.4	30.7
	93.9	71.8	97.8	85.8	76.9	41.6	74.9	39.7
	97.3	82.5	99.0	91.0	82.2	48.7	80.3	46.6
	98.4	87.1	99.3	92.8	88.6	59.7	87.6	58.4
	99.5	94.2	99.9	97.4	95.1	75.2	91.9	67.2
	100.0	100.0	100.0	100.0	100.0	100.0	100.0	100.0

*May not sum due to rounding.

Notes: A = input-output technology D = size distribution of income
  J = employment coefficients Y = level and composition of final demand
  (a)–(c) refer to Figure 10–1.

How much more employment could have been generated if the economy had been frozen at its 1953 employment and interindustry structure, yet met the 1963 level and composition of final demand? In effect, we are asking that the earlier preindustrialized structure deliver the output demanded in a later decade, as if technological change and productivity had been prohibited.[13] Under these hypothetical conditions, total employment would have risen from the 1953 base of 548,500 to 1,006,440 (Table 10-1). Female employment would have increased especially in the operative category. Even with the 1953 productivity levels maintained, a smaller proportion of farm managers and laborers would have been employed due to change in the composition of the 1963 final demands.

A second model (Table 10-1, column 3) assumes that the 1953 employment and income coefficients are still frozen, but that the interindustry technology is allowed to advance to the 1963 structure. This situation represents a partial technological transformation which would have generated 856,300 jobs and a relatively equal income distribution (see Figure 10-1, curve c), implying that the changes in the input-output structure account for a 15 percent reduction from the potential levels of employment under conditions of straight growth considered above. A third step, in which the technology, productivity, and final demand are all represented at the 1963 levels, is in fact the actual 1963 economy, which offered an observed 606,200 jobs.

How much employment would have been generated by the economy if growth had not accompanied the modernization of labor productivity and technology? If the level and mix of the 1953 final demand and interindustry technology had remained unaltered, the introduction of 1963 labor productivity would have resulted in a 20 percent decline of employment from the actual 1963 level, a further increase in male over female opportunity, and a more unequal personal income distribution as well (Table 10-1, column 4). This model is a mirror image of the previous experiment (column 3) in which 1963 input-output technology and growth were applied to 1953 productivity. These two simulations reveal the full range of the impact of changing technology and productivity on employment. They give us a precise accounting of the cost of modernizing: new factories without growth would have led to a cut in employment by over half the levels of employment that might have resulted from growth without the productivity increases.

---

13. This unlikely alternative corresponds to the complete domination of work-rules by a rigid, unchanging industry and may reflect the conditions of non-Western societies in which output is increased by replication of the basic productive unit. Certain plantation structures in the Caribbean, such as Haiti and Jamaica, have undergone only minor adaptations while facing increases in export demand. For Puerto Rico this alternative highlights the upper limit of hypothetical job creation.

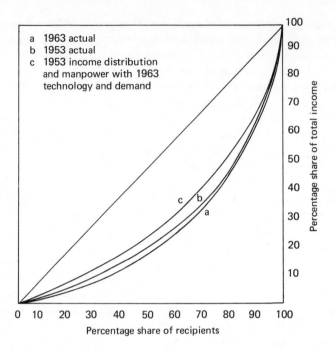

a 1963 actual
b 1953 actual
c 1953 income distribution
   and manpower with 1963
   technology and demand

Figure 10-1. Lorenz Curves for Puerto Rico.

Alternative Growth Paths

What might the Puerto Rican economy have looked like by 1970 had a different growth strategy been followed? Our objective here is to evaluate the employment accomplishments by contrasting the actual trajectory of growth to a number of the alternative paths that might have been pursued. Since the actual set of policies is embedded in the input-output relationships and in the occupational distribution of the simulation model, we retroactively alter some of the historical choices in the 1963 economy, and test out the consequences of those choices on the simulated growth of employment and income.[14]

One alternative strategy deals with the promotion of industries oriented toward import substitution during the export expansion. This type of policy could have been carried out by imposing variable excise taxes on selected commodities, such as consumer durables, ostensibly for the purpose of raising revenue, however, adjusted to encourage domestic production of a number of traditionally imported goods. While such policies might result in the short-term rise in relative prices of these domestically produced goods, we test here only for the net income-generating effect of import substitution at competitive prices.

14. The operations involved in these adaptations are described in the chapter appendixes.

A second series of alternatives examines the effects on growth and employment under different consumption patterns growing out of an aggressive and egalitarian policy of income redistribution.

Import Substitution with Export Promotion

In testing a sequence of import substitution programs, we found that a reduction in the household sector's consumption of direct imports by 20 percent with no further restriction imposed on interindustry procurement would have resulted in an 8.2 percent rise in employment and an 8.1 percent rise in national income (Table 10-2). If a similar 20 percent import reduction had been extended to interindustry procurement as well as household consumption, employment would have increased by 25.8 percent and income by 26.8 percent above the actual 1970 levels. The comparison of these two schemes demonstrates the high dependence of Puerto Rican industry on imported intermediate inputs from the mainland and the full multiplier effects which remain to be captured by increasing the linkages between domestic sectors.

Next, we posited a more traditional concept of import substitution as practiced by the deliberate promotion of selected domestic industries, especially in the food and clothing sectors. In this scheme, the household units faced no option other than to consume all domestically made products from the first thirteen sectors, and intermediate goods imports of these commodities were limited to 10 percent of total intermediate sales. This experiment yielded slightly higher employment but similar income levels as the trajectory generated by a 20 percent overall import substitution strategy.[15]

Input-output simulation imposes a step-like static quality which moves proportionately, machine-like, through time. Nevertheless, the dramatic results of both the 20 percent overall and selected import substitution schemes on national income and employment are highly suggestive of the additional dynamic gains that might accrue from a more rational mixture of export promotion and import substitution policies.

Income Redistribution: The Egalitarian Society
with Different Consumption Patterns

One hypothesis [5] associated with the structuralist school of political economy in Latin America suggests that the redistribution of income to the lower classes would reduce imports and spark a high domestic growth multiplier

15. No substitution between sectors was permitted despite the expected changes in relative prices. The sectors include Agriculture, n.e.c., Sugarcane and Sugarmilling, the six food and beverage activities, Tobacco products, Textiles, Apparel, and Leather.

These models rest upon the assumption of an instantaneous and infinitely elastic supply of costless capital. Although the supply of capital is in no sense costless, the attraction of foreign firms to plug the import sieve represents no net drain to Puerto Rico. The selective import substituting programs could be negotiated with the skillful manipulation of differential incentives.

Table 10-2. Results of Import Substitution and Income Redistribution Schemes, 1970

Development Strategy	Totals		Absolute Increases		Percentage Increases	
	Employ-ment (thousands)	Income Per Capita (dollars)	Employ-ment (thousands)	Income Per Capita (dollars)	Employ-ment	Income Per Capita
	(1)	(2)	(3)	(4)	(5)	(6)
1. Actual economy, 1970	715.5	1,357	—	—	—	—
2. Import substitution: 20% household consumption only	774.2	1,467	58.7	111	8.2	8.1
3. Import substitution: 20% household and intermediate demands	900.1	1,720	184.6	364	25.8	26.8
4. "Selected" import substitution: 100% household and 90% intermediate demands, sectors 1–13	919.3	1,710	203.7	354	28.5	26.1
Import substitution of 20% overall (row 3) and redistribution to mean income with:						
5. Consumption pattern for class 5	881.1	1,727	165.6	371	23.2	27.3
6. Consumption pattern for lowest class 1	892.5	1,703	177.0	346	24.7	25.5
7. Consumption pattern for highest class 15	896.5	1,687	181.0	330	25.3	24.3

due to both the higher domestic content and labor intensity of lower-class wage goods. An egalitarian society was therefore "imposed" on the Puerto Rican model, which was already partially closed by a policy of 20 percent import substitution of household and intermediate demand. All individuals were given the mean income and then were postulated to dispose of their family income in a manner that had been empirically recorded as characteristic of the mean income class of 1963. (See Table 10-3, column 2.)[16]

That the expenditures patterns of one era could possibly apply after such massive redistributions requires an assumption of inertia with respect to life styles. Surely any tampering with the existing structure of income classes would at once alter the consumption pattern of every family. To the extent that the current middle-class life style was developed in emulation of the upper groups, the imposition of an egalitarian living standard would, with time, lessen the imitative needs and the tendency toward conspicuous consumption.

However, since total personal savings in Puerto Rico has in past years been negative and since capital formation is more closely linked with international rather than domestic factors, it appears more relevant to focus on the direct and indirect effects of distinct consumption alternatives on production, imports, employment, and income.

The results of the Puerto Rican experiments are topsy-turvy and shed important light on the nature of small, dependent economies which, despite some efforts to substitute imports, remains extremely open to trade. The imposition of egalitarian income that is spent in the average pattern of the former era leads to a slightly *lower* level of employment at a slightly *higher* level of income than the results of the simple import substitution program alone with no redistribution! More than 881,000 workers would have been employed at income levels of $1727 per capita under the redistributive policies (Table 10-2) compared with an alternative hypothetical employment of 900,100 at $1720 per capita with no redistribution.

In further experiments, the expenditures patterns of the lowest and highest classes (Table 10-3, columns 1 and 3) were imposed on the egalitarian population. In adopting the consumption proportions of the lowest income class as the norm, employment rose to a higher level and income fell to a lower level than those achieved at the mean expenditures pattern (Table 10-2). When the consumption pattern of income class 15 was imposed, employment rose to the

16. These expenditures patterns and the conversion of family budget commodities into input-output industries represent the largest single innovation in this study. Linear functions were fitted to the aggregated budget industries for the 2500 families. The expenditures coefficients for classes 1, 5, and 15, that is, the poorest, mean, and richest are presented in Table 10-3, columns 1-3.

Note also that the expenditures-savings ratios are carried over from each of the classes. Thus in the experiments we assume that the newly created egalitarian society both consumes and saves in the manner selected from the past, although the absolute size of the baskets is altered.

Table 10-3. Distributions of Expenditures and Imports for Three Consumption Patterns (in percentages)

Sector^a	Distribution of Expenditures by Sector			η_{ie} Expenditure Elasticity at Mean	Distribution of Direct Household Imports by Sector			Direct Import Share of Sectoral Expenditures
	Class 1	Class 5	Class 15		Class 1	Class 5	Class 15	
1. Agriculture, n.e.c.^b	0.3	0.4	0.3	0.77	3.8	4.6	4.6	27.1
4. Alcoholic beverages	0.4	0.8	0.8	0.99	0.3	0.6	0.8	7.4
5. Nonalcoholic beverages	0.4	0.3	0.1	0.33	0.2	0.2	0.1	7.5
6. Beer & malt	0.8	0.8	0.5	0.68	0.3	0.3	0.3	3.9
9. Processed foods	45.2	32.6	15.1	0.44	24.2	18.9	11.6	53.2
10. Tobacco products	1.9	1.3	0.5	0.36	3.4	2.5	1.3	78.8
11. Textiles	1.6	1.1	0.4	0.37	7.0	5.1	2.8	80.9
12. Apparel	11.7	8.2	3.6	0.41	11.6	8.8	5.1	51.9
13. Leather	2.7	1.7	0.6	0.30	5.8	4.1	1.9	73.4
15. Furniture	3.3	2.8	1.7	0.60	2.1	1.9	1.5	24.4
16. Paper products	0.5	0.4	0.2	0.52	0.8	0.7	0.5	71.7
17. Printing & publishing	1.1	1.2	0.9	0.74	0.5	0.5	0.5	26.1
18. Chemicals	4.2	3.1	1.5	0.46	8.6	6.9	4.4	56.3
19. Petroleum & coal	1.4	2.1	1.8	0.88	0.7	1.1	1.2	12.8
20. Mineral products	0.3	0.2	0	0.35	0.6	0.4	0.2	65.5
21. Primary metals	0.1	0.1	0.1	0.82	0.1	0.2	0.2	85.6
22. Fabricated metals	0.2	0.3	0.3	0.88	0.8	1.3	1.5	85.5
23. Machinery, n.e.c.	0.7	0.6	0.3	0.57	1.5	1.3	1.0	79.0
24. Electrical machinery	4.4	3.3	1.6	0.47	7.3	6.0	3.9	69.3
25. Transport equipment	0	5.6	12.1	1.69	0	8.8	25.2	88.4
26. Scientific instruments	0.7	0.5	0.3	0.54	1.3	1.2	0.9	37.8
27. Other manufacturing	2.0	1.8	1.1	0.62	5.9	5.8	4.7	70.0
29. Construction	0.3	0.1	1.0	1.08	0	0	0	0
33. Transportation	0	3.0	3.9	1.23	0	3.8	6.6	17.6
34. Communication	0	0	0.8	1.15	0	0.1	0.2	8.4
35. Banking	0	0	12.1	5.79	0	0	8.0	0
36. Insurance	0	2.2	6.9	2.06	0	1.9	0	75.7
37. Real estate	7.6	6.4	3.7	0.57	0	0	0	0
38. Personal services	3.1	3.9	3.2	0.81	0	0	0	0

39. Business services	0	0	0	0.49	0	0	0	0
40. Medical services	0.5	3.1	3.7	1.14	0	0	0	0
41. Services, n.e.c.	0	3.0	10.0	2.07	0	0	0	0
42. Hotels & restaurants	0	0.5	2.4	2.43	0	0	0	0
43. Recreation	0	1.4	2.0	1.31	0	0	0	0
44. Electricity & gas	2.6	2.2	1.3	0.58	0	0	0	0
45. Water & sanitation	0.9	0.8	0.5	0.63	0	0	0	0
46. Commonwealth government	1.1	1.7	1.5	0.88	0	0	0	0
47. Household industry	0	1.3	3.1	1.79	0	0	0	0
48. Federal government	0.2	0.2	0.1	0.64	13.3	13.1	11.0	82.3
Totals	100.0	99.8	100.0	0.98[c]	100.1	100.1	100.0	—
Overall economy	3.5	10.1	5.9	1.01[d]	41.8	35.2	28.1	39.5
Subsets:								
9 Primary sectors 1, 4–6, 9–13	72.2	52.4	24.3	0.17[c]	56.6	45.1	28.5	42.7[e]
13 Durables sectors 14–27	18.9	22.0	21.9	0.21[c]	30.2	36.1	45.7	59.4[e]
16 Service sectors 29, 33–48	16.1	30.2	56.2	0.59[c]	13.3	18.9	25.8	11.5[e]
Range (income per capita)	$1–200	$801–1,000	> $4,801					
Mean expenditure per capita	$239	$998	$6,514					
Mean income per capita	$132	$893	$15,261					
Net domestic expenditure coefficient	0.870	0.657	0.427					

[a]Sectors whose purchases account for at least 0.1 percent of total expenditure of the income class. Excludes imputations. Totals may not sum exactly due to rounding.

[b]Not elsewhere classified.

[c]Weighted by budget shares, e_i/e (where e_i = expenditure on each sector i).

[d]Refers to elasticity of total expenditure on all sectors with respect to income calculated at the mean of income class 5, or $\bar{\eta}_{e \cdot y}$.

[e]Subset entries represent averages for the sectoral groups, rather than sums as in other columns.

Note: The other sectors that do not appear in this table are as follows: 2. Sugarcane; 3. Sugarmilling; 4. Alcoholic beverages; 7. Dairy products; 8. Baked products; 28. Mining; 30. Trade; 31. Excise taxes; 32. Import duties; and 49. Municipal government.

Source: Sectors are based on materials provided to the author by the Input-Output Division, Puerto Rican Planning Board.

highest level yet and income fell to the lowest level compared with the other consumption experiments.

These results at first glance run counter to structuralist intuition. In the economy examined, production for an upper-class style of consumption yields the highest net employment multiplier and lowest domestic income generator, while production for the lower-class consumption bundle results in a lower employment multiplier at higher income levels. The retention, or rather extension, of a bourgeois standard yields the lowest employment levels and the highest per capita income levels of all!

These striking results may be explained by recalling first that the structuralist hypothesis had been developed for an economy more self-sufficient in food, clothing, and other wage commodities and more responsible for its own capital formation. Both the income leakage to imports associated with lower-income-class expenditures and the labor intensity of upper-class expenditures combine to yield results that are the reverse of those hypothesized for the larger, more autonomous nations of Latin America. In the Puerto Rican case, the consumption bundle of the poor is composed to a large measure of commodities, such as synthetic textiles, processed foods, and light appliances, which are either produced locally in the high-wage manufacturing sectors or imported from abroad; this results in a low domestic employment multiplier and high income leakage to imports. On the other hand, the expenditures pattern of the upper class consists of heavy outlays for domestically produced services and remitted savings. The former leads to high domestic employment, while the latter weakens the domestic income multiplier.[17] Ironically, the imposition of the middle standard yields the highest income multiplier and the lowest employment multiplier. The former is the consequence of the low savings ratio, while the latter is due to the high wage and high labor productivity associated with the manufacture of these commodities.

The relative unresponsiveness of the Puerto Rican economy to the shock of major income redistribution demonstrates the isolation of industrial production from local needs. Even with the imposition of import substitution policies, the island economy is geared primarily for export. More than simply a partial closing of the existing structure or major shifts in expenditures proportions are apparently required to stimulate real growth.

The Testing of Industrial Policy: Employment Projections, 1970–1980

17. Mean expenditures and incomes for each of the three income classes appear in the next-to-last rows of Table 10–3. Negative aggregate savings for Puerto Rico is sustained by the continued renewal of consumer credit from North America validated by rapidly rising incomes.

The net effect of losses due to remitted savings and direct imports for each income class is shown on the bottom line of Table 10–3.

If Puerto Rico continues to grow in the decade 1970–1980 at rates similar to the past decade, what employment levels and distribution can be expected? Does the society have much of a choice in its ability to create jobs for an increase in population?

A series of experiments was devised to assist in the prediction of the effects of a continuation of current growth policies. Simulations were performed by projecting levels of exports and exogenous investment to 1980 on the basis of current trends and monitoring their feedback on interindustry flows, employment, and consumption.[18]

The 1963 general equilibrium model was first calibrated by simple annual charting of industrial growth and employment to 1970 by the application of annual final demand figures for the three major components, which are considered to be exogenous to the economy.[19] Since overall final demand grew at the rate of 12.7 percent a year in constant prices, rates were varied from 10.0 percent to 15.0 percent for the three major components of final demand (see Table 10-4). The growth rates of the construction and export components of final demand were also varied differentially.

The results of these alternatives provide us with estimates of the employment range that might be expected in Puerto Rico by 1980. The levels vary from a low of 829,100 for a 10 percent annual balanced growth rate to 1,358,400 achieved at a 15 percent annual growth rate.

Compared with the actual 1970 distribution, the 1980 projections of the distribution of occupational needs present an alarming picture. The most significant change is reflected in the sharp decline in the share of laboring men from 13.7 to 8.5 percent and the somewhat smaller decline in the share of managerial men. Both of these compositional changes are associated with the continued deterioration of the agricultural sector. The slack is taken up by men and women in the service occupations and by women in the operative, clerical, and professional categories. All programs reveal the relative decrease in male relative to female employment opportunity, as summarized in the decline of the man/woman employment ratio from 2.6 in 1970 to 2.4 for the construction boom and 2.1 for the export boom (Table 10-4). These results point to the likelihood of continued out-migration of substantial numbers of unemployable male laborers, despite the rise in overall employment.

---

18. A key assumption of the model, built into the fixed coefficients, is the infinite and instantaneous wage elasticity of supply for different skill classes of labor. This may not be too unrealistic, given the availability of mainland managers and the return migration. No attempt in this study has been made to evaluate the impact of wage differentials between the mainland and Puerto Rico in attracting or severing workers. The model is pulled by demand and assumes that trained labor appears instantaneously, ready to fill the positions created by the alternative paths.

19. Discrepancies between a simple straight–line projection of employment and actual employment between 1963 and 1970 were attributed to changes in productivity which were continued to 1980.

Table 10–4.   Percentage Distribution of Employment by Occupation: Seven Alternative Projections for 1980 (adjusted for productivity changes)

	Actual 1970	Projections						
			Balanced Growth		Construction Boom		Export Boom	
		I	II	III	IV	V	VI	VII
Annual growth rate:								
Overall exogenous demand	12.7[a]	10.0	12.7[a]	15.0	12.7[a]	12.7	12.7	12.7
Construction investment	16.7[a]	10.0	12.7	15.0	16.7[a]	20.0	12.7	12.7
Export demand	11.6[a]	10.0	12.7	15.0	12.7	12.7	11.6[a]	14.0
Employment projected (percent):								
Men:								
Professional	5.1	5.9	5.9	5.8	5.8	5.7	6.0	5.8
Managerial	9.5	8.5	8.6	8.6	8.4	8.3	8.5	8.6
Clerical	5.7	6.4	6.3	6.3	6.1	5.8	6.4	6.2
Sales	7.4	6.9	7.0	7.1	6.8	6.6	6.9	7.1
Crafts	12.3	12.6	12.5	12.5	13.7	14.8	12.7	12.3
Operatives	11.4	11.4	11.6	11.6	11.6	11.7	11.4	11.8
Service	6.4	7.5	7.4	7.3	7.1	6.8	7.5	7.2
Laborers	13.7	8.6	8.5	8.5	9.1	9.7	8.6	8.4
Not reported	0.7	0.7	0.7	0.7	0.7	0.7	0.7	0.7
Women:								
Professional	3.7	4.5	4.5	4.5	4.4	4.4	4.5	4.5
Managerial	1.2	1.2	1.2	1.2	1.2	1.2	1.2	1.2
Clerical	6.2	7.1	7.0	7.0	6.7	6.5	7.1	6.9
Sales	1.5	1.3	1.4	1.4	1.3	1.3	1.3	1.4
Crafts	0.4	0.5	0.5	0.5	0.5	0.4	0.5	0.5
Operatives	8.3	9.3	9.4	9.4	8.9	8.4	9.0	9.8
Service	5.6	6.8	6.8	6.8	6.7	6.7	6.8	6.7
Laborers	0.2	0.2	0.2	0.2	0.2	0.2	0.2	0.2
Not reported	0.7	0.7	0.7	0.7	0.7	0.7	0.7	0.7
Totals[b]	100.0	100.0	100.0	100.0	100.0	100.0	100.0	100.0
Employment (thousands)	715.5	829.1	1093.6	1358.4	1185.8	1287.5	1040.7	1157.3
Percentage increase in employment 1970–1980	—	15.9	52.8	89.9	65.7	77.9	45.5	61.8
Men/women ratio	2.6	2.2	2.2	2.2	2.3	2.4	2.2	2.1

[a]Denotes historic annual growth rate from 1963 to 1970.

All the straight-line projections except the 10 percent balanced growth program imply a demand for labor that could easily cope with a 3 percent annual growth in the labor force. However, should the Puerto Rican industrial growth rate slow, especially, with a downturn of the U.S. economy, or should the mix of new industries be considerably less labor demanding than the industries previously promoted, or should the first generation of high employment factories leave Puerto Rico for other low-wage, tax-exempt islands, then the actual achieved employment for 1980 is likely to fall far short of the optimistic projections in Table 10–4. At the time of this revision (1975), all three of these effects are acting as brakes on net job creation; and, with the deepening recession in North America, Puerto Rico's return migration swells the ranks of the unemployed and augments the natural growth of the labor force.

Concluding Speculation on Future Policies

If the national goal is the achievement of an economy capable of providing jobs for the current labor force on the island rather than on the mainland, then a radical strategy of development may be needed that builds on the actual industrial structure. The current dilemma lies in choosing the direction of future activity.

The pursuit of an import-substitution policy and the termination of the export-promotion strategy may be a practical alternative in the search for real job creation, especially in light of the array of sophisticated manufacturing already carried out in Puerto Rico. While other developing countries have found technology accessible and skills easily transferable in the early phases of import substitution, later stages involving backward integration into primary production and the exportation of industrial products have proved to be more difficult.

Puerto Rico, however, approaches the development trajectory in reverse. Having created a skilled labor force and having already mastered several complex phases of production, the economy has already overcome the classic difficulties of import substitution. What remains is to move forward in the production process and design an operational set of incentives which will encourage the substitution of domestic products for imports without jeopardizing Puerto Rico's current market arrangement with the United States. One major drawback may lie in the anticipated cost increases of the import-substituting industries while local producers learn to compete with international imports. An excise tax on imported luxury models could protect local production and concentrate demand on basic consumer goods and away from the proliferated models now popularized through extensive franchising of mainland companies. Differential and preferential tax incentives could be offered to attract those industries to supply local needs, and the payment of even nominal corporate profits taxes by other industries could be used as transfers to the less competitive local industries, enabling them to match international prices. It is toward such programs to create net domestic employment at decent income levels that future policy and empirical research must be directed.

References

1. Baer, Werner. "Puerto Rico: An Evaluation of a Successful Development Program." *Quarterly Journal of Economics* 73, no. 4 (November 1959): 645–671.

2. Carter, Anne P. *Structural Change in the American Economy.* Cambridge, Mass.: Harvard University Press, 1970.

3. Conrad, Alfred H., and John R. Meyer. *The Economics of Slavery and Other Studies in Econometric History.* Chicago: Aldine Publishing Company, 1964.

4. Friedlander, Stanley. *Labor Migration and Economic Growth.* Cambridge, Mass.: MIT Press, 1965.

5. Furtado, Celso. "Development and Stagnation in Latin America: A Structuralist Approach." *Studies in Comparative International Development,* Vols. I & II. (1965 Original Series 011.) Pp. 159–175.

6. Galbraith, John K., and Richard H. Holton. *Marketing Efficiency in Puerto Rico.* Cambridge, Mass.: Harvard University Press, 1955.

7. Goodsell, Charles T. *Administration of Revolution: Executive Reform in Puerto Rico Under Governor Tugwell, 1941–1946.* Cambridge, Mass.: Harvard University Press, 1965.

8. Guerra y Sánchez, Ramiro. *Sugar and Society in the Caribbean: An Economic History of Cuban Agriculture.* New Haven: Yale University Press, 1964.

9. Hanson, Earl Parker. *Transformation: The Story of Modern Puerto Rico.* New York: Simon and Schuster, 1955.

10. Ingram, J.C. "Some Implications of the Puerto Rican Experience." In *International Finance.* Edited by Richard N. Cooper. Harmondsworth, England: Penguin, 1969.

11. Lewis, Gordon K. *Puerto Rico: Freedom and Power in the Caribbean.* New York: Monthly Review Press, 1963.

12. Puerto Rico Department of Labor. *Employment and Unemployment in Puerto Rico.* San Juan: Puerto Rico Department of Labor, monthly and annually.

13. Puerto Rico Department of Labor. *Incomes and Expenditures of Families in Puerto Rico in 1953.* San Juan: Puerto Rico Department of Labor, 1956.

14. Puerto Rico Department of Labor. *Incomes and Expenditures of Families in Puerto Rico in 1963.* San Juan: Puerto Rico Department of Labor, 1966.

15. Puerto Rico Department of Labor, Puerto Rico Planning Board. *Income and Product, 1960.* San Juan: Puerto Rico Department of Labor, 1962.

16. Puerto Rico Department of Labor, Puerto Rico Planning Board. Worksheets of Social Accounts and Input-Output Divisions for various years.

17. Reynolds, Lloyd G., and Peter Gregory. *Wages, Productivity, and Industrialization in Puerto Rico.* Homewood, Illinois: Richard D. Irwin, Inc., 1965.

18. Ross, David F. *The Long Uphill Path.* San Juan: Talleres Gráficos Interamericanos, 1966.

19. Stead, William H. *Fomento–The Economic Development of Puerto Rico.* Planning Pamphlet 103. Washington, D.C.: National Planning Association, March 1958.

20. Thomas, Piri. *Down These Mean Streets.* New York: Alfred A. Knopf, Inc., 1967.

21. Tugwell, Rexford Guy. *The Stricken Land: The Story of Puerto Rico.* Garden City, New York: Doubleday & Company, Inc., 1947.

22. U.S. Department of Commerce, Bureau of the Census. *U.S. Census of Population: 1950–1960. General Social and Economic Characteristics, Puerto Rico.* Washington, D.C.: U.S. Government Printing Office, 1952 and 1962.

23. Weisskoff, Richard, and Adolfo Figueroa. "Traversing the Social Pyramid: A Comparative Review of Income Distribution in Latin America." *Latin American Research Review* 11, no. 2 (summer 1976).

24. Weisskoff, R. "A Multi-Sector Simulation Model of Employment, Growth, and Income Distribution in Puerto Rico: A Re-evaluation of 'Successful' Development Strategy." U.S. Department of Labor, Manpower Administration, Research Report, July 1971.

Historical Comparisons, 1953–1963, and a Simulation Model of Alternative Paths

Historical Comparisons

Historical comparisons are based on the reconciliation of two complete sets of accounts for 1953 and 1963:

$$X_i = [I - A]^{-1} Y_i \qquad (10A-1)$$

where

X_i = vector of gross output values by sector

A = matrix of technical coefficients

Y_i = vector of final demands by sector

$i,j = 1, \ldots, 8$

Total value added is related to gross output:

$$V_j = 1 \cdot \hat{X}\hat{Q} \qquad (10A-2)$$

where

V_j = row vector of value added by sector

$\hat{Q}$ = diagonal matrix of value added coefficients

A portion of the value added is either received by families as earnings and profits (W_f) or retained and remitted abroad (W_r). All personal income received by families is distributed (S_{ki}) according to different income levels and the sector of household head.

$$W_{f_j} = V_j \hat{R} \tag{10A-3}$$

where

W_{f_j} = row vector of value added received by families originating in sector *j*

$\hat{R}$ = diagonal matrix of ratios of family income to value added by sector

$$W_{r_j} = V_j - W_{f_j} \tag{10A-4}$$

where

W_{rj} = row vector of residual value added not distributed to families by sector

$$S_{ki} = D\hat{W}_{f_j} \tag{10A-5}$$

where

S_{ki} = matrix of total family income received by income class *k* from each sector *i*

k = 1, ... , 9

D = coefficient matrix of family income by income class and sector

$$G_{ki} = \hat{H}^{-1}S_{ki} \tag{10A-6}$$

where

G_{ki} = matrix of the number of people in each income class by sector

k = 1, ... , 9

$\hat{H}$ = diagonal matrix of income per person by sector of household head and by income class

The matrix of the size distribution of income generated to families by each sector (*D*) summarizes the earning and owning practices for each industry. The matrix *H* expresses a fixed scale in the distribution of relative incomes; and the number of people that are supported varies directly with the level of sectoral output, as does the amount of employment:

$$N_{li} = JX_i \tag{10A-7}$$

where

J = matrix of employment coefficients by sex and by occupation per dollar of sectoral output

$l = 1, \ldots, 18$.

A polar formulation of job and income determination could restrict the absolute number of workers per sector, with rising sectoral output leading to higher absolute incomes across the entire distribution. The assumption of infinite elasticity of labor supply as expressed in equations (10A-6) and (10A-7) was preferred in view especially of the high geographic and occupational mobility. Actually, most sectors reflect changes in both the levels and the distribution of personal income originating in the sector during the period.

The shares of recipients ordered by income class, G_{ki}, and their corresponding income shares, S_{ki}, are summarized in the Lorenz curves and the Kuznets and Gini coefficients of Table 10-1 for different historical substitutions:

$$G_{ki}^{stu} = [\hat{H}^s]^{-1} D^s [I - A^t]^{-1} \hat{Y}_{ij}^u \hat{Q}^t \qquad (10A-6a)$$

In Table 10-1, columns 3-5, the hypothetical combination of the employment matrix J, of year s, the interindustry technology, A, of year t, and final demand, Y, of year u determine the potential employment, N^{stu}:

$$N_l^{stu} = J^s [I - A^t]^{-1} Y_i^u \qquad (10A-7a)$$

where the superscripts s, t, and u refer to either 1953 or 1963.

Simulation Model of Alternative Paths:
Import Substitution, Income
Redistribution, and Growth

The model used for charting alternative paths from 1963 to 1970 and the different growth projections to 1980 follows the formulation given earlier, with several augmentations. First the scale of analysis is more disaggregated:

$$i,j = 1, \ldots, 49; k = 1, \ldots, 15; \text{ and } l = 1, \ldots, 18$$

Second, the 1963 vector of final household expenditures by sector is disaggregated by income class, E_{ik}, using the 400-commodity by 49-industry input-output codes for Puerto Rico as a guide to the regrouping of 2500 budget surveys for 1963. Total household consumption for each industry was distributed across expenditures classes according to a system of estimated linear expenditures functions and aggregate expenditures income ratios by class

$$E_k = \lambda_k \hat{H} \tag{10A-8}$$

where

λ = vector of expenditures–income ratios per person for each income class

E_k = vector of expenditures per person for each income class k

$$E_{ik} = \alpha 1 + \beta E_k \tag{10A-9}$$

where α and β are vectors of constants and slopes for linear expenditures functions by sector and class.

$$C_{ik} = E_{ik} \hat{G}_k \tag{10A-10}$$

where $\hat{C}_{ik}$ is total household consumption of final demand. Let $\bar{A}$ be the augmented matrix of the 49-order interindustry flows extended downward by the distribution of value added to families into 15 income classes and extended laterally by the allocation of household consumption to 15 expenditures classes. The separation of direct imports of household consumption, M_d, and imports for intermediate consumption, M_i, completes the specification of the endogenous and exogenous components of final demand.

From equation (10A-1),

$$\bar{X} = \left[\begin{array}{c|c} I - M_i - A & M_d - C \\ \hline -V & I \end{array} \right]^{-1} \bar{Y}$$

where $\bar{Y}$ includes the exogenous components of final demand for domestic output (capital formation, inventory change, exports, and government expenditures).

Part Three

Regional and Interregional Studies

Chapter Eleven

An Interindustry Interregional
Table of the French Economy

Raymond Courbis
Dominique Vallet

Since the First French Plan (1947–1950) was initiated, the planning process for the French economy has been extensively developed, and the scope of the projections made for the Plan has been steadily widened. An important step was the building in 1967–1968 of a simulation model, the physical-financial (FIFI) model [3;4]. In a simultaneous and interdependent treatment, the FIFI model analyses the national economic growth, from both the physical and financial points of view, but at the national level only.

The first spatial analysis was made in 1960–1962, with the preparation and execution of the Fourth Plan, but the main concern was with the regionalization of the national Plan. Although the regional work done for the Fifth Plan [9] dealt mainly with demographic variables and labour-force data (in order to improve the breakdown among regions of the public investment funds), the regional development disparities were then more clearly recognized. A similar approach was used for the Sixth Plan [11]. Improvements were made in the administrative process and methodology as a result of consultations with regional authorities and an experimental regional projection of households and local government accounts.

Nevertheless, the regional planning process has had, until now, only a limited impact on the development of the national French Plan. Regional projections cover an incomplete economic area. Although the national results were separated by regions, these national results were not modified after this regional decomposition. Thus, a dichotomy was introduced between regional and national results. By implication, the spatial location of the work force and industries was assumed to have but a very limited impact on the national development; consequently, the regional policy had only a minor role in the national planning process.

The principal author is indebted to Dominque Vallet for her collaboration in writing the paper, to Ch. Pommier and D. Bonnet in constructing the Table of Exchanges Among Industries and Regions (TEIR), and to C. Le Van for the corresponding computer program.

The avoidance of this dichotomy between regional and national planning analysis was the basic theme of the *Regional-National* (REGINA) model proposed in 1971 by Courbis and Prager [8]. In early 1972 the project was agreed to by the French Planning Office (Commissariat Général du Plan), and work was begun at the Group for Applied Macroeconomic Analysis (GAMA) at Paris-X Nanterre University under the direction of R. Courbis. The model was fully developed by the end of 1975 and will thus be operational for the preparation of the second part of the Seventh Plan.

As indicated by the acronym, the purpose of REGINA is the simultaneous and interdependent analysis of regional and national problems, which should improve both national and regional projections. For the simultaneous analysis of national and regional problems, it was impossible to work at the institutional level of the 22 regions used for the execution of the French Plan. The size of the model would have been much too large and, in any case, statistical information was lacking for a number of variables at this level. Consequently, a breakdown into five large regions[1] was used, as shown in Figure 11-1 and in Table 11-1.

1. Parisian Region—the national capital area, overdeveloped and almost fully urbanised, but congested
2. Parisian Basin—the six regions surrounding Paris, a natural area of decentralisation for Paris
3. North and East France—an old industrial area under reconversion, directly exposed to foreign competition
4. Mediterranean Delta—a rapidly growing area
5. West and South-West France—a more agricultural region, less developed than the other four regions

Such a breakdown was thought to be more relevant than a more detailed one for the description of many economic relationships, as well as for taking into consideration the effects of economic regional factors on national growth. Moreover, with this breakdown, the outputs of the model are more significant and allow for a clearer choice of the main paths of regional development by the national decision makers.

At both the regional and national levels, the input-output technique is the main tool for the analysis of demand and supply. This paper describes the regional input-output aspects of the REGINA model. Other parts of the model are described by Courbis et al. [6].

The intersectoral analysis of flows between industries and regions, and more precisely the projection of an interindustry and interregional table of the French economy (TEIR, for Table of Exchanges Among Industries and Regions), raised many problems, and above all a statistical problem: obviously, a projection into the future of such a table had to be done on the basis of a known table for the

1. For a more detailed explanation of the choice of the five regions, see Courbis et al. [6, ch. 2].

Figure 11-1. Reconciliation Between Planning Regions and REGINA Regions.

past. Unfortunately, there was none, and the GAMA, as part of its work on the REGINA model, had to build a TEIR for the years 1969 and 1970.[2]

The construction of the table, which was done at the GAMA in 1972–1974, will be described in the first part of this paper. The second part of the paper will deal with the projection of this interindustry interregional table within the framework of the REGINA model and with its role in the model.

2. Concerning the statistical information available in France for regional analysis, see Courbis [2].

Table 11-1. REGINA Regions and Planning Administrative Regions

REGINA Regions	Great Planning Regions (ZEAT)[a]	French Planning Administrative Regions
Parisian Region	Parisian Region	Parisian Region
Parisian Basin	Parisian Basin	Picardie; Champagne-Ardennes; Centre: Haute-Normandie; Basse-Normandie; Bourgogne
North and East France	North France	Nord
	East France	Lorraine; Alsace; Franche-Comté
West and South-West France	West France	Bretagne; Pays de la Loire; Poitou-Charentes
	South-West France	Limousin; Aquitaine; Midi-Pyrénées
	Center East	Auvergne; Rhône-Alpes[b]
Mediterranean Delta	Mediterranean Region	Languedoc-Roussillon; Provence-Côte d'Azur; Corse

[a]The 22 French planning administrative regions are grouped in 8 great planning regions, called ZEAT (Zones d'Études et d'Aménagement du Territoire, that is, zones of studies and land policy).
[b]Rhône-Alpes is in the Mediterranean Delta REGINA region.

The Building of an Interindustry Interregional Table for 1969 and 1970

At the national level, input-output tables are the main tool for the analysis of interrelationships between demand and supply. At the regional level, the need for such a table is obvious.

Purposes and Guidelines

A 1954 interindustry interregional table (TEIR) for 16 industries and 7 regions had already been built by Jeanneney [10], but it was built only in terms of value added; the regional breakdown was unreconcilable with the one used for REGINA. Moreover, the regional statistical information available 20 years ago was much more limited than it is today. Although the table was a pioneer methodological work, it was outdated. Thus, the GAMA had to build for the REGINA model a TEIR of the French economy for a more recent year, and a year for which sufficient regional information was available. First, 1969 was chosen, and a table was built for that year. However, since the base year of the

Seventh Plan was 1970, a second table was constructed, using new data [7]. The 1969 table is now being revised for consistency with the 1970 table.[3]

These tables allow for the regional treatment of interindustry relationships and of equilibrium between demand and supply. Also, interregional flows of goods and services are described. The regional breakdown has already been presented. The industrial classification and final demand sectors are listed in Table 11A-1.

At the regional level, the input-output framework is identical to the national table, except for the addition of one row and one column to take into account imports and exports of each region from and to the other regions. For each category of output, the regional tables are completed by an interregional-flow table, which—from the economic point of view—allows for the analysis of links between regions and—from the statistical point of view—insures the compatibility of the five regional input-output tables.

The methodology used varies from entry to entry, but four general guidelines have been followed.

1. Consistency with the national table: By construction, the aggregation of the regional tables leads to the national one; it was not possible for us to question national figures, even when they seemed dubious—for example, because of not taking into account variations in regional price discrepancies.

2. Systematic research and exploitation of basic data: This was required to estimate regional statistics directly and to avoid, as far as possible, simple breakdowns of national results. Large-scale efforts were undertaken by the GAMA for the gathering and use of regional information issued by the various government departments and local administrations and by economic consulting offices, large firms, and professional unions.

3. Choice of the most appropriate aggregation level for intermediate statistics: Even with a general framework based on five regions and ten industries, the work was very often done at a more detailed level (29 industries and 22 regions), but the final comparisons and reconciliations were made at the more aggregate level of five regions and ten industries.

4. Use of different methods and data for evaluation: Various methods were used to double-check the estimates. As the methodology used for the construction of the regional tables differs widely for each sector or industry, it will not

3. The revision of the 1969 table will be completed in 1975, and a detailed report on the methodology used for constructing both the 1969 and 1970 tables and on the results obtained will be written by the GAMA.

be possible in this short paper to present its various aspects in detail; only the main aspects of the work can be discussed.[4] They will be presented in the following order: final demand, intermediate demand, production, and trade flows.

Determination of Regional Final Demand

Regional components of final demand were calculated at a detailed level for goods and services, sectors, and regions (very often at the 22-region level).

Regional household consumption was estimated on the basis of an annual survey of the National Institute of Statistics and Economic Studies (INSEE) on "Household Standard of Living." But this survey gives information on the consumption of households located in a given region, whereas the expenditures may have been made in different regions. No direct information is given on domestic regional consumption, that is, the total consumption in each region made both by the region's households and households from other regions or abroad. Thus, it was necessary to estimate the expenditures of households outside of their regions and the expenditures of tourists in order to obtain internal regional consumption of goods and services.

Investment of the producing sector was calculated for each of the 29 industries by using regional results of the annual survey of manufactures conducted by the Department of Industrial Development. Statistical data issued by the Bureau for Economic Information and Forecast (BIPE) on demand and supply of building materials and construction were also used, as well as information from censuses on trade, services, and transportation. Also, fiscal data and, in some cases, the accounts of some large public firms, were used. For the agricultural sector and for railway transportation, purchases of equipment were first determined directly in physical units and then transferred into value units.

Investment in residential dwellings was determined on the basis of the survey of the Department of Equipment on housing starts and completions in each region. The prices given for each kind of dwelling vary from region to region.

Current and capital expenditures of administrations and banking and other financial institutions are derived from public accounts, data of the BIPE, and specific information from various other sources.

Determination of Regional Intermediate Demand

In this case, we avoided reproducing the national input coefficients at the regional level. As far as possible, we tried to estimate regional intermediate demand directly on the basis of different methods according to the kind of intermediate demand.

1. For agriculture, the regional intermediate demand was given by the regional accounts of agriculture (jointly established by the Department of Agriculture and

---

4. A first methodological presentation, with the results for the 1970 table, is given in Courbis and Pommier [7]. As indicated earlier, a more detailed methodological report (with results both for 1969 and 1970) is being prepared by the GAMA.

the INSEE); but the decomposition by input was not the same as that in our classification, and so it was necessary to make a bridge between these two classifications.

2. For some specific categories of consumption, regional data were also available. For example, regional intermediate purchases of construction and of energy could be estimated directly from data on the corresponding producing industries (obtained for construction from the BIPE and for energy from the research center on energy, CEREN).

3. In some cases, proxies were available which allowed for a regional breakdown. This was the case for food expenditures by hotels and restaurants (for which results of the services censuses were used).

4. For transportation costs, the basic information was given by the statistical data on transportation (within and between regions) in physical units. From these data, interregional flows by commodity in physical units were estimated; from those estimates, transportation expenditures of regions were calculated and then allocated to the various industries. This was done for each of the transported groups of commodities.

5. Estimates of total regional intermediate demand for some products (energy, communications) were made from estimates of total demand and total final demand (previously calculated). This total regional intermediate demand was then allocated to the various industries by taking into account the inputs already obtained and the values of national input coefficients. In this process, regional input coefficients were differentiated from the national ones (due to the double constraint on total regional demand and total national industry demand).

6. When no regional data were available, the national input coefficients were used. But regional price discrepancies on inputs and outputs were taken into account; thus, for the same industry, regional input coefficients at current prices have the same value only when input and output prices are identical in every region.

Determination of Regional Outputs

Regional outputs were determined at a detailed level (more than 29 industries) from various sources.

1. Agriculture: Regional estimates of the Department of Agriculture were used for the agricultural sector.

2. Agro- and Food-Industries: A regional allocation of the national data, based upon sales or employment figures, was made at the level of ten subindustries of this sector. In some cases, regional figures were used directly.

3. Energy: Regional statistics of the CEREN and specific information from the public sector on gas and electric power and from the Producers' Petroleum

Committee were used to determine regional output of four subindustries (coal, gas, electric power, and petroleum).

4. Manufacturing: The annual survey of manufactures and some taxation statistics were used for a breakdown of national output at a detailed level (17 manufacturing industries).

5. Construction: Regional output was determined from statistics of the BIPE.

6. Transportation: A detailed analysis was made of the subindustries of this sector, based upon specific regional information (turnovers, engine stocks, employment figures, etc.). It was considered that the production was linked to the location (from the management point of view) of the factors of production (labour and capital). Therefore, transportation was regarded as a service that may be imported and exported. Thus, there is a consistency between production and the factors of production on the one hand, and between production and related incomes distributed in a region on the other hand.

7. Communications: Regional output was determined from estimates of regional demand.

8. House rental: Regional estimates of the INSEE were used.

9. Services: A regional breakdown of output was made at the level of four groups of services, based upon the services census made by the INSEE.

10. Trade: For the trade margins, results on the basis of the trade's census were compared with those calculated by allocating to each purchaser the national trade margin rate. It was thus possible to alter the trade margin rates from region to region for each category of purchases.

Determination of Interregional and
International Trade Flows
For each region, regional customs statistics of the Department of Finance were used for a direct appraisal of exports and imports to or from foreign countries, but no information was available on internal interregional flows between French regions. Previous research in the area dealt only with specific products and regions, and the results were outdated.[5] A more recent analysis by Rudeau [12] of flows between the 21 planning regions (based upon transportation statistics) dealt with the total flows, but there was no differentiation between products.

5. In particular, a regional accounting attempt was made under the direction of J.M. Jeanneney at the National Foundation of Political Sciences 15 years ago.

To appraise interregional flows of each category of products, various sources were exploited.

1. Transportation statistics on weights carried by railways, trucks, and canalboats—The export prices of the corresponding products were applied to the figures obtained, after correction to take into account the impact of value added taxes and the eventual discrepancies between domestic and export prices.
2. Specific statistics on agricultural products (food supplies for Paris, interregional flows of cereals, specific statistics on agricultural products, etc.) provided direct information on a part of the interregional flows (in physical terms).
3. Specific statistics on energy (flows of gas, electric power, and oil transported by pipeline) were directly determined (first in physical terms) on the basis of available statistical data.

From these sources, flows at current prices were calculated for 13 products,[6] which were aggregated into the first four sectors of the ten-industry classification, viz, Agriculture; Agro- and food-industries; Energy; and Manufacturing industries. For the other goods and services (House rental; Construction; Communications; Trade), flows were assumed to be nonexistent or were not estimated. Thus, for Transportation and Services, only regional trade balances were calculated. This was done by calculating the difference between demand and supply. A priori judgment could be used for construction of a flow matrix compatible with the obtained margins. (Such an approach would be very simple for Services, which it can be assumed only the Parisian region is exporting.)

With the direct estimates of demand and supply on the one hand and of exports and imports on the other hand, regional trade balances were independently calculated twice. By comparing and then reconciling the two estimates, we corrected demands, supplies, and trade flows according to the degree of reliability of the initial results. In fact, the differences were relatively small, and mainly only flows were adjusted (except for manufactured goods, for which both outputs and flows were corrected). Thus, the first results were improved, and complete compatibility between demand, supply, and trade flows was insured.

The Projection of the Interindustry Interregional Table in the REGINA Model

We shall now turn to the projection of the interindustry interregional table (TEIR), but first we should review the main features of the REGINA model and the role played by the TEIR in this model.

6. Agricultural products; products of the agro- and food-industries; electric power; oil; gas; coal; building materials and glass; iron and steel; nonferrous metals and ores; metal products; chemicals; textile products; wood; paper; and others.

General Features of the REGINA Model and the
Role of the Projection of the TEIR

As previously stated, the purpose of the REGINA project is the simultaneous and interdependent analysis of regional and national problems. Such an approach will allow for estimating the impacts of spatial factors on national growth, which leads to improvements in the national forecasts, and building of spatial forecasts for each of the REGINA regions, which may be used for more detailed regional analysis (for example, at the 22-region level).

The breakdown of the French territory into the five large regions presented above is not the only one used in the model. In fact, as the impact of urban growth is very important for the analysis of many variables, each of our five regions has been, in turn, broken down into three "zones," according to criteria related to the degree of urbanisation:

a. urban conglomerations with more than 60,000 inhabitants in 1968;
b. urban conglomerations with fewer than 60,000 inhabitants in 1968; and
c. rural areas.

Thus, the present project will allow for the integration of urban, regional, and national planning. Owing to the three cases, the variables of the REGINA model were analysed at different levels.

Zonal level (rural and urban areas): The variables that were analysed at this level are the following: employment by industry; working labour force; demographic variables; migration and foreign immigration; and wages paid by industry.

Regional level: Here, the variables of the zonal level were determined by aggregation. The following were determined directly: input-output regional tables; trade flows (between regions and with foreign countries); interregional migration; wage rates; social security taxes; household accounts; local government accounts; and agricultural sector accounts.

National level: The variables calculated at the zonal or regional levels were determined by aggregation. The following were calculated: accounts of nonagricultural firms and price changes; accounts of central administrations, banks, and insurance companies.

The REGINA model is a static medium-term model of the French economy in which many variables are analysed directly at the spatial level (regional and rural-urban). National values for those variables are calculated afterwards by simple aggregation. All the variables determined by the FIFI model (at the national level only) are also calculated by REGINA. The breakdown into 5 regions and 15 zones and the number of economic variables create a model of considerable size (about 8000 equations).

Given regional demands by internal and external sectors and regional investments, the projection of the TEIR determines the regional equilibrium. In turn,
this equilibrium has an impact on regional or national demands as well as on the
level of the productive investment in the region. Thus, an iteration process is
necessary for the determination of regional (and national) growth.

As we will explain later, the five regional input-output tables are calculated
simultaneously, given the final demand. This is why it is necessary to project
directly an interregional interindustry table that describes both regional interindustry flows and interregional flows of goods and services. This simultaneity
is the result of the effective interdependence between regions, with regional
production and equilibrium depending not only upon regional factors, but also
upon development in other regions and the nation. National development conditions, therefore, have an impact on regional development.

Conversely, in the REGINA model, national growth depends upon equilibrium
and disequilibrium in regions. The main advantage in using the REGINA model
is precisely that it allows the user to take into account the impact of spatial
(regional and zonal) factors on national growth. This integration of spatial factors
is made at two levels.[7]

On the supply side, the impact of the regional and urban factors on national
development is taken mainly into account by the levels of the following variables: (a) working population (participation rates are calculated at the zonal
level); (b) agricultural labour force (this variable is a function of nonagricultural
jobs created in rural areas with hidden unemployment); (c) interregional migration (this is a function of wage discrepancies between regions, availability of
jobs, and number of dwellings); (d) wage rates (these are calculated using a
regional Phillips curve approach and by taking into account the leading role of
the wage increase in the Parisian region); and (e) input-output coefficients,
capital–output ratios, and transportation costs (transportation costs are determined in relationship with interregional flows of commodities).

On the demand side, the impact of regional and urban factors on national
development is introduced mainly with the following variables: (1) household
aggregate and detailed consumption (regionally determined according to specific
income level and consumption habits in the region); (2) household residential
investment (calculated as a function of regional incomes, demographic variables,
and interest rates and maturity limits on loans); and (3) local government investments (which will be endogenous and determined at the regional level).

Under these conditions, there is a complete interdependence between regional
(or subregional) and national results.

Analysis of the Productive Sectors

At the regional level, the projection of the regional input-output table presents
a two-fold interest: on the one hand, it is the basic element for the determina-

7. For more details, see Courbis [5].

tion of intermediate demand (and thus for the determination of the total regional demand); on the other hand, it is the main tool used to enforce compatibility between regional demand, supply, and trade flows (with other regions and foreign countries).

Due to the fact that the supply and market area of most firms is larger than the geographic space covered by one region, the projection of the five regional tables has to be done interdependently. In other words, the analysis must take into consideration the existence of multiregional firms, whose activities are spread over two or more regions. Thus, the model has to describe the behaviour of those firms regarding the location of their activities. This behaviour has an impact on national equilibrium and growth determination as a consequence of imperfect factor mobility (labour, in particular) and also because geographical location decisions have an effect upon the position of the domestic producers vis-à-vis their foreign competitors.

Moreover, the description of the location behaviour is essential for a genuine integration of regional factors. The alternative would lead to a mere juxtaposition of partial models, each corresponding to a geographical area. The method followed by many existing interregional models corresponds to demand models, in which trade flows between regions are described on the implicit assumption of complementarity and specialisation of regions. Interregional trade flows are calculated directly through appropriate structural relationships; regional equilibrium is then derived by input-output techniques. The interregional flows are determined in three ways: (1) the production of each region in the total national demand (and, thus, in the total supply) is calculated as a given share; (2) the production of the different regions is calculated as a given share in the demand of each region; and (3) the interregional trade flows are determined by a gravity model.

But in the medium term, such assumptions cannot hold, and a different approach must be used, especially in a country the size of France. Consequently, three types of industries, A, B, and C, are to be distinguished according to the kinds of variables determining their location:

Type A: Geographical factors determine the location of these industries, which use at least one immobile factor of production—such as the land for agriculture and mines.

Type B: Demand determines the location of these industries; they must locate close to their customers because of the transportation cost or the nature of their products.

Type C: The location of these industries (which include most of the manufacturing industries) is determined by neither geographical factors nor regional demand; it is the result of a decision process based upon opportunity considerations of investment in different regions.

The distinction between "restricted-location industries" (types A and B) and "nonrestricted-location industries" (type C) is a basic feature of the REGINA model. For the restricted-location industries, regional factors determine production; the level of output of the corresponding industries is regionally calculated through input-output techniques.

Conversely, the level of output of nonrestricted-location industries does not depend only upon regional demand or regional factors. The level of output is linked to the investment opportunities in each region, and thus to the location behaviour of the multiregional firms (concerning their investments). The level of investment carried out in each region results from location choices between regions on the basis of variables concerning all the regions, and it determines, in turn, the level of production achieved in the medium term in each region. The regional production of nonrestricted-location industries depends upon supply factors; thus, for their products, there is no regional equality between local demand and local supply. Medium-term equilibrium is then achieved through trade flows, and a complete substitutability exists between regionally produced goods and externally (from other countries and regions) produced goods.[8]

Such a treatment of nonrestricted-location industries generalizes the treatment used in the FIFI model by Courbis [3; 4] for "exposed" sectors.[9] For these sectors, the level of output is determined by investment, and local products and imports are competing on the domestic market. In the REGINA model, for nonrestricted-location industries, the same competition prevails between intraregional firms and outside producers.[10]

According to the type of industry, production is calculated as follows (see Figure 11-2):

A. Exogenously.
B. As a function of the regional demand or of the localised demand corresponding to a share of regional demand (production of services for firms is not entirely determined by local demand). The corresponding production is calculated by means of regional input-output tables.
C. As a function of the location behaviour of nonrestricted-location industries. Two possibilities are distinguished here:
1. A breakdown is made among regions of total demand and total production and determines the regional production.
2. The location behaviour has a direct impact on interregional allocation of investment. National investment and regional investment opportunities

---

8. For export markets, a complete substitutability between exports of the region and exports of other regions and countries is also assumed for the products of the nonrestricted-location industries.

9. Concerning the notions of "exposed" and "sheltered" sectors, see Courbis [1].

10. Nevertheless, some differences exist: (1) In REGINA, competing imports may come from other regions or from foreign countries. (2) Regional investment of nonrestricted-location industries is determined in REGINA by the location behaviour of firms; in FIFI, it is the financial possibilities and the "self-financing behaviour" of firms that determine investment.

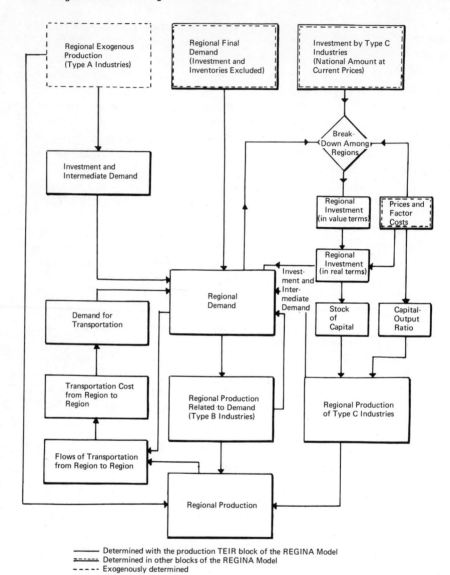

Figure 11-2. Determination of Regional Production.

determine regional investment and regional stock of capital. In the medium term, for an average year, the utilization rate of capital stock can be assumed "normal"; given the value of the capital–output ratio in each region, the regional level of output is calculated from the regional stock of capital. Thus, for type C2 industries, regional production is determined, through the location behaviour, by the amount of national investment at current prices.

At the national level, two alternatives have to be considered for the determination of investment of nonrestricted-location industries in the case of C2: First, the industry corresponds to a "sheltered" (from foreign competition) sector or to an internationally strong competitor. In this case, production and investment depend upon effective demand. But, due to the fact that the capital–output ratios vary from region to region (see above), the national investment depends upon the breakdown of production between regions. And second, the industry corresponds to an "exposed" (to international competition) sector. In this case, the amount of national investment is determined by the self-financing possibilities (which are limited by the foreign competition) and the external financing possibilities.[11]

Projection of the TEIR in the REGINA Model
Because the production of nonrestricted-location industries has a direct impact on that of restricted-location industries, the five regional input-output tables are very strongly interdependent and must be simultaneously projected. The projection process is a very complex one, and many problems have arisen in trying to obtain convergence of the equations and a solution. A detailed presentation would be beyond the scope of this discussion. Accordingly, only the main points will be given here.

The approach that is being used tries to benefit from the decomposability of the system and is accomplished in seven steps:[12]

Step One: Total investment of exposed sectors (calculated in the iteration loop, including all the model blocks) is assumed to be known and allows for a determination of regional investment and regional production of these industries.

Step Two: The regional production of type B industries is determined in matrix terms and in relationship with the regional production of nonrestricted-location industries, given the value of regional final demand.

Step Three: The production of industries for which output is determined by national demand (type C1 industries) is calculated. The interdependence between regions is taken into account to reflect the influence of nonrestricted-location industries on the regional equilibrium (thus also on national demand). In this way, both the production of industries depending upon national demand and the production of type B industries are derived as functions of regional productions of type C2 industries.

11. See Courbis [1, chs. 1 and 7].
12. It is the same method that was used for price determination in the FIFI model [4, pp. 62–65].

Step Four: National investment of type C2 industries that are sheltered from foreign competition is calculated. A regional allocation of the national investment then provides regional investment and production. This production, as well as the regional outputs of exposed industries, will, in turn, allow for a complete determination of all other regional outputs. For determining the investment of sheltered nonrestricted-location industries, an iterative process on the level of investment allowing for a national equilibrium between supply and demand could be used, but it would lead to very laborious calculations. Therefore, a direct solution of the linearized equation system has been used.[13] A first solution leads to a set of values for which the system is once again linearized; a new iteration then gives a new solution, and so on. (This process proved to converge very quickly.)

Step Five: The regional levels of output of all the industries are now determined. In the case of nonrestricted-location industries, however, the level of output is not directly linked to the regional demand; regional equilibrium between demand and supply is reached through the external trade of the region, either with other regions or with foreign countries. The regional trade balances are given by the projection of regional demand and supply and allow for a complete determination of interregional flows of goods.

Step Six: This calculation of interregional trade flows allows for the determination of the corresponding transportation expenditures from region to region and for each group of transported goods. With the intraregional transportation expenditures, it is then possible to derive the total of transportation expenditures for a given region and for each group of users (industries, trade, or final demand sectors); thus, transportation input coefficients depend upon interregional (and intraregional) flows, hence on demand and production location.

Step Seven: Investment of restricted-location industries, inventory changes, and external trade with foreign countries (for sheltered or exposed industries) are calculated and lead to new values of final demand.[14] A new calculation of regional and interregional input-output tables is necessary, and so on until the calculations converge.

The projection of the regional input-output tables is thus strongly interdependent. By aggregation of the regional tables, it is then possible to obtain the national input-output table, which takes into account the impact of spatial

13. Linearization is necessary, due to the fact that the relationship between regional production and total national investment of nonrestricted-location industries is nonlinear.
14. The other components of regional final demand are endogenous (household consumption and investment and government current expenditures) or exogenous.

factors, both at the level of production, investment, and intermediate demand and at the level of regional final demand.

References

1. Courbis, R. "Competitivité et Croissance en Economie Concurrencée" [Competitiveness and Growth in an Economy Exposed to a Strong Foreign Competition]. Ph.D. dissertation, University of Paris-I, January 1971. Paris: Dunod, 1975.

2. Courbis, R. "La Comptabilité Régionale Française" [The French Regional Accounting]. (Paper presented to the Second IARIW Latin American Conference, Rio de Janeiro, January 9–12, 1974.) *Economie Appliquée* XXVIII, no. 2–3 (1975): 279–330.

3. Courbis, R. "The FIFI Model Used in the Preparation of the French Plan." *Economics of Planning* 12, no. 1–2 (1972): 37–78.

4. Courbis, R. "Le Modèle FIFI de Simulation à Moyen Terme" [The Medium-Term Simulation FIFI Model]. *Les Collections de l'INSEE,* Series C, no. 22 (June 1973): 13–77.

5. Courbis, R. "Le Modèle REGINA d'Analyse Interdépendante des Problèmes Régionaux et Nationaux" [The REGINA Model of Interdependent Analysis of Regional and National Problems]. (Paper presented to the Montpellier meeting on regional models, Montpellier, June 7–8, 1973.) *Aménagement du Territoire et Développement Régional,* no. 7. Paris: Documentation Française, 1974. Pp. 137–162.

6. Courbis, R.; J. Bourdon; D. Bonnet; Ch. Pommier; D. Vallet; G. Cornilleau; and F. de Massougnes. "Le Modèle REGINA. Analyse Economique du Modèle" [The REGINA Model. Economic Analysis of the Model]. GAMA Paper No. 43. Report on the 1972–1973 Works on the REGINA Model made for the French Planning Office under the direction of Professor Courbis, October 1973.

7. Courbis, R., and Ch. Pommier. "Un Tableau d'Echange Inter-industriels et Inter-régionaux de l'Economie Française pour 1970" [An Interindustry Interregional Table of the French Economy for 1970]. GAMA Paper No. 86. December 1974.

8. Courbis, R., and J.C. Prager. "Analyse Régionale et Planification Nationale: Le Projet de Modèle REGINA d'Analyse Interdépendante" [Regional Analysis and National Planning: The REGINA Model Project of Interdependent Analysis. (Paper presented to the First French-Soviet Conference on Planning Models, Paris, October 11–15, 1971.) *Les Collections de l'INSEE,* Series R, no. 12 (May 1973): 5–32.

9. INSEE. "Méthodes de Programmation dans le Ve Plan" [Methods of Programming in the Fifth Plan]. Part 3, Chapter 3, "Projections et Problèmes Régionaux" [Projections and Regional Problems]. *Etudes et Conjoncture* 21, no. 12 (December 1966): 93–100.

10. Jeanneney, J.M., and S. Quiers-Valette. *Essai d'une Comptabilité Interrégionale Française pour 1954* [Essay on French Interregional Accounting for 1954]. Paris: Armand Colin, 1968–1971.

11. Rousselot, M. "La Régionalisation du VIe Plan" [The Regionalization of the Sixth Plan]. *Aménagement du Territoire et Développement Régional,* no. 6. Paris: Documentation Française, 1973. Pp. 39–96.

12. Rudeau, J. "La Comptabilisation des Flux Economiques Interrégionaux" [Accounting of Economic Interregional Flows]. Ph.D. dissertation, Lyon University, May 1968.

Appendix 11A

Table 11A-1.   Industrial Classification and Final Demand Sectors in the
REGINA Model

Industry		Final Demand Sector	
Number	Title	Number	Title
1	Agriculture	1	Household consumption
2	Agro- & Food-industries	2	Government consumption (for 6 groups*)
3	Energy	3	Banking & insurance company consumption
4	Manufacturing industries		tion
5	Construction industries	4	Producing sector investment (for 10
6	Transportation		industries)
7	Communications	5	Household investment
8	House rental	6	Government investment (for 6 groups*)
9	Services	7	Banking & insurance company investment
10	Trade	8	Inventories
		9	External foreign trade (imports & exports)
		10	External regional trade (imports & exports)

*State government; Civil expenditures; Army; Social security; Local public authorities;
Semi-public agencies for economic intervention.

Chapter Twelve

Design for Commodity-by-Industry Interregional Input-Output Models

R. B. Hoffman
J. N. Kent

In this paper we do not attempt to develop an interregional model. Rather, we propose a mathematical structure of computational framework with which a family of interregional input-output models can be constructed.

This family of interregional input-output models encompasses the well-known class of static models that are used to analyse the propagation of demand throughout an economic system disaggregated both regionally and industrially. Among the most familiar models of this class are the national–intranational model of Leontief [8], the Leontief-Strout gravity model [9], and those associated with Chenery [2], Isard [7], and Moses [11].

In our view, it is useful to consider an interregional model as a disaggregation of a national model, rather than as a formal linking of individual regional models. Many of the data required to construct input-output accounts are available at the national level, but not at the subnational level. This is particularly true of interregional trade data and some elements on the income side of the national income and expenditure accounts. The approach of disaggregation does not require estimation of the complete network of interregional trade flows nor allocation of all income to each region. The national input-output accounting framework, which serves as the starting point in the development of the interregional input-output model framework proposed in this paper, is the commodity-by-industry accounting framework associated with Statistics Canada input-output models [3; 12]. The essence of the accounting framework is the recognition of two spaces: an institutional space where institutions are grouped into industries, households, governments, and a foreign sector; and a transaction or commodity space that distinguishes intermediate flows or flows of produced goods and primary flows or factor inputs. The accounts show the production of commodities by industries; they also show foreign imports and the use of both as intermediate inputs

This study is the result of the combined efforts of members of the Structural Analysis Division of Statistics Canada. In particular, the authors wish to acknowledge the contribution of C. Gaston, who developed the computer algorithm.

or objects of final expenditure. Each industry may produce more than one commodity and each commodity may be produced by more than one industry.

Figure 12-1 represents such a set of national input-output accounts for a fictitious economy that consists of three industries, four commodities, two factors, and four final demand sectors. The accounts "balance" in two ways—the total supply of commodities is equal to the total disposition of commodities, and the total industry outputs are equal to the total industry inputs.

Mathematical Structure

From this commodity-by-industry accounting framework, the parameters for an input-output model under the assumptions of industry technology, fixed domestic market shares, and fixed import shares can be calculated [4; 12]. The model consists of three basic equations:

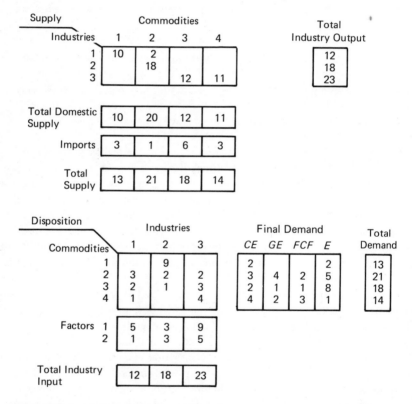

Figure 12-1. A Set of National Input-Output Accounts. *CE* and *GE* are, respectively, consumer and government expenditures; *FCF* is fixed capital formation; and *X* is exports.

$$Q + M = AX + Y + E \tag{12-1}$$

$$X = DQ \tag{12-2}$$

$$M = \hat{\mu}(AX + Y) \tag{12-3}$$

where

Q = vector of domestic output by commodities

M = vector of imports by commodities

A = matrix of input coefficients

X = vector of domestic outputs by industries

Y = vector of domestic final demand by commodities

E = vector of exports by commodities

D = matrix of domestic market share coefficients

$\hat{\mu}$ = diagonal matrix of import share coefficients

The first equation states that the total supply of commodities, $Q + M$, must be equal to their total disposition which consists of intermediate demand, AX, and final demand, $Y + E$. The A coefficients reflect the assumption of industry technology and are calculated by dividing the intermediate inputs of commodities by the appropriate industry outputs, that is,

$$A = U\hat{X}^{-1}$$

where U is the matrix of inputs into industries.

The second equation states that the output of domestically produced commodities is allocated among industries according to the market share coefficients D. They are obtained by dividing each element of the output matrix by the appropriate elements of total domestic output, that is,

$$D = V\hat{Q}^{-1}$$

where V is the matrix of outputs by commodities and industries.

The third equation states that imports are a share of total domestic demand, $AX + Y$. The import share coefficients are obtained by dividing imports by total domestic demand, that is,

$$\mu = (\hat{Z})^{-1}M$$

where $Z = AX + Y$.

These three equations form an input-output model that can be solved for X, Q, and M in terms of Y and E. The solution for X is given by:

$$X = [I - D(I - \hat{\mu})B]^{-1} D(I - \hat{\mu}) Y + DE \qquad (12\text{-}4)$$

A computational framework or computer algorithm has been developed for solving models of this mathematical structure. The most distinguishing characteristic of the computer algorithm is that it does not calculate or make use of an inverse or impact table such as that set out in equation (12-4). Rather, the computer system is used to calculate a specific solution. (No general solution is obtained.) This approach was chosen for reasons of computational efficiency and flexibility in changing parameter arrays. The large arrays of parameters required by the model—namely, the input coefficients and the domestic market share coefficients—are stored and manipulated in "compact" form. The main feature of the compact form is that only the non-zero elements in the arrays are handled. A matrix is represented by three vectors: a vector of the nonzero elements taken row by row; a vector whose elements are the column identification of the corresponding elements in the first vector; and a vector whose elements are the number of elements in each row of the matrix. The number of elements in each of the first two vectors is equal to the number of nonzero elements in the original matrix, and the number of elements in the third vector is equal to the number of rows in the original matrix. The expression of matrices in compact form is significant for input-output calculations because the coefficient arrays are extremely sparse. Since inverse matrices are by nature not sparse, it is more efficient to store sparse parameter matrices and to calculate the single solutions that use them rather than to store and manipulate inverse matrices.

It is to be noted, as well, that the use of a single-solution procedure avoids the necessity of recalculating an inverse matrix each time the coefficient arrays are changed. Accordingly, the single-solution system is convenient for analysing the impact of changes in the *structure* of the economy.

The solution of the model is achieved by means of the iterative process set out in Figure 12-2. Block 1 of the figure allocates final demand among direct imports, M, and domestic output by commodities, Q.

Block 3 allocates the domestic outputs by commodities, $\bar{Q}$, among industries according to the domestic market share coefficients. Block 6 then calculates the indirect domestic commodity production required as inputs in order to satisfy the additional demands. These additional demands, ΔQ, for domestic output by commodities are allocated among industries in Block 3.

The system iterates over Block 3 to Block 6, inclusive. At each iteration, the increments to industry outputs, ΔX, are accumulated in the X vector. This occurs in Block 4. Intuitively, convergence is assured, insomuch as the increments to outputs by industries diminish from iteration to iteration because of the leakages

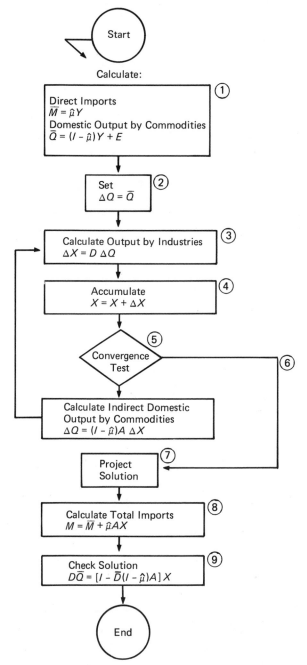

Figure 12-2. The Solution of the Model.

to imports and primary inputs that take place at each iteration. A mathematical proof of convergence is available [12].

The iterations proceed until a measure of the average increment in industry outputs is approximately equal to the increment in each industry output. More precisely, when a prespecified tolerance,

$$\epsilon \geqslant \sum_{j=1}^{n} \frac{e_j}{1 - e_j} \Delta x_{ij} \div \sum_{j=1}^{n} \Delta x_{oj}$$

where

$j = 1, \ldots, n$ industries

$i = 1, \ldots, k$ iterations

and

$$x_j = r_j - \bar{r}$$

where

$$r_j = \frac{\Delta x_{ij}}{\Delta x_{i-1,j}} \qquad \text{and} \qquad r = \frac{\displaystyle\sum_{j=1}^{n} \Delta x_{ij}}{\displaystyle\sum_{j=1}^{n} \Delta x_{i-1,j}}$$

convergence is assured and a solution is calculated in Block 7. The solution for industry outputs is the sum of the increments to industry outputs up to the iteration in which the tolerance is met plus a projected increment. For industry j,

$$x_j = \sum_{i=1}^{k} \Delta x_{ij} + \frac{r_j}{1 - r} \Delta x_{kj}$$

where k is the iteration in which the tolerance is met.

Given industry outputs, X, Block 8 calculates total imports by adding direct requirements to indirect requirements.

Block 9 checks the solution by running the system in reverse, that is, by calculating domestic final demand from the calculated industry output levels.

The mathematical structure and computational framework that have been described thus far have two features that are pertinent for interregional models.

The commodity-by-industry accounting framework facilitates the separation of supply or marketing relationships from input or technological relationships. The mathematical structure we have chosen may be interpreted as follows: at each iteration, demand is pooled and then allocated among sources of supply. This notion of "pooling" will lead to the definition of subnational "pools" and separate patterns of supply for each pool.

The use of compact parameter arrays and a single-solution algorithm makes it feasible to handle efficiently very large matrices, recognizing that these matrices are apt to be extremely sparse. The limiting characteristic from the computational point of view is not the dimensions of the matrices, but the number of non-zero numbers. This feature is important especially for interregional models, in which the dimensions of the coefficient matrix are usually the product of the number of industries and the number of regions.

The strategy adopted for introducing the regional dimension into such a framework is simply that of disaggregation within the existing mathematical structure. Thus we proceed by redefining the industry and commodity spaces.

Disaggregation in Industry Space

Because the industry space in the national input-output accounts is institutional, the "industries" may be redefined to be industries in regions. Accordingly, the mix of products and the pattern of inputs for each industry may vary from region to region.

Furthermore, the regional disaggregation of industries may be *selective*.

Certain industries may be designated as "national" industries and therefore need not be disaggregated at all. For industries, such as transportation and communications, that involve a national network and for which the assignment of outputs and inputs to a particular region is at best arbitrary, the "national" industry concept is appropriate.[1]

There are many industries for which only selected inputs and outputs can be given a regional dimension. For instance, in industries subject to an establishment-based survey or census, information on shipments, raw materials, and labour is usually available at the regional level; but information on service inputs, overhead costs, depreciation, and profits is not available. Where only partial regional-

---

1. Even for national industries, primary inputs, such as labour, can be regionally disaggregated by introducing new rows of primary inputs. This is necessary for household income if the model is to be closed with respect to consumer expenditures.

ization is possible, the dummy industry technique may be used to allocate in total the flows for which there is no regional information.

Figure 12-3 is the national accounting framework depicted in Figure 12-1 after disaggregation to distinguish by region.

Industry 1 is a national industry, and therefore remains unchanged in Figure 12-3. Industry 2 has been completely regionalized, thus becoming industries 2.1 and 2.2 in Figure 12-3, where the digit to the right of the decimal specifies the region. Industry 3 has been only partially regionalized in that inputs of commodities 3 and 4 and factor 2 could not be regionalized. Therefore, a dummy industry, 3.d, has been set up, which produces commodity 5. Commodity 5 is then purchased by industries 3.1 and 3.2.

It is to be noted that the final demand is the same in Figure 12-1 and Figure 12-3, and that there is no direct accounting for interregional trade flows.

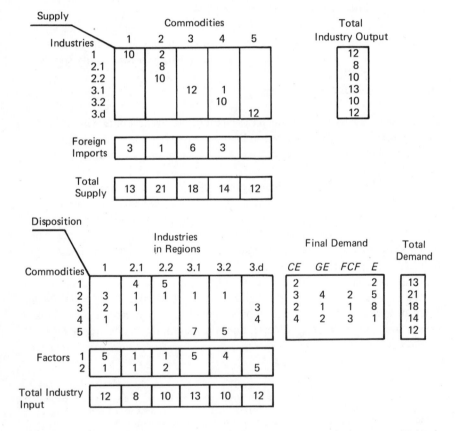

Figure 12-3. National Input-Output Accounts with Regional Disaggregation in Industry Space.

The parameters for the model outlined above could be estimated from this new set of accounts. In this case, the market share coefficients serve to allocate demand to regions as well as industries. However, demand is pooled at the national level; therefore, demand originating in one region is met by the same pattern of supply as demand for the same commodity originating in another region.

We turn now to possibilities of disaggregation in commodity space that allow the introduction of alternative models of distribution.

Disaggregation in Commodity Space

Region-specific or customer-specific patterns of supply are introduced by means of disaggregation in commodity space. With the introduction of customer-specific shares, a number of demand pools may be created for each commodity. Each pool takes the form of a separate row in the disposition matrix. For each row in the disposition matrix there is a corresponding column in the output matrix that gives rise to a pattern of supply. In this way, customer-specific shares are introduced as a simple disaggregation in commodity space, leaving the mathematical structure of the model unchanged.

Let us consider the second commodity of Figure 12-3. Under the assumption of a model formed from the accounts in Figure 12-3, domestic demand, that is, demand originating as intermediate inputs into industries or as domestic final demands, is supplied as follows: 1/16 is imported; that which is supplied domestically is shared among industries 1, 2.1, and 2.2 in the ratio of 2:8:10.

Let us assume that we have information that demands originating in industries 2.1 and 3.1 are always supplied by industry 2.1. This information can be introduced into the model by first disaggregating the second row of the disposition matrix, as shown in Figure 12-4, and then by disaggregating the output matrix, as shown in Figure 12-5.

When share coefficients are formed, domestic demand for commodity 2.1 is supplied as follows: 1/14 is imported; that which is supplied domestically is shared among industries 1, 2.1, and 2.2 in the ratio of 2:6:10. Demand for commodity 2.2 is supplied totally by industry 2.1.

Customer-specific shares may be used to depict a range of interregional trading behaviour within the context of the basic model. In fact, each commodity

Commodities	Industries						CE	GE	FCF	E	Total
	1	2.1	2.2	3.1	3.2	3.d					
2.1	3		1		1		3	4	2	5	19
2.2		1		1							2

Figure 12-4. Disaggregation of the Second Row of Disposition Matrix.

Commodities

Industries 2.1   2.2

	2.1	2.2
1	2	
2.1	6	2
2.2	10	
3.1		
3.2		
3.d		

Foreign Imports

1	

Total

19	2

Figure 12–5. Disaggregation of the Output Matrix.

market may be considered separately. Certain commodities may be designated as local commodities for which production occurs in the region where the demand originates. In this case, demand is pooled by region, and the corresponding market share coefficients direct the demand to industries in the same region. Such commodities as personal services and retail trade may be considered as local commodities.

At the other end of the scale, certain commodities may be treated as national commodities, for which the pattern of supply does not depend upon the region or sector in which the demand originates. This is the behaviour implicit in the basic model. Accordingly, commodities for which this behaviour is held to be true need not be disaggregated at all. This assumption is probably valid for commodities with national distribution networks, where brand name is important and transportation costs are a relatively small portion of the value. A number of consumer durables and semidurables would fall into this category.

For a large number of commodity markets, the distribution patterns are neither "local" nor "national." This is particularly true of many intermediate commodities for which the distribution patterns are influenced by institutional arrangements. For these commodities, customer-specific shares may be used to incorporate information on interregional flows that may be available from transportation statistics or interregional trade surveys. Alternatively, customer-specific shares may be used to incorporate analytic assumptions about trade flows. For example, given sources of supply and location of demand in the base year, customer-specific shares can be calculated in such a way as to minimize transportation costs for particular commodities.

Customer-specific shares may be used selectively and may incorporate fragmentary information on trading patterns. In principle, each nonzero element in the disposition matrix may have its own supply pattern. In the context of an interregional model, it is expected that market shares will be regional-specific for non-national commodities only.

If customer-specific shares are to be introduced in such a way that the base-period activity levels can be replicated by a solution of the model using base-period final demand, the commodities in the flow matrices should be disaggregated so as to preserve the accounting identities of the system. For each demand pool, the total supply must equal the total disposition of the commodity. In the disposition matrix and the output matrix, the sum of the output or disposition in each subset of demand pools must be equal to the corresponding commodity in the account of the basic model.

Implementation

A model within the framework presented in this paper is being implemented by the Structural Analysis Division of Statistics Canada. Work is well advanced on the regionalisation of the 1966 input-output table for Canada. These national input-output tables distinguish more than 650 commodities and 200 industries. It is expected that this degree of detail will be maintained in the regionalized version.

Initially, regionalization means provincialization (ten provinces and two territories). It is recognized, of course, that political boundaries need not coincide with economic boundaries. It is certainly feasible within the context of this model to push regionalization to any level of geographic detail within the limits imposed by the availability of data.

Plans are being made to regionalize the 1971 input-output tables for Canada. Many more commodities are being distinguished in the 1971 tables—as many as 1700. Information on finer levels of geographical detail is being preserved, as well, so that it will be possible to distinguish regions according to a number of criteria.

References

1. Bureau de la Statistique du Québec et Laboratoire d'Econometrie, Université Laval. *Le Système de Compatibilité Economique du Québec.* Vol. III, *Les Utilisations* [The System of Economic Accounting for Quebec. Vol. III, The Uses]. Bureau de la Statistique du Québec, 1970.

2. Chenery, H.; P.G. Clark; and V. Cao Pinna, *The Structure and Growth of the Italian Economy.* Rome: U.S. Mutual Security Agency, 1953.

3. Dominion Bureau of Statistics. *The Input-Output Structure of the Canadian Economy, 1961.* Vol. I. DBS Catalogue No. 15–501. Ottawa: The Queen's Printer for Canada, 1969.

4. Gigantes, T. "The Representation of Technology in Input-Output Systems." In *Input-Output Techniques.* Vol. 1, *Contributions to Input-Output Analysis.* Edited by A.P. Carter and A. Bródy. Amsterdam: North-Holland Publishing Company, 1970. Pp. 270–290.

5. Gigantes, T., and R. Hoffman. "A Price-Output Nucleus for Simulation Models." In *Input-Output Techniques.* Edited by A. Bródy and A.P. Carter. Amsterdam: North-Holland Publishing Company, 1972. Pp. 319–339.

6. Gigantes, T.; R. Hoffman; A. Lemelin; T. Matuszewski; and M. Truchon. "A New Approach to the Structural Analysis of a National Economy and Corresponding Data Strategies." Paper read at the Annual Meeting of the Econometric Society, New York, December 1973.

7. Isard, W. "Interregional and Regional Input-Output Analysis: A Model of a Space Economy." *The Review of Economics and Statistics* 33, no. 4 (November 1951): 318–328.

8. Leontief, W. "Interregional Theory." In W. Leontief et al., *Studies in the Structure of the American Economy.* New York: Oxford University Press, 1953. Pp. 93–115.

9. Leontief, W., and A. Strout. "Multiregional Input-Output Analysis." In *Structural Interdependence and Economic Development.* Edited by T. Barna. London: MacMillan, 1963. Pp. 119–150.

10. Matuszewski, T. "Partly Disaggregated Rectangular Input-Output Models and Their Use for the Purposes of a Large Corporation." In *Input-Output Techniques.* Edited by A. Bródy and A.P. Carter. Amsterdam: North-Holland Publishing Company, 1972. Pp. 301–318.

11. Moses, L.N. "Stability of Interregional Trading Patterns and Input-Output Analysis." *American Economic Review* 45, no. 5 (December 1955): 803–832.

12. Statistics Canada. "Structural Economic Models: A Users' Guide." Ottawa, 1974.

Chapter Thirteen

Interregional Trade Effects in Static and Dynamic Input-Output Models

M. Jarvin Emerson

Most regional input-output models have been constructed on the basis of two fundamental and interrelated assumptions of fixed technical coefficients and stable trading relationships. The assumption of trade coefficient stability in regional input-output models has seldom been challenged despite extensive construction and use of such models. This seems odd because, as Richardson has pointed out,

> The major problem in the development of interregional I-O models arises from the fact that I-O analysis itself has no mechanism for explaining trade patterns, yet the derivation of interregional trade flows is the key distinctive feature of the interregional model. [14, p. 56]

Conventional regional and interregional input-output models contain the assumption that trade coefficients are constant. Isard's essentially a priori considerations [8] and the results of Moses' highly aggregated test model [12] have been the primary support for this assumption. Neither of these approaches is very conclusive. More recently, Riefler and Tiebout have found evidence of trade coefficient instability [15].

The Moses test was conducted with a five-commodity, three-region model of the United States over a three-year interval using Interstate Commerce Commission 1 percent waybill statistics. Although instability was found, Moses concluded that "they [the waybill statistics interregional trade flows] have exhibited sufficient stability to warrant their being subjected to further statistical evaluation on various levels of regional and commodity aggregation." As implied, the broad levels of industrial and geographic aggregation in the test model and the short time span cast considerable doubt on the conclusiveness of the tests. Nonetheless, numerous studies have cited the Moses study as proof of trade coefficient

The author gratefully acknowledges financial assistance of the National Science Foundation.

stability. In a pioneering effort to formulate an interregional input-output system, Isard expected certain instability of trade coefficients, but observed that stability would be present in highly aggregated models [8]. The interregional model of California and Washington by Riefler and Tiebout [15] was constructed from survey data input-output tables for the two states and an import and export matrix for Washington, while the remaining coefficients and coefficient changes were estimated from secondary data. The test indicated that there was substantial instability of the trade coefficients. Of the 27 industries tested, only 8 had errors of less than 10 percent.

Subsequently, Beyers [1] examined the 1963 and 1967 Washington input-output models for stability in the import coefficients as well as the regional input coefficients. Somewhat surprisingly, he found that more import coefficients increased than decreased during the time interval.

Trade Coefficients

This paper focuses on the stability of the import coefficients in a regional input-output model. A gross import coefficient is the ratio of a sector's imports (out-of-region purchases) to its total output. The gross import coefficient may be disaggregated to indicate import coefficients for each sector as well as region of origin.

GROSS IMPORT COEFFICIENT

$$_tm_j = {_tM_j}/{_tX_j}$$

INDUSTRY-OF-ORIGIN IMPORT COEFFICIENT

$$_tm_{ij} = {_tM_{ij}}/{_tX_j}$$

where

$_tM_j$ = gross imports from rest of the world by regional sector j in year t

$_tM_{ij}$ = imports from rest of the world sector i to regional sector j in year t

$_tX_j$ = gross output of regional sector j in year t

This formulation corresponds to the usual regional input-output model containing a gross import row consisting of both competitive and noncompetitive imports. In such models, the coefficients $_tm_j$ are assumed to be stable. In interregional models, where the import row is disaggregated into an import matrix, the coefficients $_tm_{ij}$ are assumed to be stable.

Sources of Variation in Import Coefficients

Explanations for variations in import coefficients in regional input-output models may stem from either economic theory or statistical methodology. Also, as with technical coefficients and input coefficients, trade coefficients may be affected by technological change. In theories concerning the spatial distribution of firms, supply (or market) areas are assumed to be responsive to changes in relative prices and transportation costs. Industrial organization, for example, horizontal or vertical integrations, may explain certain trading patterns. From a macroeconomics viewpoint, import substitution is a vehicle of import coefficient change. Statistical aggregation, both industrial and geographic, may influence the degree of import coefficient stability.

Technological Change

A change in the technology of an industry can change import coefficients as well as input coefficients. For most regional input-output formulations, the relationship between input and import coefficients can be expressed as

$$A = R + M$$

where

A = matrix of technical input coefficients for regional industries

R = matrix of regional input coefficients (inputs supplied by regional industries)

M = matrix of regional input coefficients (inputs imported from industries outside the region)

Any a_{ij} is the sum of a corresponding r_{ij} and m_{ij}. A change in either technology or relative imports will affect the r_{ij} values and, therefore, $(I - R)^{-1}$.

Supply Areas

Cost-price relationships, capacity limits, variations in production, or a sudden increase in demand may initiate major shifts in supply locations, which could result in either increasing or decreasing import coefficients. In the construction industry, for example, for which demand is markedly unstable, the import coefficients can be extremely unstable. Some manufacturing activities, such as aircraft manufacturing, exhibit a similar pattern of oscillation.

Industrial Structure

Large corporations with branch plant operations may exert a different influence on trade coefficients than do their nonbranch counterparts, at least insofar as intracompany linkages have a stabilizing effect on inputs from outside the region.

Industrial Aggregation

Economic data are frequently aggregated, and the level of aggregation may influence the behavior of the data. For aggregation into producing sectors, firms are usually grouped according to their products. Since each firm has a unique technology structure, such aggregation results in combining data of firms with different product mixes and different technologies. Thus, while one buyer in a region may purchase its supply of a product from intraregional sources, another buyer in the region may import the same product. Each firm in an industry may have substantially different import coefficients. If some of the firms expand more rapidly than others, import coefficients will change.

Regional Delineation

The spatial distribution of firms within a region may affect the size and behavior of import coefficients. If distance influences the shipments of a good, firms located near the center of the region will have lower import coefficients than like firms located near the border. Similar differences in trade coefficients may occur.

Although there are no compelling arguments in support of trade coefficient stability, major theoretical arguments based upon relative price stability, industrial structure, technological change, or simple inertia have been made to support the assumption of stable trade coefficients. But these arguments can be made with at least equal force for an assumption of instability.

Comparative Statics

The problem of trade coefficient stability is essentially an empirical one. However, for lack of data, few such empirical tests have been conducted. We now turn to two empirical investigations of trade coefficient behavior over time.

The availability of two survey-data input-output tables for the same region permits a comparison of trade coefficients over a five-year interval. A survey-data input-output table was constructed by the author for 1965 for the state of Kansas [3] and for 1970 [4]. Each table contains 69 processing sectors, 5 payments sectors, and 7 final demand sectors. The tables also include an import matrix and an export matrix for each year, constructed from survey data. This permitted a comparison of the 1965 and 1970 import matrices as well as the aggregate import coefficient for each sector.

The Kansas model falls short of an Isard interregional model [7], but given the dearth of empirical testing of trade coefficients, it does have the capacity to illuminate partially the gray area of trade coefficient behavior over time.

The gross import coefficients, m_j's, for 1965 and 1970 for each industry are shown in Table 13-1. Of the 68 nonzero coefficients, 32 increased and 36 decreased during the 1965-1970 period. These less than conclusive results differ from those of Beyers' Washington state study [1], in which more import coefficients increased than decreased between 1964 and 1967. The reasons for variations in the Kansas coefficients are examined below.

The largest changes in coefficients occurred in Industry 41, Electrical machinery, Industry 45, Trailer coaches, and Industry 31, Petroleum & coal. Although the manufacturing sectors accounted for all of the coefficient changes in excess of 0.06, the import coefficients for the three new construction industries (Industries 18-20) also exhibited sizeable changes.

Table 13-1. Kansas Imports, 1965, and Import Coefficients, 1965 and 1970

| Industry | | Imports 1965 ($ thousands) | Import Coefficients | | Difference |
Number	Title		1965	1970	1970 - 1965
Agriculture					
1	Corn	17,239	.1940	.2138	.0198
2	Sorghum	25,365	.1420	.1274	-.0146
3	Wheat	54,305	.1689	.1513	-.0176
4	Other grains	1,098	.1156	.1278	.0122
5	Soybeans	6,089	.1451	.1526	.0075
6	Hay	9,576	.0781	.0721	-.0060
7	Dairying	5,611	.0776	.0961	.0185
8	Poultry	2,561	.1124	.1093	-.0031
9	Cattle	81,088	.1358	.1652	.0294
10	Hogs	10,509	.1042	.1125	.0083
11	Other agriculture	2,433	.1219	.1095	-.0124
12	Agricultural services	14,893	.2554	.2884	.0330
Mining					
13	Crude oil	58,977	.1335	.1251	-.0084
14	Oil & gas field services	3,048	.0656	.0912	.0256
15	Nonmetallic mining	10,531	.1440	.1447	.0007
16	Other mining	3,884	.0828	.0833	.0005
Construction					
17	Maintenance & repair	0	.0	.0	.0
18	Building construction	72,210	.1966	.1727	-.0239
19	Heavy construction	19,969	.1598	.2134	.0536
20	Special trade construction	161,804	.4693	.4272	-.0421
Manufacturing					
21	Meat products	53,141	.0899	.1526	.0627
22	Dairy products	22,034	.1955	.1809	-.0146
23	Grain mill products	100,153	.3001	.3221	.0220
24	Other food	104,139	.5028	.5957	.0929
25	Apparel	19,440	.5107	.4218	-.0889

· (continued)

Table 13-1 continued

Industry		Imports 1965 ($ thousands)	Import Coefficients		Difference 1970 - 1965
Number	Title		1965	1970	
Manufacturing continued					
26	Paper	39,485	.5224	.5153	-.0071
27	Printing & publishing	54,908	.4611	.4424	-.0187
28	Industrial chemicals	74,482	.4847	.5120	.0273
29	Agricultural chemicals	10,321	.6216	.6809	.0593
30	Other chemicals	134,776	.5862	.6441	.0579
31	Petroleum & coal	165,492	.2852	.3971	.1119
32	Rubber & plastic	103,451	.6819	.6023	-.0796
33	Cement & concrete	19,331	.2538	.2565	.0027
34	Other stone & clay	44,592	.4619	.4332	-.0287
35	Primary metals	17,758	.5655	.5034	-.0621
36	Fabricated metals	38,260	.5472	.4996	-.0476
37	Other fabricated metals	41,690	.5554	.5566	.0012
38	Farm machinery	23,683	.4588	.4932	.0344
39	Construction machinery	23,669	.4948	.4890	-.0058
40	Food products machinery	13,067	.4881	.4807	-.0074
41	Electrical machinery	25,739	.5935	.4277	-.1658
42	Other machinery	61,547	.4874	.4391	-.0483
43	Motor vehicles	109,058	.4885	.4915	.0030
44	Aerospace	223,954	.3999	.3002	-.0097
45	Trailer coaches	24,541	.5780	.4231	-.1549
46	Other transportation equipment	38,096	.8591	.7864	-.0727
47	Other manufacturing	31,640	.5323	.4813	-.0510
Transportation					
48	Railroad transportation	59,244	.2371	.2363	-.0008
49	Motor freight	56,591	.4117	.3694	-.0423
50	Other transportation	13,342	.3635	.3608	-.0027
Communications & Utilities					
51	Communications	3,863	.0241	.0419	.0178
52	Utilities	6,757	.0237	.0428	.0191
Wholesale Trade					
53	Groceries	7,618	.1672	.1653	-.0019
54	Farm products	7,358	.0905	.1358	.0453
55	Machinery & equipment	14,076	.1705	.1635	-.0070
56	Other wholesale	9,673	.0763	.0768	.0005
Retail Trade					
57	Farm equipment dealers	275	.0090	.0125	.0035
58	Gas service stations	6,349	.0854	.0846	-.0008
59	Eating & drinking	41,473	.2385	.2301	-.0084
60	Other retail	52,563	.1253	.1233	-.0020
Finance, Insurance, & Real Estate					
61	Banking	5,459	.0328	.0539	.0211
62	Other finance	43,042	.1362	.1370	.0008
63	Insurance & real estate	86,976	.2203	.2247	.0044

(continued)

Table 13-1 continued

Industry		Imports 1965 ($ thousands)	Import Coefficients		Difference
Num-ber	Title		1965	1970	1970 - 1965
Services					
64	Lodging	8,722	.2543	.2521	-.0022
65	Personal services	21,601	.0904	.0856	-.0048
66	Business services	13,402	.3066	.2827	-.0239
67	Medical & health services	38,246	.1270	.1318	.0048
68	Other services	17,637	.2185	.2225	.0040
69	Education	53,916	.0995	.0994	-.0001

Source: M. Jarvin Emerson, *The Interindustry Structure of the Kansas Economy*, Topeka: State of Kansas, 1969; and "The 1970 Kansas Input-Output Tables" (unpublished).

The scatter diagram of Figure 13-1 illustrates the changes in gross input coefficients for coefficients greater than 0.1. The numbers correspond to the industry numbers in Table 13-1. If a point lies on the line in Figure 13-1, this indicates that the import coefficient for that industry was unchanged between 1965 and 1970. If a point lies above the line, the import coefficient was larger in 1970 than 1965 and, conversely, if a point lies below the line, the size of the gross import coefficient for that industry decreased between 1965 and 1970.

Of prime importance is the absolute magnitude of change in the import coefficients. The difference between the coefficients in the two periods will be reflected in the regional input matrix and in subsequent calculations from it. Table 13-2 indicates the magnitude of these coefficient changes.

An alternative summary of the change in the m_j's during the period 1965-1970 is presented in Table 13-3. Of the 68 nonzero m_j's, 35 percent changed less than 5 percent and 62 percent changed less than 10 percent. Relatively few coefficients decreased by a substantial percentage, none more than 30 percent. However, 13 percent of the coefficients increased more than 30 percent.

Because most of the data were obtained from surveys, explanations for the coefficient changes are possible. Industry 25, Apparel; Industry 32, Rubber & plastic; Industry 41, Electrical machinery; and Industry 45, Trailer coaches, were manufacturing industries that had grown rapidly and either attracted supplier firms or became more vertically integrated. The meat-packing industry (Industry 21) experiences annual instability in supply patterns which reflects sizeable price shifts for livestock and feed grain. This phenomenon is also reflected in the import coefficient for Industry 9, Cattle.

The vagaries of the construction industry are such that large changes in the import coefficients are more the rule than the exception. The aerospace industry is similar to the construction industry in that the composition of its output and therefore of its inputs is highly variable.

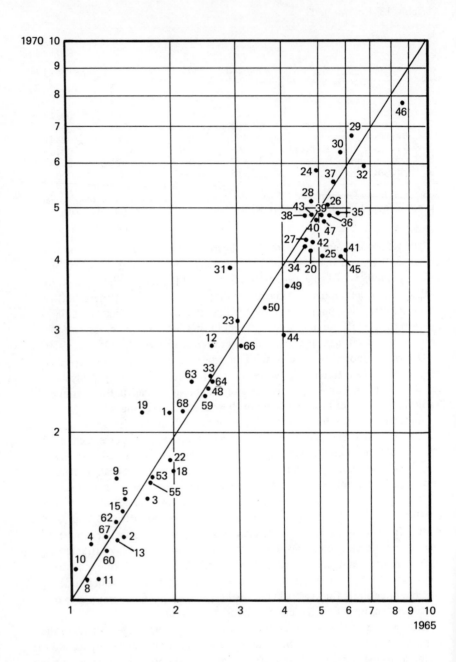

Figure 13-1.   Kansas Import Coefficients Greater Than 0.1, 1965 and 1970.

Table 13-2. Changes in Kansas Import Coefficients, m_j's, 1965 to 1970

Difference	*Number of Sectors*	
$70m_j - 65m_j$	$70m_j > 65m_j$	$70m_j < 65m_j$
0–.009	13	16
.01–.019	5	5
.02–.029	5	3
.03–.039	2	0
.04–.049	1	4
.05–.059	3	1
.06–.069	1	1
.07–.079	0	2
.08–.089	0	1
.09–.099	1	1
> .10	1	2
Total	32	36

Table 13-3. Percentage Change in Gross Import Coefficients, Kansas, 1965 to 1970

	Percent of Coefficients	
Percent Change	$65m_j < 70m_j$	$65m_j > 70m_j$
0– 4.9	14.7	20.6
5– 9.9	10.3	16.2
10–19.9	5.9	11.8
20–29.9	2.9	4.4
30–39.9	5.9	0
> 40	7.3	0
Total	47.0	53.0

The petro-chemical complex experienced shifts in raw material supply sources stemming from declining production in the state. This affected the petroleum industry as well as the industrial and agricultural chemical industries. The necessity to purchase more raw materials outside the state increased the import coefficients.

The magnitudes of changes in the m_{ij}'s and the reasons for them are reflective of the foregoing discussion of the m_j's, because they are disaggregates. Of primary concern is the effect of these variations on the R and $(I-R)^{-1}$ matrices. A comparison test was conducted to indicate the magnitude of the effect of changes in the R matrix. A 1970 final demand vector was multiplied by the $(I-R)^{-1}$ and $(I-R^*)^{-1}$ matrices, where R^* is the original 1965 regional input coefficient matrix adjusted for the changes in imports between 1965 and 1970. The results for selected industries are given in Table 13-4. Gross output of the state's industries would be underestimated by $1022 million without adjusting for import

Table 13-4. Gross Industry Outputs with Regional Input Matrices Unadjusted and Adjusted for Import Variations

Industry		Gross Outputs		
		($ millions)		
Num-ber	Title	$_{70}X$	$_{70}X^*$	$(_{70}X^*/_{70}X) \cdot 10^2$
1	Corn	114.3	107.1	93.7
2	Sorghum	220.5	232.4	105.4
3	Wheat	454.9	468.6	103.0
4	Other grains	8.3	8.0	96.4
5	Soybeans	52.2	49.8	95.4
6	Hay	137.3	141.5	103.1
7	Dairying	91.7	85.3	93.0
8	Poultry	23.8	24.7	103.8
9	Cattle	901.1	885.0	98.2
10	Hogs	154.0	149.6	97.1
11	Other agriculture	36.3	39.2	108.0
12	Agricultural services	87.2	82.3	94.4
13	Crude oil	383.4	394.5	102.9
14	Oil & gas field services	32.7	28.9	88.4
15	Nonmetallic mining	90.4	90.3	99.9
16	Other mining	89.5	89.2	99.7
17	Maintenance & repair	222.6	225.3	101.2
18	Building construction	513.8	570.7	111.1
19	Heavy construction	225.7	201.0	89.1
20	Special trade construction	483.6	490.6	101.4
21	Meat products	861.1	802.7	93.2
22	Dairy products	160.2	165.4	103.2
23	Grain mill products	407.9	397.8	97.5
24	Other food	303.8	286.1	94.2
25	Apparel	173.2	193.8	111.9
26	Paper	112.6	113.2	100.5
27	Printing & publishing	189.7	199.6	105.2
28	Industrial chemicals	200.7	190.9	95.1
29	Agricultural chemicals	25.1	23.2	92.4
30	Other chemicals	435.6	403.6	92.7
31	Petroleum & coal	740.2	680.9	92.0
32	Rubber & plastic	310.1	347.3	112.0
33	Cement & concrete	101.6	99.8	98.2
34	Other stone & clay	110.4	105.3	95.4
35	Primary metals	58.7	64.1	109.2
36	Fabricated metals	119.5	131.7	110.2
37	Other fabricated metals	142.4	141.8	99.6
38	Farm machinery	95.7	93.2	97.4
39	Construction machinery	82.1	82.9	101.0
40	Food products machinery	31.4	32.1	102.2
41	Electrical machinery	70.7	88.6	125.3
42	Other machinery	180.6	199.4	110.4
43	Motor vehicles	270.4	270.1	100.0
44	Aerospace	361.4	446.3	123.5
45	Trailer coaches	79.5	93.6	117.7
46	Other transportation equipment	55.8	61.3	109.9
47	Other manufacturing	436.9	475.5	108.8
48	Railroad transportation	314.1	312.3	99.4

(continued)

Table 13-4 continued

	Industry	Gross Outputs		
Num-		($ millions)		
ber	Title	$_{70}X$	$_{70}X^*$	$(_{70}X^*/_{70}X) \cdot 10^2$
49	Motor freight	220.8	239.8	108.6
50	Other transportation	51.6	51.1	99.0
51	Communications	216.9	213.2	98.3
52	Utilities	374.2	369.6	98.8
53	Groceries	71.5	71.9	100.6
54	Farm products	110.2	105.4	95.6
55	Machinery & equipment	129.4	131.3	101.5
56	Other wholesale	194.1	193.2	99.5
57	Farm equipment dealers	43.2	41.7	96.5
58	Gas service stations	106.7	107.2	100.5
59	Eating & drinking	315.6	322.8	102.3
60	Other retail	534.9	541.7	101.3
61	Banking	270.8	263.5	97.3
62	Other finance	478.8	475.2	99.2
63	Insurance & real estate	504.5	497.1	98.5
64	Lodging	58.1	59.9	103.1
65	Personal services	297.6	311.4	104.6
66	Business services	76.1	82.6	108.5
67	Medical & health services	427.9	420.5	98.3
68	Other services	124.8	120.0	96.2
69	Education	661.3	664.2	100.4
	Total	16,027.8	17,049.8	

changes. Alternatively stated, the adjusted output is 6.4 percent higher than the unadjusted output. Variations in individual industries are more substantial, as indicated in the table.

Dynamic Simulation

An alternative approach to the problem of trade coefficient stability is a simulation of anticipated changes in trade coefficients to determine the effect on industry output. Such a simulation was performed with the Kansas model cast in a dynamic framework. The dynamic regional input-output model is similar to Miernyk's regional adaptation [11] of the Leontief dynamic inverse [9].

The direct interdependence within the economy in any two successive years can be described by the following general dynamic equation:

$$_tX - _tR_t X - _{t+1}B(_{t+1}X - _tX) = _tC \tag{13-1}$$

where

$_tX$ = a column vector of sectoral outputs produced in year t

$_tC$ = a column vector of deliveries to final demand in year t

$_tR$ = an $n \times n$ regional input coefficient matrix

$_tB$ = an $n \times n$ capital coefficient matrix

Then, substituting

$$_tA = {_tR} + {_tM} \tag{13-2}$$

and

$$_tR = {_tA} - {_tM} \tag{13-3}$$

where

$_tA$ = an $n \times n$ regional technical coefficient matrix

$_tM$ = an $n \times n$ import coefficient matrix,

into equation (13-1) yields

$$_tX - ({_tA} - {_tM})_t X - {_{t+1}B}({_{t+1}X} - {_tX}) = {_tC} \tag{13-4}$$

Two different sets of plausible import coefficient changes were introduced, and industry growth in outputs was simulated and compared with growth where no change occurred in import coefficients. The first set was an extension of the results of the comparative static analysis discussed above. The second was based on the best-practice-firm technique extended to import coefficients where the import coefficients of the most efficient firms were employed to represent future import coefficients.

Simulations using import coefficient changes based on the best-practice-firm technique resulted in wider differences than the simulations incorporating import coefficient changes stemming from the actual changes between 1965 and 1970.

Examples of the simulations are given in Figures 13-2 and 13-3 for two industries: Motor vehicles and Electrical machinery, respectively. For both industries, the growth rate after import coefficient changes had been introduced was higher than it would have been if the import coefficient had been constant. Also, in both cases the best-practice-firm technique resulted in larger simulated outputs.

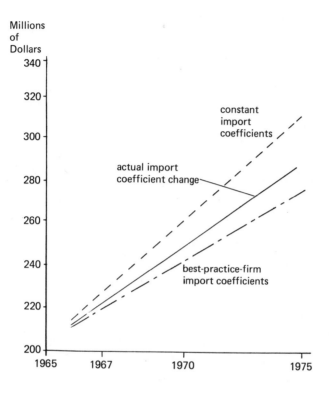

Figure 13-2. Projected Output of Motor Vehicles Sector with Different Import Coefficient Assumptions.

Summary

Comparison of the two primary-data input-output models suggests that the trade coefficient stability problem is not acute but that it is of sufficient importance to warrant concern about the stability of import coefficients and regional input coefficients. The stability problem is best assessed with the use of survey data.

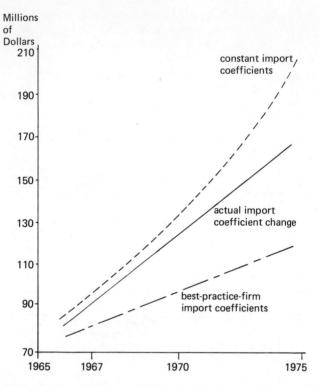

Figure 13-3. Projected Output of Electrical Machinery Sector with Different Import Coefficient Assumptions.

References

1. Beyers, W.B. "On the Stability of Regional Interindustry Models: The Washington Data for 1963 and 1967." *Journal of Regional Science* 12, no. 3 (December 1972): 363–374.

2. Chenery, H.B. "Interregional and International Input-Output Analysis." In *The Structural Interdependence of the Economy.* Edited by T. Barna. New York: MacMillan, 1956. Pp. 341–356.

3. Emerson, M.J. *The Interindustry Structure of the Kansas Economy.* Topeka: State of Kansas, 1969.

4. Emerson, M.J. "The 1970 Kansas Input-Output Tables." Unpublished manuscript, 1973.

5. Emerson, M.J.; F.C. Lamphear; and L.D. Atencio. "Toward a Dynamic Regional Export Model." *Annals of Regional Science* 3, no. 2 (December 1969): 127–138.

6. Greytak, D. "Regional Impact of Interregional Trade in Input-Output Analysis." *Regional Science Association Papers* 25 (1970): 203–217.

7. Isard, W. "Interregional and Regional Input-Output Analysis: A Model of a Space Economy." *The Review of Economics and Statistics* 33, no. 4 (November 1951): 318–328.

8. Isard, W. "Regional Commodity Balances and Interregional Commodity Flows." *American Economic Review* 43, no. 2 (May 1953): 167–180.

9. Leontief, W. "The Dynamic Inverse." In *Input-Output Techniques.* Vol. 1, *Contributions to Input-Output Analysis.* Edited by A.P. Carter and A. Bródy. Amsterdam: North-Holland Publishing Company, 1970. Pp. 17–46.

10. Leontief, W., and A. Strout. "Multiregional Input-Output Analysis." In *Structural Interdependence and Economic Development.* Edited by T. Barna. London: MacMillan, 1963. Pp. 119–150.

11. Miernyk, W.H., et al. *Simulating Regional Economic Development: An Interindustry Analysis of the West Virginia Economy.* Lexington, Mass.: D.C. Heath and Company, 1970.

12. Moses, L. "The Stability of Interregional Trading Patterns and Input-Output Analysis." *American Economic Review* 45, no. 5 (December 1955): 803–832.

13. Polenske, K.R. "The Implementation of a Multiregional Input-Output Model for the United States." In *Input-Output Techniques.* Edited by A. Bródy and A.P. Carter. Amsterdam: North-Holland Publishing Company, 1972. Pp. 171–189.

14. Richardson, H.W. *Input-Output and Regional Economics.* New York: John Wiley and Sons, 1972.

15. Riefler, R., and C.M. Tiebout. "Interregional Input-Output: An Empirical California-Washington Model." *Journal of Regional Science* 10, no. 2 (August 1970): 135–152.

16. Suzuki, K. "Observations on the Stability of the Structure of the Interregional Flow of Goods." *Journal of Regional Science* 11, no. 2 (August 1971): 187–209.

17. Wilson, A.G. "Interregional Commodity Flows: Entropy Maximizing Approaches." Center for Environmental Studies, Working Paper 19, 1968.

Chapter Fourteen

An Operational Nonsurvey Technique for Estimating a Coherent Set of Interregional Input-Output Tables

D. Vanwynsberghe

The first regional input-output tables were constructed in the early 1950s for the United States; later on, regional tables were constructed for Japan and for Holland and other European countries. Given the high cost of a direct survey, various nonsurvey techniques have most often been chosen to develop statistics for these tables. Each of these techniques leads to a different type of link between the regional and national tables and determines the nature of the conclusions that can be reached.

First, there are individual regional tables, which are frequently based on technical coefficients derived from a national table. The link with the national table is achieved by adding two vectors: a column vector of exports to the rest of the nation and a row vector of competitive imports from the rest of the nation. The column vector is a part of the final demand section of the table; the row vector is a part of the primary inputs section.

Second, there are multiregional tables that are obtained by partitioning a nation into a number of regions. These tables give the regional destination of the national output of each sector without specifying the regional origin (gross-balance method). In this type of table, total regional demand and total regional supply of each sector are known, and their balance forms the link with the national table. Such a multiregional table does not give the technological structure of individual regions. Also, it does not provide exact interregional flows of goods and services but only a positive or negative balance—it shows only the tip of the iceberg of interregional relations. (See the Dutch tables [1; 2] and Van Waterschoot [15] for examples of this type of table.)

Leontief et al. [8] developed an interesting balanced multiregional model. It makes a distinction between regional sectors and national sectors. Supplies of regional sectors are consumed in the producing region, and supplies of national sectors are consumed wherever demand exists in the nation, in proportion to regional production.

An intermediate solution between multiregional and interregional input-output tables is a multiregional intraregional input-output table based upon the gross-balance method. Such tables lead to intraregional structural coefficients instead of technical coefficients, because the intermediate inputs for each region are split into the inputs from the region itself and the inputs from abroad. The first remain in the intermediate matrix; the second are only given in an aggregate form and added to the regional primary inputs. Due to the intraregional structural coefficients, these tables theoretically add a very crucial element to the description of the sectoral structure of the region, because they show how much each sector of a region delivers to each other sector of the region. The interregional links, however, are still specified as gross rather than net flows and act as a balance. Combined with the often-used assumption that regional outputs return by preference to the producing region as inputs (Moore and Petersen [10] and Derwa [4], among others), they lead to erroneous conclusions and are contradictory to regional specialisation.

If one decides to weaken this assumption, then much more can be gained by constructing interregional tables. These tables were first conceived by Isard et al. [7]. The Isard model contains the most complete set of detailed data, but it is also the most difficult to implement because of the large number of data required. This interregional input-output model is an elaboration of a national model, as each of the m sectors in each of the n regions becomes a sector in its own right, thus requiring the identification of $(m \times n)$ equations, involving a possible $(m \times n)^2$ intersectoral relationships.

Chenery [3] and Moses [11] developed methods that are similar to the Isard model but that only define aggregate interregional flows. Purchases of a commodity by a particular region are assumed to be drawn from the various supplying regions in fixed proportions, which are independent of the purchasing sector. So the full $(mn \times mn)$ matrix of input coefficients, relating inputs and outputs of each sector in each region, is treated as the product of two matrices. The first shows for each region the technical relationships between sectors; the second describes the interregional purchasing pattern for the product of each sector.

Leontief and Strout [9] have proposed that the flows of a particular commodity should be treated as proportional both to the size of the regional demand pools and to the size of the regional supply pools of the commodity. Polenske [12; 13] has also considered this case as well as the case where flows are proportional only to the size of the supply pools and another where the flows are proportional to the size of the demand pools, and has compared the efficiency of the three forms in forecasting situations.

Because of data assembly difficulties, the Isard model was not implemented until the late 1960s. In Japan, it was first applied in 1967, when the Japanese Ministry for International Trade and Industry used it to assemble data for an interregional input-output table for Japan. Similar projects have been undertaken in England by Gordon [6] and in Holland by the Essor Working Group [5]. The present study is the first attempt to implement this model in Belgium.

Through an investigation of the different approaches, a new method was developed that integrates features from several other studies. It is based upon widely accepted assumptions and makes use of existing regional data. It was successfully used to separate the Belgian national table into a table for three domestic regions—Brabant, Flanders, and Wallonia—and one international region. The result was an interregional approach for both intermediate and final demand, combining elements of the Chenery-Moses model and the Isard model. The value added inputs are attributed to the regions in which they are produced, and competitive foreign imports are allocated to the regions in which they are consumed. In this way, no interregional dimension is introduced in the primary inputs.

Methodology

This section concentrates on the methodology used and gives special attention to the underlying hypotheses. The inadequacy of the gross-balance method is shown. At the same time, the steps that are necessary to arrive at interregional flows instead of balances are explained.

The Gross-Balance Method

Separating the columns of a national input-output table according to the regional consumption (intermediate and final) results in regional tables linked together by a balance vector. Since the starting point of the division of the national columns is a table with total data (that is, supplies to a given sector in a given region contain both the goods produced domestically and the imported goods), the national primary inputs must also be separated into regional gross value added and regional imports of competitive goods to determine the regional balance for each sector. The balance for each sector is defined as the total demand of the region (row sum) compared with the total resources available in the region (column sum). The column sum contains the competitive imports, which can be found in the primary inputs of the sector under consideration. Of course, it also contains the intermediate imports of all other sectors. The row sum contains all supplies of competitive goods, separated according to the intermediate and final demand vectors that are using them.

Therefore, there is a fundamental problem with respect to the competitive imports. These are calculated in two different ways: for the column, proportionally to the region's own production in the sector under consideration; and for the row, proportionally to the production of all consuming sectors in the region. The total, defined in this way, in each row and column can be equal only by chance. Consequently, the balances calculated with this method are biased by the imports. (We will return to this matter in the next section and suggest an improved method.) Aside from the bias thus created, the nature of these balances must be closely analysed, in view of a possible division of the supplies according to the region of origin.

The regional balances obtained from the matrix with total data, by separating the national columns, are the result of a certain number of flows. In a version with three regions, they are the result of imports from the other two regions and the exports to the other two regions. Although the exports from region 1 to region 2, for instance, are equal to the imports of region 2 from region 1, the system remains insoluble. Let M = imports, E = exports, P = production, D = demand, 1, 2, and 3 = domestic regions, and a = abroad. Then we have

for region 1: $M_{21} + M_{31} + P_1 = D_1 + E_{12} + E_{13} + E_{1a}$

for region 2: $M_{12} + M_{32} + P_2 = D_2 + E_{21} + E_{23} + E_{2a}$

for region 3: $M_{13} + M_{23} + P_3 = D_3 + E_{31} + E_{32} + E_{3a}$

in which case $P_1, P_2, P_3, D_1, D_2, D_3, E_{1a}, E_{2a}, E_{3a}$ are known, and

$$M_{12} = E_{12} \quad M_{13} = E_{13}$$

$$M_{21} = E_{21} \quad M_{23} = E_{23}$$

$$M_{31} = E_{31} \quad M_{32} = E_{32}$$

such that the system of 3 equations with 12 endogenous variables is reduced to a system with 3 equations with 6 endogenous variables and takes the following form:

$$P_1 - D_1 - E_{1a} = B_1 = \text{balance of domestic trade in region 1}$$

$$P_2 - D_2 - E_{2a} = B_2 = \text{balance of domestic trade in region 2}$$

$$P_3 - D_3 - E_{3a} = B_3 = \text{balance of domestic trade in region 3}$$

where $B_1 + B_2 + B_3 = 0$.

It is evident that the B regional flows cannot be deduced from the regional balances, even if the balances are not biased by competitive imports.

The Nonsurvey Flow Technique: Row-Column
Coefficient (Rococo) Method
Applying the gross-balance method to a national table does not allow interregional conclusions to be drawn. It also leads to biased results due to the imports, as explained in the preceding section.

The *row-column co*efficient (Rococo) method, which will be developed, results in the regional division of an input-output table according to the region of origin and the region of destination of each flow of goods. It clearly indicates the importance of each sector in each region and shows the interdependence of each sector with each other sector in each region.

To arrive at interregional flows by the Rococo method, the following consecutive steps were taken:

Preparatory phase: An analysis of the existing regional statistical data was required in order to define the regions. The sectors to be taken into account were selected. For essential information that was not available, limited pilot studies were carried out, and the base year was chosen.

Dividing columns and rows: During this phase, the following operations were carried out:

1. The national data were separated into a Belgian table with domestic data only and a Belgian table with import data only.
2. The columns of both the domestic and imported tables were separated for each region using the gross-balance method.
3. A technique was developed that established an equilibrium in each region between regional demand and regional supply of the domestic goods for each sector. The result of this technique gives a set of interregional market shares for each sector in each region. Such a set allows a given domestic flow from one sector to another in a given region to be divided into three flows according to the regional origin of the goods concerned.
4. The market shares of each region were applied to the regional input-output table, that is, to the columns that had been separated from the domestic data.
5. The interregional input-output table was constructed using interregional input-output data and regional import data.

Allocating the entries in each column of the national table to regions only leads to regional input-output tables that are divided according to the use of the regional production, without distinguishing the region of origin. The regional tables were obtained as follows:

For the final demand sectors (private consumption, collective consumption, investments, foreign exports, etc.), some gaps were filled in the existing regional statistics through interpolations and extrapolations of regional statistical series.

For the productive supplies of intermediate sectors, the following basic assumption was made: on the average, the structure of inputs (cost-price structure) for a given sector does not differ much between regions. Using this assumption, the aggregation of the sectors was done separately for each region after the national rows and columns had been divided among the regions. This allowed different cost structures to be distinguished for each region.

The Regional Allocation of Domestic and Imported Goods: As has been indicated above, the division of the columns requires a specific calculation for the competitive imports. It is indeed difficult to sustain the assumption of the gross-balance method that the imports of competitive goods might be divided proportionally to the production of the same goods in each region and that there is a constant proportion between the production of domestic and imported goods for each sector throughout the regions. Given the fact that competitive imports in Belgium are mainly used as intermediate inputs rather than for final consumption, the following solution has been used. In the national input-output table, imports are treated separately, both for the intermediate and final demand sectors. The division of the national columns was carried out for a domestic goods input-output table and an imported goods input-output table. Therefore, after the regional allocation, the imported goods input-output table contains, in each row, goods supplied from abroad to each sector in the region. Accordingly, total supplies from abroad to each region for each sector are found as the totals of the rows. They have been added as an import row to the primary input table, thus replacing the proportional imports that had been calculated through the splitting-up of the total-data columns. The differences for some sectors proved to be rather important, as is shown in Table 14-1.

Table 14-1. Comparison of 1965 Regional Competitive Imports for Brabant in Selected Sectors Using Two Methods (millions of Belgian francs)

Sector		*Proportional to the Production*	*Through the Structure of Intermediate and Final Demand*
Number	*Title*		
1	Agriculture & forestry	5,453.1	8,388.7
10	Refined oil products	485.7	2,913.2
13	Textiles	1,420.4	3,933.7
20	Iron & steel	1,545.7	3,089.7
39	Air transport	493.5	151.2

Source: D. Vanwynsberghe. *The Interregional and Intersectoral Structure of the Brabant Economy: An Input-Output Approach.* (Brussels: Regional Economic Council for Brabant), vol. 2, April 1974, p. 25.

These differences gave rise to the revision of available resources for each sector and for each region and also of the obtained balances. At the same time, a first step has been achieved in the regionalisation according to origin. Indeed, for each region and for each sector, each input has been divided into two amounts: the first coming from Belgium, the second coming from abroad. In the next step, each sectoral supply coming from Belgium has to be separated for each region according to the region of origin—in our case, Brabant, Flanders, or Wallonia.[1]

The Division of Domestic Goods: The division of the Belgian input-output table of domestic goods leads to a regional supply and regional demand of domestic goods for each sector in each region. This regional supply and demand together form a first system of constraints (according to sector and to region).

This first system of constraints is then transformed by subtracting from the regional supply of domestic goods and from the regional demand a part of the regional demand, namely, the regional exports to other countries of the region's own goods. The remainder of the regional demand can be geared to the rest of the region's own resources and to the remainder of the regional supply by the other regions. The remaining demand has been called "own regional consumption" and the remaining supply has been called "regional available resources." In a market system, both should of course be brought into balance. Therefore, the part of each region in each regional sectoral market has to be estimated in order to be able to divide the rows according to regional origin.

It is obvious that all regional solutions must be consistent with the national data. In turn, these national data must be obtained by summation of the regional data.

The Basic Assumptions: The assumptions on which the regional division of domestic goods according to origin are based are the following:

1. As a starting point, it is necessary to use a general method that does not differ according to sector or region, so that the observed differences, as well as the final results, cannot be attributed to the method.
2. Each sectoral regional market functions as a whole.
3. Once a regional market share has been defined for a given sector, the division according to the respective consumption of the demanding sectors can be carried out.
4. Since the concern here is with aggregated sectors (that is, sectors containing specialised regional production), this means that solutions such as "everything from the own region and nothing from the other region and vice versa" have to be rejected.
5. Because real transportation or communication advantages exist, the solutions will have to imply a relative preference for the own region within the framework of the constraints and assumptions set forth here.

1. Taking into consideration some constraints of the economic history of Belgium and given the available statistical data, the homogeneity of regions was best achieved by dividing the country into a northern region (Flanders), a central region (Brabant), and a southern region (Wallonia).

Method of Calculating Domestic Market Shares: Within the framework of a general method, different attempts were made in the present study to calculate the sectoral market shares. Solutions that were theoretically very attractive and that were functions of the regional consumption and of the regional available resources were examined. Both direct calculations and iterative procedures were used. None of these approaches yielded a satisfactory result for all of the assumptions and constraints. Finally, the following method was employed:

Solution 1:   As a starting point, a solution was calculated in which a preference for the own region was explicitly present. This solution reduces to satisfying by preference the own demand and to obtaining the balance by regional imports or regional exports. Such a solution, which has already been used in some countries, has the disadvantage that assumption 4 is not operative. It does not take into account the specialisations of regional production and therefore cannot be sustained within the general framework of economic theory. It is important, however, as an extreme solution, since it allows further precision of the constraints on the market shares. For each sector, it allows the indication of a maximum for the market share of the own region and a minimum for the market share of the other regions.

Solution 2:   As a second step, a solution was chosen in which there was no relative preference for the own region. This means that each region appeared on each market with its available resources and provided for the regional consumption proportionally to these resources. Assumption 5 does not apply for this solution, and this means that communication costs are not taken into account. Also, the solution cannot be upheld within the framework of economic theory. It is, however, interesting as a second extreme solution, since it makes the constraints concerning the regional market shares more precise, that is, it sets a minimum for the market shares in the own region and a maximum for the market shares in the other regions.

Solution 3:   Both the first and second solutions fulfill the requirements of the constraints, but, as noted, the first does not fulfill those of assumption 4, and the second does not fulfill those of assumption 5. They are to be considered as extreme solutions defining the set of feasible solutions. Since a general method has to be found, the solution has to be defined unequivocally as one not linked to a particular sector. The lack of objective information does lead to an average solution—the third solution—between the two extreme market values as defined according to the first two solutions.

The Model

In this section, a short presentation of the final results of the regionalisation of a national input-output table with the Rococo method for three domestic regions and a fourth international region is given. All vectors are defined as column vectors. The matrices are regionally grouped. In a $(3n \times 3n)$ matrix, the first n rows and columns refer to region 1, the $n + 1$ through $2n$ columns and rows refer to region 2, and so on. In a $(3n \times 1)$ vector, the first n elements concern the n sectors in region 1, the $n + 1$ through $2n$ elements concern the same n sectors in region 2, and so on. The following notations are used:

X = gross output vector with $3n$ sectors for the 3 domestic regions

M = vector of competitive imports from other countries for the 3 domestic regions $(3n \times 1)$

Z_k = final demand matrix of domestic region k, without specification of the regional or international origin of the goods for the s final demand components $(n \times s)$. The regional exports to other countries are excluded from this final demand

Y_k = matrix corresponding to Z_k, but for goods of domestic origin only $(n \times s)$

N_k = matrix corresponding to Z_k, but for goods of international origin only $(n \times s)$

$Z_k = Y_k + N_k$

$\hat{Y}$ = block diagonal matrix with the final demand (domestic goods) for each of the domestic regions, Y_k $(3n \times 3s)$

$\hat{N}$ = block diagonal matrix with the final demand (international goods) for each of the domestic regions, N_k $(3n \times 3s)$

$\hat{Z} = \hat{Y} + \hat{N}$

E_k = export vector $(n \times 1)$ for region k

$\hat{E}$ = diagonal matrix with the exports, E_k, grouped by region $(3n \times 3n)$

C_k = technological input coefficients for region k $(n \times n)$

A_k = structural input coefficients for region k $(n \times n)$ for domestic goods only

B_k = structural input coefficients for region k $(n \times n)$ for imported goods from the international market only

$C_k = A_k + B_k$

$\hat{A}$ = block diagonal matrix with the regional structural input coefficients, A_k $(3n \times 3n)$

$\hat{B}$ = block diagonal matrix with the regional structural input coefficients, B_k $(3n \times 3n)$

$\hat{C} = \hat{A} + \hat{B}$

G = matrix with the market shares for domestic goods only, grouped in the columns by sector and region of destination and in the rows by region of origin (this matrix consists of (3 × 3) blocks of diagonal matrices with each n element on the main diagonal if ι represents a vector with units of appropriate dimension, then $\iota' G = \iota$)

I = unit matrix

The interregional model for the domestic market can be summarized as

$$G\hat{A}X + G\hat{Y}\iota + \hat{E} = X \tag{14-1}$$

so that

$$(I - G\hat{A})X = G\hat{Y}\iota + \hat{E} \tag{14-2}$$

or

$$(I - G\hat{A})^{-1} G\hat{Y}\iota + (I - G\hat{A})^{-1}\hat{E} = X \tag{14-3}$$

and if we define $R = (I - G\hat{A})^{-1}$, then equation (14-3) becomes

$$RG\hat{Y}\iota + R\hat{E} = X \tag{14-4}$$

The interregional model for the international market can be summarized as

$$\hat{B}X + \hat{N}\iota = M \tag{14-5}$$

so that with the help of equation (14-4) we can rewrite (14-5) as

$$\hat{B}(RG\hat{Y}\iota + R\hat{E}) + \hat{N}\iota = M \tag{14-6}$$

It follows from equations (14-4) and (14-6) that the domestic model (14-4) is of the Chenery-Moses type and that through its combination with (14-5) the total model becomes a mixture of the Chenery-Moses type and the Isard type.

Conclusions

Given the fact that a general method was used, independent of the sectors and regions, the striking differences that have been observed between the structures of the regional economies are very significant and offer a clear description of reality. These differences can also be partly explained by location theory and are confirmed by other existing information. To evaluate the quality of the method used, we will first summarise the results for each of the regional economies and then discuss the method itself.

The Structure of the Regional Economies

In 1965, one could distinguish in Belgium three regions with rather important differences in sectoral structure, regional autonomy, and interregional links.

Flanders has, as a whole, the most nearly autonomous economy of the three regions, that is, it is best able to fulfill its total needs with its own production. The imports from abroad, however, are relatively more important in Flanders than in the other regions. For its inputs, industry is dependent on its own production for 40 percent, on other countries for 40 percent, and on the other Belgian regions for 20 percent. As far as total output is concerned, 53 percent remains in the region itself, 23 percent goes to other countries, and 24 percent goes to the other regions. In relation to gross output, total wages are much lower in Flanders than in the other regions, and the net indirect taxes are proportionally heavier. The region has a negative balance of trade with foreign countries and a positive balance of trade with Brabant and Wallonia. Although Flanders is the most nearly autonomous region of the country, it has very strong links with the other regions. The part of its output that goes to the regional markets is of the same magnitude as the part that goes to the international market. Also, the amount of output recorded as intermediate transactions in Flanders is less than the intermediate transactions in Wallonia. This is also evident when we look at the marginal influence of the sectors of Brabant and Wallonia on the economy of Flanders. This influence is greater than the influence of the sectors of Flanders on the economy of the other regions. Summarising, it can be said that, although Flanders is less dependent for its inputs on the other Belgian regions, it has strong links with these regions for its output.

The amount of output recorded as intermediate inputs in Wallonia is greater than that of the other two regions. Its intermediate structure is dependent on its own output for 45 percent, on the other regions for 27.5 percent, and on foreign countries for 27.5 percent. As far as its output is concerned, 49 percent remains in the region itself, 23 percent goes to other countries, and 28 percent goes to the other regions. In relation to its gross output, Wallonia consumes more intermediate inputs and pays higher wages than the other regions. It is the only region having a positive balance of trade with other countries. This positive balance, however, is cancelled out completely by its negative balances with the other two regions.

The situation in Brabant is more or less the opposite of that in Wallonia. Only one-third of Brabant's output is oriented towards intermediate demand; two-thirds is geared to final demand. The amount of output recorded as intermediate transactions is the lowest of the three regions. One-third of the intermediate demand of Brabant originates in the region itself, one-third in the other two regions, and one-third in other countries. Of its output, 49 percent remains in Brabant, 36 percent goes to the other two regions, and 15 percent to the international markets. Outputs originate mainly in tertiary and final sectors. These sectors sell mainly on the domestic market. As a consequence, the export ratio of Brabant is considerably lower than the ratio of the other two regions. The exports to other countries originate mainly in secondary and intermediate sectors. This results in a very small number of intermediate transactions, comparable to the other regions only for some tertiary sectors. Consequently, Brabant has an economy oriented towards the tertiary sectors, not only as far as its output is concerned, but also for its own inputs. This region, situated in the central part of the country, clearly has the strongest links with the other regions and the weakest with foreign countries. As a result, it has a central place in the Belgian economy and forms a bridge between the regions by means of a negative balance of trade with Flanders and a positive balance of trade with Wallonia. On the basis of the analysis of the 1965 data, it can be said that its possibilities for growth are dependent on efforts to increase its exports to foreign countries (in particular in tertiary sectors) and on attempts to build a more diversified economic structure, which, in turn, could lead to a higher degree of self-sufficiency. Regionalisation of certain tertiary sectors could have a negative influence on the balances of trade with the other regions. This ought to be compensated by creating new sectors, adapted to the typical structure of the region. This adaptation should take into account the existing intermediate links and the existing quality of the production factors.

Validity of the Method

The interregional flows in Belgium, as estimated by the Rococo method, are on the average of the same magnitude as the known international flows. Given the openness of the Belgian economy, this seems to be an acceptable result. Indeed, one can theorize that two phenomena are at work in opposite directions: the absence of political borders leads theoretically to larger flows on the interregional market, and the smaller price differences between regional markets result in smaller flows. If the interregional and intersectoral influences are measured on the basis of the decrease of the technical coefficients, very striking differences can be observed between sectors and between regions. Table 14-2 gives the results for a 32-sector version for Brabant. It shows that a relative decrease of the international influence results in a relative increase of the interregional influence, the break-even point being approximately 33 percent. In Flanders, this point is approximately 30 percent; in Wallonia, it is approximately 27 percent. This phenomenon can be explained by certain elements of location theory, which were not integrated in the method used, but which became apparent during the analysis of the results. First, location theory would suggest a greater dependence of Flanders on foreign imports, because it has major seaports. The method used in the present study also indicates that Flanders imports

Table 14-2. Decrease of Aggregate Technical Coefficients in Brabant Due to Imports from Abroad and from the Other Two Regions (percent)

Producing Sector		Decrease Due to Imports from Abroad	Decrease Due to Regional Imports
Number	*Title*		
1	Agriculture	16.2	38.7
2	Extractive industry	30.7	32.0
3	Food industry	31.0	39.0
4	Textile industry	45.6	34.9
5	Apparel & leather industry	51.7	28.8
6	Lumber, wood, & furniture	34.5	33.0
7	Paper industry	44.6	20.5
8	Printing & publishing	50.6	18.2
9	Chemical industry	52.3	21.4
10	Iron & steel industry	17.8	35.5
11	Nonferrous metals industry	84.0	7.4
12	Stone, clay, & glass	28.8	39.8
13	Fabricated metal products machinery	58.9	17.6
14	Construction industry	24.3	37.3
15	Garages	24.4	27.1
16	Other industries	70.8	14.7
17	Power & water	22.9	54.4
18	Transportation services by waterway	44.8	30.6
19	Transportation services by land	24.0	39.7
20	Transportation services by air	35.3	29.2
21	Communication	17.6	34.8
22	Finance	20.6	30.2
23	Insurance	24.6	31.0
24	Trade	21.6	35.8
25	Hotels & the like	17.9	29.0
26	Real estate	0.0	33.1
27	Private education services	18.7	34.1
28	National health services	16.9	37.5
29	Private services	23.1	31.1
30	Government	48.5	31.0
31	National education services	16.4	48.3
32	Private household services	0.0	0.0

Source: D. Vanwynsberghe: *The Interregional and Intersectoral Structure of the Brabant Economy: An Input-Output Approach.* (Brussels: Regional Economic Council for Brabant), vol. 3, April 1974, p. 88.

relatively more from abroad than do the other regions. Indeed, sectors using a higher proportion of imports from abroad usually have a higher coefficient of specialisation in Flanders. Some examples are chemicals, refined oil products, oils and fats, textiles, and apparel.[2] Second, in accordance with location theory, our method shows that those sectors using the highest proportion of inputs from their own region often have a coefficient of specialisation that is higher than the

2. The sector names used in the text refer to subcategories of the 32 sectors given in Table 14-2.

average. This phenomenon is very clear in Brabant. Examples for Flanders are textiles, apparel, glass, and transportation; for Wallonia, iron and steel and construction materials; for Brabant, finance, real estate, hotels, garages, government, communication, education, private services. Third, nearly all the sectors that have a higher coefficient of specialisation in Brabant are sectors for which interregional feedbacks are weak and which do not show significant regional differences attributable to feedback. This confirms the widely held view that sectors for which location factors are negligible are located most often in the centre of the country close to final demand.

Another important element in evaluating the merits of the method is the absence of an influence of the relative importance of the regional economies on the market shares. Indeed, as one of the extreme solutions used to arrive at the final solution was dependent on this factor, a certain bias could be expected. Table 14-3 gives the origin of the average intermediate inputs for each of the regions and the regional destination of the average regional outputs. If one knows that the average importance of Flanders is approximately 45 percent, that of Wallonia approximately 30 percent, and that of Brabant approximately 25 percent, then Table 14-3 shows that there is no bias due to the relative importance of each of these economies. Indeed, the market share of Flanders in Wallonia is 15.5 percent and the market share of Brabant in Wallonia is 12.0 percent. The output share of Flanders that goes to Brabant is 12.1 percent, and that of Wallonia to Brabant is also 12.1 percent. Finally, it appears that on the average the intraregional multipliers are 20 percent higher than the direct effects (input coefficients) and that the interregional multipliers are on the average 30 percent higher. The order of magnitude of interregional feedbacks is therefore approximately 10 percent. Although these results are different for each sector and each region, they are generally consistent with the accepted ideas on the magnitude of interregional feedbacks.

Table 14-3. Regional Origin of Average Intermediate Inputs and Regional Destination of Average Outputs (percent)

| | Origin of Inputs | | | Destination of Outputs | | | | |
Region	Flanders	Wallonia	Brabant	Flanders	Wallonia	Brabant	Abroad	Total
Flanders	41.3	15.5	17.8	52.6	12.3	12.1	23.0	100.0
Wallonia	9.6	44.9	13.3	16.4	48.8	12.1	22.7	100.0
Brabant	9.0	12.0	35.7	20.0	16.0	48.5	15.5	100.0
Abroad	40.1	27.6	33.2	48.3	24.6	22.7	4.4	100.0
Total	100.0	100.0	100.0					

Source: D. Vanwynsberghe: *The Interregional and Intersectoral Structure of the Brabant Economy: An Input-Output Approach.* (Brussels: Regional Economic Council for Brabant), vol. 3, April 1974, p. 18d.

It appears from the results for Belgium that this nonsurvey method offers a satisfactory approach to studying the interregional structure of the economy. The results are much better than those obtained by the gross-balance method and the intraregional method. Indeed, they show not only the balances of trade between the regions but estimate quite accurately the real flows. Furthermore, they are not biased by the imports from abroad. As the average estimate between maximum and minimum is used, they also are not biased by the relative importance of a sector or a regional economy. The technique is also very well suited for fully automated electronic data processing.

References

1. Central Bureau of Statistics. *Regional Accounts 1960.* Vols. I and II. The Hague: Central Bureau of Statistics, 1968.

2. Central Bureau of Statistics. *Regional Accounts 1965.* Vols. I and II. The Hague: Central Bureau of Statistics, 1970.

3. Chenery, H.B. "Interregional and International Input-Output Analysis." In *Structural Interdependence of the Economy.* Edited by T. Barna. New York: John Wiley and Sons, 1956. Pp. 341–356.

4. Derwa, L. "Une Nouvelle Méthode d'Analyse de la Structure Economique" [A New Method for Analysing the Economic Structure]. In *Revue du Conseil Economique Wallon.* Namur: Economic Council for Wallonia, September 1957. Pp. 16–42.

5. Essor Working Group. *Het Economisch Structuurmodel van Rijnmond* [The Economic Structural Model for Rijnmond]. Rotterdam: Rijnmond, 1973.

6. Gordon, I.R. "A Gravity Flows Approach to an Interregional Input-Output Model for the U.K." Canterbury: University of Kent, 1972.

7. Isard, W., et al. *Methods of Regional Analysis: An Introduction to Regional Science.* Cambridge, Mass.: M.I.T. Press, 1960. Published jointly with John Wiley and Sons, New York.

8. Leontief, W., et al. *Studies in the Structure of the American Economy.* New York: Oxford University Press, 1953.

9. Leontief, W., and A. Strout. "Multiregional Input-Output Analysis." In *Structural Interdependence and Economic Development.* Edited by T. Barna. London: MacMillan, 1963. Pp. 119–150.

10. Moore, F.T., and J.W. Petersen. "Regional Analysis: An Inter-Industry Model of Utah." *The Review of Economics and Statistics* 37, no. 4 (November 1955): 368–383.

11. Moses, L.N. "The Stability of Interregional Trading Patterns and Input-Output Analysis." *American Economic Review* 45, no. 5 (December 1955): 803–832.

12. Polenske, K.R. "A Case Study of Transportation Models Used in Multiregional Analysis." Ph.D. thesis, Harvard University, Cambridge, Massachusetts, 1966.

13. Polenske, K.R. "The Implementation of a Multiregional Input-Output Model for the United States." In *Input-Output Techniques.* Edited by A. Bródy

and A.P. Carter. Amsterdam: North-Holland Publishing Company, 1972. Pp. 171–189.

14. Vanwynsberghe, D. *De Brabantse Economie in een Interregionaal en Intersectorieel Perspectief. Een Input-Output Benadering* [The Interregional and Intersectoral Structure of the Brabant Economy. An Input-Output Approach]. 3 volumes. Brussels: Regional Economic Council for Brabant, April 1974.

15. Waterschoot, V.J. *Regionale Input-Output Tabellen voor 1965* [Regional Input-Output Tables for 1965]. Louvain: C.E.S., 1973.

Part Four

Industrial Applications

Chapter Fifteen

The INFORUM Model

Margaret B. Buckler
David Gilmartin
Thomas C. Reimbold

The INFORUM, *In*terindustry *For*ecasting at the *U*niversity of *M*aryland, project uses an input-output model to make long-term forecasts of the American economy. The project, directed by Clopper Almon, has been in existence for nine years. The maintenance of the model and the continuing research to improve it are supported by about fifteen private companies. Recently, several agencies of the United States government and groups from two foreign countries have also become sponsors of the model.

The model divides the economy into 185 product sectors and forecasts the output of each sector and its sales to each intermediate and final demand purchaser. The structure of the model, its performance, and recent extensions of it to include prices and wages will be briefly reviewed here. Several applications will be described, including a forecast with assumptions to reflect the "energy crisis." Finally, future directions of our research will be discussed.

The INFORUM Model

The workings of the model—the theory behind it, several applications using it, and a recent forecast with it—have been published in Almon et al. [1], so only a brief description of the forecasting model need be given here. Annual forecasts of sales for the next fifteen years are made in real terms. Overall exogenous controls include projections of population, labor force, households, interest rates, and government purchases. The model is not a crystal ball—it is not able to determine whether 1985 will be a boom or a recession year. Rather, the user of the model assumes some level of economic activity, as reflected in the employment rate, and then runs the model to determine the effect.

This paper was combined from three separate papers presented at the Sixth International Input-Output Conference, namely, "Applications of the INFORUM Model" (Buckler), "Price Forecasting in an Input-Output Model" (Gilmartin), and "Testing a Dynamic Input-Output Model by Simulation" (Reimbold).

Final demand equations, which utilize this exogenous information, as well as information generated by the model, have been estimated. Personal consumption expenditures per capita for each product depend upon income, relative prices, and a time trend. Investment spending by 90 sectors (aggregates of the 185 sectors) to maintain a desired capital stock is determined from the levels of output in the five preceding years and the current year and from the cost of capital. This investment spending is then converted into purchases of producer durable equipment from the 185 product sectors by means of a capital matrix. Stock adjustment equations and other methods are used to forecast the 28 types of construction expenditures, which are translated into purchases of construction materials by assembling a construction matrix. Imports for each product depend upon domestic demand and the relative foreign-to-domestic price for that product.[1] Exports also depend upon this relative price and lagged domestic output. Inventory change for each product is a function of the inventory stock and the domestic supply of the product such that the inventory–domestic supply relation is maintained.[2] Once final demands for each product have been determined, the input-output matrix is used to solve for output.[3] Interindustry coefficients are not fixed but change over time to follow a logistic curve.

The labor force provides the limit for the size of the forecast economy. Employment is determined from five types of productivity equations estimated by industry.

Simulation Testing

The performance of many parts of the model has been tested by simulating the period 1966-1971. Consumption, equipment investment, productivity, and across-the-row coefficient changes were intensively examined.[4] By requiring them to have satisfactory simulations as well as satisfactory regression fits, significant improvements were made in many of the equations.

To test the INFORUM model, a number of initial calculations were required. In particular, all equations to be used in the forecast simulation of the entire model required individual testing. Complete final demand and cost-of-input data are required to balance the input-output matrices for each year of the simulation. With these matrices, we are able to separate the individual components of the total error of the simulated forecasts. The matrix balancing was performed by the RAS method.[5]

---

1. Domestic demand = output + imports − exports.
2. Domestic supply = output + imports + exports.
3. The Seidel iterative solution method has been adapted to solve the simultaneous equations for outputs, imports, and inventory change.
4. Some of the results are given in the book by Almon et al. [1].
5. The balancing method is explained by Almon et al. [1].

The simulation period is from 1967 through 1971. All major stochastic equations of the model are, therefore, estimated through 1966 and then used to forecast the remaining years. The simulation study is designed to answer the following questions:

1. How accurate and reliable are forecasts generated by input-output models?
2. Since input-output forecasts depend as much on the prediction of input-output coefficients as on the forecasts of final demand, what portion of the total errors stems from incorrectly specified coefficients and how much is contributed by the final demand estimation?
3. How much feedback error is generated within the model and how does it affect the convergence process? (Feedback here refers to the fact that output affects investment, which in turn affects output.)

To answer these questions, four simulation tests were carried out, the results of which are shown in Table 15-1, (a) with constant 1965 base-year coefficients; (b) with logistic curve, equiproportional changes across each row; (c) with completely balanced matrices; and (d) with completely balanced matrices and final demand calculated from actual output. Test (b) represents the actual forecasting model, and its results are compared with the behavior of the other three simulations.

For each of the four simulations, the errors are recorded in Table 15-1 for four items: personal consumption expenditures (PCE), producer durable equipment (PDE), inventory change, and output. The errors are measured as a percent of actual output and represent cumulative averages over the five-year simulation period, 1967-1971. A positive error implies under-prediction, and vice versa:

$$e_i = \sum_{t=1967}^{1971} \frac{a_{it} - p_{it}}{q_{it}} \cdot 100 \qquad i = 1, 2, \ldots, 185 \qquad (15\text{-}1)$$

where a refers to actual value, p refers to predicted value, and q stands for output.

The analysis of Table 15-1 is divided into three parts: overall behavior of the model; sector analysis of five-year average errors; and sector analysis of year-by-year results.

Overall Behavior of the Model

In the two bottom lines of Table 15-1, the overall errors of the simulations are given. The "weighted cumulative error" (WCE) measures the average aggre-

Table 15-1. Average Cumulative Simulation Errors as a Percent of Actual Output for 1967–1971: Energy Crisis Forecast

Sector No.	Title	(a) Constant Coefficient and Predicted Output				(b) Predicted Coefficient and Predicted Output				(c) Balanced Coefficient and Predicted Output				(d) Balanced Coefficient and Actual Output			
		PCE	PDE	Inventory	Output	PCE	PDE	Inventory	Output	PCE	PDE	Inventory	Output	PCE	PDE	Inventory	Output
1	DAIRY FARM PRODUCTS	1.0	.0	2.3	1.5	1.0	.0	2.5	4.0	1.0	.0	2.0	-.4	1.0	.0	2.0	-.4
2	POULTRY AND EGGS	2.2	.0	.1	-.6	2.2	.0	-.2	-2.6	2.2	.0	.4	6.0	2.2	.0	.4	6.0
3	MEAT ANIMALS, OTH LIVESTK	.1	.0	.6	18.0	.1	.0	.5	-7.2	.1	.0	.5	6.2	.1	.0	.5	6.2
4	COTTON	.0	.0	-1.8	-104.3	.0	.0	2.7	-30.2	.0	.0	4.5	2.4	.0	.0	4.5	2.4
5	GRAINS	.0	.0	-.4	-.4	.0	.0	-.4	-5.6	.0	.0	-.4	3.9	.0	.0	-.4	3.9
6	TOBACCO	1.0	.0	-5.7	-5.5	1.0	.0	-5.7	-2.2	1.0	.0	-5.4	-2.6	1.0	.0	-5.4	-2.6
7	FRUIT,VEGETABLES,OTH CROPS	.0	.0	.1	-2.2	.0	.0	-.2	-1.9	.0	.0	-.1	2.7	.0	.0	-.1	2.7
8	FORESTRY + FISHERY PROD.	-3.2	.0	.1	6.7	-3.2	.0	-.2	17.0	-3.2	.0	-.3	-2.0	-3.2	.0	-.3	-2.1
9	NO DEFN.	.0	.0	.0	.0	.0	.0	.0	.0	.0	.0	.0	.0	.0	.0	.0	.0
10	AGR,FORESTRY+FISH SERVICES	.1	.0	-.2	15.8	.1	.0	-.2	22.2	.1	.0	.1	3.3	.1	.0	.1	3.2
11	IRON ORES	.0	.0	.3	-14.0	.0	.0	.7	-5.9	.0	.0	1.3	7.4	.0	.0	1.3	6.4
12	COPPER ORE	.0	.0	.1	3.6	.0	.0	.1	2.1	.0	.0	.2	4.1	.0	.0	.2	7.1
13	OTHER NON-FERROUS ORES	.0	.0	.2	-2.6	.0	.0	.2	-4.6	.0	.0	.2	8.0	.0	.0	.2	2.8
14	COAL MINING	.6	.0	.2	4.3	.6	.0	-.1	2.6	.6	.0	-.2	3.1	.6	.0	-.2	3.1
15	CRUDE PETROLEUM, NAT. GAS	.0	.0	-.1	1.8	.0	.0	-.1	-4.8	.0	.0	-.1	1.2	.0	.0	-.1	1.1
16	STONE AND CLAY MINING	-.1	.0	-.3	-15.5	-.1	.0	-.2	-13.2	-.1	.0	-.1	3.8	-.1	.0	-.1	3.6
17	CHEMICAL FERTILIZER MINING	.0	.0	.3	3.8	.0	.0	-.1	-.4	.0	.0	.5	.0	.0	.0	.5	.0
18	NEW CONSTRUCTION	.0	.0	.0	.5	.0	.0	.0	.5	.0	.0	.0	.5	.0	.0	.0	.5
19	MAINTENANCE CONSTRUCTION	.0	.0	.0	.0	.0	.0	.0	.0	.0	.0	.0	.0	.0	.0	.0	.0
20	COMPLETE GUIDED MISSILES	.0	.0	-.2	-2.5	.0	.0	.0	-1.5	.0	.0	.0	2.3	.0	.0	.0	2.3
21	AMMUNITION	.9	.0	.9	6.0	.9	.0	.9	6.0	.9	.0	.9	.1	.9	.0	.9	.1
22	OTHER ORDNANCE	-.7	.0	-.0	1.5	-.7	.0	-.1	1.2	-.7	.0	-.1	-.7	-.7	.0	-.1	-.7
23	MEAT PRODUCTS	5.4	.0	-.1	5.2	5.4	.0	-.1	6.5	5.4	.0	-.1	6.4	5.4	.0	-.1	6.4
24	DAIRY PRODUCTS	-3.7	.0	-.2	-7.7	-3.7	.0	-.2	-7.8	-3.7	.0	-.2	-4.4	-3.7	.0	-.2	-4.4
25	CANNED AND FROZEN FOODS	-.4	.0	.7	-5.1	-.4	.0	.7	-1.2	-.4	.0	.7	.5	-.4	.0	.7	.5
26	GRAIN MILL PRODUCTS	2.8	.0	-.0	2.6	2.8	.0	-.0	5.1	2.8	.0	-.0	4.8	2.8	.0	-.0	4.8
27	BAKERY PRODUCTS	-5.0	.0	-.0	-6.0	-5.0	.0	-.0	-5.1	-5.0	.0	-.0	-4.9	-5.0	.0	-.0	-4.9
28	SUGAR	5.4	.0	.7	13.4	5.4	.0	.7	11.0	5.4	.0	.7	10.8	5.4	.0	.7	10.8
29	CONFECTIONERY PRODUCTS	1.3	.0	-.0	-.4	1.3	.0	-.0	2.8	1.3	.0	-.0	1.5	1.3	.0	-.0	1.5
30	ALCOHOLIC BEVERAGES	4.5	.0	.0	3.4	4.5	.0	.1	6.2	4.5	.0	.1	5.2	4.5	.0	.1	5.1
31	SOFT DRINKS AND FLAVORINGS	5.3	.0	.1	4.3	5.3	.0	.1	5.1	5.3	.0	.1	6.3	5.3	.0	.1	6.2
32	FATS AND OILS	.5	.0	.2	-4.4	.5	.0	-.2	-5.0	.5	.0	-.2	3.1	.5	.0	-.2	3.1
33	MISC FOOD PRODUCTS	2.9	.0	.3	.3	2.9	.0	-.3	2.5	2.9	.0	-.3	3.1	2.9	.0	-.3	3.1
34	TOBACCO PRODUCTS	1.1	.0	1.5	-.4	1.1	.0	1.3	2.7	1.1	.0	1.5	3.3	1.1	.0	1.5	3.0
35	BROAD AND NARROW FABRICS	-.2	.0	2.0	-9.0	-.2	.0	1.7	-8.9	-.2	.0	1.7	3.3	-.2	.0	1.6	3.3
36	FLOOR COVERINGS	10.2	2.3	-.3	19.3	10.2	-1.8	1.7	14.8	10.2	1.9	1.7	14.9	10.2	1.2	1.6	14.1
37	MISC TEXTILES	.3	.0	-.3	-13.0	.3	.0	-.0	6.7	.3	.0	-.0	3.5	.3	.0	-.0	3.3
38	KNITTING	2.5	.0	-.1	20.1	2.5	.0	-.0	-2.0	2.5	.0	-.0	-.6	2.5	.0	-.1	-1.6
39	APPAREL	-10.1	.0	.4	-11.6	-10.1	.0	-.0	-11.7	-10.1	.0	-.1	-10.7	-10.1	.0	-.4	-10.7
40	HOUSEHOLD TEXTILES	.9	.0	1.1	-1.5	.9	.0	1.3	1.2	.9	.0	1.5	3.1	.9	.0	1.5	3.0
41	LUMBER AND WOOD PRODUCTS	-.1	.0	-.1	-4.3	-.1	.0	.6	8.3	-.1	.0	.4	2.3	-.1	.0	.4	2.2
42	VENEER AND PLYWOOD	.0	.0	.4	2.2	.0	.0	.3	.9	.0	.0	1.0	5.9	.0	.0	1.0	5.6
43	MILLWORK AND WOOD PRODUCTS	.8	.0	.4	12.7	.8	.0	-.0	13.0	.8	.0	-.2	2.7	.8	.0	-.2	2.6
44	WOODEN CONTAINERS	.8	.0	3.5	-41.2	.8	.0	9.8	13.8	.8	.0	10.7	13.8	.8	.0	10.7	13.5
45	HOUSEHOLD FURNITURE	-5.8	-.4	-.2	-7.9	-5.8	-1.4	.1	-5.8	-5.8	-1.2	.1	-6.3	-5.8	-1.2	.1	-6.3
46	OTHER FURNITURE	.8	11.1	.2	10.6	.8	9.0	.1	9.4	.8	7.5	.1	8.9	.8	5.7	.1	7.0

#	Industry	C1	C2	C3	C4	C5	C6	C7	C8	C9	C10	C11	C12	C13	C14	C15
48	PAPER AND PAPERBOARD MILLS	1.4	.1	.0	-.0	1.6	.1	.0	-.0	-6.9	-.3	.0	-.0	-5.7	.0	-.0
49	PAPER PRODUCTS, NEC	.8	.2	.0	-.4	2.9	.2	.0	-.4	-5.1	-.3	.0	-.4	-3.6	.0	-.4
50	WALL AND BUILDING PAPER	2.7	.3	.0	-.0	2.8	.3	.0	-.0	-4.1	-.3	.0	-.0	-8.0	.0	-.0
51	PAPERBOARD CONTAINERS	1.5	-.0	.0	.2	1.6	-.0	.0	.2	-3.0	.0	.0	.2	-1.5	.0	.2
52	NEWSPAPERS	2.0	-.1	.0	.8	2.1	-.1	.0	.8	-.6	-.0	.0	.8	.9	.0	.8
53	PERIODICALS	2.6	1.1	.0	1.6	2.7	1.1	.0	1.6	-.9	.4	.0	1.6	-6.0	.0	1.6
54	BOOKS	-1.1	1.1	.0	-2.0	-1.1	1.1	.0	-2.0	-6.7	1.1	.0	-2.0	-10.9	.0	-2.0
55	INDUSTRIAL CHEMICALS	2.1	.3	.0	.2	2.4	.3	.0	.2	-8.1	.2	.0	.2	-1.8	.0	.2
56	BUSINESS FORMS,BLANK BOOK	1.0	-.1	.0	.6	1.2	-.1	.0	.6	-7.5	-.2	.0	.6	7.8	.0	.6
57	COMMERCIAL PRINTING	1.7	.0	.0	.3	1.8	.0	.0	.3	-2.8	.0	.0	.3	.0	.0	.3
58	OTHER PRINTING, PUBLISHING	3.1	.4	.0	2.4	3.2	.4	.0	2.4	.2	.3	.0	2.4	1.3	.0	2.4
59	FERTILIZERS	2.9	.6	.0	-.2	2.9	.6	.0	-.2	-13.5	-.3	.0	-.2	-10.5	.0	-.2
60	PESTICIDES + AGRIC. CHEM.	2.6	.5	.0	.1	2.6	.5	.0	.1	7.0	.4	.0	.1	-17.5	.0	.1
61	MISC CHEMICAL PRODUCTS	2.2	.2	.0	.2	2.2	.2	.0	.2	-3.4	.1	.0	.2	18.5	.0	.2
62	PLASTIC MAT'LS. + RESINS	1.9	.0	.0	.0	2.2	.0	.0	.0	-17.4	-.0	.0	.0	.3	.0	.0
63	SYNTHETIC RUBBER	5.6	.3	.0	.0	5.9	.3	.0	.0	-.7	-.0	.0	.0	.0	.0	.0
64	CELLULOSIC FIBERS	-1.3	.4	.0	-.0	-1.3	.4	.0	-.0	-6.4	.2	.0	-.0	1.5	.0	-.0
65	NON-CELLULOSIC FIBERS	1.3	.3	.0	.0	1.5	.3	.0	.0	5.0	.7	.0	.0	-31.0	.0	.0
66	DRUGS	3.2	.4	.0	1.7	3.2	.4	.0	1.7	-3.3	.2	.0	1.7	10.2	.0	1.7
67	CLEANING + TOILET PROD.	2.4	.2	.0	2.0	2.4	.2	.0	2.0	-.6	.7	.0	2.0	-2.0	.0	2.0
68	PAINTS	1.9	.2	.0	-.7	2.2	.2	.0	-.7	6.0	.2	.0	-.7	-10.7	.0	-.7
69	PETROLEUM REFINING	.2	.2	.0	-.7	.4	.2	.0	-.7	-5.2	-.1	.0	-.7	.2	.0	-.7
70	FUEL OIL	.9	-.0	.0	-.7	.4	-.0	.0	-.7	-9.0	-.0	.0	-.7	9.3	.0	-.7
71	PAVING AND ASPHALT	7.1	.8	.0	3.7	7.9	.8	.0	3.7	2.6	.8	.0	3.7	3.1	.0	3.7
72	TIRES AND INNER TUBES	3.7	.5	.0	.9	4.2	.5	.0	.9	6.2	-.1	.0	.9	12.7	.0	.9
73	RUBBER PRODUCTS	2.6	.0	.0	.3	2.8	.0	.0	.3	3.7	.8	.0	.3	-.1	.1	.3
74	MISC PLASTIC PRODUCTS	-.9	-.1	.0	-.4	-.8	-.1	.0	-.4	-3.7	-.1	.0	-.4	21.7	.1	-.4
75	LEATHER + IND LTHR PROD	2.9	.1	.0	-.2	2.9	.1	.0	-.2	-13.6	-.1	.0	-.2	-18.6	.0	-.2
76	FOOTWEAR(EXC. RUBBER)	2.6	-.0	.0	.1	2.8	-.0	.0	.1	-6.7	-.1	.0	.1	1.2	.0	.1
77	OTHER LEATHER PRODUCTS	-2.8	.2	.0	-3.4	-2.1	.2	.0	-3.4	1.2	.2	.0	-3.4	-9.3	.0	-3.4
78	GLASS	3.0	.3	.0	-.1	3.2	.3	.0	-.1	-.9	.2	.0	-.1	5.7	.0	-.1
79	STRUCTURAL CLAY PRODUCTS	3.5	.3	.0	-.1	3.5	.3	.0	-.1	-10.0	.7	.0	-.1	-13.1	.0	-.1
80	POTTERY	3.8	.3	.0	-.8	4.2	.3	.0	-.8	1.4	.1	.0	-.8	1.9	.0	-.8
81	CEMENT, CONCRETE, GYPSUM	1.2	.1	.0	-.0	2.2	.1	.0	-.0	-10.6	.2	.0	-.0	-7.6	.0	-.0
82	OTHER STONE + CLAY PROD.	1.9	-.2	.0	-.1	4.6	-.2	.0	-.1	-4.0	-.2	.0	-.1	-3.0	.0	-.1
83	STEEL	3.8	.2	.0	-.0	4.6	.2	.0	-.0	1.8	-.0	.0	-.0	-6.7	.0	-.0
84	COPPER	3.3	.1	.0	-.0	4.0	.1	.0	-.0	-20.3	.1	.0	-.0	1.9	.0	-.0
85	LEAD	5.1	1.3	.0	-.0	5.8	1.3	.0	-.0	-20.5	1.0	.0	-.0	-42.2	.0	-.0
86	ZINC	6.4	1.6	.0	-.0	7.3	1.6	.0	-.0	3.6	1.4	.0	-.0	-27.0	.0	-.0
87	ALUMINUM	7.0	1.5	.0	-.0	7.7	1.5	.0	-.0	18.3	1.3	.0	-.0	9.1	.0	-.0
88	OTH PRIM NON-FER METALS	5.7	.4	.0	-.0	6.7	.4	.0	-.0	4.1	.1	.0	-.0	24.1	.0	-.0
89	OTH NON-FER ROLL + DRAW	3.2	-.1	.0	-.0	4.2	-.1	.0	-.0	4.1	-.1	.0	-.0	6.7	-.0	-.0
90	NON-FERROUS WIRE DRAWING	1.8	.1	.0	.0	2.2	.1	.0	.0	2.4	.6	.0	.0	-7.8	.2	.0
91	NON-FER CASTING + FORGING	3.4	.4	.0	.0	4.4	.4	.0	.0	2.9	-.0	.0	.0	12.6	.0	.0
92	METAL CANS	2.8	.1	.0	.0	2.8	.1	.0	.0	6.0	.3	.0	.0	6.9	.1	.0
93	METAL BARRELS AND DRUMS	1.9	.3	.0	-.0	2.3	.3	.0	-.0	2.3	.3	.0	-.0	-14.1	.0	-.0
94	PLUMBING + HEATING EQUIP.	2.3	-1.1	.0	.5	2.3	-1.1	.0	.5	-5.7	-1.0	.0	.5	-12.9	.0	.5

Table 15-1 continued

Sector No.	Title	(a) Constant Coefficient and Predicted Output				(b) Predicted Coefficient and Predicted Output				(c) Balanced Coefficient and Predicted Output				(d) Balanced Coefficient and Actual Output			
		PCE	PDE	Inven-tory	Out-put	PCE	PDE	Inven-tory	Out-put	PCE	PDE	Inven-tory	Out-put	PCE	PDE	Inven-tory	Out-put
95	STRUCTURAL METAL PRODUCTS	-.0	1.9	.4	7.2	-.0	1.6	.1	-6.0	-.0	2.1	.3	3.1	-.0	1.8	.3	2.6
96	SCREW MACHINE PRODUCTS	-.0	.0	.7	9.4	-.0	.0	.6	6.7	-.0	.0	.3	5.9	-.0	.7	.3	4.9
97	METAL STAMPINGS	-.3	.0	.4	7.2	-.3	.0	.6	6.1	-.0	.0	.3	5.3	-.3	.0	.3	4.8
98	CUTLERY,HAND TOOLS,HARDWR	.9	.1	-.8	-.7	.9	.1	-.8	6.1	.9	.1	-.3	3.4	.0	.0	-.3	3.0
99	MISC FABRICATED WIRE PRODU	-.2	.0	-.7	-11.3	-.2	-.0	-.6	5.7	-.2	-.1	-.3	2.2	-.3	-.8	-.3	1.7
100	PIPES, VALVES, FITTINGS	-.0	-3.8	.2	2.8	-.2	-3.3	-.2	1.9	-.3	.3	-.3	1.7	-.2	-.8	-.3	-.7
101	OTH FABRICATED METAL PROD.	-.1	.1	.6	8.6	-.1	.1	.3	3.2	-.1	.4	.2	3.9	-.1	-.1	.3	3.3
102	ENGINES AND TURBINES	-.1	5.8	.8	26.0	-.1	5.3	.0	8.8	-.2	6.2	.2	8.3	-.3	5.5	.3	7.0
103	FARM MACHINERY	3.4	-4.1	3.0	2.4	3.4	-1.6	3.4	5.4	3.4	.6	3.8	8.7	3.4	-1.9	3.5	5.7
104	CONSTR-MINE-OILFIELD MACH	.0	1.1	-.1	-3.3	-.1	.2	-.1	.2	.0	1.1	-.2	1.7	.0	.9	-.6	1.1
105	MATERIALS HANDLING MACH.	-.0	5.8	.8	11.5	.0	3.6	.1	3.1	.0	5.0	.7	6.6	.0	2.2	.6	3.3
106	MACH. TOOLS, METAL CUTTING	.1	8.4	1.4	10.6	.1	7.0	1.2	9.3	.0	5.6	1.4	6.5	.1	4.0	2.0	2.4
107	MACH TOOLS, METAL FORMING	-.2	9.0	2.6	16.0	.1	8.2	2.4	13.3	.0	8.3	2.4	12.3	.4	4.2	2.0	7.2
108	OTHER METAL WORKING MACH	-.2	1.3	-.6	6.4	-.2	8.7	.5	5.7	-.2	1.2	.6	6.3	-.1	-.1	.6	4.3
109	SPECIAL INDUSTRIAL MACH	-.0	4.0	-1.2	2.7	-.0	2.2	-1.1	.6	-.0	4.6	-1.3	3.9	-.0	3.2	-1.5	3.2
110	PUMPS,COMPRESSORS,BLOWERS	-.0	4.2	-1.5	7.5	-.0	3.1	-.5	3.2	-.0	5.5	-.5	6.0	-.0	3.1	-.5	3.9
111	BALL AND ROLLER BEARINGS	-.0	.0	-.4	-1.9	-.0	.0	-.4	-3.0	-.0	.0	-.3	5.5	-.0	.0	-.4	3.2
112	POWER TRANSMISSION EQUIP	-.0	.0	.4	4.3	-.0	.0	.9	3.3	-.0	.0	.6	4.7	-.0	.0	.4	5.3
113	INDUSTRIAL PATTERNS	.0	6.0	-.8	4.3	.0	6.1	-.3	8.4	.0	6.6	1.3	9.4	.0	3.1	1.1	5.3
114	COMPUTERS + RELATED MACH.	-.0	.6	-.2	1.5	-.1	.5	-.3	-.1	-.1	.7	.2	.1	-.1	4.5	3.8	9.1
115	OTHER OFFICE MACHINERY	-.0	8.0	3.8	12.4	-.1	6.1	3.6	9.6	-.1	6.7	.7	11.6	-.2	2.3	-.3	5.7
116	SERVICE INDUSTRY MACHINERY	2.3	4.4	.1	18.4	2.3	3.1	.0	3.1	2.3	3.5	.1	7.2	2.3	.1	-.3	4.2
117	MACHINE SHOP PRODUCTS	-.0	-.0	-.9	31.8	-.0	.2	-.4	13.4	-.0	-.0	-.2	5.1	-.0	.0	-.3	6.0
118	ELECTRICAL MEASURING INSTR	-.0	8.2	.9	14.7	-.0	6.7	.2	11.7	-.0	6.9	.2	18.4	-.0	4.5	.3	16.4
119	TRANSFORMERS + SWITCHGEAR	-.0	17.1	1.2	21.5	.0	16.1	.9	13.1	-.0	16.6	1.4	4.8	-.0	15.0	.9	3.0
120	MOTORS AND GENERATORS	-.0	1.0	.3	2.5	-.0	.7	.5	6.4	-.0	1.8	.8	8.8	-.0	1.0	.3	6.1
121	INDUSTRIAL CONTROLS	-.0	1.2	-.7	18.1	-.0	1.0	.7	3.7	-.0	3.7	.7	7.3	-.0	1.5	.7	4.5
122	WELDING APP, GRAPHITE PROD	-.0	3.1	-.6	.6	-.0	2.5	-.7	-.8	-.0	1.1	1.1	1.9	-.0	.9	-.7	3.0
123	HOUSEHOLD APPLIANCES	1.1	.3	-.6	2.0	1.1	1.2	.4	.8	1.1	.8	-.8	1.7	1.1	.2	-.8	1.4
124	ELEC LIGHTING + WIRING EQ.	-.8	.3	1.0	5.4	-.8	.3	-.9	-3.3	-.8	.3	.8	1.7	-.8	.2	-.8	3.9
125	RADIO AND TV RECEIVING	-2.8	-.2	.7	-.6	-2.2	-.4	.9	3.0	-2.2	-.1	-.0	4.1	-2.2	-.0	-2.2	3.9
126	PHONOGRAPH RECORDS	14.3	.0	-2.1	17.1	14.3	.0	-2.1	17.1	14.3	.0	-2.2	12.9	14.3	.0	-2.2	12.8
127	COMMUNICATION EQUIPMENT	-.1	3.5	.2	14.3	-.0	2.5	.1	3.1	-.0	2.8	.6	4.1	-.1	1.8	.6	2.6
128	ELECTRONIC COMPONENTS	-.0	.2	.7	-.7	-.0	1.8	-.1	-.1	-.7	.2	.7	4.2	-.1	.9	.1	3.2
129	BATTERIES	-.3	2.0	1.4	9.1	-.3	1.5	.9	2.5	-.3	1.7	.9	4.2	-.3	1.0	.9	9.9
130	ENGINE ELECTRICAL EQUIP.	-.1	.0	5.9	22.8	-.1	1.8	4.8	13.0	-.1	1.0	5.4	10.4	-.1	.1	5.3	9.9
131	X-RAY, ELEC EQUIP,NEC	-2.9	-.7	-.5	-2.4	-2.9	-1.0	-.5	-5.9	-2.9	-1.8	-.4	-4.6	-2.9	-2.7	3.9	-5.6
132	TRUCK, BUS, TRAILER BODIES	.0	7.2	5.0	15.0	.8	5.0	4.8	12.6	-2.0	7.2	4.1	11.5	4.7	4.7	3.9	8.8
133	MOTOR VEHICLES	3.4	1.0	.5	8.6	3.4	.5	.4	7.4	3.4	.8	2.9	7.0	3.4	.5	2.5	6.5
134	AIRCRAFT	.3	7.3	3.0	10.7	.3	7.0	3.1	10.3	.3	4.0	2.9	7.2	3.0	1.0	2.5	6.5
135	AIRCRAFT ENGINES	-.0	.1	3.0	5.9	-.0	.3	.1	5.9	-.0	.0	.3	2.3	-.0	.3	.3	1.8
136	AIRCRAFT EQUIPMENT, NEC	-.2	9.7	.1	18.4	.0	-18.2	.2	8.7	.8	9.8	.2	2.6	.8	-9.8	.3	1.5
137	SHIP AND BOAT BUILDING	.8	-19.7	-.4	-12.5	.8	-8.8	-.2	-14.4	.8	9.8	.2	-9.0	.2	-5.3	-.2	-9.0
138	RAILROAD EQUIPMENT	.0	-9.9	-.1	-15.4	.8	-5.3	-1.0	-11.3	.8	-5.2	-1.0	-3.9	.8	-2.7	1.0	-6.5
139	CYCLES, TRANS EQUIP NEC	33.6	1.0	1.0	37.6	33.6	1.0	.5	32.9	33.6	1.0	1.0	39.9	33.6	1.0	1.5	39.3
140	TRAILER COACHES	34.6	1.0	.5	35.2	34.6	.5	.5	34.2	34.6	.5	.5	36.1	34.6	2.4	.5	35.9
141	ENGR. + SCIENTIFIC INSTR.	-.0	2.0	.5	2.6	-.0	1.8	.7	7.3	.0	2.1	.4	4.0	.0	1.4	.4	2.6

SECTOR TITLES

Sector	C1	C2	C3	C4	C5	C6	C7	C8	C9	C10	C11	C12	C13	C14	C15
142 MECH. MEASURING DEVICES	-.1	3.1	-.1	.8	3.2	1.0	9.8	-.1	3.7	.9	7.4	-.1	3.0	.9	6.1
143 OPTICAL + OPHTHALMIC GOODS	4.0	3.6	4.0	29.8	1.1	9.9	26.9	4.0	4.1	9.9	19.1	4.0	2.7	9.8	17.5
144 MEDICAL + SURGICAL INSTR.	1.0	-1.1	1.0	1.8	-2.3	.6	.4	1.0	-2.9	.5	1.0	1.0	-3.0	.6	-.2
145 PHOTOGRAPHIC EQUIPMENT	-.3	-.6	-.3	10.6	-1.0	-.2	-5.0	-.3	-.4	-.5	-1.0	-.3	-1.0	-.6	-.4
146 WATCHES AND CLOCKS	8.5	.0	8.5	10.9	.0	-2.0	1.3	8.5	.0	-2.0	-1.9	8.5	-1.0	-2.0	-2.0
147 JEWELRY AND SILVERWARE	-4.7	-.3	-4.7	7.1	-.0	.0	7.0	-4.7	-1.1	.0	9.1	-4.7	-1.0	.0	9.1
148 TOYS,SPORT,MUSICAL INSTR.	.3	1.2	.3	-6.6	-.1	-.1	-5.3	.3	.7	-.1	-5.9	.3	.6	-.1	-5.9
149 OFFICE SUPPLIES	-.8	.0	-.8	-9.2	.0	.4	-9.3	-.8	.6	-.1	.3	-.8	.6	-.1	-.0
150 MISC MANUFACTURING, NEC	.3	.0	.3	-.3	.0	.0	-3.5	.3	.7	.0	.3	.3	.3	.0	.3
151 RAILROADS	3.6	.0	3.6	-10.0	.0	.0	5.7	3.6	.0	.0	4.5	3.6	3.6	.0	4.5
152 BUSSES AND LOCAL TRANSIT	.0	.0	.0	-9.8	.0	.0	-9.8	.0	.0	.0	2.5	3.6	.0	.0	2.7
153 TRUCKING	.0	.0	.0	8.4	.0	.0	-2.0	.0	.0	.0	2.9	.0	.0	.0	-2.9
154 WATER TRANSPORTATION	-1.9	.0	-1.9	-21.2	.0	.0	-.1	-1.9	.0	.0	-1.1	-1.9	-.3	.0	-2.0
155 AIRLINES	-5.7	.0	-5.7	16.5	.0	.0	12.9	-5.7	.0	.0	7.9	-5.7	5.7	.0	-.1
156 PIPELINES	-5.7	.0	-5.7	-9.5	.0	.0	-14.9	-5.7	.0	.0	-5.4	-5.7	-5.7	.0	7.8
157 FREIGHT FORWARDING	2.4	.0	2.4	-2.1	.0	.0	7.1	2.4	.0	.0	7.1	-5.7	-5.7	.0	-5.5
158 TELEPHONE AND TELEGRAPH	1.0	.7	1.0	6.1	.3	.0	5.8	2.4	.5	.0	3.5	2.4	2.4	.0	2.2
159 RADIO AND TV BROADCASTING	.6	.0	.6	3.4	.0	.0	1.6	1.0	.0	.0	1.8	1.0	1.0	.0	3.2
160 ELECTRIC UTILITIES	.0	.0	.0	3.6	.0	.0	3.5	.0	.0	.0	1.8	1.0	1.0	.0	3.6
161 NATURAL GAS	-.4	.0	-.4	2.0	.0	.0	-3.5	-.4	.6	.0	1.3	-.4	-.4	.0	1.6
162 WATER AND SEWER SERVICES	-.8	.6	-.8	4.2	.4	.0	.4	-.8	.6	.0	.1	-.8	-.8	.0	1.7
163 WHOLESALE TRADE	.0	.0	.0	6.2	.0	.0	.0	.0	.6	.0	.1	-.1	-.1	.0	-.1
164 RETAIL TRADE	.2	-.1	.2	8.4	-.1	.0	-1.0	.2	.2	.0	.8	.2	.2	.0	-.2
165 BANKS,CREDIT AGEN.,BROKERS	-.8	.0	-.8	12.1	.0	.0	6.0	-.8	.0	.0	1.4	-.8	-.8	.0	-.6
166 INSURANCE	-2.7	.0	-2.7	1.4	.0	.0	.5	-2.7	.0	.0	-3.1	-2.7	-2.7	.0	1.3
167 OWNER-OCCUPIED DWELLINGS	1.4	.0	1.4	1.4	.0	.0	1.7	1.4	.0	.0	1.4	1.4	1.4	.0	3.1
168 REAL ESTATE	1.3	.0	1.3	-5.8	.0	.0	1.7	1.3	.0	.0	1.4	1.3	1.3	.0	1.4
169 HOTEL AND LODGING PLACES	-3.1	.0	-3.1	-5.8	.0	.0	-3.2	-3.1	.0	.0	-2.6	-3.1	-3.1	.0	1.9
170 PERSONAL + REPAIR SERVICES	-1.9	.0	-1.9	-1.7	.0	.0	-1.8	-1.9	.0	.0	-1.7	-1.9	-1.9	.0	-2.7
171 BUSINESS SERVICES	.6	.0	.6	11.4	.0	.0	9.3	.6	.0	.0	1.7	.6	.6	.0	-1.7
172 ADVERTISING	.0	.0	.0	-4.4	.0	.0	-1.0	.0	.0	.0	1.9	.0	.0	.0	1.5
173 AUTO REPAIR	1.7	.0	1.7	3.1	.0	.0	3.4	1.7	.0	.0	2.4	1.7	1.7	.0	1.7
174 MOVIES + AMUSEMENTS	2.7	.0	2.7	4.0	.0	.0	5.1	2.7	.0	.0	3.7	2.7	2.7	.0	2.3
175 MEDICAL SERVICES	4.2	.0	4.2	4.1	.0	.0	4.3	4.2	.0	.0	4.2	4.2	4.2	.0	3.7
176 PRIVATE SCHOOLS + NPO	-4.3	.0	-4.3	-3.4	.0	.0	-3.6	-4.3	.0	.0	-4.3	-4.3	-4.3	.0	4.2
177 POST OFFICE	-.3	.0	-.3	-.3	.0	.0	1.2	-.3	.0	.0	1.2	-.3	-.3	.0	4.3
178 FEDERAL GOV. ENTERPRISES	.0	.0	.0	3.1	.0	.0	-.8	.0	.0	.0	1.5	.0	.0	.0	1.0
179 NO DEFN.	.0	.0	.0	.0	.0	.0	.0	.0	.0	.0	.0	.0	.0	.0	1.4
180 ST+LOC ELECTRIC UTILITIES	2.7	.0	2.7	-14.2	.0	.0	-10.5	2.7	.0	.0	3.6	2.7	2.7	.0	3.5
181 NON-COMPETITIVE IMPORTS	3.6	.0	3.6	-10.5	.0	.0	-10.0	3.6	.0	.0	3.7	3.6	3.6	.0	3.7
182 BUSINESS TRAVEL(DUMMY)	.0	.0	.0	8.1	.0	.0	5.6	.0	.0	.0	1.9	.0	.0	.0	1.6
183 OFFICE SUPPLIES(DUMMY)	.0	.0	.0	-17.2	.0	.0	-17.4	.0	.0	.0	.3	.0	.0	.0	-.1
184 UNIMPORTANT IND.(DUMMY)	.0	.0	.0	-11.0	.0	.0	-13.0	.0	.0	.0	4.2	.0	.0	.0	3.5
185 COMPUTER RENTAL(DUMMY)	.0	.0	.0	38.3	.0	.0	35.8	.0	.0	.0	1.9	.0	.0	.0	1.5
WTD. CUM. ERROR	.6	.3	.6	3.3	.2	.1	.4	.6	.3	.2	2.1	.6	.2	.1	1.8
WTD. ABS. ERROR	1.5	.4	1.5	6.5	.3	.2	4.3	1.5	.4	.2	3.1	1.5	.3	.2	2.8

gate prediction error, and the "weighted absolute error" (WAE) reflects the average size of the errors.

$$WCE = \frac{\displaystyle\sum_{i=1}^{185} (e_i q_i)}{\displaystyle\sum_{i=1}^{185} q_i} \tag{15-2}$$

$$WAE = \frac{\displaystyle\sum_{i=1}^{185} (|e_i| q_i)}{\displaystyle\sum_{i=1}^{185} q_i} \tag{15-3}$$

where e is defined in equation (15-1), and q stands for output in 1971. A quick comparison of the four different runs shows that the final demand errors remain approximately the same. But before we can conclude that output errors have little or no feedback effect on the final demand prediction, the result must be analyzed in further detail.

The general improvement as we go from test (a) to test (d) is clear; however, a large portion of the total prediction error can be attributed to coefficient misspecifications, as may be seen clearly when the overall output errors are graphed, as in Figure 15-1. In this figure, a, b, c, and d, refer to the four different simulations that were made.

Since PCE is not a function of output, its error column is the same for all four runs. The overall weighted absolute error (1.5 percent) is the largest of the three final demand components. But the fact that the average PCE error is larger than the one of PDE (0.4 percent) or inventory changes (0.2 percent) does not indicate inferior PCE equations but rather reflects the fact that PCE is a much larger component of total final demand then PDE or inventory change. Indeed, the errors for PDE are zero in many sectors simply because some of those particular sectors do not produce capital goods at all.

Because more and more of the forecasting error is removed as we introduce more precise coefficients, the test results in Table 15-1 help to isolate individual error components. The next section, therefore, contains a sector analysis of the simulated forecasts. The behavior of test (b), the model with the across-the-row changed coefficients (which reflects the performance of the standard INFORUM model), will be evaluated by comparing its results with both the constant and balanced coefficient simulations. Finally, the fourth simulation, which uses

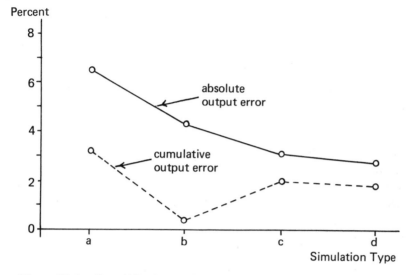

Figure 15-1. Overall Prediction Errors of Complete Model Simulations.

exogenous outputs in the final demand equations, will be used to evaluate the effect of feedback errors.

Sector Analysis of Five-Year Average Errors

Only six PCE sectors show relatively large forecasting errors. But the inadequate forecasting behavior of each equation can be understood, for these sectors are affected by data problems, style-determined shifts, introduction of new products, and changes in taste. All other PCE equations are well behaved and only a few show any consistent underpredicting or overpredicting. Also, the across-sector offsetting effect is quite strong, as is proven by the small weighted cumulative error. If a given industry is underpredicted, a related industry will be overpredicted. In short, if measured as a percent of actual output, the overall PCE error is only 0.6 percent (cumulative) and 1.5 percent (absolute). These rather small aggregate errors occur despite the relatively large errors of the six sectors.

There are about 45 sectors that sell more than 10 percent of their output to PDE. Nine of these are equipment-supplying sectors and show unsatisfactory simulation results. Comparisons of simulations (a) and (b) show, however, that the across-the-row changes remove a substantial portion of the errors. Still, a large portion of these errors stems from a few inadequate investment functions, notably from those for Sector 160, Electric utilities (which affect PDE for Sector 119, Transformers & switchgears), and Sectors 163, Wholesale trade, and 164, Retail trade (which affect PDE for Sector 46, Other furniture). Eight sectors (103, 104, 105, 109, 114, 116, 127, and 133) show less than 10 percent error. When comparing the PDE column with the PCE column, however, we must bear in mind that the PCE share of many sectors is larger than the PDE portion of output and that all errors are measured as a percent of actual output. This definition makes all errors additive, so that it is possible to analyze each final demand component's contribution to the total output error. In short, the analysis of the PDE errors has shown that only a few investment equations are responsible for a large portion of the PDE errors, and that at the same time a significant portion of the errors is caused by the constant-coefficient assumption.

The individual errors of the inventory equations are small when measured as a percent of actual output. But again, we must realize that inventory change is a small portion of total output. The percentage error of the inventory equations is quite high. It is, however, well accepted that the change in inventory is the most difficult final demand component to forecast; but because it is a relatively small portion of final demand, the large percentage prediction errors can be tolerated. When measured as a percent of actual output, very few sectors show larger than 3 percent errors, and most of the significant errors belong to small sectors. For example, Sector 133, Motor vehicles, one of the large-inventory sectors, only misses by 0.5 percent, while the largest error—10.2 percent—belongs to Sector 143, Optical & ophthalmic products, a rather small sector accounting for only 0.06 percent of total output. Although the overall behavior of the inventory change errors is satisfactory (0.1 percent average output error), we must note that the equations are estimated through 1971, and therefore this test is not an altogether reliable indication of how well they forecast.

An examination of the output error columns shows a large number of sizeable underpredictions and overpredictions. Fortunately, the largest errors belong to the small, volatile output sectors, such as Sector 4, Cotton (-104.3 percent—probably a data problem) and Sector 44, Wooden containers (-41.2 percent). These sizeable final demand errors naturally result in output errors. But sectors that sell chiefly to intermediate use will have output errors arising from both the final demand errors of their customer sectors and the errors in the input-output co-efficients. It is therefore these sectors from which we can best evaluate the across-the-row change technique. With this technique, all coefficients in a row are changed in the same proportion, and that proportion is determined from a logistic curve. The curve is fitted to the ratio of actual intermediate use to what intermediate use would have been had coefficients remained constant. The curves were fitted over the period for which data were available—1958–1971. They are used in the INFORUM model on rows where annual time series on individual coefficients are not available. Their effect is shown graphically in Figure 15-2, where the vertical axis shows the percent output error from Table 15-1, while the horizontal axis represents the four tests (a) through (d). Sectors with large output errors and large intermediate use were selected for these plots.

All of the industries shown respond favorably to the coefficient-change technique, test (b). The strongest improvement is shown by Sector 3, Meat animals &

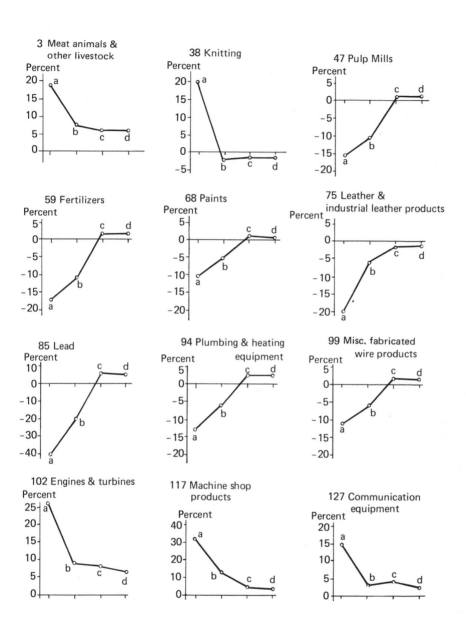

Note: The horizontal axis refers to the four simulations.

Figure 15-2.   Selected Output Errors of Complete Model Simulations.

other livestock products; Sector 38, Knitting; Sector 75, Leather & industrial leather products; Sector 102, Engines & turbines; Sector 117, Machine shop products; and Sector 127, Communication equipment. For the remaining sectors, improvement from across-the-row changes is about one-half of the potential error reduction. This conclusion follows from the fact that the prediction error of test (b)—across-the-row changes—is about halfway between the constant-coefficient and the balanced-coefficient error. Finally, the feedback error effect seems to be rather insignificant: tests (c) and (d) give very similar results. Using the actual output instead of the output predicted by the model in the final demand equations does not appreciably change the forecasts.

Developing an Income Side

The model forecasts sales in real terms. Substantial progress has been made toward completing the wage, price, and income side of the model. Industry wages are estimated as a function of the consumer price index, the unemployment rate, productivity, and the level of employment. Prices are estimated as a function of unit labor and materials costs and a distributed lag on output.[6]

Prices

The price computations rely on the quantity forecasts and, once made, enter into the forecasts of consumer demands and of input-output coefficients. Prices are calculated monthly, so that they can respond quickly and dramatically to a change in supply or demand; annual simulations would sleep through the interesting action. In every industry, the specification of the price equation is the same:

$$P_{jt} = c_j + \sum_{k=1}^{18} u_k (UMC_{j,t-k} + ULC_{j,t-k}) + \sum_{k=1}^{18} v_i Q_{j,t-k} \qquad (15\text{-}4)$$

where

c_j = constant

P_{jt} = price index for industry j in month t (1967 = 1.0)

Q_{jt} = constant-dollar output of industry j in month t

---

6. Brian O'Connor, a former research student at the University of Maryland, has estimated the other components of income. When his work has been coordinated with the estimates of the present INFORUM model, disposable income, now exogenous, can be generated within the model. Alternatively, we will be able to test whether the present tax structure generates a disposable income that is consistent with a desired level of employment.

UMC_{jt} = unit material cost of industry j in month t

ULC_{jt} = unit labor cost of industry j in month t

u_k, v_k = distributed lag weights

k = time lag in months

A basic requirement for each industry is that it set a price to cover its costs. The prices of materials and labor are determined by forces beyond the control of the industry. The industry adjusts by choosing the mix of inputs and by setting the price of output. But the adjustment is not made immediately or all at once. In the simulations, it occurs over an 18-month period. When the adjustment is fully registered, the price may have risen proportionately less than cost or proportionately more. This characteristic—the elasticity of price with respect to cost—varies from industry to industry, as does the pattern of the response over time. The shape and sum of these distributed lags are estimated by making a regression analysis of each industry's experience. The analysis will be described later.

The forecasting of prices requires forecasting of the unit materials and labor costs for each industry. But the unit materials cost of an industry is nothing else than the ratio of the average price of the inputs to the price of the output. These input prices are the very same product prices that are the subject of the forecast. The industry's input column of the input-output matrix gives the weights for forming the appropriate average. An important feature to note is that this calculation is not a simultaneous determination of all materials costs and prices. The simultaneity is broken by making one month's prices depend on past months' costs, not on the current month's cost. An industry price is set at the beginning of each month on the basis of prior experience. Once this month's prices are in hand, 185 unit cost figures can be formed with the updated input-output table and set aside for the next month's price computations.

To each industry's unit materials cost must be added its unit labor cost, calculated as the ratio of average wage to labor productivity. Labor productivity is generated in the quantity model to arrive at employment by industry. The wages are the dependent variables of another set of equations and are discussed below.

Cost push is half the story. Demand conditions are the other half. If demand for an industry's product is strong, producers will pass along cost increases. Slack demand will eat away at the cost-induced increases in price, making the observed price rise less than would otherwise be expected. To incorporate this effect into price forecasts, changes in outputs are allowed to have a transitory effect on prices; the long-run effects are near zero, in accord with the idea that the production occurs on a relatively flat portion of the long-run average-cost curves. The distributed lag specification allows both the short-run and long-run characteristics; the weights are positive on recent increments in output to reflect the bidding-up of price and negative on increments of more distant months as long-run adjustments are made. The outputs that enter the industry price equations for forecasting are derived from the quantity model.

Wages

The industry wages are the subject of regression analysis. The explanatory variables are the consumer price index, the national unemployment rate, aggregate labor productivity, and employment in the particular industry. In each of the four variables, a change is allowed 12 months to have its full effect on the wage. Three of these variables are forecast in the quantity model; the fourth, the consumer price index, is an average of all the prices and is calculated from the forecasts. Again, the simultaneity is broken by excluding the current month's consumer price index from the wage computation and making wages depend wholly on lagged values.

The consumer price index and aggregate productivity are included in the wage equations to set the overall wage level; workers in all industries participate in increases coming from these two forces. The reciprocal of the unemployment rate enters to catch the short-term pressures of the labor market.

For all four variables, polynomial distributed lags were estimated. In the forecast, the wages are thereby made to reflect recent price experience as well as technological progress, productivity, and the varying levels of industry demand. The unit labor cost can then be added to the unit materials cost to complete the measure of unit production cost used in the price equations.[7]

The Simulations

The computations simulate several interactions that are important in any effort to anticipate price changes. Money wages rise roughly in proportion to aggregate productivity increase plus inflation. For industries whose prices have risen more than the average, household demand declines relative to what would otherwise have occurred. Producers substitute relatively cheaper inputs for relatively more expensive ones where possible. Thus, both intermediate and final demands respond to relative prices, and output levels are affected. These results are carried into the investment decisions. Because the capital stock needed for production will decline with output in industries experiencing rapid price increases, productivity will grow more slowly and employment more quickly. Meanwhile, all the prices will be felt by the producing industries as costs of production. Thus, inflated prices cause further inflation. As they work through demand adjustments, they create self-correcting forces. The complete simulations show the net effect as it appears over a period of several years.

7. The wage equations were estimated by David Belzer, a research student at the University of Maryland. He is completing the integration of the income side into the real model.

Regression Analysis

Before discussing some of the simulations, it would be appropriate to present the results of the regression analysis of the historical behavior of industry prices. To estimate the lags between unit cost and price and between output and price, monthly times series were needed for three variables for each input-output sector: the price, the total payroll, and the quantity of output. Prices came from the U.S. Department of Labor. Wholesale prices were used where possible; consumer prices were used for all services. Industry payrolls were taken from the U.S. Department of Labor data on employment, earnings, and hours. Payrolls were made as comprehensive as possible, including overtime pay. Since the salaries of supervisors and executives are not covered, these employees were counted in at the same average earnings as production workers. This method gave the derived unit labor cost at the more nearly correct magnitude, although the variable certainly fails to reflect shifts between these two classes of employees. The third set of industry data, monthly output, comes from the Board of Governors of the Federal Reserve System's Industrial Production Index program. Both seasonalized and unadjusted series were used, the latter for the denominator of the unit labor cost and the former for output, the independent variable. The other explanatory variable, unit cost, was formed for each month by weighting all prices for the month according to the industry's input coefficients and adding payroll per unit of output, that is, by adding unit materials costs to unit labor costs. Where the price variable was missing, there could not, of course, be an equation. The period covered by the data was generally 1958 to 1971. The results of the regression are shown in Table 15-2 for typical sectors. The first column shows the $\bar{R}^2$; the second column, the rho or autocorrelation coefficient of the errors. Since the data are monthly, and no lagged values of the dependent variable are used, it is not surprising that the rho values are high. They are used to move the forecasts gradually from the last actual value back to the value forecast in the equation.

Table 15-2. Characteristics of Price Equations

Sector				Unit		
Num-ber	Title	$\bar{R}^2$	rho	Cost Elasticity	Average Lag	Output Elasticity
7	Fruits, vegetables, & other crops	.548	.55	.75	15.4	.22
15	Crude petroleum, natural gas	.547	.91	.75	11.4	.08
16	Stone & clay mining	.985	.94	1.01	7.3	.25
17	Chemical fertilizer mining	.646	.96	1.14	13.6	.25
21	Ammunition	.935	.84	.98	11.5	-.11

(continued)

Table 15-2 continued

Number	Title	$\bar{R}^2$	rho	Unit Cost Elasticity	Average Lag	Output Elasticity
25	Canned & frozen foods	.950	.92	1.08	6.9	.17
26	Grain mill products	.725	.86	.75	3.9	.25
27	Bakery products	.966	.94	1.25	3.8	.13
28	Sugar	.602	.83	1.01	5.4	.25
29	Confectionery products	.808	.87	.89	4.4	.23
30	Alcoholic beverages	.963	.91	.75	9.9	-.00
31	Soft drinks & flavorings	.982	.88	1.25	10.4	.23
32	Fats & oils	.562	.80	1.25	3.6	-.12
35	Broad & narrow fabrics	.581	.95	.94	10.3	-.02
36	Floor coverings	.818	.95	.75	4.8	-.10
38	Knitting products	.849	.95	.75	3.6	-.16
39	Apparel	.972	.92	1.24	7.5	.18
40	Household textiles	.689	.94	.75	7.1	.03
43	Millwork & wood products	.901	.98	.80	5.3	.13
44	Wooden containers	.973	.76	.75	9.2	-.01
45	Household furniture	.885	.94	1.04	8.3	.19
46	Other furniture	.986	.87	.83	9.7	.20
47	Pulp mill products	.538	.95	.75	13.1	.07
48	Paper & paperboard mills	.962	.94	.75	9.9	.19
59	Fertilizers	.968	.85	.91	9.2	.23
61	Misc. chemical products	.704	.98	.75	15.3	.25
65	Noncellulosic fibers	.484	.94	.75	8.4	-.07
66	Drugs	.832	.95	.75	2.3	-.06
67	Cleaning & toilet products	.986	.91	.75	7.1	.13
69	Petroleum refining	.621	.86	1.08	5.6	-.12
74	Misc. plastic products	.757	.93	.75	13.3	.17
75	Leather & industrial leather products	.653	.95	1.25	12.0	.24
76	Footwear (except rubber)	.990	.74	1.25	6.0	.22
77	Other leather products	.974	.74	.90	8.0	-.02
78	Glass	.916	.96	1.25	5.4	.14
82	Other stone & clay products	.853	.95	1.25	6.0	-.01
83	Steel	.917	.95	1.25	10.1	.25
88	Primary nonferrous metals	.490	.99	.75	6.2	.25
93	Metal barrels & drums	.952	.85	1.05	7.4	.12
94	Plumbing & heating equipment	.898	.92	.97	2.6	-.00
95	Screw machine products	.923	.98	1.25	4.2	.25
98	Cutlery, hand tools, hardware	.953	.86	1.07	7.1	.21
100	Pipes, valves, fittings	.936	.94	1.25	13.0	.07
102	Engines & turbines	.961	.95	.94	3.4	.22
103	Farm machinery	.979	.95	1.03	5.9	.24
104	Construction, mine, oilfield machinery	.991	.92	1.18	12.3	.25
106	Machine tools, metal cutting	.993	.71	1.16	9.8	-.25

(continued)

Table 15-2 continued

Sector					
Num-ber	Title	$\bar{R}^2$	rho	Unit Cost Elasticity	Average Lag	Output Elasticity
107	Machine tools, metal forming	.978	.60	.75	8.8	-.15
108	Other metal working machines	.949	.97	1.07	9.3	.16
110	Pumps, compressors, blowers	.946	.99	1.25	9.0	.25
112	Power transmission equipment	.768	1.00	1.25	5.2	.25
113	Industrial patterns	.961	.97	1.25	6.9	.25
114	Computers & related machines	.468	.87	.75	11.1	-.14
117	Machine shop products	.893	.95	1.25	5.8	.25
118	Electrical measuring instruments	.940	.70	.86	11.8	.25
119	Transformers & switch-gears	.472	.98	.88	2.3	-.04
121	Industrial controls	.782	.95	1.22	10.0	-.10
123	Household appliances	.926	.90	.84	4.4	.03
124	Electrical lighting & wiring equipment	.889	.92	1.25	15.9	.20
126	Phonograph records	.429	.98	.75	4.9	.25
127	Communication equipment	.905	.86	.75	3.9	.22
129	Batteries	.704	.97	.75	14.9	.13
131	X-Ray & other electrical equipment, n.e.c.	.947	.82	1.08	8.0	.25
133	Motor vehicles	.965	.74	.82	12.0	-.05
138	Railroad equipment	.817	.97	1.25	8.3	.25
139	Cycles & transportation equipment, n.e.c.	.529	.98	.75	6.5	.03
145	Photographic equipment	.886	.97	.75	15.4	.17
148	Toys, sport, musical instruments	.985	.91	.94	11.8	.13
149	Office supplies	.420	.85	.75	10.9	.13
150	Misc. manufacturing, n.e.c.	.932	.91	.75	16.0	.24
155	Airlines	.912	.87	.88	13.8	.13
158	Telephone & telegraph	.549	.81	.75	14.5	.03
160	Electric utilities	.918	.88	.75	15.8	.10
161	Natural gas	.743	.95	.75	12.7	.25
162	Water & sewer services	.976	.93	1.11	10.8	.25
165	Banks, credit agencies & brokers	.863	.98	.88	11.3	.25
166	Insurance	.978	.97	1.25	2.9	.25
167	Owner-occupied dwellings	.994	.85	.85	3.7	.09
168	Real estate	.950	.98	.75	15.1	.07
170	Personal & repair services	.984	.98	1.03	9.0	.25

Note: n.e.c. = not elsewhere classified

The unit cost, output, and price were all represented as index numbers with the average value during 1967 set to unity. The sum of the individual lags could therefore be interpreted as the elasticities. If the sum of the 18 weights on unit cost is 0.9, then 90 percent of cost increases will be permanently recorded in a higher price for the output. Such a result would imply that between 1958 and 1971 the industry had been unable to pass along all increases in cost; that inability is carried forward into the forecasts. The third column of Table 15-2 shows these elasticities of price with respect to cost. The estimation method constrained them to lie between 0.75 and 1.25. The weighted average length of lag in months, $\Sigma k u_k / \Sigma u_k$ is shown in the fourth column.

When it comes to the output variable, the weights have the analogous interpretation, and so does the sum of the weights. However, the elasticities of price with respect to output, shown in column 5 of Table 15-2, are much less than unity. They should be near zero, meaning that if enough time is allowed for installing new capacity, a much greater quantity could be provided at nearly as low a price. In the months immediately following an increase in output, the price may rise, but the effect is transitory.

Oil and Food in the U.S. Inflation

The price-wage model will be illustrated by using it to answer the question of how much of the 1973 inflation can really be traced to uncontrollable factors in the agricultural and crude oil sectors. To answer this question, it is necessary to simulate the economy under the hypothetical condition that price increases in these sectors did not occur. In the government price control program, the fourth quarter of 1972 was adopted as a base period for measuring cost changes. The simulations use November 1972 to match this base. The hypothetical case, then, consisted of making a complete simulation forecast for the years 1971 to 1976, but for seven sectors—Dairy farms (raw milk); Poultry & eggs; Meat animals; Cotton; Grains; Fruits & vegetables & other crops; and Crude petroleum & natural gas (crude oil)—the results from the price equations were replaced after November 1972 by that month's price. Under this assumption, it appears that wholesale prices would have risen only 5 percent in 1973. The actual increase was over 18 percent. The comparison is misleading, however, for the model cannot quite reproduce the actual rate. If the second simulation forecast is made using actual raw materials price movements during 1973, wholesale prices appear to rise 15 percent instead of 18 percent. This difference is the error of the model. The difference between 5 percent and 15 percent is attributable to inflation in the raw materials sectors whose prices were allowed to change.

A third simulation (in which agricultural prices remain at their November 1972 levels, but inflation is allowed to occur in crude oil prices) traces out a path between the first two. Under these conditions, wholesale prices would have risen 6 percent during 1973. Compared with 5 percent, the additional aggregate effect is much less dramatic than the headlines and price quotations of November and December 1973. During 1974, however, a strong effect can be expected. The first simulation led to a prediction of 9 percent, compared with the original 4 percent. Since the second simulation differs from the third only by the agricultural price changes, the further observation can be made that those price changes will increase this 9 percent to 14 percent. The best prediction for 1974 is this 14 percent inflation, a rate hardly less than the rate for 1973. In each year, two-thirds of the increase is traceable to raw goods; but in 1973, oil played a negligible part, while in 1974, its part will be as large as that of the agricultural sectors. The full course of the simulation is shown in Figure 15-3.

Applications of INFORUM

Forecasts with the INFORUM model have been used to aid business and government planning. A model such as this one provides a consistent framework for assessing the performance of various sectors of the economy. Altering various assumptions under which the model is run and comparing the effects on demand and employment is a simple application of the model. Although this approach suggests answers to some of the questions that concern users of the model, the standard format is often an incomplete answer to many specific problems. In many cases, the model can be expanded and tailored to the problem at hand. Several questions to which the model has been adapted include forecasting company profits, selecting a merger partner, increasing the product detail, and assessing environmental impacts. These areas have been fully described by Almon

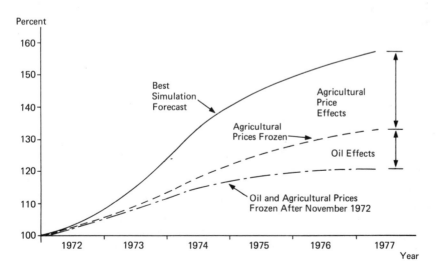

Figure 15-3. Wholesale Price Index Simulations, 1972-1977.

et al. [1], and will be only briefly outlined here. A topic of more current interest—the energy crisis—will then be discussed in the context of the INFORUM model.

One sponsor has used the model with a profit model of its own to evaluate the effect of alternative assumptions and government policies on the company's profits. Its specific products are related to one of the 185 sectors in the INFORUM model, or to particular cells in the row of that sector. This relationship is used to determine the growth sales of the company's products. The information is then fed into the company's model to forecast profits.

A similar approach was used to aid another company in the selection of a merger partner. Here, the sales of various product lines of prospective partners were related to the sectors in the INFORUM model. Then a composite sales forecast was made for each company. This type of approach was also used to study diversification and the sensitivity of the products under consideration to cyclical effects. The use of quadratic programming enabled us to specify a trade-off between rapid growth and risk aversion. We hope to apply this technique to the analysis of portfolio management.

Often many business decisions require knowledge of the demand for a product at a much more detailed level than it is possible to incorporate into a standard model. For example, investment decisions by a paper company may depend not merely on how much paper will be required by book printing, but on what kind of paper—whether it is a grade used to make paperbacks, or a much higher quality used to make textbooks. In such a case, when detailed product information on end use is available, coefficients can be derived to show how much of that product is sold to each of the 185 sectors in the model. In this way, the number of rows in the model can be expanded in areas of special interest. When information on such coefficients is available over time, trends in the coefficients can be estimated. Future demand for the products is obtained from the forecast coefficients and the forecasts of outputs of the 185 sectors of the model. Studies of this nature have been done for paper and plastics.

The Environmental Protection Agency has developed a model known as SEAS—Strategic Environmental Assessment System—to study the impact of different growth policies and compositions on the environment. The INFORUM model is the "front end," which provides forecasts of outputs to this system. The SEAS model then forecasts the generation of pollutants and their regional impacts.

The Energy Crisis

The Arab oil embargo, shortages of domestic refinery capacity, and rapid growth in the demand for petroleum products combined in late 1973 to create an "energy crisis." Predictions of a severe recession were commonplace. Quite naturally, many users of the INFORUM model wished to know what the model had to say about the consequences of this energy crisis. Accordingly, imports of crude and refined petroleum were revised to reflect the embargo. Crude imports were reduced by about 20 percent; refined petroleum imports were reduced by 18 percent. The 1974 price of crude petroleum was exogenously introduced at double its 1973 level and fed into the price model to determine the effect on other prices. This new price forecast was introduced into the real model. Hence, the consumption forecasts were altered to reflect the revised relative prices according to their respective price elasticities.

As it was then structured, the model's results were not encouraging. It required an unreasonably large increase in domestic crude petroleum production to meet the needs of the economy for 1974. Alternatively, if all demands were reduced to a level of possible crude petroleum production, a large amount of unemployment was generated. However, the model had not taken a significant factor into account. It had assumed a zero elasticity of intermediate demand with respect to the relative price of petroleum. Certainly there are opportunities for the substitution of coal for oil, and of less petroleum-intensive products and services for those relatively more petroleum-intensive. There are other potentials for conserving, such as reducing fuel oil used for space heating. Because we lacked specific information about the magnitudes of the elasticities, we introduced some assumptions. These assumed elasticities are shown in Table 15-3.

Rerunning the model with the assumed elasticities permitted intermediate demand to react to relative price changes. Now, with a 112 percent increase in the price of crude petroleum, domestic production is kept to 2.7 percent of its 1973 level. Tables 15-4 and 15-5 and Figure 15-4 show the format of the INFORUM forecasts. Table 15-4, which shows the forecast made in April 1974, lists final demands, employment, and prices. It also lists the important assumptions that were exogenous to this forecast. Table 15-5 lists the sales of energy-related sectors to the important purchasers. Figure 15-4 shows historical and forecast energy outputs.

Some problems with the data should be noted here. The base year of the model is 1971, the most recent year for which we have complete information on

Table 15-3.   Assumed Relative Price Elasticities for Intermediate Demand

Energy-Related Sector	Substitute	Elasticity
Fuel oil used for electricity	Coal	−2.0
Fuel oil used for process heat	Coal	−0.3
Fuel oil used for space heat[a]	None	−0.3
Gasoline and other petroleum products	None	−0.1
Trucking	Railroads	−0.2
Electric utilities	None	−0.2
Noncellulosic fibers	Cellulosic fibers	−0.2

[a] Alan M. Strout, "Weather and the Demand for Space Heat," *The Review of Economics and Statistics* 43, no. 2 (May 1961): 185–192.

Table 15-4. GNP Summary

TABLE 4.

ENERGY CRISIS FORECAST   GNP SUMMARY (BILLIONS OF 1971$)

	1971	1972	1973	1974	1975	1976	1978	1980	1983	1985
GROSS NATIONAL PRODUCT	1050.36	1099.12	1159.96	1182.80	1237.67	1285.28	1362.86	1440.53	1548.44	1612.89
PERSONAL CONSUMPTION EXPENDITURES	664.90	692.02	730.84	742.48	768.26	794.73	854.37	911.81	992.99	1041.79
DURABLE GOODS	103.48	112.09	120.89	114.90	119.00	122.95	132.38	141.17	153.91	161.18
NONDURABLE GOODS	278.12	284.83	299.87	304.98	313.12	324.27	344.78	364.57	393.75	412.36
SERVICES	283.30	296.07	312.47	322.09	335.12	346.66	375.40	403.24	441.89	464.33
GROSS PRIVATE DOMESTIC INVESTMENT	151.97	170.28	188.16	186.67	207.52	218.08	220.01	231.77	246.44	254.92
STRUCTURES	80.94	89.32	91.67	87.97	94.59	99.74	98.75	102.64	107.66	110.29
RESIDENTIAL	42.58	50.98	49.04	38.37	43.68	47.77	46.66	49.75	52.80	54.30
PRODUCERS' DURABLE EQUIPMENT	67.41	75.22	84.39	89.74	100.55	106.06	112.13	120.10	130.18	136.73
AGRICULTURE	5.37	5.42	5.57	5.72	6.61	6.79	6.83	6.76	7.06	7.34
MINING	2.40	2.51	2.66	2.84	3.22	3.47	3.69	3.91	4.22	4.46
CONSTRUCTION	2.53	2.96	3.19	3.31	3.79	4.03	4.15	4.40	4.58	4.78
NONDURABLE GOODS	7.80	8.51	9.84	11.17	11.82	12.25	12.87	13.57	14.34	15.10
DURABLE GOODS	7.81	9.30	10.97	12.71	14.20	15.41	15.10	15.38	16.18	17.04
TRANSPORTATION	4.29	5.61	5.70	5.83	7.38	7.67	8.25	9.01	10.30	10.96
COMMUNICATION	7.76	8.91	9.87	10.89	11.72	12.53	13.88	15.34	17.26	18.23
UTILITIES	7.24	7.49	8.30	9.53	9.92	10.37	11.39	12.35	13.71	14.41
TRADE	8.53	9.31	10.07	10.69	12.24	13.23	14.31	16.06	17.67	18.91
FINANCE AND SERVICES	6.64	7.37	9.85	8.14	10.48	10.77	11.48	12.25	12.81	12.97
INVENTORY CHANGE	3.60	5.69	11.95	8.81	12.18	12.08	8.95	8.84	8.39	7.69
EXPORTS OF GOODS AND SERVICES	66.13	66.55	71.75	78.43	82.95	90.32	100.47	106.78	117.19	124.16
MERCHANDISE	36.88	36.17	39.03	43.15	45.40	49.90	55.43	57.96	62.31	65.11
MARGINS AND SCRAP	5.90	5.50	5.93	6.55	6.89	7.56	8.39	8.77	9.42	9.84
TRAVEL	2.46	2.85	3.11	3.39	3.77	4.06	4.44	4.69	5.05	5.30
PASSENGER FARES, OTH TRANSPORT	3.71	4.05	4.36	4.49	4.67	4.92	5.28	5.56	6.00	6.28
OTHER PRIVATE SERVICES	1.97	2.03	2.21	2.47	2.62	2.90	3.26	3.42	3.70	3.88
INVESTMENT INCOME	12.01	12.90	14.07	15.29	16.58	17.91	20.67	23.58	28.22	31.49
GOVERNMENT	3.21	3.24	3.24	3.24	3.24	3.24	3.24	3.24	3.24	3.24
IMPORTS OF GOODS AND SERVICES	-65.41	-66.27	-71.85	-70.33	-72.18	-74.77	-80.90	-89.02	-101.68	-110.25
MERCHANDISE	-47.77	-47.09	-52.14	-49.56	-50.36	-51.39	-54.32	-59.42	-67.33	-72.70
NON-COMPETITIVE MERCHANDISE	-3.10	-3.21	-3.33	-3.38	-3.52	-3.64	-3.88	-4.10	-4.42	-4.61
MARGINS AND SCRAP	5.32	5.89	6.52	6.19	6.30	6.43	6.81	7.45	8.45	9.13
TRAVEL	-4.29	-4.44	-4.79	-4.97	-5.25	-5.50	-6.11	-6.66	-7.36	-7.72
PASSENGER FARES, OTH TRANSPORT	-4.30	-4.32	-4.69	-4.81	-4.98	-5.22	-5.71	-6.24	-7.11	-7.68
OTHER PRIVATE SERVICES	-.87	-.96	-.96	-.93	-.94	-.95	-.99	-1.06	-1.16	-1.23
INVESTMENT INCOME	-3.06	-3.86	-4.53	-5.25	-6.03	-6.83	-8.53	-10.36	-13.33	-15.46
GOVERNMENT	-7.42	-7.42	-6.82	-6.22	-5.62	-5.62	-5.62	-5.62	-5.62	-5.62
FOREIGN LONG-TERM CAPITAL TO U.S.	2.27	2.31	2.50	2.69	2.88	3.00	3.23	3.46	3.81	4.04
U.S. LONG-TERM CAPITAL ABROAD	-6.35	-6.59	-6.96	-7.32	-7.69	-7.91	-8.35	-8.79	-9.45	-9.89
U.S. GOVT. LONG-TERM CAPITAL FLOWS	-2.19	-3.84	-3.82	-3.80	-3.79	-3.79	-3.79	-3.79	-3.79	-3.79
GOVERNMENT PURCHASES	232.76	235.33	239.90	244.28	249.76	255.57	267.51	277.86	292.32	301.24
PUBLIC CONSTRUCTION	30.10	28.19	28.41	30.05	30.97	31.78	33.08	34.20	35.73	36.71
NATIONAL DEFENSE	69.71	66.54	65.40	64.30	63.19	63.82	65.07	66.32	68.19	69.44
NON-DEFENSE FEDERAL	24.10	25.98	26.46	27.83	29.20	29.94	31.42	32.90	35.29	36.88
STATE AND LOCAL	108.85	114.53	119.48	121.89	126.13	129.75	137.60	144.06	152.67	157.74
EDUCATION	52.54	54.93	57.82	58.68	60.48	61.94	64.56	66.18	68.49	70.23
PRODUCTIVITY ($1000 PER EMPLOYEE)	12.64	12.88	13.25	13.31	13.68	13.89	14.18	14.53	15.04	15.37

	1971	1972	1973	1974	1975	1976	1978	1980	1983	1985
EMPLOYED PERSONS (MILLIONS)	81.96	84.14	86.32	87.63	89.23	91.27	94.76	97.79	101.52	103.50
PRIVATE INDUSTRY	65.61	67.70	69.70	70.89	72.23	73.96	76.82	79.52	82.32	83.82
CIVILIAN GOVERNMENT	13.53	13.96	14.18	14.36	14.66	14.98	15.62	16.16	16.91	17.40
DEFENSE	1.14	1.09	1.03	.97	.91	.91	.91	.91	.91	.91
MILITARY	2.81	2.48	2.43	2.39	2.34	2.33	2.32	2.31	2.29	2.28

AGGREGATE PRICE FORECASTS

	1971	1972	1973	1974	1975	1976	1978	1980	1983	1985
WHOLESALE PRICE INDEX (1967=100)	114.14	121.02	136.69	153.98	163.18	170.36	178.47	181.86	187.37	197.75
GROSS NATIONAL PRODUCT	143.02	151.53	164.38	183.02	197.23	208.86	221.34	227.44	231.64	231.08
PERSONAL CONSUMPTION EXPEND.	121.67	129.17	139.80	156.55	168.41	178.49	189.53	195.26	205.85	224.89
DURABLE GOODS	113.98	118.54	124.57	133.49	145.59	155.83	168.23	173.21	175.29	174.06
NONDURABLE GOODS	133.38	142.60	162.13	185.77	196.04	201.95	209.66	213.34	215.62	215.06
SERVICES	148.25	157.47	166.91	186.08	201.86	216.92	232.38	240.98	248.21	248.75
GROSS PRIVATE FIXED INVESTMENT	141.47	149.18	160.07	174.52	190.18	201.53	212.87	217.07	218.40	216.04
BUSINESS STRUCTURES	164.05	173.05	186.43	207.00	225.60	237.86	247.52	250.75	251.19	247.67
PRODUCERS DURABLE EQUIPMENT	127.98	133.88	141.81	153.54	168.38	180.06	193.12	198.12	200.02	198.24
RESIDENTIAL CONSTRUCTION	148.35	155.34	175.29	190.09	204.20	213.16	220.97	203.77	224.39	221.77
EXPORTS	126.47	132.46	152.93	171.28	180.42	189.66	199.25	203.25	204.99	203.73
GOVERNMENT	174.19	183.91	199.24	223.43	240.94	253.30	266.19	271.66	274.57	272.75
FEDERAL	172.06	182.25	198.41	220.52	237.06	249.31	262.02	267.18	269.87	268.24
STATE AND LOCAL	176.98	186.41	201.90	226.71	244.62	257.08	270.80	276.99	280.57	278.95
PUBLIC CONSTRUCTION	194.51	205.37	219.46	251.39	273.02	287.01	298.85	303.03	304.24	300.59

EXOGENOUS ASSUMPTIONS

	1971	1972	1973	1974	1975	1976	1978	1980	1983	1985
CONSUMPTION										
DISPOSABLE PER CAPITA INCOME 58$	2679.00	2770.00	2889.00	2940.00	3030.00	3104.00	3286.67	3440.00	3610.00	3680.00
POPULATION - SERIES E (MILLIONS)	207.05	208.80	210.50	212.16	213.92	215.79	219.79	224.13	231.04	235.70
SCHOOL AGE POPULATION	59.91	59.61	59.18	58.75	58.32	57.97	56.32	54.62	53.35	53.46
PLANT AND EQUIPMENT INVESTMENT										
LONG-TERM INTEREST RATE	.02	.03	.02	.02	.03	.03	.02	.02	.02	.02
SHORT-TERM INTEREST RATE	-.00	-.00	.02	.02	.02	.02	.02	.01	.01	.01
RENT/CONSTRUCTION COST INDEX	.79	.76	.75	.77	.80	.80	.80	.80	.80	.80
HOUSEHOLDS (MILLIONS)	64.37	66.67	67.64	68.87	70.08	71.54	74.44	77.30	81.45	84.21
INVESTMENT TAX CREDIT	.00	.07	.07	.07	.07	.07	.07	.07	.07	.07
FOREIGN TRADE										
AVERAGE FOREIGN CURRENCY PRICE	1.00	1.01	1.03	1.05	1.09	1.12	1.13	1.13	1.12	1.11
EMPLOYMENT										
LABOR FORCE (MILLIONS)	86.93	88.99	90.58	92.17	93.78	95.39	98.62	101.81	105.69	107.72
CIVILIAN UNEMPLOYMENT RATE	5.90	5.60	4.83	5.05	4.97	4.43	4.00	4.03	4.02	3.99

NUMBERS HAVE BEEN SCALED TO 1971 PUBLISHED LEVELS AND MAY NOT ADD TO TOTALS

Table 15-5. Selected Interindustry Sales

SELLER 14 COAL MINING

BUYER	1971	1973	1974	1980	1985
14 COAL MINING	897.8	942.5	1105.6	1311.7	1433.7
35 BROAD AND NARROW FABRICS	22.8	25.3	26.8	32.0	34.1
48 PAPER AND PAPERBOARD MILLS	146.0	158.1	172.0	210.2	228.6
55 INDUSTRIAL CHEMICALS	136.1	155.1	160.1	214.4	251.8
81 CEMENT, CONCRETE, GYPSUM	128.2	135.7	140.3	172.1	190.8
83 STEEL	772.4	859.6	866.3	918.0	910.4
133 MOTOR VEHICLES	24.2	27.7	25.4	31.2	34.5
160 ELECTRIC UTILITIES	1618.9	1714.1	2162.3	2644.1	2960.3
SUM OF INTERMEDIATE FLOWS	4106.9	4407.4	5063.1	6036.2	6607.1
SALES TO FINAL DEMAND					
186 PERSONAL CONSUMPTION	137.2	103.1	85.2	21.1	.0
187 DEFENSE EXPENDITURES	41.2	41.2	41.2	45.3	49.4
189 EDUCATION	22.6	26.8	27.4	32.2	34.7
193 CHANGE IN INVENTORIES	-44.8	-72.0	-31.8	14.2	10.0
194 EXPORTS	565.3	560.0	760.0	900.0	1000.0
SUM OF SALES TO FINAL DEMAND	738.8	679.9	904.3	1043.8	1131.4
TOTAL	4845.7	5087.3	5967.4	7079.9	7738.4

SELLER 15 CRUDE PETROLEUM, NAT. GAS

BUYER	1971	1973	1974	1980	1985
15 CRUDE PETROLEUM, NAT. GAS	118.6	124.2	127.5	160.9	188.8
69 PETROLEUM REFINING	15830.0	17705.1	17154.7	21627.9	25201.9
160 ELECTRIC UTILITIES	104.4	116.4	120.1	150.0	173.5
161 NATURAL GAS	3308.1	3523.5	3598.2	4211.9	4821.6
SUM OF INTERMEDIATE FLOWS	19412.9	21524.9	21056.6	26227.4	30481.2
SALES TO FINAL DEMAND					
193 CHANGE IN INVENTORIES	-193.0	.0	50.0	46.6	45.8
195 IMPORTS	-2555.1	-4106.1	-3200.0	-3680.0	-4010.0
SUM OF SALES TO FINAL DEMAND	-2708.1	-4034.6	-3100.0	-3568.4	-3884.2
TOTAL	16704.7	17490.3	17956.6	22658.9	26597.1

SELLER 69 PETROLEUM REFINING

BUYER	1971	1973	1974	1980	1985
69 PETROLEUM REFINING	3070.5	3434.2	3327.5	4195.1	4888.4
3 MEAT ANIMALS, OTH LIVESTK	141.2	148.0	155.4	178.2	198.7
5 GRAINS	691.1	697.9	716.2	871.9	995.2
7 FRUIT,VEGETABLES,OTH CROPS	270.8	307.3	320.9	392.2	447.4
19 MAINTENANCE CONSTRUCTION	211.2	243.7	242.7	306.5	356.0
68 PAINTS	145.5	166.2	169.3	195.8	210.0
70 FUEL OIL	4823.1	5774.0	5412.6	6383.3	7420.6
71 PAVING AND ASPHALT	342.8	398.7	411.8	551.5	666.2
83 STEEL	138.6	167.4	160.0	171.2	172.2
152 BUSSES AND LOCAL TRANSIT	215.5	287.2	286.0	346.7	386.0
155 AIRLINES	1258.0	1635.1	1742.9	2594.0	3272.8
158 TELEPHONE AND TELEGRAPH	140.0	161.5	156.9	218.1	272.7
163 WHOLESALE TRADE	1369.1	1594.8	1524.9	2022.6	2452.0
164 RETAIL TRADE	909.2	1047.1	998.3	1291.2	1536.0
170 PERSONAL + REPAIR SERVICES	156.4	175.7	168.4	208.7	236.0
171 BUSINESS SERVICES	176.1	213.0	209.1	276.8	333.1
173 AUTO REPAIR	177.5	193.8	183.2	221.2	255.1
SUM OF INTERMEDIATE FLOWS	16870.2	19723.3	19220.4	24169.8	28332.8
SALES TO CONSTRUCTION ACTIVITIES					
18 HIGHWAYS	455.9	407.2	424.7	419.2	414.7
20 CONSERVATION & DEVELOPMENT	254.0	246.3	277.5	363.8	436.5
SUM OF SALES TO CONSTRUCTION	1357.5	1390.6	1456.6	1649.8	1793.3
SALES TO FINAL DEMAND					
186 PERSONAL CONSUMPTION	10364.0	10872.3	10400.7	13133.0	15275.1
187 DEFENSE EXPENDITURES	229.3	229.3	229.3	252.2	275.2
189 EDUCATION	270.2	320.2	326.9	385.0	414.9
194 EXPORTS	378.8	439.4	375.0	440.0	505.0
195 IMPORTS	-588.2	-786.0	-650.0	-750.0	-800.0
SUM OF SALES TO FINAL DEMAND	11113.3	11702.3	11119.2	14267.7	16585.5
TOTAL	29340.9	32816.2	31796.3	40087.3	46711.5

(continued)

Table 15-5 continued

SELLER 70 FUEL OIL

BUYER	1971	1973	1974	1980	1985
5 GRAINS	56.3	66.6	71.6	86.6	97.7
48 PAPER AND PAPERBOARD MILLS	75.4	103.7	95.7	120.1	135.4
55 INDUSTRIAL CHEMICALS	25.9	37.5	39.1	52.4	61.5
81 CEMENT, CONCRETE, GYPSUM	26.3	35.4	32.3	40.4	46.1
83 STEEL	94.9	134.2	120.6	130.2	132.6
151 RAILROADS	360.8	496.4	551.7	669.0	748.1
152 BUSSES AND LOCAL TRANSIT	85.3	133.2	134.7	163.1	181.6
153 TRUCKING	746.6	1022.9	1049.9	1466.1	1822.2
154 WATER TRANSPORTATION	478.7	526.8	472.9	473.2	473.1
160 ELECTRIC UTILITIES	476.9	736.1	370.6	517.2	696.7
163 WHOLESALE TRADE	46.8	63.9	60.1	80.1	98.2
164 RETAIL TRADE	196.0	264.5	248.0	322.4	387.7
165 BANKS,CREDIT AGEN.,BROKERS	34.5	48.7	45.6	60.9	72.0
166 INSURANCE	38.4	46.8	42.6	53.4	62.6
171 BUSINESS SERVICES	49.2	69.7	67.3	89.6	109.0
175 MEDICAL SERVICES	52.8	69.2	65.3	82.8	98.1
176 PRIVATE SCHOOLS + NPO	69.3	97.7	93.6	120.3	141.2
SUM OF INTERMEDIATE FLOWS	3372.8	4576.4	4170.1	5289.2	6241.5
	SALES TO FINAL DEMAND				
186 PERSONAL CONSUMPTION	2635.0	2845.0	2589.5	2800.0	3150.0
189 EDUCATION	85.9	101.8	90.3	45.6	24.3
192 GENERAL STATE + LOCAL GOV.	50.7	58.0	51.9	28.5	16.1
194 EXPORTS	49.0	29.4	30.0	30.0	30.0
195 IMPORTS	-1395.1	-1865.0	-1545.0	-1825.0	-2050.0
SUM OF SALES TO FINAL DEMAND	1450.3	1197.6	1242.5	1094.2	1179.1
TOTAL	4823.1	5774.0	5412.6	6383.3	7420.6

outputs, in this case from the *Annual Survey of Manufactures: 1971* [3]. However, we have drawn on other statistics published in the *Survey of Current Business (SCB)* [5] to update the energy sectors. We introduced data on personal consumption expenditures, inventory change, imports, and exports. In mid-April of 1974, complete data for 1973 had not been published in the *SCB*; therefore, many of these 1973 numbers are estimates based on data through October. While domestic production of refined products increased almost 13 percent between 1971 and 1973, domestic supply (production plus imports) of crude petroleum increased only 5.7 percent. Domestic production of crude fell by more than 2 percent.

With output of refined petroleum and imports and inventory change of crude petroleum in agreement with published statistics, the model generates domestic crude petroleum demand that is 7 percent higher than published crude petroleum production in 1973. Statistics on crude imports are likely to be accurate, because this information reported in the *SCB* is collected by the Tariff Commission. There was essentially no change in reported inventory stocks. A negative change of more than a billion dollars would have been necessary for the output generated by the model to conform with published data. We feel it would be even more unrealistic to assume that the sales of crude per unit of refined petroleum declined drastically. Indeed, preliminary reports of the *Census of Manufactures, 1972* [4, Table 4] indicate a slight increase in the historical trend of this coefficient. For these reasons, we have not forced the 1973 output generated by the

Figure 15-4. Historical and Forecast Energy Outputs

Inforum April 1974 Forecast

14 Coal Mining

	1955	1956	1957	1958	1959	1960	1961	1962	1963	1964	1965	1966
Output (+) ——	4240.	4576.	4475.	3729.	3738.	3752.	3632.	3793.	4123.	4356.	4552.	4724.
Consumption (•) — —	641.	588.	431.	431.	352.	368.	366.	341.	284.	237.	231.	241.
Imports (0) —··—	0.	0.	0.	-6.	-6.	-4.	-4.	-6.	-6.	-6.	-4.	-4.
Exports (X) ······	0.	0.	0.	622.	449.	422.	412.	459.	575.	564.	581.	559.

	1967	1968	1969	1970	1971	1972	1973	1974	1975	1976	1977	1978
Output (+)	4880.	4810.	4933.	5290.	4846.	5205.	5087.	5967.	6275.	6494.	6613.	6759.
Consumption (•)	207.	184.	178.	145.	137.	116.	103.	85.	71.	57.	48.	37.
Imports (0)	-6.	-4.	-2.	-2.	-2.	-2.	-2.	-2.	-2.	-2.	-2.	-1.
Exports (X)	551.	552.	601.	730.	565.	560.	560.	760.	800.	820.	840.	860.

	1979	1980	1981	1982	1983	1984	1985
Output (+)	6905.	7080.	7228.	7373.	7518.	7640.	7738.
Consumption (+)	29.	21.	13.	6.	0.	0.	0.
Imports (0)	-1.	-1.	-1.	-1.	-1.	-1.	-1.
Exports (X)	880.	900.	920.	940.	960.	980.	1000.

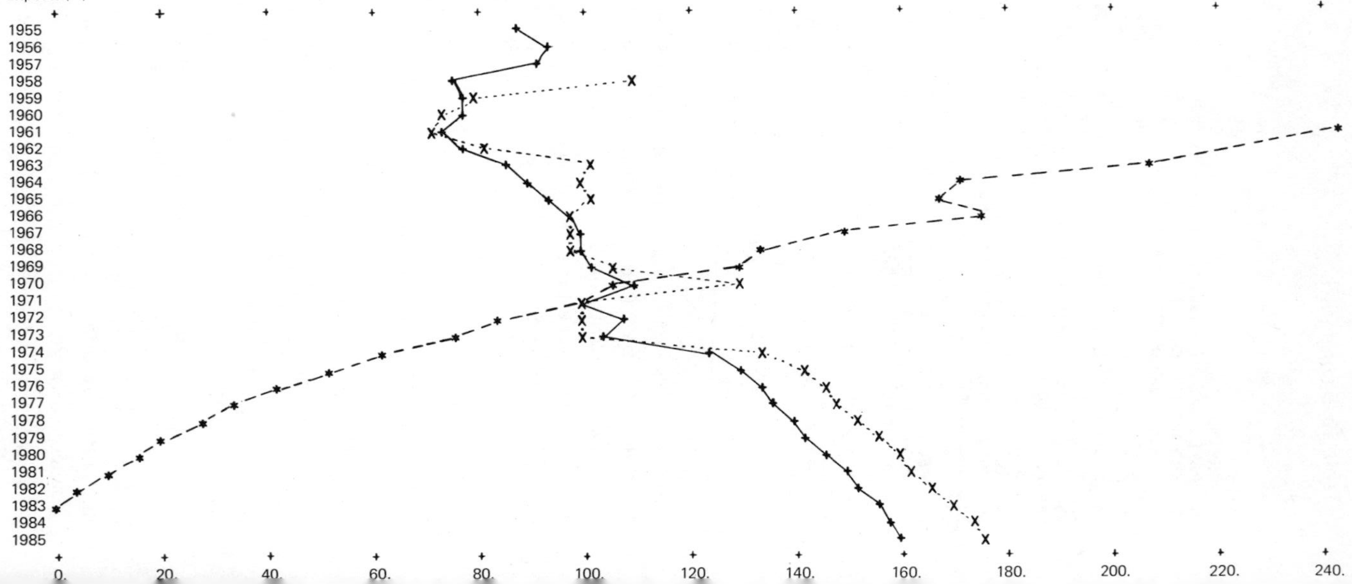

15 Crude Petroleum, Nat. Gas

Inforum   April 1974 Forecast

	1955	1956	1957	1958	1969	1960	1961	1962	1963	1964	1965	1966
Output (+) ——	10061.	10726.	10679.	10046.	10842.	11164.	11495.	11897.	12357.	12609.	13001.	13948.
Imports (0) – – –	0.	0.	0.	-1302.	-1302.	-1354.	-1431.	-1604.	-1646.	-1735.	-1802.	-1786.
Exports (X) · · · · ·	0.	0.	0.	32.	15.	13.	14.	11.	11.	10.	12.	26.

	1967	1968	1969	1970	1971	1972	1973	1974	1975	1976	1977	1978
Output (+)	14844.	15414.	15699.	16812.	16705.	17055.	17490.	17957.	18904.	19681.	20479.	21183.
Imports (0)	-1731.	-1897.	-2048.	-2066.	-2555.	-3075.	-4106.	-3200.	-3350.	-3416.	-3482.	-3548.
Exports (X)	134.	49.	32.	51.	40.	68.	72.	50.	50.	53.	56.	59.

	1979	1980	1981	1982	1983	1984	1985
Output (+)	21888.	22659.	23430.	24168.	24977.	25795.	26597.
Imports (0)	-3614.	-3680.	-3746.	-3812.	-3878.	-3944.	-4010.
Exports (X)	62.	65.	68.	71.	74.	77.	80.

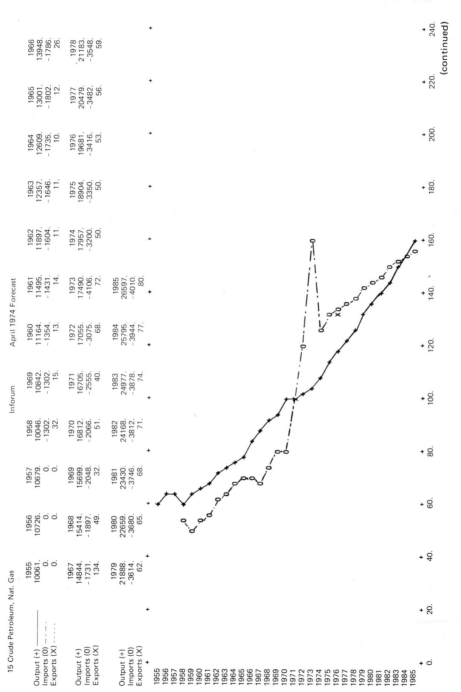

(continued)

Figure 15-4 continued

69 Petroleum Refining

	1955	1956	1957	1958	1959	1960	1961	1962	1963	1964	1965	1966
Output (+) ———	16780.	17581.	17443.	18553.	19680.	19949.	19787.	20523.	20966.	23269.	23259.	24160.
Consumption (*) — — —	5607.	5896.	5894.	6316.	6672.	6787.	6728.	6949.	7033.	7933.	7987.	8332.
Imports (0) —·—·—	0.	0.	0.	-241.	-211.	-178.	-181.	-225.	-259.	-252.	-302.	-324.
Exports (X) ·······	0.	0.	0.	359.	331.	350.	344.	344.	370.	403.	358.	383.

	1967	1968	1969	1970	1971	1972	1973	1974	1975	1976	1977	1978
Output (+)	24793.	26397.	27728.	29104.	29341.	30454.	32816.	31796.	33087.	34713.	36241.	37526.
Consumption (*)	8549.	9207.	9830.	10346.	10364.	10499.	10872.	10401.	10687.	11246.	11732.	12256.
Imports (0)	-305.	-392.	-449.	-563.	-588.	-667.	-786.	-650.	-700.	-710.	-720.	-730.
Exports (X)	384.	421.	384.	399.	379.	430.	439.	375.	375.	388.	401.	414.

	1979	1980	1981	1982	1983	1984	1985
Output (+)	38764.	40087.	41394.	42639.	43999.	45366.	46712.
Consumption (*)	12688.	13133.	13573.	13976.	14400.	14854.	15275.
Imports (0)	-740.	-750.	-760.	-770.	-780.	-790.	-800.
Exports (X)	427.	440.	453.	466.	479.	492.	505.

Inforum   April 1974 Forecast

70 Fuel Oil

Inforum   April 1974 Forecast

Output (+) ——————
Consumption (+) — — —
Imports (0) — · — · —
Exports (X) · · · · · ·

	1955	1956	1957	1958	1959	1960	1961	1962	1963	1964	1965	1966
Output (+)	3261.	3418.	3389.	3606.	3758.	3513.	3575.	3581.	4036.	3812.	4016.	4145.
Consumption (+)	2142.	2248.	2224.	2394.	2416.	2474.	2338.	2285.	2247.	2351.	2489.	2515.
Imports (0)	0.	0.	0.	-752.	-761.	-743.	-771.	-819.	-811.	-855.	-970.	-1007.
Exports (X)	0.	0.	0.	162.	128.	105.	75.	81.	119.	78.	60.	48.

	1967	1968	1969	1970	1971	1972	1973	1974	1975	1976	1977	1978
Output (+)	4656.	4870.	4901.	4712.	4823.	5156.	5774.	5413.	5511.	5698.	5919.	6055.
Consumption (+)	2746.	2864.	2787.	2609.	2635.	2742.	2845.	2589.	2550.	2600.	2650.	2700.
Imports (0)	-1043.	-1125.	-1157.	-1291.	-1395.	-1582.	-1865.	-1545.	-1600.	-1645.	-1690.	-1735.
Exports (X)	63.	26.	45.	51.	49.	33.	29.	30.	30.	30.	30.	30.

	1979	1980	1981	1982	1983	1984	1985
Output (+)	6215.	6383.	6574.	6759.	6971.	7188.	7421.
Consumption (+)	2750.	2800.	2870.	2940.	3010.	3080.	3150.
Imports (0)	-1780.	-1825.	-1870.	-1915.	-1960.	-2005.	-2050.
Exports (X)	30.	30.	30.	30.	30.	30.	30.

model to conform with published data. Rather, it seems more realistic to assume that the published data are inaccurate.

There are still limitations to this forecast. The model has not addressed itself to the problem of complementary goods—how does the price of gasoline affect the demand for automobiles? The consumption equation for automobiles had an upward taste-change factor of 0.6 percent per year. We have removed this factor. There are problems of time lags in the shift to a substitute energy source.

All in all, we feel that the elasticities are realistic and that, with a little allowance for adjustment problems, the forecasts show that the economy could operate at a high level of employment within the limits of available petroleum. (Layoffs in the automotive industry have come, not from a lack of fuel to *produce* the cars, but from a shift in demand to cars that the industry was not equipped to make.)

Future Directions—A System of World Input-Output Models

Any model, to remain useful, must be adapted to address new questions, such as the energy crisis, and be improved where it is weak. During the last several years, we have devoted some effort to a more reasonable specification of the foreign trade equations, particularly to take fluctuating currencies into account. Although we are satisfied with the import equations, problems remain with exports. Currently, exports are related to lagged domestic output and the relative foreign to domestic price. Obviously, they should instead be related to foreign demand. Although this task is simple enough in the historical period, in order to forecast exports we would need to forecast world demand by product.

We are planning, therefore, to construct a system of input-output forecasting models for the major countries, which are interconnected through their trade sectors. Previous experience with an input-output model of Austria convinced us that our approach is feasible, provided we have the help and cooperation of economists in those countries.

References

1. Almon, Clopper; Margaret Buckler; Lawrence C. Horwicz; and Thomas C. Reimbold. *1985: Interindustry Forecasts of the American Economy*. Lexington: Lexington Books, D.C. Heath and Company, 1974.

2. Strout, Alan M. "Weather and the Demand for Space Heat." *The Review of Economics and Statistics* 43, no. 2 (May 1961): 185–192.

3. U.S. Bureau of the Census. *Annual Survey of Manufactures, 1971: General Statistics for Industry Groups and Industries*, M71(AS)-1. Washington, D.C.: U.S. Government Printing Office, 1973.

4. U.S. Bureau of the Census. *Census of Manufactures, 1972: Preliminary Reports—Industry Series.* Washington, D.C.: U.S. Government Printing Office, 1974.

5. U.S. Department of Commerce. "Current Business Statistics." *Survey of Current Business* 54, no. 2 (February 1974): S1–S40.

Chapter Sixteen

The Use of Input-Output Analysis in Industrial Planning

A. George Gols

This paper briefly explores the topic of the industrial applications of input-output analysis in the United States, particularly in corporate planning. An unpublished survey, conducted by Arthur D. Little, Inc., in 1971, showed that there were two hundred, out of several thousand, corporations in the United States that, at one time or another, have used input-output analysis in some form in their corporate-planning work. Of these two hundred corporations, all of which had sales in excess of $500 million annually, sixty firms indicated that they used input-output analysis regularly and intended to continue to do so. From some other informal questionnaires that Arthur D. Little, Inc., circulated among fifty or so major U.S. corporations for which it had undertaken input-output studies, it was found that input-output analysis was typically used in connection with forecasting work. A few other types of application seem also to have been made and, judging from various input-output conferences held in the United States, it has become evident that there are beginning to be more applications that tie directly into all aspects of corporate-planning activity.

We can best understand the new inroads that input-output analysis is making if we examine and define the corporate-planning process. The first section of this paper delineates the functions of corporate planning. The second section classifies types of input-output classifications and relates them to the corporate-planning functions. The third section lists some of the principal barriers that have to be overcome to speed acceptance of input-output analysis in corporate planning and provides an illustration of the details of analysis that make applications cumbersome. The final section considers the prospect for greater acceptance of input-output analysis in private-industry planning.

This is a slightly modified version of an article published in *Business Economics,* vol. X, no. 3 (May 1975) pp. 19–27.

Concept and Functions of Corporate Planning

To fully understand what comes under the rather broad heading of corporate planning could obviously, in itself, be a lifetime job. There is certainly ample literature on the subject [8]. Also, it is a dynamic concept constantly undergoing change. First, we must point out that, like input-output analysis, corporate planning is young; its pioneers in the United States (George Steiner, Russell Ackoff, Peter Drucker, et al.) did not actually start spreading the corporate planning "gospel" until the early 1950s. Unlike the slow spread of the use of input-output techniques by corporations, the conversion of corporations to systems of formal planning turned out to be very fast and widespread indeed. A survey in 1960 of the chemicals processing industry in the United States—which is one of the most progressive users of modern management techniques and methods—showed that upwards of 90 percent of the chemical firms used a system of formal planning—particularly of the long-range variety—while practically none used such a system as recently as 1948 [2]. There are, of course, still a few large corporations that have not yet instituted formal planning systems and procedures, but they are in a distinct minority. Also, the actual planning processes, systems, and styles do vary greatly in content and organization from one firm to another.

Second, like any other new discipline, or science, corporate planning has organized itself around a few key concepts, approaches, and tools. Basically, corporate planning has become a collection of methods and approaches drawing heavily, though not exclusively, on certain management-science tools, particularly those usually associated with operations research. As George Steiner puts it, "During the past ten years, the rapid expansion of comprehensive corporate planning has been matched only by the great dynamism with which new techniques, methods, and approaches have been injected into it" [8, p. vii].

In that sense, it is, of course, clear that corporate planning is a discipline that is continually embracing new management tools. This is, indeed, the principal reason why the input-output technique should be considered a natural candidate for membership in this exclusive corporate-planning-tools club. Let us now briefly explain how planning fits into the management decision process of a modern corporation and how input-output can relate to this process. Figure 16-1 shows the corporate management cycle divided into five key stages. The corporate planning functions that support each of these stages are shown in the lower half of each of the five stages.

Opportunity Search and Threat Response
This first stage is, so to speak, the "hub" of the management wheel. Since the business corporation embodies an organization of focused activity designed to identify and realize commercial opportunities and to respond to threats that would frustrate the realization of such opportunities, this first stage reflects the

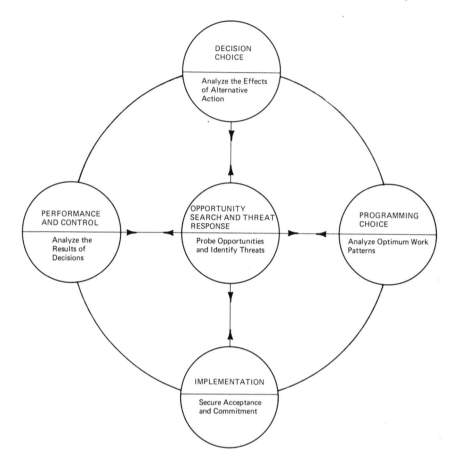

Figure 16-1. Management Decision Cycle.

raison d'être of the corporation. Our questions are: What can input-output studies contribute to this particular planning function? Are there any unique ways in which input-output analysis can be brought to bear on the planning function that other methods cannot? We shall return to those questions later, as we look at specific input-output applications.

Decision Choice

This stage is where the merits of various alternative action courses are evaluated. It is one that traditionally has been the principal preserve of the management science practitioners. A great number of management science tools, such as simulation and linear programming models, are used to analyze the consequences of alternative financial or resource allocation possibilities, given predetermined choice criteria. It would seem to be an area where input-output analysis should find some application, and indeed it does. But the great problem that continues to attend the use of many management science tools and models in this area lies in making them less abstract for application to particular practical business problems. If input-output analysis is to find a useful role in this area, it, too, will have to respond to this challenge.

Programming Choice

This is a stage of management where decisions are translated into specific action patterns for implementation. The primary management tasks in this phase are: (1) scheduling activities in support of decisions; (2) budgeting or assigning and scheduling resources in support of decisions; (3) establishing patterns of work flow in the firm; (4) establishing patterns of authority and responsibility; and (5) establishing communication flow networks.

This stage of the management cycle is where planning was born. Many corporate planners today will argue that programming, or the problem of defining and laying out optimum work patterns, is the core and the substance of corporate planning work and that the major job of planners is to catalyze activities, integrate the inputs received from the rest of the organization, and interpret results for management. Dynamic programming and decision-tree analysis are beginning to take a foothold in this area. If input-output analysis is to make a substantial mark in corporate planning, it will have to come to the assistance of the planner in this basic area.

Implementation

This stage of the management decision cycle deals with implementation and is probably the most time consuming. It consists of: (1) disseminating information about the plans and programs; (2) securing acceptance by responsible participants; (3) triggering organizational action; (4) providing coordination among related activities; and (5) providing leadership and otherwise motivating the participants. The planner's attention is focused mainly on (1) and (2). It would seem an unlikely place for input-output analysis to find a role, and yet there may be possibilities of application even here. For example, insofar as acceptance of the corporate planner's programs and plans by department heads and plant managers depends on good communications, it may be useful to organize planning data on output targets, materials usage, market distribution, or production cost structure along input-output lines. This could provide a new perspective on how the various components of particular work plans are interlocked. If this promotes a better understanding of plans by managers who must implement them, it may also promote a better execution of such plans.

Performance and Control

Historically, the staff responsibility for this stage has been lodged with the controller and finance branch of the firm. Since business planners usually report directly to top operating management, their function is often parallel to, rather than coupled with, the controller's. Though the organizational implications remain to be resolved, planners are becoming increasingly concerned with designing activity programs in ways that will expedite effective performance measurement and control. Since the planner is entering this area, there is also likely to be room for the input-output analysts.

In sum, the management decision wheel shows that some planning activity is involved in all stages of corporation management decision making. To better understand where input-output analysis can serve in the various functions of the planning process, let us now appraise input-output analysis from an applications point of view. We will identify various forms of usage and see how they fit into the individual planning functions described above.

Input-Output Applications

In sifting through the rather sparse literature of existing input-output applications relating to private industry, we find that there is no book, no collection of essays—only a few papers. But it appears that there are perhaps at least four principal types of input-output applications. They are: forecasting; sensitivity testing; flow and structural analysis; and sorting and screening. To some extent, these applications overlap or are interdependent, but for purposes of discussion, let us consider them separately.

Forecasting

Forecasting seems to have been the mainstay of past input-output applications in corporate planning. Most likely, it will remain such. Some of the early applications in the United States originated with work done in the early 1950s at the Western Electric Company. Later, Arthur D. Little, Inc.; Clopper Almon at the University of Maryland; and the Battelle Institute; as well as other organizations and individuals, launched more ambitious and comprehensive research efforts in this area. This was done by assembling groups of corporations to jointly sponsor forecasting studies [6; 7].

At Arthur D. Little, Inc., where the principal activity is in management consulting work for private business firms, input-output application work during the last five years has progressed to the point where an input-output model, somewhat similar to the one used at the University of Maryland, is used every year to provide, on a regular basis, forecasts of the U.S. economy to a group of 30 to 40 corporate clients. The forecasts are made of output growth of 215–230 individual industries for the year ahead (in current and constant dollars) and for the next five to ten years (in constant dollars). The key job here is to update and project the final demand data, the structure of the technical coefficient matrix, and other exogenous variables that are used in implementing the input-output model. In addition, it is necessary to interpret results in a way meaningful to the average corporate planner, who may be unfamiliar with input-output definitions, data, and methods, and to help apply them in the planning work. Input-output forecasting has been useful in several areas of corporate planning, but its prime application has been in the function we call corporate opportunity search. Here, the information is used, together with other inputs, to assist corporate planners to identify acquisition, or diversification and general investment, opportunities. This is done by screening forecasts of industry growth or decline derived with the input-output model, and by determining which industries are, on the average, likely to grow at a more or less rapid rate than the economy as a whole over the long term. If realistic forecasts are to be obtained, it is essential to develop quantitative estimates of the likely structural shifts that will take place in the economy over time and to represent these in the input-output matrix. These shifts indicate the expected changes in the size and position of individual industry markets. We determine what these shifts are likely to be by assessing probable changes in the technology and competition of various products in different industry sectors. As has been explained by others [1; 3], there are various ways in which this can be, and has been, done.

There are also one-year, or even quarterly, input-output forecasts that can help the planner focus particular attention on more immediate business problems, arising from very unexpected alterations in the business environment. The alterations may emerge from a suddenly announced new government policy or a business cycle change, or from some external event, such as the international energy crisis. The results of this type of input-output forecast become useful in setting up or changing corporate work schedules and programs. Input-output forecasts can also be useful in the performance monitoring and controls function where corporations evaluate profit centers in terms of how actual results compare with planned results. A discussion of how an input-output forecast is used in this context was given in a paper presented by Yost and Stowell [10]. In their paper, Yost and Stowell discuss in detail a method by which the input-output analysis results are adapted to evaluate corporate profit-center operations. By profit centers, Yost and Stowell mean individual corporate operating units for which separate profit and loss accounts are developed to gauge the relative performance between different units. In essence, they tell us that input-output forecasts, if sufficiently detailed, can be used to adjust actual performance measures of profit centers to reflect actual changes in the business environment, in order to more objectively measure the "real" performance progress of profit centers.

Sensitivity Testing

This type of input-output analysis is, in some respects, simply a variant of the more standard forecasting work. But it differs from the more traditional forecasts produced with input-output models in that it is geared principally to test the consequences of alternative hypotheses concerned with changes in the economic environment. Specifically, it deals with "what if" questions, that is, "What if the growth of the economy goes this way or that way?" "What if the structure of an industry shifts along this direction instead of that direction?" "What happens if we have, or do not have, the introduction of a specific new product in an industry next year—what difference does it make?" Here, input-output analysis can help to draw the boundary lines of the likely effects on industry and company growth of alternative hypotheses. Such hypotheses may set out different final parameters of growth or component mixes in the gross national product, or alternative hypotheses about changes in the market structure and/or technology. For example, a couple of years ago, North American Rockwell Corporation, a major aircraft-producing company, wishing to understand the impact on U.S. industry of the introduction of a space shuttle in the United States, undertook an input-output analysis to better define the dimensions of such an impact [5].

In making sensitivity tests, the input-output technique is often particularly useful in demonstrating the indirect effects of specific changes. For example, a change in the mix of a nation's exports, due to a currency revaluation or devaluation, obviously directly influences the growth of corporations that export goods and services. But the change in exports also affects the growth of corporations that import their materials and supply products either to the corporations that do the exporting or to the enterprises that are major suppliers to the exporting corporations. In such a case, input-output analysis can be instrumental in showing up hidden but often significant indirect effects. Similar questions about impacts arise when a change in an industry's production technique changes the input patterns of another industry that is not directly involved in this change. The recent energy shortage in the United States provides a good example. In many cases, the materials and components inputs to the mining equipment, shipbuilding, and transportation equipment building industry have to be changed to respond to changing equipment needs of the mining sector that arise, for example, as mining activity shifts its emphasis from on-shore to off-shore oil drilling.

With the profusion of seismic tremors that seem to be continually reverberating through the world economic environment these days, and the increasing number of multinational companies that are involved in all types of activities all over the world, the greatest potential for using the input-output technique will lie in quick evaluations of the likely industry impacts and ramifications of international and complex events. It is clear that the input-output application possibilities for sensitivity analysis span both the first and second functions of the corporate planning process. In many cases, it can also provide services to the third corporate planning function, that is, it can help in shaping programs. This is particularly true if the results of the input-output analysis show that the environmental parameters used as an assumption in a corporation's work program are no longer valid.

Flow and Structural Analysis

The input-output concept provides, of course, one of the best frameworks for analyzing some of the key flow patterns of goods and materials and services in the economy. The determination of flow patterns or the identification of the network by which goods move through the economy can provide very perceptive insights into possible bottlenecks, strategic connections, and ways in which specific markets are coupled to each other. For example, in carrying out plant and product feasibility studies for corporations, patterns of materials input hierarchies and input mixes of different industries can be used in determining which particular materials supplies should be given priority. This has some resemblance to the theoretical types of input-output analysis described by some as structural analysis [9, p. 86]. In practice, however, a good understanding of the potential for coefficient analysis in this area seems to be most critical to progress, since coefficients define the flow relationships.

How useful the analysis of the pattern by which products and materials flow through the economy is to corporations is still to be determined, but at least one recent event has proven it a very useful tool. For example, when recent energy developments in the United States pointed out a possible lack of feedstocks for the petrochemical industry, input-output analysis was used by Arthur D. Little, Inc., to determine what petrochemical inputs the chemical industries directly require, and what industrial and employment repercussions would occur if these inputs proved to be in short supply [4]. Knowledge of the flow network of the petrochemical industry in the United States was obviously one of the most essential ingredients of this evaluation process. Second, it was necessary to make the evaluation within the framework of all industries operating in the national economy in order to determine how dependent the overall economy was on this industry.

There is, in addition, the possibility that flow analysis along input-output lines can also be used to identify flow patterns of materials between different entities within a given corporate enterprise. This is beginning to be looked at by some very large chemical corporations with substantial intracompany product flows, and may yet turn out to be an important application for input-output analysis as more corporations move toward intensifying the vertical integration of their operations.

Sorting and Screening

Here, input-output analysis serves primarily as an ordering tool, by which markets and industries can be arrayed according to size, category, and other criteria. Recently, Arthur D. Little, Inc., and other organizations have arrayed industries on the basis of their energy intensiveness or usage. Similarly, we could array key markets of the metal-producing or chemical-producing or food-processing industries on the basis of size or categories of suppliers, or order industries on the basis of their similarity of principal materials inputs (which to some extent is the basis of the U.S. Standard Industrial Classification—SIC—code). At Arthur D. Little, Inc., we now can array over 40,000 markets by perhaps as many as 20 different key configurations. The possible different ordering configurations are theoretically almost limitless. This type of information is most useful for almost all of the first three functions of corporate planning. It can be a key ingredient in determining the priorities that should be given to different markets or materials supplies. It can enter into determining employment needs within production units in corporations or in sales departments. It can be useful even in the corporate planning function, where implementation through communications and commitments are made. Here, input-output analysis results can be used heuristically to communicate and demonstrate how or why management has reached certain decisions about allocating resources or establishing priorities.

In sum, there are many possible applications of input-output analysis that can be related to various corporate planning functions. Table 16-1 attempts to broadly summarize the possible interfaces that may exist between applications of input-output analysis and the different functional stages of corporate planning. We would expect that in the future this grid will be much enlarged and more finely divided.

Overcoming Barriers

Why, if there are all these possibilities for using input-output analysis in the corporate planning process, has there not been more widespread use of it by businesses? There are at least three major barriers that must be overcome:

1. *Better information.* Unless input-output studies can be extended to include work with more detailed up-to-date information, they will remain academic exercises and useless to the highly specific information needs of the planner.

Table 16-1. Relationships Between Corporate Planning and Input-Output Analysis Functions

	Input-Output Functions			
Planning Functions	*Forecasting*	*Sensitivity Testing*	*Flow and Structural Analysis*	*Sorting and Screening*
Opportunity search and threat response	Very applicable	Very applicable	Moderately applicable	Moderately applicable
Decision choice	Moderately applicable	Very applicable	Moderately applicable	Moderately applicable
Programming choice	Moderately applicable	Very applicable	Moderately applicable	
Implementation		Moderately applicable		Moderately applicable
Performance and control	Very applicable	Moderately applicable		Moderately applicable

2. *More work on very detailed applications.* There is a reluctance of the input-output analyst to deal with the very detailed aspects of applying input-output to business problems. Input-output specialists will also have to learn more about the decision-making and planning process in corporations.
3. *Better interpretation.* There is a need to translate the abstract and theoretical formulations of input-output analysis into operational terms that the average business planner—indeed, the average businessman—can understand.

A Concrete Illustration

The above statements are best understood by referring to concrete illustrations. So let us briefly consider at least one scenario of a planning situation confronting a typical major manufacturing corporation.

A manufacturing corporation in the United States has diversified interests in various business areas and a yearly sales volume of around $1 billion. The individual divisions of the corporation are engaged in manufacturing products in three key areas: plastics, metals, and electronics. These products are sold to various markets, but in the main to the automotive, appliances, and machinery industries. The management of the company is venturesome and aggressive; it wants to expand—possibly, but not necessarily, into new products. Obviously, it wants to avert a decline in profitability and sales. It feels there is a need not only to enlarge its share of existing markets (which financial analysis shows leads to higher profits or return on investments) but also to look for opportunities in new areas where risks are high, but potential returns are also better.

The planning department has been asked by the management to systematically investigate future growth opportunities in the economy to determine how they might be tied into existing operations and the resources and experience of the company. This is typical of the kind of opportunity-search work that is carried out by thousands of individual companies in the United States periodically, if not continuously. How does input-output analysis enter into the process?

The Company Seeks Opportunities

The planner starts by drawing up a business environment scenario of the U.S. economy for the next ten to fifteen years. This will, he hopes, provide him with some of the key ingredients with which to determine the economic environment and the assumptions needed to undertake more detailed opportunity-search work. He consults with the company's economist, who provides some of these inputs, such as long-range gross national product (GNP) forecasts, population trend forecasts, and market forecasts in key industries and products. However, this does not prove to be comprehensive enough for the planner. He also wants to identify opportunities in key areas with which the internal staff and in-house economists are relatively less familiar and lack the overall analytical framework by which to cross-check the consistency of the analysis results. The planner consults the literature and collects various articles; he interviews various marketing managers and marketing research staffs inside and outside the company; but he has a problem in linking it all together. As the matter comes to a head, his information search confirms a suspicion already held by the management— namely, that a small compact car will perhaps soon replace the full-sized vehicle that has been traditionally produced by the auto industry. This would, at first glance, imply substantial decreases in the demand for the company's plastics and metal products. But how much impact will it have and what offsetting opportunities may arise? The corporate divisional market research managers also have become increasingly aware of this threat, but they have done little to analyze the industry-wide or company-wide repercussions. The planner knows he needs to do this. He goes back to the economist. The economist now indicates that it is necessary to develop a rather elaborate framework to determine all the possible repercussions that might arise from such a fundamental change in the company's markets. Especially tricky is the problem of arriving at quantitative estimates of the impact, particularly if it is desirable to measure not only the direct, but also the indirect effects on materials demands, since it appears that the production of the small car will involve not only the substitution of materials for each other, but also the introduction of new technologies (pollution control and electronics equipment) into the car. This obviously raises the possibility that new markets will be created for electronics and other components. It raises the question of whether other industries and materials needs will evolve as a consequence of these more direct changes that are now anticipated. The economist, a resourceful person, well informed about the new tools of his trade, recommends the use of input-output analysis. He reasons that the planner can thereby not only forecast the impact of economic and technological change, but also learn something about how and to what degree other industries will be affected, and to what extent these effects will represent opportunities for the corporation.

The Company Analyzes

Because the corporation's in-house economic research capabilities are inadequate to handle this kind of study, the corporate planner and the economist decide to contract with an independent research organization to provide long-range forecasts to help analyze the problem. It is thought that the information would be most meaningful if the change could be analyzed by using in the input-output analysis the GNP forecasts already developed by the corporation's economist. The research organization concedes that this can be done, but points out that there is a need also to have at least reasonably up-to-date detailed data on present materials usage in cars and to forecast new materials usage patterns in the auto and related industries. This requires engineering and survey data from many industries. The research organization thus proposes a more significant exercise than had earlier been anticipated by the planner or the economist. The planner and the economist reconcile themselves and their budget to this situation, but their real problems have only begun. As the first forecasts roll out of the model, the planner compares the results with data with which he is familiar. He finds inconsistencies having to do with reconciling information from different sources. This is not necessarily peculiar to input-output, but it complicates the assessment work.

A more fundamental problem is to determine what it is precisely that the planner wants to know about materials demand. Does he want to measure demand in physical or value-of-output terms? Does it make a difference to him? Why is it critical? It so happens that the engineering data show that the small car or compact car will be structurally quite different from the large car. It will contain significantly more plastic and significantly less steel. It will contain new types of pollution-control components and electronic devices that have never existed before to improve the braking, warning signal, and motor operations of the vehicle. The auto would cost the same, but weigh only half as much as the traditional large-sized car. Now, should the input-output analysis measure the demand for plastics, electronics, pollution-control components, steel, etc., in tons, dollars, capacity, or what? The planner wants to know them all. The input-output analyst must decide whether to run a constant dollar or current dollar model, or both; short-term or long-term model, or both. Also, he must decide how to measure coefficient changes.

The problem of how to measure technical coefficient changes in physical or value terms is, in itself, worth some discussion. It can be illustrated by drawing attention to Tables 16–2 and 16–3, which outline hypothetical computations of alternative input-output coefficients of steel usage in the average automobile and in the auto industry as a whole. The tables first show steel usage in cars before any change takes place. The average car uses one ton of steel. Coefficients are

Table 16–2. Hypothetical Computation of Alternative Input-Output Coefficients, in Physical Terms (steel inputs to automobiles)

	Alternative Technologies		
	A	*B*	*C*
Steel usage per vehicle	1.0 tons	0.8 tons	0.3 tons
Total weight per vehicle	2 tons	2 tons	1 ton
Total amount used (in 10 million vehicles)	10 million tons	8 million tons	3 million tons
Total weight of all cars produced	20 million tons	20 million tons	10 million tons
Input-output coefficient	1/2 = 0.5	0.8/2 = 0.4	0.3/1 = 0.3
Physical coefficient change		−20 percent	−40 percent
Total steel demand change		−20 percent	−70 percent

A = Before substitution and technological change.
B = After substitution of plastics for steel and price changes in standard-sized cars.
C = After introduction of electronics, pollution control equipment, and plastics substitutes in compact cars.

Table 16–3. Hypothetical Computation of Alternative Input-Output Coefficients, in Value Terms (steel inputs to automobiles)

	Alternative Technologies		
	A	*B*	*C*
Cost per ton	$200	$250[a]	$250[a]
Steel cost per vehicle	$200	$200 = 0.8 × $250	$75 = 0.3 × $250
Total cost of steel (for 10 million vehicles)	$2,000 million	$2,000 million	$750 million
Total cost of vehicle	$2,000	$2,000	$2,000
Total cost of 10 million vehicles	$20,000 million	$20,000 million	$20,000 million
Input-output coefficient	0.10[b]	0.10[b]	0.04
Value coefficient change		+0.0 percent	+60.0 percent
Total steel demand change		+0.0 percent	+62.5 percent

[a]25 percent price increase.
[b]$2 billion/$20 billion.
A = Before substitution and technological change.
B = After substitution of plastics for steel and price changes in standard-sized cars.
C = After introduction of electronics, pollution control equipment, and plastics substitutes in compact cars.

given in physical and value terms as 0.5 and 0.1, respectively. That is, if 10 million tons of steel are used to produce 20 million tons of cars, or one ton of steel is used to produce a two-ton car, the physical coefficient measures 0.5. On the other hand, if the total cost of steel used in 10 million vehicles (at $200 a ton) is $2 billion, if the average vehicle costs $2000, and if 10 million vehicles are produced, the industry's total value of output equals $20 billion. The value coefficient is thus $2 billion divided by $20 billion, or 0.1. Thus, we have a choice of using a value or physical coefficient and this, in turn, depends on whether the planner wants to measure demand changes in physical or value dimensions. Let us further analyze this by looking at the situation where there is a substitution of plastics for steel, but no changes in the size of the car. Usage of steel per vehicle drops 0.8 tons; plastics are substituted for steel (not shown in the table). Cost per ton of steel was formerly $200 and is now $250 because the newer type of steel has a higher tensile strength and is more corrosion-resistant. But this increases the price of steel by 25 percent. If we now use only 0.8 tons of steel, which costs 25 percent more, the inputs of steel in cost terms remain the same, at $200. The price of a car also does not change significantly because, while there is an increase in plastics usage, plastics prices decrease proportionately more than plastics usage increases. Thus, neither the value coefficient of plastics nor the value coefficient of steel changes. But the physical input of steel and plastics changes. The steel usage has dropped to 0.8, and steel demand now stands at 8 million tons. The total weight of the car has not changed, since the plastics which displace the steel are equally heavy, so the physical input coefficient of steel has now dropped to 0.4, or by 20 percent. This is important for planning, because physical demand changes affect plant capacity utilization rates in both the steel and plastics divisions of the company.

But the problem has only started. The design of the car is changed radically, as the size of the car is significantly reduced. Because of this, even more plastics and less steel are used in the compact car. The physical coefficient of steel drops to 0.3, or by 40 percent. The value of steel input is now $75. But the cost of the car stays the same because of the additions of high-cost electronic and antipollution equipment. The value coefficient of steel drops to 0.04, or by 60 percent. In physical terms, the demand for steel has dropped from 10 million tons to 3 million tons, or by 70 percent. In dollar terms, it has dropped from $2 billion to $750 million, or by 63 percent.

The planner really needs to know all these things. He needs to know the steel usage in physical terms because it influences plant capacity utilization rates, and he needs to know the value of steel sold because it affects the corporation's revenues and cash-flow profits. But he also needs to know the demand for electronic and other components in physical and value terms, because they promise new opportunities. He also wants comparable information for all the other industry sectors that make up the input-output model. But the problem of measurement can get even more difficult there. What do we do about measurement in the electronics and other sectors, such as machinery, where perhaps performance capacity, instead of weight, has to be used to lend a meaningful physical dimension to coefficient changes?

Emerging from all of this is the insight that perhaps the key stumbling block to the use of input-output analysis in corporate planning is that the assumptions and definitions concerning technological change, structural change, pricing, and demand sensitivity—on which the input-output coefficient changes are based—are of very great interest to the planner and of perhaps least interest to the input-output analyst; in fact, most input-output analysts tend to sweep these assumptions under the analytical rug, because they interfere with the mathematical elegancies of the input-output model or the simplicity of the analysis task.

The Future

If the input-output analyst cannot demonstrate sympathy and a full understanding of what is important to the corporate planner, the planner is not likely to accept the results of any input-output analysis. The kind of fundamental analysis problem just illustrated is duplicated and magnified in the application of input-output analysis in almost all the various stages of corporate planning.

Widespread acceptance of input-output analysis in corporate planning thus awaits better solutions to dealing with the very detailed, vexing, but very real, problems attending the practical use of input-output models. Some progress is being made by those who have the interest and patience to tackle these problems; but it is not the most fashionable pursuit among input-output analysts. So progress is slow in coming.

References

1. Carter, Anne P. *Structural Changes in the American Economy.* Cambridge, Mass.: Harvard University Press, 1970.

2. *Chemical Week* 86 (June 1960).

3. Elliott-Jones, M.F. *Economic Forecasting and Corporate Planning.* Conference Board Report No. 585. New York: Conference Board, 1973.

4. Ficcaglia, V., and G. Hegeman. "United States Petrochemical Industry Import Analysis." A report to the Petrochemical Energy Group, Arthur D. Little, Inc., Cambridge, Massachusetts, November 1973.

5. Gibson, T.A., and C.M. Merz. "Impact of Space Shuttle Program on the Economy of Southern California." El Segundo, California: Space Division, North American Rockwell, September 1971.

6. "The Growing Use of Input-Output Models." *EDP Analyzer* 7, no. 7 (July 1969): 1–14.

7. Stäglin, Reiner. "Zur Anwendung der Input-Output Rechnung." [The Application of Input-Output Accounting]. *Konjunkturpolitik* 16, no. 6 (1970): 327–366.

8. Steiner, G.A. *Top Management Planning.* New York: MacMillan Co., 1969.

9. Yan, C. *Introduction to Input-Output Economics.* New York: Holt, Rinehart and Winston, 1969.

10. Yost, S. W., and C.E. Stowell. "Using Input-Output Analysis for Evaluating Profit Center Performance." Paper presented at the Institute for Management Sciences Eighteenth International Conference, London, July 1–30, 1970.

Chapter Seventeen

The Use of Input-Output Computer Information in Programming for Chemical Processes

Thomas Vietorisz

The first programming models for the chemical industry, some fifteen years back, were of the heuristic type, because their nonconvex features could not be practicably handled by the optimizing algorithms and computer programs then available. These problems have been overcome, and large-integer programming models for the chemical sector have been built and solved. Now, heuristic models are becoming attractive again, but for different reasons.

Methods of standard economics are now undergoing a process of critical revision and expansion. As the focus of sectoral policy decisions widens from resource allocation to technological capability, environmental impact, institution building, and the amount and kind of foreign dependency, it is becoming increasingly urgent to interface resource allocation models with broader policy considerations. Heuristic models, which allow a continuous interaction of policymakers and technical specialists with the evolving program, can provide the needed interface.

This also overcomes one of the main faults of large optimizing models, namely, that they are opaque. They require compiling all data in advance, pouring them into the computer, and then allowing the algorithm to grind out blindly a solution. This makes error control difficult and prevents adapting technical detail to the requirements of an evolving solution. And policymakers are suspicious of end-results produced in a manner they cannot follow step by step.

The objective of this paper is to discuss the principles of a heuristic modeling system for the chemical industries, designed to be implemented on a computer in the time-sharing mode. It will define a heuristic, nonoptimizing yet efficient computer-based mode of using process-level input-output information for planning the chemical sector.[1]

1. For chemical industry planning, see two reports published by the United Nations [10; 12].

Shortcomings of the Formal Modeling Approach

Sectoral planning models using process-level input-output information are typically set up as formal input-output or mathematical programming systems.[2] Derivation of the inverse matrix or of optimizing and parametrically optimizing solutions is then accomplished by algorithms incorporated in large computer programs. In concrete applications, several problems arise with this approach.

First, it does not permit including in the planning process information that is either qualitative, unquantified, or quantified in a manner not conforming to model structure. Yet such considerations often dominate resource allocation decisions around which formal models revolve. For example, in a recent study of engineering industry development in Mexico [13;15], day-to-day production and technological change have been found to be so intertwined as to make formal resource allocation models incomplete or even misleading. This work has also raised doubts about the comparative advantage concept implicit in such models, and has suggested the need for interfacing them with historical development sequences. A heuristic, nonoptimizing approach to sectoral modeling uses process-level input-output data in a step-by-step fashion and thus permits taking into account supplementary information of many kinds as sectoral programs are gradually pieced together.

A second problem with formal models arises from the predetermined categories that are needed for setting them up. In concrete applications, it is generally not known in advance which detailed item will turn out to be critical. Small amounts of impurities in ethylene or hydrogen feedstocks can be ruinous to some processes and a matter of concern to others. Thus, the formal model is either defined in painstaking detail, most of which will turn out to be redundant, or omits detail which may turn out to be vital. Even worse, detail that is critical for the model may never be identified as such since modeling consists of two non-overlapping phases: information gathering and computation. Heuristic models, on the contrary, are built up from processes step by step. The procedure is transparent, can be followed by engineering specialists, and permits infusing additional qualitative or quantitative technical information *as it becomes identified as critical.*

A third problem with formal models is that the larger they get, the more their workings take on the nature of a mechanism working inside a black box. Policymakers rightly detest black boxes. The more opaque a large model becomes, the more chance there is for severe distortion arising from undetected keypunching errors, technical mistakes in the definition of a few among the thousands of coefficients, uncontroled biases inherent in mixing engineering data of various levels of reliability, or failure to include relevant items of information. For example, in linear programming models, two alternative processes are treated on a par even though the data for one may be derived from past

2. Recent examples of such work will be found in Goreux and Manne [3] and Stout-jesdijk and Westphal [8].

experience while the data for the other may represent unconfirmed engineering estimates. In a large, opaque model, it is impossible to keep track of biases of this kind. Heuristic models, on the other hand, are completely transparent and therefore particularly suited to detecting technical errors as processes are built into programs, adding information as needed, keeping track of the reliability of data, and representing the inner logic of complex process combinations for the appraisal of policymakers.

Advantages of Heuristic Models

The heuristic system rests upon a data bank that is set up so that it can grow and expand in use. In what follows, the principles of organizing such a data bank will be explained, and its application to heuristic modeling tasks will be laid out. A published data base for the chemical industry [14] will be used for illustrative purposes.

A far more cumbersome version of the heuristic method discussed here was used some years ago to define chemical industry development possibilities in Puerto Rico [5] and in Latin America [9; 17]. The main reason for bypassing formal models in these early experiments was the absence of powerful computer programs for the solution of large-integer programming problems. With the advances in mathematical programming and computing techniques, these problems have become amenable to formal solution. Integer programming models of the chemical sector have been explored in simplified models [16] and, lately, in large and complex ones [3; 8].

In the meantime, however, the emerging new perspective in economics and its planning applications has undermined naive faith in such formal models and in the underlying view of development as a matter of resource accumulation. Overriding concern with efficiency in resource allocation, which is the motivating force behind formal models, thus gives way to concern for the possibilities of interfacing resource-allocation problems with broader (and more important) questions of technological, institutional, and political strategies of development. The wheel thus swings back to the techniques that provided the first systematic approach to sectoral planning for the chemical industries. The approach discussed here is now being implemented in a concrete policy context.

Organization of Process-Level Input-Output Data

The heuristic approach to modeling the chemical industries rests on organizing process-level input-output data and supplementary information into a data bank. This data bank must be flexible in use, and capable of expansion and growth while it is being applied to a specific planning problem, because a concrete problem will typically generate new information that has not yet been included in the data bank. A time-shared computer system offers the needed virtues of rapid information-processing capability and great flexibility of data input and data format modification.

The Data Base Needed for Sectoral Programming
The tasks of sectoral programming are:

1. tracing the most important technological and economic linkages between different branches of the chemical sector, regardless of the subdivision of the sector between individual enterprises;
2. tracing the technological and economic linkages between the chemical sector and its supply, raw material, and institutional base; and
3. tracing the technological and economic linkages between the chemical sector and its key markets in other domestic sectors and abroad.

The data base required for these tasks must define the input-output structure of processes and products and must provide complementary information on the local economy: production capacities, imports, and prices. The major components of this data base are discussed in the following sections.

Organization of the Data Bank
The organization of the data follows closely the principles set out in "Programming Data Summary for the Chemical Industry" [14]. This source contains detailed technical information on 90 processes, organized in a uniform manner. Other *sources* of chemical process information are: *Chemical Engineering* [1], current issues; *Oil and Gas Journal,* current issues; Faith, Keyes, and Clark [2]; Hahn [4]; Noyes Development Corporation [6]; Shreve [7]; and United Nations [11].

Each of the following *directories* is required for the data bank and can be maintained manually in an alphabetical card file. In the computerized version, each directory converts into an array stored in memory. The directories cover: (1) process codes and names; (2) item codes and names; and (3) unit-of-measurement codes and names. Directories must be updated whenever a process is added to the data bank, modified, or deleted.

The *process bank* consists of a set of processes; each process has a full name and a process code (maintained in an alphabetical directory). Two processes that differ in any respect, for example, units of measurement used, comments, etc., must have separate process codes. Each individual process is maintained in the process bank in the following format:

> Process code
> Item code
>   Item information

Item code
Item information

.

.

.

The number of items in each process is open. Thus, a simple process may consist of only six or eight items, a complicated process of twenty or more. Each process is headed by a process code (PC) which is a string of eight alphanumeric characters beginning with 0 (zero). The code may terminate in blanks. For example, the process of manufacturing ammonia from natural gas, shown below, is coded as 0A10.

Individual items within a process may be of four kinds: (1) scale-related resources ("resources"); (2) indirect inputs; (3) institutional requirements; and (4) general comments on the process as a whole. Each item is introduced by an item code, which consists of a string of eight alphanumeric characters which may terminate in blanks, with the first character being 1 to 4, depending on the four classes just specified. Thus, for example, ammonia may be coded as 1NH3. The initial 1 identifies this item as a resource.

Scale-Related Resources

These resources are outputs, shown as positive amounts, or inputs, shown as negative amounts. They always vary as a function of the *scale* of the process as a whole. The scale of the process is measured by a scaling resource selected for this purpose. For example, in ammonia production, the output of the resource, ammonia, is used to measure the process scale. In petroleum refining, generally, the input of the resource, crude oil, is used as the measure of scale.

Resource inputs may vary linearly or nonlinearly with scale. Four standard functional relationships are specified to record this variation: proportionality; constant elasticity with respect to scale; a step function; or a piecewise linear input function. For example, in the case of constant elasticity, the amount of the resource X varies as a fixed power, E, of the scaling resource, S:

$$(X/X_0) = (S/S_0)^E$$

where the subscript 0 refers to the base level of each variable, and E is a *constant* exponent, termed scale elasticity. Thus, in the production of ammonia from natural gas, the requirement for plant investment varies nonlinearly, with scale. S_0 = 36 thousand tons per year of ammonia; X_0 = 5 million dollars; $E = 0.73$. Therefore, $(X/5) = (S/36)^{0.73}$. If the scale of production is 50 thousand tons per year,

$$X = (5) (50/36)^{0.73} = (5) (1.389)^{0.73} = (5) (1.27) = 6.35$$

Note that proportionality can be regarded as a special case of constant elasticity, with $E = 1$. The step function can be regarded as a special case of constant elasticity within the range of each individual step, with $E = 0$.

Indirect Inputs

Indirect inputs are estimated (generally in money-value units) from two specific resource inputs, direct labor and plant investment. The most important indirect inputs are maintenance, depreciation, and overhead. Maintenance and depreciation are estimated as percentages of plant investment; overhead is estimated as a percentage of direct labor cost plus a percentage per year of plant investment. For example, say overhead is 80 percent of direct labor cost plus 11 percent per year of plant investment. The labor and plant investment requirements for the given scale are first determined; then the labor input is costed out (by multiplication by the wage rate); and finally the respective percentages are applied to labor cost and to plant investment. Occasionally the percentages vary as a step function of process scale.

Institutional Requirements

The chemical industry depends for its technological advance on the existence of supporting institutions. These include: engineering education at the undergraduate and postgraduate levels; research laboratories; development and pilot-plant facilities; consulting engineering firms; professional associations; industry and trade associations; labor-training institutions; productivity institutes; export-promotion associations and facilities; and many others.

While it is often not possible to associate the requirements for specific institutions with particular processes, whenever the need for high-level technology or specific institutional support is clear-cut, provision can be made to include this type of information in the data bank. Generally the information is only semi-quantitative: the *amount* of required service by specific institutions is impossible to establish; therefore, the need is registered simply on a zero–one basis.

General Comments

In many cases, comments must be attached to the data on given processes. When comments refer to the grade, purity, etc., of particular resources, they can be included with the item referring to the resource. Each general comment that refers to the process as a whole is given an item code of its own.

An important kind of general comment refers to the range between minimum and maximum economical scales. Another important kind of general comment gives information for the conversion of units. For example, in order to convert tons per day to tons per year, the number of operating days per year is needed. This information can be given in a general comment.

Information Given for Individual Items

Five classes of information can be recorded for various items: (1) item code
(all items); (2) resource specifications (for resources only); (3) scaling parameters
(for resources only); (4) indirect parameters (for indirect inputs only); and (5)
item comments (any item). No one item can have every class of information
recorded. For example, institutional-requirement items omit all but the item
code and (possibly) a comment. Use of the principles discussed above make it
possible to work out a specific coding system for all processes and items in the
data bank.

Use of Process Data in Heuristic Models

The basic concepts needed for using data from the process bank in order to prepare heuristic development programs for the chemical industry are the following: (1) process vector; (2) technology tree; (3) program matrix; (4) complex
vector; (5) capacity evaluation; and (6) cost evaluation. These concepts will be
discussed both in relation to the design of a computerized system and in relation
to a simple manual system that can be used for experimentation prior to com-
puterizing the heuristic approach.

Process Vector

The purpose of maintaining a process bank is to be able to *rapidly* represent
(on a cathode ray tube display or as a printout) the resource flows, plant investment, indirect input requirements and other relevant information for any process
(1) for any desired scale and (2) on an annual basis.

The scale of a process is generally defined by market conditions—for the
production of products marketed outside the chemical industry—or by processing requirements—for intermediate products. Once the scale is known, all
resource flows are fixed and can be calculated from the relevant scaling functions.
For programming use, quantities given by shift (for example, labor) or on a daily
basis must be annualized.

For example, the process vector of the ammonia process 0A10, operated at a
scale of 36 thousand tons per year, will appear as columns (1), (2), and (3) of
Table 17-1, with rows 2, 6, and 7 omitted.

When a process vector is required in the manual system, it must be calculated
at the proper scale. In the computerized system, the scaling computation is
automatic, and the process vector can be displayed—ideally, on a cathode ray
tube, or, alternatively, in the form of a printout. In the computerized display of
the process vectors, the coded comments may be appended as desired.

The units of measurement (as used in Table 17-1) must be included in the
directory of units of measurement; for example:

Table 17-1.   Program Matrix for Production of 36,000 Tons of Ammonia and 10,000 Tons of Nitric Acid

Process and Item Codes	Unit of Measurement Codes	Ammonia (0A10)	Nitric Acid (0A03)
(1)	(2)	(3)	(4)
1NH3	KTONPY	+36.000	-2.90
1HNO3	KTONPY	—	+10.00
1NATGAS	MM3PY	-54.000	—
1NAOH	KTONPY	-0.144	—
1CCR	KDOLPY	-72.000	—
1MR	KDOLPY	—	-60.00
1STEAM	KTONPY	—	+7.50
1ELECT	MWHPY	-4320.000	-1900.00
1WATER	MM3PY	-0.900	-0.90
1LABOR	KMHPY	-56.000	-16.00
1SUP	KMHPY	-16.000	-8.00
1PLANT	MDOLLAR	-5.000	-0.65
2MAINT	KDOLPY	-150.000	-19.50
2DEPREC	KDOLPY	-400.000	-39.00
2OHLAB	KMHRPY	-56.000	-16.00
2OHKAP	KDOLPY	-550.000	-58.50

MM3PY   millions M3 per year

KDOLPY   thousand dollars per year

MWHPY   megawatt-hours per year

KMHRPY   thousand manhours per year

Overhead appears not in *one* but in *two* rows. The first is that part which depends on direct labor; it has the units of labor and, for costing purposes, it has to be evaluated at the wage rate of direct labor. The second part depends on capital (plant investment) and is obtained directly in thousands of dollars per year. These overhead concepts are coded as 2OHLAB and 2OHKAP, respectively. In a manual system, it is convenient to maintain a file of such process vectors at the minimum economic scale, in order to save computations.

Technology Tree

Process vectors can be organized into technology trees by indicating their interrelations in the process of production. For example, the production of ammonium nitrate can be represented by the technology tree shown in Figure 17-1. In this tree, ammonia can be produced either from fuel oil, using process A-10, or from natural gas, using process A-11 (see [14]). Ammonia converts into nitric acid, using process A-3, giving steam as a by-product; then ammonia and nitric acid combine to form ammonium nitrate, using process A-47. (All quantities indicated are measured in kilotons per year.)

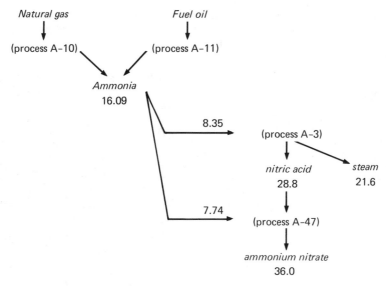

Figure 17-1. Technology Tree for Ammonium Nitrate.

The technology tree can be quantified by choosing a scale, for example, 36 kilotons per year, for the final output (ammonium nitrate) and producing intermediates (ammonia and nitric acid) in the amounts needed for conversion. The key questions at this stage are:

1. At what scale can the production of the final output be justified by market conditions?
2. Are the final output and intermediates to be produced at scales exceeding the minimum economic scale?

The information needed to answer these questions is relatively limited. It consists of the necessary inputs of the major intermediate resources and of the minimum economic scale of production for both final and intermediate products.

In Figure 17-1, the scale of production of the final product, ammonium nitrate, is chosen to correspond to the minimum economic scale of 36 kilotons per year. The intermediate, nitric acid, is required well above its minimum economic scale of 10 kilotons per year. Ammonia is needed as a direct input (7.74 kilotons per year) and indirectly for nitric acid production (8.35 kilotons per year). The combined amount is 16.09 kilotons per year, but the minimum economic scale for ammonia production is 36 kilotons per year, which exceeds the combined ammonia requirement by a factor of 2.24. Consequently, the ammonium nitrate process would have to be operated at an annual scale of

(36.0) (2.24) = 80.64 kilotons per year before the ammonia intermediate could be produced at the minimum economic scale. This, however, is subject to the proviso that there is no other need for ammonia that could utilize part of the output of the minimum-sized ammonia plant.

With the aid of the process bank, technology trees can be constructed rapidly and efficiently, yet a large amount of computation is involved when many alternatives are under consideration. It is worthwhile to computerize these tasks in order to increase efficiency and to obtain not only feasibility information based on minimum scales, but also—and equally rapidly in the computerized system—costing information that is much more time consuming to obtain manually. While the technology tree can be constructed by concentrating just on the most important intermediate inputs, for costing purposes more exact computations are needed to obtain every process vector at the precise scale at which it fits into each trial version of each technology tree.

The relationships that appear in Figure 17–1 are essential for programming development of the industry. In every case, resources connect with each other through the processes; and processes connect with each other through the resources. The technology tree is thus a *chromatic graph* with two types of nodes: resources and processes. There are five types of key relationships.

1. *Sequential relations*—The output of one process becomes input to another; for example, the output of the ammonia process A-10 becomes input into the nitric acid process A-3. Such sequential relations are used to trace back intermediates for a final output.
2. *Joint inputs*—The outputs of two or more processes combine as inputs into another; for example, the ammonia process A-10 and the nitric acid process A-3 produce outputs that combine to produce ammonium nitrate by process A-47. Sequential relations and joint inputs tie processes together into a complex.
3. *Alternative sources*—Two processes are alternatives when they produce the same output needed by another process. For example, the ammonia processes A-10 (from natural gas) and A-11 (from fuel oil) are alternatives for producing nitric acid and ammonium nitrate. Processes providing alternative sources for an input will generally *compete* with each other but sometimes (especially in cases of raw material shortage) they may *supplement* each other.

   For most intermediates, imports form an alternative to domestic production. Exceptions exist when the intermediate is difficult or expensive to transport in industrial quantities, for example, ethylene or acetylene. Imports as an alternative are essential when an input is needed in an amount that is not sufficient to justify domesic production at the minimum feasible scale.

In order to distinguish joint inputs from alternative inputs in the representation of the technology trees, joint inputs are shown as arrows terminating in a process; an arrow then leads from the process to the output commodity.

4. *Joint outputs*—A single process may produce more than one output; the outputs can then connect sequentially to separate processes. An important example is the joint production of caustic (NaOH) and chlorine (Cl_2) by electrolysis of salt (NaCl). In the illustrative tree, nitric acid and steam are joint outputs of process A-3; nitric acid then feeds into process A-47. Joint outputs are shown graphically as originating from a single process. In the programming of chemical industry development, joint outputs often raise problems of economic utilization. Further processes may be added to convert such joint products into marketable end-products.

5. *Alternative outlets*—Two or more processes may form alternative outlets for the output of a given process. For example, in the illustrative tree, processes A-3 and A-47 are alternative outlets for ammonia production. Alternative outlets may compete with each other for a scarce intermediate product; but more typically in the programming of chemical-industry development they will *supplement* each other in bringing a production process up to a more economic scale. Often it is necessary to search for supplementary outlets in order to make a group of processes economical. Then several additional processes are typically included in the complex, in order to convert critical intermediate products—whose production would otherwise not reach the minimum economical scale—into other kinds of useful end-products.

Program Matrix

A program consists of two or more processes, each at a specified scale. The program matrix is a table whose columns are the individual process vectors. For an example of the matrix of a program consisting of the production of 36,000 tons per year of ammonia and 10,000 tons per year of nitric acid, see columns (1) to (4) of Table 17-1.

In the illustrative technology tree, the ammonia and nitric acid processes are in a sequential relationship; that is, the output of one (ammonia) becomes input to the other (nitric acid). In the matrix (see the 1NH3 row), the corresponding entries are +36.0 and -2.9. The scales chosen for this program have so far been arbitrary except that in each case the scale chosen has been the minimum economic scale. When two processes in a program are in a sequential relationship, however, in planning for the sector it is desirable to balance the connecting resource—in this case, ammonia. This can be done by choosing the scales of the two processes so that the positive ammonia entry for the ammonia process will be offset by the negative ammonia entry for the nitric acid process.

For example, if the scale of the ammonia process remains 36 kilotons per year, there is now a large ammonia surplus (+36.0 against -2.9). Therefore, we increase the scale of nitric acid production in the ratio 36.0/2.9 = 12.414. Then ammonia input into the nitric acid process will be -36.0, and the matrix will be as in Table 17-2.

Complex Vector

A third column of numbers has been introduced in the last matrix to show the algebraic sum of each row item. This column is the complex vector. It treats a group of two or more processes as an integrated chemical-industry complex and represents it by a single set of input and output figures. The complex shown in Table 17-2 produces an enormous amount of nitric acid.

The nonlinear items associated with the nitric acid process have been derived by assuming that several near-maximal-sized plants are used (the maximum shown in "Programming Data Summary for the Chemical Industry" [14] is 46,000 tons per year). If there were three nitric acid plants, each producing one-third the given output, the scale of each would be 41,380 tons per year—near the maximum.

In any realistic chemical-industry development plan, this amount of nitric acid could rarely be marketed directly. It is therefore necessary to search for other ways of utilizing ammonia. In the illustrative technology tree, the ammonium nitrate process, which uses additional ammonia and also uses up the nitric acid produced, is added. Choose the scales of ammonium nitrate and nitric acid production so that: (1) ammonia is produced in a minimum-sized plant (36,000

Table 17-2. Program Matrix for Production of 36,000 Tons of Ammonia and 124,140 Tons of Nitric Acid

Process and Item Codes	Unit of Measurement Codes	Ammonia (0A10)	Nitric Acid (0A03)	Complex
(1)	(2)	(3)	(4)	(5)
1NH3	KTONPY	+36.000	-36.000	0.000
1HNO3	KTONPY	–	+124.140	+124.140
1NATGAS	MM3PY	-54.000	–	-54.000
1NAOH	KTONPY	-0.144	–	-0.144
1CCR	KDOLPY	-72.000	–	-72.000
1MR	KDOLPY	–	-744.840	-744.840
1STEAM	KTONPY	–	+93.105	+93.105
1ELEC	MWHPY	-4,320.000	-23,586.600	-27,906.600
1WATER	MM3PY	-0.900	-11.173	-12.073
1LABOR	KMHPY	-56.000	-48.000	-104.000
1SUP	KMHPY	-16.000	-48.000	-64.000
1PLANT	MDOLLAR	-5.000	-4.711	-9.711
2MAINT	KDOLPY	-150.000	-141.300	-291.300
2DEPREC	KDOLPY	-400.000	-282.600	-682.600
2OHLAB	KMHRPY	-56.000	-57.600	-113.600
2OHKAP	KDOLPY	-550.000	-339.200	-889.200

tons per year); (2) ammonia is balanced; (3) nitric acid is balanced. Then the scale of the ammonia process will be 36,000 tons per year, the scale of the nitric acid process will be 64,430 tons per year, and the scale of the ammonium nitrate process will be 80,530 tons per year.

These scales for nitric acid and ammonium nitrate production are still very large. They can be cut in half if half the ammonia output can be partly channeled into the production of urea fertilizer. Then the scales will be: ammonia, 36,000 tons per year; nitric acid, 32,215 tons per year; ammonium nitrate, 40,265 tons per year; and urea, 31,034 tons per year (see process A-49 for urea in [14]). This program matrix and the corresponding complex vector can be readily constructed by the methods discussed above. The corresponding technology tree is also easy to derive; it will have a structure similar to the one given, but the urea process will be added on at the end of one more arrow leading away from the resource of ammonia.

As shown above, defining candidate complexes for chemical industry development makes use of both technology trees and program matrices. The basic principles of constructing candidate complexes for subsequent evaluation are the following:

1. Start with an end-product whose domestic production is of interest. Fix its scale of production at a reasonable projected market size.
2. Work back through intermediate inputs to processes in a sequential relation with the first. Fix the scale of each process so as to balance key intermediates. Avoid both deficits (which would imply supplementary imports) and surpluses (which would imply a marketing dilemma) whenever possible.
3. When the scales of production of key intermediates are below minimum economic scales, search for additional outlets for these intermediates. Survey all possible processes that use the intermediates and see if these processes can lead, through a sequence of other processes, to marketable end-products.
4. When nothing else helps, a low-scale intermediate can be imported.
5. Whenever joint products appear, search for outlets as under point (3).
6. The sequencing steps and outlet-finding steps will quickly lead to a proliferation of large program matrices with correspondingly complicated technology trees. Alternative processes will further expand the range of possibilities.
7. Evaluate candidate complexes as discussed below.

Capacity Evaluation

In evaluating candidate complexes, the first consideration is the relationship of the complex to existing domestic production capacity. Some of the required intermediates may already be domestically produced and will often have large excess capacities. If so, the complex will make use of these excess capacities and thereby confer external benefits on existing industries.

Whenever a process that is not yet used in domestic production appears in a candidate complex, the key consideration in capacity evaluation is the projected scale of production of the process in relation to the minimum economic scale. In addition, capacity evaluation also takes into account institutional requirements. Since these are registered in the data bank on a zero–one basis, the question that arises is whether the institutional base needed for the success of a productive process is or is not present in the country. When a particular set of institutions appears again and again as a bottleneck in the development of particular chemical-industry complexes, this constitutes a clear incentive for establishing the missing institutions.

The construction of complexes and the capacity evaluation are *not* independent but interact continually. Instead of starting the programming task with an end-product that appears attractive for import substitution, one might as well start with an intermediate that has a large excess capacity, and proceed as shown under step (3) of the preceding section.

Capacity Monitoring

When a task force is assigned the responsibility of continuously monitoring the development of the chemical industry, one of the key tasks is to set up, and keep up-to-date, two files that are useful in program construction and capacity evaluation.

1. The *plant and product capacity file* includes: what is produced, where, in what amounts, and how much excess capacity exists.
2. The *domestic market and import file* includes: what major products are now imported, in what amounts, at what prices, for what use, and when the possibility of import substitution has last been considered.

These files are the starting point for the construction and evaluation of candidate complexes. The work needs to be undertaken on a continuing basis for the industry as a whole, since individual productive enterprises typically do not consider the entire range of industry-wide possibilities and opportunities.

Cost Evaluation

Cost evaluation consists of applying *prices*—either market prices or opportunity costs—to the input and output items of a complex vector. Output items multiplied by their prices become revenues of the complex; input items multiplied by their prices become costs. The balance of revenues and costs is the gross profit, which must be divided by total investment to arrive at the rate of return of the complex in question.

If all intermediates of a complex are balanced, then the only required prices are those of end-products and of primary inputs. Primary inputs should be costed both at market and at opportunity cost. Raw materials, such as natural gas, petroleum, refinery streams, sulfur, salt, limestone, phosphate rock, coal, or agricultural commodities, often have a substantially higher market price than their opportunity cost. Then a chemical complex based on these can confer a large national benefit even in the presence of a modest commercial profitability.

At times, certain raw materials appear with extremely high costs based on very limited domestic production. For example, salt may be produced from sea water on a handicraft basis for table use. The cost of this process is no proper basis for evaluating the feasibility of a chlorine-and-caustic process based on salt electrolysis. Whenever such situations arise, it is necessary to add a process to the technology tree that represents the production of the raw material on an industrial scale, using modern technology. This may carry the representation of technology slightly beyond the bounds of the chemical industry itself, but otherwise represents no new departure as compared with what has been discussed before.

End-products and imported intermediates should be accounted for at c.i.f. cost, including import duties for market-price evaluation, but without such duties for social cost-benefit evaluation. Intermediates drawing on excess domestic capacity should be costed *both* at market price and for social cost-benefit evaluation at marginal cost.

The computations needed for cost evaluation are elementary: First, construction of the complex vector from individual process vectors; and second, multiplication of the complex vector by a price vector. The first has been discussed before; the second is an item-by-item multiplication followed by one summation. All computations can in principle be readily performed in a manual system for any single-candidate complex. The manual system is, however, not well suited to performing a large number of repetitive calculations for a great variety of candidate complexes based on an extensive data bank. To cope with these conditions, computerization is required.

The Computerized System

The manual system is cumbersome to operate unless it is of restricted size and unless the number of candidate complexes to be evaluated is quite small, for, while the computations are simple, they are very numerous. Also, it is difficult to manually keep track of a large number of alternatives; beyond a certain point, there is a tendency to drown in endless repetitive calculations as worksheets become a threatening tidal wave. The training and supervision of computing clerks becomes extremely onerous. Yet unless these are managed exceptionally well, the computations are subject to errors and risky to use in concrete policy decisions.

The computerized system must have the following capabilities:

1. Directories: assemble and update from process input; modify codes; modify names; sort; convert units of measurement; display.

2. Process bank: input new processes; modify and erase existing processes; convert units of measurement of existing processes; display a stored process; graphically display the variation of specified inputs with process scale; display a process vector at any scale in any desired units, with or without appended comments.

3. Technology tree: find alternative source processes for producing a resource, and alternative major outlet processes for disposing of a resource; sequence specified processes at appropriate scales; flag process scales that fall outside of economical-scale limits; construct a technology tree corresponding to a specified program matrix; display a specified technology tree graphically, with or without comments supplied.

4. Program matrix and complex vector: construct a matrix of specified processes at specified scale; delete a process; compute complex vector; display program matrix and complex vector with or without comments.

5. Complex evaluation: compare a specified complex vector with a list of excess domestic capacities, with a list of available institutions, and with scale limits for potential production, and display results; find sequences connecting the complex vector with a list of desired import contributions, and display results; multiply complex vector by a vector of prices to be used for costing purposes; display revenues and costs item by item, algebraically summed, or as a return on investments (net social benefit ratio when using opportunity costs).

The following files complement the process data bank.

1. Directory of items: resources; indirect inputs; institutions; general-comment items.

2. Directory of units of measurement: includes conversion rules.

3. Plant and product capacity file: organized by product—what is produced and where; total capacity; current production; excess capacity; projection of excess capacity.

4. Domestic market and import file: organized by product—current imports; projected imports; destination (use); has import substitution been considered? When, and by whom?

5. Import price file for chemical products: organized by product—the cif (cost, insurance and freight) price before and after customs duties and other governmental charges. Needed for all chemical products, not only for those now imported.

6. Domestic price file: organized by products, raw materials, and other input and output items. Both market cost and opportunity cost needed.

Conclusion

The system described here embodies a philosophy of sectoral planning and policymaking that is broader than any specific manual or computerized programming system. This philosophy stresses the need to interface technical planning information with questions of a qualitative nature that are often of overriding policy importance. It also recognizes that in such a policy environment, mathematical models that allocate scarce economic resources within a precise quantitative framework give the illusion but not the substance of optimality.

Concrete policy decisions must cope with the emergence of new dimensions as the past unfolds into the future. A good policy design is more than just the answer to a preconceived problem; it is creative to the extent that it clarifies and transcends earlier formulations. This creative quality can grow only out of a "dialogue" between the aspirations of the policymaker and the data he works with, representing technical land organizational possibilities.

This is, then, the ultimate reason why the heuristic technique, which permits continual interaction between the policymaker and his information base, is deemed superior to formal programming methods. In the system that has been presented, this interaction can in part be channeled through a time-shared computer installation that embodies a steadily growing data bank. The policymaker— with engineers, marketing specialists, and often technical experts standing behind his shoulder—can then continually explore a wide range of sectoral planning designs as the development process of the sector unfolds. Each alternative is judged for technical completeness, qualitative idiosyncrasies, economic attractiveness, and higher-order policy considerations as it emerges. At the same time, additional information is channeled into the data bank as new complexes are being defined.

Such planning systems must undergo a period of growth—in regard to the data bank they contain, the back-up information attached to them, and the personnel working with them. They must, moreover, be interfaced with other related policy problems. These concern other sectors: for example, the construction of new chemical plants will almost always provide a stimulus for the development of the engineering industries. They concern regional development, particularly questions of transportation and urbanization. They involve institution building, most notably with a view to research, development, and higher technical education, all of which are essential to technological autonomy. And they interface with economy-wide policy decisions concerning growth, social equity, and the quality of life.

The heuristic programming approach discussed in this paper grows out of such a philosophy. It is intended as a guide to the building of sectoral planning and policymaking systems responding to the needs of particular countries and regions.

References

1. Chemical Engineering. *Manual of 124 Flowsheets.* London: McGraw-Hill (no date, approximately 1965).

2. Faith, W.L.; D.B. Keyes; and R.L. Clark. *Industrial Chemicals.* 3rd ed. London: John Wiley and Sons, 1965.

3. Goreux, L.M., and A.S. Manne. *Multi-Level Planning: Case Studies in Mexico.* Amsterdam: North-Holland Publishing Company, 1973.

4. Hahn, A.V., in collaboration with R. Williams and H. Zabel. *The Petrochemical Industry: Market and Economics.* New York: McGraw-Hill, 1970.

5. Isard, W.; E.W. Schooler; and T. Vietorisz. *Industrial Complex Analysis and Regional Development.* Cambridge, Mass.: Technology Press of the Massachusetts Institute of Technology, 1959. Published jointly with John Wiley and Sons, New York.

6. Noyes Development Corporation. "Chemical Process Monograph Series." 118 Mill Road, Park Ridge, New Jersey, 07656

7. Shreve, R.N. *Chemical Process Industries.* 2nd ed. New York: McGraw-Hill, 1956.

8. Stoutjesdijk, A., and L. Westphal. *Industrial Planning with Economies of Scale.* Washington, D.C.: International Bank for Reconstruction and Development, forthcoming, 1975.

9. United Nations. *La Industria Quimica en America Latina* [The Chemical Industry in Latin America]. Mexico: United Nations, 1963.

10. United Nations. *Industrialization of Developing Countries: Problems and Prospects: Chemical Industry.* (By T. Vietorisz.) UNIDO Monographs on Industrial Development, Number 8. New York: United Nations, 1969. (Sales Number E.69.II.B.39, vol. 8.)

11. United Nations. *Studies in Petrochemicals.* Vols. I–II. New York: United Nations, 1966. (Sales Number 67.II.B.2.)

12. United Nations. *Techniques of Sectoral Economic Planning: The Chemical Industries.* (By T. Vietorisz.) New York: United Nations, 1966. (Sales Number 66.II.B.1.)

13. Vietorisz, T. "Planning at the Micro Level: The Heavy Electrical Equipment Industry in Mexico." In *Industrial Planning with Economies of Scale.* Edited by A. Stoutjesdijk and L. Westphal. Washington, D.C.: International Bank for Reconstruction and Development, forthcoming, 1976.

14. Vietorisz, T. "Programming Data Summary for the Chemical Industry." *Industrialization and Productivity,* Bulletin 10. New York: United Nations, 1966, pp. 7–56. (Sales Number 66.II.B.8.)

15. Vietorisz, T. "Structure and Change in the Engineering Industries." Paper presented at the Fifth International Input-Output Conference, Geneva, 1972.

16. Vietorisz, T., and A.S. Manne. "Chemical Industries, Plant Location, and Economies of Scale." In *Methods of Process Analysis.* Edited by A.S. Manne and H.M. Markowitz. New York: John Wiley and Sons, 1963, chap. 6, Pp. 136–158.

17. Vietorisz, T., and Z. Szabo. "El Mercado Comun y La Industria Quimica en America Latina" [The Common Market and the Chemical Industry in Latin America]. 3 vols. Report of a joint working party of the United Nations Economic Commission for Latin America and the Chilean Development Corporation, Santiago, Chile, 1969.

Part Five

Studies on Energy and the Environment

Chapter Eighteen

Empirical Application of Input-Output Models to Environmental Problems

John H. Cumberland
Bruce N. Stram

Continuing concern about environment, energy, and growth confirms the importance of analyzing basic relationships between economic activity, waste generation, waste treatment, and environmental quality. An earlier paper presented by Cumberland at the Fifth International Conference on Input-Output Techniques described an interindustry model which was extended to link environmental with economic relationships [3]. That paper emphasized the importance of (a) tracing waste flows explicitly through treatment processes, recycling loops, and alternative paths; (b) basing economic–environmental models on a materials-balance concept; and (c) using a broad systems approach to define major economic-environmental relationships. The purpose of this paper is to discuss the subsequent development of the model and to present some of the empirical results that have been obtained.

An Economic-Environmental Systems Approach

Although it is possible here to deal in detail with only a few aspects of a total economic-environmental systems model, it may be helpful to present a symbolic representation of the total system (see Figure 18-1). Part A of the figure represents the traditional interindustry model, which describes the economic flows of the system. Economic activities draw resources from the environment (Part F) and ultimately return the same resources, usually in altered form, to the physical environment. Part B represents the gross residual or gross wastes that result from all production and consumption activities. Data from this submodel are emphasized in the paper. Part C represents the alternative technical options for treating, recycling, or otherwise handling the wastes produced by the system. Part C also measures treatment costs. Treating wastes requires inputs of real resources, and thus involves economic costs. Typically, these costs are assumed to be an increasing function of the percentage of waste removed, as is suggested by the asymptotically rising cost function sketched in Part C. These technical treat-

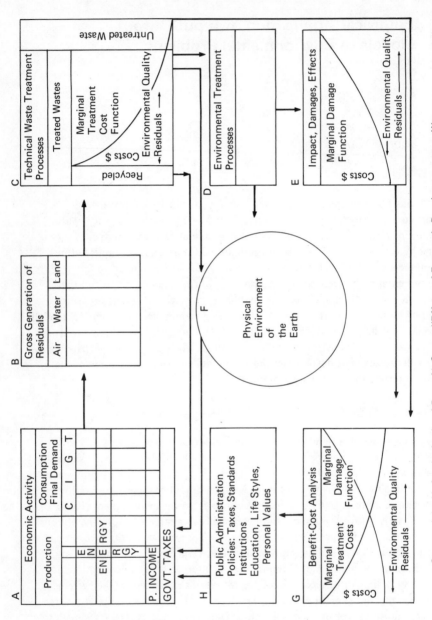

Source: John H. Cumberland and Bruce N. Stram, "Effects of Economic Development upon Water Resources," University of Maryland Water Resources Research Center, College Park, Maryland, Technical Report No. 18, Spring, 1974.

ment processes transform, dilute, transport, or modify wastes; but because of the physical laws of nature, are incapable of eliminating or destroying the wastes. Therefore, treated and untreated wastes flow from these processes and are discharged into environmental receptors, as shown in Part D. The environment is also capable of transporting, diluting, recycling, assimilating, and otherwise transforming wastes. Waste resulting from these environmental processes, after passing through the environmental processes, affects human beings and other species related to human interests, as shown in Part E. These impacts are assumed to be an increasing function of the quantities involved, as is indicated by the conventional damage function, which suggests that damages are a nonlinear function of the amount of wastes and residuals. In addition to impacting upon human beings and related species, wastes and residuals are ultimately returned to the physical environment, as shown in Part F.

Marginal cost functions can be derived from the data required in Part C and marginal damage functions (and, therefore, marginal functions for the benefits of damages prevented) can be derived from the data in Part E. These two functions are brought together in Part G, which symbolizes traditional benefit-cost analysis and which can be used to derive optimal levels of waste treatment in order to equate the benefits and costs of environmental management at the margin. This benefit-cost analysis can then be used to suggest appropriate policy instruments for enforcing optimal environmental standards or optimal levels of waste treatment. The instruments available for achieving these optima, as suggested in Part H, are taxes, subsidies, standards, controls, and related measures. These control instruments in turn affect the interindustry input-output flows by acting upon decisions concerning consumption; investment; government programs; regulations; trade; and, in the longer run, upon tastes; life styles; population size; and technology. The result is a closed general equilibrium system, as shown in the figure.

Although the total system is visualized as closed, its individual subcomponents are open, individual modules. This approach permits the analyst to operate the model flexibly, in steps, by using the output of one component as input into another component. It also permits the analyst to intervene in the operation at any point rather than being dependent upon a purely mechanical operation of the model.

This paper deals primarily with Parts A, B, and D of Figure 18-1, but the total system is sketched in the figure to indicate what is needed for an overall approach and where the work reported on in this paper fits into the total system.

The Model

The input-output component (Part A) of this model is specified in conventional form as

$$X = (I - A)^{-1} Y \tag{18-1}$$

where

X = vector of gross outputs

$(I - A)^{-1}$ = the Leontief inverse matrix

Y = vector of final demand estimates

The output of this step of the model, estimates of gross output, X, is used in Part B to estimate gross residuals, GR, and gross residual coefficients, GRC, as follows:

$$GR = (X)(GRC) \qquad\qquad (18\text{-}2)$$

where

X = vector of gross outputs

GRC = matrix of grc_{ij}

grc_{ij} = gross residual coefficient relating residual of type j to gross output of industry i

gr_{ij} = amount of gross residual of type j produced in industry i

where

$j = 1, \ldots, m$ types of residual

$i = 1, \ldots, n$ industries

Outputs from these components are, in turn, entered into Part C to trace out the amounts and flows of wastes through various alternative treatment routines.

Waste Generation

One of the most important responses by economists to environmental problems has been to extend the application of input-output models to the examination of relationships between economic activity and the emission of pollutant materials. Various interindustry tables have been augmented with additional rows and columns, thereby providing an accounting system which delineates materials flows through economic processes, making it possible to estimate withdrawals of materials from the environment and the discharge of wastes. Papers describing these efforts are cited in the reference list at the end of the chapter [1; 3-9; 12-13].

The obvious next step is to convert such a table into a static model of economic-environmental flows after the fashion of standard input-output techniques. Previously, the authors have presented such an accounting structure and have indicated some means by which it could be converted to a static linear model of the pollutant-emissions process [7].

Most production and consumption activities give rise to material joint products that have no positive economic value, that is, they cannot be sold or further processed at a profit. These materials—of many different types—which we label as gross residuals, would be immediately discharged into the environment by the unrestrained profit maximizer. Of course, such discharge imposes costs upon others, and an opportunity exists for government to initiate policies to encourage further processing of such material when the damage imposed by discharge is greater than the costs of further processing.

Consistent with the input-output methodology, it is assumed that the quantity of each gross residual bears a proportional relationship to the level of activity of the industry that generates the residual; consequently, it is appropriate to calculate a gross residual coefficient

$$grc_{ij} = \frac{gr_{ij}}{x_i} \tag{18-3}$$

where

i $= 1, \ldots, n$ activities

j $= 1, \ldots, m$ residual types

gr_{ij} $=$ gross residual of type i from industry j

x_i $=$ total production of industry i

Each gross residual is initially transferred to one of three categories, indicating whether it is to be immediately discharged into the environment, to receive treatment, or to be transferred to some external activity (that is, a public or private agency that carries out the treatment operation thereby incurring a cost). Expressed as a materials-balance tautology

$$GR = GU + GT + DE \tag{18-4}$$

where

GU $=$ untreated gross residuals discharged into the environment

GT $=$ internally treated gross residuals

DE $=$ externally transferred gross residuals

Again, these accounting categories are converted to coefficients

$$guc_{ij} = \frac{gr_{ij}}{x_i} \tag{18-5}$$

$$gtc_{ij} = \frac{gi_{ij}}{x_i} \tag{18-6}$$

$$dec_{ij} = \frac{de_{ij}}{x_i} \tag{18-7}$$

The externally transferred residuals become gross residuals for the receiving activity. The treated gross residuals are acted upon by various abatement processes. The residuals from this treatment process may be discharged into the environment, transferred to a second treatment process, transferred to an external activity, or recycled. The consequences of these processes may also be expressed as a materials-balance tautology

$$GT \equiv TU + TT + TE + TR \tag{18-8}$$

where

TU = treatment of residuals discharge

TT = treatment-to-treatment transfer of residuals

TE = treatment residuals transferred to an external activity

TR = treatment residuals recycling

Those categories are also transformed into coefficients

$$tuc_{ij} = \frac{tu_{ij}}{x_i} \tag{18-9}$$

$$ttc_{ij} = \frac{tt_{ij}}{x_i} \tag{18-10}$$

$$tec_{ij} = \frac{te_{ij}}{x_i} \tag{18-11}$$

$$trc_{ij} = \frac{tr_{ij}}{x_i} \tag{18-12}$$

The use of final products by households, governments, and investors also generates waste residuals. These waste residuals can be entered into the same accounting framework as production residuals, and coefficients can be similarly calculated. For example

$$pgrc_{ij} = \frac{pgr_{ij}}{pce_i} \tag{18-13}$$

where

pgr_{ij} = gross residual of type j generated by households' use of product i

pce_i = personal consumption expenditures for product i

These coefficients can be used in conjunction with a regional or national input-output structure to estimate the impact of economic activity and change upon the level of gross residuals generation. The gross residuals coefficients can be used to estimate the pollutants generated directly by the growth of production in any industry. However, the growth of any one industry implies that the suppliers of that industry must also increase production. In order to capture all of these effects, the following calculation can be made

$$DIC = (I - A)^{-1}(GRC) \tag{18-14}$$

The $(I - A)$ inverse indicates the total direct and indirect production necessary to produce a dollar's worth of output in each industry. Multiplication by the gross residuals coefficient matrix yields an estimate of the residuals generated by all direct and indirect production for each industry, DIC.

In a similar manner, residuals generation of both production and consumption activity can be allocated to product categories

$$DIPC = (I - A)^{-1}(GRC) + PGRC \tag{18-15}$$

This calculation estimates the total gross residuals of each type generated in the production and use of each product. The resulting coefficients show the residual impact of the consumption pattern, and analogous calculations can be made for other categories of final demand.

The coefficients may also be used to forecast residual generation for future years.

$$GR^* = \hat{X}^* \cdot GRC \tag{18-16}$$

where

$\hat{X}*$ = diagonal matrix of forecast production

$GR*$ = forecast gross residual

or

$$GR* = [(I - A)^{-1} \hat{Y}*] \; GRC \qquad (18\text{-}16')$$

where

$\hat{Y}*$ = diagonal matrix of forecast final demand.

Before presenting some examples of these calculations, it is important to examine the validity of converting the accounting structure to a static linear model and using such a model to portray the emissions process. Consider the generation of gross residuals in the context of ordinary static input-output analysis. In particular, it is assumed that each activity requires a fixed set of purchases to produce a dollar's worth of output. We postulate a vector expressing the precise elemental composition of the output of each activity. The following materials-balance relationship holds for all activities, k (ignoring atomic reactions)

$$\sum_{j=1}^{p} e_{jk} + \sum_{i=1}^{n} \sum_{j=1}^{p} a_{ijk} = \sum_{i=1}^{n} \sum_{j=1}^{p} a_{kij} + \sum_{j=1}^{p} y_{kj} + \sum_{j=1}^{p} gr_{kj} \qquad (18\text{-}17)$$

where

e_{jk} = environmental inputs

a_{ijk} = intermediate inputs

a_{kij} = output to other industries

y_{kj} = outputs to final demand

gr_{kj} = gross residual

i = $1, \ldots, n$ industries

j = $1, \ldots, p$ elements

This simply says that the weight of materials inputs is identically equal to the weight of materials outputs. (Note that for this particular exercise, all materials are described simply in terms of the chemical elements that constitute them.)

If it is true that any change in the materials composition of inputs and/or outputs implies a shift in relative prices, then to assume that input coefficients remain stable implies that materials inputs and outputs remain stable. In general, we would expect this hypothesis to hold with regard to input substitution. That is, if inputs are substituted to take advantage of lower costs, then both the input and gross residuals coefficients will change. Substitution of inputs implies a change in input materials, which would very likely cause a change in the composition and weight of both product and gross residual. Of course, it is conceivable that input substitution could occur without change in the gross residual, and vice versa, but it is doubtful that such occurrences are significant in quantity and/or in the nature of the pollutants. A more serious problem is that in the absence of a full materials-balance specification for the relevant activities, we cannot accurately estimate the impact upon the gross residual of a known input substitution. A simple substitution of inputs could have a substantial effect on the gross residual, or a complex substitution could have a minor effect.

Despite these problems, use of the gross residual coefficient as a constant parameter is suggested as a reasonable first approximation to reality in a broad range of industries, such as agriculture, food processing, extraction, refining, fuel, and energy processing, which produce large quantities of pollutants. Materials inputs and outputs and the gross residual can be regarded as stable, at least in the short run.

To summarize, a gross residual coefficient resembles a technological coefficient representing the existing mix of production processes and may reasonably be used for projection and prediction purposes in conjunction with the input-output coefficients that measure the economic determinants of that mix of production processes. The data to be presented here represent an attempt to provide some elementary analyses and projections of these technological relationships, based on the gross residual coefficients. Of course, these analyses of gross residuals provide only a fraction of the total information required for environmental management, as discussed below.

Residuals Treatment

After measuring residuals, the next task is to link the generation of gross residuals with treatment processes and with emissions into the environment. The quantity and type of residual material discharged by an industry or activity may vary with two distinct sets of parameters, representing two distinct sets of decisions about the emissions process. These may be identified as: (1) treatment versus nontreatment decisions, $(GR \equiv GR + GT + DE)$; and (2) treatment-processing decisions, $(GT \equiv TU + TT + TE + TR)$.

In the absence of specific regulations governing the emission of each major pollutant, the decision to treat a gross residual or simply to discharge it into the environment must be regarded as an exogenous variable. Similarly, the choice of treatment processes and consequently the level of treatment must also be regarded as exogenous. Within the context of a modeling procedure designed to optimize treatment levels or to examine the response to hypothesized emissions regulations and/or taxes, such decisions could be considered endogenous. In particular, the choice of treatment process and level of treatment should be determined by least-cost combinations of processes that would involve less social cost than the emissions prevented, or that are required to meet emissions standards, or that are less expensive than emissions taxes. For the 1967 data that have been collected largely before enforcement of environmental regulations, however, these decisions are predominately parameters and are included in the static model derived from the accounting structure. The technological parameters and functions describing treatment processes are of more significance.

We define treatment as any processing of gross residual material. By the definition of gross residual, these processes must be undertaken at a loss. Since residuals materials must generally be removed from the production site in order to avoid costly interference with production processes, such simple collection procedures are assumed to be profit motivated and are not considered as treatment processes.

As indicated by Ayres and Kneese [1] and amplified by the present authors [6] and others, simple materials-balance considerations imply that for practical purposes no process, including treatment, can alter the quantity of materials upon which that process acts. This implies that the amount of material left after treatment is equal to the quantity of gross residual (or may be greater if the treatment process adds materials to gross residual). In particular, the same chemical elements, in the same quantities, that appear in the gross residual must be present in treatment residuals. What the treatment process can do is alter certain specific characteristics of the material. At one extreme, a treatment process may transform a potentially harmful gross residual into relatively inert and/or harmless substances which do not adversely affect the environment or interfere with any human activities. Thus, organic wastes that might disastrously reduce the oxygen dissolved in lakes or streams can be oxidized to carbon dioxide and water. This is not generally the case, however. Often, some harmful gross residual escapes a treatment process or is not affected by the process. Further, even the materials that have been successfully acted upon may be harmful, and it is even possible that the treatment residual can be more harmful than the original gross residual.

However, the potential harmfulness of the gross residual or the treatment residual is irrevelant to the profit-maximizing firm. The treatment process simply represents the least-cost method of meeting regulations or of avoiding charges. This implies that an emissions-control strategy should be comprehensive. Even though treatment processing may permit a residual to be recycled, thereby reducing the total quantity of residual that must be discharged, it is still the case that most residuals, in some form, will be discharged into the environment.

A control strategy that concentrates upon a small set of pollutants or a single receptor medium may engender treatment processes that transform the residual (so as to meet the regulations) without effectively reducing the harmfulness of the residual. Similarly, any accounting of, or modeling of, the emissions process should also include a full specification of residuals from treatment processes. The accounting structure presented here is constructed to provide for a complete materials-balance accounting structure.

This structure has been converted into a simple static model by assuming that treatment residuals and treatment costs are a fixed proportion of gross residual (or of activity levels). This is equivalent to assuming that a dollar's expenditure on treatment activity (that is, a dollar's worth of a fixed set of economic inputs) results in the conversion of a fixed quantity of gross residuals to a fixed quantity of treatment residuals.

This input-output approach is, however, not nearly so appropriate for the study of treatment processing of residuals as it is for the study of residual generation. Treatment processes may be nonlinear with respect to input and output, or may be linear only within fairly narrow limits of operation. Moreover, the likely necessity for further processing of many already-treated residuals indicates that a residual might flow through alternative treatment paths. If an analysis of residuals management attempts to simulate the response to alternative policy tools, or alternative damage weighting of the pollutants, a range of alternative treatment paths must be considered.

For these reasons, we would include the treatment processes in a submodel structure linked to the economic model both by gross residuals generation and by the market input requirements of the treatment process. This may be outlined in Figure 18-2, which is derived from Figure 18-1. Exogenously determined final demand generates the gross residuals and induces production activity, which generates additional gross residuals. This gross residual is acted upon by the treatment submodel to optimize residual levels or meet policy goals. This treatment activity requires market inputs and will probably alter relative prices. Unless

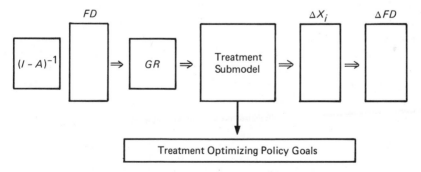

Figure 18-2. Treatment Process Submodel.

there is substantial excess capacity to begin with, the additional production requirements will exceed the appropriate restraints. Thus, as one alternative, final demand must be determined so as to be consistent with capacity restraints, treatment process requirements, and the altered price vector. This will, of course, change the gross residual generated by final demand and change the total production vector and its generated gross residual, which will alter the treatment requirements, and so on.[1] The solution would be determined by successive interactions, which should converge.

Some work based upon this approach has been pursued at the University of Maryland on a regional basis by Korbach [11] and others. The present data available on a state or national level fall short of the requirements for implementing such a structure.

Residuals Loadings

As indicated previously, the conservation of matter implies that the aggregate weight of the gross residuals differs from the aggregate weight of residuals discharged into the environment only in that the latter may be reduced by recycling and increased by treatment-process inputs.

Appendix Table 18A-1 shows activities ranked by the aggregate gross residuals for air, water, and solid waste generated by the direct and indirect production necessary to produce one dollar's worth of output. Table 18A-2 shows the gross residuals generated by production and consumption of particular product categories. (Only industries whose products directly reach consumers are ranked in Tables 18A-2 and 18A-4.) The ranking shows those products whose use and production involve the generation of the largest residual per dollar of product. Again, aggregate airborne, waterborne, and solid residual categories are used. These products are those which involve the greatest generation of residuals, and, if recycling is minimal, must also involve the greatest discharge of residuals. Table 18A-3 and Table 18A-4 are analogous to the above tables. Rankings have also been made for other specific residual categories.[2]

The activities that generate the most pollution per dollar are energy, raw material supplies, and foodstuffs. While this should come as no great surprise, it should be abundantly clear that antipollution policy initiatives will infringe most heavily upon these industries, and because their products and activities are basic to the economy, the effects of such policies will be felt throughout the economy.

Projections

In order to present a compact, aggregative indication of the growth of residual generation relative to other residuals and relative to economic growth, a ratio

---

1. If it is assumed that the composition of a product varies somewhat by purchaser, then transferring delivery of an industry's product from final demand to intermediate or treatment requirements will alter the aggregate gross residual. If this is not the case, then only a change in absolute production levels could alter the gross residual.

2. More complete data tables can be found in Cumberland and Stram [6].

between percent change in consumption-generated residual and percent change in personal consumption expenditures (PCE) was calculated for each residual. The results of this calculation for a subset of the 130 residuals which are most significant and for which relatively complete data are available are presented in Tables 18-1 and 18-2.[3] Table 18-1 contains these ratios for direct and indirect production residuals. These ratios are similar to income elasticities in that numbers greater than one indicate growth of residuals greater than growth of PCE and numbers smaller than one indicate generation of waste at rates lower than for PCE. However, growth rates for wastes of less than one are not necessarily reasons for optimism. Any residual that is growing at all is growing relative to fixed space, and even a residual that is not growing may exceed the assimilative capacity of that fixed space. But it is clear that any residual that continues to grow must eventually exceed that assimilative capacity.

Table 18-2 contains the results of similar calculations for treatment residuals discharged into the environment. These are materials that have received at least one stage of treatment and are actually rather than potentially discharged into the environment. Clearly, some of them could be dangerous, and they are growing. (It should be noted that these numbers do not include the additional increases in residuals resulting from treatment of presently untreated gross residuals.)

Looking at the aggregate residuals, airborne residuals are growing much more rapidly than PCE; solid residuals, mainly mine wastes, at a rate about equal to PCE; and waterborne residuals at a rate substantially less than PCE. Since waterborne residuals data are limited here to those for foods and food processing, it is no surprise that they grow relatively slowly. The airborne residuals tend to be related to energy use in those industries that at the time these calculations were made were projected to be high-growth industries. If in response to the energy crisis the quantity produced (in physical units, not dollars) is significantly retarded in its growth, of course these numbers would be relatively smaller. But this factor could be more than offset by a substitution of "dirty" energy for "cleaner" energy, the increased use of soft coal and relaxation of controls on petroleum fuels.

3. The numbers that refer to radionuclides are not calculated according to the simple linear methods outlined in this chapter. Because those subactivities that are involved with radioactive materials represent, in 1967, a very small but very rapidly growing portion of those aggregate activities used in the input-output structure, the data for radionuclides have been calculated directly from data given in a report by Battelle Pacific Northwest Laboratories [2]. This document provides gross residuals and emissions estimates from 1967-1980.

While the "elasticity" numbers for radioactivity are quite large, it should be noted that they grow from a very small base. If the nuclear component of electric energy were growing at the same rate as total electric energy, elasticity of the radionuclides gross residual would be 1.02, while that of net emissions would be 1.13.

It should also be noted that the Battelle report includes the following qualification: "The number of curies should not be interpreted as a measure of the radiation hazard presented by the various waste streams. In no cases have human exposures exceeded, or even approached, current radiological protection criteria" [2, p. 1.1].

Table 18-1.   Growth of Projected Gross Residual Relative to Projected Personal Consumption Expenditures for Production Residuals for Selected Residuals and Aggregates, 1967–1985

Residual Type	Elasticity
Particulate matter	1.151430
Hydrocarbons	1.188071
Sulfur oxides	1.234396
Carbon monoxide	1.162683
Nitrogen oxides	1.262441
Fluorine	0.790913
Total solids	0.579813
Biological oxygen demand	0.587152
Chemical oxygen demand	0.504262
Lube oil	1.156645
Acids	0.861477
Soluble metallic ions	0.504655
Emulsions	1.156645
Coke plant chemical	1.156545
Phenols	0.812786
Sulfides	0.812786
Carbohydrate	0.808783
Chromate	0.992752
Phosphate	0.992752
Fluoride	0.992752
Monoethanolamine	0.992752
Sulfate	0.992752
Oil	0.992752
Bases	1.257342
Nonmetallic ions	1.257342
Radionuclides	165.000000
Agricultural chemicals	0.584531
Mining wastes	1.012717
Pesticides	0.633705
Aggregate airborne residual	1.186821
Aggregate waterborne residual	0.607994
Aggregate solid waste	1.012665
Aggregate residual	0.672126

The reader may note in comparing Tables 18-1 and 18-2 that the selected residuals listed are exactly the same. Earlier in this paper it was emphasized that treatment processes do not eliminate residuals but rather transform them into other substances. The materials listed in Table 18-2 are similar to those in Table 18-1 because they represent materials that have escaped the treatment processes and remain in their original form. Treatment residuals other than such escapements are generally not reported and consequently cannot be included. Some such treatment residuals are included in aggregate solid waste (collected particulate matter, for example) but are not specified in sufficient detail to be useful. If we were to attempt to estimate the elasticity of net emissions, expansions of treatment practices would cause the elasticity of primary residuals to be quite low. However, unless recycling expands, the elasticity of net emissions must be

Table 18-2. Growth of Projected Treatment Residual Emissions Relative to Projected Personal Consumption Expenditures for Production Residuals for Selected Residuals and Aggregates, 1967-1985

Residual Type	*Elasticity*
Particulate matter	0.936285
Hydrocarbons	1.188888
Sulfur oxides	1.239038
Carbon monoxide	1.164323
Nitrogen oxides	1.262441
Fluorine	1.134872
Total solids	0.569360
Biological oxygen demand	0.545707
Chemical oxygen demand	0.501724
Lube oil	1.156645
Acids	1.009909
Soluble metallic ions	0.451884
Emulsions	1.158645
Coke plant chemical	1.156645
Phenols	0.000000
Sulfides	0.000000
Carbohydrate	0.808783
Chromate	0.000000
Phosphate	0.000000
Fluoride	0.000000
Monoethanolamine	0.000000
Sulfate	0.000000
Oil	0.000000
Bases	0.000000
Nonmetallic ions	0.000000
Radionuclides	120.000000
Agricultural chemicals	0.548471
Mining wastes	1.020349
Pesticides	0.662405
Aggregate airborne residual	1.196122
Aggregate waterborne residual	0.557241
Aggregate solid waste	1.020148
Aggregate residual	0.602585

exactly the same in the aggregate as are gross residuals. In other words, the elasticity of treatment residuals other than escapements will be quite high. This of course is simply another way of stating the basic implication of matter conservation, that is, that, except for recycling, net emissions will have the same aggregate weight as gross residuals. In Table 18-3 projections are made for these gross residual quantities, based upon gross residual coefficients and output projections for 1985.

Conclusions

The findings reported here represent only a modest beginning in constructing the waste generation component of a more comprehensive economic-environ-

Table 18-3. Gross Residual for 1985 by Selected Residual and Aggregates, Production Residuals Only

Residual Type	(Thousand Tons)
Particulate matter	70,983.254
Hydrocarbons	8,970.903
Sulfur oxides	92,799.671
Carbon monoxide	26,760.808
Nitrogen oxides	7,070.514
Fluorine	604.410
Total solids	458,776.645
Biological oxygen demand	54,389.761
Chemical oxygen demand	135,154.172
Lube oil	213.754
Acids	1,863.260
Soluble metallic ions	8,628.099
Emulsions	44.079
Coke plant chemical	13.737
Phenols	0.134
Sulfides	0.026
Carbohydrate	812.525
Chromate	145.540
Phosphate	121.111
Fluoride	1,632.097
Monoethanolamine	40.097
Sulfate	4,132.034
Oil	1,864.516
Bases	5.490
Nonmetallic ions	0.345
Radionuclides (curies)	3,360,000,000.000
Agricultural chemicals	41,420.628
Pesticides	504.339
Mining wastes	816,194.852
Aggregate airborne residual	207,189.557
Aggregate waterborne residual	544,402.547
Aggregate solid residual	7,228,678.625
Aggregate residual	7,185,054.250

mental system model sketched at the beginning of the paper. Interdisciplinary research is urgently needed in translating the gross-residuals data into damage functions needed for assessing efficient levels of pollution treatment and control. However, despite their tentative and incomplete nature, some of our estimates raise disturbing questions about man's stewardship in managing his environmental resources. For example, the estimates shown in Table 18-3 indicate that the gross generation of radionuclides from energy production is expected to rise to the level of 3.36 billion curies by 1985. Although this is a staggering figure, it should be noted on the optimistic side that many of these curies are short lived, that they are gross residuals, and that if the Faustian bargain we have struck with nuclear technologists can be honored [10], then most of these gross emissions will be safely contained, though some will inevitably escape into the general environment.

Although most radioactive material has always existed in the crust of the earth, and our generation is merely concentrating it in potentially dangerous forms, nuclear energy and weapons technologies produce large amounts of new, man-made radionuclides, especially plutonium, which has a long halflife and which is highly toxic in minute quantities. The fact must be faced that these estimates of gross generation of 3.36 billion curies of radionuclides in nuclear energy production by 1985 warn of sharp increases in the potential exposure of human beings to radiation. The magnitude of the problem is suggested by the comparison with the pre-World War II era, when the total amount of radioactivity from radium refined on the earth was reckoned in single curies, and the accidental loss of a single microcurie was then a matter of grave concern. Furthermore, the estimates presented here refer only to the radionuclides produced in the United States for nonmilitary purposes, and radioactive wastes are only a single dramatic example of the total wastes that are accumulating. Although very little information on the generation of radioactivity and other environmental damage by military programs has been released, the mere examination of the magnitude of the military budget as a percentage of total economic activity, without regard to its content, suggests that military activities constitute a major environmental threat over which civilian environmental management efforts have little influence.

The estimates we have been able to make to date concerning the generation of radioactive and other pollutants suggest an urgent need to design and evaluate alternative systems of energy generation, economic development, and environmental management consistent with sustainable long-run maintenance of the earth's delicate life-support systems.

Input-output economic models, because of their logical structure and consistency with the physical concept of mass balance, provide a promising basis upon which to build models needed to evaluate alternative economic-environmental options for the future.

References

1. Ayres, Robert U., and Allen V. Kneese. "Production, Consumption, and Externalities." *American Economic Review* 59, no. 3 (June 1969): 282–297.

2. Battelle Northwest Laboratory. "Data for Preliminary Demonstration Phase of the 'EQUIPS' System." Prepared for the Office of Environmental Affairs, Atomic Energy Commission, December 1971.

3. Cumberland, John H. "Application of Input-Output Technique to the Analysis of Environmental Problems." Paper prepared for the Fifth International Conference on Input-Output Techniques, Geneva, January 1971.

4. Cumberland, John H. "A Regional Interindustry Model for Analysis of Development Objectives." *Regional Science Association Papers* 17 (1966): 65–94.

5. Cumberland, John H., and Robert J. Korbach. "A Regional Interindustry Environmental Model." *Regional Science Association Papers* 30 (1973): 61–75.

6. Cumberland, John H., and Bruce N. Stram. "Effects of Economic Development upon Water Resources." University of Maryland Water Resources Research Center, Technical Report No. 18, Spring 1974.

7. Cumberland, John H., and Bruce N. Stram. "An Interindustry Approach to Modeling Economic–Environmental Systems." *Systems, Man, and Cybernetics* SMC-3, no. 6 (November 1973): 562–567.

8. Daley, Herman E. "On Economics as a Life Science." *Journal of Political Economy* 76, no. 3 (May/June 1968): 392–406.

9. Isard, Walter, et al. "Ecologic-Economic Analysis for Regional Development." *Regional Science Association Papers* 21 (November 1968): 79–99.

10. Kneese, Allen V. "The Faustian Bargain." *Resources* no. 44 (September 1973): 1–5.

11. Korbach, Robert J. "A Regional Environmental Input-Output Model." Ph.D. thesis, University of Maryland, 1973.

12. Leontief, Wassily. "Environmental Repercussions and the Economic Structure: An Input-Output Approach." *The Review of Economics and Statistics* 52, no. 3 (August 1970): 262–271.

13. Victor, Peter A. *Pollution: Economy and Environment.* Toronto: University of Toronto Press, 1972.

Rankings of Gross Residuals

Table 18A-1. Rankings by Industry of Gross Residuals Generated Directly and Indirectly per Million Dollars in 1967 (output in 1967 prices, Almon industries)

Residual		Industry	Tons per $ millions
	85	Lead	13,295
	160	Electric utilities	2,615
	129	Batteries	2,187
Aggregated	81	Cement, concrete, & gypsum	1,764
Airborne	84	Copper	1,240
Residuals	47	Pulp mills	1,125
	70	Residuals fuel oil for heating	989
	59	Fertilizers	958
	83	Steel	910
	14	Coal mining	534
	3	Meat, animals, & miscellaneous livestock products	22,013
	23	Meat products	14,210
	1	Dairy farm products	10,161
Aggregated	162	Water & sewer services	6,875
Waterborne	24	Dairy products	4,771
Residuals	2	Poultry & eggs	4,359
	25	Canned & frozen foods	3,226
	5	Grains	2,068
	37	Miscellaneous textiles	1,992
	4	Cotton	1,908
	14	Coal mining	1,259,643
	12	Copper ore	872,138
	17	Chemical fertilizer mining	687,744
Aggregated	11	Iron ores	416,982
Solid	84	Copper	203,810
Residuals	13	Other nonferrous metal ores	166,396

(continued)

Table 18A-1 continued

Residual		Industry	Tons per $ millions
Aggregated	59	Fertilizers	103,057
Solid	86	Zinc	77,605
Residuals,	160	Electric utilities	67,675
continued	90	Nonferrous wire drawing & insulating	66,756

Table 18A-2. Rankings by Product of Gross Residual Generated in Direct and Indirect Production Plus Household Consumption of Million Dollars of Product (output in 1967 prices, Almon industries)

Residual		Industry	Tons per $ Millions
	14	Coal mining	23,675
	69	Petroleum refining & related products	4,814
	160	Electric utilities	2,680
Aggregated	129	Batteries	2,187
Airborne	81	Cement, concrete, & gypsum	1,764
Residuals	59	Fertilizers	958
	83	Steel	910
	90	Nonferrous wire drawing & insulating	534
	26	Grain mill products	486
	180	State and local electric utilities	380
	3	Meat, animals, & miscellaneous livestock products	22,013
	23	Meat products	14,397
	24	Dairy farm products	10,161
Aggregated	162	Water & sewer services	6,975
Waterborne	24	Dairy products	4,957
Residuals	2	Poultry & eggs	4,358
	25	Canned & frozen foods	3,413
	37	Miscellaneous textiles	1,992
	7	Fruits, vegetables, & other crops	1,637
	60	Pesticides & other agricultural chemicals	1,392
	14	Coal mining	1,159,643
	59	Fertilizers	103,057
	160	Electric utilities	67,675
Aggregated	90	Nonferrous wire drawing & insulating	66,756
Solid	83	Steel	65,453
Residuals	16	Stone & clay mining	47,987
	55	Industrial chemicals	35,516
	81	Cement, concrete, & gypsum	32,271
	94	Plumbing & heating equipment	29,616
	60	Pesticides & other agricultural chemicals	29,065

Table 18A-3. Rankings by Industry of Gross Residual Generated by Million Dollars of Direct and Indirect Production for Selected Residuals and Aggregates for 1967 (output in 1967 prices, Almon industries)

Residual		Industry	Tons per $ millions
	85	Lead	3,157
	81	Cement, concrete, & gypsum	1,708
	160	Electric utilities	1,278
	70	Residual fuel oil for heating	943
Particulates	59	Fertilizers	584
	129	Batteries	528
	14	Coal mining	453
	26	Grain mill products	449
	83	Steel	368
	47	Pulp mills	236
	83	Steel	110
	93	Metal barrels, drums, & pails	47
	92	Metal cans	45
	138	Railroad equipment	40
Hydrocarbons	99	Miscellaneous fabricated wire products	32
	95	Structural metal products	30
	97	Metal stampings	28
	111	Ball & roller bearings	25
	139	Cycles & parts, transportation equipment	25
	103	Farm machinery	23
	85	Lead	10,132
	129	Batteries	1,650
	84	Copper	1,116
	160	Electric utilities	1,063
Sulfur Oxides	90	Nonferrous wire drawing & insulating	436
	89	Nonferrous rolling & drawing	263
	21	Ammunition	203
	55	Industrial chemicals	182
	86	Zinc	161
	68	Paints	157
	47	Pulp mills	773
	83	Steel	334
	64	Cellulosic fibers	176
	93	Metal barrels, drums, & pails	141
Carbon	92	Metal cans	137
Monoxide	138	Railroad equipment	120
	99	Miscellaneous fabricated wire products	98
	95	Structural metal products	92
	48	Paper & paperboard mills	92
	97	Metal stampings	85
	160	Electric utilities	264
	180	State & local electric utilities	28
Nitrogen	50	Wall & building paper	11
Oxides	17	Chemical fertilizer mining	10

(continued)

Table 18A-3 continued

Residual		Industry	Tons per $ Millions
Nitrogen	12	Copper ore	10
Oxides	14	Coal mining	9
continued	16	Stone & clay mining	9
	55	Industrial chemicals	9
	13	Other nonferrous metal ores	9
	176	Private schools & nonprofit organizations	8
	3	Meat, animals, & miscellaneous livestock products	19,936
	23	Meat products	12,737
	1	Dairy farm products	8,683
	162	Water & sewer services	5,865
Total Solids	24	Dairy products	3,898
	2	Poultry & eggs	3,283
	37	Miscellaneous textiles	1,719
	5	Grains	1,459
	6	Tobacco	1,452
	182	Business travel	1,287
	3	Meat, animals, & miscellaneous livestock products	22,123
	23	Meat products	14,323
	85	Lead	13,355
Agricultural	1	Dairy farm products	10,296
Chemicals	162	Water & sewer services	7,032
	24	Dairy products	4,875
	2	Poultry & eggs	4,623
	25	Canned & frozen foods	3,328
	160	Electric utilities	2,673
	129	Batteries	2,336
	4	Cotton	89
	7	Fruits, vegetables, & other crops	21
	32	Fats & oils	15
	6	Tobacco	14
Pesticides	35	Broad & narrow fabrics	10
	5	Grains	9
	28	Sugar	7
	1	Dairy farm products	5
	3	Meat, animals, & miscellaneous livestock products	5
	26	Grain mill products	5
	14	Coal mining	1,259,641
	12	Copper ore	872,137
	17	Chemical fertilizer mining	587,743
	11	Iron ores	416,979
Mining	84	Copper	203,809
Wastes	13	Other nonferrous metal ores	166,394
	59	Fertilizers	103,058
	86	Zinc	77,504
	160	Electric utilities	67,675
	90	Nonferrous wire drawing & insulating	66,754

Table 18A-4. Rankings by Product of Gross Residual Generated in Direct and Indirect Production Plus Household Consumption of Million Dollars of Product for Selected Residuals and Aggregates (output in 1967 prices, Almon industries)

Residual		Industry	Tons per $ Millions
	14	Coal mining	12,631
	81	Cement, concrete, & gypsum	1,708
	160	Electric utilities	1,287
	59	Fertilizers	584
Particulates	129	Batteries	528
	26	Grain mill products	449
	83	Steel	366
	2	Poultry & eggs	223
	180	State & local electric utilities	203
	99	Miscellaneous fabricated wire products	120
	14	Coal mining	769
	69	Petroleum refining & related products	340
	83	Steel	110
	99	Miscellaneous fabricated wire products	32
Hydrocarbons	95	Structural metal products	30
	97	Metal stampings	28
	139	Cycles & parts, transportation equipment	25
	103	Farm machinery	23
	96	Screw machine products	21
	102	Engines & turbines	19
	14	Coal mining	5,835
	129	Batteries	1,650
	160	Electric utilities	1,063
	90	Nonferrous wire drawing & insulating	436
Sulfur Oxides	69	Petroleum refining & related products	331
	21	Ammunition	203
	55	Industrial chemicals	182
	68	Paints	157
	180	State and local electric utilities	131
	94	Plumbing & heating equipment	129
	69	Petroleum refining & related products	3,868
	14	Coal mining	3,820
	83	Steel	334
	99	Miscellaneous fabricated wire products	98
Carbon	95	Structural metal products	92
Monoxide	48	Paper & paperboard mills	92
	97	Metal stampings	85
	155	Airlines	79
	139	Cycles & parts, transportation equipment	76
	103	Farm machinery	71
Nitrogen	14	Coal mining	621
Oxides	160	Electric utilities	320

(continued)

Table 18A-4 continued

Residual		*Industry*	*Tons per $ Million*
Nitrogen Oxides continued	69	Petroleum refining & related products	204
	161	Natural gas	57
	180	State & local electric utilities	28
	55	Industrial chemicals	9
	16	Stone & clay mining	9
	176	Private schools & nonprofit organizations	8
	59	Fertilizers	8
	81	Cement, concrete, & gypsum	7
Total Solids	3	Meat, animals, & miscellaneous livestock products	19,936
	23	Meat products	12,908
	24	Dairy farm products	8,683
	162	Water & sewer services	5,865
	24	Dairy products	4,168
	2	Poultry & eggs	3,289
	37	Miscellaneous textiles	1,718
	7	Fruits, vegetables, & other crops	1,209
	32	Fats & oils	1,068
	48	Paper & paperboard mills	981
Agricultural Chemicals	14	Coal mining	24,041
	3	Meat, animals, & miscellaneous livestock products	22,123
	23	Meat products	15,064
	24	Dairy farm products	10,296
	162	Water & sewer services	7,032
	43	Millwork & wood products	6,430
	41	Lumber & wood products	6,408
	24	Dairy products	5,817
	69	Petroleum refining & related products	4,884
	2	Poultry & eggs	4,623
Pesticides	7	Fruits, vegetables, & other crops	21
	32	Fats & oils	15
	35	Broad & narrow fabrics	10
	28	Sugar	7
	1	Dairy farm products	5
	3	Meat, animals, & miscellaneous livestock products	5
	26	Grain mill products	5
	2	Poultry & eggs	4
	36	Floor coverings	4
	40	Household textiles	3
Mining Wastes	14	Coal mining	1,259,641
	59	Fertilizers	103,056
	160	Electric utilities	67,675
	90	Nonferrous wire drawing & insulating	66,754
	83	Steel	65,452
	16	Stone & clay mining	47,982
	55	Industrial chemicals	35,515
	81	Cement, concrete, & gypsum	32,270
	94	Plumbing & heating equipment	29,615
	60	Pesticides & other agricultural chemicals	28,064

Chapter Nineteen

Pollution, Pollution Abatement, and the Economic Structure of the Netherlands

H. den Hartog
A. Houweling

The impact of man on his natural environment as a result of his economic activities is, generally speaking, related to (1) the occupation of space, (2) the extraction of raw materials, and (3) the discharge of residuals. The negative effects of
the last activity are now a significant, if not new, feature of environmental
problems experienced by industrialised economies in particular. This is considered
a sufficient justification to deal in this paper with the generation and elimination
of residuals, or rather, with pollution only, with respect to the Netherlands.

Pollution generation stems from two primary sources, the production of goods
and services and the consumption of goods and services. Automobiles not only
create air pollution in their use—and solid waste when this usage is terminated—
but also generate gaseous, liquid, and solid residuals during their production. It
is this latter type of waste generation, pollution from production, and its elimination or abatement, that are examined in this paper. More precisely, the paper
deals with an extension of the input-output framework that enables the Netherlands to cover more than the production and intermediate use of conventional
goods and services: viz., the generation and elimination of pollutants, and the
shifting of the pollution-abatement burden and its incidence.

Leontief and Ford [4] analyse the integration of the first of these into the
input-output system and anticipate its empirical implementation. Their analytical results are taken here as a point of departure. In addition, the introduction
of the "polluter pays" principle into the input-output framework is considered.
This permits analyses of effects that are likely to occur from shifting the burden
of pollution abatement and its incidence to the polluter.

The "polluter pays" principle is characteristic of Dutch environmental legislation enacted up to now. Analytically, it provides a device to include in the
input-output matrix not only the column coefficients or input requirements of

The authors are indebted to members of the staff of the Central Planning Bureau,
specifically to P.H. Gommers, H.D. Nagtegaal, and Th. F.L. de Waal for their cooperation
and assistance with the research reported in this paper and C. Kwinkelenberg for his able
programming on the Univac 1108 and Control Data Corporation 6600 computers.

pollution-abatement activities, but also row coefficients of those sectors representing the inputs "purchased" by other sectors to abate pollution generated directly by these other sectors. In this approach, the elimination of pollutants generated by abatement activities themselves and the connected costs are explicitly taken into consideration.

This line of thought was pursued earlier by den Hartog, Houweling, and Tjan [2] in the application of a comprehensive economic model with four conventional sectors and one abatement sector to the problem of water pollution. It will be carried on in this paper with emphasis on the input-output framework and applied to more sectors, conventional as well as abatement sectors.

The Model

Preceding its empirical implementation, a formal description of the expanded input-output system is given here.

Leontief and Ford [3; 4] have presented an expanded input-output system in which the conventional system is extended to cover the intermediate inputs of pollution elimination as well as the generation or output of pollutants in physical terms. This system can be summarised as follows:[1]

For outputs of conventional sectors

$$X = AX + ES + Y \tag{19-1}$$

where

$X = (n \times 1)$ column vector of outputs of conventional sectors, x_i

$S = (m \times 1)$ column vector of eliminated amounts of pollutants by type, s_k

$Y = (n \times 1)$ column vector of deliveries to final demand[2] by conventional sectors, y_i

$A = (n \times n)$ matrix of interindustry coefficients, a_{ij}, defining inputs from (conventional) sector i per unit of output of (conventional) sector j

$E = (n \times m)$ matrix of coefficients, e_{il}, defining inputs from conventional sectors i per unit of eliminated pollutant l

For the gross generation of pollution,

$$T = PX + QS + R \tag{19-2}$$

1. The number of conventional sectors (industries) is n (row subscript i and column subscript j). The number of abatement activities is m (row subscript k and column subscript l).
2. Final demand here is defined as deliveries to domestic final sectors (consumption, investment, and stockbuilding) plus exports minus competing imports.

where

$T = (m \times 1)$ column vector of total pollution by type of pollutant, t_k

$R = (m \times 1)$ column vector of pollution by type of pollutant generated by final sectors, r_k

$P = (m \times n)$ matrix of pollution coefficients, p_{kj}, defining quantities of pollutant k generated per unit of output of (conventional) sector j

$Q = (m \times m)$ matrix of pollution coefficients, q_{kl}, defining quantities of pollutant k generated per unit of eliminated pollutant l

For the net generation of pollution,

$$U = T - \hat{\alpha}T \tag{19-3}$$

where

$U = (m \times 1)$ column vector of net pollution by type of pollutant, u_k

$\hat{\alpha} = (m \times m)$ diagonal matrix, with the vector of predetermined relative levels of pollution abatement of type k, α_k, along the main diagonal

For the quantities of eliminated pollutants,

$$S = \hat{\alpha}T \tag{19-4}$$

If pollution abatement is nonexistent, that is, if the vector of predetermined abatement levels, α, is a null vector, then S is a null vector. Consequently, the net generation of pollution, U, equals the gross generation of pollution, T. The equations (19-1) and (19-2) reduce to

$$X = AX + Y \tag{19-5}$$

and

$$T = PX + R \tag{19-6}$$

yielding the solution

$$X = (I - A)^{-1}Y \tag{19-7}$$

$$T = P(I - A)^{-1}Y + R \tag{19-8}$$

If pollution abatement is introduced—in other words, if α is *not* a null vector—the solution of equations (19-1) through (19-4) is somewhat more involved than the one given by equations (19-7) and (19-8). It is obvious that this is due to the circumstance that pollution abatement itself contributes to the generation of pollutants, not only directly by its own activity, but also indirectly through the purchase of inputs from other sectors. The solution of the system (19-1) through (19-4) is in fact

$$X = [(I - A) - E\hat{\alpha}(I - Q\hat{\alpha})^{-1}P]^{-1} [Y + E\hat{\alpha}(I - Q\hat{\alpha})^{-1}R] \tag{19-9}$$

$$T = [(I - Q\hat{\alpha}) - P(I - A)^{-1} E\hat{\alpha}]^{-1} [P(I - A)^{-1} Y + R] \tag{19-10}$$

$$U = (I - \hat{\alpha})[(I - Q\hat{\alpha}) - P(I - A)^{-1}E\hat{\alpha}]^{-1} [P(I - A)^{-1}Y + R] \tag{19-11}$$

$$S = \hat{\alpha}[(I - Q\hat{\alpha}) - P(I - A)^{-1}E\hat{\alpha}]^{-1} [P(I - A)^{-1}Y + R] \tag{19-12}$$

The shifting of the pollution-abatement burden and its incidence can be introduced into the input-output framework by assuming that the total burden of abatement by type of pollutant is represented by the (real) value of output of abatement activities. This implies that the raising of funds for investment in abatement facilities is left out of consideration. Insofar as it is necessary to catch up with appreciable backlogs in pollution abatement, however, the re-allocation of resources to, and thus, investment in abatement activities is a very important, if not overwhelming, economic problem, not only on the macro-economic level, but also on the sectoral level (compare den Hartog et al. in [2]). In this context, only a partial analysis of the shifting of the burden of pollution abatement and its incidence is presented, namely, for that part of the incidence that is connected with the current operation of abatement activities.

The "polluter pays" principle as it is implemented in Dutch environmental legislation enacted up to now is based on a general prohibition against discharging residuals into the environment, which in practice amounts to an obligation to abate pollution. Disregarding the transitional problems, such as catching up with the backlog, the "polluter pays" principle thus would imply that the costs of the current operation of abatement activities are charged directly to polluters in proportion to the amount of pollution generated by them.[3]

Given the (real) elimination costs (primary and secondary) per unit of eliminated pollutant k, ϕ_k (vector ϕ), it is possible to define the vector of (real) values of outputs of abatement activities, Z, for a given level of abatement, α:

$$Z = \hat{\phi}S = \hat{\phi}\hat{\alpha}T \tag{19-13}$$

---

3. If the alternative were to pollute and be fined for it, the polluter could compare the cost of the abatement and nonabatement alternatives. In this case, and analysis presented here could help to determine the fines for pollution.

Substitution of equation (19–2) for T in (19–13) yields

$$Z = \hat{\alpha}(\hat{\phi}PX + \hat{\phi}QS + \hat{\phi}R) \tag{19-14}$$

Redefining S in terms of Z according to equation (19–13) and substituting in equation (19–14) gives for the (real) output values of abatement sectors

$$Z = \hat{\alpha}(\hat{\phi}PX + \hat{\phi}Q\hat{\phi}^{-1}Z + \hat{\phi}R) \tag{19-15}$$

Accordingly, redefining S in equation (19–1) in terms of Z gives

$$X = AX + E\hat{\phi}^{-1}Z + Y \tag{19-16}$$

The matrices $\hat{\phi}P$, $\hat{\phi}Q\hat{\phi}^{-1}$ can be interpreted as matrices of input coefficients of conventional and abatement activities, respectively, representing the required cost per unit of output for abating pollution generated by that unit of output. The matrix $E\hat{\phi}^{-1}$ stands for secondary inputs of abatement activities from conventional sectors per unit of output value (in contrast to "per unit of eliminated pollutant").

Introducing a shorthand notation for the three last-mentioned matrices, the matrix $Q\hat{\phi}^{-1}$, and the vector $\hat{\phi}R$,

$$
\begin{aligned}
E\hat{\phi}^{-1} &= B \\
\hat{\phi}P &= C \\
\hat{\phi}Q\hat{\phi}^{-1} &= D \\
Q\hat{\phi}^{-1} &= H \\
\hat{\phi}R &= G
\end{aligned}
\tag{19-17}
$$

the expanded input-output framework may be written as

$$X = AX + BZ + Y \tag{19-18}$$

$$Z = \hat{\alpha}(CX + DZ + G) \tag{19-19}$$

$$T = PX + HZ + R \tag{19-20}$$

$$S = \hat{\alpha}T \tag{19-21}$$

$$U = T - \hat{\alpha}T \tag{19-22}$$

The solution of the output vectors X and Z in terms of the final demand vectors Y and G runs as follows:

$$X = [(I - A) - B(I - \hat{\alpha}D)^{-1}\hat{\alpha}C]^{-1} [Y + B (I - \hat{\alpha}D)^{-1}\hat{\alpha}G] \qquad (19\text{-}23)$$

$$Z = [(I - \hat{\alpha}D) - \hat{\alpha}C(I - A)^{-1}B]^{-1} [\hat{\alpha}C(I - A)^{-1}Y + \hat{\alpha}G] \qquad (19\text{-}24)$$

From these, straightforward solutions for T, S, and U may be obtained by substituting equations (19-23) and (19-24) in equation (19-20) and consequently in equations (19-21) and (19-22).

Formally speaking, the last system does not differ from the system embodied in equations (19-1) through (19-4). Economically, however, there is a significant difference. The simple reformulation of S in money terms means that abatement activities are *economically valued* at their costs. The "polluter pays" principle charges these costs directly to polluters according to their rate of pollutant generation. This is not essential for the resulting output levels X and Z, but it is essential for shifting the burden of pollution abatement to sectors (intermediate and final) other than those that are charged directly through the application of the "polluter pays" principle. In fact, the significance of the introduction of this principle into an input-output framework lies in the circumstance that it is possible to specify the ultimate price effects of shifting on the charges. This applies not only to prices of conventional sectors but to prices (costs) of abatement activities as well.

Following conventional input-output analysis, the price change, $\Delta\Pi$, as the ultimate result of some initial cost-push, W, in the system described by equations (19-18) and (19-19) can be ascertained as follows.

Enforcing pollution abatement to a certain degree of elimination, $\hat{\alpha}$, and charging the cost to polluters according to the "polluter pays" principle represents such an initial cost-push. It follows from equation (19-15) and the interpretation of the matrices $\hat{\phi}P$ and $\hat{\phi}Q\hat{\phi}^{-1}$ that premultiplication of these matrices by the degree of abatement, $\hat{\alpha}$, and summation over rows (column totals) would indicate the total initial cost-push per sector. That is, for conventional and abatement sectors, respectively

$$W' = \alpha'(\hat{\phi}P, \hat{\phi}Q\hat{\phi}^{-1}) \qquad (19\text{-}25)$$

Using the notation (19-17), this reduces to

$$W' = \alpha'(C, D) \qquad (19\text{-}26)$$

This is an initial cost-push of purely domestic origin. Describing the ultimate price change resulting from it, it is necessary to decompose the technological coefficient matrices A and B into two matrices each, one pertaining to input requirements of domestically produced intermediate goods and services and one pertaining to imported intermediate goods and services:

$$A = \bar{A} + \tilde{A}$$

$$B = \bar{B} + \tilde{B}$$

The bar, ‾, refers to domestically produced intermediate inputs and the swung dash, ~, to imported intermediate inputs. The resulting price change of an initial (and autonomous) cost-push introduced into the system embodied in equations (19-18) and (19-19) is

$$(\Delta\Pi)' = (\Delta\Pi)' \begin{bmatrix} \bar{A} & \bar{B} \\ \hat{\alpha}C & \hat{\alpha}D \end{bmatrix} + (\Delta\tilde{\Pi}) \begin{bmatrix} \tilde{A} & \tilde{B} \\ 0 & 0 \end{bmatrix} + \alpha'(C, D) \tag{19-28}$$

where

$(\Delta\tilde{\Pi}) = 1 \times (m + n)$ vector of import price changes

$0 \quad = $ a null matrix

The price change equation (19-28) allows us to trace the effects of price changes of imported intermediate goods and services as well. This is of some significance insofar as such price changes may come about as a result of abatement policies abroad. Purely by way of hypothesis, it is assumed that in this respect import prices follow domestic prices to some degree:

$$(\Delta\tilde{\Pi})' = (\Delta\Pi)'\hat{\beta} \tag{19-29}$$

where $\hat{\beta}$ is a $(m + n) \times (m + n)$ scalar matrix, indicating the degree of correspondence. Substitution of equation (19-29) in equation (19-28) and solving for $(\Delta\Pi)$ yields:

$$(\Delta\Pi)' = \alpha'(C, D) \begin{bmatrix} (I - \bar{A} - \beta\tilde{A}) & -(\bar{B} + \beta\tilde{B}) \\ -\hat{\alpha}C & (I - \hat{\alpha}D) \end{bmatrix}^{-1} \tag{19-30}$$

The foregoing still looks like the result of "the flight of the model builder's theoretical fantasy." The real advance of knowledge and of understanding will depend not primarily on this fantasy, but on the progress of systematic fact-finding efforts. Therefore, before discussing the empirical results of computations with the model, an account is given of the data used.

Statistics and Fact Finding

Sectoral classification of the conventional sectors is based on the International Standard Industrial Classification (ISIC) of all Economic Activities of the Statistical Office of the United Nations [5; 6]. This classification is specified in

Appendix 19A, together with the corresponding ISIC (major) division or group numbers. The grouping of sectors in this way is usual in sectoral analyses of the Dutch Central Planning Bureau.

The sectoral classification of abatement activities is still preliminary and by no means exhaustive. It is determined by the results of fact finding up to now. Table 19-1 specifies seven different pollution abatement activities covering the most urgent problems of pollution in the Netherlands. In terms of pollutants to be eliminated, the classification is not completely unambiguous. This applies particularly to abatement activities 30, Adaptation of passenger cars, and 31, Adaptation of trucks and vans, in which elimination is not restricted to one specific pollutant. In contrast, one and the same pollutant (SO_x) is eliminated in activities 27, Desulphurization of gas oil, and 28, Desulphurization of residual oil. Differences in elimination techniques justify the distinction between these two activities. The distinction between activities 25, Public waste-water treatment, and 26, Private waste-water treatment and sanitation, on the other hand, is based on a difference of administration and management of the abatement facilities, causing differences in the scale and technique of elimination (treatment as against sanitation of production processes), this in turn leading to different levels of unit cost of elimination.

This approach to abatement activities requires a definition of the units of pollutants concerned. Table 19-1 also provides this information.

There are two main sources of data—or rather, two institutes responsible for the collection of data from numerous, scattered, other sources. Needless to say, this paper benefited from the activities of these institutes. One is the Central Bureau of Statistics of the Netherlands, the other the Central Planning Bureau.

Table 19-1. Pollution Abatement Activities and Units of Measurement of Pollutants

Abatement Activities[a]		
Num- ber	*Title*	*Unit of Measurement of Pollutant[b]*
25	Public waste-water treatment	1000 of population equivalents BOD^{20}_5
26	Private waste-water treatment and sanitation	1000 of population equivalents BOD^{20}_5
27	Desulphurisation of gas oil	100 tons of gas oil
28	Desulphurisation of residual oil	100 tons of residual oil
29	Solid-waste management	1000 tons of solid waste
30	Adaptation of passenger cars	100 passenger cars
31	Adaptation of trucks and vans	100 trucks or vans (commercial vehicles)

[a]The numbers 25–31 correspond to the row numbers given these activities in the expanded input-output table.
[b]BOD^{20}_5 = biological oxygen demand during 5 days at a temperature of 20 degrees centigrade.

The latter institute has initiated some environmental fact-finding activities[4] in cooperation with the Central Bureau of Statistics for its own analytical and forecasting purposes to serve the Steering Group on Macro-Economic Analysis of Environmental Policies (Steering Group MEAM). This group itself contributed to the fact finding, also, by facilitating access to sources otherwise difficult to reach. Most of the groundwork resulting in the pollution and pollution-abatement data presented here is accounted for in unpublished reports to the Steering Group MEAM. This is not to say that the data gathered so far are in any way definitive. In many instances they are still subject to revision and in some instances they still cannot be considered to be truly representative. Hence the results of the computations based on these data are to be taken with the same provisos.

The 24-order technological matrix A and its decomposition into the matrix of requirements of domestically produced intermediate inputs, $\bar{A}$, and the matrix of requirements of imported intermediate inputs, $\tilde{A}$, are derived from a conventional 35-sector input-output table prepared by the Central Bureau of Statistics for the year 1968 [1].

The (7×24) matrices of total gross generation of pollutants per conventional sector, $\bar{P}$, and of pollution coefficients per sector, $P = \bar{P}\hat{X}^{-1}$, are derived mainly from the Central Planning Bureau reports to the Steering Group MEAM. The last matrix is given in full in Table 19-2.

The matrix of direct pollution coefficients of abatement activities, H, presented in Table 19-3, is very provisional indeed. It is based on engineering estimates of the prevailing 1973 technology of abatement. The determination of the matrix of input requirements of abatement sectors per unit of output, B ($=E\hat{\phi}^{-1}$), given in Table 19-4, is equally provisional. Still more speculative is the decomposition of matrix B into $\bar{B}$, standing for domestically produced input requirements, and $\tilde{B}$, representing imported input requirements. For the sake of completeness, this decomposition was carried out on a provisional basis; but it is not presented here, as it seems it does not play a dominant role in the accuracy of the calculations, though this remains a matter for further consideration.

The last line of Table 19-4 specifies the cost of abatement per unit of pollutant eliminated in million guilders at 1973 prices. This is the vector ϕ. Given this vector, it is possible to determine matrices C and D, using the notations from (19-17):

$$C = \hat{\phi}P \qquad \text{and} \qquad D = \hat{\phi}H$$

---

4. The fact-finding team at the Central Planning Bureau consists of P.H. Gommers, A. Houweling, H.D. Nagtegaal, and Th. F.L. de Waal.

Table 19-2.   Direct 1973 Pollution Coefficients for Conventional Input-Output Sectors

Num-ber	Conventional Sector — Title	Type of Pollutant[a]						
		25	26	27	28	29	30	31
1	Agriculture	0	0.1587	0.1309	0.6292	0.0202	0.0141	0.0101
2	Coal mining	0.0153	0	0	0	0	0.1174	0.0102
3	Other mining	0	0.0462	0	0.0865	0.1742	0.0053	0.0033
4	Animal foods	0.2793	0.3481	0.0233	0.0676	0.0077	0.0109	0.0062
5	Other foods	0.1655	1.1648	0.0182	0.0643	0.0279	0.0221	0.0074
6	Beverages & tobacco	0.3078	0.4823	0.0174	0.1473	0.0107	0.0144	0.0073
7	Textiles	0.5120	0.0402	0.0294	0	0.1671	0.0312	0.0065
8	Clothing & footwear	0.0079	0	0	0.2045	0.0358	0.0876	0.0041
9	Paper & paper products	0.4269	0.9088	0.0186	0.2017	0.0186	0.0247	0.0028
10	Chemicals	0.2242	0.5007	0.1286	3.6981	0.0527	0.0185	0.0027
11	Oil refining	0.0343	0.0743	0	0.4486	0.0085	0.0025	0.0006
12	Basic metals	0.0109	0.0421	0.0234	0.0197	0.0418	0.0091	0.0011
13	Metal products & machinery	0.0119	0	0.0195	0.0270	0.0388	0.0431	0.0077
14	Electrical goods & machinery	0.0120	0	0.0274	0.0085	0.0258	0.0330	0.0050
15	Transport equipment	0.0666	0.0084	0.0241	0.1303	0.0541	0.0512	0.0122
16	Other industries	0.0339	0	0.1577	2.4712	0.0700	0.0462	0.0065
17	Public utilities	0.0051	0.2691	0.0384	0.4936	0.0071	0.0156	0.0042
—	Manufacturing	0.1193	0	0.0466	0	0.0434	0.0272	0.0055
18	Construction	0.0080	0	0.1037	0.0040	0.1275	0.0529	0.0129
19	Wholesale & retail trade	0.0104	0	0.0526		0.0113	0.0879	0.0342
20	Ownership of dwellings	0	0	0	0	0	0.0035	0.0003
21	Ocean & air transport	0.0026	0.0098	0.0210	0.0014	0.0034	0.0178	0.0303
22	Other transport	0.0014	0.0007	0.0458	0.0036	0.0041	0.0622	0.0624
23	Other services	0.0764	0.0017	0.0657	0.0049	0.0055	0.0777	0.0020
—	Services	0.0313	0	0.0506	0.0038	0.0069	0.0704	0.0242
24	Not elsewhere specified	0	0	0	0	0	0	0
	Total (excl. abatement activities)	0.0706	0.1447	0.0586	0.2870	0.0379	0.0431	0.0127

[a]The numbering of the type of pollutant refers to abatement activities; this and the units of pollutant measurement are defined in Table 19-1.
Note: Gross pollution per million guilders of output at 1973 prices; matrix $P' = (\bar{P}\hat{X}^{-1})'$.

Table 19-3.   Direct 1973 Pollution Coefficients for Abatement Activities

Abatement Activity		Type of Pollutant[a]						
Num-ber	Title	25	26	27	28	29	30	31
25	Public waste-water treatment	0	0	0	0	1.4604	0	0.0102
26	Private waste-water treatment and sanitation	0	0	0	0	7.1990	0	0.0485
27	Desulphurisation of gas oil	0	0	0	8	0	0.0024	0.0006
28	Desulphurisation of residual oil	0	0	0	8	0	0.0024	0.0006
29	Solid-waste management	4.1016	0	0	0	0	0	0.1057
30	Adaptation of passenger cars	0	0	0	0	0	0	0
31	Adaptation of trucks and vans	0	0	0	0	0	0	0

[a]The numbering of the type of pollutant refers to abatement activities; this and the units of pollutant measurement are defined in Table 19-1.

Note: Pollution generated per million guilders of output; matrix H'.

Table 19–4.   Input Requirements Per Unit of Output of Abatement Activities from Conventional Input-Output Sectors and Abatement Costs

Num-ber	Conventional Sector — Title	25	26	27	28	29	30	31
1	Agriculture	0	0	0	0	0	0	0
2	Coal mining	0	0	0	0	0	0	0
3	Other mining	0	0	0	0.0230	0	0	0
4	Animal foods	0	0	0	0	0	0	0
5	Other foods	0	−0.2400	0	0	0	0	0
6	Beverages & tobacco	0	0	0	0	0	0	0
7	Textiles	0	0	0	0	0	0	0
8	Clothing & footwear	0	0	0	0	0	0	0
9	Paper & paper products	0	0	0	0	0	0	0
10	Chemicals	0	0	0.0300	0.0300	0.0140	0	0
11	Oil refining	0	0	0.1110	0.1110	0.0230	0.4000	0.4000
12	Basic metals	0	0	0	0	0	0	0
13	Metal products & machinery	0.0040	0.0400	0.0100	0.0100	0.0200	0	0
14	Electrical goods & machinery	0	0	0	0	0.0150	0	0
15	Transport equipment	0	0	0	0	0.0160	0	0
16	Other industries	0.0040	0.0400	0.0050	0.0050	0.0250	0.1000	0.1000
17	Public utilities	0.0780	0.2000	0.0070	0.0070	0.0200	0	0
18	Construction	0.0240	0.0200	0.0060	0.0060	0.0040	0	0
19	Wholesale & retail trade	0.0040	0.0400	0.0130	0.0130	0.0040	0	0
20	Ownership of dwellings	0	0	0	0	0	0	0
21	Ocean & air transport	0	0	0	0	0	0	0
22	Other transport	0.0040	0	0.0070	0.0070	0.0190	0	0
23	Other services	0	0	0	0	0.0300	0	0
24	Not elsewhere specified	0	0	0	0	0	0	0
	Abatement cost per unit of pollutant eliminated (million guilders in 1973 prices)	0.04930	0.00500	0.00106	0.00195	0.01780	0.03000	0.04000

Header over columns 25–31: *Abatement Sector* [a]

[a]The numbering of the type of pollutant refers to abatement activities; this and the units of pollutant measurement are defined in Table 19–1.

Note: Measured in 1973 prices; matrix B and vector ϕ', respectively.

The decomposition of matrices $A = \bar{A} + \tilde{A}$ and $B = \bar{B} + \tilde{B}$ being available, it is possible also to carry out the most relevant calculations using the input-output framework set forth in the preceding section.

Of course, the fact finding concerning pollution and its abatement is still far from complete. Up to now, the input-output application for the Netherlands does not cover *thermal* pollution; the discharge of *heavy metals*; air pollution *generated from nonenergetic* sources; the discharge of *chemical and radioactive* wastes; or *noise* and *odor* pollution. Work on these areas is being continued. Once appropriate sets of pollution and abatement coefficients for these "sectors" in the environmental field have been compiled and other sets of coefficients have been revised, a more comprehensive study of environmental repercussions can be undertaken for the Netherlands within the framework of the input-output system that is being implemented here on a more provisional basis.

Results of Computations

Preliminary to a discussion of the computational results,[5] some consideration must be given to the assumptions used concerning the degree of abatement, α, and the degree of correspondence between prices of domestic inputs and prices of competing imported inputs, β.

The degree of pollution *abatement* as defined in the preceding section coincides with the degree of *elimination* of pollution [compare equations (19-3) and (19-4)]. In practice, however, this is not necessarily the case. The abatement activities considered here may treat all pollution generated, but, given the prevailing technology, may not eliminate all of it. This difference is disregarded here for the time being.

Given this assumption, only three alternatives for the degree of abatement vector are considered. These are: α being either a null vector (absence of abatement) or a unit vector (complete abatement) or a vector indicating the degree of abatement already existing for the different types of pollution. The last-mentioned alternative assumes the following values:

$$\alpha' = (0.22, 0.18, 0.40, 0.00, 0.24, 0.10, 0.10)$$

To limit the number of combinations of the last two alternatives with possible values of the vector β, the case of α being a unit vector is always combined with β being a unit vector as well, while the last-mentioned alternative of the α vector is always combined with $\beta = 0.5$. These two cases are denoted by the long-run case and the intermediate case, respectively.

In the absence of abatement (i.e., $\hat{\alpha} = 0$), the amounts of the different kinds of pollution generated in connection with the increase in level of all outputs contributing directly or indirectly to delivery to final users of one million

5. Computations were performed on a Univac 1108 computer and a Control Data Corporation 6600 computer.

guilders output of each conventional input-output sector are represented by the matrix product $P(I - A)^{-1}$ [compare equation (19-8)]. The results of such a computation are shown in Table 19-5.

Analytically, the same kind of cumulated gross pollution coefficients can be established for conventional as well as abatement activities if abatement activities are introduced. If abatement is complete (i.e., if $\hat{\alpha} = I$), then cumulated gross pollution coefficients (or rather "potential" pollution coefficients, since net pollution will be nil) are represented for each sector and each type of pollution by the matrix expression

$$(P, H) \begin{bmatrix} (I - A) & -B \\ -C & (I - D) \end{bmatrix}^{-1}$$

This expression may be derived from the solution of T resulting from the substitution of equations (19-23) and (19-24) in equation (19-20), being the matrix premultiplying the vectors Y and G. The results of this computation are shown in Table 19-6.

The coefficients in Table 19-6 are greater than those in Table 19-5. This illustrates the fact that abatement facilities developed to cope with pollution generation by conventional sectors create additional pollution and consequently a need for more abatement facilities than are required considering pollution by conventional sectors only. Even so, the situation underlying the figures in Table 19-6 implies, of course, a state of much greater "cleanliness" than the situation where abatement facilities are nonexistent (Table 19-5).

Given the cumulated pollution coefficients, the question arises whether or not in an open economy like the Netherlands the pattern of exports and imports contributes on balance to the level of pollution generated. A rough indication of an answer to this question is contained in Table 19-7.

The figures in Table 19-7 are computed on the assumption that the pollution content of competitive imports is equal to the pollution content of final output of the competing domestic sector. This assumption is relevant insofar as the question raised boils down to asking whether import substitution in one sector and more exports in another would lead, on balance, to less pollution.

The table indicates that, roughly speaking, pollution connected with exports and imports balances for air pollution by sulphur dioxide and automotive transport. The structure of foreign trade seems detrimental, however, to the level of water pollution and favourable to the amount of solid waste otherwise generated. Apart from policy questions and other practical problems involved, simply rearranging the pattern of exports and imports would not, in general, lead to a reduction of pollution by just one type of pollutant. Rather, an increase of pollution by other pollutants would occur as well. Linear programming could

Table 19-5. Cumulated 1973 Pollution Coefficients in the Absence of Abatement

Number	Title	25	26	27	28	29	30	31
		Conventional Sector			Pollutant per Million Guilders[a]			
1	Agriculture	0.1264	0.7793	0.2031	0.9892	0.0593	0.0485	0.0215
2	Coal mining	0.0583	0.0737	0.0386	0.1393	0.0224	0.1546	0.0169
3	Other mining	0.0317	0.0949	0.0293	0.1900	0.1976	0.0295	0.0094
4	Animal foods	0.4344	1.0764	0.2064	1.0172	0.0671	0.0628	0.0280
5	Other foods	0.3439	2.0438	0.1374	0.6924	0.0796	0.0704	0.0255
6	Beverages & tobacco	0.3796	0.7125	0.0613	0.2629	0.0317	0.0363	0.0144
7	Textiles	0.9577	0.3483	0.1336	0.6313	0.3158	0.0867	0.0207
8	Clothing & footwear	0.3589	0.1632	0.0781	0.3214	0.1633	0.1479	0.0119
9	Paper & paper products	0.7311	1.5365	0.0850	0.6348	0.0636	0.0730	0.0147
10	Chemicals	0.3734	0.8253	0.2159	0.7202	0.1045	0.0578	0.0116
11	Oil refining	0.0754	0.1700	0.0334	3.9877	0.1206	0.0276	0.0078
12	Basic metals	0.0627	0.1571	0.0914	1.2984	0.1389	0.0593	0.0125
13	Metal products & machinery	0.0612	0.0838	0.0735	0.4089	0.0919	0.0835	0.0168
14	Electrical goods & machinery	0.0629	0.0799	0.0770	0.2956	0.0668	0.0695	0.0130
15	Transport equipment	0.1267	0.0721	0.0807	0.2965	0.1091	0.1005	0.0234
16	Other industries	0.1439	0.1909	0.2382	0.4394	0.1235	0.0900	0.0167
17	Public utilities	0.0316	0.0480	0.0628	2.8206	0.0516	0.0413	0.0094
18	Construction	0.0727	0.0988	0.1888	0.2895	0.1856	0.0991	0.0232
19	Wholesale & retail trade	0.0461	0.0537	0.0819	0.1644	0.0263	0.1148	0.0469
20	Ownership of dwellings	0.0140	0.0182	0.0335	0.0519	0.0320	0.0217	0.0044
21	Ocean & air transport	0.0684	0.0645	0.0719	0.2339	0.0251	0.0687	0.0390
22	Other transport	0.0332	0.0464	0.0740	0.2742	0.0253	0.0873	0.0693
23	Other services	0.1253	0.0984	0.0975	0.1752	0.0220	0.0989	0.0071
24	Not elsewhere specified	0.1288	0.1265	0.0996	0.2299	0.0279	0.0952	0.0139

[a] The numbering of the type of pollutant refers to abatement activities; this and the units of pollutant measurement are defined in Table 19-1.

Note: Gross pollution generated directly and indirectly per million guilders of each sector's final demand; matrix $[P(I - A)^{-1}]'$.

Table 19-6. Cumulated 1973 Pollution Coefficients with Full Abatement

Number	Title	Pollutant per Million Guilders[a]						
		25	26	27	28	29	30	31
1	Agriculture	0.1335	0.7779	0.2033	1.0153	0.0972	0.0486	0.0220
2	Coal mining	0.0607	0.0740	0.0387	0.1518	0.0298	0.1548	0.0171
3	Other mining	0.0467	0.0949	0.0295	0.1971	0.2045	0.0296	0.0099
4	Animal foods	0.0445	1.0744	0.2068	1.0494	0.1382	0.0632	0.0289
5	Other foods	0.3567	2.0396	0.1377	0.7200	0.1791	0.0707	0.0266
6	Beverages & tobacco	0.3858	0.7112	0.0616	0.2771	0.0854	0.0365	0.0150
7	Textiles	0.9874	0.3484	0.1344	0.6627	0.4002	0.0873	0.0222
8	Clothing & footwear	0.3736	0.1635	0.0785	0.3415	0.1966	0.1482	0.0176
9	Paper & paper products	0.7437	1.5336	0.0855	0.6637	0.1730	0.0734	0.0158
10	Chemicals	0.3853	0.8239	0.2163	0.7449	0.1623	0.0580	0.0123
11	Oil refining	0.0854	0.1702	0.0337	4.0590	0.1332	0.0278	0.0082
12	Basic metals	0.0739	0.1572	0.0915	1.3267	0.1502	0.0594	0.0129
13	Metal products & machinery	0.0687	0.0840	0.0737	0.4230	0.1002	0.0836	0.0171
14	Electrical goods & machinery	0.0685	0.0800	0.0772	0.3068	0.0749	0.0696	0.0132
15	Transport equipment	0.1359	0.0724	0.0809	0.3110	0.1218	0.1007	0.0237
16	Other industries	0.1545	0.1909	0.2385	0.4573	0.1418	0.0902	0.0171
17	Public utilities	0.0360	0.0484	0.0629	2.8721	0.0562	0.0414	0.0096
18	Construction	0.0872	0.0990	0.1891	0.3045	0.1958	0.0993	0.0237
19	Wholesale & retail trade	0.0487	0.0541	0.0821	0.1775	0.0321	0.1149	0.0471
20	Ownership of dwellings	0.0165	0.0183	0.0335	0.0548	0.0339	0.0217	0.0045
21	Ocean & air transport	0.0710	0.0647	0.0720	0.2456	0.0328	0.0688	0.0391
22	Other transport	0.0356	0.0468	0.0742	0.2891	0.0299	0.0875	0.0694
23	Other services	0.1280	0.0985	0.0977	0.1863	0.0350	0.0990	0.0073
24	Not elsewhere specified	0.1320	0.1265	0.0997	0.2423	0.0423	0.0954	0.0141
25	Public waste-water treatment	0.1143	0.0087	0.0120	0.2437	1.4789	0.0076	0.0147
26	Private waste-water treatment & sanitation	0.4657	-0.4605	0.0021	0.4866	7.2229	0.0069	0.0622
27	Desulphurisation of gas oil	0.0263	0.0507	0.0164	0.6445	0.0288	0.0125	0.0032
28	Desulphurisation of residual oil	0.0263	0.0507	0.0164	8.6445	0.0288	0.0125	0.0033
29	Solid-waste management	4.1465	0.0318	0.0229	0.2600	0.3169	0.0160	0.1124
30	Adaptation of passenger cars	0.0477	0.0753	0.0216	1.6547	0.0655	0.0212	0.0057
31	Adaptation of trucks & vans	0.0477	0.0753	0.0216	1.6547	0.0655	0.0212	0.0057

[a]The numbering of the type of pollutant refers to abatement activities; this and the units of pollutant measurement are defined in Table 19–1.

Note: Gross pollution generated directly and indirectly per million guilders of each sector's final demand; matrix

Table 19-7. Pollution Content of Domestic Final Demand and Exports Minus Imports, 1968

Pollution	Unit	Domestic Final Demand	Exports Minus Imports
Water pollution by degradable organic matter	1000 BOD_5^{20}	44,110	2,502
Air pollution by sulphur dioxide generated by fuel combustion in stationary sources	1000 tons SO_2	639	5
Solid waste	1000 tons	8,871	−672
Air pollution by automotive transport	1000 cars	1,180	32

give a more specific answer to this problem provided that the amounts of different pollutants can be brought on a common denominator (for instance, abatement cost).

As shown earlier, the introduction of the "polluter pays" principle has price effects that can be ascertained rather precisely within an input-output framework. It is interesting to note that in the approach followed here, not only prices of conventional sectors change (that is, rise), but also prices of abatement activities, or rather the "polluter pays" charges per unit of eliminated pollutant. The results of computations for the intermediate and long-run cases are summarised in Table 19-8 for different categories of final demand. Resulting price changes per sector are presented in Table 19-9.

Leontief and Ford [4] expressed the suspicion that assuming the matrices E and Q (or, alternatively, the matrices B and D) to be zero matrices results in a general underestimation of the repercussions on the industrial price structure of pollution-abatement measures. This suspicion is strongly confirmed by the empirical results of the computations for the Netherlands. This, of course, is already apparent from the differences found between cumulated (gross) pollution coefficients with and without pollution abatement. The results of computations for price repercussions reinforce this conclusion, because prices of eliminating a unit of pollutant rise, as well. It is particularly striking that the price increase per sector is largest for the abatement activities. From Table 19-9, it appears that this price effect is concentrated in solid-waste management, which activity requires relatively expensive inputs from the waste-water-treatment sector in order to prevent water pollution.

Conclusion

Economic aspects of environmental analysis can be dealt with adequately within the framework of conventional input-output analysis. The "polluter pays" prin-

Table 19–8. Percentage Change of Final Demand Prices as a Consequence of the Enforcement of Pollution Abatement

	Intermediate Case	Long-run Case
Private consumption	0.25	1.84
Private investment	0.14	1.19
Exports	0.32	2.23
Total final demand[a]	0.23	1.74

[a]Includes stockbuilding.

Table 19–9. Percentage Changes of Output Prices of Each Sector as a Consequence of the Enforcement of Pollution Abatement

Sector		Intermediate Case	Long-run Case
Number	Title		
1	Agriculture	0.22	1.67
2	Coal mining	0.10	0.96
3	Other mining	0.12	0.81
4	Animal foods	0.59	3.51
5	Other foods	0.53	3.57
6	Beverages & tobacco	0.47	2.64
7	Textiles	1.00	6.25
8	Clothing & footwear	0.33	2.86
9	Paper & paper products	0.84	5.16
10	Chemicals	0.47	2.99
11	Oil refining	0.11	1.65
12	Basic metals	0.12	1.21
13	Metal products & machinery	0.11	0.97
14	Electrical goods & machinery	0.09	0.84
15	Transport equipment	0.19	1.39
16	Other industries	0.22	1.56
17	Public utilities	0.06	1.03
18	Construction	0.18	1.30
19	Wholesale & retail trade	0.11	0.90
20	Ownership of dwellings	0.03	0.25
21	Ocean & air transport	0.08	0.86
22	Other transport	0.09	0.86
23	Other services	0.18	1.12
24	Not elsewhere specified	0.11	1.19
25	Public waste-water treatment	0.67	3.35
26	Private waste-water treatment & sanitation	3.14	15.29
27	Desulphurisation of gas oil	0.03	1.94
28	Desulphurisation of residual oil	0.03	1.94
29	Solid-waste management	4.55	21.57
30	Adaptation of passenger cars	0.06	0.80
31	Adaptation of trucks & vans	0.06	0.80

ciple serves as a closing piece for integrating the impact of the burden and its incidence into the input-output framework. The input-output system set forth on this basis is applied to empirical data for the Netherlands.

The computations presented disclose noticeable effects of the introduction of pollution abatement. These effects, however, do not appear to be very drastic, at least not at the level of aggregation considered in the analysis here. This is because the total output of abatement activities is relatively small compared with the output of other activities and because, compared with the input structure of conventional sectors, the ratio of secondary inputs to primary inputs is relatively low in abatement activities.

Of course, this is not to say that the enforcement of pollution abatement does not cause problems. At the firm level, such problems may in some instances be serious, if not insurmountable. Generally speaking, transitional problems remain important. And this still does not take into account the macroeconomic problem of providing the investment funds to throw into gear pollution-abatement facilities needed to catch up with the backlog in abatement, at least in the Netherlands. This problem is of particular interest in view of the high level of capital intensity in abatement activities as compared with that level in most of the conventional sectors.

Though the empirical data used are not in all instances truly representative and therefore the computations presented here are preliminary, further advance in this empirical inquiry will depend not only on a revision of the data used, but even more on an extension of the inquiry to other kinds of pollution and pollution abatement.

References

1. Central Bureau of Statistics of the Netherlands. *De Produktiestructuur van de Nederlandse Volkshuishouding.* Deel VI, *Input-Output Tabellen 1968–1970* [The Structure of Production of the Netherlands Economy. Vol. VI, Input-Output Tables 1968–1970]. The Hague: Central Bureau of Statistics, 1974.

2. Den Hartog, H.; A. Houweling; and H.S. Tjan. *The Economic Impact of Pollution Abatement: The Case of Water Pollution by Degradable Organic Matter.* Occasional Papers No. 1/1973. The Hague: Central Planning Bureau, 1973.

3. Leontief, W. "Environmental Repercussions and the Economic Structure: An Input-Output Approach." *The Review of Economics and Statistics* 52, no. 3 (August 1970): 262–271.

4. Leontief, W., and D. Ford. "Air Pollution and the Economic Structure: Empirical Results of Input-Output Computations." In *Input-Output Techniques.* Edited by A. Bródy and A.P. Carter. Amsterdam: North-Holland Publishing Company, 1972. Pp. 9–30.

5. United Nations, Statistical Office. *International Standard Industrial Classification of All Economic Activities.* Statistical Papers, Series M, no. 4, rev. 1. New York: United Nations, 1958.

6. United Nations, Statistical Office. *International Standard Industrial Classification of all Economic Activities.* Statistical Papers, Series M, no. 4, rev. 2. New York: United Nations, 1968.

Appendix 19A

Table 19A-1. Sector List

Number	Title	ISIC 1958[a]	ISIC 1968[b]
	Conventional Sector		
1	Agriculture	01, 02, 04	1
2	Coal mining	11	21
3	Other mining	13, 14, 19	22, 23, 29
4	Animal foods	pt. 20	pt. 311, pt. 312
5	Other foods	pt. 20	pt. 311, pt. 312
6	Beverages & tobacco	21, 22	313, 314
7	Textiles	23	321
8	Clothing & footwear	24	322, 324
9	Paper & paper products	27	34
10	Chemicals	31	35 (excl. 353, 355)
11	Oil refining	32	353
12	Basic metals	34	37
13	Metal products & machinery	35, 36	38 (excl. 383, 384, 385)
14	Electrical goods & machinery	37	383
15	Transport equipment	38	384
16	Other industries	25, 26, 28, 29, 30, 33, 39	323, 355, 385 33, 36, 39
17	Public utilities	51, 52	4
–	Manufacturing	11, 13, 14, 19–39, 51, 52	3, 4
18	Construction	40	5
19	Wholesale & retail trade	61	61, 62
20	Ownership of dwellings	64	831
21	Ocean & air transport	pt. 71	pt. 712, pt. 713
22	Other transport	pt. 71, 72, 73	71 (excl. pt. 712, pt. 713), 72
23	Other services	62, 63, 82, 83, 84	631, 632; 8 (excl. 831), 9

(continued)

Table 19A–1 continued

	Conventional Sector	ISIC 1958[a]	ISIC 1968[b]
Num-ber	Title		
–	Services		6, 7, 8, 9
24	Not elsewhere specified		00

[a]United Nations, Statistical Office. *International Standard Industrial Classification of All Economic Activities.* Statistical Papers, Series M, no. 4, rev. 1. New York: United Nations, 1958.

[b]United Nations, Statistical Office. *International Standard Industrial Classification of All Economic Activities.* Statistical Papers, Series M, no. 4, rev. 2. New York: United Nations, 1968.

Chapter Twenty

A Generalized Input-Output Model
for Residuals Management

Rainer Thoss

This is a progress report on the construction of a generalized input-output
linear programming model for environmental policy.[1] The purpose of the model
is to provide decision makers who are concerned with residuals management
with a means of finding targets that will be generally accepted and of finding the
proper levels of the instrument variables required to reach those targets.

In recent years it has become obvious that to improve the quality of life,
societies must not only accept certain environmental limits on the production of
goods and services, but must also conserve natural resources for present and
future generations. And it is here that conflicts of interest arise. How much of
scarce factors of production should be used to avoid damage to persons or to the
biosphere (and thus indirectly to persons)? It is clear that structural change must
be channeled in a direction that allows certain economic requirements to be met,
while at the same time keeping ecological damage within tolerable bounds, and
equally clear that the final objective of any environmental protection policy must
be to accomplish this in the most efficient way.

To find such a mutually balanced set of generally accepted economic and
environmental targets is a very difficult task. But not an impossible one, given
that decision makers use policy models with flexible targets to provide reliable
information about the opportunity costs of various social-economic alternatives.[2]
Shadow prices and sensitivity analysis can provide them with a rational basis for
determining acceptable targets. An iterative procedure can be used to review and
revise the original value judgements.

The author acknowledges the help of K. Wiik and A. Hermann with computations and of
H.P. Döllekes and P. Brasse with data collection and estimation of parameters.

1. In previous reports on our model, water pollution and air pollution were treated
separately. See Thoss and Wiik [23] and Thoss and Döllekes [22].

2. See Tinbergen [24, pp. 7–14]; Theil [20, pp. 385–395]; and Hickman (Ed.) [7, pp.
2–6].

General Features of the Model

Before presenting the model equations, some general characteristics of the model should be outlined.

Unlike most other input-output models, the purpose of the model is not to forecast the probable future structure of the German economy, but rather to search for possibilities of structural change that will reduce environmental pollution.[3] Hence a closed input-output model was used as the central part of the equation system. The open model was closed by adding a number of equations and inequalities that link the components of final demand to the value added of particular production sectors. Without specification of additional conditions, however, only relative amounts of output by sector (or commodity) could be determined. We therefore needed an additional method of determining absolute levels of output.

It is customary in most input-output studies to assume that each sector produces only one commodity (or one product mix) and that the same commodity is produced by only one sector. For most sectors, we followed this convention. For energy, however, we made an exception in that 34 commodities (types of energy) may be produced by 34 processes (as main products or as by-products) in 6 sectors. In this respect, our model is quite similar to the Isard [8, p. 85] and Victor [28, p. 53] models.

Our model contains two types of joint production: that of the 34 types of energy and that of pollution. Most of the energy sectors produce more than one energy commodity in fixed proportions (gas and coke in cokeries, or gasoline, light oil, and heavy oil in refineries, for example). Wherever joint production is specified, more than one positive coefficient must appear in the column of the respective sector, commodity, or process.

The basic aim of our analysis is to allow for substitution of inputs rather than to force inputs to be used in fixed proportions. This has the following three consequences: First, whenever more than one sector contributes to total domestic output of a commodity, the proportions among commodities are allowed to vary. (Each process is assumed, however, to use commodities in fixed proportions.) The sector that employs the cleaner technology should increase its market share. Such technological flexibility (change in product mix) can become a possible means of restructuring the economy.

Second, there is the possibility of substitution between different processes within the same sector. As in the first case, the assumption of fixed proportions is maintained for each process, but a possibility of choice exists between processes that differ with respect to the relative size of negative (input) or positive (output) coefficients. We treat as cases of process substitution the installation of

3. For a comparative survey of environmental input-output models, see Victor [28, pp. 25–50].

in-plant devices for environmental protection as well as the substitution of inputs of raw materials by recycled products.[4] In other words, we assume that for each sector a choice can be made between several processes (each using commodities in fixed proportions), each with different amounts of undesired by-products to be discharged into the environment.

Third, there is the possibility of unlimited substitution. This can only occur for energy-input commodities in electricity generation, for which the assumption of fixed proportions of energy sources is dropped. Inclusion of substitution options in a generalized input-output framework means that there must be more than one positive coefficient in the respective rows of the transactions matrix.[5]

The model is static in that changes in output levels are not related to changes of capital stocks. This assumption implies that any sector can expand production without augmenting fixed capital and that, on the other hand, sectors receiving capital goods need not expand output. (At a later stage, attempts will be made to relax this rather unrealistic assumption.) The only factor of production explicitly related to output is labour. For this factor of production, recursive relations which permit the time path of structural development to be simulated are included in the model.[6]

Productive activities and treatment activities are interconnected by "pollutants-balance equations," a system of accounts that shows the origins of the different residuals and that determines the levels of any pollution-abatement activities [9; 14, p. 262; 15, p. 9]. Quantities of pollutants not eliminated are assumed to be discharged into the natural environment (air, water) and there to cause damage either to the elements of the ecosystems or directly to human beings. It would be appropriate to specify in the pollutants balances the regenerative effect of the environment, as well. In addition, the harmful effects on the elements of the ecosystem measured per unit of pollution could be included. In this way, a feedback into the economic system through the ecologic system could be constructed. We have not, however, been able to estimate such damage functions.[7] This means that externalities are not considered in the results furnished here.

Even in a model with damage functions, the optimal structure of the economy could not be determined entirely by comparing economic benefits and environmental costs. Rather, certain environmental restrictions must be imposed on the solution, because any solution that depends on the benefit-cost criterion alone may lead to a considerable amount of pollution if the benefits are only large enough to exactly compensate for the damages.[8] In Germany, the people seem

4. See the remarks on recycling in Victor [28, pp. 49–50].
5. See Chenery and Clark [4, p. 111]; Koopmans [11, pp. 33–97]; and Georgescu-Roegen [6].
6. For the methodology of recursive programming, see Day [5].
7. But see, for example, Lave and Seskin [13, p. 723].
8. See Turvey [25, p. 310].

to prefer pollution abatement even if costs are higher than benefits. For this reason, we introduced effluent constraints for the amounts of pollution. If those constraints are set low enough, economic activity has only negligible adverse effects on the ecological and economic systems, so that the omission of damage functions does not create severe difficulties.

In a closed input-output model, absolute levels of production have to be determined exogenously. One way would be to minimize cost while guaranteeing a certain level of output. This approach is frequently applied in sectoral and microeconomic studies, because in partial analyses it can be assumed that saving of resources will not lead to unemployment in general, but will only make those resources available to other sectors.[9] On the other hand, for the economy as a whole, it seems more logical to look for solutions that will provide full employment of available factors. Maximization of output subject to full employment and environmental quality constraints provides an economic structure and production techniques that most efficiently protect the environment and enhance economic welfare.

Activities

Four groups of activities were defined: production sectors, energy commodities, pollution abatement, and pollution.

For the specification of the target composition of final demand, Y, we use the variables defined by the following vectors:

C_{pr} = private consumption

C_{st} = public consumption

ΔK = investment

E = exports

M = imports

ΔV = change of stocks

The economy is disaggregated into 56 production sectors, as shown in Table 20A-1, with X_i describing the amount of output of sector i in millions of Deutsche marks. Six sectors produce energy commodities, namely

2 Electricity & heat

3 Gas & water

4 Coal

7 Petroleum & natural gas

10 Iron & steel production

15 Petroleum refining

9. See, for example, Kneese and Bower [10, pp. 92–93] and Russell [16, pp. 20–21].

The 34 commodities produced by the 6 energy sectors are listed in Table 20A-2. They are measured in 100 tons of coal-equivalent units.

For the six industrial sectors shown in Table 20-1, alternative production technologies are available. They either have different input-output relations (efficiency levels) with respect to inputs or outputs of energy commodities or lead to different amounts of pollutants per unit of output. The latter may be caused either by recycling or installation of pollution-abatement devices.

Because unlimited substitution exists between energy inputs in the four processes of electricity production, activities must be defined that convert different types of energy into alternative inputs for electricity generation. Choice of inputs of energy then determines choice of activities. Such activities use one unit of input of an energy commodity, p ($p = 1, \ldots, 34$), and transform it into one unit of input for the processes of Sector 2, Electricity & heat.

Table 20-1. Alternative Production Processes

Sector		*Process*	
Number	*Title*	*Number*	*Main Characteristic of Process*
2	Electricity & heat	2.1	Main input: Fossils (low efficiency)
		2.2	Main input: Fossils (medium efficiency)
		2.3	Main input: Fossils (high efficiency)
		2.4	Main input: Fossils (output heat)
		2.5	Main input: Nuclear power
		2.6	Main input: Water power
4	Coal	4.1	Main output: Coke
		4.2	Main output: Coal
		4.3	Main output: Brown coal
		4.4	Main output: Brown-coal briquettes
		4.5	Main output: Pitch coal
7	Petroleum & natural gas	7.1	Main output: Oil
		7.2	Main output: Gas
10	Iron & steel production	10.1	Main input: Ore
		10.2	Main input: Scrap
		10.3	Main output: Low pollution per unit of output
13	Nonferrous metals	13.1	Main input: Ore
		13.2	Main input: Scrap
		13.3	Main output: Low pollution per unit of output
18	Pulp & paper	18.1	Main input: Wood
		18.2	Main input: Waste paper
		18.3	Main output: Low pollution per unit of output

Formal Structure of the Model

Figure 20-1 shows the structure of the system of equations and inequalities. Different final demand components are kept as a fixed proportion of the gross national product (GNP). Therefore, GNP (which is designated as Y) is defined as the sum of value added in all sectors (or processes)

$$Y = \sum_i \sum_k w_i^k X_i^k \qquad i = 1, \ldots, 56 \tag{20-1}$$

where

i = sector

k = process of production

w_i^k = amount of value added per unit of output

X_i^k = level of output produced by sector i with process k.

Recently, the government of the Federal Republic of Germany published target values for the composition of the GNP [3], which we use as a standard. The shares of private consumption (C_{pr}) and public consumption (C_{st}), private and public investment (ΔK), and the trade balance ($E - M$)—exports minus imports—must be within certain upper and lower limits of the GNP:

$$0.54Y \leqslant C_{pr} \quad \leqslant 0.57Y \tag{20-2}$$

$$0.14Y \leqslant C_{st} \quad \leqslant 0.17Y \tag{20-3}$$

$$0.26Y \leqslant \Delta K \quad \leqslant 0.29Y \tag{20-4}$$

$$0.01Y \leqslant E - M \leqslant 0.02Y \tag{20-5}$$

Constraints (20-1) to (20-5) are shown in the upper left part of Figure 20-1.

The next section of Figure 20-1 shows the interindustry relations [18]. The input-output matrix describes the interdependencies between the 56 production sectors

$$\sum_k X_i^k = \sum_j \sum_k a_{ij}^k X_j^k + c_i C_{pr} + d_i C_{st} + b_i \,\Delta K + e_i E + \Delta V_i \quad i = 1, \ldots, 56 \tag{20-6}$$

The total gross output of a sector i (produced by all processes k) is denoted as the $\sum_k X_i^k$. The a_{ij}^k's are the constant input coefficients. The constant coefficients $c_i, d_i, b_i,$ and e_i indicate the sectoral composition of private and public consumption, investment, and exports, respectively. The final demand variables,

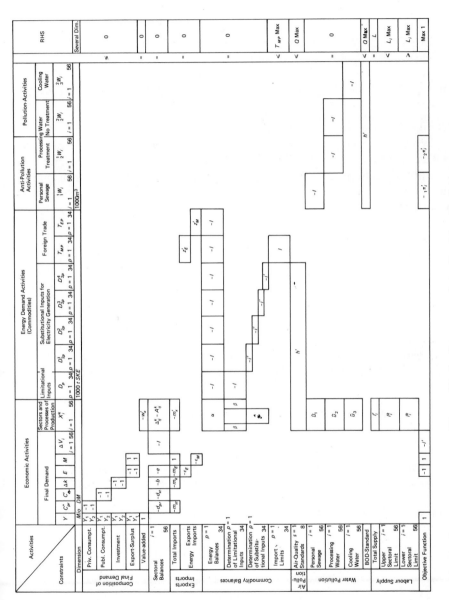

Figure 20-1. Structure of the Decision Model.

C_{pr}, C_{st}, ΔK, E, and ΔV_i, have already been defined. As mentioned earlier, to introduce alternative "clean" processes without augmenting the number of equations increases the degrees of freedom. Summation over k in equation (20-6) means that outputs of different processes are substitutable.

Equation (20-7) defines total imports, M, assuming that sectoral imports are fixed proportions, m_i, of gross output

$$M = \sum_i \sum_k m_i^k X_i^k + m_C(C_{pr} + C_{st}) + m_K \Delta K + m_E E + m_V \Delta V \qquad (20\text{-}7)$$

The difference between exports and imports is determined, by constraint (20-5).

Demand for energy is one of the most important causes of environmental pollution. Thus, substitution of clean energy processes for polluting ones must be a primary concern in environmental protection planning. We therefore introduce the possibility of choice between different energy commodities, each of which is supplied either from domestic production or from imports. The total amount of energy must equal the energy inputs for electricity production plus those required for all other purposes

$$\sum_k \sum_j \alpha_{pj}^k X_j^k + T_{Mp} - T_{Ep} = D_p + \sum_k D_{2p}^k \qquad p = 1, \ldots, 34 \qquad (20\text{-}8)$$

where T_{Mp} and T_{Ep} are quantities of all goods of type p imported and exported, and α_{pj}^k is the amount of output per unit of activity j. Of course, some of these activities may produce several types of output, so that there may be several positive coefficients α_{pj}^k in some of the columns. Fortunately, the necessary statistical information about supply of and demand for energy is available in the form of energy balances.[10]

The energy balances may be used to determine the necessary output levels for each commodity if demand (and foreign trade) is known. The next step, then, is to determine demand by another set of constraints. To allow substitution in the electricity sector, total demand for energy commodities is split into two parts. The first part is energy used in Sector 2, Electricity. For all processes in this sector, it is assumed that unlimited substitution of energy sources is feasible

$$\gamma^k X_2^k = \sum_p D_{2p}^k \qquad k = 1, 2, 3, 4 \qquad (20\text{-}9)$$

The second part is energy demanded by all other sectors (processes), which use energy inputs in fixed proportions

$$\sum_j \sum_k \beta_{pj}^k X_j^k = D_p \qquad \begin{aligned} p &= 1, \ldots, 34 \\ j &\neq 2 \end{aligned} \qquad (20\text{-}10)$$

10. See Arbeitsgemeinschaft Energiebilanzen [1].

where β_{pj}^k is the (constant) amount of energy of type p used per unit of output of process k in sector j.

To secure consistency of sectoral balances and commodity balances with respect to foreign trade, we have to define

$$\sum_i e_i E = \sum_p z_p T_{Ep} \qquad (20\text{-}11)$$
$$i = 2, 3, 4, 8, 10, 15$$
$$\sum_i m_i X_i = \sum_p z_p T_{Mp} \qquad (20\text{-}12)$$

where z_p is the average price of one unit of commodity p.

The explicit differentiation of imports by commodities is of special interest in periods of energy shortage. A reduction of petroleum imports, for instance, must be compensated for by increasing production of substitutable energy commodities. Information about likely structural change as a consequence of a reduction of energy imports is a useful by-product of our model. To study those effects on the economy and the ecology of our country, we must introduce alternative import constraints

$$T_{Mp} \leqslant (1 - \sigma_p) T_{Mp} (t-1) \qquad p = 1, \ldots, 34 \qquad (20\text{-}13)$$

where σ_p is the anticipated decrease in imports.

A comprehensive model would have to contain all factors of production that are scarce during the planning period or that will become scarce in the future. So far, however, we have not succeeded in incorporating capital and land into our model; all these factors are treated as if they were not scarce. Real fixed capital is produced by the system, but no set of equations specifies the need of this factor in the different sectors of the economy. This, of course, is a serious short-coming, because not all costs of production are considered in the calculation of the optimal solution. One way to incorporate capital and improve the model would be to include capital as part of a dynamic input-output model.[11] Another way to introduce capital would be to incorporate sectoral production functions that allow for substitution between capital and labour.[12] According to our experience, this would give a more realistic picture of the German economy [21, p. 66]. In this present version of the model, however, only labour is considered as a scarce factor, and both total and sectoral labour supply are limited

$$\sum_i \sum_k l_i X_i^k \leqslant L \qquad (20\text{-}14)$$

Change of employment in each sector is limited to ±20 percent within a period:

---

11. See Sugiyama [19].
12. See Schumann [17, p. 417].

$$1.2L_i(t-1) \geqslant \sum_k l_i X_i^k \geqslant 0.8 L_i(t-1) \qquad i = 1, \ldots, 56 \qquad (20\text{-}15)$$

These constraints guarantee that sectoral employment cannot expand or drop too rapidly, which is an important social condition of structural change.

The dependence of the discharge of residuals on industrial production and on the consumption of energy commodities is expressed by constant discharge coefficients. Production and energy consumption pollute the natural environment by emissions of noxious substances. Pollutants balances show the sources of those substances and their impacts on other parts of the system. The following nine residuals, s, are considered:

1	Carbon monoxide	6	Fluorides
2	Carbon dioxide	7	Chlorides
3	Hydrocarbons	8	Particulates
4	Sulfur dioxide	9	Biochemical oxygen demand
5	Nitrogen oxides		

The first eight residuals are discharged into the air, the ninth into surface water.

The total amount of air pollution is found by adding the amounts resulting from energy consumption and from production.[13] For each residual, s, this total sum should not be greater than the effluent standards, Q_s. This leads to

$$\sum_j \sum_k H_{sj}^k X_j^k + \sum_p h_{sp} D_p + \sum_k \sum_p h_{sp} D_{2p}^k \leqslant Q_s \qquad s = 1, \ldots, 8 \qquad (20\text{-}16)$$

where

s = type of pollutant

j = sectors

k = processes

p = energy type

h_{sj}^k = (constant) amount of pollutants of type s emitted per unit of output

h_{sp} = (constant) amount of pollutants of type s emitted per unit of energy consumed

Like all input-output coefficients, the coefficients h_{sj}^k and h_{sp} represent certain techniques of production and certain methods of environmental protection in establishments. The latter show the impacts of the installation of a certain technology that destroys, detoxicates, or reduces waste materials and/or

13. For a more detailed model of air pollution, see Thoss and Döllekes [22, pp. 77-106].

recycles them back to the production process. They are estimated as constant proportions of the corresponding consumption of energy commodities, p, and gross production values of the emitting sectors, j, respectively, and are measured in physical terms. They were derived from technical and business literature and from discussions with experts in industry.

In order to depict the relationship between water pollution by organic and toxic material (measured as biochemical oxygen demand—BOD) and the economic system, we define three types of waste-water balances: personal sewage, processing water, and cooling water.[14] For the personal sewage, treatment is obligatory. For processing water, the system contains a possibility of choice between discharging with or without treatment (according to factor constraints and environmental standards), even though the discharge of untreated processing water causes pollution of streams by organic materials (and toxic substances). For cooling water, no treatment is required.

As noted earlier, pollution-abatement activities for public sewage treatment are specified only for waste water and are measured in terms of units of sewage treated (millions of cubic metres). These activities use "waste water" as an input and produce "treated waste water" with a substantially reduced BOD load. Thus, they eliminate one pollutant and produce another. For simplicity in the present version of this model, the demands for intermediate and primary inputs by pollution-abatement activities are not explicitly specified. Rather, an a priori estimate of the opportunity cost of waste-water treatment (quantity of goods and services forgone by allocating resources to the treatment of sewage) is subtracted in the objective function.

These sets of waste-water balances link economic activities and BOD production

$$W_H + \sum_k {}_1u_i^k X_{i\cdot}^k = {}_1^1 W_i \tag{20-17}$$

$$\sum_k {}_2u_i^k X_i^k = {}_1^1 W_i + {}_2^2 W_i \tag{20-18}$$

$$\sum_k {}_3u_i^k X_i^k = {}_3^2 W_i \tag{20-19}$$

where $i = 1, \ldots, 56$ for $i \neq 55$. Superscript 1 = pollution-abatement activity; superscript 2 = pollution activity; subscript 1 = personal sewage; subscript 2 = processing water; and subscript 3 = cooling water. The amount of household sewage, W_H, is given exogenously. In these balances, ${}_1^1 W_i$ stands for (treated) personal sewage, ${}_2^1 W_i$ for (treated) processing water, ${}_2^2 W_i$ for (untreated) processing water, and ${}_3^2 W_i$ for (untreated) cooling water. The constant coefficients ${}_1u_i$,

14. For a multiregional study of water pollution in the Ruhr Basin with more detailed treatment of pollutants, see Thoss and Wiik [23, pp. 21, 104–141].

$_2 u_i$, and $_3 u_i$ give the amounts of waste water per unit of output per day. For these activities, no other inputs are specified, so that some correction π_i has to be made in the objective function. The value of π_i depends on the quantity of BOD removed per unit of waste water.

The supply of dissolved oxygen from atmospheric re-aeration and the capacity of streams for self-purification are mainly functions of the load of organic material, which determines the total metabolism of river water as a water-quality criterion. The total amount of BOD discharged into the rivers should be smaller than or equal to the BOD standard, Q_9

$$\sum_i \left[{_1^1} h_{i1} W_i + {_2^1} h_{i2} W_i + {_2^2} h_{i2} W_i + {_3^2} h_{i3} W_i \right] \leqslant Q_9 \tag{20-20}$$

where h is the content of organic material per cubic metre of waste water.

In order to find the limits to growth (subject to the economic and ecological constraints listed), we must maximize production, but we want the least possible amount of resources to be devoted to exports, stocks, and pollution-abatement activities. The objective function for the model is to maximize

$$\text{Max } Z = Y - (E - M) - \sum_i \Delta V_i - \sum_i {_1} \pi_{i1}^1 W_i - \sum_i {_2} \pi_{i2}^1 W_i \tag{20-21}$$

This gives a solution in which the gross national product, Y, is as large as possible, but in which the export surplus, the (involuntary) increase of stocks, and the expenses for water treatment—the last four terms on the right-hand side of equation (20-21)—are as small as possible.

Results

With the model just presented, we calculated the optimal structure of the West German economy according to a preliminary set of constraints and compared it with the observed structure to find the optimal direction of structural change. As is well known, however, activity analysis also provides valuable information for the revision of the preliminary constraints, because the opportunity costs of all constraints can be studied.

Structural Change (Primal Variables)

As pointed out earlier, adjustment of the economy to new situations is only possible on a step-by-step basis. In this respect, there is no important difference between adjustment to new constraints (such as environmental protection) and adjustment to new supply conditions of raw materials (such as oil). In any case, adaptation takes time, because structural relations change slowly.

To compare changes in the relative sizes of different sectors, it is most convenient to use employment figures, $l_i X_i$. Table 20-2 shows the percentage differences between the calculated and actual 1970 employment.

Table 20-2. Optimal Change of Employment (compared with 1970)

Sector	Change (percent)	Sector	Change (percent)	Sector	Change (percent)
1	+8.26	21	+9.89	41	−20.00
2	+20.00	22	+4.13	42	+4.41
3	+13.36	23	+13.33	43	+7.18
4	+8.91	24	+6.76	44	+0.00
5	+20.00	25	+8.70	45	+17.46
6	+10.99	26	+13.59	46	+11.36
7	+20.00	27	+10.32	47	+6.68
8	+20.00	28	+9.80	48	+10.21
9	+14.78	29	+9.63	49	+7.47
10	+0.32	30	+9.68	50	−1.40
11	+13.44	31	+6.23	51	+10.88
12	+11.73	32	+9.09	52	+9.86
13	+6.66	33	+10.12	53 } 54	−5.19
14	+9.47	34	+9.28	55	+20.00
15	+10.82	35	+6.10	56	+7.31
16	+9.64	36	+7.79		
17	+13.71	37	+7.48		
18	−20.00	38	+9.51		
19	+16.06	39	+6.00		
20	+12.61	40	+12.96		

Table 20-3. Optimal Change in the Market Shares of the Energy Commodities

Commodity	Change (percent)	Commodity	Change (percent)	Commodity	Change (percent)
C1	+13.5	C13	−3.3	C25	−0.7
C2	−12.7	C14	−6.5	C26	+69.3
C3	+19.7	C15	−4.3	C27	+0.0
C4	−7.5	C16	−19.4	C28	+82.7
C5	−18.3	C17	+7.7	C29	+0.0
C6	+87.2	C18	+9.0	C30	+73.5
C7	+23.5	C19	+0.0	C31	−86.2
C8	+103.5	C20	−19.0	C32	+105.3
C9	−4.0	C21	−49.0	C33	−1.4
C10	−6.6	C22	+72.0	C34	+0.0
C11	−12.8	C23	−2.5		
C12	+77.0	C24	−29.0		

In order to reduce pollution, the 1970 commodity mix of the energy sectors shown in Table 20-3 should be changed. The table shows that the use of clean energy like C1, Electricity, and C3, Gas, should be expanded.

Because of the close relationship between commodities and processes in the energy sectors, there are also substantial changes in the process mix of those sectors. Under the conditions specified by the model, the following substitutions of processes should be carried out:

Sector 2, Electricity & heat: Levels of processes 2 (Fossils, medium efficiency) and 6 (Water power) should be extended; levels of the other four processes (1, 3, 4, and 5) should remain unchanged.

Sector 4, Coal: Levels of processes 1 (Coke), 4 (Brown-coal briquettes), and 5 (Pitch coal) should be extended; levels of processes 2 and 3 (Coal and Brown coal) should be reduced as much as possible because of serious pollution problems.

Sector 7, Petroleum & natural gas: It would be preferable to produce more oil (process 1) instead of natural gas (process 2). This finding is probably due to the by-products of petroleum refining.

Sector 10, Iron & steel: Processes 1 and 2 (use of Ore and Scrap) should contribute equally to total output, whereas the "clean" process 3 should not be used at all.

Sector 13, Nonferrous metals: Only the "clean" process 3 should be used.

Sector 18, Pulp & paper: Only the "clean" process 3 should be used.

Of special interest is the process mix suggested for Sector 10, Iron & steel. At first sight, it would seem plausible that in this sector special emphasis should be given to a direct reduction of pollution by applying process 3. However, by using processes 1 and 2, the input of coke and the output of sulfur dioxide can be reduced substantially, and since the model is especially sensitive to sulfur dioxide (with present standards), those processes are to be preferred.

The BOD standard, Q_9, in the Federal Republic of Germany is not very strict at present. Therefore, although treatment of personal and household sewage is universally obligatory, treatment of processing water is obligatory for only a few sectors: namely, Sector 4, Coal (50 percent); Sector 6, Potash; Sector 14, Chemicals; Sector 15, Petroleum refining; and Sector 24, Electrical and electronics. About 50 percent of the processing water may go without treatment in Sector 4 because the present BOD standard does not require a higher level of the treatment activities.

Opportunity Costs of Constraints (Dual Variables)
For the discussion and revision of preliminary constraints, the dual solution of the model is of great importance because it shows the consequences of any relaxation or tightening of the constraints.

Environmental Constraints: Of the nine pollutants considered in the model, only the three shown in Table 20-4 are relevant in terms of the environmental restrictions: 1, Carbon monoxide; 4, Sulfur dioxide; and 9, Biochemical oxygen demand. (The other substances are not produced in amounts large enough to reach the environmental limits.)

If decision makers would allow one additional unit of sulfur dioxide to be discharged into the biosphere, for example, an additional 0.00607 million Deutsche marks' worth of GNP could be produced. Keeping economic activity low enough so as not to exceed the effluent standards for these pollutants means that the economy as a whole has to give up goods and services that otherwise could be produced. This is the price that society must pay for environmental protection. Naturally, negative external effects also would rise considerably if standards were relaxed, whereas if they were strictly enforced, the social welfare gained by avoiding the negative effects of pollution would probably be greater than the social welfare lost as a result of the GNP forgone.

Economic Constraints: Not only do the environmental restrictions keep the economy from reaching a higher GNP, but also some of the economic targets are in conflict with this objective. For instance, a decrease in private consumption by one unit would lead to an increase of GNP by 0.145 units, and a decrease in the export surplus would lead to an increase of 1.153 units. Also, protection of employment in some sectors is in conflict with the maximization of output, as specified by the objective function (20-21). The opportunity costs of protecting sectoral employment from rapid decline are shown in the top part of Table 20-5. The reason for those costs is that employment in these sectors is not available for alternative—ecologically and economically more efficient—employment opportunities, and therefore must be regarded as a loss to society.

Scarcity of Labour Supply: In five sectors, employment should be increased by more than 20 percent, but the labour market cannot provide the number of workers that would be required. The sectors are shown in Table 20-5. If employment condition (20-11) is relaxed by one unit—for instance, by permitting immigration of 1000 foreign workers—, then the gross national product of the Federal Republic of Germany could be augmented by 5.93 million Deutsche

Table 20-4. Opportunity Costs for Pollutants (million Deutsche marks)

Pollutant	Opportunity Cost
1 Carbon monoxide	.00476
4 Sulfur dioxide	.00607
9 Biochemical oxygen demand	.07407

Table 20-5. Opportunity Costs of Sectoral Employment (million Deutsche marks per 1000 persons)

Sector		Opportunity Cost
Num-ber	Title	
	Sectors Where Employment Should be Decreased	
8	Other mining	28.46
18	Pulp & paper	79.11
41	Brewing & malting	60.80
	Sectors Where Employment Should Be Increased	
2	Electricity & heat	89.07
5	Iron ore mining	79.43
7	Petroleum & natural gas	2024.16
55	Government	1.29

marks per year. This is the opportunity cost of the social and political goal to limit the inflow of foreign workers into the Federal Republic.

Waste-Water Discharge: The shadow prices of the waste-water balances are of special interest for the political discussion of measures to improve the quality of surface water. If it were possible to reduce discharge coefficients, u_i, enough to cut ceteris paribus waste-water discharge by one unit, the GNP could be increased without any decline in the quality of the environment. The dual variables therefore indicate the priority that should be given to sectoral pollution-abatement policy. As an example, shadow prices for processing water and personal sewage are listed in Table 20-6.

Extensions

As was pointed out in the beginning, this is a report on a long-term research project. In our further work, we will attempt to improve the model, especially by including regional, dynamic, and ecologic relations.

Regional Analysis

Construction of regional models is clearly one of the preconditions of realistic environmental decision making. The solution of such a model not only answers the questions of what, how much, and how to produce, but also answers the question of where to locate establishments. In the study of water pollution cited above [23], we worked with a four-region model. In the UNESCO programme "Man and Biosphere," work on a regionalized model will be continued. For this

Table 20-6. Opportunity Costs of Processing Water and Personal Water
(Deutsche marks)

Sector Number[a]	Processing Water	Personal Water	Sector Number[a]	Processing Water	Personal Water
1	–	–	19–25	10[b]	40[c]
2	–	10	26	70	40
3	–	10	27	10	40
4	90	40	28	20	40
5	30	40	29	20	40
6	40	40	30	20	40
7	20	40	31	20	40
8	10	40	32	30	40
9	20	40	33	40	40
10.1	30	40	34	20	40
10.2	30	40	35	60	40
10.3	10	–	36	150	40
11	60	40	37	10	40
12	40	40	38	20	40
13.1	30	40	39	60	40
13.2	70	40	40	180	40
13.3	30	40	41	120	40
14	300	40	42	30	40
15	80	40	43	90	40
16	30	40	44	–	40
17	90	40	45–56	–	10[b]
18.1	180	–			
18.2	30	40			
18.3	30	40			

[a]Numbers to the right of the decimal indicate the process number.
[b]The opportunity cost of each sector is equal to 10.
[c]The opportunity cost of each sector is equal to 40.

programme, we are constructing a model with 21 regions for the Frankfurt metropolitan area [26].

Dynamic Analysis

Neglect of the capacity effects of capital formation and of land use have already been mentioned as serious limitations to the applicability of the optimal results of this present version of the model. The possibility of structural change by substitution in the course of time should be studied in the future. Dynamic analysis is also necessary because of the existence of cumulative effects, which cannot be analysed in a static setting. For the study of such problems, knowledge about the time path of development must be obtained, and time lags and repercussions of policy measures must be studied. Thus augmented, the model lends itself to the simulation of decisions on still another type of choice: the question of when to interfere.

Ecological Analysis

The last extension to be mentioned is work on providing a better linkage to the ecosystem. This work must follow three lines of research.[15] The first has to do with our model's pollutants balances, in which the regenerative capacity of the environment has to be included explicitly, because some elements of the ecosystem act similarly to pollution abatement activities, as they have the capacity to dilute or destroy pollutants. This capacity can be used to save resources without any damage to the environment.

The second is completion of materials balances, describing the deliveries of natural resources to the economy by a system of equations. This set of equations is quite similar to the pollutants balances, except that now the outputs of the ecosystem and the inputs of the economy have to be described.

The third is a study of the destruction of elements of the ecosystem by excessive discharge of pollutants. This has to be considered, because it affects nature's capacity to regenerate and supply natural resources in later periods.

Regional, dynamic, and ecological features may easily be incorporated into the framework of generalized input-output analysis. Further work in this direction, therefore, seems to be a promising contribution to the improvement of structural and environmental policy.

References

1. Arbeitsgemeinschaft Energiebilanzen [Committee on Energy Accounts], ed. *Energiebilanzen der Bundesrepublik Deutschland* [Energy Balances of the Federal Republic of Germany]. Frankfurt: 1971.

2. Bródy, A., and A.P. Carter, eds. *Input-Output Techniques.* Amsterdam: North-Holland Publishing Company, 1972.

3. Bundesministerium für Wirtschaft und Finanzen [Federal Department of Economy and Finance]. "Perspektiven des Wirtschaftswachstums in der BRD bis zum Jahre 1985" [Perspectives of Economic Growth in the Federal Republic of Germany up to 1985]. *Vierteljahresbericht* III (1970): 27–28; BMWF-Dokumentation, vol. 145 (Oktober 1971), Appendix.

4. Chenery, H.B. and P.G. Clark. *Interindustry Economics.* New York: John Wiley and Sons, 1959.

5. Day, R.H. *Recursive Programming and Production Response.* Amsterdam: North-Holland Publishing Company, 1963.

6. Georgescu-Roegen, N. "Some Properties of a Generalized Leontief Model." In *Activity Analysis of Production and Allocation.* Edited by T.C. Koopmans. New York: John Wiley and Sons, 1951, pp. 165–176.

7. Hickman, B.G. "Introduction." In *Quantitative Planning of Economic Policy.* Edited by B.G. Hickman. Washington, D.C.: Brookings Institution, 1965. Pp. 2–6.

15. The schedule we follow in the construction of such a combined economic-ecological decision model was developed by UNESCO [27].

8. Isard, W. "Some Notes on the Linkage of Ecologic and Economic Systems." *Regional Science Association Papers* 22 (1969): 56–96.

9. Kneese, A.V.; R.U. Ayres; and R.C. d'Arge. *Economics and the Environment: A Materials Balance Approach.* Baltimore: Johns Hopkins Press, 1970 (for Resources for the Future).

10. Kneese, A.V., and B.T. Bower. *Managing Water Quality: Economics, Technology, Institutions.* Baltimore: Johns Hopkins Press, 1971 (for Resources for the Future).

11. Koopmans, T.C. "Analysis of Production as Efficient Combination of Activities." In *Activity Analysis of Production and Allocation.* Edited by T.C. Koopmans. New York: John Wiley and Sons, 1951. Pp. 33–97.

12. Koopmans, T.C., ed. *Activity Analysis of Production and Allocation.* New York: John Wiley and Sons, 1951.

13. Lave, L., and E. Seskin. "Air Pollution and Human Health." *Science,* 109 (1970): 723.

14. Leontief, W. "Environmental Repercussions and the Economic Structure: An Input-Output Approach." *The Review of Economics and Statistics,* 52, no. 3 (August 1970): 262–271.

15. Leontief, W., and D. Ford. "Air Pollution and the Economic Structure: Empirical Results of Input-Output Computations." In *Input-Output Techniques.* Edited by A. Bródy and A.P. Carter. Amsterdam: North-Holland Publishing Company, 1972. Pp. 9–30.

16. Russell, C.S. *Residuals Management in Industry: A Case Study of Petroleum Refining.* Baltimore: Johns Hopkins Press, 1973.

17. Schumann, J. "An Input-Output Model with CES Production Functions." *Zeitschrift für die gesamte Staatswissenschaft* 124 (1968): 417–429.

18. Stäglin, R., and H. Wessels. *Input-Output Rechnung für die Bundesrepublik Deutschland 1954, 1958, 1962, 1966* [Input-Output Accounts for the Federal Republic of Germany 1954, 1958, 1962, 1966]. Berlin: Duncker and Humbolt, 1973. Appendix VII.

19. Sugiyama, K. "Dynamic Simulation on Environmental and Economic Behavior of the Japanese Islands." *Journal of Earth Science* 21 (1973): 1–42.

20. Theil, H. *Economic Forecasts and Policy.* Amsterdam: North-Holland Publishing Company, 1970.

21. Thoss, R. "Resolving Goal Conflicts in Regional Policy by Recursive Linear Programming." *Regional Science Association Papers* 33 (1974): 59–76.

22. Thoss, R., and H.P. Döllekes. "Energy and Environmental Planning." In *Energy and Environment.* Edited by OECD. Paris: OECD, 1974. Pp. 77–106.

23. Thoss, R., and K. Wiik. "A Linear Decision Model for the Management of Water Quality in the Ruhr." In *The Management of Water Quality and the Environment.* Edited by J. Rothenberg and I.G. Heggie. London: MacMillan, 1974. Pp. 104–141.

24. Tinbergen, J. *Centralization and Decentralization in Economic Policy.* Amsterdam: North-Holland Publishing Company, 1954.

25. Turvey, R. "On Divergences Between Social Cost and Private Cost." *Economica* 30 (1963): 370.

26. UNESCO. "Final Report, Expert Panel on Project 11: Ecological Aspects of Energy Utilization in Urban and Industrial Ecosystems." MAB Report Series No. 13.

27. UNESCO. "Final Report, Expert Panel on Project 13: Perception of Environmental Quality." MAB Report Series No. 9.

28. Victor, P.A. *Pollution: Economy and Environment.* London: Allen and Unwin, 1972.

Appendix 20A

Table 20A-1. Production Sectors

Sector Number	Title	Sector Number	Title
1	Agriculture	29	Glass
2	Electricity & heat	30	Timber products
3	Gas & water	31	Musical instruments, sports equipment, toys, & jewelry
4	Coal		
5	Iron ore	32	Paper products
6	Potash	33	Printing
7	Petroleum & natural gas	34	Artificial fibres
8	Mining of other materials	35	Leather
9	Quarrying	36	Textiles
10	Iron & steel production	37	Clothing
11	Iron & steel founding	38	Milling
12	Sheet metal & cables	39	Edible oils & margarine
13	Nonferrous metals	40	Sugar
14	Chemicals	41	Brewing & malting
15	Petroleum refining	42	Tobacco
16	Rubber & asbestos	43	Food
17	Timber	44	Crafts
18	Pulp & paper	45	Building
19	Steel construction	46	Wholesale trading
20	Light engineering	47	Retail trading
21	Motors	48	Railways
22	Aerospace	49	Shipping
23	Shipbuilding	50	Transport (excluding 48 and 49)
24	Electrical & electronics	51	Post
25	Fine mechanical & optical products	52	Banking & finance
		53	Housing
26	Steel manufacturing	54	Services
27	Iron, plate, & metal products	55	Government
		56	Households
28	Pottery		

Table 20A-2. Energy Commodities

Commodity Number	Title	Commodity Number	Title
C1	Electricity	C19	Other petroleum products
C2	Area heating	C20	Solid waste
C3	Town gas	C21	Peat
C4	Blast-furnace gas	C22	Firewood
C5	Natural gas	C23	Bituminous coal and anthracite
C6	Natural-oil gas	C24	Coke
C7	Refinery gas	C25	Coke briquettes
C8	Fluid gas	C26	Crude tar, pitch
C9	Crude oil	C27	Other coal products
C10	Petrol (automobile)	C28	Crude benzene
C11	Petrol (aero)	C29	Crude brown coal
C12	Crude petrol	C30	Brown-coal briquettes, heavy coke, powdered coal
C13	Paraffin		
C14	Aero engine turbine oil	C31	Hard brown coal
C15	Diesel oil	C32	Pitch coal
C16	Light heating oil	C33	Nuclear energy
C17	Heavy heating oil	C34	Water energy
C18	Petroleum coke		

Chapter Twenty-One

Multiregional Interactions Between Energy and Transportation

Karen R. Polenske

Energy is a word that has taken on new and dramatic meaning in the United States, as elsewhere, within the last few years. This country's current energy problems are closely interconnected with its other economic problems: transportation, urban development, environmental, and so on. Therefore, as efforts are made to understand and solve some of the energy problems, the need for a comprehensive and systematic analysis of energy at a multiregional level, where the interconnection with related economic problems among all regions of the country can be observed most accurately, becomes increasingly evident. The impact of almost all changes in the demand for and supply of energy varies significantly among different industries and regions. As will become apparent later in this chapter, the interconnection between energy and transportation is most effectively studied within a multiregional framework.

At the regional level, the tools and data required to analyze energy and transportation problems have not been readily available. At the national level, they have not only been available, but they have also been constantly refined; therefore, relatively small amounts of time and funds are necessary for the national studies. Many of the conclusions of these studies, however, so far as a given region is concerned, are misleading or inapplicable.[1] Now, industry, government officials, and the general public have become vitally interested in having these policies analyzed with specific reference to their impact on particular areas of the country, as well as the repercussions among regions.

Paul F. Levy did the calculations for the paper and assisted with interpreting the data.

The research reported in this paper is financed with funds from Contract No. DOT-OS-30104 between the University Research Program, U.S. Department of Transportation, and the Department of Urban Studies and Planning, Massachusetts Institute of Technology, Cambridge, Massachusetts. The author takes full responsibility for the conclusions, which are not necessarily those of the sponsoring agency.

1. In Paul F. Levy's study *The Residential Demand for Electricity in New England,* for example, the elasticity of demand for electricity (with respect to price or income) obtained for New England is significantly different from that obtained in national studies [8].

The present study has two purposes. The first is to explain why and to show how the multiregional input-output (MRIO) model can be useful for analyzing energy and transportation policies in general. The second is to show through a specific study how the MRIO framework is used to examine the economic interactions between electricity, coal, and freight transportation created by changes in technology and trade flows.[2]

Defining the Scope of the MRIO Energy and Transportation Studies

The multiregional input-output model is a comprehensive multipurpose tool that can be used for systematic studies of regional economic policies in general and of energy and transportation policies in particular. It provides a consistent framework for describing and analyzing the sales and purchases of the energy and transportation industries in every region of the economy and can be used to measure the direct and indirect effects of variations in these economic activities throughout the country.

For the present study of the multiregional interactions between energy and transportation, the analysis has been restricted to the inputs of coal into the private electric-power industry and the resulting derived demand for the transportation of coal. The investigation has been conducted using the column-coefficient version of the MRIO model to obtain both regional outputs and interregional trade flows. Although a static version of the basic MRIO model has been used for this analysis, it is of course evident that a dynamic version of the model and supplemental multiregional models will have to be developed and additional data will have to be assembled if an analysis in greater depth is required. A modal-split model, for example, can be developed and linked into the MRIO model. This could be used for an intensive analysis of the impact of a specific energy policy on substitutions among modes of transportation, which basically affects the rail, water, and truck modes of shipping, or to analyze the impact that modal shifts have upon the supply of and demand for energy.

The calculations for this paper were not disaggregated by mode of transportation. Also, the analysis is restricted to the period 1963 through 1970. At present, base-year MRIO data are available only for 1963, and projections of the gross regional product figures have been made to 1970 and 1980. (The methodology used to assemble these data is explained in a series of five volumes published by Lexington Books, D.C. Heath and Company [12-16].) Although all of the MRIO data are available for 79 industries and 51 regions—50 states plus the District of Columbia—for this study, the data were aggregated to 18 industries and 9 regions (refer to Appendix 21A). In general, those industries that are large users of coal

---

2. Full explanations of all components of the study are contained in DOT Report No. 8 by Karen R. Polenske and Paul F. Levy entitled "Multiregional Economic Impacts of Energy and Transportation Policies" [11].

were kept separate, and the 9 U.S. census regions were used because regional controls were frequently available at this level when the data were originally assembled. The data for the 9 census regions may therefore be more accurate than those for some other regional aggregation.

Extensions and expansions of the MRIO model and the development of supplemental multiregional models will be needed to improve the comprehensiveness and accuracy of the results of energy and transportation studies using the MRIO framework. Even without this additional work, however, a large number of regional economic policies relating to energy and transportation can be studied within the MRIO framework, and the results obtained from the studies will be unique in many respects.[3] Extensions and expansions of the model would thus add to an already powerful tool of economic analysis.

The next section presents background information on electricity and transportation that will be useful in interpreting the results of this study.

Generation of Electricity

The processes used to generate electricity vary widely from one region of the country to another. In the West, where ample water supplies are available, the principal process is hydroelectric generation. In the West South Central region, gas-burning generators are used almost exclusively. In the East North Central and East South Central regions, coal-burning generators are dominant; while in New England, oil is now the principal fuel.

In 1963, coal provided the largest share—65 percent—of BTU's used for fossil-fuel generation in the country. In 1970, it still provided the largest share, but the percentage had dropped to 56 percent, as shown in Table 21-1. The fuel mix varies drastically from region to region, however, because the energy-supply market is quite different in each part of the country. No coal is used for fossil-fuel electricity generation in either the West South Central or Pacific regions, while coal represents approximately 90 percent of the fossil fuel used by electric utilities in both the East North Central and East South Central regions. The only two regions that show an increase in the use of coal relative to oil and natural gas from 1963 to 1970 are the West North Central and Mountain regions.

In addition to a discussion of fuel mix, a complete picture of electric-power production should account for the relative position of fossil fuels in total electricity generation and the regional distribution of fossil-fuel generating plants. These distributions for 1963 and 1970 are shown in Tables 21-2 and 21-3, respectively. In 1970, for example, 97.2 percent of the electricity in Region 2 was produced by fossil-fuel generating plants, and this represented 22.5 percent of the total 1970 U.S. fossil-fuel production. Table 21-2 shows that most regions were highly dependent upon fossil fuels for production of electricity in both

3. Examples of economic policies and some of the unique aspects of the studies are given in the report by Polenske and Levy [11].

Table 21-1. 1963 and 1970 Distribution of Fuel Use: Steam-Electric
Generating Plants (percent)

Region		1963		1970	
Num- ber	Name	Coal	Oil and Natural Gas	Coal	Oil and Natural Gas
1	New England	63	37	16	84
2	Middle Atlantic	75	25	55	45
3	East North Central	96	4	90	10
4	West North Central	49	51	57	43
5	South Atlantic	79	21	66	34
6	East South Central	92	8	89	11
7	West South Central	0	100	0	100
8	Mountain	40	60	56	41
9	Pacific	0	100	0	100
	United States	65	35	56	44

Note: Percentages are based upon BTU's used for fossil-fuel steam electric generation.
Source: Thomas D. Duchesneau, *Interfuel Substitutability in the Electric Industry*.
Washington, D.C.: Federal Trade Commission, February 1972. *Electric Utility Sector of
the U.S. Economy*. Staff report.

1963 and 1970. (The fossil-fuel percentages range between 83 and 97 percent.)
The only two exceptions were Regions 8 and 9 where "hydro" had a large
share—44.9 and 59.4 percent, respectively, in 1963. Although nuclear-power
plants were just beginning to make a significant contribution to electricity generation in 1963, by 1970 a number of atomic units had been constructed. It
should be noted, however, that even in New England, where nuclear power is
more dominant than elsewhere, electricity generated by such plants amounted
to only 7.9 percent of the total in the region.[4] Both nuclear and hydroelectric
power plants are geographically isolated. Nuclear plants are located mainly in the
three regions in the Northeast and on the West Coast, and over 65 percent of the
hydroelectric generating capacity is located in the Mountain and Pacific regions.
Given the long lead time (ten years) needed for nuclear-power plant construction
and the lack of suitable locations for additional hydroelectric plants, fossil-fuel
plants will undoubtedly continue to predominate as the main source of electricity
in most of the country for at least the next decade. Thus, choices among coal- or
oil- or gas-generating plants will continue to be important. Conversion of plants
from oil- and gas-fired units to coal is of course receiving increasingly serious
consideration as a result of the 1973–1974 oil embargo imposed by the Arab
nations and the unilateral price increases set by the Organization of Petroleum
Exporting Countries.

4. No reason could be found for the decrease in the percentage of electricity generated
by nuclear power in the West North Central region from 0.1 percent in 1963 to zero in 1970.

Table 21-2. 1963 and 1970 Regional Distribution of Electricity by Generation Process (percent)

| Region | | 1963 | | | | | 1970 | | | | |
Number	Name	Fossil	Hydro	Nuclear	Other	Total	Fossil	Hydro	Nuclear	Other	Total
1	New England	83.8	12.9	2.7	0.6	100.0	83.8	7.7	7.9	0.6	100.0
2	Middle Atlantic	84.4	14.7	0.7	0.1	100.0	83.9	12.1	3.9	0.2	100.0
3	East North Central	97.6	1.4	0.5	0.5	100.0	97.2	1.3	1.0	0.4	100.0
4	West North Central	84.0	12.8	0.1	3.1	100.0	84.2	13.5	–	2.2	100.0
5	South Atlantic	90.3	9.4	0.0	0.3	100.0	94.8	5.0	0.0	0.2	100.0
6	East South Central	84.1	15.9	–	0.0	100.0	87.1	12.9	–	0.0	100.0
7	West South Central	97.4	1.4	–	1.2	100.0	96.9	2.6	–	0.5	100.0
8	Mountain	54.0	44.9	0.1	1.1	100.0	62.5	37.0	–	0.5	100.0
9	Pacific	40.4	59.4		0.1	100.0	37.4	60.0	2.5	0.1	100.0
	United States	81.1	18.0	0.3	0.5	100.0	82.0	16.2	1.4	0.4	100.0

0.0 Less than 0.05 percent
–   Zero generation

Note: Totals may not add to 100 percent due to rounding. Percentages are based upon BTU's used for electricity generation.

Sources: Edison Electric Institute. *Statistical Bulletin of the Electrical Industry, 1963 and 1970* (New York: Edison Electric Institute, 1964 and 1971).

Table 21-3. 1963 and 1970 Generation-Process Distribution of Electricity by Region (percent)

Region Number	Name	1963 Fossil	Hydro	Nuclear	Other	Total	1970 Fossil	Hydro	Nuclear	Other	Total
1	New England	3.9	2.7	29.3	4.2	3.8	4.1	1.9	22.1	6.1	4.0
2	Middle Atlantic	15.6	12.3	29.5	4.0	15.0	14.2	10.4	37.6	6.0	13.9
3	East North Central	25.2	1.7	32.9	17.5	20.9	22.5	1.5	14.0	19.7	18.9
4	West North Central	6.4	4.4	2.3	34.7	6.1	6.6	5.4	—	36.5	6.4
5	South Atlantic	15.7	7.4	0.0	7.7	14.1	18.6	5.0	0.0	8.1	16.1
6	East South Central	11.6	9.9	—	0.4	11.2	10.2	7.6	—	0.2	9.6
7	West South Central	11.1	0.7	—	21.0	9.3	13.5	1.8	—	14.9	11.5
8	Mountain	3.1	11.5	—	9.0	4.6	3.6	10.8	—	5.4	4.7
9	Pacific	7.5	49.6	6.0	1.5	15.0	6.8	55.6	26.4	3.1	15.0
	United States	100.0	100.0	100.0	100.0	100.0	100.0	100.0	100.0	100.0	100.0

0.0 Less than 0.05 percent

— Zero generation

Note: Figures may not add to 100 percent due to rounding. Percentages are based upon BTU's used for electricity generation.

Sources: Edison Electric Institute. *Statistical Bulletin of the Electrical Industry, 1963* and *1970* (New York: Edison Electric Institute, 1964 and 1971).

Factors Influencing the Future Use of Coal

Projections of the future use of coal by electric utilities depend mainly upon three factors: (1) ability of generating plants to use coal; (2) transport-system capability; and (3) federal coal-mining policy.

Ability of Generating Plants to Use Coal: As was mentioned earlier, coal supplied 56 percent of the BTU's needed for fossil-fuel electricity generation in 1970. While this is a fairly large percentage, there is a potential for expanding coal's share either by building new plants capable of burning coal or by converting existing plants from oil to coal. The construction of coal-fired plants will probably become predominant in the next decade, especially in states bordering the newly productive Mountain coal region. In addition, some utilities may convert existing gas or oil plants to coal. The Federal Power Commission considered this alternative during the fuel-oil shortage in the winter of 1973 and estimated that the total oil-fired generation capacity that could be converted to coal at that time was 23,697 megawatts, or about 44 percent of the total oil-fired steam-electric capacity [5, p. 5].

Several basic alternatives are open to utilities that will enable them to reduce their dependence on oil and use coal for electricity generation. Two of the most important of these are explained here.

Utilization of low-sulfur coal reserves: Federal ambient air-quality standards established by the Clean Air Act Amendments of 1970 set limits, equivalent to about 0.7 percent sulfur content of the coal used, on the amount of sulfur oxides emitted by fossil-fuel steam-generating plants. Low-sulfur coal reserves are found principally in the western states of Montana, Wyoming, North Dakota, and New Mexico, although limited quantities are available in West Virginia, Virginia, and eastern Kentucky. For the western states, projections indicate that coal production may grow by a factor of 10 in the two decades from 1970 to 1990 [10, p. 17]. The use of western coal presents certain problems, however, namely, the inadequacies of transport links to the market and possible restrictions on strip-mining activity, the predominant form of mining in this region.

Removal of sulfur from coal: A long-run policy of strict sulfur-pollution restrictions will of course force managers of electricity-generating plants to invest in various means of removing sulfur from coal. Four major methods are now available: stack-gas scrubbing (removal of sulfur as the gas is burned); physical desulfurization (removal of sulfur pyrites by subjecting crushed coal to froth flotation); chemical desulfurization (removal of sulfur through a variety of techniques, leaving the coal in the form of a solid, liquid, or gas—depending upon the process employed); fluidized-bed construction (removal of sulfur by the use of a boiler designed to mix coal with a layer of granular particles that move about as air is passed rapidly upward).[5]

5. A paper by Carl R. Strauss explains the four techniques in more detail [17].

Either of the two options discussed above will involve substantial increases in the amount of bulk coal transported from the mines to the utilities, and the first option will involve new corridors of movement from the western states to the East. Thus, the question is whether or not the transportation industry will be able to handle this burden.

Transportation-System Capability: Transportation-system inadequacies are likely to stand in the way of increased use of coal by electric utilities. Freight-car shortages, poor track and roadbed conditions, and inefficient delivery systems affect the amount of coal that can be moved by rail. Because a substantial long-term market has not been guaranteed, railroads have been reluctant to invest in equipment and to introduce new train routes. On the other hand, electric utilities are wary of committing themselves to coal unless it can be delivered on time and at the stated cost, and coal companies will not start full production on a mine unless a long-term buyer and a means to move the coal are guaranteed.

Federal Coal-Mining Policy: There are two main areas in which the federal government is involved in coal mining. One is its concern for the health and safety of coal miners, and the other is its concern for the environmental effects of strip mining. The Federal Coal Mine Health and Safety Act passed in 1969 has been an important influence on mining operations in the United States. Surface-mining regulations will have their primary impact on the newly developed and as yet to be developed low-sulfur coal fields of Montana, North Dakota, and Wyoming; but they will also have an effect on the older fields in Appalachia. The advantages of surface mining—less time and capital to open, lower operating costs, less specialized labor required, and higher recovery—will be offset to a certain degree by federal (and state) regulations requiring recontouring of strip-mined fields to their original topography.

Production, Consumption, and Transportation of Coal

The five principal producers of bituminous coal in 1963 were West Virginia, Pennsylvania, Kentucky, Illinois, and Ohio, which together produced 80.6 percent of the total. Consumption of coal was more widely dispersed, with the five major consumers (Pennsylvania, Ohio, Illinois, Indiana, and Michigan) accounting for only 44.3 percent of the total [20]. Seventy-two percent of the bituminous coal was shipped by railroad; and coal movements accounted for 24.8 percent of the total tonnage carried by rail and 12.4 percent of the railroads' freight receipts [9]. Most of the consumption of coal is at considerable distances from the mines—coal is generally mined in rural areas and is then moved to centers of greater density and industrialization. Thus, transportation is an important link between production and consumption.

Following World War II, coal began to lose what had amounted to a monopoly energy position in the United States. By 1963, diesel had replaced bituminous coal as the fuel for railroad locomotives, for diesel had proved to be a more economical fuel. Coal still retained great importance in other markets, however. For example, the demand for coal by electric utilities actually accelerated after World War II, growing from 72 million tons in 1945 (13 percent of total coal consumption) to 174 million tons in 1960 (46 percent of total consumption) [24, p. 4]. The iron and steel, paper, and stone and clay industries also continued to use a considerable amount of coal [18]. These three industries, together with the utilities, purchased almost 60 percent (in dollar terms) of the coal produced in 1963 in the United States.

The background information just presented shows why the production, consumption, and transportation of coal should be studied. Because policy makers must evaluate many different policies, an important aid will be the availability of a method of analysis that allows for quick studies, using different combinations of assumptions and policies.

Policy Alternatives for Regions

The present prototype study is designed to show how the MRIO model can be used to investigate policy issues related to the energy and transportation industries, with particular reference to the use of coal for the generation of electricity. A specific study that could be done, for example, would be an examination of the impact on New England of converting from coal-fired to oil-fired generators during the period 1963 to 1970, which resulted in changes both in the technology inputs into the electricity industry and in the trade flows of coal into the region. Another policy study might be to determine the impact on the East North Central region of buying coal from the Mountain region instead of from the Midwest and Appalachian regions. Although no specific policies were analyzed in this study because of time, data, and financial limitations, the experience gained from this research will provide the framework for more intensive future investigations.

The present analysis indicates the value of conducting regional, rather than national, studies of energy and transportation. First, the results of changing technologies by region and over time for the electricity industries are assessed. In this part of the analysis, insight is provided into the extent of regional and industrial repercussions that can be anticipated if significant changes occur either in the technologies currently being used to generate electricity or in the regional mix of the present technologies. Second, the results of altering trade coefficients for coal using 1970 instead of 1963 shipments are examined This part of the analysis shows the importance of considering changes in shipping origins and destinations for coal and also shows the regional and industrial impacts that can be expected if a significant quantity of the total coal used is mined west of the Mississippi River.

Adjustments to the MRIO Data

Before the MRIO model could be implemented for this study of energy and transportation, four major adjustments were made to the original set of 1963 technology and trade data:

1. *Process-Mix Variation for Generation of Electricity:* The IO-68.01, Electricity, portion of IO-68, Electricity, gas, water, & sanitary services, was subdivided into four electricity-generating processes: fossil fuel, hydro, nuclear, and other (mainly internal combustion), using special estimates of the national technologies assembled by Rudyard Istvan [6] and 1963 and 1970 regional outputs [2; 3; 23].

2. *Product-Mix Variation:* The 1963 national direct coefficients for IO-68.02, Gas, and IO-68.03, Water & sanitary services [19], the other two subcomponents of IO-68, were weighted by the two respective sets of regional outputs [4; 23] to reflect differences in the product mix of the two subindustries in each region.

3. *Fuel-Input Variation:* The national fossil-fuel generation coefficients estimated by Istvan [6] were adjusted to reflect differences in the amounts of coal (IO-7, Coal mining) and oil and natural gas (IO-8, Crude petroleum & natural gas) used in each region [1].

4. *Trade Flow Adjustment:* The 1963 transportation flows for coal (Industry 3) were adjusted to reflect the 1970 distribution of the product, using shipments data obtained from a Bureau of Mines publication [22] for bituminous coal and lignite and the *Minerals Yearbook, 1970* [21] for anthracite. The two sets of data were added and multiplied by prices per ton published in the *Minerals Yearbook, 1970* to obtain estimates in terms of dollars. The 1963 and 1970 trade flows for coal represent coal used by all industries, rather than coal used only by electric utilities.

After the first and second adjustments had been completed, the regional input data for the four generation processes were aggregated to 18 industries and 9 regions. The fuel-input variation adjustment was then made, and the inputs into the four generation processes were summed for each of the 18 industries in each of the 9 regions and added to the respective input data for gas and water (which had also been aggregated to 18 industries and 9 regions) to form one column of purchases for Industry 18, Electricity, gas, water, & sanitary services. This procedure was followed for both 1963 and 1970. These purchases were then divided by the respective 1963 and 1970 total regional outputs of Industry 18 to obtain regional input coefficients for the industry. The two sets of coefficients are given in Tables 21–4 and 21–5, respectively.

Table 21-4. 1963 Adjusted Regional Technology Coefficients: Industry 18, Electricity, Gas, Water, & Sanitary Services

Num-ber	Title	1 New England	2 Middle Atlantic	3 East North Central	4 West North Central	5 South Atlantic	6 East South Central	7 West South Central	8 Moun-tain	9 Pacific
1	Livestock & livestock products	0.000	0.000	0.000	0.000	0.000	0.000	0.000	0.000	0.000
2	Other agricultural products	0.000	0.000	0.000	0.000	0.000	0.000	0.000	0.000	0.000
3	Coal mining	0.056	0.049	0.054	0.045	0.067	0.076	0.000	0.045	0.000
4	Crude petroleum & natural gas	0.067	0.078	0.082	0.089	0.065	0.053	0.137	0.094	0.128
5	Other mining	0.0	0.0	0.0	0.0	0.0	0.0	0.0	0.0	0.0
6	Construction	0.035	0.033	0.032	0.032	0.034	0.036	0.033	0.031	0.035
7	Food & tobacco	0.001	0.001	0.001	0.001	0.001	0.000	0.001	0.001	0.001
8	Fabrics, apparel, & footwear	0.000	0.000	0.000	0.000	0.000	0.000	0.000	0.000	0.000
9	Transport equipment & ordnance	0.000	0.000	0.000	0.000	0.000	0.000	0.000	0.000	0.000
10	Lumber & paper	0.000	0.001	0.000	0.001	0.000	0.000	0.000	0.000	0.000
11	Petroleum & related industries	0.017	0.015	0.015	0.014	0.018	0.020	0.016	0.015	0.018
12	Plastics & chemicals	0.009	0.007	0.007	0.007	0.009	0.010	0.008	0.007	0.009
13	Glass, stone, & clay products	0.000	0.000	0.000	0.000	0.000	0.000	0.000	0.000	0.000
14	Primary iron & steel manufacturing	0.001	0.001	0.001	0.001	0.001	0.001	0.001	0.001	0.001
15	Primary nonferrous manufacturing	0.0	0.0	0.0	0.0	0.0	0.0	0.0	0.0	0.0
16	Machinery & equipment	0.000	0.000	0.000	0.000	0.000	0.000	0.000	0.000	0.000
17	Services	0.129	0.135	0.095	0.107	0.084	0.077	0.078	0.088	0.095
18	Electricity, gas, water, & sanitary services	0.210	0.226	0.241	0.243	0.217	0.204	0.237	0.251	0.210

0.000 Coefficient smaller than 0.0005

0.0 Zero coefficient

Table 21-5.   1970 Regional Technology Coefficients: Industry 18, Electricity, Gas, Water, & Sanitary Services

Number	Title	1 New England	2 Middle Atlantic	3 East North Central	4 West North Central	5 South Atlantic	6 East South Central	7 West South Central	8 Mountain	9 Pacific
1	Livestock & livestock products	0.000	0.000	0.000	0.000	0.000	0.000	0.000	0.000	0.000
2	Other agricultural products	0.000	0.000	0.000	0.000	0.000	0.000	0.000	0.000	0.000
3	Coal mining	0.047	0.049	0.054	0.052	0.072	0.075	0.000	0.052	0.000
4	Crude petroleum & natural gas	0.077	0.079	0.082	0.082	0.057	0.055	0.133	0.086	0.128
5	Other mining	0.0	0.0	0.0	0.0	0.0	0.0	0.0	0.0	0.0
6	Construction	0.035	0.033	0.032	0.032	0.036	0.036	0.034	0.032	0.036
7	Food & tobacco	0.001	0.001	0.001	0.001	0.000	0.000	0.001	0.001	0.000
8	Fabrics, apparel, & footwear	0.000	0.000	0.000	0.000	0.000	0.000	0.000	0.000	0.000
9	Transport equipment & ordnance	0.000	0.000	0.000	0.000	0.000	0.000	0.000	0.000	0.000
10	Lumber & paper	0.000	0.001	0.000	0.000	0.000	0.000	0.000	0.000	0.000
11	Petroleum & related industries	0.018	0.015	0.015	0.015	0.020	0.020	0.018	0.015	0.019
12	Plastics & chemicals	0.009	0.008	0.007	0.007	0.010	0.010	0.009	0.007	0.010
13	Glass, stone, & clay products	0.000	0.000	0.000	0.000	0.000	0.000	0.000	0.000	0.000
14	Primary iron & steel manufacturing	0.001	0.001	0.001	0.001	0.001	0.001	0.001	0.001	0.001
15	Primary nonferrous manufacturing	0.0	0.0	0.0	0.0	0.0	0.0	0.0	0.0	0.0
16	Machinery & equipment	0.000	0.000	0.000	0.000	0.000	0.000	0.000	0.000	0.000
17	Services	0.116	0.125	0.092	0.099	0.081	0.076	0.076	0.085	0.090
18	Electricity, gas, water, & sanitary services	0.206	0.229	0.242	0.238	0.206	0.207	0.219	0.245	0.206

0.000   Coefficient smaller than 0.0005 .

0.0   Zero coefficient

To calculate 1963 and 1970 column trade coefficients, each column of the matrices containing the 1963 and 1970 transportation flows of coal (described in adjustment 4 above) was divided by the respective column sum. These coefficients then reflected the amount of coal shipped into a region as a fraction of the total consumption in the region. Both sets of coefficients are given in Table 21-6.

Implementation of the MRIO Model

Calculations for the present energy and transportation study were made using the column trade coefficient version of the MRIO model. All of the calculations will be represented in the remainder of this report in matrix notation, defined as follows:

n = number of industries—in the present calculations, 18.

m = number of regions—in the present calculations, 9.

* = adjusted coefficients.

^ = block diagonal matrix.

X = column vector ($mn \times 1$) giving total production. Each element describes the amount of output of commodity i produced in region g.

Y = column vector ($mn \times 1$) giving total final demand. Each element describes the total amount of commodity i consumed by final users in region g regardless of the place where the good was produced.

$\hat{A}$ = block diagonal matrix ($mn \times mn$) with n square matrices ($n \times n$) of input coefficients along the diagonal describing the structure of production in each region.

$\hat{A}_*$ = block diagonal matrix ($mn \times mn$) with the same basic information as $\hat{A}$, but with the 1963 column of coefficients for IO-68, Electric, gas, water, & sanitary services, adjusted using the procedures described earlier.

$\hat{A}_o$ = block diagonal matrix ($mn \times mn$) with the same basic information as $\hat{A}$, but with the 1970 column of coefficients for IO-68, Electric, gas, water, & sanitary services.

C = square matrix ($nm \times nm$) filled with diagonal matrices ($n \times n$). Each element c_i^{gh} describes the fraction of total consumption of commodity i in region h that is imported from region g. The sum of each column of this matrix must equal 1, since the coefficients are proportions of total consumption. It is assumed that each industry within region h will consume the same fraction as imports:

$$c_i^{gh} = c_{i1}^{gh} = c_{i2}^{gh} = \ldots = c_{in}^{gh}$$

Table 21-6.   1963 and 1970 Column Trade-Flow Coefficients: Industry 3, Coal Mining

Shipping Region		1 New England	2 Middle Atlantic	3 East North Central	4 West North Central	5 South Atlantic	6 East South Central	7 West South Central	8 Moun- tain	9 Pacific
1 New England	1963	.004	.000	.0	.0	.0	.0	.0	.0	.0
	1970	.0	.0	.0	.0	.0	.0	.0	.0	.0
2 Middle Atlantic	1963	.426	.716	.069	.002	.184	.0	.0	.0	.140
	1970	.601	.550	.036	.001	.127	.0	.0	.0	.0
3 East North Central	1963	.0	.005	.488	.580	.019	.093	.087	.0	.0
	1970	.059	.126	.591	.427	.024	.068	.058	.0	.0
4 West North Central	1963	.0	.0	.0	.214	.0	.0	.040	.000	.0
	1970	.0	.0	.000	.293	.0	.0	.073	.0	.0
5 South Atlantic	1963	.460	.263	.274	.131	.579	.152	.318	.256	.594
	1970	.330	.284	.185	.038	.468	.215	.194	.0	.0
6 East South Central	1963	.110	.016	.169	.070	.218	.755	.524	.0	.0
	1970	.010	.040	.183	.048	.381	.717	.123	.0	.0
7 West South Central	1963	.0	.0	.0	.002	.0	.0	.031	.066	.0
	1970	.0	.0	.000	.104	.0	.0	.552	.005	.0
8 Mountain	1963	.0	.0	.0	.001	.0	.0	.0	.627	.239
	1970	.0	.0	.005	.069	.0	.0	.0	.978	.901
9 Pacific	1963	.0	.0	.0	.0	.0	.0	.0	.051	.027
	1970	.0	.0	.0	.020	.0	.0	.0	.017	.099
Total 1963/1970		1.000	1.000	1.000	1.000	1.000	1.000	1.000	1.000	1.000

.000 Coefficient smaller than .0005
.0   Zero coefficient

Sources: 1963–John M. Rodgers. *State Estimates of Interregional Commodity Trade, 1963.* Lexington: Lexington Books, D.C. Heath and Company, 1973. 1970–U.S. Department of Interior, *Minerals Yearbook,1970*, U.S. Government Printing Office, 1971. U.S. Department of Interior, Bureau of Mines, Division of Fossil Fuels, *Bituminous Coal and Lignite Distribution, Calendar Year 1970*, U.S. Government Printing Office, 1971.

C_* = square matrix ($nm \times nm$) with the same basic information as C, but adjusted to represent the 1970 trade flows of coal.

Three basic sets of calculations, represented by equations (21-1), (21-2), and (21-3), were performed using the adjusted technology and trade data with the column trade coefficient model

$$X = (C^{-1} - \hat{A})^{-1} Y \tag{21-1}$$

$$X = (C^{-1} - \hat{A}_*)^{-1} Y \tag{21-2}$$

$$X = (C^{-1} - \hat{A}_o)^{-1} Y \tag{21-2'}$$

$$X = (C_*^{-1} - \hat{A}_o)^{-1} Y \tag{21-3}$$

Only the 1963 and 1970 final demands were used for the calculations discussed in this report, although final demand data are also available for 1947, 1958, and 1980.

Calculation 1, Base-Year Estimates: The first calculation of regional outputs, represented by equation (21-1), was made to determine the 1963 base-year outputs before alterations were made to the technology and trade data. The 1963 base-year technology and trade coefficients were combined with the final demands for each of the two years to obtain estimated regional outputs for the two years. The 1963 regional outputs were calculated using national, rather than regional, technologies for Industry 18, Electricity, gas, water, & sanitary services.

Calculation 2, Adjusted Industry 18 Technology: The second calculation of regional outputs is represented by equation (21-2) above. For this calculation, the 1963 technology coefficients for Industry 18 were adjusted to account for regional differences. A comparison of the results of the first and second calculations is shown in Table 21-7. Not surprisingly, the industries most affected by the use of regional, rather than national, technologies are those relating to coal, petroleum, and electricity (Industries 3, 4, and 18, respectively) with some changes also occurring for Industry 11, Petroleum & related industries, and Industry 12, Plastics & chemicals. This table, however, does not provide all the information available from the set of calculations.

To study the effects of these interindustry, interregional repercussions, a comparison matrix was formed. The comparison matrix was obtained by multiplying the difference between the inverse matrix before adjustment (Calculation 1) and the inverse matrix after adjustment of Industry 18 technologies (Calculation 2) by the 1963 final demands for each respective column. The result was a 162 × 162 matrix, giving changes in values (in terms of dollars) occurring for each commodity in each region. If the comparison matrix is divided into 81 sub-

Table 21-7.   Percent Differences Between 1963 Regional Outputs Resulting from Adjusted Electricity-Generation Technology Coefficients

Number	Title	1 New England	2 Middle Atlantic	3 East North Central	4 West North Central	5 South Atlantic	6 East South Central	7 West South Central	8 Mountain	9 Pacific
1	Livestock & livestock products	0.0	0.0	0.0	0.0	0.0	0.0	0.0	0.0	0.0
2	Other agricultural products	0.0	0.0	0.0	0.0	0.0	0.0	0.0	0.0	0.0
3	Coal mining	64.9	35.3	40.7	33.0	29.2	34.8	10.6	12.2	3.9
4	Crude petroleum & natural gas	8.5	8.0	9.1	11.7	7.0	4.3	7.4	11.9	18.7
5	Other mining	0.3	0.3	0.3	0.3	0.3	0.4	0.4	0.2	0.2
6	Construction	0.3	0.4	0.2	0.3	0.3	0.4	0.5	0.2	0.3
7	Food & tobacco	0.0	0.0	0.0	0.0	0.0	0.0	0.0	0.0	0.0
8	Fabrics, apparel, & footwear	0.0	0.0	0.0	0.0	0.0	0.0	0.0	0.0	0.0
9	Transport equipment & ordnance	0.0	0.0	0.0	0.0	0.0	0.0	0.0	0.0	0.0
10	Lumber & paper	0.1	0.1	0.1	0.1	0.1	0.1	0.2	0.1	0.1
11	Petroleum & related industries	1.7	1.6	1.7	1.3	2.0	2.3	1.6	1.6	1.7
12	Plastics & chemicals	0.8	0.8	0.8	0.9	0.8	0.9	1.0	1.0	1.0
13	Glass, stone, & clay products	0.2	0.3	0.2	0.3	0.2	0.3	0.5	0.3	0.3
14	Primary iron & steel manufacturing	0.4	0.4	0.4	0.4	0.5	0.6	0.7	0.6	0.4
15	Primary nonferrous manufacturing	0.1	0.1	0.1	0.1	0.1	0.1	0.1	0.1	0.1
16	Machinery & equipment	0.1	0.2	0.2	0.2	0.1	0.1	0.1	0.1	0.1
17	Services	0.6	0.6	0.5	0.6	0.2	0.2	0.3	0.2	0.1
18	Electricity, gas, water, & sanitary services	3.0	5.4	6.6	7.5	4.3	3.6	7.1	8.0	5.5

divisions (9 shipping regions times 9 receiving regions), each subdivision being 18 × 18 (representing the 18 producing and the 18 purchasing industries in each of the 9 regions), and if each row of each subdivision is summed, the total changes in interregional requirements of each commodity are obtained.

The changes for coal are reproduced in Table 21-8 and represent the effect that final demands for the products of all industries in the regions listed at the top of the table have upon the coal output in the regions listed at the left of the table, given the alterations in Industry 18 technologies. Thus, the interregional and interindustry repercussions are clearly shown by these data. According to Table 21-7, total coal production in each region increased as a result of using regional, rather than national, technical coefficients for Industry 18. But, as shown especially by the negative changes in columns 7 and 9 in Table 21-8, final demands in Regions 7 and 9 created a lower requirement for coal production in most of the regions. This partly reflects the extremely small amounts of coal used for electricity generation in the two regions.

Changes in direct requirements have substantial effects on total production, but they have equally important effects on interregional trade patterns. (Although the figures in Table 21-8 do not represent shipments between regions, those shipments can be determined using the regional trade coefficients and regional consumption data.) Thus, this comparison indicates the value of a multiregional model, such as MRIO, for analyzing future shifts in the relative distribution of electricity-generation processes among regions or for analyzing the regional repercussions of significant shifts in the types of generation processes used throughout the country.

Calculation 3, 1970 Technology for Industry 18; 1970 Trade Coefficients for Coal: The third calculation of regional outputs is represented by equation (21-3). It was made to compare the results of altering the trade flows for coal to reflect 1970 coal shipments (described previously as adjustment 4) in addition to using 1970 regional technology coefficients for Industry 18. A comparison of these outputs with those obtained from equation (21-2′), that is, the outputs estimated from the 1963 coal trade flows and the 1970 regional technology coefficients, is given in Table 21-9. These results show that the greatest impact is on the coal industry. The amount of coal produced declined by more than 20 percent in the Middle Atlantic and South Atlantic regions. In all other regions, except New England, the outputs increased, the largest increases occurring in the West South Central, Mountain, and Pacific regions.

The repercussions that changes in the trade flows of coal can have on all industries were again calculated and put into summary form.[6] Detailed region-

6. Calculation 3 was made using 1970 final demands and altering only the trade coefficients for coal; therefore, these particular results do not reflect what actually occurred between 1963 and 1970, but they do indicate how shifts in coal shipments have directly and indirectly influenced production in each industry.

Table 21-8. 1963 Interregional Changes in Coal Requirements Resulting from Adjusted Electricity-Generation Technology Coefficients (thousands of 1963 dollars)

Receiving Region	1	2	3	4	5	6	7	8	9
Shipping Region	New England	Middle Atlantic	East North Central	West North Central	South Atlantic	East South Central	West South Central	Mountain	Pacific
1 New England	204	17	8	2	6	1	2	1	5
2 Middle Atlantic	29,906	135,091	28,350	3,698	43,044	2,489	2,382	1,355	-5,574
3 East North Central	2,019	8,606	107,246	37,819	8,382	10,325	-1,570	1,398	4,106
4 West North Central	69	239	449	12,019	97	98	-1,626	106	193
5 South Atlantic	29,200	62,002	72,887	12,991	103,288	16,893	-12,759	10,416	-31,417
6 East South Central	8,497	11,731	47,765	7,906	45,830	66,238	-25,066	1,211	2,354
7 West South Central	-10	-23	5	125	-32	-21	-1,399	2,281	62
8 Mountain	59	241	374	405	158	73	397	21,417	-13,126
9 Pacific	2	12	22	22	8	4	27	1,723	-1,516

Table 21-9. Percent Differences Between 1970 Regional Outputs Resulting from Adjusted Coal Trade-Flow Coefficients

Num-ber	Title	1 New England	2 Middle Atlantic	3 East North Central	4 West North Central	5 South Atlantic	6 East South Central	7 West South Central	8 Moun-tain	9 Pacific
1	Livestock & livestock products	-0.0	-0.0	0.0	0.0	-0.0	0.0	0.0	0.0	0.0
2	Other agricultural products	-0.0	-0.0	0.0	0.0	-0.0	-0.0	0.0	0.0	0.0
3	Coal mining	-100.0	-27.6	30.1	42.1	-23.7	13.7	670.2	142.7	97.0
4	Crude petroleum & natural gas	-0.0	-0.1	0.1	0.0	-0.1	-0.0	-0.0	0.1	0.0
5	Other mining	-0.0	-0.0	0.0	0.0	-0.0	-0.0	0.0	0.0	0.0
6	Construction	-0.0	-0.0	0.0	0.0	-0.0	0.0	0.0	0.0	0.0
7	Food & tobacco	-0.0	-0.0	0.0	0.0	-0.0	0.0	0.0	0.0	0.0
8	Fabrics, apparel, & footwear	-0.0	-0.0	0.0	0.0	-0.0	-0.0	0.0	0.0	0.0
9	Transport equipment & ordnance	-0.0	-0.0	0.0	0.0	-0.0	0.0	0.0	0.0	0.0
10	Lumber & paper	-0.0	-0.0	0.0	0.0	-0.0	0.0	0.0	0.1	0.0
11	Petroleum & related industries	-0.0	-0.1	0.0	0.0	-0.1	0.0	-0.0	0.1	0.1
12	Plastics & chemicals	-0.0	-0.0	0.0	0.0	-0.1	0.0	0.0	0.1	0.1
13	Glass, stone, & clay products	-0.0	-0.0	0.0	0.0	-0.0	0.0	0.1	0.1	0.0
14	Primary iron & steel manufacturing	-0.0	-0.0	0.0	0.0	-0.1	-0.0	0.0	0.3	0.0
15	Primary nonferrous manufacturing	-0.0	-0.0	0.0	-0.0	-0.0	0.0	0.0	0.0	0.0
16	Machinery & equipment	-0.0	-0.0	0.0	0.0	-0.1	0.0	0.0	0.1	0.0
17	Services	-0.0	-0.0	0.0	0.0	-0.1	0.1	0.0	0.1	0.0
18	Electricity, gas, water, & sanitary services	-0.0	-0.2	0.1	0.0	-0.2	0.2	0.0	0.3	0.0

to-region changes for Industry 3, Coal mining, are reproduced in Table 21-10. Using 1970 rather than 1963 shipments of coal has the effect of reducing all requirements of coal from Region 5, except for coal required by Region 6, which is increased slightly. The largest reduction is in the intraregional coal requirements for Region 5 itself, which declined by $95,541 thousand. However, the largest change for any region is the intraregional requirement of coal in Region 2, which decreased by $172,214 thousand. This is partially offset by a significant increase in the requirement from Region 3 of $114,468 thousand.

Of the remaining industries, the direct and indirect requirements for Industry 17, Services, are the most affected by changes in the trade flows of coal. These changes are reproduced in Table 21-11. Again, the largest change for any region is the intraregional requirement for services in Region 2, which decreased by $25,006 thousand. Also, almost all of the services required from Region 5 decreased, the exception being Region 6. This particular table illustrates very clearly the interregional repercussions that occur. An assumption of the model is that there are no interregional shipments of services. Transportation flows were estimated only for those industries that produced goods that are shipped by the regular modes of transportation, such as rail and truck. Even so, it is evident that demands in one region are affecting the amounts of services produced in other regions. The model is specially constructed so as to pick up the interregional as well as the interindustry interactions that occur.

Conclusions

The regional nature of electricity-generation processes is obvious from the background information presented in this report. Both fuel mix and the distribution of types of generation vary from region to region, depending on economic and geographical factors. Because it is likely that the increased use of coal by electric utilities will receive more and more consideration in the future, this study has focused on that fuel.

A number of economic, physical, and technological factors must be considered when determining whether or not more coal should be used to generate electricity. Current and proposed energy, transportation, and environmental policies will affect the use of coal by electricity-generating plants. Of the different energy-related issues, the most important ones affecting coal are those associated with the availability and price of oil and the mix of generating processes. One of the main transportation issues pertaining to the use of coal is whether or not rail freight transportation can be revitalized, especially in the Northeast. Two major environmental issues affect the use of coal, the first being air-quality standards in general and sulfur-pollution restrictions in particular and the second being the strip-mining restrictions under consideration by the Environmental Protection Agency. All of these issues will have to be considered seriously by policy makers.

Table 21-10. 1970 Interregional Changes in Coal Requirements Resulting from Adjusted Coal Trade-Flow Coefficients (thousands of 1963 dollars)

Shipping Region \\ Receiving Region	1 New England	2 Middle Atlantic	3 East North Central	4 West North Central	5 South Atlantic	6 East South Central	7 West South Central	8 Mountain	9 Pacific
1 New England	-537	-71	-36	-11	-29	-7	-15	-6	-23
2 Middle Atlantic	13,737	-172,214	-54,034	-8,892	-74,615	-5,491	-10,294	-4,923	-31,931
3 East North Central	16,571	114,468	94,889	-22,710	21,631	-1,294	4,176	2,661	10,919
4 West North Central	275	976	1,333	15,999	650	515	4,062	416	765
5 South Atlantic	-20,796	-15,681	-84,851	-29,417	-95,541	7,572	-24,013	-33,326	-79,201
6 East South Central	-11,118	31,656	16,759	-4,882	134,853	-7,228	-39,122	-1,523	465
7 West South Central	1,399	4,721	4,845	22,478	3,845	2,650	50,475	-3,811	2,773
8 Mountain	1,485	5,153	9,297	16,892	3,518	1,422	5,289	40,084	77,098
9 Pacific	101	335	402	4,062	219	125	305	-2,859	7,016

Table 21-11.   1970 Interregional Changes in Services Requirements Resulting from Adjusted Coal Trade-Flow Coefficients (thousands of 1963 dollars)

Shipping Region \ Receiving Region	1 New England	2 Middle Atlantic	3 East North Central	4 West North Central	5 South Atlantic	6 East South Central	7 West South Central	8 Mountain	9 Pacific
1 New England	9	-227	-118	-60	-182	-3	-50	-26	-99
2 Middle Atlantic	1,955	-25,006	-8,032	-1,521	-11,140	-786	-1,690	-819	-4,922
3 East North Central	2,167	15,152	12,520	-3,128	3,016	-188	339	371	1,412
4 West North Central	34	236	241	1,537	195	47	394	126	253
5 South Atlantic	-2,701	-2,119	-11,018	-3,857	-12,247	965	-3,199	-4,330	-10,308
6 East South Central	-1,434	3,986	2,002	-656	16,915	-902	-4,964	-226	-30
7 West South Central	119	493	444	2,524	533	300	5,707	-445	261
8 Mountain	199	710	1,247	2,221	472	187	702	5,258	10,130
9 Pacific	20	59	92	603	29	27	91	-92	1,335

The prototype study reported here was designed to show how information on the alternative regional technologies for the electricity industry and alternative transportation movements of coal could be incorporated into the basic sets of MRIO data and how the results of implementing the column trade coefficient version of the MRIO model could then be analyzed. For future studies, supplemental multiregional models should be formulated, and regional technology and interregional commodity shipments coefficients should be projected and data on capital requirements assembled for use in implementing a dynamic version of the MRIO model. In addition, either the present static or the suggested dynamic version of the MRIO model should be extended with the use of regional employment data to determine the effect on employment of changes in energy and transportation policies. There is a basic need to make multiregional analyses of regional disparities that occur through existing energy and transportation policies and to assess the effect of proposed new policies on these disparities.

The present study has indicated which industries and regions would be most affected by changes in electricity technology as well as trade shipments of coal. It has also provided a first approximation of the extent of the regional economic impact on the various industries and regions of these changes.

References

1. Duchesneau, Thomas D. *Interfuel Substitutability in the Electric Utility Sector of the U.S. Economy.* Staff Report. Washington, D.C.: Federal Trade Commission, February 1972.

2. Edison Electric Institute. *Statistical Bulletin of the Electrical Industry, 1963.* New York: Edison Electric Institute, 1964.

3. Edison Electric Institute. *Statistical Bulletin of the Electrical Industry, 1970.* New York: Edison Electric Institute, 1971.

4. [Jack] Faucett Associates, Inc. "Unreconciled 1963 Production Estimates—IO-68, Electric, Gas, Water, and Sanitary Services." Unpublished, n.d.

5. Federal Power Commission, Bureau of Power. *Staff Report on the Potential for Conversion of Oil-Fired and Gas-Fired Electric Generating Units to Use of Coal.* Washington, D.C.: Federal Power Commission, November 6, 1973 (revised).

6. Istvan, Rudyard. "1980 Inputs for Private Electric Utilities." Prepared for the Interagency Growth Project, Bureau of Labor Statistics, August 1972.

7. Istvan, Rudyard. "Outputs and Growth in the Electric Utilities." Unpublished undergraduate thesis, Harvard University, Cambridge, Massachusetts, 1972.

8. Levy, Paul F. *The Residential Demand for Electricity in New England.* Report No. MIT-EL 73–017. Cambridge, Mass.: Department of Urban Studies in Association with the Energy Laboratory, Massachusetts Institute of Technology, November 1973.

9. *Moody's Transportation Manual, 1963.* New York: Moody's Investors Service, Inc., 1963.

10. *1973 Keystone Coal Industry Manual.* New York: McGraw-Hill, Inc., Mining Information Services, 1973.

11. Polenske, Karen R., and Paul F. Levy. "Multiregional Economic Impacts of Energy and Transportation Policies." DOT Report No. 8. Prepared for the University Research Program, U.S. Department of Transportation, June 1974.

12. Polenske, Karen R., et al. *State Estimates of the Gross National Product, 1947, 1958, 1963.* Lexington, Mass.: Lexington Books, D.C. Heath and Company, 1972.

13. Polenske, Karen R., et al. *State Estimates of Technology, 1963.* Lexington, Mass.: Lexington Books, D.C. Heath and Company, 1974.

14. Rodgers, John M. *State Estimates of Interregional Commodity Trade, 1963.* Lexington, Mass.: Lexington Books, D.C. Heath and Company, 1973.

15. Rodgers, John M. *State Estimates of Outputs, Employment, and Payrolls, 1947, 1958, 1963.* Lexington, Mass.: Lexington Books, D.C. Heath and Company, 1972.

16. Scheppach, Raymond C., Jr. *State Projections of the Gross National Product, 1970, 1980.* Lexington, Mass.: Lexington Books, D.C. Heath and Company, 1972.

17. Strauss, Carl R. "A Study of Air Pollution and Coal: Sulfur Emissions and the Electric Utilities." DOT Supplementary Paper No. 1. Unpublished, June 1974.

18. U.S. Department of Commerce, Office of Business Economics. "Input-Output Structure of the U.S. Economy: 1963." *Survey of Current Business* 49, no. 11 (November 1969).

19. U.S. Department of Commerce, Office of Business Economics. *Input-Output Structure of the U.S. Economy: 1963.* Vol. 2, *Direct Requirements for Detailed Industries.* Washington, D.C.: U.S. Government Printing Office, 1969.

20. U.S. Department of the Interior, Bureau of Mines. *Minerals Yearbook, 1963.* Washington, D.C.: U.S. Government Printing Office, 1964.

21. U.S. Department of the Interior, Bureau of Mines. *Minerals Yearbook, 1970.* Washington, D.C.: U.S. Government Printing Office, 1972.

22. U.S. Department of the Interior, Division of Fossil Fuels. *Bituminous Coal and Lignite Distribution, Calendar Year 1970.* Washington, D.C.: U.S. Government Printing Office, March 1971.

23. U.S. Department of Labor, Bureau of Labor Statistics. "1970 Subcomponents of IO-68." (Unpublished data obtained by phone, March 1974.)

24. U.S. Senate, Committee on Interior and Insular Affairs. *Factors Affecting the Use of Coal in Present and Future Energy Markets.* Washington, D.C.: U.S. Government Printing Office, 1973.

Appendix 21A

Table 21A-1. Multiregional Input-Output Classification for Eighteen Industries

MRIO	BEA	Industry Title
1	1	Livestock & livestock products
2	2	Other agricultural products
3	7	Coal mining
4	8	Crude petroleum & natural gas
5		Other mining
	5	Iron & ferrous ores mining
	6	Nonferrous metal ores mining
	9	Stone & clay mining
	10	Chemical & fertilizer mineral mining
6		Construction
	11	New construction
	12	Maintenance & repair construction
7		Food & tobacco
	14	Food & kindred products
	15	Tobacco manufactures
8		Fabrics, apparel, & footwear
	16	Fabrics
	17	Textile products
	18	Apparel
	19	Misc. textile products
	33	Leather tanning & products
	34	Footwear, leather products
9		Transportation equipment & ordnance
	13	Ordnance & accessories
	59	Motor vehicles, equipment
	60	Aircraft & parts
	61	Other transportation equipment
10		Lumber & paper
	20	Lumber & wood products
	21	Wooden containers
14	37	Primary iron & steel manufacturing
15	38	Primary nonferrous manufacturing
16		Machinery & equipment
	39	Metal containers
	40	Fabricated metal products
	41	Screw mach. products, etc.
	42	Other fabricated metal products
	43	Engines & turbines
	44	Farm machinery & equipment
	45	Construction machinery & equipment
	46	Materials hand. machinery & equipment
	47	Metalworking machinery & equipment
	48	Special machinery & equipment
	49	General machinery & equipment
	50	Machine shop products
	51	Office, computing machines
	52	Service industry machines
	53	Electricity transmission equipment
	54	Household appliances
	55	Electric lighting equipment
	56	Radio, TV, etc., equipment
	57	Electronic components
	58	Misc. electrical machinery
	62	Professional, scientific instruments
	63	Medical, photo equipment
	64	Misc. manufacturing
17		Services
	3	Forestry & fishery products
	4	Agriculture, forestry, & fishery services
	65	Transportation & warehousing

	22	Household furniture
	23	Other furniture
	24	Paper & allied products
	25	Paperboard containers
	26	Printing & publishing
11	31	Petroleum, related industries
12		Plastics & chemicals
	27	Chemicals, selected products
	28	Plastics & synthetics
	29	Drugs & cosmetics
	30	Paint & allied products
	32	Rubber, misc. plastics
13		Glass, stone, & clay products
	35	Glass & glass products (18)
	36	Stone & clay products

66	Communications, excl. broadcasting
67	Radio & TV broadcasting
69	Wholesale & retail trade
70	Finance & insurance
71	Real estate & rental
72	Hotels; repair services, excl. auto.
73	Business services
74	Research & development
75	Automobile repair & services
76	Amusements
77	Medical & educational services, nonprof. organ
78	Federal government enterprises
79	State & local government enterprises
68	Electricity, gas, water, & sanitary services

Table 21A-2. MRIO Regional Classification

Regions (9)	Census Region	States (51)	Regions (9)	Census Region	States (51)
1	New England	6 Connecticut 18 Maine 20 Massachusetts 28 New Hampshire 38 Rhode Island 44 Vermont	6	East South Central	1 Alabama 16 Kentucky 23 Mississippi 41 Tennessee
2	Middle Atlantic	29 New Jersey 31 New York 37 Pennsylvania	7	West South Central	3 Arkansas 17 Louisiana 35 Oklahoma 42 Texas
3	East North Central	12 Illinois 13 Indiana 21 Michigan 34 Ohio 48 Wisconsin	8	Mountain	2 Arizona 5 Colorado 11 Idaho 25 Montana 27 Nevada 30 New Mexico 43 Utah 49 Wyoming
4	West North Central	14 Iowa 15 Kansas 22 Minnesota 24 Missouri 26 Nebraska 33 North Dakota 40 South Dakota	9	Pacific	4 California 36 Oregon 46 Washington 50 Alaska 51 Hawaii
5	South Atlantic	7 Delaware 8 District of Columbia 9 Florida 10 Georgia 19 Maryland 32 North Carolina 39 South Carolina 45 Virginia 47 West Virginia			

Part Six

International Trade Studies

Chapter Twenty-Two

Structures of Trade, Production, and Development

K. Tokoyama
Y. Kobayashi
Y. Murakami
J. Tsukui

In two of his books [15; 16] Nurkse casts doubt on the effectiveness of the nineteenth-century prescription for growth through trade. His insistence is that any country trying to "take off" and then to sustain a steady rate of growth should diversify production, rather than specialize in outputs of particular commodities, say, primary materials, in accordance with some international comparative advantage. The classical theory of comparative advantage, according to Nurkse, has lost relevance to reality in the contemporary developing countries. First, the theory of international trade, or its modern version, the Heckscher-Ohlin theorem, is one of comparative statics dealing with what happens to autarkic economies when trade is suddenly freed. But the problem that the developing countries now confront is how to realize a self-sustained rapid rate of growth comparable to that of the developed countries; and this is a problem that should be analyzed in a dynamic framework. Second, the classical theory assumes full employment of production factors, while Nurkse's factual observations strongly suggest that, contrary to the generally accepted observations, the developing countries are abundant not only in labor but also in capital, so that the theory is not applicable to these countries. It is a sluggish expansion of demands, not a scarcity of capital, that hinders developing countries from "take off." Hence, they should diversify production to provide markets for one another domestically. This argument has led to the Nurksean concept of balanced growth.

The first point, which seems to be persuasive, demands reconstruction of the theory in a dynamic setting. However, the second point is not fully pertinent, since what really impedes growth is not the scarcity of capital in general, but of capital available for production. In other words, the true obstacle is a lack of long-term prospects that will encourage capital invest-

The authors wish to thank M. Kondo of the Economic Planning Agency for his computational assistance.

ment. Thus, a country, though abundant in capital, may not have a strong engine for growth. There can be two alternative ways of breakthrough, namely, domestic production and imports. Which alternative an economy should choose depends upon its dynamic comparative advantage. In some circumstances, specialization may enjoy a comparative advantage; in others, diversification may. That is to say, Nurkse's prescription is not a logical necessity.

The present paper attempts to show that, even in a dynamic setting, the optimal composition of outputs may vary from diversification to specialization with changing terms of trade. The model used here is an optimizing version of a multisectoral linear model. Since many models focusing on the relation between patterns of trade and development have been predecessors of the present one,[1] it is necessary to justify constructing still another such model. Most of the earlier models are single-period models that are static in character and have little relevance to the present concerns. Even in those models that are intended to be dynamic, artificial exogenous constraints are imposed from practical considerations. Thus, exogenous effects inevitably mingle in the optimal solutions, so that they may not reflect a true dynamic comparative advantage to be determined by production functions and factor endowments. The model presented below is dynamic in the exact sense of the term and is not subject to any artificial exogenous restrictions.

A Dynamic Trade and Development Model

Consider a developing country that has n industries. Let the country be very small, in the sense that its exports and imports have little effect on world prices. It follows that the country can freely change the amount of its production without affecting the terms of trade. Moreover, it is assumed that the economy is so abundant in labor that the limit to growth is not due to scarcity of labor. These two conditions seem to be common to all the less-developed countries in the stage preceding "take off." The following discussion will be conducted within this framework.

The formulation of the model essentially follows an earlier model by Murakami et al. [14], which is a linear programming version of the dynamic Leontief model. The demand-supply conditions will be expressed as follows:

$$X_t + M_t \geqslant AX_t + K_t + C_t + E_t \tag{22-1}$$

$$d + PE_t \geqslant QM_t + RX_t \tag{22-2}$$

---

1. Discussions of this work will be found in, among others, Bruno [3]; Bruno, Dougherty, and Fraenkel [4]; Chenery and Raduchel [7]; Chenery and Uzawa [8]; Eckaus and Parikh [9]; Mann and Weisskopf [13]; and Tendulkar [17].

where $K_t = B(X_{t+1} - X_t)$, and X_0, C_0, M_0, and E_0 are given by initial conditions. All variables must be nonnegative. A summary of the notation follows.

Variables:

X_t = column vector of outputs in period t

C_t = column vector of consumption in period t

K_t = column vector of investment in period t

E_t = column vector of exports in period t

M_t = column vector of competitive imports in period t

Parameters:

A = matrix of input coefficients

B = matrix of stock-flow coefficients

P = row vector of export prices, with each element p_i representing the price of a unit of exports of commodity i in terms of foreign exchange (row)

Q = row vector of competitive import costs, with each element q_i representing the cost of a unit of competitive imports of commodity i in terms of foreign exchange

R = row vector of noncompetitive import costs, with each element r_i representing the cost of imported materials required per unit of domestic production in terms of foreign exchange

d = trade deficit or foreign aid (scalar)

Further notation is introduced as required.

The meanings of equations (22-1) and (22-2) are self-evident. Equation (22-1) requires that production plus imports be sufficient to meet intermediate and final demands plus exports. Foreign trade is restricted by requiring that the trade deficit should not exceed a predetermined amount d. It is assumed below that an economy cannot expect to be receiving foreign aid or loans over a long period of time; consequently, $d = 0$. (A relaxation of this constraint, $d = 0$, would not be difficult and would not significantly affect our conclusion.)

Although the problem of development programming is conventionally formulated as the maximization of the utility sum derived from the consumption achievable subject to the constraints described above, we will not follow this line. The reason is that the application of linear programming as a practical algorithm for solving the problem necessitates a linearization of the utility function, and this is apt to result in a flip-flop solution, unless modified by some relationships. Another approach is to limit the changes in variables exogenously, as in most of the earlier models mentioned. As previously noted, however, it is desirable to dispense with exogenous restrictions as far as possible. An alternative way is to reduce the degrees of freedom in the model by changing consumption from being a control variable to being a dependent variable and to replace utility as the maximand by the value of final stocks. Thus, consumption is assumed to be a linear function of national income

$$C_t = C_m VX_t \tag{22-3}$$

where C_m is a vector representing marginal propensity to consume for each commodity and V is a vector standing for value-added ratios by industry. The maximand becomes UBX_T, where U is a valuation vector, with each element u_i representing the preference for commodity i in the terminal period.

Inserting equation (22-3) in equation (22-1) and treating all commodities, including foreign exchange, alike, our programming problem can now be simply expressed as follows:
Maximize

$$U^*B^*X_T^* \tag{22-4}$$

subject to

$$[A^* + B^*]X_t^* - B^*X_{t+1}^* \geq 0 \qquad (t = 0, 1, \ldots, T-1) \tag{22-5}$$

$$X_t^* \geq 0$$

where A^* and B^* are $(n + 1) \times 3n$ extended matrices and X_t^* is an extended $3n$-dimensional vector; that is,

$$A^* = \begin{bmatrix} I - A - C_m V & I & -I \\ -R & & -Q & P \end{bmatrix} \qquad B^* = \begin{bmatrix} B & 0 & 0 \\ 0 & 0 & 0 \end{bmatrix} \qquad X_t^* = \begin{bmatrix} X_t \\ M_t \\ E_t \end{bmatrix} \qquad U^* = [U \ \ 0]$$

Foreign exchange is a special commodity in the sense that it can be easily turned into any commodity through international trade, and vice versa. Thus, alternative production processes exist for each commodity: two processes (domestic production and imports) for an ordinary good and n processes (exports) for foreign exchange.

It is clear that the extended programming problem is a special case of the system developed by Tsukui [18]; therefore, his turnpike theorem can be applied to the model.[2] In other words, with any $U^* \geq 0$, any solution to the problem must remain in a certain neighborhood of the turnpike during most of the periods except those near the beginning and the end. In actuality, simulations strongly suggest that in most cases the sensitivity of a solution with respect to the change in valuation vector is imperceptible except for the final few periods.[3] It follows that arbitrariness in setting up a valuation vector does not give rise to difficulties.

Turnpike here is defined as follows: Let A_σ^* and B_σ^* be $(n + 1) \times (n + 1)$ matrices composed of $(n + 1)$ column vectors, each of which is selected from A^* and B^* so as to be among the activities possible for each industry. Matrices A_σ^* and B_σ^* are called the "σ technology." The number of σ-technologies is $2^n n$. Referring to the Frobenius theorem, it is seen that for each technology, with the assumption that A_σ satisfies the Hawkins-Simon's condition, there exists a nonnegative eigenvalue λ_σ and a nonnegative vector X_σ^* such that

$$[\lambda_\sigma I^* - (A_\sigma^*)^{-1} B_\sigma^*] X_\sigma^* = 0$$

Let λ_* be the minimum value among λ_σ. Let X_*^* be the eigenvector accompanied with λ_*. The inverse of λ_* gives the maximal growth factor feasible for the economy, and X_*^* is the turnpike. Matrices A_*^* and B_*^*, which give λ_* and X_*^*, will be called the "turnpike technology."

It would not be legitimate to approximate the empirical consumption function by a homogeneous function as in equation (22–3). Therefore, in the computations the following nonhomogeneous linear consumption function was used:

$$C_t = \bar{C} + C_m V X_t$$

where $\bar{C}$ is a vector representing for each commodity the basic (subsistence) consumption. Thus, the computational model is:

Maximize

$$\alpha z + \beta$$

subject to

$$[A^* + B^*] X_t^* - B^* X_{t+1}^* + S_t^* - S_{t+1}^* \geq \bar{C}^* \qquad (t = 0, 1, \ldots, T - 2)$$

---

2. If formally stated, the sufficient conditions for the existence of a turnpike given in his paper are not satisfied in this system. However, as will be seen later, the existence is empirically guaranteed.

3. For example, see Murakami et al. [14].

$$[A^* + B^*]X^*_{T-1} - B^* Z^* z + S^*_{T-1} \geqslant \bar{C} + B^* \bar{X}^*$$

where

$$\alpha = U^* B^* Z^* \qquad \beta = U^* B^* \bar{X}^* \qquad \bar{C} = \begin{bmatrix} \bar{C} \\ 0 \end{bmatrix} \qquad \bar{X}^* = \begin{bmatrix} (I - A - C_m V)^{-1} \bar{C} \\ 0 \\ 0 \end{bmatrix}$$

The positive constant vector, Z^*, and the valuation vector, U^*, may be arbitrarily determined, since a version of turnpike theorem holds in this nonhomogeneous case.[4] The vector $\bar{X}^*$ stands for the production level in the stationary state. Stock activity, S^*_t, is introduced to allow unemployed capital to be transferred to the next period, not simply discarded.

Data for the Model

Since our concerns are centered on the problem of the relationship between trade structure and economic growth in developing countries, it may be desirable to use data of those countries. However, those data are difficult to find. Parameters could be estimated only with a rather wide margin of error, if at all. Thus, it was decided tentatively to use data for the Japanese economy, which may not be so unreasonable as it appears to be at first sight. There seem to be several justifications for this. First of all, the technology that has been adopted by an economy must be accessible to all economies because of that technology's universality. In other words, the production process employed by Japan belongs to the technology set feasible for a developing country. Needless to say, the choice of the technology must have depended upon the prices of commodities, and ultimately those of factors. However, considering that a superfluity of labor has prevailed in Japan for many years, her choice is likely to reflect that of a developing country with a similar grouping of factor endowments.

It may be less appropriate to apply the consumption pattern of one economy to that of another country, since natural environment and historical influences that differ from country to country are the leading economic determinants. On the level of aggregation of the present study, however, it may be expected that a similar pattern will be observed in all countries. Thus, it was decided to make use of the Japanese consumption pattern as a first approximation.

The 8-sector classification used is as follows:

1. Primary industry
2. Light industry
3. Heavy industry
4. Construction

5. Energy
6. Transportation
7. Services and trade
8. Foreign exchange

4. See Tsukui and Kobayashi [19].

Although the definition of sectors is self-evident, it is to be noted that mining is classified as heavy industry. This classification is not inappropriate in Japan, since domestic mining production is negligible.

The preparation of data follows the work by Murakami et al. cited above [14]; hence, brief explanations will suffice. Consumption functions were estimated from the 56-order flow tables of 1960 [11] and 1965 [12]. Value-added ratios were calculated from the table of 1965. Estimated parameters and constants are shown in Table 22-1. Input-output coefficients were calculated from the flow table of 1965 and the 56-order capital-stock table of 1965 prepared by the Economic Planning Agency [10]. Stock-flow coefficients were calculated through the aggregation of the 56-order stock-flow table of 1965 [10]. Tables 22-2 and 22-3 show these coefficients.

Coefficients p_i and q_i need further discussion. When commodities are measured in terms of one yen's worth, we have

$$p_i = \frac{\rho p_i^e}{p_i^d} \quad \text{and} \quad q_i = \frac{\rho p_i^m}{p_i^d} \tag{22-6}$$

where ρ is the rate of exchange and p_i^d are domestic prices; p_i^e and p_i^m are export prices fob (free on board) and import prices cif (cost, insurance, and freight) including custom duties. For simplicity, it is assumed in the following computations that p_i and q_i are the same among all commodities, and moreover, that each q_i is unity, that is, domestic prices are equal to import prices valued in terms of the home currency. This simplification can be safely employed if domestic prices are proportionate to the world prices for whatever reason—free trade, for example. Thus

$$P = \pi(1, 1, \ldots, 1) \quad \text{and} \quad Q = (1, 1, \ldots, 1)$$

Table 22-1. Estimated Parameters and Constants

Industry		Parameters			Constants	
Number	Title	C_m	V	R	C	X_0
					(billion yen)	
1	Primary industry	.014659	.659117	.003060	711	4746
2	Light industry	.150892	.287734	.057217	2510	15071
3	Heavy industry	.055625	.325535	.027484	−441	18035
4	Construction	.139149	.376694	.000307	−896	6640
5	Energy	.009365	.568278	.192887	104	2619
6	Transportation	.029400	.657749	.000034	220	4552
7	Services & trade	.253034	.777157	.000232	4075	17323

Source: Tsukui, J., and Y. Kobayashi, "Economic Development and the Change of Industrial Structure" (in Japanese, unpublished, no date).

Table 22-2. Input-Output Matrix, 1965

Producing Industry		Purchasing Industry						
Num-ber	Title	1	2	3	4	5	6	7
1	Primary industry	.116899	.188811	.003319	.003582	.006194	.000779	.001539
2	Light industry	.087401	.246524	.054727	.222182	.017587	.060089	.028709
3	Heavy industry	.093050	.115793	.481436	.264585	.109449	.172828	.049409
4	Construction	.033417	.008376	.012027	.002362	.058102	.048656	.060035
5	Energy	.017296	.022948	.041981	.018002	.100152	.055104	.020653
6	Transportation	.015895	.034280	.030384	.046730	.033421	.088958	.051639
7	Services & trade	.038797	.070129	.072233	.087566	.041962	.059793	.082744
	Total	.402755	.686861	.696107	.645009	.366867	.486207	.294728

Source: Tsukui, J., and Y. Kobayashi, "Economic Development and the Change of Industrial Structure" (in Japanese, unpublished, no date).

Table 22-3. Stock-Flow Matrix, 1965

Producing Industry		Purchasing Industry						
Num-ber	*Title*	*1*	*2*	*3*	*4*	*5*	*6*	*7*
1	Primary industry	.216970	.007923	.000744	.000626	.000581	.000049	.010257
2	Light industry	.023753	.057351	.031642	.049529	.051854	.020233	.055729
3	Heavy industry	.427369	.229705	.351573	.203747	.985380	.618917	.134825
4	Construction	1.273637	.173703	.191152	.060755	1.328698	1.183269	.582351
5	Energy	.003946	.001016	.002852	.003115	.011856	.000442	.010480
6	Transportation	.008600	.005863	.008337	.010599	.019320	.019095	.024567
7	Services & trade	.061611	.024732	.033679	.037475	.079375	.090713	.071292
	Total	2.015886	.500293	.619979	.365846	2.477964	1.842005	.889501

Source: Tsukui, J., and Y. Kobayashi, "Economic Development and the Change of Industrial Structure" (in Japanese, unpublished, no date).

The scalar π will be parametrically changed to assess its possible effect on the structures of production and trade.

There may be several explanations of the meaning of the parameter π. Let p_i^w and $\hat{p}_i^w$ be the world prices of the commodities with their origin in the home country and those of the identical commodities with their origin in the rest of the world, respectively. Then.

$$p_i^w = p_i^e + f_i^e \qquad \text{and} \qquad p_i^m = \hat{p}_i^w + f_i^m + t_i^m \tag{22-7}$$

where f_i^e and f_i^m are the international transportation costs charged by non-resident enterprises and t_i^m is the import tax. From equation (22-7)

$$p_i^m - p_i^e = (\hat{p}_i^w - p_i^w) + (f_i^e + f_i^m) + t_i^m$$

That is, the difference between import prices and export prices is decomposed into three components: the discrepancy in valuation in the world markets of the identical commodities with different origins, the transportation costs paid abroad, and customs duties.

Let the home country be a developing country. Then, her backwardness in the international transportation services will cause the major portion of the transportation costs to be paid to the rest of the world, say, to the developed area; hence, $f_i^e + f_i^m > 0$. The country may also impose heavy import taxes to protect her infant industries; hence $t_i^m > 0$. The discrepancy in valuation is ascribed to several causes. It may be a reflection of the disparity in quality as well as good will value. It may also be the consequence of certain policies adopted by the developing country. For example, the country in question may artificially fix the rate of exchange or pay subsidies so as to reduce export prices for promoting the exports. Therefore, the discrepancy is likely to be positive. Thus, for the developing country, p_i^m is not less than p_i^e, which means that $\pi \leqslant 1$. In any case, the parameter π, called the "terms of trade" below, may be considered to be an index of the degree of development.

The model covers a time span of ten periods. It should be noted that Industry 4, Construction; Industry 6, Transportation; and Industry 7, Services & trade, are assumed to be nontraded overseas because of the nature of these commodities.

Numerical Results and Analysis

For the execution of the computations, π and Z^* need to be specified. Since the purpose of the present study is to assess the effect of changes in the terms of trade on the structure of the economy, it is necessary to obtain solutions for various values of π. For a developing country, it can be safely assumed that π is not greater than 1, as the foregoing interpretation suggests. Computations have been conducted for the following four cases: $\pi = 0.6, 0.8, 0.9,$ and $1.0.$ The value of Z^* was adjusted so as to be equal to the turnpike ratio. The initial conditions are the actual 1965 Japanese values. Numerical results are shown in Tables 22-4 through 22-7.

There are some interesting observations to be made concerning the results shown in these tables. First, it is to be noted that it takes several periods, though varying from case to case, for the optimal paths to attain a sustained growth. Deteriorations in the terms of trade result in lengthening the adjustment periods and lowering the rate of sustained growth. The sustained growth is a turnpike, which is suggested by observing that the composition of the computed outputs less basic outputs—X_t^* - $\bar{X}^*$—becomes identical to that of the eigenvector given by the efficient technology at the end of adjustment periods and thereafter stays constant. Needless to say, efficient technologies differ from case to case. In every case, the activities selected are identical through a sustained growth. In the cases where π = 0.6 and 0.8, domestic production is efficient for every commodity, so that a country should diversify its production under such unfavorable terms of trade. Only noncompetitive material goods should be imported; the foreign exchange required is obtained by exporting commodities produced by heavy or light industry.

It is paradoxical that heavy industry plays an important role in leading growth in the lowest stage of development. The paradoxical aspect is strengthened when it is noted that, contrary to the generally accepted theories, at the higher stages, light industry has to replace heavy industry as the leading sector. At the higher stages, importing becomes an efficient activity for several commodities. For example, when π = 0.9, the domestic production of energy should be shut down and imported energy substituted. At the highest stage, domestic production has to be discontinued for two further industries, namely, the primary and heavy industries. In light industry, whose products in part are exported, domestic production becomes specialized and this provides the foreign exchange required for both competitive and noncompetitive imports.

Almost all the actual observations, qualitatively, meet the theoretical expectations, since the effect of decreasing π is formally equivalent to that of increasing input-output coefficients. An advantage of the present study lies in establishing this conjecture quantitatively. It is also impressive that an improvement in the terms of trade brings about a progressive increase in the rate of sustained growth.

Conclusion

The above discussions may be summarized as follows: Nurkse's prescription for growth—the so-called balanced-growth prescription—is not a universal remedy. It can be applied only to the lower stage of development. There may be the case where a specialization of production is efficient at a higher stage of development.

Table 22–4. Optimal Path for π = 0.6

Num-ber	Title	Period 0	1	2	3	4	5 (Billion Yen)	6	7	8	9	10
1	Primary industry	4,764	4,699	5,030	4,947	4,949	4,975	5,003	5,035	5,073	5,120	5,180
2	Light industry	15,071	13,196	16,134	15,607	15,564	15,656	15,757	15,868	15,994	16,151	16,486
3	Heavy industry	18,036	13,920	22,430	21,235	21,113	21,295	21,496	21,715	21,945	22,131	21,843
4	Construction	6,648	2,910	8,305	6,605	6,298	6,364	6,436	6,516	6,610	6,744	7,149
5	Energy	9,619	5,526	0	2,331	2,774	2,793	2,814	2,837	2,863	2,890	2,915
6	Transportation	4,552	3,681	4,324	4,240	4,241	4,268	4,299	4,333	4,370	4,414	4,494
7	Services & trade	17,323	16,416	18,618	18,352	18,361	18,459	18,567	18,687	18,819	18,970	19,213
8	Foreign exchange	--	3,704	2,603	3,246	3,379	3,402	3,428	3,457	3,488	3,520	3,548
	Rate of growth (%)	--	(1, 3) -12.5	(3) 24.0	(3) -2.0	(3) 0.0	(3) 0.7	(3) 0.7	(3) 0.8	(3) 0.9	(3) 1.0	(3) 1.1

Note: Figures in parentheses are the code numbers of industries whose products are exported
- - means not applicable to base period

Table 22-5. Optimal Path for π = 0.8

Num-ber	Industry Title	Period										
		0	1	2	3	4	5	6	7	8	9	10
							(Billion Yen)					
1	Primary industry	4,746	6,055	2,745	5,242	5,671	5,768	5,876	5,995	6,124	6,243	6,237
2	Light industry	15,071	26,210	0	16,409	18,887	19,245	19,644	20,089	20,587	21,154	21,816
3	Heavy industry	18,038	10,722	17,714	21,210	16,266	16,727	17,242	17,820	18,475	19,235	20,136
4	Construction	6,648	0	7,852	9,138	6,713	6,927	7,164	7,429	7,717	8,037	8,358
5	Energy	9,619	3,055	4,908	0	2,658	2,716	2,780	2,851	2,932	3,025	3,148
6	Transportation	4,552	3,731	3,408	4,335	4,244	4,330	4,427	4,535	4,656	4,797	5,001
7	Services & trade	17,323	16,458	15,464	18,650	18,331	18,636	18,977	19,357	19,783	20,269	20,932
8	Foreign exchange	3,008	1,377	1,931		2,580	2,636	2,698	2,768	2,846	2,936	3,045
			(3,5)	(3)	(3)	(2)	(2)	(2)	(2)	(2)	(2)	(2)
	Rate of growth (%)		-4.0	-21.4	44.0	-3.0	2.2	2.4	2.6	2.8	3.1	3.5

Note: Figures in parentheses are the code numbers of industries whose products are exported.

- - means not applicable to base period

Table 22-6. Optimal Path for $\pi = 0.9$

Num-ber	Title	Period										
		0	1	2	3	4	5 (Billion Yen)	6	7	8	9	10
1	Primary industry	4,746	4,688	5,607	6,763	6,960	7,181	7,430	7,708	8,008	8,273	8,161
2	Light industry	15,071	13,518	16,972	23,562	24,308	25,148	26,094	27,161	28,364	29,772	31,218
3	Heavy industry	18,038	11,920	21,195	18,640	19,471	20,407	21,464	22,663	24,050	25,869	28,187
4	Construction	6,648	3,994	8,922	7,634	8,012	8,437	8,916	9,449	10,048	10,438	12,360
5	Energy	9,619	5,677	0	2,722[a]	2,818[a]	2,926[a]	3,047[a]	3,184[a]	3,340[a]	3,527[a]	3,791[a]
6	Transportation	4,552	3,711	4,445	4,669	4,825	5,001	5,199	5,422	5,674	5,973	6,364
7	Services & trade	17,323	16,483	19,070	19,835	20,384	21,003	21,700	22,486	23,374	24,416	25,667
8	Foreign exchange	- -	2,462	1,753	5,123	5,303	5,505	5,734	5,992	6,285	6,640	7,097
	Rate of growth (%)	- -	(3)[b] −13.0	(3) 27.0	(2) 6.4	(2) 3.5	(2) 3.8	(2) 4.2	(2) 4.5	(2) 4.9	(2) 5.0	(2) 6.9

[a]The commodity is imported and its domestic production has been discontinued.

[b]Figures in parentheses are the code numbers of industries whose products are exported.

- - means not applicable to base period

Table 22-7. Optimal Path for $\pi = 1.0$

Num-ber	Title	Period 0	1	2	3	4	5 (Billion Yen)	6	7	8	9	10
1	Primary industry	4,746	6,598[a]	13,103[a]	13,872[a]	14,761[a]	15,786[a]	16,969[a]	18,336[a]	19,908[a]	21,746[a]	24,354[a]
2	Light industry	15,071	28,634	61,760	65,588	70,005	75,105	80,991	87,788	95,592	104,893	112,300
3	Heavy industry	18,038	7,896[a]	14,868[a]	15,963[a]	17,228[a]	18,688[a]	20,372[a]	22,320[a]	24,536[a]	27,329[a]	30,473[a]
4	Construction	6,648	4,058	8,867	9,592	10,429	11,394	12,510	13,789	15,344	16,501	23,778
5	Energy	9,619	5,240	2,869[a]	3,037[a]	3,230[a]	3,454[a]	3,711[a]	4,009[a]	4,352[a]	4,756[a]	5,284[a]
6	Transportation	4,552	4,081	5,714	6,047	6,432	6,975	7,387	7,979	8,660	9,464	10,273
7	Services & trade	17,323	17,327	22,269	23,366	24,632	26,093	27,780	29,728	31,971	34,622	37,336
8	Foreign exchange	--	13,024	34,382	36,634	39,234	42,234	45,698	49,699	54,278	59,847	66,522
	Rate of growth (%)	--	(2, 5)[b] −8.0	(2) 55.3	(2) 6.1	(2) 6.6	(2) 7.1	(2) 7.7	(2) 8.3	(2) 8.8	(2) 9.2	(2) 11.0

[a]The commodity is imported and its domestic production has been discontinued.
[b]Figures in parentheses are the code numbers of industries whose products are exported.

-- means not applicable to base period

Paradoxically, the strategy for industrial growth appears to be to stress heavy industries in the early stage and light ones in the late stage.

These conclusions need some qualifications, of course. The two most important ones are: First, the present analysis provides only a pilot research for more meaningful studies. The structures of technology and consumer preference used here reflect only the particular environment in which Japan is situated. Japan is a resource-poor country and as a result must import almost all resources noncompetitively. Japan is also a dramatic case of land-poor agriculture. The domestic production processes open to a developing country that is richer in resources will differ from those of Japan and may, therefore, require a different pattern of development. In such cases, we can substitute indigenous data for the Japanese data, and proceed to the next stage of analysis. Second, it has been assumed throughout the present study that labor is abundant. However, the modern technology of production requires not labor in general, but labor by skill category, which may be scarce in the less-developed countries. To handle this problem, labor constraints have been introduced explicitly and the final stocks as maximand have been replaced by the sum of utilities or consumptions—which, incidentally, will open a road to preventing a flip-flop solution. This is a possible step to take in a future study.

References

1. Adelman, I., and E. Thorbecke, eds. *The Theory and Design of Economic Development.* Baltimore, Maryland: Johns Hopkins Press, 1966.

2. Arrow, K.; L. Hurwicz; and H. Uzawa, eds. *Studies in Linear and Nonlinear Programming.* Stanford, California: Stanford University Press, 1958.

3. Bruno, M. "Optimal Patterns of Trade and Development." *The Review of Economics and Statistics* 49, no. 4 (November 1967): 545–554. (Reprinted in 8.)

4. Bruno, M.; C. Dougherty; and M. Fraenkel. "Dynamic Input-Output, Trade and Development." In *Input-Output Techniques.* Vol. 2, *Applications of Input-Output Analysis.* Edited by A.P. Carter and A. Bródy. Amsterdam: North-Holland Publishing Company, 1970. Pp. 48–69.

5. Carter, A.P., and A. Bródy, eds. *Input-Output Techniques.* Vol. 2, *Applications of Input-Output Analysis.* Amsterdam: North-Holland Publishing Company, 1970.

6. Chenery, H.B., ed. *Studies in Development Planning.* Cambridge, Mass.: Harvard University Press, 1971.

7. Chenery, H., and W. Raduchel. "Substitution in Planning Models." In *Studies in Development Planning.* Edited by H.B. Chenery. Cambridge, Mass.: Harvard University Press, 1971. Pp. 29–47.

8. Chenery, H., and H. Uzawa. "Non-linear Programming in Economic Development." In *Studies in Linear and Non-linear Programming.* Edited by K. Arrow, L. Hurwicz, and H. Uzawa. Stanford, California: Stanford University Press, 1958. Pp. 203–229.

9. Eckaus, R., and K. Parikh. *Planning for Growth.* Cambridge, Mass.: MIT Press, 1968.

10. Economic Planning Agency. "Estimates of Capital Coefficients." *Keizai Bunseki* 35 (1972): 1–39. (In Japanese.)

11. Economic Planning Agency et al. "Inter-Industry Tables, 1960." Government of Japan, 1964. (In Japanese.)

12. Economic Planning Agency et al. "Inter-Industry Tables, 1965." Government of Japan, 1969. (In Japanese.)

13. Manne, A.S., and T.E. Weisskopf. "A Dynamic Multisectoral Model for India, 1967–75." In *Input-Output Techniques.* Vol. 2, *Applications of Input-Output Analysis.* Edited by A.P. Carter and A. Bródy. Amsterdam: North-Holland Publishing Company, 1970. Pp. 70–102.

14. Murakami, Y.; K. Tokoyama; and J. Tsukui. "Efficient Paths of Accumulation and the Turnpike of the Japanese Economy." In *Input-Output Techniques.* Vol. 2, *Applications of Input-Output Analysis.* Edited by A.P. Carter and A. Bródy. Amsterdam: North-Holland Publishing Company, 1970. Pp. 24–47.

15. Nurkse, R. *Equilibrium and Growth in the World Economy.* Cambridge, Mass.: Harvard University Press, 1961.

16. Nurkse, R. *Patterns of Trade and Development.* Oxford: Basil Blackwell, 1961.

17. Tendulkar, S. "Interaction Between Domestic and Foreign Resources in Economic Growth: Some Experiments for India." In *Studies in Development Planning.* Edited by H.B. Chenery. Cambridge, Mass.: Harvard University Press, 1971. Pp. 122–154.

18. Tsukui, J. "Turnpike Theorem in a Generalized Dynamic Input-Output System." *Econometrica* 34, no. 2 (April 1966): 396–407.

19. Tsukui, J., and Y. Kobayashi. "Economic Development and the Change of Industrial Structure." (In Japanese, unpublished, no date.)

Chapter Twenty-Three

A Multilateral Model of
Japanese-American Trade

Peter A. Petri

The empirical analysis of international trade flows has been recently advanced along two important avenues of research. On one hand, the world-wide effort of Project Link [2] appears to have made substantial progress in modelling the international interdependence of macroeconomic aggregates. On the other hand, several independent researchers have recently obtained quite promising estimates of import functions at relatively fine product detail [11]. This study attempts to fuse these trends in an effort to develop a product-disaggregated system of multilateral interdependence.

The present model deals specifically with the trade network connecting the United States, Japan, and the rest of the world. Dissatisfaction with earlier results based on a linear programming strategy has led to a formulation that combines econometrically estimated demand functions with an input-output system of production. The approach is similar to that proposed by Barker [3].

The empirical model is still in an exploratory stage, and the purpose of this report is to highlight some of the issues involved in its formulation and estimation. Though important refinements remain to be made, promising results were achieved in a simple simulation of multilateral adjustments to variation in exchange rates.

Some fundamental assumptions are discussed in the following section. The next three sections deal with the output, price, and trade equations, respectively. The remaining sections show how the model was applied to simulate the impact of exchange rate variations on the U.S. and Japanese economies.

Background Assumptions

Assumptions about product homogeneity are central to all empirical research on international trade: imported products and their domestically produced counter-

The author wishes to thank Professor Iwao Ozaki for providing important Japanese data at various stages of this analysis.

parts can be regarded either as perfect substitutes—essentially indistinguishable—or as imperfect substitutes with many similarities and some differences.

The assumption that imports and domestic products are perfect substitutes leads to a set of models in which imports appear as the balancing residual between domestic supply and demand *at world export prices.*[1] These models are typically solved by linear programming methods, and prove to be inherently inaccurate in predicting, or even reproducing, actual trade flows. A close look at their structure often reveals arbitrary constraints on domestic production—restrictions designed specifically to tame unreasonable trade behavior. In the short run, these constraints (the frequently used limits on the expansion and contraction rates of industries, for example) may be justified, but they are unacceptable in models covering longer periods of time.

The assumption of product heterogeneity, or that imports are merely imperfect substitutes for domestic goods of the same product category, suggests a more realistic approach. In the resulting models, import shares depend on consumer preferences (conditioned by prices and incomes), and shares between 0.0 and 1.0 are no longer poised on a knife-edge. This strategy also admits cross-hauling, the important empirical fact that countries often export *and* import products falling into the same product category.

Unfortunately, the "heterogeneous" approach cannot be implemented directly, because the precise differentiating characteristics of imported goods are not easily identified, even at extremely fine levels of product detail. A practical alternative, suggested by Armington [1], Rhomberg [12], and others, is to regard the place of production of goods as their prime differentiating characteristic. In some cases, the place of production is in fact important in a purchasing decision, as for tailor-made products and those that involve considerable servicing by the manufacturer. In most cases, however, the place of production is used as a proxy for other, unobserved differentiating characteristics. This approach is adopted in the present study; its implications will be discussed later.

In order to simplify implementation of the present model, another strong assumption was added: while products *within* each sector are considered substitutes, products originating in different sectors are treated as strict complements. Introducing intersectoral substitutions would greatly complicate the solution strategies, since a new set of nonlinear functions would then have to replace the model's present input-output core. Compromises that permit limited intersectoral substitution have yet to be explored.

Output Equations

While this study deals primarily with Japanese-American trade, a Rest-of-the-World (ROW) sector is included to account for third-partner relationships. For

1. See, for example, Bruno [4], Evans [6], and Werin [13].

this sector, certain key economic variables are assumed to be known. In particular, price and domestic demand equations are developed in detail only for the United States and Japan (in the notation used below, $i = 1$ and 2, respectively); ROW product prices and overall import demands are treated exogenously. Distinct trade equations are specified for all three "countries" of the system ($i = 1, 2, 3$); thus, the American and Japanese shares of ROW imports are endogenously determined.

The basic input-output balance equations (23-1) are assumed to govern production in each of the two endogenous economies

$$X_i = A_i X_i + C_i Y_i + \sum_j E_{ij} - \sum_j M_{ij} \qquad i = 1, 2 \qquad (23\text{-}1)$$

where

X_i = $(n \times 1)$ output vector of country i

Y_i = $(k \times 1)$ vector of expenditures by final demand category in country i

E_{ij} = $(n \times 1)$ vector of exports—from country i to country j

M_{ij} = $(n \times 1)$ vector of imports—of country i from country j

A_i = $(n \times n)$ matrix of technical coefficients in country i

C_i = $(n \times k)$ matrix of final demand coefficients in country i

n = number of products

Summations in equation (23-1) and in subsequent equations implicitly run across trading partners, that is, $j = 1, 2, 3$ for $i \neq j$.

In accordance with conventions for input-output accounts in producers' values, exports are valued at fob (free on board) prices, and imports are valued at cc (customs clearance) prices, that is, with freight, insurance, and duties included. International consistency then requires

$$M_{ij} = \hat{V}_{ij}^e E_{ji} \qquad j = 1, 2, 3; \ i = 1, 2, 3; \ i \neq j \qquad (23\text{-}2)$$

where V_{ij}^e is an $(n \times 1)$ vector of cc/fob valuation converters for imports of country i from country j (that is, from fob into cc prices) and $\wedge$ indicates a diagonal matrix.

It is convenient to express imports as shares of total domestic demand, defined as the sum of final and intermediate demands

$$D_i = A_i X_i + C_i Y_i \qquad i = 1, 2, 3 \qquad (23\text{-}3)$$

where D_i is an $(n \times 1)$ vector of domestic total demand in country i.

The shares then become

$$\hat{S}_{ij} = \hat{M}_{ij}\hat{D}_i^{-1} \qquad i = 1, 2, 3; \quad j = 1, 2, 3; \quad i \neq j \tag{23-4}$$

where S_{ij} is an $(n \times 1)$ vector of shares of country j in country i's domestic demand.

Using equation (23-4), equation (23-1) can be solved for the outputs, X

$$X_i = [I - (I - \hat{S}_i)A_i]^{-1}[(I - \hat{S}_i)C_iY_i + \Sigma E_{ij}] \qquad i = 1, 2 \tag{23-5}$$

where

$$S_i = \sum_j S_{ij}$$

Equation (23-5) would also follow from the assumption that all activities obtain the same uniform proportions (S_i) of their input vectors from abroad, but the derivation of (23-5) offered here does not require this assumption. The interindustry destination of imports does not need to be known in order to determine output, though in formulating the price system, uniform import proportions are later assumed for all domestic activities. The trade effects of slowly changing patterns in interindustry demands will be captured instead in the equations estimated to describe the movement of total import shares.

Once outputs are known, the employment levels of primary factors can be readily obtained

$$L_i^* = L_iX_i \qquad i = 1, 2 \tag{23-6}$$

where

L_i^* = $(f \times 1)$ vector of factor employments

L_i = $(f \times n)$ matrix of factor input coefficients

f = number of primary factors

Through alternative specifications of factor inputs the model could reflect a wide range of assumptions about the interindustry mobility of productive resources. At the Ricardian extreme, factors can be defined uniquely by industry. The equilibrium prices of such factors represent scarcity rents, which might be zero when capacity is not fully employed. At the opposite extreme, the simulations reported here assume perfect primary-factor mobility and substitutability. The implications of this approach are analyzed later.

Price Equations

The dual of the share formulation set out in equation (23-5) determines prices that, in turn, affect the import shares themselves. In a model based on imperfect product substitutability, import prices may differ from domestic prices, and some assumption about the interindustry demand for imports has to be made before prices can be determined. In the most general case, all buyers of a product could have different preferences (or technical requirements) for imports relative to domestic goods. In this case, the estimation of share functions for domestic demand as a whole would not be valid. However, aside from theoretical complications, the data base is simply not rich enough to support the estimation of industry-specific import demand relationships. The only workable strategy, then, was to assume that imports are similarly substituted for corresponding domestic goods in all domestic activities.[2]

The price of domestic products is accordingly given by

$$P_i = A_i'(I - \hat{S}_i)P_i + L_i'W_i + A_i' \sum_j \hat{S}_{ij}P_j r_{ij} \qquad i = 1, 2 \qquad (23\text{-}7)$$

where

$P_i = (n \times 1)$ vector of domestic prices in country i

r_{ij} = exchange rate, units of i's currency needed to buy a unit of country j's

$W_i = (f \times 1)$ matrix of factor returns to country i.

The first two terms on the right side of equation (23-7) represent the cost of domestic materials and primary factors, respectively, while the third term shows the cost of imported inputs.

Equation (23-7) can be readily solved for domestic prices

$$P_i = [I - A_i'(I - \hat{S}_i)]^{-1} [L_i'W_i + A_i' \sum_j \hat{S}_{ij}P_j r_{ij}] \qquad i = 1, 2 \qquad (23\text{-}8)$$

The overall level of factor payments, as distinct from relative levels in the case of several factors, is given by

$$G_i = W_i'L_i^* \qquad i = 1, 2 \qquad (23\text{-}9)$$

where G_i is gross domestic income (including indirect taxes) in country i.

---

2. Allowance could have been made for base-level differences in import share in the input structures of various activities. A full import matrix does exist for Japan, but not for the United States, and this modification was left for future work.

Relative levels can be determined using supply equations for the several factors. As suggested earlier, the present simulation is based on a particularly simple formulation: the supply of a single factor (value added) is assumed to be totally inelastic at full employment levels.

Once prices are determined, the merchandise balance can be derived as

$$B_i = P'_i \sum_j E_{ij} - \sum_j r_{ij} P'_j V^m_{ij} M_{ij} \qquad i = 1, 2 \qquad (23\text{-}10)$$

where V^m_{ij} are cif/cc valuation converters and the balance is expressed on a cif (cost, insurance and freight) import basis, in keeping with standard international accounting procedures, which, however, do not correspond to the fob valuation commonly used in U.S. statistics.

Trade Determination

Thus far, three assumptions have been made:

1. Products falling into different sectors cannot be substituted for each other.
2. Products of different countries falling into the same sector are imperfect substitutes.
3. All domestic activities have identical "preference" functions for imports relative to domestic goods.

These assumptions lead to tolerably simple equations for imports

$$M_{ij} = f(D_i; P_j; r_{ij}; Z) \qquad i = 1, 2, 3; \ j = 1, 2, 3; \ i \neq j \qquad (23\text{-}11)$$

where Z is a matrix of other exogenous determinants of imports. The value of exports corresponding to this import flow can be found using the cc/fob valuation adjustments set out in equation (23-2). Assumption (1) justifies the omission from equation (23-11) of prices in other sectors. Assumption (2) explains the presence in (23-11) of three price and exchange rate terms—each price represents the cost of a competing product. Assumption (3) assures that imports, M_{ij}, are single-valued functions of domestic demand, D_i.

Functional Form

The trade equations are general demand relationships for substitute commodities, and there is an extensive literature that deals with the functional form of such equations. In the standard formulation, demand depends on relative prices (assuming the absence of money illusion) and on real income. If the present assumption of complementarity among products of different sectors is correct, the size of total domestic demand is an ideal proxy for real income.

The share of each imported product in each country should, ideally, depend on the prices of all its competitors. If the price of each country's domestic product is arbitrarily chosen as the *numeraire*, each import equation should then account for as many *relative* prices as there are trading partners. In fact, in the equations estimated, only a given import's own relative price was found to be statistically significant. This happened partly because the simultaneous nature of imports from different sources was not directly recognized in this first round of estimation.[3] Cross-substitution effects among imports may in fact be quite small. If imports substitute for domestic products and other imports with roughly similar price elasticities, the large volume of domestic products on domestic markets will dominate the overall effects of a price change. Still, the omission of import-to-import price relatives may have introduced some upward bias into our elasticity estimates since, using American imports from Japan as an example, (P_J/P_{US}) and (P_J/P_{ROW}) are correlated, and therefore the effects of (P_J/P_{ROW}) are captured by (P_J/P_{US}) in its absence.

Some 66 equations were estimated for imports of 11 traded product groups k in each of three markets i (United States, Japan, and the Rest-of-the-World), from each of the three suppliers j.[4] Time series data from 1955–1971 were used to estimate the demand functions, though the time subscript is suppressed

$$m_{ijk} = \alpha_{ijk} \left(\frac{p_{jk} r_{ij}}{p_{ik}} \right)^{\beta_{ijk}} d_{ik}^{\delta_{ijk}} \epsilon_{ijk} \tag{23-12}$$

where

α, β, δ are parameters, and

$\epsilon \quad$ = error terms

$i \quad$ = markets = 1, 2, 3 $\left. \begin{array}{l} \\ \\ \end{array} \right\} \; i \neq j$

$j \quad$ = suppliers = 1, 2, 3

$k \quad$ = products = 3, . . . , 13

Estimation Technique

First, the least squares method was used to estimate all import equations in log-linear form. These equations were adopted as the final estimate, provided

3. Some evidence suggests that this distortion is small, since no appreciable *inverse* relationship seems to exist between the error terms obtained from the equations of competing imports. In several cases, some positive correlations were noted, indicating that similar unknown variables may have been omitted from both competitors' equations.

4. No equations were estimated for Sectors 1 and 2, Agriculture and Natural resource products. In place of these equations, subjective a priori guesses were adopted on the basis of estimates by Moriguchi and Tatemoto [9] and on the basis of Petri [10].

that the Durbin-Watson statistic did not indicate serial correlation in the error terms. When substantial serial correlation was present (DW ≤ 1.7), the generalized differencing approach suggested by Cochrane and Orcutt [5] was applied.

When significant, a trend term was introduced to absorb various omitted effects, such as gradual changes in product quality, in trade restrictions, and in the activity pattern of demand. In some equations, the size of the exporter's own domestic market was included as a proxy for supply effects. Dummy variables were introduced for the American import quotas for steel and textiles; and, starting with 1968, the relative price ratios were adjusted for tariff reductions negotiated in the Kennedy Round.

The two major explanatory variables, relative price and market size, generally affect imports with some lag—consumers and producers may not immediately adjust to long-run equilibrium levels implied by current prices and markets. Direct introduction of lagged price and market terms is not possible, since these variables are highly correlated with their unlagged values, and a large number of observations would be needed to resolve this collinearity.

Some studies have used the simple Koyck lag function, assuming that the impact of the explanatory variables declines geometrically with time. This model is appealing because the entire lag function can be estimated with a single additional explanatory variable: lagged imports. However, it is subject to possibly serious biases [8], and imposes identical lag forms on all explanatory variables.

The strategy adopted here was to limit the lag function to a few possible shapes for each explanatory variable, based on a priori judgments about acceptable forms. A choice was then made by comparing the fits of the different standard forms. This procedure requires no additional variables in estimating delayed response, though a degree of freedom is lost since "fit" plays a role in the selection of the shape itself. The resulting equations provide primarily long-run elasticities. While impact elasticities can be recalculated from the chosen lag function, they are highly sensitive to the initial judgments that restricted the shape of the lag. The lag shapes are shown in Figure 23-1. Forms B, C, and D

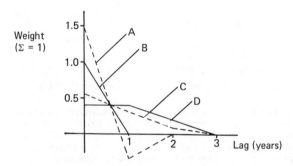

Figure 23-1. Alternative Lag Forms.

allow for increasingly slow responses, with average lags of 0.5, 1.0, and 1.3 years, respectively. In addition to specifying a short reaction lag, Form A also accounts for some transitory changes in import shares as a result of sudden shifts in total domestic demand.

Estimation Results

The estimated trade relationships are interesting in their own right, and a more detailed cross-sectional analysis of these parameters will be undertaken in the future. In general, the estimated price elasticities were more significant and typically larger than those found in more aggregative studies. The overall price elasticities of trade (the weighted averages of commodity-by-commodity elasticities) reported in Table 23-1 easily satisfy the Marshall-Lerner conditions for exchange rate stability in each of the three "countries" of the system.

These fairly uniform and sedate overall price elasticities mask a great deal of product-to-product variability. As Table 23-2 shows, some relatively standardized products, such as iron and steel, chemicals, and textiles, are unusually sensitive to exchange rate variations, and substantial sectoral dislocations may result from a radically new exchange rate regime. The fact that the effects of exchange rate variations differ so substantially from sector to sector clearly illustrates a need for detailed interindustry studies of international linkage.

Of the six bilateral trade relations analyzed, the flow of Japanese goods to the United States shows the greatest price sensitivity, while most of the other flows are characterized by elasticities in the neighborhood of unity. As a result, in the simulation described in the next section, roughly equal but opposite changes in American and Japanese exchange rates produce a reallocation of trade balances between these two countries without substantially changing their joint balance vis-à-vis the rest of the world.

Table 23-1. Trade-Weighted Price and Total Demand Elasticities

	Importer		
Exporter	*United States*	*Japan*	*Rest-of-the-World*
United States	–	1.28, 1.65	0.61, 1.04
Japan	3.41, 1.52	–	2.16, 1.43
Rest-of-the-World	1.49, 1.15	0.97, 1.94	–

Note: The first number in each cell is the elasticity of the trade flow with respect to the exporter's price; the second, the elasticity with respect to the importer's total domestic demand. Of the 66 underlying price elasticities, 40 were significant at the 0.05 level. Of the 66 demand elasticities, 54 were significant at the 0.05 level.

Table 23-2. Average Commodity Elasticities

Sector			
Num-ber	Title	Price Elasticity	Total Domestic Demand Elasticity
1	Agriculture, food, etc.[a]	0.50	1.17
2	Natural resources[a]	0.20	1.75
3	Textiles, apparel, etc.	3.38	1.05
4	Wood products, paper	2.53	1.31
5	Chemicals	3.87	1.18
6	Stone, clay, & glass	0.85	1.43
7	Iron & steel	5.78	1.62
8	Nonferrous metals	2.17	1.77
9	Metal products	3.18	1.03
10	Machinery, instruments	1.50	1.55
11	Electrical machinery	2.32	1.53
12	Transport equipment[b]	1.55	0.92
13	Miscellaneous manufacturers	0.83	1.14

[a]A priori estimates.

[b]Excludes U.S.–Canada auto trade.

Note: These are simple averages based on the six bilateral trade equations estimated for each commodity.

Model Specification for Simulation

A condensed summary of the model's equations and variables is presented in Table 23-3. The table shows clearly that the system set out so far is under-determined: it has only $24n + 2f + 4$ equations in terms of its $26n + 4f + 8$ variables. The remaining gaps are left to be filled with assumptions and information suited to the specific objectives of each new application. There is even some choice as to which variables should be exogenous, and which endogenous, though obviously not every set of $2n + 2f + 4$ exogenous values leads to a sensible solution or, for that matter, to any solution at all.

Of special current interest is the model's ability to simulate the overall effects of variations in exchange rates in a multicountry general-equilibrium framework. For the purposes of this simulation, the required values of the exogenous variables were determined by assuming:

1a. full employment of a single primary factor;
2a. no inflation or deflation in the nominal levels of gross domestic income;
3a. unchanged ROW prices; and
4a. constant ROW total imports, used as a proxy for the ROW's "total domestic demand."

The remaining specification gaps were filled by parametrically varied exchange rate values. Using 1971 as a base, the model was solved to reflect the various

Table 23-3. Model Summary

Equation No.	Equations Description	Number[a]	Symbol	Variables Description	Number[a]
2	Export/import conversions	$6n$	e	Exports	$6n$
3	Domestic demand definition	$2n$	d	Total domestic demand	$3n$
4	Import share definition	$6n$	s	Import shares	$6n$
5	Output solution	$2n$	x	Outputs	$2n$
6	Primary factor demand	$2f$	l	Primary factor employment	$2f$
8	Price solution	$2n$	p	Prices	$3n$
9	Gross domestic income account	2	g	Gross income levels	2
10	Merchandise balance account	2	b	Merchandise balances	2
11	Import determination	$6n$	m	Imports	$6n$
			w	Factor prices	$2f$
			r	Exchange rates	2
			y	Final demand levels	2
	Total $= 24n + 2f + 4$			Total $= 26n + 4f + 8$	

[a] In the present application, $n = 13 =$ number of commodities, $f = 1 =$ number of primary factors. The model's 8 nontraded sectors were omitted from this accounting.

combinations of 0, 5, 10, and 15 percent devaluations by the United States with 0, 5, 10, and 15 percent revaluations by Japan.[5]

As assumption (1a) indicates, provisions are here made for only a single primary factor: value added. This approach implicitly assumes that (i) all factor inputs that comprise value added are perfect substitutes, and (ii) resources can move freely among industries without creating bottlenecks in expanding sectors and temporary surpluses (unemployment) in declining sectors. As a result, the present simulations provide only an upper bound on the effectiveness of exchange rate variations—at least with respect to the primary factor side of industry production functions.

Consider an alternative specification that distinguishes among several distinct, imperfectly substitutable primary factors. In response to a devaluation, shifting patterns of outputs will exert pressures on the demand for and prices of factors most directly involved in producing exports and import replacements. The consequent increases in the domestic prices of exports and import replacements will then partly offset the first-round changes induced by the devaluation itself. Versions of the model with primary factors specified in more detail can be useful in gauging the effectiveness of currency devaluations in correcting trade imbalances.

The model was solved using the iterative process illustrated in Figure 23-2. An interesting feature of this process is that several of its steps resemble policy actions of governmental authorities. For example, after each new computation of trade flows, the level of domestic aggregate demand had to be adjusted upward for the revaluing country (Japan) and downward for the devaluing country (the United States). This operation is similar to the fiscal policy offsets that would neutralize the impact of the changed trade balance on domestic employment. An oversimplified equivalent of monetary policy is introduced in a step that determines nominal levels for total factor income. This feature of the model could in turn be used to study the international transmission of inflation.

Results and Conclusions

The principal results of this analysis, the comparative static changes on merchandise trade account (assuming no changes on service account and in the United States–Canada automobile trade balance), are illustrated in Figure 23-3. The grid of this figure identifies alternative combinations of exchange rates, while its axes indicate the corresponding changes in the merchandise balances of Japan and the United States in 1971 U.S. dollars. For example, a 10 percent devaluation of the dollar combined with a 15 percent revaluation of the yen

5. Alternate specifications of this model might, for example, fix consumption goals or balance-of-trade goals and search for the exchange rate or employment policies needed to achieve these. A good deal more analysis remains to be done in exploring other versions based on different choices of exogenous and endogenous variables.

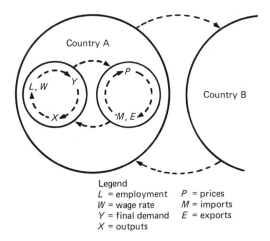

Legend
L = employment   P = prices
W = wage rate   M = imports
Y = final demand E = exports
X = outputs

Figure 23-2. Iterative Solution Strategy.

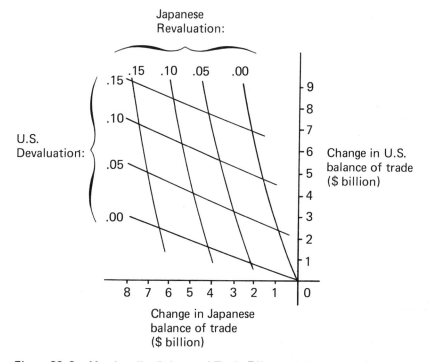

Figure 23-3. Merchandise Balance of Trade Effects of Alternative Exchange Rates.

(implying a 28 percent change in the dollar-yen exchange rate) would produce a $7.1 billion improvement in the American balance and a $7.2 billion deterioration in the Japanese balance.

Aside from the changes in merchandise balances, the model also produced detailed information on changes in outputs, product prices, and trade. Some specific effects of a 10 percent devaluation by the United States and a 15 percent revaluation by Japan are reported in Figure 23–4. Since only a single

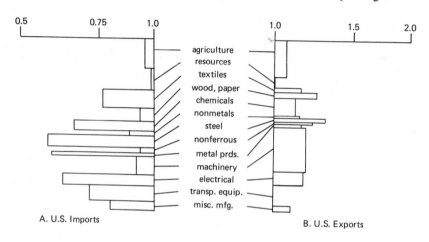

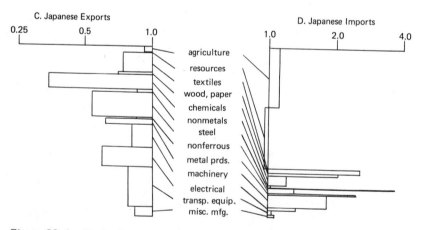

Figure 23–4. Trade Effects of 10 Percent U.S. Devaluation Coupled with 15 Percent Japanese Revaluation. (The base of each bar represents the relative importance of the product in trade. The length of each bar shows the ratio of the simulated trade flow to the corresponding actual 1971 flow. The scale is logarithmic.)

primary factor was present, and its price was held constant, product price changes reflect only the increased (decreased) cost of imported inputs. Thus, price changes in both countries were minor—a maximum of 0.7 percent in non-ferrous metals in the United States, a minimum of -2.8 percent in nonferrous metals in Japan. In both countries, the prices of traded products were affected relatively more than prices of nontraded products, indicating that both countries trade commodities that are relatively intensive in their use of imported inputs.

Since the model did not account for supply bottlenecks, the physical system absorbed nearly all of the impact of the exchange rate variations. Steel outputs were affected most dramatically; they increased by 6.6 percent in the United States and decreased by 13.8 percent in Japan. Real consumption fell by 1.1 percent in the United States and rose by 4.9 percent in Japan.

Since the model was estimated entirely on pre-Smithsonian data, its ability to simulate the actual impact of the dramatic exchange realignments that followed is of obvious interest. During the 1971–1973 period, the U.S. dollar devalued by about 17 percent against the Special Drawing Rights, while the Japanese yen revalued by approximately 7 percent. The full effects of these changes were certainly not felt by the end of 1973, especially since about half of the U.S. devaluation occurred in early 1973. Using a 12 percent U.S. devaluation and a 7 percent Japanese revaluation as crude measures of the average rates in effect during the period, the model predicts a $6 billion improvement in the United States' merchandise balance, and a $5 billion deterioration in Japan's. The actual changes were +$3.1 billion and -$4.1 billion, respectively.

A rigorous comparison cannot, however, be made on the basis of the present simulations. The exchange rate impacts mapped out in Figure 23-3 were based on several ceteris paribus assumptions (including zero inflation in the United States, Japan, and the Rest-of-the-World), and dealt with comparative static changes in a system of 1971 economies. Most importantly, the model was not "told" about the radical shifts in raw material prices that were already evident in 1973. In principle, the model is sufficiently detailed to be able to accept exogenous information about all of these factors, and might, to some extent (for example, with regard to the international transmission of inflation), be able to shed light on what actually happened. This more ambitious task is the chief objective of further refinements now under way.

References

1. Armington, P.S. "A Theory of Demand for Products Distributed by Place of Origin." *IMF Staff Papers* 16, no. 1 (March 1969): 159–178.

2. Ball, R.J., ed. *The International Linkage of National Economic Models*. Amsterdam: North-Holland Publishing Company, 1973.

3. Barker, T.S. "Foreign Trade in Multisectoral Models." In *Input-Output Techniques.* Edited by A. Bródy and A.P. Carter. Amsterdam: North-Holland Publishing Company, 1972. Pp. 111–126.

4. Bruno, M. "A Programming Model for Israel." In *The Theory and Design of Economic Development.* Edited by I. Adelman and E. Thorbecke. Baltimore: Johns Hopkins Press, 1966. Pp. 327–354.

5. Cochrane, D., and G.H. Orcutt. "Application of Least Squares Regressions to Relationships Containing Auto-Correlated Error Terms." *Journal of the American Statistical Association* 44, no. 245 (1949): 32–61.

6. Evans, H.D. *A General Equilibrium Analysis of Protection.* Amsterdam: North-Holland Publishing Company, 1972.

7. Kravis, I.B., and R.E. Lipsey. *Price Competitiveness in World Trade.* New York: Columbia University Press, 1971.

8. Leamer, E.E., and R.M. Stern. *Quantitative International Economics.* Boston: Allyn and Bacon, 1970.

9. Moriguchi, C., and M. Tatemoto. "An Econometric Analysis of a Bilateral Model of International Economic Activity: Japan and USA." In *The International Linkage of National Economic Models.* Edited by R.J. Ball. Amsterdam: North-Holland Publishing Company, 1973. Pp. 367–393.

10. Petri, P.A. "The Structural Determinants of Japanese Imports, 1955–1970." Paper delivered at the Japan Economic Seminar, Cambridge, Massachusetts, 1974.

11. Price, J.E., and J.B. Thornblade. "U.S. Import Demand Functions Disaggregated by Country and Commodity." *Southern Economic Journal* 39, no. 1 (July 1972): 46–57.

12. Rhomberg, R.R. "Possible Approaches to a Model of World Trade and Payments." *IMF Staff Papers* 17, no. 1 (March 1970): 1–27.

13. Werin, L. *A Study of Production, Trade and Allocation of Resources.* Stockholm: Almqvist and Wiksell, 1965.

Appendix 23A

Table 23A-1.   Sectoral Alignment Scheme

Model Sector		United States 1967 Input-Output Sectors	Japan 1970 Input-Output Sectors	Standard International Trade Classification
Number	Title			
1	Agriculture, food, etc.	1-4, 14-15	1-6, 12-17	0, 1, 2 n.e.s., 4
2	Natural resources	5-10, 31	7-11, 31-32	27, 28, 3
3	Textiles, apparel, etc.	16-19, 33-34	18-21, 26	61, 65, 83-85
4	Wood products, paper	20-25	22-24	243, 251, 63-64, 82
5	Chemicals	27-30, 32	27-30	231, 266, 5, 62
6	Stone, clay, & glass	35-36	33	66
7	Iron & steel	37	34-35	67
8	Nonferrous metals	38	36	68
9	Metal products	13, 39-42	37	69, 81
10	Machinery, instruments	43-52, 62-63	38, 41	71, 86
11	Electrical machinery	53-58	39	72
12	Transport equipment	59-61	40	73
13	Miscellaneous manufactures	26, 64	25, 42	89
14	Construction	11-12	43-44	
15	Utilities	68, 78-79	45-47	
16	Wholesale, retail trade	69	48	
17	Financial, insurance	70	49	
18	Real estate	71	50-51	
19	Transport, communication	65-67	52-53	
20	Services	72-77	54-57	
21	Unallocated	—	60	

Chapter Twenty-Four

A Multisectoral and Multicountry Model for Planning ECAFE Production and Trade

V. R. Panchamukhi

There is now a growing awareness among the developing countries of the world of the need for closer cooperation in their economic relationships. Some efforts are being made to form groups or associations of nations (such as the Association of South East Asian Nations) with the objective of bringing about better coordination in their development plans so as to fully realise the economic complementarities among them. The will for increased economic cooperation is growing rapidly in the developing countries of the Economic Commission for Asia and the Far East (ECAFE) region. There is, however, a need for a systematic analysis of the implications of the strategy of cooperation, of the production activities in each country, and of the trade flows among them—in particular, a need to analyse the effects of increased cooperation on the processes of industrialisation and development in the different countries.

It is the purpose of this paper to develop an integrated framework for deriving a consistent plan of production and trade for the countries of the ECAFE region. First, a brief review of the existing production and trade structures in these countries is given. Various indices of the stages of development are used to show the divergences in the development processes of the various countries and the need for coordination in their development plans. Second, alternative models for analysis of the interdependence among the ECAFE countries are developed. Two types of models are presented: a multiregional and multisectoral consistency model and a multiregional and multisectoral optimisation model. The models are designed with a view to examining the implications of the following alternative strategies of cooperation: (1) import substitution at the regional level; (2) expansion of intraregional trade so as to balance the incremental trade and/or improve the overall level of trade reciprocity between pairs of countries;

Mr. Santanam helped in reclassifying the input-output tables of the different countries to a comparable basis; Mr. Ramanathan provided research and computer assistance; Miss Vasanthakumari and Mrs. Balan statistical assistance; and Mr. Bhakathavalsalan gave secretarial assistance. Thanks to all of them.

Table 24-1.   Consumption, Investment, Exports, Imports, and Trade, 1960,
1965, and 1970 (percentage of gross domestic product)

Country	Consumption			Gross Fixed Capital Formation		
	1960	*1965*	*1970*	*1960*	*1965*	*1970*
India	86.70	84.39	–	13.43	16.69	–
South Korea	99.14	93.35	83.99	10.82	14.73	25.72
Malaysia	74.09	79.35	–	11.25	15.03	–
Pakistan	91.74	88.12	–	11.75	14.29	–
Philippines	86.12	80.67	79.76	11.46	18.29	18.99
Thailand	82.59	79.36	–	14.07	18.98	–
Japan	65.78	65.67	59.24	30.18	30.46	35.03

(3) gradual reduction or elimination of tariff and other trade barriers for intra-regional trade; (4) shifting the location of some new investments and technologies from the countries in relatively advanced stages of industrialisation to those less advanced; and (5) introducing unrestricted mobility for the primary factors of production, in particular, skilled labour, entrepreneurial labour, and capital—in other words, moving towards the goal of a common market for the ECAFE region. It is obvious that some of these strategies of cooperation may imply complete convertibility of national currencies. This aspect, however, is not brought into these models. Third, the results of the models, with projections for the years 1975 and 1980, and a discussion of the results are presented. The projections derived from the models are compared with those obtained from models in which interdependences among the countries are not explicitly recognised. Fourth, a brief summary of the results of the study is given, along with its limitations and suggestions for further work in this area.

Patterns of Development of the ECAFE Countries

The ECAFE region consists of developing countries that differ from one another in several characteristics, such as area; population size; per capita income; growth rate of gross domestic product; share of agriculture, industry, and exports in the national income; and pattern of investment. Tables 24-1 and 24-2 present a broad picture of the disparities in the stages of development, based upon some macroeconomic indicators. Annual growth rates of the gross domestic product (GDP) range from 2.4 percent to 9.8 percent; those of exports from –10.9 percent to 40.1 percent; those of imports from –8.1 percent to 23.1 percent. The share of exports in the GDP ranges from 3 percent to 45 percent, the share of investment in the GDP from 14 percent to 19 percent. The trade gap as a proportion of the GDP ranges from 2 percent to 9.6 percent.

Table 24-1 continued

Exports			Imports			Trade Gap		
1960	*1965*	*1970*	*1960*	*1965*	*1970*	*1960*	*1965*	*1970*
5.18	3.94	–	8.24	6.62	–	–3.06	–2.08	–
3.35	8.59	15.04	12.66	16.15	25.35	–9.31	–9.56	–10.31
52.89	44.33	–	39.13	38.74	–	+13.76	+5.59	–
5.81	5.93	–	10.09	9.41	–	–4.28	–3.48	–
11.59	16.05	19.70	10.70	16.96	20.26	+0.89	–0.91	–0.56
17.41	18.27	–	18.89	19.57	–	–1.48	–1.30	–
11.04	10.77	11.16	10.56	9.32	9.83	+0.48	+1.45	+1.33

Source: United Nations. *Year Book of National Accounts Statistics, 1971.* New York: United Nations.

Table 24-2. Annual Growth Rates of the Gross Domestic Product, Exports, and Imports, 1960-1966 (percent)

	Annual Rate of Growth		
Area	*GDP at 1960 Market Prices*	*Exports*	*Imports*
Brunei	–	–1.9	17.9
Burma	2.3	–2.6	–8.1
Cambodia	4.6	–0.7	2.6
Ceylon	3.3	–1.3	–0.6
Taiwan	9.8	21.8	13.1
Hong Kong	–	11.5	9.5
India	2.8	3.2	3.3
Indonesia	2.4	–3.5	0.1
Iran	6.4	7.6	6.0
South Korea	7.5	40.1	13.0
Laos	–	–6.5	23.1
Malaysia			
West Malaysia	6.1	1.1	3.4
East Malaysia			
Sabah	–	8.2	9.8
Sarawak	–	–1.0	3.7
Pakistan	5.3	7.3	5.5
Philippines	5.0[a]	6.9	6.3
Singapore	–	–0.5	–0.1
Thailand	7.2	9.3	17.1
South Vietnam	5.1	–10.9	22.5
Western Samoa	–	–6.3	1.3
Total Developing ECAFE	4.1	4.4	6.0

[a]1962-1966: revised national product estimates.

Source: ECAFE Secretariat, Bangkok (United Nations), and several national sources of statistics.

In order to identify the degree of complementarity among different countries, various factors need to be examined: (1) the correspondence between commodity composition of export supplies of one country and import requirements of another country; (2) the pattern of consumption demand; (3) the sectoral structure of capital formation; (4) the growth rates of industrial sectors; and (5) the pattern of industrial linkages realised in each country. Although these indices are obviously not comprehensive enough to fully reflect the economic disparity between any two countries, they can provide a broad picture of complementarity.

Coefficients of commodity correspondence, ω^{kr}, have been derived by the following formula: [1]

$$\omega^{kr} = \frac{\sum\limits_{i=1}^{n} e_i^k m_i^r}{\sqrt{\sum\limits_{i=1}^{n} (e_i^k)^2} \ \sqrt{\sum\limits_{i=1}^{n} (m_i^r)^2}}$$

where

e_i^k = proportion of the export of commodity i in the total exports of country k

m_i^r = proportion of the import of commodity i in the total imports of country r

These coefficients indicate the degree to which the structure of export supplies of one country matches that of import requirements of another country. As can be seen in Table 24–3, the coefficients show that except for Japan, ECAFE countries have a rather poor correspondence among commodities. [2] This evidence suggests that the first step towards increased cooperation among the developing countries is to bring about a better coordination between their production and domestic demand structures.

Analysis of the commodity composition of consumption and the sectoral structure of capital formation and growth rates of selected industrial sectors in the ECAFE countries shows that there are considerable divergencies in the demand and growth structures among them and hence that there are ample possibilities for achieving complementarity among these countries. Rankings of industries by linkage indices also differ among the countries [4]. Relationships between estimated sectoral linkages and realised sectoral growth rates are also not uniform. This indicates that the different countries have exploited the linkage potentials to different degrees and thus a proper streamlining of the production technologies and the product mix within a sector could improve the realisation of linkage potentials.

1. For further discussion and use of this measure, see Linnemann [2].
2. A detailed discussion of similar results is given in [5].

Table 24-3. Coefficients of Commodity Correspondence Between Exports and Imports, 1965

Exporting Countries	India	South Korea	Philip-pines	Malaysia	Taiwan	Japan	Australia
				Importing Countries			
India	–	.0998	.0723	.2199	.0973	.1695	.2048
South Korea	.0881	–	.1395	.3435	.1403	.1260	.1793
Philippines	.0306	.1735	–	.1800	.2422	.3880	.0515
Malaysia	.0453	.0899	.0632	–	.0730	.1413	.0805
Taiwan	.1242	.1252	.2185	.3553	–	.1621	.1225
Japan	.3220	.3050	.2546	.4842	.4952	–	.5095
Australia	.3010	.2163	.1309	.1271	.0276	.5396	–

An examination of the trade balances of the different countries within the developing ECAFE region and the rest of the world, as presented in Table 24-4, brings out the fact that the ECAFE countries generally have trade deficits in regional trade and that cooperation in export trade could help them reduce their trade deficits within the region. This may imply some import substitution at the regional level and trade diversion from developed ECAFE to developing ECAFE countries. The countries of the region also have divergent trade policies. India and Pakistan stand at one extreme, with rigid import controls, exchange rate policies, etc.; Malaysia stands at the other extreme, with greatly liberalised trade. South Korea and the Philippines have adopted import control policies with varying degrees of intensity for short periods. All the countries have adopted various export promotion policies. A study of the effective rates of protection resulting from the various trade policies in these countries indicates that the distortions in the patterns of resource allocation caused by trade policies differ widely from country to country [3;6]. Trade policies in each country should be suitably modified so that prospects of cooperation among the countries are increased.

The foregoing paragraphs have provided a brief review of the divergences that exist in the different developing countries of the ECAFE region with respect to the various aspects of development. These points emphasize the need for dealing with the problem of cooperation among them in a framework that explicitly recognises their interdependence and still retains specific features of each country. Further, the framework should be such that it is possible to work out the implications of the various schemes of cooperation by suitable manipulations. Such a framework is provided by an interregional and multisectoral model, which will be developed in the next section.

The Models

Two types of models are developed: a consistency model and an optimisation model. Formulation of the models is based, in part, on considerations of data

Table 24-4.   Trade Balance of ECAFE Countries with ECAFE Region and Rest-of-the-World (millions of U.S. dollars at current prices)

Country		Average of 1963-1965			Average of 1966-1968		
		Exports	Imports	Balance	Exports	Imports	Balance
India	(a)	5,032.2	8,009.7	-2,977.5	4,966.7	7,950.8	-2,984.1
	(b)	1,056.3	1,266.3	-210.6	1,122.0	1,231.2	-109.2
	(c)	533.6	633.9	-100.3	467.3	575.1	-107.8
Taiwan	(a)	1,207.0	1,337.8	-130.8	1,957.3	2,316.5	-359.2
	(b)	784.9	617.0	+167.9	1,020.4	1,217.6	-197.2
	(c)	392.5	108.1	+284.4	624.3	208.0	+416.3
Philippines	(a)	2,233.8	2,450.8	-217.0	2,504.1	3,408.6	-904.5
	(b)	685.1	862.3	-177.2	1,020.4	1,417.5	-397.1
	(c)	76.9	283.6	-206.7	173.5	316.9	-143.4
South Korea	(a)	381.2	1,428.1	-1,046.9	1,025.6	3,181.5	-2,155.9
	(b)	191.1	567.2	-376.1	383.4	1,740.5	-1,357.1
	(c)	82.1	105.8	-23.7	126.0	346.3	-220.3
Ceylon	(a)	2,253.6	1,944.1	+109.5	1,020.1	1,145.2	-125.1
	(b)	255.0	483.8	-228.8	242.0	513.6	-271.6
	(c)	147.5	347.1	-199.6	142.5	379.9	-237.4
Pakistan	(a)	1,488.0	2,922.3	-1,434.3	1,919.3	2,990.7	-1,071.4
	(b)	524.4	546.1	-21.7	565.2	674.9	-109.7
	(c)	389.6	292.5	+97.1	396.3	308.9	+87.4
West Malaysia	(a)	2,714.7	2,246.6	+468.1	3,023.6	2,609.9	+413.7
	(b)	1,109.3	1,256.6	-147.3	1,376.2	1,469.9	-93.7
	(c)	591.7	866.6	-274.9	908.9	875.0	+33.9
Japan	(a)	20,583.4	22,854.5	-2,271.1	33,185.3	34,171.0	-985.7
	(b)	6,634.0	6,616.9	+17.1	10,932.1	10,319.9	+612.2
	(c)	5,770.0	4,795.2	+974.8	9,665.5	7,580.7	+2,084.8

Notes: (a) Trade balance with respect to total trade with Rest-of-the-World.
(b) Trade balance with respect to total trade with ECAFE countries.
(c) Trade balance with respect to total trade with developing ECAFE countries.

Source: United Nations. *Foreign Trade Statistics of Asia and the Far East* (1963-1968).

availability. The models are of static or comparative static type. First to be presented is the consistency model—with some variants—which differ in the treatment of the trade flows among the countries of the region explicitly included in the model. Only those countries that have input-output tables are included. For the purpose of this part of the study, the ECAFE region is divided into three groups: (1) developing countries explicitly included in the model— India, South Korea, Taiwan, Malaysia, the Philippines; (2) other developing countries of the region; and (3) developed countries of the region—Japan, Australia, New Zealand. The countries outside the ECAFE region are referred to as Rest-of-the-World.

The mathematical formulations of the models use the following notations:

VARIABLES

x_i^k = output of sector i in country k

m_i^k = imports of sector i in country k

c_i^k = consumption demand for sector i in country k

d_i^k = demand for capital formation of sector i in country k

d^k = total capital formation in country k

e_i^{kj} = exports of sector i from country k to country j, in fob (free on board) prices

m_i^{jk} = imports of sector i from country j to country k in cif (cost, insurance, and freight) prices

Note: The superscript j may be replaced by

r = developing country explicitly included in the model

DE = other developing countries

DD = developed ECAFE countries

RW = rest-of-the-World

$RE = DE + DD$

x_i^{oo} = total output of sector i in all the developing ECAFE countries explicitly introduced in the model

t_{mi}^r = implicit tariff on import sector i in country r (Implicit tariff is the divergence between the domestic price and international price as a proportion of the latter.)

s_{ei}^r = implicit subsidy on export sector i in country r

l^k = supply of labour in country k

$\hat{M}^k$ = diagonal matrix of m_{ii}^k coefficients linking imports of sector i with domestic output i in country k

T^k = minimum tariff revenue desired for country k

$(\text{aid})_R$ = total aid available to the developing countries of the region explicitly introduced in the model

PARAMETERS

a_{ij}^k = input-output coefficient in country k

A^k = matrix of a_{ij}^k coefficients

θ_i^{rk} = ratio of cif price to fob price of products of sector i exported from country r to country k

ϵ_{il}^{rk} = partial coefficients in the export demand equation

γ_{il}^k = partial import coefficients relating imports to the different determinants of import-demands (This refers only to the countries included in the model.)

m_i^{REk} = ratio of imports of sector i products from rest of ECAFE (RE) to country k to the output of sector i in country k

m_i^{RWk} = ratio of imports of sector i products from Rest-of-the-World (RW) to country k to the output of sector i in country k

v_i^k = ratio of value added in sector i to its output in country k

α_i^k = labour-output ratio in sector i of country k

β_i^k = capital-output ratio in sector i of country k

$\hat{\lambda}^{kr}$ = ratio of trade reciprocity between countries k and r

μ_i = coefficient of import dependence of the developing ECAFE region (included in the model) on extraregional imports

ϕ_i = intraregional trade ratio

t_i^k = nominal tariff rate on products of sector i in country k

$\lambda_{\min}^{kr}$ and $\lambda_{\max}^{kr}$ are, respectively, the prescribed minimum and maximum trade reciprocity ratios.

Consistency Model

The consistency model is composed of balance equations for each sector in each country. A typical balance equation for sector i in country k is

$$x_i^k - \sum_j a_{ij}^k x_j^k + m_i^k - \sum_r e_i^{kr} = \sum_{DE} e_i^{kDE} + \sum_{DD} e_i^{kDD} + e_i^{kRW} + c_i^k + d_i^k \qquad (24\text{-}1)$$

There are mn balance equations, where m is the number of countries introduced in the model and n is the number of sectors in each input-output table. In this formulation, exports from country k are separated into four parts: (i) those to country r explicitly included in the model (e_i^{kr}); (ii) those to other developing ECAFE countries (e_i^{kDE}); (iii) those to developed ECAFE countries (e_i^{kDD}); and (iv) those to Rest-of-the-World (e_i^{kRW}).

Several variants of this model can be considered, depending on the way in which the trade flows, e_i^{kr}, are explained. In the first variant, they are determined by the demand factors (demand-based trade flows); in the second variant, they are determined by the supply factors (supply-based trade flows); in the third variant, they are determined by both supply and demand factors. In each of these variants, in addition to the demand/supply factors, government policy variables of import control and export promotion may also be introduced as additional explanatory variables. The mathematical formulation of only the first variant will be presented here. (The empirical study in the paper is also confined to this variant.)

The determinants of import-demand for a commodity are generally (i) domestic production of that commodity, (ii) total investment, and (iii) total consumption expenditures. The relevance of some or all of these determinants depends upon the nature of the imported commodity. However, in general, the function for trade flows based on demand factors can be written as

$$e_i^{kr} = f(x_i^r, d^r, c^r)$$

In linear form,

$$e_i^{kr} = \epsilon_{i1}^{kr} x_i^r + \epsilon_{i2}^{kr} d^r + \epsilon_{i3}^{kr} c^r \tag{24-2}$$

where ϵ_{il}^{kr} ($l = 1, 2, 3$) can be derived as regression coefficients on the basis of the historical data.

Total imports of sector i products by country k, viz., m_i^k, is given by

$$m_i^k = \sum_r m_i^{rk} + m_i^{DEk} + m_i^{DDk} + m_i^{RWk} \tag{24-3}$$

Since

$$m_i^{rk} = \theta_i^{rk} e_i^{rk}$$

The total imports of sector i products by country k from all the other countries included in the study is

$$\sum_r m_i^{rk} = (\sum_r \theta_i^{rk} \epsilon_{i1}^{rk}) x_i^k + (\sum_r \theta_i^{rk} \epsilon_{i2}^{rk}) d^k + (\sum_r \theta_i^{rk} \epsilon_{i3}^{rk}) c^k \tag{24-4}$$

or this may be written as

$$\sum_r m_i^{rk} = \gamma_{i1}^k x_i^k + \gamma_{i2}^k d^k + \gamma_{i3}^k c^k \tag{24-5}$$

where

$$\gamma_{il}^k = \sum_r \theta_i^{rk} \epsilon_{il}^{rk} \qquad (l = 1, 2, 3)$$

Using similar demand-determined trade-flow equations for m_i^{DEk}, m_i^{DDk}, m_i^{RWk} one can write the total import equation as

$$m_i^k = \bar\gamma_{i1}^k x_i^k + \bar\gamma_{i2}^k d^k + \bar\gamma_{i3}^k c^k \tag{24-6}$$

where

$$\bar\gamma_{il}^k = \gamma_{il}^k + \gamma_{il}^{DEk} + \gamma_{il}^{DDk} + \gamma_{il}^{RWk} \qquad (l = 1, 2, 3)$$

$\bar\gamma_{il}^k$ are the final import coefficients relating the imports to the domestic output, investment, and consumption expenditures. Substituting equations (24-2) and (24-6) into equation (24-1) gives

$$x_i^k - \sum_j a_{ij} x_j^k + \bar\gamma_{i1}^k x_i^k - \epsilon_{i1}^{kr} x_i^r = f_i^k \tag{24-7}$$

where

$$f_i^k = \sum_{DE} e_i^{kDE} + \sum_{DD} e_i^{kDD} + e_i^{kRW} + \sum_r \epsilon_{i2}^{kr} d^r + \sum \epsilon_{i3}^{kr} c^r$$

$$+ d_i^k + c_i^k - \bar\gamma_{i2}^k d^k - \bar\gamma_{i3}^k c^k$$

$$i = 1, 2, \ldots, n$$

$$k = 1, 2, \ldots, m$$

The model in matrix notation takes the form,

$$
\begin{bmatrix}
I - A^1 + \hat M^1 & -\hat E^{12} & -\hat E^{13} & \cdots & -\hat E^{1K} \\
-\hat E^{21} & I - A^2 + \hat M^2 & -\hat E^{23} & \cdots & -\hat E^{2K} \\
& \cdot & \cdot & & \cdot \\
& \cdot & \cdot & \cdot & \cdot \\
& \cdot & \cdot & \cdot & \cdot \\
-\hat E^{K1} & -\hat E^{K2} & -\hat E^{K3} & \cdots & I - A^K + \hat M^K
\end{bmatrix}
\begin{bmatrix}
X^1 \\ X^2 \\ \cdot \\ \cdot \\ \cdot \\ X^K
\end{bmatrix}
=
\begin{bmatrix}
F^1 \\ F^2 \\ \cdot \\ \cdot \\ \cdot \\ F^K
\end{bmatrix}
$$

or

$$\Omega X = F \tag{24-8}$$

where

$\hat{E}^{kr}, \hat{M}^k$ = the appropriate diagonal matrices, respectively, of the trade coefficients e_{i1}^{kr} and γ_{i1}^{k}

$F^1, F^2, \ldots, F^k$ = the vectors of f_i^k s, as defined in equation (24-7)

Ω = the matrix of the coefficients on the left side

X = the vector of outputs.

The endogenous variables of this model are the mn outputs of the n sectors of each of the m countries included in the model. Trade flows for the countries included in the model are also endogenously determined through the trade coefficients, e_{il}^{kr}, and the outputs. The exogenous variables are: (1) exports to the rest of the developing ECAFE countries; (2) exports to the developed ECAFE countries; (3) exports to the Rest-of-the-World; (4) sectoral private and public consumption demands; and (5) sectoral fixed and inventory capital formation. Since the capital-coefficient matrices are not available for all the countries, no attempt is made to treat capital formation as endogenous in the model. Since c_i^k and d_i^k are exogenously determined for each country, that portion of the trade flow, e_i^{kr}, that is determined by them can also be regarded as exogenous in the model. The alternative approaches adopted in deriving the projections of the exogenous elements will be described later.

One interesting modification of the trade-flow equation in this model could be obtained by introducing government policy variables. It is difficult to measure all the policy variables of the government, because some are purely institutional in nature. However, it is conceivable that most of the policies are reflected in the form of a disparity between the domestic prices and the international prices. This disparity as a proportion of the international price is generally called an "implicit tariff" in the case of imports (t_m) and "implicit export subsidy" in the case of exports (S_e). These implicit price effects could be taken as proxy variables to measure government policies. Alternatively, the estimates of effective rates of protection for each industry (ERP) in the importing country could be used as summary measures of all types of protection policies and introduced as explanatory variables in the trade-flow equation.

Thus,

$$e_i^{kr} = f\left(x_i^r, d^r, c^r, t_{mi}^r, s_{ei}^r\right)$$

or

$$e_i^{kr} = f\left(x_i^r, d^r, c^r, (ERP)_i^r\right) \tag{24-9}$$

Given the exogenous elements, the model can be solved to derive consistent production plans for the different countries and the trade flows among them. The model can be reworked for several alternative levels of investment and consumption in the different countries. Thus the implications of locations of final demands for production activity in the different countries can be studied. We will now introduce three concepts: (i) trade reciprocity between pairs of countries; (ii) regional import substitution; and (iii) intraregional trade diversion.

Trade reciprocity, λ^{kr}, between pairs of countries in terms of incremental trade can be defined by the ratio of incremental imports to incremental exports. Thus

$$\lambda^{kr} = \frac{\sum\limits_{i} \Delta e_i^{kr}}{\sum\limits_{i} \Delta e_i^{rk}} \tag{24-10}$$

After deriving the output vectors, changes in them from the base-year levels can be derived, as well as the incremental trade induced by the output changes. With Δe_i^{kr}'s, the trade reciprocity ratio implied by the results of the models can be studied. It is possible to extend this concept by considering multilateral rather than bilateral trade.

Import dependence at the regional level is defined as the ratio of imports of the countries included in the model from the Rest-of-the-World and their total output. Thus

$$\mu_i = \frac{\sum\limits_{k} m_i^{RWk}}{\sum\limits_{k} x_i^k} \tag{24-11}$$

This is defined only for the countries included in the model, as the data on outputs, x_i^k, are not available for the other countries. This is therefore a subregional index. Change in μ_i indicates the import substitution at the subregional level. A fall in μ_i implies that the subregional imports from RW rise at a lower rate than the subregional output. The value of μ_i can be specified to realise a desired level of import substitution at the subregional level.

The ratio of intraregional imports to the imports from the Rest-of-the-World outside ECAFE is a broad index of the relative importance of the intraregional trade. Expansion of the intraregional trade may be encouraged also by trade diversion from extraregional to regional sources of import supply. Thus, the desired level of trade diversion can be specified by fixing the level of the intra-regional trade ratio, ϕ_i:

$$\phi_i = \frac{\sum_k \sum_r m_i^{rk} + \sum_k m_i^{REk}}{\sum_k m_i^{RWk}} \tag{24-12}$$

Using these concepts, we impose three sets of conditions on the solutions of the models, so that the solutions conform to the desired levels of trade reciprocity, regional import substitution, and regional trade diversion. The equations giving these conditions are

$$\lambda^{kr} = \lambda^{*kr} \tag{24-13}$$

(These are $\binom{m}{2}$ in number, where m is the number of the countries included in the model.)

$$\mu_i = \mu_i^* \qquad (i = 1, 2, \ldots, n) \tag{24-14}$$

and

$$\phi_i = \phi_i^* \qquad (i = 1, 2, \ldots, n) \tag{24-15}$$

In these equations, $\lambda^{*kr}, \mu_i^*, \phi_i^*$ indicate the desired or target levels of the respective ratios. It is easy to show by using equations (24-2) and (24-6) that equations (24-13), (24-14), and (24-15) can be expressed as linear functions in x_i^k's.

The model is solved in the following manner. For given exogenous elements, solve equation (24-7) for the x's. Substitute these x's in (24-13), (24-14), and (24-15). If these are not satisfied, change the trade coefficients, ϵ_{il}'s and γ_{il}'s, so that these are satisfied. Use these new sets of parameters in equation (24-8) and derive new output levels, to be used again in equations (24-13), (24-14), and (24-15), and check again. Thus the system is solved by the process of iteration, and there may not be a unique solution. If the process does not converge in a few iterations and/or the desired changes in the parameters imply values that are not feasible, then the targets in regard to the trade reciprocity ratio and other regional parameters may have to be changed.

Optimisation Model

In order to derive an optimum plan of production and trade, an optimisation model is developed in this section. The objective function is formulated to maximise the total income in the region. The minimisation of the regional trade balance can also be considered as an objective of the regional plan. The model is presented below:

Maximise (regional income)

$$\sum_{k,i \in R} v_i^k x_i^k \qquad (24\text{-}16)$$

subject to the following constraints:

1. Constraints for Each Country

COMMODITY BALANCE CONSTRAINTS
FOR ALL COUNTRIES SEPARATELY

$$\Omega X \geqslant F \qquad (24\text{-}17)$$

LABOUR CONSTRAINT

$$\sum_i \alpha_i^k x_i^k \leqslant l^k \qquad (24\text{-}18)$$

CAPITAL CONSTRAINT

$$\sum_i \beta_i^k x_i^k \leqslant d^k \qquad (24\text{-}19)$$

TARIFF REVENUE CONSTRAINT

$$\sum_i t_i^k m_i^{REk} x_i^k + \sum_i t_i^k m_i^{RWk} x_i^k \geqslant T^k \qquad (24\text{-}20)$$

For examining the implications of factor mobility, the labour and capital constraints will be introduced at the regional level as follows:

2. Constraints with Factor Mobility Within the Region

$$\sum_k \sum_i \alpha_i^k x_i^k \leqslant \sum_k l^k \qquad (24\text{-}18')$$

$$\sum_k \sum_i \beta_i^k x_i^k \leqslant \sum_k d^k \qquad (24\text{-}19')$$

3. Constraints for Each Region

REGIONAL IMPORT SUBSTITUTION CONSTRAINT

$$\sum_k m_i^{RWk} x_i^k - \bar{\theta}_i \sum_k x_i^k \leqslant 0 \qquad (i = 1, 2, \ldots, n) \qquad (24\text{-}21)$$

REGIONAL TRADE DIVERSION CONSTRAINTS

$$\phi_i(x_i^k) \geqslant \bar{\phi}_i \qquad (i = 1, 2, \ldots, n) \tag{24-22}$$

TRADE-RECIPROCITY CONSTRAINTS

$$\lambda_{min}^{kr} \leqslant \lambda^{kr} \leqslant \lambda_{max}^{kr} \qquad [\binom{m}{2} \text{ constraints}] \tag{24-23}$$

REGIONAL TRADE BALANCE CONSTRAINT

$$\sum_k \sum_i m_i^k - \sum_k \sum_i e_i^k \leqslant (\text{aid})_R \tag{24-24}$$

Endogenous variables of the model are $\Big\}$ x_i^k's $(i = 1, 2, \ldots, n)$

All the constraints are linear in $\Big\}$ x_i^k's $(k = 1, 2, \ldots, m)$

For examining the implications of removal of tariffs and trade barriers, implicit subsidies, etc., the model will be calculated (i) with the existing tariff structures and (ii) with the modified parameter values for the situation when implicit tariffs and subsidies for intraregional trade are eliminated. The input-output coefficients, a_{ij}, several trade coefficients, and the consumption structure will have to be modified so as to conform to the relative price structure of the new trade-policy system. The implications of complete factor mobility within the region can be studied by calculating the model with and without constraints (24-18') and (24-19').

Data Sources and Limitations
At the present stage of the research, only the first variant of the consistency model with one modification has been calculated. Work on the optimisation model is now in the last phases of completion, but the results are not reported here. In the trade-flow equations (24-2), the variables d^r, c^r are not introduced and instead, only x's are considered. Thus the trade coefficient, e^{kr}, now becomes only a trade-output ratio. The countries listed in Table 24-5, for which input-output tables were readily available, have been included. Other countries of the ECAFE region are treated as rest of ECAFE, of which Japan, New Zealand, and Australia constitute developed ECAFE. All these input-output tables are in domestic producers' prices. The table for Pakistan is for 1960-1961 and is in purchasers' prices; it is therefore not included in the first phase of the work. The input-output tables for Ceylon (1968) and Indonesia (1969) have

Table 24-5.   Countries with Input-Output Tables Included in the Study

Country	Year to Which Input-Output Table Refers	Number of Sectors in the Original Table
India	1964–65	77
South Korea	1966	43
Taiwan	1966	55
Malaysia	1965	30
Philippines	1965	51

only recently become available, and work in extending the matrix so as to include these tables and the corresponding trade coefficients is now in progress. The input-output tables of the five countries listed in Table 24-5 are first reduced to a common sectoral classification of 31 sectors, including services. The average geographical structure of trade (geographical shares) as derived from the trade volume is applied to the absolute export value recorded in the input-output tables. These estimated geographical trade flows are combined with the sectoral output data to obtain the ϵ_{il}^{rk} coefficients. The import coefficients, γ_i^k, are obtained from the data on imports and output in the input-output tables.

The limitations of an empirical study of such a huge magnitude as the present one arise from various sources. First, no price adjustments are made in using the trade statistics of 1964–1966 with the data from the input-output tables, which referred to 1964, or 1965, or 1966. Second, sectoral correspondence between the different input-output tables cannot be perfect, as the definitions of sectors often vary from one country to another. Third, the effects of exchange rate changes (for example, the 1966 devaluation in India) on the parameter values are not considered, nor is the further role of exchange rates and convertibility of currencies in fostering trade cooperation analysed. Fourth, time series data required to fully estimate the trade-flow functions are not available; hence some approximations are made in the formulation and estimation of the functions.

Projections of Exogenous Variables

The model is implemented for the years 1975 and 1980. This implies first projecting the exogenous variables of the model, viz.: sectoral consumption demands; sectoral capital formation; and exports to the rest of the world, rest of developing ECAFE, and developed ECAFE. For making these projections, a macroeconomic model is implicitly assumed for each country. The gross domestic product is projected on the basis of an assumed growth rate. An overall marginal propensity to consume is used to obtain the total consumption expenditures of the projection period. Base-year proportions of private and public consumption are applied to this total and then sectoral shares in total consumption of the base period are applied to these total private- and public-consumption levels. The assumption of constant commodity composition implies unitary expenditures elasticity for all sectors, which is not, of course, very realistic. When expenditures elasticity data are available, these should be used. Total investment is estimated by using an overall capital-output ratio, while sectoral structure of capital formation is derived by using the constant composition of the base year, viz., the year of the table. This procedure is used both for the fixed and inventory capital formation. Projections of exports to the rest of ECAFE and the rest of the world are based on country shares and assumed growth rates of total regional trade. Country shares in the total regional trade are derived from the average trade data of 1964, 1965, and 1966 for the different sectors [8]. There can be two approaches here: assume the shares and growth rates constant as in the past; or make adjustments in them for the future periods. At present, only the first approach has been used. Feasible growth rates of the GDP, values of the marginal propensity to consume, and capital-output ratios are mostly taken from the studies of ECAFE [7] ;

Output Structure and Trade Flows—1975, 1980

The results of the model for the 1975 and 1980 sectoral output pattern for the five countries of the model are presented in Tables 24-6 and 24-7. It should be pointed out that these results are tentative, and examination of the sensitivity of the results to the various alternative assumptions regarding different parameter values is necessary before finalizing the results. The projected outputs between 1975 and 1980 imply varying growth rates for the different sectors, as presented in Table 24-8. A comparison is made between the growth rates derived from the results of this multiregional, multisectoral model with those derived from the separate models of each country, as worked out in the ECAFE studies [6]. The projections bring out that about 80-90 percent of the output in most of the sectors is induced by the location—by country—of demands for final consumption and capital formation. However, in the case of some predominantly export sectors—for example, Sector 8, Leather & leather products, in India; Sector 3, Forestry & logging, in the cases of Malaysia and the Philippines; and Sector 21, Mining, in the case of the Philippines—the shares of export-induced components of the sectoral outputs are substantial [as indicated by the difference between the figures in row (b) and row (a) in Tables 24-6 and 24-7].

The two sets of growth rates reported in Table 24-8 differ considerably for most of the countries. The multiregional model predicts higher sectoral growth rates than do the models for each country in 7 out of 18 comparable sectors in India, 8 out of 27 in South Korea, 23 out of 26 in Taiwan, 10 out of 20 in Malaysia, 11 out of 24 in the Philippines. Except in the case of Taiwan, the ECAFE studies for each country seem to have overestimated the sectoral growth rates in the majority of the sectors of the different countries. To put this differently, this result seems to suggest that failure to take account of the inter-

Table 24-6.   Projections of Sectoral Outputs for 1975 (millions of 1965–1966 U.S. dollars)

Sector Num-ber	Title		India	South Korea	Taiwan	Malaysia	Philippines
1	Palay and corn	(a)	23,374.9	2,384.8	638.6	567.8	758.4
		(b)	23,516.6	2,408.9	722.2	593.7	843.6
2	Other agriculture	(a)	13,267.8	1,439.2	885.2	152.2	779.4
		(b)	13,931.5	1,458.9	1,018.7	390.1	943.5
3	Forestry & logging	(a)	825.6	237.5	109.2	59.9	214.9
		(b)	862.9	251.0	186.6	370.7	1,071.3
4	Livestock & fishery	(a)	5,897.0	184.1	360.6	71.0	1,018.9
		(b)	6,086.0	412.3	391.6	85.2	1,056.9
5	Beverages	(a)	247.9	264.3	128.7	25.1	214.3
		(b)	323.7	265.4	129.7	25.5	220.9
6	Tobacco & manufacturing	(a)	1,736.8	203.0	181.7	116.2	355.8
		(b)	1,802.1	206.6	184.5	116.2	388.8
7	Food manufacturing	(a)	8,963.2	819.9	515.3	321.0	2,383.6
		(b)	9,852.8	841.4	667.9	352.5	2,671.3
8	Leather products	(a)	582.6	67.4	12.1	1.6	14.9
		(b)	1,006.1	88.8	26.6	2.7	15.4
9	Rubber products	(a)	298.3	104.0	41.2	62.8	91.8
		(b)	322.6	110.2	46.8	86.6	99.6
10	Paper, paper products, & printing	(a)	948.8	492.7	200.4	38.8	227.0
		(b)	975.8	517.9	221.8	45.3	239.9
11	Wood, furniture, & nonmetallic mineral products	(a)	1,648.0	453.1	370.1	161.8	277.9
		(b)	1,773.3	545.4	495.6	268.4	399.9
12	Textile manufacturing	(a)	8,846.4	1,055.1	429.3	21.4	331.6
		(b)	10,203.1	1,144.1	486.7	22.3	339.1
13	Chemicals	(a)	2,238.0	262.7	440.9	134.4	373.1
		(b)	2,400.6	280.9	516.5	157.5	421.2
14	Petroleum products	(a)	377.7	154.7	313.5	47.1	255.0
		(b)	408.5	180.0	345.1	89.0	322.8
15	Metallic products	(a)	1,817.8	118.0	26.6	117.5	183.5
		(b)	1,860.3	179.3	37.4	133.0	194.9

16	Basic metals	(a)	2,159.5	246.6	316.8	67.1	99.8
		(b)	2,319.1	323.2	376.3	1,334.6	116.5
17	Machinery, except electrical	(a)	950.8	16.8	217.4	70.2	40.4
		(b)	1,054.9	29.3	231.2	1,417.1	42.1
18	Electrical machinery	(a)	797.5	107.3	135.3	–	95.6
		(b)	908.6	178.9	446.9	6.2	98.0
19	Transport equipment	(a)	1,809.1	134.0	197.3	82.9	175.3
		(b)	1,865.9	137.7	200.2	158.6	179.0
20	Other minerals & scrap	(a)	310.3	164.7	76.7	616.8	0.2
		(b)	527.0	328.6	94.2	1,136.1	1.8
21	Mining	(a)	525.1	278.0	115.9	212.6	91.9
		(b)	619.3	297.3	138.2	243.0	507.1
22	Electricity & water	(a)	–	180.9	216.8	34.4	157.5
		(b)	–	199.4	244.5	39.7	167.3
23	Construction	(a)	6,276.8	1,448.2	840.5	–	1,026.3
		(b)	6,276.8	1,452.7	845.0	–	1,027.4
24	Transportation	(a)	2,502.3	560.6	327.3	71.4	500.2
		(b)	2,669.4	584.6	349.4	84.3	1,029.2
25	Miscellaneous manufacturing	(a)	745.4	144.6	19.7	813.5	49.5
		(b)	802.6	487.2	136.9	940.7	60.9
26	Communication	(a)	–	89.3	60.5	901.5	50.7
		(b)	–	95.1	65.7	918.2	54.9
27	Banking & insurance	(a)	–	492.1	186.8	319.8	1,539.3
		(b)	–	506.4	195.3	446.6	1,579.5
28	Trade	(a)	–	1,332.9	1,041.8	187.5	1,691.0
		(b)	–	1,419.3	1,140.9	187.5	1,771.0
29	Government & private services	(a)	–	979.6	2,020.1	–	2,380.4
		(b)	–	999.9	2,111.7	–	2,442.3
30	Unallocated	(a)	–	93.3	104.9	–	28.9
		(b)	–	111.3	118.0	–	92.0
31	Storage & warehousing	(a)	–	–	12.5	–	28.9
		(b)	–	–	14.6	–	30.4

Notes: Figures in row (a) give output induced by total of private consumption, government consumption, fixed capital formation, and inventory change. Figures in row (b) give total output of the sector. Difference between rows (b) and (a) gives the outputs induced directly and indirectly by all the exogenous components of export demand.

Table 24-7.   Projections of Sectoral Outputs for 1980 (millions of 1965-1966 U.S. dollars)

Num-ber	Title		India	South Korea	Taiwan	Malaysia	Philippines
1	Palay and corn	(a)	29,455.8	3,482.2	937.5	759.1	1,009.3
		(b)	29,712.5	3,528.9	1,098.9	853.1	1,108.4
2	Other agriculture	(a)	15,348.0	2,083.1	1,301.0	212.2	1,037.3
		(b)	16,231.6	2,113.1	1,466.0	310.2	1,196.5
3	Forestry & logging	(a)	1,090.7	346.8	163.9	81.0	293.5
		(b)	1,169.8	373.7	343.4	781.2	2,237.2
4	Livestock & fishery	(a)	7,480.0	267.1	529.4	94.5	1,358.1
		(b)	8,002.4	298.6	625.9	148.7	1,414.2
5	Beverages	(a)	248.5	383.6	188.9	33.4	285.2
		(b)	381.6	385.9	191.6	34.2	297.1
6	Tobacco & manufacturing	(a)	1,737.3	294.7	266.6	155.0	473.3
		(b)	2,323.2	300.7	270.5	155.2	542.8
7	Food manufacturing	(a)	9,207.7	1,192.4	756.9	428.2	3,172.0
		(b)	9,689.9	1,231.8	938.9	469.2	3,504.7
8	Leather products	(a)	583.3	97.9	18.1	2.3	18.7
		(b)	1,499.0	145.6	55.6	264.4	19.6
9	Rubber products	(a)	327.2	151.7	61.3	85.8	122.4
		(b)	386.3	169.6	87.9	149.0	165.2
10	Paper, paper products, & printing	(a)	738.9	727.1	295.7	54.2	302.1
		(b)	805.6	812.8	271.2	74.7	328.6
11	Wood, furniture, & nonmetallic mineral products	(a)	2,054.2	674.3	554.0	224.3	364.3
		(b)	2,316.6	867.2	868.2	547.5	594.0
12	Textile manufacturing	(a)	9,386.8	1,539.0	633.6	28.8	441.6
		(b)	1,132.1	1,669.8	743.6	36.1	452.8
13	Chemicals	(a)	2,428.4	384.1	652.4	183.9	496.9
		(b)	2,603.5	439.0	905.0	243.1	608.5
14	Petroleum products	(a)	433.2	225.7	462.4	66.1	338.5
		(b)	514.2	270.9	551.2	154.5	1,008.9
15	Metallic products	(a)	2,071.5	174.1	40.1	164.0	244.1
		(b)	2,185.8	533.6	93.4	208.1	270.2

16	Basic metals	(a)	2,809.8	366.8	476.4	93.0	131.6
		(b)	3,312.3	720.7	780.6	1,485.3	177.5
17	Machinery, except electrical	(a)	1,326.0	24.8	326.6	97.7	55.1
		(b)	1,701.4	72.3	359.1	1,301.0	59.9
18	Electrical machinery	(a)	1,068.9	159.1	227.1	–	131.2
		(b)	1,863.1	801.6	2,450.5	43.6	137.0
19	Transport equipment	(a)	2,341.3	199.4	294.8	114.4	237.3
		(b)	2,487.1	205.4	303.8	238.2	246.3
20	Other minerals & scrap	(a)	295.4	243.9	113.5	858.3	0.3
		(b)	2,162.0	757.4	167.9	2,439.2	2.4
21	Mining	(a)	605.8	404.6	172.0	291.6	121.8
		(b)	772.2	459.7	231.0	368.2	1,352.5
22	Electricity & water	(a)	–	264.3	320.4	46.5	209.6
		(b)	–	328.5	426.5	62.8	232.5
23	Construction	(a)	9,034.3	2,165.7	1,261.4	–	1,313.1
		(b)	9,034.3	2,181.4	1,275.4	–	1,315.5
24	Transportation	(a)	3,048.1	816.4	482.9	101.1	665.7
		(b)	4,325.9	893.1	565.7	132.6	730.8
25	Miscellaneous manufacturing	(a)	882.8	211.4	29.2	1,095.7	66.2
		(b)	1,011.3	1,310.6	401.4	1,399.9	98.6
26	Communication	(a)	–	130.1	89.0	1,205.7	67.0
		(b)	–	256.7	111.0	1,250.9	76.6
27	Banking & insurance	(a)	–	714.0	274.7	481.9	2,057.8
		(b)	–	759.9	356.8	789.2	2,145.2
28	Trade	(a)	–	1,942.9	1,531.1	249.4	2,251.2
		(b)	–	2,225.7	2,009.6	249.4	2,413.5
29	Government & private services	(a)	–	1,421.1	2,967.5	–	3,165.8
		(b)	–	1,489.7	3,207.9	–	3,309.5
30	Unallocated	(a)	–	136.4	155.5	–	117.9
		(b)	–	169.0	211.8	–	126.1
31	Storage & warehousing	(a)	–	–	18.4	–	38.6
		(b)	–	–	26.0	–	40.9

Note: Figures in row (a) give output induced by total of private consumption, government consumption, fixed capital formation, and inventory change. Figures in row (b) give total output of the sector. Difference between figures in (b) and (a) gives the outputs induced directly and indirectly by all the exogenous components of export demand.

Table 24-8.   Sectoral Growth Rates of the Projected Outputs During 1975–1980

Num-ber	Sector Title	India	South Korea	Taiwan	Malaysia	Philippines
1	Palay & corn	4.8 (4.2)	7.9 (6.8)	8.8 (5.9)	7.5 (8.4)	5.6 (5.0)
2	Other agriculture	3.1 (4.2)	7.7 (6.8)	7.5 (5.9)	-4.5 (1.4)	4.8 (5.0)
3	Forestry & logging	6.3 (4.2)	8.3 (9.9)	13.0 (8.3)	16.1 (6.2)	15.9 (5.8)
4	Livestock & fishery	5.6 (4.2)	-6.2 (8.8)	9.9 (5.3)	11.8 (7.0)	6.0 (5.1)
5	Beverages	3.4 (4.2)	7.8 (12.9)	8.1 (6.1)	6.1 (8.8)	6.1 (5.1)
6	Tobacco & manufacturing	5.2 (4.2)	7.8 (12.9)	8.0 (5.8)	5.9 (8.8)	6.9 (5.1)
7	Food manufacturing	-0.3 (4.8)	7.9 (8.4)	7.0 (7.8)	5.9 (8.8)	5.6 (5.1)
8	Leather products	8.3 (6.4)	10.4 (12.3)	15.9 (7.6)	150.2 (–)	4.9 (5.9)
9	Rubber products	3.7 (6.4)	9.0 (22.1)	13.4 (8.5)	11.5 (9.5)	10.6 (7.5)
10	Paper, paper products, & printing	-3.8 (6.5)	9.4 (11.5)	4.1 (7.4)	10.5 (5.0)	6.5 (10.2)
11	Wood, furniture, & nonmetallic mineral products	5.5 (–)	9.7 (10.1)	11.9 (8.5)	15.3 (5.5)	8.2 (8.1)
12	Textile manufacturing	2.1 (5.0)	7.9 (12.7)	8.8 (8.5)	10.1 (11.7)	5.9 (5.9)
13	Chemicals	1.6 (8.5)	9.3 (12.2)	11.9 (6.9)	9.1 (8.0)	7.6 (8.9)
14	Petroleum products	4.7 (–)	8.5 (–)	9.1 (–)	11.7 (7.0)	25.6 (7.3)
15	Metallic products	3.3 (8.3)	24.4 (11.0)	20.1 (8.5)	9.4 (11.0)	6.8 (8.3)
16	Basic metals	7.4 (7.9)	17.4 (11.1)	15.7 (8.6)	2.1 (6.4)	8.8 (12.2)
17	Machinery, except electrical	10.0 (8.3)	19.8 (13.1)	49.2 (9.1)	-1.7 (11.0)	7.3 (8.5)
18	Electrical machinery	15.5 (8.3)	35.0 (13.1)	40.5 (9.1)	47.7 (11.0)	6.9 (8.3)
19	Transport equipment	5.9 (8.3)	8.3 (13.1)	8.7 (9.1)	8.5 (11.0)	6.6 (8.3)
20	Other minerals & scrap	32.6 (–)	18.2 (11.0)	12.3 (7.2)	16.5 (–)	5.9 (8.2)
21	Mining	4.5 (7.7)	9.1 (11.0)	10.9 (7.2)	8.7 (5.5)	21.7 (8.2)
22	Electricity & water		10.5 (11.8)	11.8 (8.8)	9.6 (7.3)	6.8 (–)
23	Construction	7.6 (–)	8.5 (9.3)	8.6 (7.9)	– (–)	5.1 (6.0)
24	Transportation	7.8 (–)	8.8 (19.6)	10.0 (7.9)	9.5 (–)	-6.6 (6.6)
25	Miscellaneous manufacturing	4.8 (–)	21.9 (10.1)	25.2 (11.2)	8.3 (–)	10.1 (5.2)
26	Communication	–	22.0 (–)	11.1 (–)	6.4 (–)	6.9 (–)
27	Banking & insurance	–	8.5 (9.7)	12.8 (–)	12.1 (–)	6.3 (–)
28	Trade	–	9.4 (10.9)	12.0 (–)	5.9 (–)	6.4 (–)
29	Government & private services	–	8.3 (–)	8.7 (5.9)	– (–)	6.3 (–)
30	Unallocated	–	8.7 (12.2)	12.4 (6.9)	– (–)	6.5 (–)
31	Storage & warehousing	–	– (–)	12.2 (–)	– (–)	6.1 (–)

Note: Figures in parentheses give the growth rates of the separate country models, based on the ECAFE studies, *Sectoral Output and Employment Projections, for the Second Development Decade, Development Programming Techniques, Series No. 8, United Nation (1970)*

dependence among the countries in the projection exercises may lead to over-estimation of the sectoral growth rates, and this would prescribe a growth pattern that does not conform to the objective of intraregional consistency in trade and production.

The intraregional trade flows implied by the projected output levels and assumed trade coefficients are presented in Table 24-9. The trade reciprocity ratios, based on total trade, range from 0.0005 to 2150.5. These have fallen in 1980 from those in 1975 for some countries, viz.: India with every other country; South Korea with the Philippines; Taiwan with South Korea and with Malaysia; Malaysia with South Korea and with the Philippines; and the Philippines with Taiwan and with Malaysia. A fall in the trade-reciprocity ratio for country A with country B indicates that country A is now importing more from country B per unit of its own exports to country B. If the initial value is greater than unity, then this fall would imply that the two countries are moving towards the stage of being equal partners in the trade. The comparison of the trade-reciprocity ratios of 1975 and 1980 shows that in 12 out of 20 cases, trade-reciprocity ratios have fallen. Thus, even with the existing trade coefficients, the countries of the ECAFE region have prospects of coming closer in trade relations, provided they plan their production patterns so as to take explicit account of their interdependences.

Concluding Remarks

An attempt has been made to integrate the development plans of the ECAFE countries within the framework of a multiregional and multisectoral model for planning production and trade. Five ECAFE countries—India, South Korea, Taiwan, Malaysia, and the Philippines—are explicitly considered, as their input-output tables are readily available. Alternative consistency models based upon different assumptions about the trade flows have been developed. Suitable measures of import-substitution at the regional level, trade reciprocity between pairs of countries, and trade diversion from non-ECAFE sources to ECAFE sources of supply of imports have also been developed. In addition, an optimisation model has been presented in which maximisation of the regional income is taken as the criterion of optimality. Empirical results of the first phase of the work using one alternative of the consistency models are presented and discussed. Projections of the output structure and trade structure of 1975 and 1980 are derived from the model. Trade-reciprocity ratios indicate that the developing countries of the ECAFE region move in the direction of increased trade cooperation, provided they plan their production by taking account of their interdependences.

The results of this paper are highly tentative, since more work on sensitivity analysis with respect to various parameter values is essential before results can be considered as final. In particular, trade coefficients need to be modified to take account of the deliberate attempts at trade cooperation. More interesting and

Table 24-9.   Intraregional Trade Flows and Trade-Reciprocity Ratios, 1975, 1980 (millions of U.S. dollars)

	1975					1980				
From ↓ To →	India	Korea	Taiwan	Malaysia	Philippines	India	Korea	Taiwan	Malaysia	Philippines
India	—	11.41 (34.58)	5.21 (28.94)	5511.78 (767.76)	129.03 (2150.50)	—	15.49 (20.38)	7.29 (22.38)	6019.66 (745.93)	145.67 (2820.88)
Korea	0.33 (0.03)	—	6.06 (0.30)	12.28 (5.51)	12.15 (0.07)	0.76 (0.05)	—	11.36 (0.30)	18.16 (6.16)	20.10 (0.06)
Taiwan	0.18 (0.03)	20.30 (3.35)	—	53.90 (1.80)	36.78 (0.17)	0.33 (0.05)	37.89 (3.34)	—	103.10 (1.77)	125.74 (0.28)
Malaysia	7.18 (0.00)	2.23 (0.18)	29.95 (0.56)	—	51.88 (11.63)	8.07 (0.00)	2.95 (0.16)	58.12 (0.56)	—	63.04 (11.12)
Philippines	0.06 (0.00)	168.32 (13.85)	214.95 (5.84)	4.46 (0.69)	—	0.08 (0.00)	350.01 (17.41)	450.60 (3.58)	5.67 (0.09)	—

Note: Values given in parentheses are trade reciprocity ratios, based on total trade.
Source: Projections of the output structure as given in Tables 24-6 and 24-7.

more useful results could be derived by using an optimisation model. In addition, other countries, such as Pakistan, Ceylon, and Indonesia, for which input-output tables now exist, should also be explicitly included in the model. Further work in these various directions is now in progress.

References

1. Leontief, W., and A. Strout. "Multiregional Input-Output Analysis." In *Structural Interdependence and Economic Development.* Edited by T. Barna. London: MacMillan and Company, Ltd., 1963. Pp. 119–150.

2. Linnemann, A. *An Econometric Study of International Trade Flows.* Amsterdam: North-Holland Publishing Company, 1966.

3. Panchamukhi, V.R. "Effective Protection and Resource Allocation—Case Studies of India, Korea, Philippines, Malaysia, and China (Taiwan)." Bombay University, Bombay, 1971. (Mimeographed.)

4. Panchamukhi, V.R. "Linkages and Industrialisation—A Study of Selected ECAFE Countries." *Journal of Development Planning,* no. 8, forthcoming.

5. Panchamukhi, V.R. "Revealed Comparative Advantage: India's Trade with the Countries of the ECAFE Region." *Economic and Political Weekly* (India) 7, no. 2 (January 1973): 65–74.

6. Panchamukhi, V.R. Separate reports prepared by the author are being published by the United Nations ECAFE Secretariat in the Development Programming Series, No. 9 (forthcoming).

7. United Nations, Economic Commission for Asia and the Far East. *Sectoral Output and Employment Projections for the Second Development Decade.* Development Programming Techniques Series, no. 8, Bangkok: United Nations, 1970.

8. United Nations. *Foreign Trade Statistics of Asia and the Far East.* New York: United Nations, 1968.

Part Seven

Optimization Models and Production Functions

Chapter Twenty-Five

A Minimal Realization of the Leontief Dynamic Input-Output Model

D. A. Livesey

In a recent paper, Kendrick [4] has reexamined the well-known difficulty of a singular capital matrix which arises in a dynamic input-output model. Quite independently, the same partitioning approach used by Kendrick was adopted in a paper by the present writer [5], which also generalized the technique so that the relationship between the normal version of the dynamic input-output model and the transformed version, which overcomes the singularity problem, is apparent. This paper concentrates on a new version of this transformation approach, which, unlike earlier versions, is, in the terminology of realization theory, a proper representation of the dynamic input-output system.

We show that the earlier work, whilst correct as far as it went, did not yield the smallest set of difference equations that can represent the entire behaviour of a dynamic Leontief system. Since the new results arise from a correct use of state-space theory, the paper also serves to illustrate some of that theory's key features and to establish its usefulness in economic planning problems, with the dynamic input-output model as an example. Primarily, however, we are concerned with finding the minimal realization of the Leontief system—in other words, the smallest set of difference equations that fully determine all the elements of the gross output vector, given the vector of final demands, excluding investment. We accordingly begin by specifying the singularity problem and earlier attempts to overcome it. The state-space theory is introduced when it is needed to guide us on our way to the new results.

A Solution to the Singularity Problem

We are considering here the multisectoral dynamic input-output model, which is normally represented by

$$X_t = AX_t + B(X_{t+1} - X_t) + Y_t \tag{25-1}$$

where

X_t = gross output levels

Y_t = final demand, excluding investment

A = Leontief technical coefficient matrix

B = capital coefficient matrix.

Since the composition of final demand, excluding investment, is taken to be exogenously determined, equation (25-1) could be written, provided that matrix B is nonsingular, as

$$X_{t+1} = B^{-1}RX_t - B^{-1}Y_t \tag{25-2}$$

where $R = I - A + B$. If we define matrix F to be $(I - A)^{-1}B$, then an alternative form of equation (25-2) is

$$X_{t+1} = F^{-1}(I + F)X_t - B^{-1}Y_t \tag{25-3}$$

an equation that we shall later find useful for purposes of comparison. In this paper, however, we are concerned with the case in which B is a nonsingular matrix and hence the transformation of equation (25-1) into equations (25-2) and (25-3) cannot be carried out directly.

Both Kendrick and this writer assumed that the singularity of the B matrix arises because some of its rows consist entirely of zero elements. By rearranging B so that the first n_1 rows are nonzero and the last $n - n_1$ rows contain all the zero rows, they were able to partition equation (25-1) as

$$\begin{bmatrix} X^1 \\ \hline X^2 \end{bmatrix}_t = \begin{bmatrix} A_{11} & A_{12} \\ \hline A_{21} & A_{22} \end{bmatrix}\begin{bmatrix} X^1 \\ \hline X^2 \end{bmatrix}_t + \begin{bmatrix} B_{11} & B_{12} \\ \hline 0 & 0 \end{bmatrix}\left(\begin{bmatrix} X^1 \\ \hline X^2 \end{bmatrix}_{t+1} - \begin{bmatrix} X^1 \\ \hline X^2 \end{bmatrix}_t\right) + \begin{bmatrix} Y^1 \\ \hline Y^2 \end{bmatrix}_t \tag{25-4}$$

The partitioning of the reordered vectors X_t and Y_t reflects the fact that those commodities that do not go into capital goods appear as the elements of the vectors X^2 and Y^2. From equation (25-4) we obtain two sets of equations, one of which is

$$[I - A_{22}]X_t^2 = A_{21}X_t^1 + Y_t^2 \tag{25-5}$$

This can be used to give an expression for X_t^2 in terms of X_t^1 and Y_t^2, which, when substituted into the other set of equations, yields[1]

1. Matrix R is as defined in equation (25-2) and has to be partitioned so that $R_{11} = I - A_{11} + B_{11}$, etc.

$$X_{t+1}^1 = P[Y_t^1 - R_{12}R_{22}^{-1} Y_t^2 + B_{12}R_{22}^{-1} Y_{t+1}^2 - (R_{11} - R_{12}R_{22}^{-1}R_{21})X_t^1] \qquad (25\text{-}6)$$

where $P = [B_{11} - B_{12}R_{22}^{-1}R_{21}]^{-1}$. As Kendrick states, the existence of equation (25-6) depends upon the nonsingularity of R_{22} and P, a condition that is ordinarily fulfilled.

Equation (25-6) can be solved for X_t^1 at any date, given its initial value and the final demands Y_t^1 and Y_t^2 over the planning period. It can then be used in equation (25-5) to yield the corresponding values for X_t^2. As a result, though, we no longer have a simple expression for gross outputs, like equation (25-3), which we get when B is nonsingular. In what follows, we show how such an expression can be obtained and we examine its properties.

The Transformation Approach

We define two transformation matrices as

$$J_1 = \left[\begin{array}{c|c} I_{n_1} & 0 \\ \hline 0 & 0 \end{array}\right] \qquad J_2 = \left[\begin{array}{c|c} 0 & 0 \\ \hline 0 & I_{n-n_1} \end{array}\right]$$

where I_k denotes the unit matrix of rank k and the partitioning corresponds to that used for the B matrix in equation (25-4). Then we may write the two sets of equations that make up equation (25-4) as

$$J_1 R X_t = J_1 B X_{t+1} + J_1 Y_t \qquad (25\text{-}7)$$

and

$$J_2 R X_t = J_2 B X_{t+1} + J_2 Y_t \qquad (25\text{-}8)$$

Since $J_2 B$ is a null matrix, it follows from equation (25-8) that, by shifting the time subscript forward one period,

$$J_2 R X_{t+1} = J_2 Y_{t+1} \qquad (25\text{-}9)$$

So that combining equations (25-7) and (25-9) yields

$$J_1 R X_t = [J_1 B - J_2 R] X_{t+1} + J_1 Y_t + J_2 Y_{t+1} \qquad (25\text{-}10)$$

which can be solved to yield X_{t+1} in terms of X_t, Y_t, and Y_{t+1}

$$X_{t+1} = [B - J_2(I - A)]^{-1} \left\{ [B + J_1(I - A)] X_t - J_1 Y_t - J_2 Y_{t+1} \right\} \qquad (25\text{-}11)$$

Note that in writing out equation (25-11) we have made use of the properties that $J_1 B = B$, $J_2 R = J_2(I - A)$, hence

$$J_1 R = B + J_1 (I - A)$$

In equation (25-11), we have merely a neater way of writing both equations (25-5) and (25-6).

Now suppose that we define

$$B^* = B - J_2(I - A) \tag{25-12}$$

and

$$F^* = (I - A)^{-1} B^* \tag{25-13}$$

then equation (25-11) becomes

$$X_{t+1} = (F^*)^{-1}(I + F^*)X_t - (B^*)^{-1}[J_1 Y_t + J_2 Y_{t+1}] \tag{25-14}$$

The result is that we now have, for the case of the singular B matrix, an equation that is equivalent to equation (25-3), and comparisons between the two forms are possible. Apart from the differences between F and F^*, and B and B^*, to which we shall return shortly, there is only the fact that $J_2 Y_{t+1}$ rather than $J_2 Y_t$ enters into equation (25-14). In effect, we have to decide upon Y_{t+1}^2 in period t so that X_{t+1}^2 can be calculated and hence the investment necessary in period t for the expansion of output in period $t + 1$ can be evaluated. This matter of the timing of policy decisions is quite important and relates to the definition of a proper realization, which we will discuss below. Using the concepts of state-space theory, it is possible to derive an alternative version of equation (25-14), which clarifies the timing of policy decisions. But first we consider the effect that changing B into B^* has upon the eigenvalues of the model.

Characteristics of the Transformed Model

An alternative way of writing the dynamic input-output model, even when the B matrix is singular, is

$$[I - A + B]^{-1} B X_{t+1} = X_t - [I - A + B]^{-1} Y_t$$

which leads to

$$\sigma \left[\frac{I}{\sigma} - B(I - A)^{-1} \right](I - A)X_t = Y_t \tag{25-15}$$

when X_t is assumed to be growing at the proportional rate σ. This is the formulation used in studies of balanced growth paths. We know that the upper bound on σ is the reciprocal of the largest characteristic root of matrix $B(I - A)^{-1}$, which we shall define to be matrix E. Since both B and $(I - A)^{-1}$ are nonnegative matrices, it follows that the characteristic vector associated with this root is nonnegative. We now show how these properties are preserved when the model is transformed in the way set out in the previous section.

From our earlier definition, it is obvious that

$$E = (I - A)F(I - A)^{-1} \tag{25-16}$$

which also defines an E^* in terms of F^*. Using the E^* and F^* version of equation (25-16), together with equations (25-12) and (25-13), yields

$$E^* = B^*(I - A)^{-1} = B(I - A)^{-1} - J_2 = E - J_2 \tag{25-17}$$

Thus,

$$E = \left[\begin{array}{c|c} E_{11} & E_{12} \\ \hline 0 & 0 \end{array}\right] \quad \text{and} \quad E^* = \left[\begin{array}{c|c} E_{11} & E_{12} \\ \hline 0 & -I \end{array}\right]$$

and we note that

$$E_{11} = P[I - A_{11} - A_{12}(I - A_{22})^{-1}A_{21}]^{-1} \tag{25-18}$$

In equation (25-18), P, the first of the two matrices that define E_{11}, also occurred in equation (25-6) and was there assumed to be nonsingular. If that assumption is incorrect, then the transformation approach is invalid and the analysis in this section is of no interest, anyway. Since $(I - A)^{-1}$ exists, then so does the matrix that postmultiplies P in equation (25-18) and hence we have established that, if the transformation is valid, then E_{11}^{-1} exists.

The modal matrix, M, of E, that is, the matrix whose columns are the eigenvectors of E, can be written as

$$M = \left[\begin{array}{c|c} N & -E_{11}^{-1}E_{12} \\ \hline 0 & I \end{array}\right] \quad \text{and} \quad M^{-1} = \left[\begin{array}{c|c} N^{-1} & N^{-1}E_{11}^{-1}E_{12} \\ \hline 0 & I \end{array}\right]$$

where N is the modal matrix of E_{11}.[2] If we define

2. This transformation is possible since, although there are multiple zero-valued eigenvalues, the matrix E_{11} is by assumption [see equation (25–18)] of full rank, that is, n_1.

$$\Lambda = \left[\begin{array}{c|c} \Phi & 0 \\ \hline 0 & 0 \end{array} \right]$$

where Φ is, in general, a diagonal matrix with elements corresponding to the distinct eigenvalues of the matrix E_{11},[3] then it follows that

$$E = M\Lambda M^{-1} \quad \text{since} \quad E_{11} = N\Phi N^{-1}.$$

When we consider E^*, we realize that the eigenvalues remain unchanged except that all those which were zero valued become -1. Hence associated with E^* are

$$M^* = \left[\begin{array}{c|c} N & -(E_{11} + I)^{-1}E_{12} \\ \hline 0 & I \end{array} \right], \quad (M^*)^{-1} = \left[\begin{array}{c|c} N^{-1} & N^{-1}(E_{11} + I)^{-1}E_{12} \\ \hline 0 & I \end{array} \right],$$

$$\Lambda^* = \left[\begin{array}{c|c} \Phi & 0 \\ \hline 0 & -I \end{array} \right] = \Lambda - J_2$$

That $E^* = M^* \Lambda^* (M^*)^{-1}$ is easily established.

It is obvious from the above analysis that the nonnegative eigenvector associated with E must in fact be associated with E_{11} and be one of the columns of the modal matrix N. Equally, the corresponding eigenvalue must be the largest diagonal element of the matrix, Φ. Both of these have been shown to apply equally to matrix E^*. We also know that, since equation (25-16) holds, E^* and F^* must have the same eigenvalues and that the modal matrix of F^* is $(I - A)^{-1}M^*$, a nonnegative transformation that preserves the nonnegative eigenvector. If λ is the maximal eigenvalue of E^*, the corresponding eigenvalue of $I + (F^*)^{-1}$ is $1 + 1/\lambda$ and hence the growth rate of X_t is $1/\lambda$. This result, as would be expected, is the same as that which follows directly from equation (25-15).

In this section we have therefore established that the transformation approach adopted in the previous section preserves the fundamental eigenvalues and eigenvectors of the dynamic input-output model.

A Proper Realization

We now turn to the problem of the timing of policy decisions, which occurred when we derived equation (25-14). In order to place our analysis within an established framework, we shall endeavour to find a state-space representation

3. Provided that E_{11} has n_1 linearly independent eigenvectors. If this is not the case one can still proceed by using a Jordan form—see, for instance, Desoer [2].

of the dynamic input-output model. In particular, we are hoping to find a version of equation (25-14) that can be written as

$$\widetilde{X}_{t+1} = U\widetilde{X}_t + V\widetilde{Y}_t \tag{25-19}$$

and

$$D_t = S\widetilde{X}_t + T\widetilde{Y}_t \tag{25-20}$$

Equation (25-19) is known as the state equation since it relates the value of the state variables in the next period, $\widetilde{X}_{t+1}$, to the value of the state, $\widetilde{X}_t$, and the control, $\widetilde{Y}_t$, variables in this period. Writing the dynamic input-output model as either equation (25-2) or (25-3) shows that given the level of gross outputs in this period, X_t, the final demand vector, Y_t, determines the level of output in the next period. This "air of determinancy"[4] results from the assumption, implicit in equation (25-1), that there is no excess capacity at any time. If we regard the final demand vector, Y_t, as a set of policy instruments, or control variables, then we only have to identify the level of gross outputs with the state variables, X_t, for equation (25-2) to be clearly seen as a state-space representation of the dynamic input-output model. It is unusual for the state-space version of an economic model to be in a form that economists can intuitively interpret. Because of its simplicity of form, the dynamic input-output model is the exception that proves the rule. We shall show later that this is also true when the B matrix is singular. Equation (25-20) is the observation equation, and we shall call the S matrix the measurement matrix since it relates the states to the vector of observed variables, D_t. V is termed the control transition matrix and U the state transition matrix.[5]

Together, equations (25-19) and (25-20) form the realization of a system and are a *minimal realization* if and only if they are both controllable and observable. If $\widetilde{X}_t$ has n elements, then the system is *controllable* if and only if the matrix

$$[V, UV, \ldots, U^{n-1}V] \tag{25-21}$$

is of rank n. If the matrix

$$[S', U'S', \ldots, U^{(n-1)'}S] \tag{25-22}$$

where a prime (') denotes transposition, is of rank n, then the system defined by equations (25-19) and (25-20) is *observable*.[6] Since the speed of computa-

---

4. Dorfman, Samuelson, and Solow [3] find it to be logically unjustified.
5. See Desoer [2] for a good introduction to this terminology.
6. Preston [6] gives a good explanation of these terms and relates them to the theory of economic policy.

tional algorithms is inversely related to the number of state variables, it is clearly desirable to reduce the order of equation (25-19) to a minimum. This is automatically achieved if we have a minimal realization,[7] hence the importance of the concept, quite apart from its implicit guarantee that the system is both controllable and observable.

Controllability implies that the policy instruments are able to influence the behaviour of every fundamental mode of behaviour of the model. In other words, by altering the level of final demands we alter both the growth path and the transient properties of the Leontief dynamic system. This will be illustrated below, as will be the concept of observability. This latter property ensures that given the observable variables—the gross outputs in our case—and the policy variables, we are able to determine the value of each state variable.

Finally, we are left with the distinction between proper and improper realizations. Equations (25-19) and (25-20) are a *proper realization* since the time subscripts on the right side of equation (25-19) are one period earlier than that on the left side, whereas all the time subscripts in equation (25-20) are the same. Clearly, equation (25-14) does not satisfy this criterion and is therefore termed an improper realization. Since the properties of a minimal realization only apply to a proper realization, it is important for us to proceed to find a proper form of equation (25-14).

To do this, let us return to equation (25-14), the transformed version of the dynamic input-output model, and consider the result of letting

$$\widetilde{X}_t = X_t + (B^*)^{-1}J_2 Y_t \tag{25-23}$$

Then equation (25-14) becomes

$$\widetilde{X}_{t+1} = (F^*)^{-1}(I+F^*)\widetilde{X}_t - [(F^*)^{-1}(I+F^*)(B^*)^{-1}J_2 + (B^*)^{-1}J]Y_t$$
$$= (F^*)^{-1}(I+F^*)\widetilde{X}_t - [(F^*)^{-1}(B^*)^{-1}J_2 + (B^*)^{-1}]Y_t \tag{25-24}$$

where

$$X_t = \widetilde{X}_t - (B^*)^{-1}J_2 Y_t \tag{25-25}$$

Since equation (25-24) now involves only Y_t and $\widetilde{X}_t$ on the right, we can identify it at once as a proper state-space representation of the dynamic input-output model, and equation (25-25) is the associated observation equation.

Whether equation (25-24) is a controllable representation depends crucially upon the control transition matrix that premultiplies the Y_t term. It can be reordered as

---

7. For ways of achieving a minimal realization for econometric models, see Preston and Wall [7].

$$(F^*)^{-1}[(B^*)^{-1}J_2 + F^*(B^*)^{-1}] = (F^*)^{-1}(B^*)^{-1}[J_2 + E^*] = (F^*)^{-1}(B^*)^{-1}E$$

which shows that its rank is no greater than the rank of E, that is, n_1. Evaluating the controllability condition (25-21) for this example is somewhat tedious. We shall therefore proceed as if equation (25-24) were controllable, a premise that we shall later prove to be false.

The state and observation equations that represent a system are not unique, since any nonsingular matrix can be used to transform the states. For example, let

$$X_t^* = B^* \widetilde{X}_t \qquad (25\text{-}26)$$

then equation (25-24) becomes the state equation in terms of the new state variables, X_t^*,

$$X_{t+1}^* = (E^*)^{-1}[I + E^*]X_t^* - [(E^*)^{-1}J_2 + I]Y_t \qquad (25\text{-}27)$$

The corresponding observation equation is

$$X_t = (B^*)^{-1}X_t^* - (B^*)^{-1}J_2 Y_t \qquad (25\text{-}28)$$

which defines the state variables as

$$X_t^* = B^* X_t + J_2 Y_t$$

$$= BX_t + J_2[Y_t - (I - A)X_t]$$

$$= BX_t \qquad (25\text{-}29)$$

That the final term in the penultimate line of equation (25-29) is zero follows from equation (25-8). We now have an obvious definition for the state variables, since the elements of the vector BX_t are the stocks of outputs that enter the implicit production function in the dynamic input-output model.

Since the controllability matrix for equation (25-27) is complex, let us once again carry out a nonsingular transformation on the state equations. This time, however, we shall use the standard technique of decomposing the model using the modal matrix, M^*, associated with the matrix E^*. Thus if we define

$$X_t^{**} = (M^*)^{-1}X_t^*$$

then equation (25-27) becomes

$$X_{t+1}^{**} = (M^*)^{-1}[I + (E^*)^{-1}]M^* X_t^{**} - (M^*)^{-1}[(E^*)^{-1}J_2 + I]Y_t$$

$$= (I + \Lambda^{-1})X_t^{**} - (M^*)^{-1}[(E^*)^{-1}J_2 + I]Y_t \qquad (25\text{-}30)$$

Armed with the expression for $(M^*)^{-1}$ from the previous section, we can establish that

$$(M^*)^{-1}[(E^*)^{-1}J_2 + I_1] = \begin{bmatrix} N^{-1} & N^{-1}(E_{11} + I)^{-1}E_{12} \\ \hline 0 & I \end{bmatrix} \begin{bmatrix} I & E_{11}^{-1}E_{12} \\ \hline 0 & 0 \end{bmatrix}$$

$$= \begin{bmatrix} N^{-1} & N^{-1}E_{11}^{-1}E_{12} \\ \hline 0 & 0 \end{bmatrix}$$

that is, it is of rank n_1. That the representation (25-30) is uncontrollable follows from noting that the matrix $(I + \Lambda^{-1})$ is a diagonal matrix. Hence the bottom rows of

$$(I + \Lambda^{-1})^k (M^*)^{-1} [(E^*)^{-1}J_2 + I]$$

a typical element of the controllability matrix, (25-21), will always have null elements, whatever the value of k. The rank of the controllability matrix is therefore n_1, not n, and hence the representation is uncontrollable.

This approach to the controllability condition is sometimes termed the coupling criterion. This follows from the observation that since the state transition matrix in equation (25-30) is diagonal, then each state variable is independent of the value of any of the other states. If the ith row of the control matrix does not have at least one nonzero element, then $\tilde{x}_{t+1}^i$, the ith element of $\tilde{X}_{t+1}$, is given by $(1 + \lambda_i)\tilde{x}_t^i$. In other words, it is completely uncoupled from the rest of the system, and the control variables, Y_t, are unable to influence its value.

It follows from the uncontrollability of equation (25-30) that equations (25-24) and (25-27) are also uncontrollable representations of the dynamic Leontief model. A valuable key is provided by equation (25-29) as to how one might best proceed. We note that writing this definition in its partitioned form,

$$\begin{bmatrix} B_{11} & B_{12} \\ \hline 0 & 0 \end{bmatrix} \begin{bmatrix} X_1 \\ \hline X_2 \end{bmatrix} = X_t^* \equiv \begin{bmatrix} K_t \\ \hline 0 \end{bmatrix} \tag{25-31}$$

defines a new vector, K_t, which has n_1 elements. Each element, k_t^i, is the stock of the ith industry's output required to produce at the level of gross output, X_t. That not all types of industrial output go into capital formation explains the zero rows in the B matrix and accounts for the zero elements of the vector, X_t^*.

Suppose, therefore, that we define

$$K_t = JX_t^* \qquad \text{where} \qquad J = \left[I_{n_1} \mid 0 \right]$$

then

$$X_t^* = J^* K_t, \qquad \text{where} \qquad J^* = \left[\begin{array}{c} I_{n_1} \\ \hline 0 \end{array} \right]$$

Thus the state equation (25-27) may be transformed into

$$\begin{aligned}
K_{t+1} &= J[I + (E^*)^{-1}] J^* K_t - J[(E^*)^{-1} J_2 + I] Y_t \\
&= \left[I + E_{11}^{-1} \right] K_t - \left[I \mid E_{11}^{-1} E_{12} \right] Y_t
\end{aligned} \qquad (25\text{-}32)$$

where the corresponding observation equation is

$$X_t = (B^*)^{-1} J^* K_t - (B^*)^{-1} J_2 Y_t \qquad (25\text{-}33)$$

Since the control matrix in equation (25-32) has a rank equal to the number of state variables, n_1, it follows that we have, at last, a controllable and proper representation of the Leontief dynamic system. There remains the question of whether the states, K_t, are observable. Since

$$(B^*)^{-1} J^* = \left[\begin{array}{c} P \\ \hline -PR_{22}^{-1} R_{21} \end{array} \right], \qquad \text{where} \qquad P = [B_{11} - B_{12} R_{22}^{-1} B_{21}]^{-1}$$

is the measurement matrix and is of rank n_1, if P exists, then we can conclude that equation (25-33) is an observable representation. Throughout this paper we have assumed that P exists. If it does not, then our original premise that the singularity of the B matrix arises entirely from the existence of rows with no nonzero elements is false.

Other Sources of Singularity

Here it will be shown that, whereas the previous section dealt successfully with a B matrix that contained rows consisting entirely of zero elements, this does not entirely remove the problem of singularity from the dynamic input-output model. By examining the way in which the B matrix is constructed from the original data, it becomes apparent that zero rows are but a small part of the problem. In particular, even if we have a 90 × 90 input-output table, the rank of the B matrix could be as small as three, if that is the largest number of different assets distinguished in our data. The implications of this result are far-reaching for the programming of dynamic input-output planning problems.

By distinguishing the vector of gross commodity outputs, X_t, from the vector of gross industry outputs, G_t, it is possible in what follows to preserve a more general analysis than the usual commodity-by-commodity or industry-by-industry approach. Once again, the starting point is the equation

$$X_t = AX_t + L_t \iota + Y_t \qquad (25\text{-}34)$$

where the row sums of the matrix L_t are the components of the final demands for commodity outputs going into capital formation, and the vector of final demands, Y_t, excludes investment demand. So that we can transform equation (25-34) into the familiar dynamic input-output model, equation (25-1), it is necessary to relate changes in commodity outputs to changes in industrial outputs. Then the changes of industrial outputs will imply, after the assumption of a particular type of production function, changes in the stock of different assets held by all the industrial sectors. A classification converter can be used to yield the commodity demands implied by these changes in the asset structure of the industries.

As a first step, assume that each of the three steps outlined above is represented by one of the following equations:

$$\Delta G_t = C \, \Delta X_t \qquad (25\text{-}35)$$

$$\Delta K_t^* = H \, \Delta \hat{G}_t \qquad (25\text{-}36)$$

$$L_t = W \, \Delta K_t^* \qquad (25\text{-}37)$$

where $\wedge$ denotes a diagonal matrix formed by the elements of the vector. Of the three equations, (25-35) is the most familiar and least controversial. Working on the basis of an industry technology assumption, the make matrix, $\widetilde{M}$, yields the market-share matrix, C. Since

$$C = \widetilde{M} \hat{X}^{-1} \qquad (25\text{-}38)$$

then

$$C \hat{X} \iota = \widetilde{M} \iota = G \qquad (25\text{-}39)$$

where ι is the unit vector and equation (25-35) follows immediately. Equation (25-36) is the most crucial of the three since it is implicitly a production function. A rough first description would be that the matrix, H, is a set of incremental capital-output ratios. The matrix K_t^* consists of elements k_{ij}^*, which are the assets of type i held by industry j. Hence the dimensions of H are the number of assets by the number of industries. Finally, we have equation (25-37), which converts the increase in the stock of assets by industry into the matrix, L, of commodity demands for investment by purchasing industry. But the total investment demand for each commodity is all that is required for the dynamic input-output model. Thus, taking the row sums of L gives

$$L\iota = WHC \, \Delta \hat{X}_t \iota$$

$$= WHC \, \Delta X_t \qquad (25\text{-}40)$$

and this therefore defines the B matrix to be WHC.

It follows at once that the rank of B is equal to the lowest rank of W, H, and C, respectively. Suppose that the number of assets distinguished is less than both the number of industries and the number of commodities. Then the conclusion, that the maximum rank of B equals the number of assets, is immediately obvious. Before considering this result, and the assumptions underlying it, it is best to proceed as though it were correct.

One method of proceeding with a dynamic input-output model when there is a singular B matrix is to work with stocks of capital assets rather than commodities or industry outputs.[8] Thus we can write

$$X = AX + W \, \Delta K^* \iota + Y \qquad (25\text{-}41)$$

subject to

$$K^* = H\hat{C}X \qquad (25\text{-}42)$$

If we assume that we are not concerned about how much of each asset is used in a particular sector, then we can work with $K = K^* \iota$ and we get

$$K = HCX = HC(I - A)^{-1} (Y + W \, \Delta K) \qquad (25\text{-}43)$$

Since the maximal rank of the matrix HC is equal to the number of assets, we cannot invert it to produce X as a function of K. One possibility, however, is to

8. See, for instance, University of Cambridge, Department of Applied Economics [8]. More recently Bergendorff, Blitzer, and Kim have looked at this problem in an unpublished paper [1]. They suggest the use of capital stock by sector of origin, which is the result found in the preceding section of this paper. Although they refer to Kendrick [4], they do not examine the concepts of controllability or minimal realizability and do not find the relationship between the two approaches.

produce such an inverse from the original incremental capital-output ratio data. Say $X = H^{**}K$, so that equation (25-43) can be written as

$$K_{t+1} = [I + (W'W)^{-1}W'(I - A)H^{**}]K_t - (W'W)^{-1}W'Y_t \tag{25-44}$$

which is thus the required state equation. In order to clarify how this equation relates to the material in the preceding section, suppose that the classification converter, W, is in fact the matrix J^*. This is equivalent to assuming that there are n_1 assets in the model and that each one is made up of a single commodity. Since

$$J' = J^*, JJ^* = I_{n_1}, \text{ and } I_{n_1}J = J,$$

then equation (25-44) becomes

$$K_{t+1} = [I + J(I - A)H^{**}]K_t - JY_t \tag{25-45}$$

Our immediate reaction is to wonder why equation (25-45) is not the same as equation (25-32). The answer is that they are the same since we have assumed that $X = H^{**}K$, which, if combined with equation (25-33), yields

$$J_2Y_t = [J^* - B^*H^{**}]K_t$$

and this, when substituted in equation (25-32), yields equation (25-45).

Since the control transition matrices in both equations (25-44) and (25-45) are of rank equal to the number of assets, we have a controllable realization. This, together with the fact that the observation equation

$$X_t = H^{**}K_t \tag{25-46}$$

satisfies the observability condition, implies that we have a minimal realization. Our demonstration that the order of the minimal realization for a dynamic input-output model is equal to the number of assets has therefore been proven. It rests on certain assumptions, and we must now examine these.

The first assumption is that, whereas capital is not shiftable in the sense that one asset cannot be converted into another asset, assets can be transferred from one sector to another. If we wished to rule out this movement of assets, we would need inequality constraints of the form

$$K^*_{t+1} > K^*_t$$

These would automatically increase the order of the model. Another assumption relates to the classification converter, W. It describes the commodity composition of each asset, but it assumes that assets have the same commodity composition regardless of their industrial location. Thus, buildings in the agricultural sector are assumed to have the same commodity composition as buildings in the service sector. Finally, we need to note that equation (25-36) makes the usual assumption that production takes place in fixed proportions and that there is assumed to be an excess supply of labour.

Conclusions

We have established here that the minimal realization of the dynamic Leontief input-output model, when the B matrix has rows with no nonzero elements, is given by equations (25-32) and (25-33). We have also established that there may be other sources for the singularity of the B matrix and have shown that these, too, may be satisfactorily dealt with. The solution in both cases is to work with the vector of capital stocks either by sector of origin or by type of asset. Any mathematical programming technique applied to such a minimal realization will be at least, if not more, efficient than if it were applied to any other representation of the Leontief model. A disadvantage of the results is that they depend upon the planner's ability to shift capital of the same type from one sector of production to another.

References

1. Bergendorff, H.G.; C.R. Blitzer; and H.K. Kim. "Applications of Control Theory to Leontief-Type Planning Models." Washington, D.C.: Development Research Center, International Bank for Reconstruction and Development, 1973.

2. Desoer, C.A. *Notes for a Second Course on Linear Systems.* New York: Van Nostrand Reinhold, 1970.

3. Dorfman, R.; P.A. Samuelson; and R.M. Solow. *Linear Programming and Economic Analysis.* New York: McGraw-Hill, 1958.

4. Kendrick, D. "On the Leontief Dynamic Inverse." *Quarterly Journal of Economics* 86, no. 4 (November 1972): 693–696.

5. Livesey, D.A. "The Singularity Problem in the Dynamic Input-Output Model." *International Journal of Systems Science* 4 (1973): 437–440.

6. Preston, A.J. "A Dynamic Generalization of Tinbergen's Theory of Policy." *Review of Economic Studies* 41, no. 1 (1974): 65–74.

7. Preston, A.J., and K.D. Wall. "Some Aspects of the Use of State Space Models in Econometrics." *I.E.E. Conference Publication* 101 (1973): 226–239.

8. University of Cambridge, Department of Applied Economics. *The Model in its Environment: A Progress Report. A Programme for Growth,* Vol. 5. Edited by Richard Stone. London: Chapman and Hall, 1964.

Chapter Twenty-Six

Use of the Wigley Production Function in a Static General Equilibrium Model Applied to France

A. Duval
G. McNeill
N. Jeantet

The Wigley production function presents a number of practical advantages for use in combination with models based on input-output techniques. These advantages are mainly related to the limited amount of data required for parameter estimation and the ease with which it can be integrated into an input-output model. Much still remains to be done to improve and expand the basic formulation proposed by Wigley [6]. A recent paper [5] describes the line of research he is at present pursuing.

We have been working on Wigley's basic function with a view to testing it and acquiring a better understanding of its implications. Our research scope is primarily limited to determining the best way in which the function can be used under conditions of limited data availability. Under these circumstances, such models can obviously be only of the static equilibrium type.

A Sector Approach to the Interpretation of the Wigley Production Function

We will limit this paper to highlighting a number of differences between our interpretation and the way Wigley has presented his function [5; 6]. At this stage of our own research, these differences do not infringe in any way on the parameter estimation techniques that Wigley has developed.

An important point to make at the start is that the function is a production function only in a rather loose sense. (We have retained this term for lack of a better one at this time. This will become clear as we pursue our exposition.) Notwithstanding this observation, the so-called Wigley production function is related to the set of ex post and vintage production functions. On the one hand, it

To illustrate part of our work, we have made use of some results contained in a Ph.D. dissertation prepared by McNeill [2], while a senior economist at the Battelle Geneva Research Centre.

describes the outcome of decisions made by producers for the introduction of new equipment or a new plant into the productive system for replacement and expansion purposes. On the other hand, it considers this process in terms of the relative efficiencies of factors of production of the new plant and the old or scrapped plant in relation to the sector considered as a whole.

The construction of the function presented by Wigley is essentially microeconomic. We have found this to be somewhat troublesome in view of the fact that a direct transposition to a semiaggregate or sector level is difficult to make. We have therefore endeavoured to establish its practical significance directly at the sector level.

Technical Change Measured in the
Wigley Production Function

We begin by assuming that we can assemble the relevant information in constant prices for a sector from observations made by producers for some given set of years. We would then obtain sector data on output and the relevant factors of production for a particular year, as shown in Table 26-1. With these measures, we can estimate the parameters of the function:

$$\frac{y_t^o}{l_t^o} = \alpha_t \frac{y_t}{l_t} \qquad \frac{y_t^n}{l_t^n} = \beta_t \frac{y_t}{l_t}$$

$$\frac{y_t^o}{c_t^o} = \bar{\alpha}_t \frac{y_t}{c_t} \qquad \frac{y_t^n}{c_t^n} = \bar{\beta}_t \frac{y_t}{c_t}$$

$$(26\text{-}1)$$

The parameters are simply relative measures of efficiency or productivity of the two factors of production, namely, labour and intermediate inputs, for the old and the new plant, in regard to the sector averages. It should be noted that the sector measures include those of the plant to be scrapped, which is still in use at time t, but exclude the new plant not yet in operation. The parameters are not parameters in the usual sense of production functions in that they do not correspond to specific technical relations.

Table 26-1. Measures of Output, Labour, and Intermediate Inputs

Activity Measures	Sector	New Plant to be Introduced in $t + 1$	Old Plant to be Scrapped in $t + 1$
Production	y_t	y_t^n	y_t^o
Labour	l_t	l_t^n	l_t^o
Intermediate inputs	c_t	c_t^n	c_t^o

Table 26-2 shows the parameters for the French steel sector calculated for 1969. Such parameters or ratios can be useful to producers, as they provide some basis for appraisal of the quality of technical change being introduced into the productive system in comparison with the average practice in use at that specific time.

In this comparison, we have a set of factor combinations associated with the new plant or the new techniques. We can assume that the new plant in question corresponds to a set of choices made within a reasonably homogeneous field of available technologies and that the plant has been set up within a reasonable period of time, say, five years. We also have factor combinations associated with the old plant and the old techniques that are impossible to specify in terms of age. Any given plant comprises equipment having different life spans due to the nature of the capital goods considered, as well as to the speed with which obsolescence is reached.

In practical terms, producers compare average sector performance against (1) the factor combinations that are expected with the set of new techniques, having a definite time reference, and (2) the factor combinations that are observed with the set of old techniques to be scrapped. For the producers, the equipment to be scrapped and vintage production functions possess similar characteristics—which are of no importance, insofar as the decision is based on both economic and physical obsolescence, and these will be particular to each specific type of capital making up the mix. The problem the producers must solve is basically that of replacing worst-practice production methods by best-practice production methods.

It is also important to note that the comparison is made in regard to performances of the old plant or techniques at the moment these techniques are to be abandoned. We have no basis for evaluating how factor combinations have evolved over the life span of the equipment to be scrapped in the following period. This is also true for new techniques in that the moment the equipment concerned is introduced into the productive system we lose track of it. The only measure of technical change we have is, in effect, how the average factor combinations are evolving over time. The change involved will be both embodied and disembodied. We cannot separate the types of changes involved. We therefore

Table 26-2. Relative Efficiency Measures Estimated for Steel, 1969

Relative Efficiencies	New Plant or Techniques	Old Plant or Techniques
Relative efficiency of labour (compared with the sector average)	1.903 (β 1969)	0.517 (α 1969)
Relative efficiency of intermediate inputs (compared with the sector average)	1.104 ($\bar{\beta}$ 1969)	0.886 ($\bar{\alpha}$ 1969)

find that the parameters so computed on a yearly basis will measure relative efficiencies in the light of the factor combinations reached at that particular time.

Medium-Term Development Policy and the Degree of Technical Change

The above observations lead us to reject Wigley's interpretation of the term $t + 1$, that is, the average age of scrapped techniques plus one. We therefore propose an alternative one. This alternative interpretation requires some assumption of how producers act to establish an expansion policy. Thus, the time process as expressed by Wigley

$$\lambda y_t = y_t^n - y_t^o$$

$$\mu l_t = l_t^n - l_t^o \tag{26-2}$$

$$\gamma c_t = c_t^n - c_t^o$$

can be written as

$$\lambda = \frac{y_t^n}{y_t} - \frac{y_t^o}{y_t}$$

$$\mu = \frac{l_t^n}{l_t} - \frac{l_t^o}{l_t} \tag{26-3}$$

$$\gamma = \frac{c_t^n}{c_t} - \frac{c_t^o}{c_t}$$

Expansion policy is based on a process of adjustment involving replacement of a scrapped plant by a new plant in such a manner as to maintain the medium-term growth rates for the next period $(t + 1)$ in the light of the activity levels attained. An interesting point to make is that the effective growth attained in $t + 1$ (say, $\lambda^*, \mu^*, \gamma^*$) may not necessarily correspond to the medium-term rates indicated here. The growth indicators correspond to measures of the medium-term development policy pursued by producers.

Obviously, any number of combinations of factors associated with old or new techniques may be selected by producers to obtain the expansion. There is, however, a rather strong hypothesis underlying the way in which development of the productive activity is envisaged by producers. It implies, through the growth indicators, that the producers have been able to establish implicit relationships between production, labour, and intermediate input development. In other words, these medium-term growth indicators correspond to a coherent view of how technical change modifies the factor combinations through time for the sector as a whole.

If this is the case, then the producers can proceed by comparing (in the light of these growth indicators) the relative degree of change taking place for the set of factors associated with a new plant or new techniques with the set associated with the old plant to be scrapped. We have

$$y_t^n = (1 + \lambda)^{T^*} y_t^o$$

$$l_t^n = (1 + \mu)^{T^*} l_t^o \qquad (26\text{-}4)$$

$$c_t^n = (1 + \gamma)^{T^*} c_t^o$$

In the case of Wigley, the term T^* corresponds to the average age of techniques plus one $(t + 1)$. We now have in T^* a measure of the degree of technical change. We must accept this measure as being identical for each component insofar as we have assumed that the constant proportional growth rates used are a consistent set of measures of medium-term development of the sector as a whole. This would appear to be a reasonable assumption to make under the circumstances.

Investment in the Wigley Production Function
Consider the central equation system before incorporation of a capital term

$$\lambda = \left(1 - \frac{\alpha_t}{\beta_t}\right) - \frac{y_t^n}{y_t} + \mu_t \alpha_t \qquad \text{(labour)}$$

$$\qquad (26\text{-}5)$$

$$\lambda = \left(1 - \frac{\bar{\alpha}_t}{\bar{\beta}_t}\right) - \frac{y_t^n}{y_t} + \gamma_t \bar{\alpha}_t \qquad \text{(intermediate inputs)}$$

In Wigley's function, a capital term is incorporated by replacing the ratio of the sector's production associated with new techniques to the sector's total production, in the following manner

$$\frac{y_t^n}{y_t} = \frac{1}{k_t^n} \frac{K_t}{y_t} \qquad (26\text{-}6)$$

with

$$k_t^n = \frac{K_t}{y_t^n}$$

where

K = a measure of the capital stock of new techniques

k^n = the capital-output ratio for new techniques

This is an addition to the function; it plays no role in the computation of the parameters. In fact, the incorporation of a capital term can be somewhat misleading in that the function does not permit us to make explicit the relations between capital and the productive activity. The function is actually an ex post one.

We preferred to introduce gross investments instead of capital stock and so compute investment-output ratios. Thus, we have an investment term that is defined in the following manner:

$$\frac{y_t^n}{y_t} = \frac{1}{k_t} \frac{\bar{u}_t}{y_t} \qquad \text{with} \qquad k_t = \frac{\bar{u}}{y_t^n} \tag{26-7}$$

where $\bar{u}$ is the gross investments of the sector.

Besides the difficulties involved in trying to establish a capital term, we have considered that investment is related to new techniques, while accepting the fact that the investment for a given year corresponds only in part to the equipment that is to be activated the coming year, given the time schedules involved for the various types of capital goods. The main advantage is that we are specifying the investment term we are directly interested in generating. The Wigley production function per se has little or no explanatory power for investment. The system needs to be extended to include an investment function that will make explicit the relations existing between the investment effort and the process of introducing new techniques.

The possibility of developing and integrating such an investment function is dependent upon the type of model into which it will be incorporated. The unit requirements of factors of production for new techniques are obtained from the parameter estimates made with the Wigley production function. The time variable is introduced to take into account the time process in investment. A static general equilibrium system based upon input-output techniques offers a highly limited framework for investment determination. This has led us to test investment functions where the investment-output ratio is related to the factor combinations of new techniques, that is

$$k_t = f\left(\frac{l^n}{y^n}, \frac{c^n}{y^n}, t \right) \tag{26-8}$$

where

k_t = the investment-output coefficient at time t associated with new techniques

$\dfrac{l^n}{y^n}$ = the labour-output coefficient of new techniques

$\dfrac{c^n}{y^n}$ = the unit-output requirements of intermediate inputs for new techniques

Parameter Estimates of the Wigley Production Function

In the present study, the procedure developed by Wigley for estimating parameters has been used. The symbols are defined in Table 26-3. Our main interest

Table 26-3. Definitions of Variables and Parameters in the Wigley Production Function

		Type of Activity	
Variables and Parameters	*Sector*	*Old Plant or Techniques*	*New Plant or Techniques*
Yearly Data			
Production	y		
Labour	l		
Intermediate inputs	c		
Gross investments	$\bar{u}$		
Production price	p		
Price of intermediate inputs	$\bar{p}$		
Ad valorem tax rates	τ_1		
Volume tax rates	τ_2		
Subsidy rates	ϵ		
Development Indicators			
Average annual growth rates of production	λ		
Average annual growth rates of labour	μ		
Average annual growth rates of intermediate inputs	γ		
Parameters			
Ratio of degree of technical changes	T^*		
Investment–output ratio			$\bar{k}$
Labour–efficiency ratios compared with the sector average		α	β
Intermediate input–efficiency ratios compared with the sector average		$\bar{\alpha}$	$\bar{\beta}$

has been centered on how it performs and on how well the proposed alternative interpretation holds up. We have been most fortunate in being able to use French input-output data prepared in current and constant 1963 prices for the period 1959–1969. Some manipulation has been required to incorporate labour and investment data, as well as the breakdown of value added, from relevant industry-based statistics. The French sector classification used is given in Table 26–4.

Estimations Made

In order to compute parameters applicable to the medium term, we have adopted Wigley's approach in that a first set of estimates was made from the averages of the input data required by the production function, namely:

1. average annual growth rates for production, labour, and intermediate inputs,
2. average shares of production-cost items (gross profits, wage bill net indirect taxes, and intermediate inputs), and
3. average investment-output coefficients for the sector as a whole.

These parameter estimates are given on the left side of Table 26–5.

We then proceeded with a second set of parameter estimates, made on a yearly basis using the annual cost structures and investment-output coefficients. For illustrative purposes, we have reproduced the estimates obtained in this manner for 1969 on the right side of Table 26–5. We have introduced two modifications of the estimation procedure used by Wigley: we have measured labour

Table 26–4. French Sector Classification

Sector Number	Sector Code	Sector Title
1	AGR	Agriculture
2	ALIM	Food and drinks
3	CMS	Coal
4	GAZEL	Gas, water, & electricity
5	PETROL	Mineral oil refining
6	MATVER	Glass & building material
7	SIDER	Iron & steel
8	NONFER	Nonferrous metal manufacturing
9	CONEM	Electrical & mechanical equipment
10	CHIMIE	Chemicals
11	TEXTIL	Textiles
12	INDIV	Miscellaneous industries
13	BTP	Building & civil engineering
14	TRANS	Transport services
15	TELEC	Communications
16	LOGE	Dwelling services
17	SERDIV	Miscellaneous services
18	COMM	Distributive trades

Table 26-5. Parameter Estimates of the Wigley Production Function for the Period 1959-1969 and for the Year 1969

Num-ber	Title	Parameter Estimates for 1959-1969						Parameter Estimates for 1969					
		T^*	α	β	$\bar\alpha$	$\bar\beta$	k	T^*	α	β	$\bar\alpha$	$\bar\beta$	k
1	Agriculture	16	.595	1.817	1.232	0.829	1.690	19	.537	2.021	1.291	0.806	1.500
2	Food & drinks	25	.592	1.628	0.911	1.078	1.077	22	.635	1.545	0.923	1.070	0.737
3	Coal	42	.691	1.953	0.999	1.002	12.490	29	.757	1.550	0.999	1.001	7.979
4	Gas, water, & electricity	27	.360	2.066	0.824	1.116	3.956	26	.376	2.026	0.831	1.113	4.821
5	Mineral oil refining	26	.386	1.812	1.090	0.959	1.063	26	.386	1.812	1.090	0.959	0.920
6	Glass & building material	16	.590	1.606	1.072	0.949	1.664	14	.637	1.529	1.061	0.954	1.413
7	Iron & steel	23	.517	1.903	0.886	1.104	2.007	21	.550	1.809	0.847	1.096	2.093
8	Nonferrous metal manu-facturing	49	.226	2.538	0.710	1.173	1.810	42	.290	2.306	0.754	1.159	2.319
9	Electrical & mechanical equip.	13	.663	1.472	1.000	1.000	0.478	10	.740	1.366	1.000	1.000	0.458
10	Chemicals	15	.601	1.564	1.075	0.948	1.660	16	.577	1.601	1.082	0.945	2.000
11	Textiles	16	.623	1.651	1.088	0.928	0.855	15	.643	1.605	1.082	0.932	0.694
12	Miscellaneous industries	16	.614	1.554	1.069	0.951	0.822	14	.658	1.484	1.058	0.955	0.623
13	Building & civil engineering	18	.599	1.521	1.115	0.928	0.592	18	.599	1.521	1.115	0.928	0.538
14	Transport services	21	.643	1.481	1.075	0.947	2.812	22	.627	1.504	1.079	0.945	3.046
15	Communications	13	.741	1.321	1.046	0.963	2.952	12	.761	1.299	1.041	0.965	2.161
16	Dwelling services	—	—	—	—	—	—	—	—	—	—	—	—
17	Miscellaneous services	37	.447	1.644	1.385	0.857	1.965	35	.471	1.615	1.355	0.861	1.283
18	Distributive trades	23	.579	1.525	1.029	0.982	1.374	27	.579	1.525	1.029	0.982	1.073

in terms of persons as opposed to number of hours worked per year, and we have introduced net indirect taxes into the cost equation. These changes obviously make comparisons with Wigley's estimates of the United Kingdom somewhat troublesome, but they have proved to be necessary for exploitation of the data at our disposal and of the multisector model into which we have incorporated the function.

Analysis of the Intermediate Input and Labour Parameter Estimates

The complete set of parameter estimates made is summarized in Figures 26–1 and 26–2, where we have related the various estimates of factor efficiency ratios $(\alpha, \bar{\alpha}, \beta, \bar{\beta})$ to the measure of the degree of technical change (T^{*}). In the figures, the solid symbols represent in each case the parameter estimates made over the whole period; the open symbols correspond to the yearly estimates. These figures are self-explanatory to a large extent. They show how well the parameter estimates fit together for any given sector and how compatible they are amongst themselves.

The relationship between the ratio of degree of technical change (T^{*}) and each of the production factor parameters is an almost perfect fit in a semi-log form. Further, we obtain symmetry between the sets of parameter estimates $(\alpha, \beta$ and $\bar{\alpha}, \bar{\beta})$. The yearly estimates correspond to the testing of the interpretation proposed above for the system. The average annual growth rates are con-

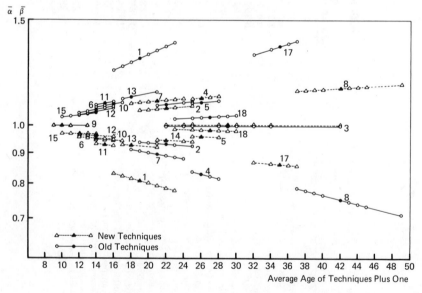

Figure 26-1. Ratios for Intermediate Inputs.

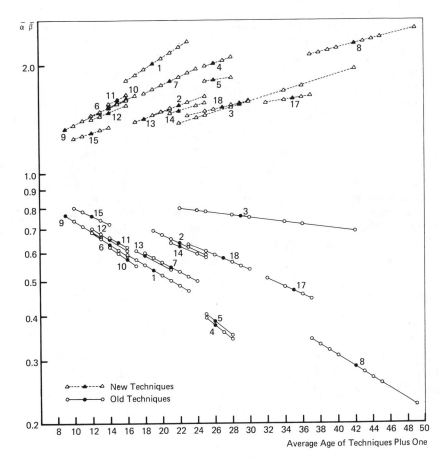

Figure 26-2. Ratios for Labour.

sidered to be the medium-term indicators to which the producers adjust the expansion process.

While the ratios obtained for labour describe well the pursuit of increased efficiency with new techniques, the coefficients for intermediate inputs tend to show a rather different picture. On the whole, old techniques are more efficient than new ones; 11 out of the 17 sectors are more efficient than the average in old techniques. To assume that there is increased wastage would appear to be an oversimplification at this stage. The rise in intermediate input requirements per unit of output would appear to be related more to the use of more elaborate production techniques needing additional commodities, in combination with an increase in the number of processing stages.

Analysis of Investment–Output Ratios

The investment–output ratios associated with new techniques can be calculated. For comparative purposes, we have reproduced in Figure 26-3 the ratios obtained, along with the capital-output ratios which can be derived from capital stock data published by INSEE (Institut National des Statistiques et des Etudes Economiques). The historical series obtained for the investment–output ratios tend to fluctuate rather drastically in a number of cases. Even so, they compare favourably with the capital–output ratio series in that the same orders of magnitude are reproduced, and the specific capital intensity of a given sector is moving in the same way over time. If we have found in this manner a way to incorporate the investment term, we must recognise that the production function has no explanatory power as to why such investment levels were reached for any given year. This has led us to seek a means of deriving an investment function directly from the results obtained from the production function.

We have noted that gross investments are concerned with the composition of the new plant to be incorporated into the productive apparatus. Given the time schedules involved, gross investments of any given year will comprise capital outlays on equipment that will be made over a number of the following periods. This has resulted in our incorporating a time variable into the investment function whose general form was given in equation (26-8). We have thus tried to give a technical explanation as to how the investment–output ratio evolves. The explanatory power of the function used has proved to be better than we expected in that the fits obtained in 11 cases out of 17 are good. The specific function forms tested were:

a. arithmetic,
b. semi-log (natural logarithms), and
c. log-log (natural logarithms).

The time term was introduced in the log cases by the element e^{bt}.

We have found the semi-log set of functions to be the more interesting and have determined that the following equation is the better general equation for a given sector

$$k_t = b_0 \left(\frac{I_t^n}{y_t^n} \right)^{b_1} \left(\frac{c_b^n}{y_t^n} \right)^{b_2} e^{b_3 t} \tag{26-9}$$

This form was used for incorporation into the multisector model.

Two other forms of the investment function were tested to see empirically if the investment effort could be more significantly related to one specific factor. Table 26-6 shows the results of using the general equation (column 1)

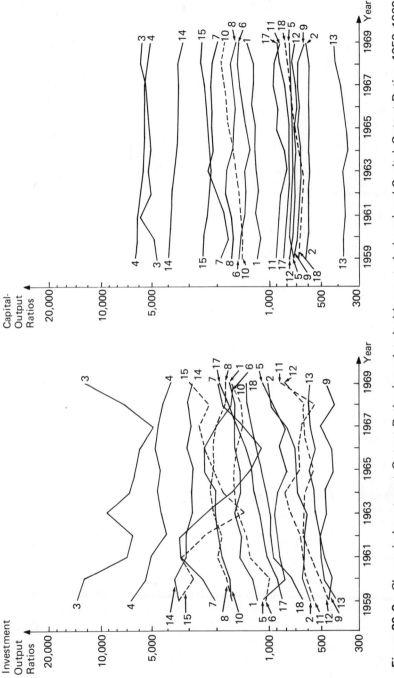

Figure 26-3. Change in Investment-Output Ratios (associated with new techniques) and Capital-Output Ratios, 1959–1969.

Table 26-6. Correlation Coefficients with Alternative Investment Functions

Sector		Factors Considered		
Number	*Title*	*Combined*	*Labour*	*Intermediate Inputs*
1	Agriculture	.853	.950	.850
2	Food & drinks	.990	.959	.980
3	Coal	.973	.993	.532
4	Gas, water, & electricity	.944	.873	.879
5	Mineral oil refining	.584	.414	.612
6	Glass & building material	.994	.973	.781
7	Iron & steel	.513	.470	.314
8	Nonferrous metal manufacturing	.695	.690	.676
9	Electrical & mechanical equip.	.343	.227	.345
10	Chemicals	.538	.483	.343
11	Textiles	.701	.592	.484
12	Miscellaneous industries	.901	.820	.749
13	Building & civil engineering	.988	.939	.987
14	Transport services	.719	.839	.693
15	Communications	.939	.938	.987
17	Miscellaneous services	.974	.981	.984
18	Distributive trades	.993	.972	.929

$$\bar{k} = f\left(\frac{l^n}{y^n}, \frac{c^n}{y^n}, t\right) \qquad b_1, b_2, b_3 \neq 0 \qquad\qquad (26\text{-}10)$$

and of considering each of the factors of production alone (columns 2 and 3)

$$\bar{k} = f\left(\frac{l^n}{y^n}, t\right) \qquad b_1, b_3 \neq 0 \quad b_2 = 0$$

$$\bar{k} = f\left(\frac{c^n}{y^n}, t\right) \qquad b_2, b_3 \neq 0 \quad b_1 = 0$$

Incorporation of the Wigley Production Function into a Static General Equilibrium Model

We have tested a variant of the Explor multisector model. This is a medium-term forecasting system applied to target years at five-year intervals (1970, 1975, and 1980, for example). A target year is considered to be representative of the position reached by the economy considered—here, France—at that moment in time with respect to a growth path along which the country is moving. The computation schedule for the model incorporates the Wigley production function. The model is static and is organized in order to compute results that are as close as possible to the expected values. To verify that this criterion is met, we follow iteratively a six-step sequence:

Step 1.   Compute the spending prices from industrial prices.
Step 2.   Compute household consumption using a linear expenditure system.
Step 3.   Compute final demand components other than household consumption
consumption.
Step 4.   Using the input-output model, compute total output.
Step 5.   Apply the Wigley production function to recompute investments,
productivity, and employment.
Step 6.   Compute industrial prices.

Return to Step 1.

The symbols are defined in Table 26-7. Earlier in the paper we noted that by
making yearly forecasts we are trying to reproduce the short-term adjustment
process pursued by producers to insure medium-term development of their productive activity. This is not the case here, as the forecasts are oriented towards
the determination of the medium-term position of sector activies. Yearly estimates, in the form in which they are compiled at present, therefore cannot be
retained. We must fall back on the parameter estimates over the whole period as
being indicative of the medium-term development of productive activities in

Table 26-7. Main Variables for Testing the Wigley Production Function

Designation	Symbol
Final Demand	
Net final demand	f
Private consumption	q
Government spending	g
Inventory changes	s
Investment by type of commodity	u
Exports	x
Imports	m
Spending Function Data on Households	
Private consumption	$\bar{q}$
Prices	$\bar{p}$
Productive Activity Data	
Production	y
Investment by users	$\bar{u}$
Labour	l
Intermediate inputs	c
Cost Equations	
Prices	p
Average annual wage rates	ω
Tax rates	τ_1, τ_2, τ_3
Subsidy rates	ϵ_1, ϵ_2

terms of the underlying changes shaping the changes in factor combinations. We will call these parameters the "medium-term parameter estimates." There still remains, however, the problem of investment generation. We have made two alternative estimates for the French economy for 1969 with the Explor model:

1. The medium-term investment–output ratio is held constant.
2. The investment–output ratio is computed with the investment function from the estimates of unit requirements of intermediate inputs (c^n/y^n) and of labour (l^n/y^n) which can be derived in the course of using the model.

The deviations obtained in percentage form between the estimates and the observations are given in Table 26-8 for each run of the model. The incorporation of the investment function does substantially improve the investment and production estimates. Labour estimates tend to deteriorate slightly, as the overall deviation is –0.6 percent as opposed to 0.3 percent.

The differences obtained correspond essentially to the underlying estimates for overall investment–output ratios ($\bar{u}/y$), which are derived in both cases. Use of the medium-term investment–output ratios for the observed period tends to generate estimates reflecting the average overall investment–output ratios, while introduction of the investment function has the advantage of coping in part with the medium-term investment movement (that is, the tendency towards an increase or decrease in capital intensity in the long run). We have reproduced the values obtained in Table 26-9.

Future Research

The results we have briefly presented were principally concerned with testing the Wigley production function. We are satisfied with the basic system, which has held up very well in our analysis. It has many limitations, however, in the simple form in which it is presented. A more elaborate estimation technique is required in order to take full advantage of the available historical data. We are working on this at present. For the moment, our orientation is centered more on a short-term adjustment process than on the elaboration of a medium-term production system incorporating an investment function. This results from the confusion of growth indicators. In terms of yearly data, we are working with a combination of medium-term growth indicators and yearly growth rates. We can derive only the latter in the case of medium-term forecasts, as these correspond to the development path the activities are following between the reference and target years. For the medium-term application, we are investigating the possibility of endogenously generating the parameters within the model for the forecast year. This approach may well offer some interesting computational methods.

Table 26-8. Deviations Obtained for 1969 Using the Wigley Production Function

Num-ber	Title	Production (millions of 1963 French francs)	Labour Force (thousands of persons)	Observations — Productive Investment (millions of 1963 French francs)	Observations — Investment Goods (millions of 1963 French francs)	Estimates without Investment Function — Production	Estimates without Investment Function — Labour Force Deviations (percent)	Estimates without Investment Function — Productive Investment	Estimates with Investment Function — Production	Estimates with Investment Function — Labour Force Deviations (percent)	Estimates with Investment Function — Productive Investment
1	Agriculture	55,488	2,842.7	7,599		-0.3	-0.9	-22.7	0.4	-0.9	-14.8
2	Food & drinks	75,648	655.7	5,190		-0.3	–	-26.2	0.3	–	6.7
3	Coal	3,515	123.3	548		-5.1	-0.3	6.8	0.6	-1.1	12.7
4	Gas, water, & electricity	18,023	134.9	6,724		-1.9	-0.2	20.6	0.2	-0.4	9.0
5	Mineral oil refining	27,020	96.7	3,145		-2.2	–	-15.4	0.3	-0.2	-8.7
6	Glass & building material	15,878	302.3	2,952		-3.2	-0.6	-12.0	0.6	-0.9	10.3
7	Iron & steel	15,337	172.1	2,157		-7.4	-1.2	0.5	0.8	-2.1	-13.1
8	Nonferrous metal manufacturing	3,476	29.5	395		-10.6	-0.3	17.0	1.1	-1.7	11.9
9	Electrical & mechanical equip.	150,187	2,169.7	9,277	64,980	-8.0	-0.3	3.2	0.8	-1.2	-18.5
10	Chemicals	31,799	406.7	6,519		-2.4	-0.1	13.9	0.3	-0.4	7.0
11	Textiles	37,822	964.9	2,863		-0.7	-0.9	-16.4	0.1	-0.9	-2.0
12	Miscellaneous industries	46,485	889.9	4,183	508	-2.0	-0.1	-20.1	0.3	-0.4	-1.8
13	Building & civil engineering	103,166	2,057.5	6,612	28,504	-2.8	-0.3	-12.0	0.6	-0.6	2.8
14	Transport services	31,854	726.1	7,119		-2.1	-0.2	3.1	0.2	-0.4	0.7
15	Communications	8,304	353.8	3,078		-1.6	-0.3	-24.6	0.2	-0.4	-1.5
16	Dwelling services	20,326	74.9	–	879	–	–	–	–	–	–
17	Miscellaneous services	103,082	2,600.6	14,526		-1.4	-0.1	-34.8	0.2	-0.2	-0.1
18	Distributive trades	91,559	2,318.8	9,966		-2.4	-0.1	-29.3	0.3	-0.4	-7.9
	Total	838,969	16,920.1	92,853	94,871	-2.9	-0.3	-12.7	0.4	-0.6	1.2

Table 26-9.   Comparison of Investment-Output Ratios by Sector

Sector		Average Values 1959-1969	Observa-tions	Estimates without Investment Function	Estimates with Investment Function
Num-ber	Title			1969	
1	Agriculture	.107	.137	.106	.117
2	Food & drinks	.051	.069	.051	.073
3	Coal	.177	.156	.176	.175
4	Gas, water, & electricity	.460	.373	.459	.406
5	Mineral oil refining	.101	.116	.101	.106
6	Glass & building material	.170	.186	.169	.204
7	Iron & steel	.155	.141	.153	.121
8	Nonferrous metal manu-facturing	.150	.114	.149	.126
9	Electrical & mechanical equip.	.069	.062	.069	.073
10	Chemicals	.239	.205	.239	.219
11	Textiles	.064	.076	.064	.074
12	Miscellaneous industries	.073	.090	.073	.088
13	Building & civil engineering	.058	.064	.058	.066
14	Transport services	.236	.223	.235	.224
15	Communications	.285	.371	.284	.364
17	Miscellaneous services	.093	.141	.093	.140
18	Distributive trades	.079	.109	.079	.100

For the time being, we can only hope that the presentation we have made may stimulate others to pursue research in this area. Methods are urgently needed at present for the generation of labour and investment in model systems using input-output techniques.

References

1. Battelle. "Econometric Methods Used in the EXPLOR-80-II Research Phase." Geneva, Switzerland, 1971.

2. McNeill, G. "Analyse de la Fonction de Production de Wigley et de Son Incorporation dans un Modèle Multisectoriel d'Equilibre Statique" [Analysis of the Wigley Production Function and Its Incorporation into a Multisectoral Static Equilibrium Model]. Mémoire de Thèse, Université de Génève, Geneva, Switzerland, 1974.

3. Mairesse, J. "L'Estimation du Capital Fixe Productif" [The Estimation of Fixed Productive Capital]. Economie et Statistique, no. 25 (July–August 1971): 33–55.

4. Mairesse, J. "L'Evaluation du Capital Fixe Productif: Méthodes et Résultats" [The Valuation of Fixed Productive Capital: Methods and Results]. *Les Collections de l'INSEE,* Series C, nos. 18–19 (November 1972).

5. Wigley, K.J. "An Investment-Production Model for Input-Output Analysis." Paper presented at the Sixth International Conference on Input-Output Techniques, Vienna, April 22–26, 1974.

6. Wigley, K.J. "Production Models and Time Trends of Input-Output Co-efficients." In *Input-Output in the United Kingdom.* Edited by W.F. Gossling. London: Frank Cass and Co., Ltd., 1970. Pp. 89–118.

Chapter Twenty-Seven

A Dynamic Optimal Plan
of Economic Growth

Iu. N. Ivanov

Any centralized economic management should incorporate planning in aggregate terms. The calculation of this plan should use a model describing the economy in aggregate terms, be subjected to some constraints, and be optimal in relation to some criterion. (All this is specified by the management structure.) In this paper, which uses a Leontief-type model, a plan is regarded as optimal if it insures that within the shortest possible time the desired levels of final consumption are achieved. In this process, certain constraints on final consumption have to be imposed. The objective is then to depict the qualitative properties of the transition path.

First, a canonical problem is defined, in which the set of characteristics for description of an aggregate economic model is minimal; then, the characteristics ignored in the canonical problem are added in succession, and changes in the pattern of the path are studied.

A Canonical Problem

The canonical problem is defined so that the transition time T, which is the criterion, is minimized

$$X(t) = AX(t) + B\dot{V}(t) + Y(t)$$

$$\begin{aligned} \dot{V}(t) &\geq 0 \\ X(t) &\leq V(t) \\ \text{at } t \in (t_0, T), \quad Y(t) &\geq Y_0 \\ \text{at } t \geq T, \quad Y(t) &\geq Y_1 \end{aligned} \qquad (27\text{-}1)$$

$$V(t_0) = V_0$$

where

$X(t)$ = gross output vector

$V(t)$ = capacity vector

$Y(t)$ = final consumption vector

A = technical coefficient matrix

B = matrix of incremental capital–output ratios

The equation defines a balance of product flows: the gross output, $X(t)$, is used for intermediate consumption, $AX(t)$, capital formation, $BV(t)$, and final consumption, $Y(t)$. The equation also gives two technological constraints, viz., that the capacity should not decrease and the output should, first, be nonnegative and, second, not exceed the capacity. The inherent constraints are: in the transition period, final consumption should not be lower than Y_0; in the transition period and later, final consumption should not be lower than a desired value Y_1. The initial condition for the vector of capacities is defined as $V(0)$.

The very first question arising from this formulation of the problem is how to reduce the variational problem, defined over a semi-infinite period, to a conventional terminal variational problem. For Y_1 = constant, this is possible, and the problem is identical to a terminal one for the vector of capacities. The condition on the right end of the interval is

$$V(T) \geqslant (I - A)^{-1} Y_1$$

Another question is the optimality condition. In the problem, $V(t)$ is the vector of phase coordinates; the control functions are the vector $\dot{V}(t)$, the rate of growth of capacity; and the vector $\Delta V = V - X$ is unused capacity. Dual-phase variables and dual-control functions are introduced. The last are combinations of dual variables and their derivatives; they help to define optimality conditions for direct-control functions. The optimality criterion incorporates two kinds of requirements, concerning both the signs of dual controls and the mutual correspondence of signs of direct and dual controls.

Analysis of the optimality criterion provides the following properties of optimal paths. Let us introduce three concepts: the state of the industry, the mode of production, and the basic sequence of production. Any industry can be characterized by two nonnegative control functions: the growth rate of capacity and the magnitude of unused capacity. It can be in any one of the following four states:

State 1. The capacity does not grow and is fully used.
$$\dot{V}_i = \Delta V_i = 0$$

State 2. The capacity does not grow and is not fully used.
$$\dot{V}_i = 0, \quad \Delta V_i > 0$$

State 3. The capacity grows and is fully used.
$$\dot{V}_i > 0 \qquad \Delta V_i = 0$$

State 4. The capacity grows and is not fully used.
$$\dot{V}_i > 0 \qquad \Delta V_i > 0$$

Control variables in the direct problem can take zero or nonzero values. In the latter case, they are determined through phase coordinates. A similar situation is valid for dual-control variables, as well.

A mode is a set of zero and nonzero components of vectors of direct and dual-control variables for which the optimality conditions are fulfilled. When control variables dictated by the former mode become nonfeasible, the mode that existed over the final part of the path is replaced by another mode. Modes can be degenerate and nondegenerate. In the latter case, each of the control variables is unambiguously defined by phase coordinates; in the former, certain linear combinations of control variables are defined unambiguously, while the control variables themselves can be arbitrarily chosen within these combinations. Modes can also be classified by their positions on the path. In this case, the following situations can be distinguished: starting, turnpike, and blind. Starting modes are not preceded by any others, as in the case, say, when one industry is in state (3) and the remaining ones are in state (2). A blind mode cannot be followed by any other mode, as in the case, say, when no industries are in state (3) and the number of industries in state (4) is equal to that in state (1). A basic sequence of modes is the longest chain of modes, beginning with the starting one and ending with a blind one; this sequence is such that any of its parts can be used on the optimal path. All basic sequences of modes determine the structure of all possible optimal paths of the problem.

Two-, three-, and five-industry problems were studied, and modes and basic sequences were found for them. The methodology employed for studying the canonical problem was as follows: the states, modes, and basic sequences were used to analyze the optimization problem for models; then characteristics describing an economy were added.

Changing the Levels of Desired Consumption in Time

In the definition of the problem, this assumption leads to the change:
$Y(t) \geqslant Y_1(t)$ at $t \geqslant T$, where $Y_1(t)$ is the vector of desired control variables. In the canonical problem, the assumption of a constant vector Y_1 was made full use of, because the problem necessarily has a solution and is always reducible to a terminal problem for the vector of capacities. An analysis was made for two industries and the case of

$$Y_1(t) = Y_1 e^{\lambda t}$$

A maximal value of the rate λ for which the transition problem still has a solution was calculated: the rate λ should be less than the inverse of the maximal eigenvalue of the matrix

$$G = (I - A)^{-1} B$$

In the space of final values of the capacity, an area is fixed that depends on the time, T, and the parameter λ. If this area is found, transition to the desired level of consumption, $Y_1 e^{\lambda t}$, is insured.

Limited Labor Resources

The canonical problem is extended by placing a constraint on the labor force, $LX(t) \leqslant l$, where l is the available labor force (scalar) and L is the row-vector of average labor costs. In another version of the constraint, $LX(t) = l$, the entire available labor force is assumed to be fully employed. The only change in the canonical problem is that there is now a constraint on the desired consumption level (if, of course, the labor constraint remains even after the level is achieved). In the first version, the desired consumption is constrained by the inequality

$$L(I - A)^{-1} Y_1 \leqslant l$$

in the second, by the equality

$$L(I - A)^{-1} Y_1 = l$$

Another change in comparison with the canonical problem is in the states of control functions, modes, and basic sequences, but only for $LX(t) \leqslant l$. An additional control, the unused labor resource,

$$\Delta l = l - LX(t)$$

is added. This control may be in either one of two states, $\Delta l(t) > 0$ or $\Delta l(t) = 0$. In other words, modes of this version can be divided into two groups: modes of the canonical problem, $\Delta l(t) > 0$, and modes of the problem with equality, $\Delta l(t) = 0$. As for basic sequences in the two-industry case, the modes $\Delta l > 0$ appear first and then $\Delta l = 0$ in all sequences.

Allowance for Delay in Formation of Fixed Assets

Allowance for delay in the formation of fixed assets causes two changes in notation: the term $B\dot{V}(t)$ is replaced by $B\dot{V}(t + \tau)$ and the initial condition $V(0) = V_0$ by $V(t) = f(t)$ at $t \in (0, \tau)$. Components of the vector $\dot{V}(t + \tau)$ are

$\dot{V}_1(t + \tau_1)$, $\dot{V}_2(t + \tau_2)$, ... The characteristics of the industry state are the same as those described in the section on the canonical problem, and the modes are extended with new transient modes whose duration does not exceed that of the delay. In the two-industry problem with delay, the number of basic sequence modes does not change, but each is extended by transient modes.

Similar qualitative conclusions are valid for representation of capital terms with delay (as in the Tinbergen case) for $B^{\tau}[V(t + \tau) - V(t)]$ —instead of $B\dot{V}(t)$ in equation (27-1). The important feature of the solution to the latter problem is the presence of discontinuities in the function $V(t)$ and the piecewise-constant form of the dual coordinates.

Allowance for Exports and Imports

Allowance for exports and imports introduces into the left side of equation (27-1) a term $M(t)$, the import flow, and into the right side a term $E(t)$, the export flow. Also, the equation system (27-1) is extended by a new condition

$$CM(t) = CE(t)$$

that is, the sum of purchases in the external market is equal in each period to the sum of sales, C, which is the row vector of international prices. The solution depends on two vectors, $\alpha = C - CA$ and $\beta = CB$. The vector α is the "production cost" of a product unit; the vector β is the average capital investment. The vector α contains both positive and negative components: $\alpha = \{\alpha_+, \alpha_-\}$. Industries are ranked according to the ratios α_i/β_i. Two hypotheses concerning the after-the-planning horizon period are considered: (1) the external trade ceases after the time $t = T$; and (2) the external trade continues infinitely, as in the transition interval. In the former case, the conditions on the right side coincide with the conditions of the canonical problem; in the latter case, they are different. The solution of the optimization problem in the former case is as follows: Industries with negative values of the parameter α_i ($\alpha_i < 0$) manufacture no products, $X_- = 0$ (consequently $\Delta V_- = V_-$); industries with positive values α_i ($\alpha_i > 0$) use their capacities fully, $X_+ = V_+$ (consequently $\Delta V_+ = 0$). Capacities grow in the following order: Initially, the industry with the greatest value of α_1/β_1 develops (the final value of its capacity may exceed the desired value); then, the second-ranking industry develops ($\alpha_2 > 0$); then the third one ($\alpha_3 > 0$); and so on. Industries with negative values of α_i ($\alpha_i < 0$) develop after those with positive values in any order. If in the after-the-planning horizon period the external trade is not restricted, the structure of the solution differs from the one above so that only the first capacity develops. This property is, however, lost if the constraints on exports ($E \leqslant E_{max}$) and imports ($M \leqslant M_{max}$) are imposed on the transition path. Detailed studies of the two-industry case show that the pattern of an optimal path simultaneously represents the features of the structure of the canonical problem and of the problem with unlimited exports and imports.

Conclusion

We have been concerned here with properties of an optimal plan of economic development. A mathematical optimization problem is formulated, to achieve a specified final consumption level over minimal time. Analysis of solutions to this problem yields the qualitative properties of an optimal plan.

References

Dubovskii, S.V.; A.N. Diukalov; Iu. N. Ivanov; V.V. Tokarev; A.P. Uzdmir; and Iu. M. Fatkin. "On Development of an Optimal Plan." *Automation and Remote Control* 33, no. 8 (1972): 100–144.

Chapter Twenty-Eight

The Role of Intersectoral Models in Determining the Discount Rate

V. Volkonskii

Models of optimal development of production and of optimal allocation of resources are prepared in the USSR for all large sectors of the economy. It can be expected that their coordination by an integrated system of optimal planning for the whole national economy will be urgent. For the purpose of such coordination, the following macroeconomic indices are important: the expected rate of economic growth, the rate of discount (the common rate of shadow-price reduction), output shares by sectors, average relative output prices by sectors, and a number of indices related to these.

Advantages and Disadvantages of Square Intersectoral Models

The advantage of models using the square input-output framework is that they give good approximate values of the sectoral outputs as well as relative price levels by sectors, while avoiding the difficult problem of the choice of the optimality criterion [2]. Intersectoral models can be formally written as optimization ones. But the square form of their basic flow matrices often results in a reduction (degeneration) of the set of feasible plans to a single plan [1] so that the solution is independent of the objective function.

But such a property is also a defect in these models in that it makes them inflexible. They do not reflect the interdependence of changes in the parameters that determine prices (in particular, changes in the discount rate) and changes in the parameters that determine the levels of production and consumption. The consequence is that several price systems corresponding to different discount rates are consistent with the same matrix of intersectoral flows and the same level of production. Moreover, the influence of changes in the discount rates on the relative sectoral price levels is rather weak. Therefore, it can be concluded that relative sectoral price levels can be determined approximately, with the help of an intersectoral model, but the discount rate cannot be. This will be demonstrated in the next section for a simple model.

The Simplest Intersectoral Model

The balance equations may be written as

$$X = AX + S + Y \qquad (28\text{-}1)$$

where

X = the vector of the sectoral outputs $(x_1, \ldots, x_n)$

A = the square matrix of current input coefficients, which include the fixed capital (assets) consumption

S = the vector of net productive investment

Y = the vector of nonproductive inputs

The vector S^t (the investment in year t) is a function of the future growth of the sectoral outputs[1]

$$S^t = \sum_{\tau > 0} B_\tau \, \Delta X^{t+\tau} \qquad (28\text{-}2)$$

where

$\Delta X^t = X^{t+1} - X^t$

B_τ = the matrix of the inputs to be made in the year t in order to achieve the increment of output in the year $t + \tau$

It is assumed that the output of each sector j increases at a constant rate

$$x_j^t = x_j^0 (1 + \alpha_j)^t$$

Then

$$\Delta X^{t+\tau} = \hat{\alpha}(I + \hat{\alpha})^\tau X^t$$

where I is the unit matrix, and

---

1. Throughout this paper, the superscript is a time index, with the exception of the expressions $(1 + \alpha_j)^t$, $(I + \hat{\alpha})^\tau$, $(I + \hat{\beta})^\tau$, etc., which are constant numbers or constant matrices of degree t or τ.

$$\hat{\alpha} = \begin{pmatrix} \alpha_1 & & 0 \\ & \cdot & \cdot & \cdot \\ 0 & & & \alpha_n \end{pmatrix}$$

Let

$$B(\hat{\alpha}) = \sum_{\tau > 0} B_\tau \hat{\alpha}(I + \hat{\alpha})^\tau$$

then

$$S^t = B(\hat{\alpha})X^t$$

Now the equation system (28-1) may be written as:

$$[I - A - B(\hat{\alpha})]^{-1}X = Y \tag{28-3}$$

Let $\alpha = (\alpha_1, \ldots, \alpha_n)$ and $\mu(\alpha) =$ the maximal eigenvalue (the spectral radius) of the matrix $A + B(\hat{\alpha})$. For each α, if $\mu(\alpha) < 1$, equation system (28-3) has a solution with positive components.

The nonproductive inputs may be written in a similar way as inputs of the productive sector

$$Y = A_0 y + B_0(\gamma)y \tag{28-4}$$

where

y	= a scalar that measures the level of inputs into the nonproductive sector, that is, the level of personal and state consumption (for example, y is the total consumption in constant prices, or the total labour income)
γ	= its growth rate
A_0 and $B_0(\gamma)$	= vectors of coefficients of current and capital inputs in the nonproductive sector

It is assumed that the input coefficients are constant over time. Now, we consider a stationary solution (the turnpike) that satisfies the following condition:

$$\alpha_1 = \ldots = \alpha_n = \gamma \tag{28-5}$$

It can be proved that (under the usual assumptions) $\mu(\gamma)$ increases only when γ increases. Let γ_1 be defined as $\mu(\gamma_1) = 1$. Then for each $\gamma < \gamma_1$, a positive solution of equations (28-3), (28-4), and (28-5) exists. Calculations made at the Central Economic-Mathematical Institute of the USSR Academy of Sciences using a model of the Soviet economy for the year 1965, disaggregated into 16 sectors, show that $\gamma_1 = 0.36$. But the growth rate, γ_1, cannot be achieved for a real economy because the limited labour resources are not considered in equation system (28-3).

Let

$$l_0 y + (L, x) = l \tag{28-6}$$

where

L = the labour input per unit of output in the productive sector = $(l_1, \ldots, l_n)$

l_0 = the labour input per unit of output in the nonproductive sector

l = the total labour force

Under these conditions, the rate of economic growth is determined both by the rate of growth of the labour force and the rate of decrease of the labour–output ratio.

If the labour input is measured by the remuneration of labour, then the labour–output ratios, l_0 and L, are almost as stable as other input coefficients, so that the assumption of their stability over time is realistic (see [10, ch. IV, §2]). It may be assumed that the rates of labour remuneration are exogenously given and increase proportionally to labour productivity. Then the stationary growth rate is equal to the growth rate of labour resources, λ, which is exogenous with respect to equations (28-3) to (28-6). This exogenous parameter, λ, has an impact on the values of all the endogenous variables.

The Dual Model

In order to determine the relative optimal prices, equations (28-1), (28-2), (28-4), and (28-6) can be written for a number of time moments, thus defining an optimization problem, provided that an objective function is known. Assuming that the objective function criterion u depends only on the level of the consumption indices

$$u = u(y^0, y^1, \ldots) \to \max \tag{28-7}$$

The vector of dual prices (Lagrangian multipliers), $P^t = (p_1^t, \ldots, p_n^t)$, corresponds then to equation (28-1) and the multiplier, w^t, corresponds to equation (28-6). The multiplier, w^t, should not be interpreted as the wage rate, but as the shadow price of labour (that is, the ratio of the total efficiency of labour to its remuneration).[2] If we write the dual equation for the optimal solution, assuming that the price, $p_i^t = p_i^0(1 + \beta_i)^{-t}$, of each sector decreases at a constant rate, β_i, we then obtain the following equation system:

$$P^t[I - A - \widetilde{B}(\hat{\beta})] = w^t L \tag{28-8}$$

$$P^t[A_0 + \widetilde{B}_0(\hat{\beta})] + w^t B_0 = g^t \tag{28-9}$$

where

$$\hat{\beta} = \begin{pmatrix} \beta_1 & & 0 \\ & \ddots & \\ 0 & & \beta_n \end{pmatrix}$$

$$\widetilde{B}(\hat{\beta}) = \sum_{\tau > 0} \hat{\beta}(I + \hat{\beta})^\tau B_\tau$$

$$\widetilde{B}_0(\hat{\beta}) = \sum_{\tau > 0} \hat{\beta}(E + \hat{\beta})^\tau B_{0\tau}$$

$$g^t = \frac{\partial u}{\partial y^t} = \text{the time–preference rate of discount}$$

Let us denote the maximal characteristic value of the matrix $A + \widetilde{B}(\hat{\beta})$ as $\mu(\beta)$, $\beta = (\beta_1, \ldots, \beta_n)$. Equations (28-8) and (28-9) have a positive solution for each β if $\mu(\beta) < 1$. Equation (28-9) may be considered as a price-determining equation (that is, fixing the price level) or as a definition of the discount rate, g^t.

It is more reasonable to use stationary solutions of the dual problem (the characteristic features of which are constant price ratios and discount rate) than stationary solutions of the primal problem. Most economic plans are prepared and economic projections made using constant prices, and comparisons of inputs and outputs for different time periods are carried out with the help of the compound interest rate.

In the model outlined earlier, the stationary condition is

$$\beta_1 = \ldots = \beta_n = \delta \tag{28-10}$$

where δ is the rate of decrease of the shadow price of labour, w^t. It should be noted that for the stationary solutions, $\widetilde{B}(\delta) = B(\delta)$. Moreover, $g^t = g^0(1 + \delta)^{-t}$,

---

2. The multiplier must be greater than one unit.

that is, the rate of decrease of the dual prices, δ, is equal to the rate of discount (that is, the rate of decrease of the coefficients g^t). It is an exogenous parameter (like the growth rate, λ) of the level of the labour force in the primal problem. If it is lower than γ_1, then a positive solution of the equation system (28-8) to (28-10) exists.

Thus, under the given assumptions, both the determination of the rate of economic growth, γ, and the determination of the rate of decrease of the prices, δ, are independent problems that cannot be solved using the input-output data only. The indices γ and λ do not influence the prices, and changes of δ do not influence the levels of output. Indeed, the optimal plan satisfying the constraints of type (28-3), (28-4), and (28-6) is the same for a wide class of objective functions, or it depends weakly on the choice of another criterion (see [1]). In particular, as noted earlier, the stationary solution of the primal problem is a single one. A change in the criterion (that is, in the discount rate), even in the stationary case, strongly influences the dual prices. On the other hand, the impact of the growth rate, γ, on prices is quite weak.

Introduction of a Dependence Between Nonproductive Inputs and Labour Productivity

The model may be modified so that the labour force is considered to be reproducible. Let the parameter l be not an exogenously given value, as earlier, but let it increase proportionally to the level of the nonproductive sector: $l = Cy$ (C is a constant). Such an assumption is close to reality in the case that labour is measured by its real remuneration, because the share of the labour remuneration in the total consumption is very stable. Then, for simplicity, the parameters l and y can be assumed to have the same value (for example, the total real remuneration of labour) and

$$l = y \tag{28-11}$$

(See [10, ch. IV, §2].)

Let

$$\bar{A}(\gamma) = \begin{pmatrix} l_0 & L \\ A_0 + B_0(\gamma) & A + B(\gamma) \end{pmatrix}$$

$$G = (g, 0, \ldots, 0) \qquad \bar{X} = (y, x_1, \ldots, x_n) \qquad \bar{P} = (w, p_1, \ldots, p_n)$$

The constraints for stationary solutions of the primal and dual problems can now be written briefly as

$$\bar{X} = \bar{A}(\gamma)\bar{X} \tag{28-12}$$

$$G + \bar{P} = \bar{P}\bar{A}(\delta) \qquad (28\text{-}13)$$

Let $\bar{\mu}(\gamma)$ be the maximal eigenvalue of the matrix $\bar{A}(\gamma)$. It increases strictly when γ increases. Let γ_2 be defined as $\mu(\gamma_2) = 1$. Under the usual assumptions, $0 < \gamma_2 < \gamma_1$. For a stationary solution, if $g^t > 0$, then γ_2 is the maximal growth rate.

If $\delta < \gamma_2$, equation (28-13) has no positive solution. In this case, the matrix $[I - \bar{A}(\Delta)]^{-1}$ exists, and all its elements are positive. Therefore, the components of the vector $\bar{P} = -G[I - \bar{A}(\delta)]^{-1}$ are negative. On the other hand, if $\delta \in (\gamma_2, \gamma_1)$, a positive solution of the equation system (28-8) to (28-10) always exists.

A special case is $\delta = \gamma_2$, when a positive solution exists only for $g = 0$. The equation $g = 0$ means that an increase of nonproductive expenditures is not desirable, nor preferable in itself, but is only serving the general economic development. This case corresponds to maximization of the economic growth rate, as in the Von Neumann model and in the turnpike theorems (see [3] and [10]). Unfortunately, it is not likely that such a hypothesis corresponds to reality; in any case, there is no better substantiation for this than for the hypothesis that $g > 0$.

Therefore, equations (28-12) and (28-13) can be considered as a generalization of the primal and dual Von Neumann models, which correspond better to reality. Calculations with the primal model (28-12) show that the maximal growth rate, γ_2, and the sectoral shares are very near to actual ones [2; 3; 10]. For calculations with the dual model (28-13), it is necessary to determine the values of δ.

Difficulties in Determination of the Discount Rate

In a stationary case, the rate of discount, δ, and the rate of economic growth, γ, satisfy the following simple relation:

$$\delta = \gamma + \frac{\pi - e}{\varphi}$$

where

$\pi = PY$ $\qquad$ = the material nonproductive expenditures

$e = wLX$ $\qquad$ = the output of labour in the productive sectors

$\varphi = P \displaystyle\sum_{\tau > 0} B_\tau (1 + \delta)^\tau X =$ the value of the productive assets

Unfortunately, this equation does not determine the value of δ, because the determination of the output of labour, e, is also a complicated problem. The output of labour, as defined in the model, cannot be accurately measured using such "natural" indices as the number of working people, manhours, or even wages, because the value e has to include the total effect of technical progress and economic management and planning.

The value of e could be determined by a production function defining final product as a function of productive assets and labour resources. But such calculations for the Soviet economy give different results, depending upon the form of the models used, the data (time series or regional statistics), degree of preliminary aggregation or smoothing of data, the way the lags are taken into account, and so on (see [4; 8]). Estimates of δ vary from 8 percent to 15 percent.

A Model with Sectoral Development Variants

The discount rate, δ, can be, however, most easily determined when the national economic plan is constructed by combining the various sectoral models. (See, for example, [3] and [8].)

Let us consider a two-period model for the periods $(-T, 0)$ and $(0, T)$. The vector X^0 is assumed to be given, and the dual prices, P^0, do not appear in the model. The prices for the years $t = T$ and $t = 2T$ satisfy the equations

$$P^t = P^t A^t + P^t B^t(\hat{\beta}) + w^t L^t \qquad t = T, 2T \tag{28-14}$$

$$\hat{\beta} = \begin{pmatrix} \beta_1 & & 0 \\ & \ddots & \\ 0 & & \beta_n \end{pmatrix} \qquad \beta_i = \sqrt[T]{\frac{p_i^T}{p_i^{2T}}} - 1 \tag{28-15}$$

The discount rate introduced exogenously in the equation results from a comparison of the time preference of nonproductive inputs for the periods $t = T$ and $t = 2T$

$$P^{2T}[A_0^{2T} + B_0^{2T}(\gamma)] + w^{2T}l_0^{2T} = (1 + \delta)^{-T}\{P^T[A_0^T + B_0^T(\gamma)] + w^T l_0^T\} \tag{28-16}$$

The general scale of the prices is determined by the equation

$$\sum_i p_i^T x_i^0 = \sum_i x_i^0 \tag{28-17}$$

Let us assume there are several development alternatives for each sector that may be obtained with the help of sectoral models. Matrices A^t, B_τ^t, and L^t are interpreted as matrices reflecting the relationship between the increase of inputs that results from an increase of outputs. Columns A_j^t, $B_{j\tau}^t$, and L_j^t of these matrices are formed as convex linear combinations of corresponding vectors that characterize the development alternative

$$A_j^t = \sum_k q_j^t(k) A_j^t(k) \qquad B_{j\tau}^t = \sum_k q_j^t(k) B_{j\tau}^t(k)$$

$$l_j^t = \sum_k q_j^t(k) l_j^t(k) \qquad \sum_k q_j^t(k) = 1$$

$$q_j^t(k) \geqslant 0; \quad j = 1, \ldots, n; \quad t = T, 2T \tag{25-18}$$

Here, k is an index of the weight, q_j^t (which is used to weight the variables). Among all the linear combinations, the optimal one is

$$A_j^t = A_j^t(k^*) \qquad B_{j\tau}^t = B_{j\tau}^t(k^*) \qquad l_j^t = l_j^t(k^*) \tag{28-19}$$

where $k^* = k^*(j, t)$ is the value of the index k that provides a minimum of the value

$$P^t[A_j^t(k) + B_j^t(\hat{\beta}, k)] + w^t l_j^t(k)$$

The model described by the equation system (28-14) to (28-19) has a positive solution, under usual assumptions, for a wide interval of values $\delta > 0$. For each given δ, a set of the best alternatives may be obtained. Then, the following primal problem must be solved:

$$X^T = A^0 X^0 + A^T (X^T - X^0) + B^T(\hat{\alpha}) X^T + [A_0^T + B_0^T(\gamma)] y^T$$

$$L^T = (L^0, X^0) + (L^T, X^T - X^0) + (l_0^T, y^T)$$

$$X^{2T} = A^0 X^0 + A^T (X^T - X^0) + A^{2T} (X^{2T} - X^T)$$

$$\qquad + B^{2T}(\hat{\alpha}) X^{2T} + [A_0^{2T} + B_0^{2T}(\gamma)] y^{2T}$$

$$L^{2T} = (L^0, X^0) + (L^T, X^T - X^0) + (L^{2T}, X^{2T} - X^T) + (l_0^{2T}, y^{2T})$$

$$\hat{\alpha} = \begin{pmatrix} \alpha_1 & & 0 \\ & \ddots & \\ 0 & & \alpha_n \end{pmatrix} \quad \alpha_j = \sqrt[T]{\frac{x_j^{2T}}{x_j^T}} - 1, \quad \gamma = \sqrt[T]{\frac{y^{2T}}{y^T}} - 1$$

Calculation of production and consumption plans for a series of discount rates, δ, makes it possible to obtain values for the pairs (π^T, π^{2T}) that correspond to each value of δ, where $\pi^t = P^t Y^t + w^t l_0^t y^t$ is a nonproductive input. Then, the curve on the plane (π^T, π^{2T}) that connects corresponding points can be constructed. This curve shows the possibilities of "substitution" between consumption at the period $t = T$ and at the period $t = 2T$ or the limits of a simultaneous increase of both indices. A choice of a desirable point on the curve determines (at the same time) the discount rate, δ, corresponding to this point.

The experiences of constructing macroeconomic dependences with the help of the calculation of variants of the optimal plan and an economic analysis of them are described in [8].

Summary

In this paper, an optimization dynamic model based on a square input-output framework and the dual to it are considered. The stationary solutions of both models, that is, solutions that are characterized by constant-in-time sectoral output or dual price ratios (Lagrangian multipliers), are described.

The economic growth rate in such models is determined by the growth (or efficiency) of the labour force; it is not connected with the technological matrices and is only weakly connected with output shares. Analogously, the discount rate (the common rate of the decreases in the dual prices) is an exogenous parameter that is not connected with the technological matrices or with production and consumption plans, and is only weakly connected with the dual price ratios.

A simple model constructed with several development alternatives for each sector, where the discount rate is connected with production and consumption plans, is described in the last part of the paper.

References

1. Belen'kii, V.Z. "O modeliakh optimal'nogo planirovaniia, osnovannykh na skheme mezhotraslevogo balansa" [On Some Optimal Models Based on Input-Output Balance]. *Ekonomika i matematicheskie metody* 3, no. 4 (1967): 534–549.

2. Belen'kii, V.Z.; V.A. Volkonskii; and N.V. Pavlov. "Dinamicheskie mezhotraslevye modeli, ikh ispol'zovanie dlia raschetov plana i tsen i ekonomicheskogo analiza" [Dynamic Input-Output Models for Plan and Price Calculations and Economic Analysis]. *Ekonomika i matematicheskie metody* 8, no. 4 (1972): 495–511.

3. Efimov, A.N., and S.M. Movshovich. "Analiz sbalansirovannogo rosta v dinamicheskoi modeli narodnogo khoziaistva" [Analysis of Balanced Growth in the Dynamic Model of the National Economy]. *Ekonomika i matematicheskie metody* 9, no. 1 (1973): 32–43.

4. Iaremenko, Iu. V.; E.B. Ershov; and A.S. Smyshliaev. "Issledovanie vzaimosviazi i faktorov rosta ekonomiki SSSR v 1950–1970 gg" [Investigation

of Interrelations and of Factors of Growth in the Economics of the USSR Between 1950 and 1970]. In *Matematicheskie metody resheniia ekonomicheskikh zadach.* Vol. 5. Moscow: Nauka Publishers, 1973. Pp. 115–132.

5. Klotsvog, F.N.; E.B. Ershov; R.A. Buzunov; A.A. Konüs; and G.M. Abdykulov. "Model' mezhotraslevogo balansa s elementami optimizatssii" [Input-Output Model with Elements of Optimization]. *Ekonomika i matematicheskie metody* 7, no. 5 (1971): 643–657.

6. *Nauchnye osnovy ekonomicheskogo prognoza* [Scientific Principles of Economic Forecasting]. Moscow: Ekonomika Publishers, 1968.

7. Pugachev, V.F. *Optimizatsiia planirovaniia (Teoreticheskie problemy)* [Optimization of Planning (Theoretical Problems)]. Moscow: Ekonomika Publishers, 1968.

8. Rimler, J.; Zs. Daniel; and J. Kornai. "Macrofunctions Computed on the Basis of Plan Models." *Acta Oeconomica* 8, no. 4 (1972): 375–406.

9. Volkonskii, V.A. *Model' optimal'nogo planirovaniia i vzaimosviazei ekonomicheskikh pokazatelei* [Model of Optimal Planning and the Interrelations of Economic Indicators]. Moscow: Nauka Publishers, 1967.

10. Volkonskii, V.A. *Printsipy optimal'nogo planirovaniia* [Principles of Optimal Planning]. Moscow: Ekonomika Publishers, 1973.

Chapter Twenty-Nine

Use of Normalized General Coordinates in Linear Value and Distribution Theory

R. M. Goodwin

The aim of this paper is not to treat input-output as such but rather to use it to discuss some old and some more recent economic issues. All the awkward empirical problems we intentionally put to one side and assume an economy completely and correctly characterized by a simple input-output system, with no joint products, only circulating capital, and only one factor, homogeneous human labour. The system is irreducible, primitive, and, being empirical, nondegenerate, that is, for n homogeneous commodities, the coefficient matrix has n distinct eigenvalues.[1] All production is of the same unit duration, taking place in one period and available as output at the beginning of the next. Thus, in the spirit of the classical economists, and of Marx, reality is represented in a highly oversimplified form with the intention of illuminating certain central features, but at a sacrifice of detail.

Representation of the Value and Output System

The value system, then, is

$$P_0[I - (1 + \pi)A] = (1 + \pi)wB_0^l \qquad (29\text{-}1)$$

---

1. In the discussion of this paper at the Sixth International Input-Output Conference, Dr. W.F. Gossling of the University of East Anglia, United Kingdom, asked whether the input-output coefficient matrix, in addition to being irreducible, should also be primitive. Comment was deferred at the time, but he and I have since discussed the question. My view is that the nondegeneracy of an empirical matrix rules out the possibility of cyclic roots, that is, those with the same modulus but different phase. He suggests, however, that it may well be that this property may not (possibly cannot) automatically include matrices with *all* eigenvalues real, positive, and equal to the dominant eigenvalue, and having an eigenvector in an eigenvector space with geometric multiplicity of one, which is positive and scalar multiple unique.

where P_0 is the price vector, A the square coefficient matrix, w the money wage rate, π the profit rate, and B_0^l the vector of direct labour inputs. The output system is

$$[I - (1 + g)A]Q_0 = (1 + g)\gamma C_0 \tag{29-2}$$

where Q_0 is the output vector, g the growth rate, C_0 a given consumption vector, and γ its scale factor.

With this sort of system it is always possible to transform to normalized general coordinates [1, pp. 77–80]. For each eigenvalue, λ_i, there exists an output eigenvector, H_i^{-1}, and a value eigenvector, H_i, making $2n$ in all. Arraying these gives $HAH^{-1} = \lambda$, where λ is a diagonal matrix. This represents a transformation to an oblique coordinate system, where we choose a set of coordinates appropriate to the system rather than the conventional axes, all normal to one another. Here the value axes are normal to the corresponding output axes, since $HH^{-1} = I$. The transformation thus preserves the simplicities of aggregation, which constitute the great attraction of macroeconomics, without sacrificing the realism of interdependence. This interdependence is specified by the technology, represented by A, which, being unchanged, can safely be set on one side in the transformation and thereby separated effectively from the value and distribution problems. The observed quantities P_0, Q_0, B_0^l, and C_0 are transformed to P, Q, B^l, and C, thus $PH = P_0$; $B^l H = B_0^l$; $H^{-1}Q = Q_0$; $H^{-1}C = C_0$, which yields the striking simplification

$$P[I - (1 + \pi)\hat{\lambda}] = (1 + \pi)wB^l \tag{29-3}$$

$$[I - (1 + g)\hat{\lambda}]Q = (1 + g)\gamma C \tag{29-4}$$

Graphically for two goods, the picture is as in Figure 29-1. Thus the transformation, representing the technology, defines n distinct, composite commodities, constituted by a technologically determined, unchanging bundle of goods; call them eigengoods. These eigengoods are actually rays, not vectors, that is determined as to proportions but not as to scale. The same process determines n eigenprices, or, rather, eigenvalues since only the price ratios, not absolute levels, are determined. The remarkable fact about these eigenrays is that each good is produced entirely out of inputs of its own product; wages in each sector are paid out of its own product; any surplus or profit consists of each good itself. It is to be understood that we take this to be in the "as if" sense, that is, we can reckon in such a way that it is as if wages, materials, and profits were actually being paid in own products. It is of course a fiction; the linear transformation is an accounting system but there is no corresponding reality. Therefore we have a universal Ricardian Corn Economy with all the clarity it embodies. The ith corn is produced by the ith corn, by labour that is paid in the ith corn,

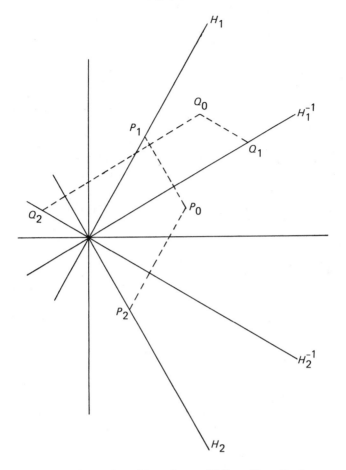

Figure 29-1. Transformation to Oblique Coordinates.

which leaves a profit in *i*th corn. In this sense it seems to share the simplicity and intelligibility of Marshall's supply and demand analysis, whilst avoiding its grave defect (that is, it takes full account of interdependence and employs no ceteris paribus). An awkward aspect of this device is that it will ordinarily involve negative and complex quantities, so that it is difficult to give commonsense interpretations to the analysis. Of course, in transforming back, these complex and negative quantities disappear. The great advantage of the transformation is that it separates value from distribution and allocation from growth, so that in each value equation, we may divide by price, and in each output equation by quantity. Consequently, it is useful to define unit labour cost as

$$\theta_i = b_{li}(w/p_i) \tag{29-5}$$

and unit consumption as

$$\delta_i = c_i(\gamma/q_i) \tag{29-6}$$

Then we can write the whole equilibrium conditions as

$$1 = (1 + \pi)(\lambda_i + \theta_i) \tag{29-7}$$

$$i = 1, 2, \ldots, n$$

$$1 = (1 + g)(\lambda_i + \delta_i) \tag{29-8}$$

Since this holds for all i and j, we have the useful result that

$$\lambda_i + \theta_i = \lambda_j + \theta_j = 1/(1 + \pi) \tag{29-9}$$

The dominant eigenvalue, λ_1, will lie between zero and one, and hence for $\pi = 0$, θ_1 will also be positive and less than unity. Consequently, as π runs from 0 to π_{max}, all $\lambda_i + \theta_i$ will be nonnegative. If λ_i be negative, θ_i will be positive and large enough to make their sum positive. A further implication is that if b_{li} be negative, so also must p_i, so that their ratio will be positive.

Since points are confined to movements along the given axes, we may ignore the orientation of the axes and present an extremely simple graphical analysis, shown in Figure 29-2, of value and distribution for a pair of typical sectors, writing σ_i for $\pi(\lambda_i + \theta_i)$. This gives distributive shares in gross product, whilst the double line gives shares in net product. It also shows that a change in shares, for example, an increase in σ_i, will reduce the share of wages in i but also in all other sectors. Hence a study of one sector gives qualitatively the result for all sectors. Likewise, it is clear that quantitatively the effect is very different. Also b_{li} and b_{lj} are constant, and any change in w is the same for all sectors, hence $\Delta p_i \neq \Delta p_j$, and we see that a change in distribution alters all price ratios. The principal virtue

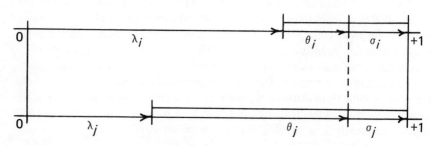

Figure 29-2. Value and Distribution for a Pair of Typical Sectors.

of the transformation is that it allows us to study the distribution problem without involving ourselves in the valuation problem, while not actually suppressing the disastrous linkage between the two. Sraffa [2] has reminded us that values are not independent of (functional) distribution. The difficulty arises because of the tight interconnection between different markets. Because normalization formally removes the interdependence (separation of variables), it neatly frees value from distribution. Thus the n eigenprices are independent of wages and profits in the sense that the proportions of prices making each eigenprice are unaffected by a change in distribution—the "direction" of each eigenray never alters even though the eigenprice itself will alter. Only one thing is known (from a theorem of Frobenius) about the eigenvalues: The largest eigenvalue is real, positive, singular, and less than unity; its output eigenvector defines Sraffa's standard commodity, which has only real, nonnegative components. None of the eigenvectors ever alter direction with a change in distribution. It is this characteristic that permits us to divide the value equations by their prices and the output equations by their quantities, the results being θ_i and δ_i, which are pure numbers less than unity, as also is λ_i by its very nature. Thus, rewriting the equations, the shares of gross output for each separately are

$$1 = \lambda_i + \theta_i + \pi(\lambda_i + \theta_i) \tag{29-10}$$

$$= \text{materials} + \text{wages} + \text{profits}$$

and

$$1 = \lambda_i + \delta_i + g(\lambda_i + \delta_i) \tag{29-11}$$

$$= \text{materials} + \text{consumption} + \text{investment}$$

Similarly for net product

$$1 = \frac{\theta_i}{1 - \lambda_i} + \frac{\pi(\lambda_i + \theta_i)}{1 - \lambda_i} \tag{29-12}$$

$$1 = \frac{\delta_i}{1 - \lambda_i} + \frac{g(\lambda_i + \delta_i)}{1 - \lambda_i} \tag{29-13}$$

giving distributive and productive shares.

The attraction of this formulation is that it joins micro and macro elements indissolubly without losing the simplicity of either. To some extent this is illusory: The complications of general interdependence are hidden in the linear transformation; likewise, the variations of the individual eigenprices and outputs are not visible. However, separating the value and the distribution problems does give a fruitful framework for the discussion of difficult issues. The test of a method is in its usefulness. Therefore, we shall try to indicate, without fully exploring, some of the ways in which it appears to be illuminating.

Separation of Value and Distribution

By stating distribution independently from valuation, the conflicting interests of workers and capitalists are not confused by complex value reactions; the greater the unit profit, the less the unit wage cost, and vice versa. Furthermore, we see clearly that cost pricing cannot and is not intended to determine distribution, so that we need a different framework for its determination.

The contrasting roles of w and π are made clear. Any change in π, regardless of whether or not w is constant, will alter distribution, whereas, by contrast, if π, regarded as mark-up, is constant, no change in w can alter shares. If all labour inputs, b_{li}, are constant, then the wage rate simply determines the price level (all prices change in proportion). If any b_{li} is changing, then the required price change is less. Thus, as a first approximation, θ_i can be taken as constant, the real wage, w/p_i, can rise pari passu with the fall in b_{li}, and p_i can rise to the extent that w rises faster than productivity.

Micro–Macro Demand

For $(1 + g)(\lambda_i + \delta_i)$ to equal unity, g must have a particular value, thus ensuring equilibrium. This is the Marxian Realization Problem and/or the Keynesian Effective Demand Problem: Evidently they are essentially the same problem, however differently they may have been formulated. If g is too small, some portion of last period's output remains unsold and profits are unrealized. Or if g is too large, stocks are reduced and realized profit is exceptional. Consequences are acceleration and deceleration of growth, unemployment, and stocks cycles.

The Invariant Measure of Value

Ricardo generated a muddle by supposing (1) that labour determined value in the sense of price ratios, and (2) that therefore labour was an invariant or otherwise desirable measure of value. Both propositions are demonstrably false. The transformation shows clearly how Sraffa solved the invariance problem. The dominant goods eigenvector is real, and its "direction" relative to all actual prices is invariant to changes in π and θ_1. Hence it can be taken as an invariant numéraire. Ignoring capital in the wage fund, letting $p_1 = 1$, and redefining units so that when $\pi = 0$, $w = 1$, and when $w = 0$, $\pi = 1$, that is, with

$$w^* = \frac{w}{(1 - \lambda_i)/b_{li}} \qquad \text{and} \qquad \pi^* = \frac{\pi}{(1 - \lambda_i)/\lambda_i}$$

then

$$\pi^* = 1 - w^*$$

which is equivalent to the Sraffa invariant distribution formula.

Marxian Value Theory

The differences between Marxian and orthodox theory become transparently clear. With a universal corn economy, the wage share in output is explicit and not masked by the valuation problem. In capitalism there is a tendency, fully accepted by Marx, to equal profit rates, so that we have the situation shown in Figure 29-3. Therefore, in the actual capitalist price mechanism, the rate of surplus value is $\sigma_i/\theta_i \neq \sigma_j/\theta_j$ due to the different cost structures; thus, there is no single rate of surplus value. This remains true even if we transform goods inputs back into labour inputs. Marx's procedure, however, was different.

"Labour embodied" is defined in Marx as direct plus indirect labour, which in normal coordinates becomes simply

$$\mathcal{L}_i = b_{li} + \mathcal{L}_i \lambda_i$$

so that

$$\mathcal{L}_i = \frac{b_{li}}{1 - \lambda_i} \qquad (29\text{-}14)$$

Marx then asked the question that follows naturally from Ricardo: If $\mathcal{L}_i$ is the labour content of output, what is the labour content of the real wage? If there is a common basket of (normalized) wage goods A^l, then the inner product $\mathcal{L}A^l = \mathcal{L}_w$ is the labour embodied in a unit of labour. It is a pure number, less than unity in

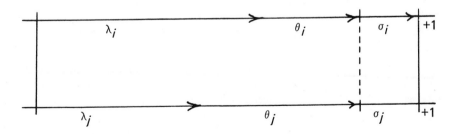

Figure 29-3. Equal Profit Rates in Capitalism.

any viable economy. The same wage basket is assumed to hold for all sectors, so we get

$$\mathcal{L}_w + \mathcal{L}_\pi = 1$$

and there is one common rate of surplus value

$$\frac{1 - \mathcal{L}_w}{\mathcal{L}_w} \qquad\qquad (29\text{-}15)$$

The objection to this procedure is that it involves the whole economy, and hence valuation, in a way the previous one did not; Marx's method lacks the desired invariance. A change in the profit rate gives two different effects which may well work in opposite directions: (1) a change in the real wage rate and hence in the rate of exploitation and (2) a change in relative prices that would lead to an alteration in the composition of the basket of goods, which complicates the direct exploitation effect. It should be noted that both procedures are simply measures of exploitation, not explanations of why any particular rate exists; both are consistent with $\pi = 0$ and nil exploitation.

The Transformation Problem

The classical economists tended to believe in the demonstrably false theory that value, meaning exchange value, was equal to labour content. Marx embraced the unfalsifiable theory that value *is* labour content. In doing so, he landed himself with the problem of relating his private definition of value to the observable values, that is, the Transformation Problem. Marxian value can be easily represented in Figure 29-4 as

$$\frac{h_i}{h_j} = \frac{b_{li}/A}{b_{lj}/B} \qquad\qquad (29\text{-}16)$$

It is evidently not, with unequal cost structures, the same as the relative price produced by equal profit rates. However, the one set of values bears a clearly defined relation to the other, and the transformation from the one to the other can always be effected.

It seems more appropriate to use the concept of labour embodied in those problems for which its definition naturally fits. Then it tells us something about what actually happens. In normal coordinates, these are the constituent labour multipliers that determine how much labour, and in which sectors, we need to produce any given set of net outputs. With any required increments or decre-

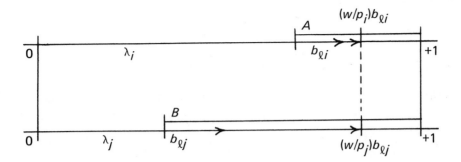

Figure 29-4. Marxian Definition of Value.

ments to net real product, $\{\delta A\}$, the labour embodied quantities yield both total labour required and its allocation by sector

$$\mathcal{L}\{\delta A\} = \delta L$$

and

$$\mathcal{L}\begin{bmatrix} \delta A_1 & 0 & . & . & . & 0 \\ 0 & \delta A_2 & . & . & . & 0 \\ . & . & . & & & . \\ . & . & & . & & . \\ . & . & & & . & . \\ 0 & 0 & . & . & . & \delta A_n \end{bmatrix} = (\delta l_1, \delta l_2, \ldots, \delta l_n)$$

The resulting sectoral employment, transformed back to actual quantities, gives the desired information. Aggregate employment is always equal in both coordinate systems, since

$$L = B^l Q = B_0^l H H^{-1} Q = L_0 \tag{29-17}$$

A Dynamic Labour Theory of Value

Consider an economy with a uniform growth rate g, including autonomous net demands, $A_i(t + 1) = (1 + g)A_i(t)$, which will result in the same growth rate in gross outputs. Then

$$[1 - (1 + g)\lambda_i]q_i = (1 + g)A_i$$

so that

$$q_i = \frac{(1+g)A_i}{1-(1+g)\lambda_i} \qquad \text{and} \qquad l_i = b_{li}q_i = \frac{(1+g)b_{li}}{1-(1+g)\lambda_i}A_i \qquad (29\text{-}18)$$

Therefore, one can, in one sense, say that in a Golden Age, the labour embodied is

$$\mathcal{L}_i = \frac{(1+g)b_{li}}{1-(1+g)\lambda_i} \qquad \text{instead of} \qquad \frac{b_{li}}{1-\lambda_i} \qquad (29\text{-}19)$$

The advantage of normal coordinates is that we need not consider the change in the output mix with a change in growth rate. This is the dual analogue of the elimination of the consideration of the value change resulting from the changed distribution. The gain here is more significant, since the growth rate, unlike distribution, changes frequently and massively.

One may therefore consider a dynamic labour theory of value with prices proportional to dynamic embodied labour, that is

$$p_i = w\mathcal{L}_i = w \frac{(1+g)b_{li}}{1-(1+g)\lambda_i} \qquad (29\text{-}20)$$

This leads to a fundamental revision of the measure of exploitation. Some profits are consumed but a large part is invested, so that $\pi > g$, and we get the result shown in Figure 29-5. Capitalist consumption per unit of product is

$$c_{\pi i} = (\pi - g)[\lambda_i + (w/p_i)b_{li}]$$

Dynamic net product is

$$\chi_i = (w/p_i)b_{li} + c_{\pi i}$$

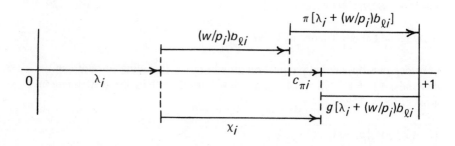

Figure 29-5.   Dynamic Labour Theory of Value.

Then the rate of exploitation in each sector is

$$\epsilon_i = \frac{c_{\pi i}}{(w/p_i)b_{li}} = \frac{(\pi - g)\,[(w/p_i)b_{li} + \lambda_i]}{(w/p_i)b_{li}} = (\pi - g)\,\frac{1 + \lambda_i}{\theta_i} \qquad (29\text{-}21)$$

which gives a strikingly reduced measure of exploitation. If $\pi = g$ (all profits invested), no exploitation occurs. For a workers' state faced with equipping a growing labour force, this gives a true representation of the real situation, and therefore seems to be the more illuminating measure of exploitation.[2]

Assuming workers spend all their income on consumption and either that no profits are consumed or that any consumption is subtracted from profits and combined with autonomous demands, then $(w/p_i)b_{li}$ is the real wage measured in good i per unit of good i and is a pure number that measures the share of workers' consumption in output. Also, it is equal to $\gamma c_{li}/q_i$. Then net output is

$$(1 - \lambda_i)q_i = \frac{1 - \lambda_i}{(1 - \lambda_i) - (w/p_i)b_{li}}\,A_i = \frac{1}{1 - \dfrac{(w/\bar{p}_i)b_{li}}{1 - \lambda_i}}\,A_i \qquad (29\text{-}22)$$

with $(w/p_i)b_{li}/(1 - \lambda_i)$ being the share of wages in output, thus giving n output multipliers in terms of distributive shares.

If $\pi = g$, distribution is determined

$$[1 - (1 + g)\lambda_i]q_i = (1 + g)(w/p_i)b_{li}q_i$$

so that the share of labour is equal to

$$\frac{1}{1 + g}\left(1 - \frac{g\lambda_i}{1 - \lambda_i}\right)$$

which is also 1 minus the share of profits. If $g = g_N$, the Harrod natural growth rate, the distribution is completely determined.

Aggregate distribution is the same in both coordinate systems

$$\frac{wB_0^l Q_0}{P_0(I - A)Q_0} = \frac{wB^l HH^{-1}Q}{PH(I - A)H^{-1}Q} = \frac{wB^l Q}{P(I - \lambda)Q} \qquad (29\text{-}23)$$

2. In the discussion at the Sixth International Input-Output Conference, Bródy took exception to this definition, commenting, correctly, that the whole of profits, regardless of reinvestment, accrued to the capitalists through their retention of ownership. They accumulate power through the plough-back of profits, and individuals may at any time disinvest and consume, but, *as a class,* they get no share in consumption (the net yield of production), if $\pi = g$, and they are simply providing equipment for an expanding population.

Say's Law

Calling value added per unit of output V and net product U, Say's Law is

$$VQ \equiv PU \tag{29-24}$$

In normal coordinates this has a very simple interpretation, as shown in Figure 29-6, since output and value eigenvalues are the same

$$v_i = (1 - \lambda_i)p_i \qquad \text{and} \qquad u_i = (1 - \lambda_i)q_i$$

so that

$$v_i/p_i = u_i/q_i$$

and hence $v_i q_i = u_i p_i$ for all i. This validates Say's Law

$$v_1 q_1 + v_2 q_2 + \ldots + v_n q_n = u_1 p_1 + u_2 p_2 + \ldots + u_n p_n \tag{29-25}$$

This establishes it also for rectangular coordinates since

$$V_0 Q_0 = VHH^{-1}Q = VQ \tag{29-26}$$

and

$$P_0 U_0 = PHH^{-1}U = PU \tag{29-27}$$

In sharp contrast to Say's Law, in normal coordinates the same result applies to each market separately since $v_i q_i = u_i p_i$.

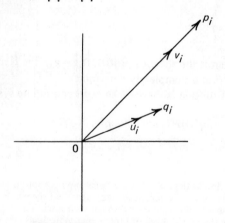

Figure 29-6. Say's Law.

There is nothing in Say's Law, or rather in its prescriptive form (which might better be called Say's Theory), that says supply will equal demand. Dropping the useful but misleading equilibrium condition, we may write

$$(1 + g)(\lambda_i + \delta_i) \gtrless 1 \qquad (29\text{-}28)$$

so that this sum may lie on either side of the positive unity point, as shown in Figure 29-7. The value of g is determined by producers and, given λ_i and δ_i, there is only one value that satisfies Say's Law. If g is too small, output is greater than demand; if too large, less than demand. This, then, is the Realization/ Effective Demand Problem. Say's Law (Theory) is violated almost all the time; yet Say has his revenge in that it cannot be violated for long in any one direction, since unbearably large stocks would accumulate, or be exhausted.

Sectoral Growth Rates

Unlike π, there is no reason to expect all growth rates to tend to equality; consequently, it is highly desirable to drop the assumption of a single g. Let $q_i(t + 1)$ replace $(1 + g)q_i(t)$ and similarly for $\gamma(t)$. Demand is

$$d_i(t) = \lambda_i q_i(t + 1) + \gamma(t + 1)c_i = (\lambda_i + \theta_i)q_i(t + 1) \qquad (29\text{-}29)$$

since

$$\gamma c_i = [(w/p_i)b_{li}]\, q_i = \theta_i q_i \qquad (29\text{-}30)$$

to which may be added $A_i(t + 1)$ for autonomous demand. Given, say by investment, the share of consumption in output, a change in taste, c_i, may alter the allocation of output, q_i, or the scale, γ, or both. If there is a common constant mark-up (and profit rate)

$$1 - (1 + \pi)\lambda_i = (1 + \pi)\theta_i$$

or

$$\frac{1}{1 + \pi} = \lambda_i + \theta_i = \lambda_j + \theta_j = \alpha < 1$$

Figure 29-7. The Marxian/Keynesian Realization Problem.

If then demand determines output

$$q_i(t + 2) = d_i(t) = \alpha q_i(t + 1) + A_i(t + 1)$$

The solution for each sector may be found recursively

$$q_i(t + 1) = A_i(t) + \alpha q_i(t)$$

$$= A_i(t) + \alpha A_i(t - 1) + \alpha^2 q_i(t - 1), \text{ etc.} \tag{29-31}$$

so that q_i is the Faltung sum of the structure and the external shocks

$$q_i(t + 1) = \sum_{\tau=0}^{\alpha} \alpha^\tau A_i(t - \tau)$$

If A is constant

$$q_i = \frac{\bar{A}_i}{1 - \alpha}$$

and if $A_i = \bar{A}_i(1 + g)^t$

$$q_i(t + 1) = \bar{A}_i(1 + g)^t \left[1 + \frac{\alpha}{1 + g} + \left(\frac{\alpha}{1 + g} \right)^2 + \dots \right] \tag{29-32}$$

$$= \frac{\bar{A}_i}{1 - [\alpha/(1 + g)]}(1 + g)^t$$

The chief advantage of a Faltung-type solution is that it reduces the structural dynamic to a triviality and thus allows concentration on the perpetually changing "initial conditions" as they are continually being varied by outside events. For it remains awkwardly true that after half a century of intensive investigation there is still no generally accepted explanation of investment behaviour. Investment, like Topsy, just grows, but unlike her does not grow in any very intelligible way. In this fashion, the baneful influence of the uniform constant growth rate can be exorcised. Different industries grow at strikingly different rates, and these various growth rates shift fitfully. Finally, this loosening of an unrealistic assumption does not intolerably complicate a general interdependence analysis. The final solution is

$$Q_0(t + 1) = H^{-1}Q(t + 1) = \sum_\tau \alpha^\tau H^{-1}A(t - \tau) = \sum_\tau \alpha^\tau A_0(t - \tau) \tag{29-33}$$

In such a general disequilibrium model, it is bound to appear grossly unrealistic to assume a constant profit rate. As is generally known, profits are ultra sensitive to the small vagaries of the market. It all depends on what is meant by profit; it is not too unreasonable to assume a constant operating profit based on revenue less prime costs (labour and materials, θ and λ). The point is that fixed costs have been explicitly excluded in this analysis, and it is they that cause the instability in profits. To some extent, profits and profit rates are figments of the accountants' imaginations. More relevant are fixed (with respect to output and revenue) outlays, that is, debt service, fixed staff, rents, etc. At some points firms have operating profits greater than these, at other points less, so that net profits being the small difference between two large quantities, revenues and costs, the proportional changes in the former are much greater than in the latter. In this way, firms easily switch from absorbing funds to injecting them into the system.

The Inventory Cycle

The inventory cycle is the best observed and most satisfactorily explicable of all dynamic behaviour. Stocks, s, will normally be held over from period to period, thus imparting flexibility to output behaviour. In this model they represent "normal" excess capacity, peak load, or stand-by capacity. Stocks transform like capacity; indeed, output becomes stock at the beginning of each period. Let $\alpha_i = \lambda_i + \theta_i$ and note that all α's lie between zero and unity even when λ_i is negative. Then

$$\Delta s_i = q_i - \alpha_i q_i - g\alpha_i q_i - A_i(t)$$

$$= (1 - \alpha_i)q_i - \alpha_i \, \Delta q_i - A_i(t) \tag{29-34}$$

The simplest and possibly the best assumption about producers is that they conform to proportional negative feed-back to regulate production so as to maintain the desired level of stocks (capacity), thus

$$\Delta q_i = -\beta(s_i - \bar{s}_i) \tag{29-35}$$

It is to be noted that there are no "normalized" producers carrying out this operation. It is, however, a correct representation of n different groups of producers, all using the same proportional control routine. Ignoring the $\alpha_i \, \Delta q_i$ term, it is easy to see in Figure 29–8 that this gives an undamped cycle of arbitrary amplitude about the equilibrium point, $\Delta s_i = 0$, $\Delta q_i = 0$, for each normalized sector. Adding the term $\alpha_i \, \Delta q_i$ results in the phase path no longer having a zero slope on the vertical dotted line (that is, $\Delta s_i \neq 0$) and hence the typical path is no longer a closed one, but rather is an outward spiral and hence unstable. On

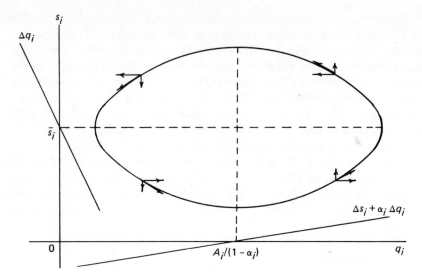

Figure 29-8.   The Stocks Cycle in Normalized Coordinates.

transforming back, the solutions become linear combinations (with weighting depending on "initial" conditions of the system) of expanding cycles. These movements will be inhibited by one or more boundaries, the most obvious one being the labour supply. This means that each cycle will be able to reach higher and higher q_i. If the $A_i(t)$ and $\bar{s}_i$ drift upward with these higher output levels, then the spiral will creep to the right and upward, thus generating a trend also. The advantage of normal coordinates is that they allow the analysis of this exceedingly complex phenomenon to proceed with the simplicity of a macro-model.

It is of some interest to note that the inventory problem resists formulation in terms of growth rates. Sectoral disequilibrium yields stable behaviour; those sectors short of stocks, by accelerating, can increase their stocks–output ratio, those long on stocks can decelerate, reducing their excess. But for general dis-equilibrium, the effort to increase stocks by acceleration only reduces them, and the effort to decrease them by deceleration only increases them. Therefore, we have Harrodian instability. This seems to be a striking case in which decentral-ized decision making leads to highly undesirable consequences. By contrast, centralized planners could regard excessive stocks as a basis for a general increase in growth rates, and deficient stocks would be a signal for slowing the pace.

A Dynamic Model

To illustrate the usefulness of normalized coordinates and at the same time to suggest the kind of theory that is required for capital and distribution analysis, we shall describe briefly a dynamic model embodying the mutual determination of wage, profit, and growth rates. Labour and productivity growth rates are given; output and capital stock adjust to them in a cyclical manner. The real profit rate determines the growth rate, which, in turn, leads to upward pressure on money wage rates. With a constant mark-up, this brings a falling real-profit rate and hence a falling growth rate. The result is a relaxation in the labour market, real-profit rates are restored, and the vigorous growth is resumed. The resulting endogenous growth path (or rather growth paths, which are then combined linearly to get the overall aggregative path) will be cyclical in the short run, exponential in the long run, with constant average shares to wages and to profits resulting from the required constant average amount of unemployment.

The parameters g, π, and w are not affected by the coordinate transformation; profit rate is proportional to growth rate, the proportion being taken as unity for simplicity. The whole structure of values, distribution, relative and absolute outputs depends, then, on the single parameter g. Consequently, it is possible to discuss a dauntingly complex problem in terms of a pair of simple difference or differential equations. There is a constant growth rate, $\bar{g}_A$, in labour productivity, and in the labour force, $\bar{g}_L$. Being scalars, they also remain unaltered by transformation. The value $\bar{g}_A$ could be treated as a weighted sum of individual growth rates, but this would complicate, without essentially altering, the analysis. The value of g must be taken as indicative of a central tendency only, so that the analysis is in some respects only semidisaggregated.

Calling total employment l, and labour force L

$$\frac{\Delta l/L}{l/L} = g - (\bar{g}_A + \bar{g}_L) \tag{29-36}$$

if we ignore the difference between differentials and differences. With fixed mark-up, $\bar{\pi}$, equal, in this type of model, to nominal profit rate, $\bar{\pi}_N$, cost in one period determines price in the next, thus

$$p_i(t + 1) = (1 + \bar{\pi}_N)[\lambda_i p_i(t) + w(t)b_{li}(t)]$$

which gives

$$\Delta p/p = (1 + \bar{\pi}_N)(\lambda + \theta) - 1 \tag{29-37}$$

where the ith sector is referred to. Since the real rate, π_R, is equal to $\bar{\pi}_N - (\Delta p/p)$

$$\bar{\pi}_N - \pi_R = (1 + \bar{\pi}_N)(\lambda + \theta) - 1 \quad \text{or} \quad \pi_R = (1 + \bar{\pi}_N)[1 - (\lambda + \theta)] = g \tag{29-38}$$

Calling labour's share in any sector β, $\beta = \theta/(1 - \lambda)$, so that

$$g = (1 + \bar{\pi}_N)(1 - \lambda)(1 - \beta) \tag{29-39}$$

$$\frac{\Delta \beta}{\beta} = \frac{\Delta \theta}{\theta} = \frac{\Delta w}{w} + \frac{\Delta b_l}{b_l} - \frac{\Delta p}{p} \tag{29-40}$$

If, as in the Phillips Curve, $\Delta w/w = \phi(l/L)$

$$\frac{\Delta \beta}{\beta} = \frac{\phi(l/L)}{L} - (1 + \bar{\pi}_N)(1 - \lambda)\beta + [1 - (1 + \bar{\pi}_N)\lambda - \bar{g}_A] \tag{29-41}$$

which determines the evolution of labour's share in net product as dependent on unemployment. The dependence of unemployment (and employment) on labour's share is given by

$$\frac{\Delta l/L}{l/L} = -(1 + \bar{\pi}_N)(1 - \lambda)\beta + (1 + \bar{\pi}_N)(1 - \lambda) - (\bar{g}_A + \bar{g}_L) \tag{29-42}$$

Such a pair of equations characterizes each of the n sectors, and they suffice each separately to determine completely the dynamic evolution of the sector. The functions, being nonlinear, do not permit analytic solutions but are easily and completely soluble graphically with the help of a phase diagram, as in Figure 29-9.

A given initial condition chooses one of the curves, and each sector spirals onto its stable equilibrium point. This point, $\Delta l/L = 0$ and $\Delta \beta = 0$, determines that degree of unemployment and the consequent distribution of income which will yield the long-run average growth rate, that is, Harrod's natural growth rate. The stability of the system results from the fact that, even with a constant markup, there will be a lagging response of prices to wage changes. This means that real wages and the share of wages move with money wages, but less rapidly so. Consequently, the share of profits, available funds for investment, and the growth rate also vary with the state of unemployment. The level lines for $\Delta \beta/\beta$ lie, as indicated, on a line sloping upward to the right, forcing the phase lines ever inward. Irregular exogenous shocks will maintain the oscillation. In their absence, real wages would tend to grow steadily in step with productivity; but, as it is, they first rise more rapidly and then more slowly than productivity.

Dynamic Interindustry Analysis:
The Key to Capital Theory

As a result of Sraffa's work, we know that there is a fatal circularity in capital theory: Distribution depends on the amount of capital but the amount of capital depends on distribution (since capital goods have to be valued). Ricardo sensed this pitfall and evaded it in his corn economy example, where valuation is exorcised since input, output, wages, and profits are all in corn. In normalized

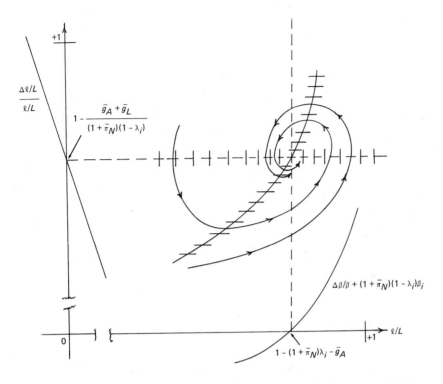

Figure 29-9. A Disaggregated Growth Cycle.

coordinates there are *n* separated corn economies giving profit rates directly as dimensionless numbers. Normalized prices, in long-run equilibrium, must be such as to equate all these sectoral profit rates. The own rate of return in all sectors, being brought into equality, becomes *the* rate of return for the economy, unambiguously determined, without any circularity of reasoning in relation to distribution.

In each sector, real capital is simply the currently available stock, last period's output plus carry-over. This still does not yield a single number for aggregate real capital, since these quantities are not summable. When they are valued for summation, the distribution problem fatally flaws the procedure. That it must be so even in normal coordinates can be seen from the fact that the aggregate value of output and stocks must be the same in both coordinate systems. So long as one keeps to heterogeneous capital goods, no problem arises, but the immediate consequence is that it is not possible to determine a quantity of homogeneous capital analogous to the quantity of homogeneous labour.

In fact, there is no separately distinguishable thing called capital in this model. There are only goods, some of which may not enter into consumption but all of which have prices determined by cost. The value of capital goods is determined like that of other goods and the rate of profit (interest) must be otherwise determined: It is a proportionality factor applying to all goods, consumption goods, capital goods, and labour alike, and it alters the value of all of them. Capital is a name applied to one of the dynamic aspects of an economy, not a separate category on its own: To look for something called capital is to commit the fallacy of misplaced concreteness; it is like trying to isolate energy.

Operationally, the capital problem resides in the necessity to accumulate out of current production the required stocks of inputs before an increase can take place. This gives rise to the dated labour analysis whereby goods inputs are recursively resolved into labour inputs (as the only unproduced good), which, in the case of normal coordinates, become a simple geometric series, easily summed, and in input-output analysis to a convergent matric-geometric series with its inverse. This shows why economists so easily lose the capital problem by suppressing interindustrial structure and speaking as if goods were produced by labour and "capital." It is precisely the necessity of producing intermediate goods, including durable capital goods, that constitutes the capital problem. By summing the geometric series, whether scalar or matric, one gets a timeless representation of the dynamic structure. For a stationary state, this is quite adequate and seems to negate the time sequence. In fact it is not so, for, without previously accumulated stocks, output cannot be increased. Correspondingly, all attempts to construct a theory of the rate of profit for a stationary state are bound to fail: The rate of profit can be anything between zero and a certain maximum value. The very real complications of durability, vintage, and choice of technique all only help to conceal this basic point. The moment we consider change, the problem and its resolution become more comprehensible. There are three types of cases to consider.

The first is the Keynesian one, in which there is unemployment of both capacity and labour. In this simple model, excess capacity takes the form of an excess of goods at the end of each period, more than is considered necessary for production plus contingencies. If this is the case in all sectors, there is no capital problem: $\alpha_i q_i(t + 1)$ can be greater than $q_i(t)$; there is no saving problem, nor is any accumulation necessary: The scale of output can be raised forthwith to any level short of removing the entire excess of stocks; both investment and consumption can rise, hence there is no "cost" to investment. Under such conditions it is not surprising that Keynes produced a special and limited theory of interest, depending entirely on arbitrary, short-run speculative positions. Of course, at some point, a constraint on expansion will arise in one or more sectors, but we cannot say that "capital" in general or in the aggregate is scarce, merely that it is so in particular sectors.

The second case is that of unemployed labour along with full-capacity operation in all or most sectors. Then acceleration can occur only if there is net saving in the form of lower consumption per head prior to the increased scale of production; the increase in stocks must be generated before the expanded scale of production can be undertaken. This is rather a special case of the Austrian analysis. It does not encompass their favourite problem of a shift to a new technique involving more goods per man in response to a lower interest rate. It is, however, open to some doubt whether that process is as important as they thought it to be. The bulk of capital accumulation relates to the growth of the labour force and improved technology, neither of which requires a fall in the profit rate—on the contrary, they tend to hold it up.

Lastly, there is the case of joint limitation by labour force and capacity. If stocks are in excess, growth in the labour force can be accommodated without saving, simply by reducing the excess stocks. The Austrians, in common with all neoclassical economists, assumed a labour market mechanism that would guarantee full employment, so there was no need to consider any other case. It is for this reason that their doctrine, as expounded by Wicksell, can reduce capital to dated labour, for, if labour is the limiting factor, then any transfer from consumption to accumulation can be, and logically should be, measured in terms of the quantity of labour embodied. The trouble with this comes in the complications of timing and compounding; these become much less serious with normal coordinates.

Whether there is full employment of labour or not, the problem of capital accumulation involves not consuming the whole of the available current output. Assuming demand equals current output

$$\lambda_i q_i(t + 1) + c_i(t) = q_i(t) \qquad (29\text{-}43)$$

from which, by recursion, we get for an arbitrary initial period n

$$q_i(t) = \left(\frac{1}{\lambda_i}\right)^{1+n} q_i[t - (1 + n)] - \sum_{\tau=0}^{n} \left(\frac{1}{\lambda_i}\right)^{1+\tau} c_i[t - (1 + \tau)] \qquad (29\text{-}44)$$

The first term tells us what output would be in the absence of any consumption at all over the periods. The others show the effects of consumption at different times. The earlier the act of saving (that is, reduction of consumption), the more potent the effect on the scale of output. Thus, dating is basic to the accumulation problem, and it involves compounding in real as well as monetary terms. The changing degrees of shortage in goods and in labour provide the basis for developing a theory of the determination of the real wage and of the rate of profit, which in turn condition the accelerations and decelerations that determine the relative shortages of goods and of labour.

References

1. Goodwin, R.M. "Static and Dynamic Linear General Equilibrium Models." *Input-Output Relations.* Proceedings of a Conference on Inter-industrial Relations held at Driebergen, Holland. Leiden: The Netherlands Economic Institute, 1953.

2. Sraffa, Piero. *Production of Commodities by Means of Commodities.* Cambridge, England: Cambridge University Press, 1960.

About the Editors

Karen R. Polenske is an associate professor in the Department of Urban Studies and Planning at the Massachusetts Institute of Technology, where she has been teaching regional economics and directing the multiregional input-output research project since 1972. She received the B.A. in 1959 from Oregon State College in home economics, the M.A. in 1961 from the Maxwell School, Syracuse University, in the joint program of public administration and economics, and the Ph.D. in 1966 from Harvard University in economics. After receiving the Ph.D. she taught for four years in the Department of Economics at Harvard University and was a research associate at the Harvard Economic Research Project until it closed in 1972. In 1970–1971, she spent the year at the University of Cambridge as a Senior Visitor at the Faculty of Economics and a Member of High Table at King's College. She belongs to the American Economic Association and the Regional Science Association. She is writing the sixth volume in a series entitled *Multiregional Input-Output Analysis*. The first five volumes have been published by Lexington Books, D.C. Heath and Company. She is the author of numerous articles and reports on input-output analysis.

Jiri V. Skolka is a research associate at the Austrian Institute for Economic Research in Vienna. Born in Czechoslovakia, he studied statistics at the Prague Technical University and received a doctorate for his study on statistical analysis of the fixed assets in the engineering industry. From 1956 to 1965 he was a research associate in the Institute of Economics of the Czechoslovak Academy of Sciences; in 1963 he was appointed Head of the macroeconomic branch of the Econometric Laboratory in the Institute, where he worked on input-output and macroeconomic planning models. Between 1955 and 1965 he was a part-time lecturer at the Technical Universities in Prague and Brno and High Schools of Economics in Prague and Bratislava and in 1965 an external associate professor at the Institute of Econometrics at the High School of Economics, Prague. From 1965 to early 1971 he was an economic affairs officer in the Programming and Planning Division of the UN Economic Commission for Europe, where his work involved comparative analysis of a set of standardized input-output tables, preparation of seminars, and exchange of information on economic research. In 1971, he was a visiting professor at the Chr. Michelsen Institute, Bergen, Norway. He belongs to the International Association for Research in Income and Wealth and to the Association Européene d'Economie Appliquée. He has written three books on input-output analysis (two in Czech, one in German) and articles in various journals.